# II SAMUEL

YALE

VOLUME 9

The Anchor Yale Bible is a fresh approach to the world's greatest classic. Its object is to make the Bible accessible to the modern reader; its method is to arrive at the meaning of biblical literature through exact translation and extended exposition, and to reconstruct the ancient setting of the biblical story, as well as the circumstances of its transcription and the characteristics of its transcribers.

The Anchor Yale Bible is a project of international and interfaith scope: Protestant, Catholic, and Jewish scholars from many countries contribute individual volumes. The project is not sponsored by any ecclesiastical organization and is not intended to reflect any particular theological doctrine. Prepared under our joint supervision, The Anchor Yale Bible is an effort to make available all the significant historical and linguistic knowledge which bears on the interpretation of the biblical record.

The Anchor Yale Bible is aimed at the general reader with no special formal training in biblical studies; yet it is written with the most exacting standards of scholarship, reflecting the highest technical accomplishment.

This project marks the beginning of a new era of cooperation among scholars in biblical research, thus forming a common body of knowledge to be shared by all.

*William Foxwell Albright*
*David Noel Freedman*
GENERAL EDITORS

THE ANCHOR YALE BIBLE

# II SAMUEL

A New Translation
with
Introduction, Notes and Commentary
by
P. KYLE McCARTER, JR.



YALE

THE ANCHOR YALE BIBLE
*Yale University Press*
New Haven & London

First published in 1984 by Doubleday, a division of Random House, Inc.
First Yale University Press impression 2010.



Printed in the United States of America.

Library of Congress Cataloging-in-Publication Data
Bible. O.T. Samuel, 2nd. English. McCarter. 1984.
II Samuel
(The Anchor Bible; v. 9)
Bibliography; p.
Includes indexes
1. Bible. O.T. Samuel, 2nd—Commentaries. I. McCarter, P. Kyle (Peter Kyle), 1945- II. Title. III. Title: 2nd Samuel. IV. Title: Second Samuel. V. Series: Bible. English. Anchor Bible. 1964; v. 9.
BS192.2.A1 1964.G3 vol. 9 [BS1323] 220.7'7s
[222'.44077] 81-43919

ISBN 978-0-300-13951-8

A catalogue record for this book is available from the British Library.

*To Frank Moore Cross*

# ACKNOWLEDGMENTS

Much of the basic research for this commentary was completed under the auspices of a Sesquicentennial Associateship awarded me by the University of Virginia. I owe special thanks to the Interlibrary Loan staff of Alderman Library and to the staffs of two nearby libraries with excellent Old Testament collections—the Woodstock Theological Library of Georgetown University and the library of Union Theological Seminary in Richmond. To David Noel Freedman, for the thoroughness and expertise with which he read every part of the manuscript, I repeat my appreciation. Portions of the text were also read by Kent Jackson and Marsha Stuckey, both of whom made helpful suggestions. Thanks also go to Eve Roshevsky, Jill Grundfest, and copy editor Henry Krawitz of Doubleday for their supervision of the production of the manuscript.

# CONTENTS

# LIST OF MAPS



*Maps by Rafael Palacios*

# PRINCIPAL ABBREVIATIONS

*AHw* — *Akkadisches Handwörterbuch,* by W. von Soden. 3 vols. Wiesbaden: Harrassowitz, 1965–.

*ANET*[3] — *Ancient Near Eastern Texts Relating to the Old Testament,* ed. J. B. Pritchard. 3d ed. with supplement. Princeton, N.J.: Princeton University Press, 1969.

*ARM* — *Archives royales de Mari.* Paris: Guenther, 1941–.

AV — Authorized Version or King James Version, 1611.

BDB — F. Brown, S. R. Driver, and C. A. Briggs, eds., *A Hebrew and English Lexicon of the Old Testament.* Oxford: Clarendon Press, [1906].

*BHK*[3] — *Biblica Hebraica,* ed. R. Kittel. 3d ed. Stuttgart: Privilegierte Württembergische Bibelanstalt, 1937.

*BHS* — *Biblia Hebraica Stuttgartensia,* ed. K. Elliger and W. Rudolph. Stuttgart: Deutsche Bibelstiftung, 1967–77. (Samuel I and II, ed. P. A. H. de Boer, 1976.)

*(bis)* — twice, two occurrences.

*CAD* — *The Assyrian Dictionary of the Oriental Institute of the University of Chicago,* ed. I. J. Gelb et al. Chicago: Oriental Institute, 1964–.

*CAH*[3] — *The Cambridge Ancient History.* 3d ed. Cambridge: Cambridge University Press, 1970–.

chap., chaps. — chapter, chapters.

*CTCA* — *Corpus des tablettes en cunéiformes alphabétiques,* ed. A. Herdner. 2 vols. Mission de Ras Shamra X. Paris: Imprimerie Nationale, 1963.†

DN — divine name.

*EA* — *Die El-Amarna Tafeln,* ed. J. A. Knudtzon. Vorderasiatische Bibliothek 2. Leipzig: Hinrichs, 1908–15.

GK[2] — *Gesenius' Hebrew Grammar,* ed. E. Kautzsch. 2d English ed., rev. A. E. Cowley. Oxford: Clarendon Press, 1910. Cited by section (§).

GN — geographical name, place name.

*IDB* — *The Interpreter's Dictionary of the Bible,* ed. G. A. Buttrick et al. 4 vols. New York: Abingdon Press, 1962.

† Ugaritic passages are cited by the *CTCA* number followed, in parentheses, by the corresponding *UT*[4] number.

| | |
|---|---|
| *IDBSup* | *The Interpreter's Dictionary of the Bible. Supplementary Volume*, ed. K. Crim et al. Nashville, Tenn.: Abingdon Press, 1976. |
| Jastrow | M. Jastrow, *A Dictionary of the Targumim, the Talmud Babli and Yerushalmi, and the Midrashic Literature.* Brooklyn, N.Y.: Traditional Press, [1903]. |
| JB | Jerusalem Bible, 1966. |
| Josephus, *Ant.* | Josephus' *Jewish Antiquities* (cited from *Josephus*, trans. H. St. J. Thackeray and R. Marcus. Vol. 5. The Loeb Classical Library. London: Heinemann, 1934). |
| *KAI* | *Kanaanäische und aramäische Inschriften*, by H. Donner and W. Röllig. 3 vols. Wiesbaden: Harrassowitz, 1962–64. |
| KB$^3$ | L. Koehler and W. Baumgartner, *Hebräisches und aramäisches Lexikon zum Alten Testament.* 3d ed. Leiden: Brill, 1967–. |
| LXX | Septuagint (cited from *The Old Testament in Greek . . .* , ed. A. E. Brooke, N. McLean, and H. St. J. Thackeray. Vol. II, pt. I. Cambridge: Cambridge University Press, 1927). |
| LXX$^A$ | Codex Alexandrinus. |
| LXX$^B$ | Codex Vaticanus. |
| LXX$^L$ | so-called Lucianic manuscripts (boc$_2$e$_2$). |
| LXX$^M$ | Codex Coislinianus. |
| LXX$^N$ | Codex Basiliano-Vaticanus. |
| LXX$^O$ | Hexaplaric witnesses, the fifth column of Origen's Hexapla. |
| mg | margin. |
| MS, MSS | manuscript, manuscripts. |
| MT | Masoretic Text (cited from *Biblia Hebraica Stuttgartensia*, ed. K. Elliger and W. Rudolph. Stuttgart: Deutsche Bibelstiftung, 1967–77). |
| NAB | New American Bible, 1970. |
| NEB | New English Bible, 1970. |
| NJV | New Jewish Version, 1977. |
| OG | Old Greek translation. |
| OL | Old Latin translations (cited from *The Old Testament in Greek . . .* , ed. A. E. Brooke, N. McLean, and H. St. J. Thackeray. Vol. II, pt. I. Cambridge: Cambridge University Press, 1927 [see also Ulrich 1980*]). |
| PN | proper name. |
| *PRU* | *Le Palais royal d'Ugarit*, ed. C. F.-A. Schaeffer. Paris: Imprimerie Nationale, 1955–. |
| RS | Ras Shamra. |

* For the full citation see the Bibliography.

| | |
|---|---|
| RSV | Revised Standard Version, 1952. |
| RV | Revised Version, 1881–85. |
| Syr. | Syriac translation or Peshiṭta (cited from *The Old Testament in Syriac according to the Peshiṭta Version*, ed. Peshiṭta Institute. Pt. II, fasc. ii. Leiden: Brill, 1978 [Samuel, ed. P. A. H. de Boer]). |
| Targ. | Targum Jonathan (cited from *The Bible in Aramaic . . .*, ed. A. Sperber. Vol. II. Leiden: Brill, 1959). |
| *THwAT* | *Theologisches Handwörterbuch zum Alten Testament*, ed. E. Jenni and C. Westermann. 2 vols. Munich: Kaiser, 1971 (vol. 1), 1976 (vol. 2). |
| *(tris)* | thrice, three occurrences. |
| *Ugaritica V* | *Ugaritica V*, by J. Nougayrol et al. Mission de Ras Shamra 16. Paris: Imprimerie Nationale, 1968. |
| *$UT^4$* | *Ugaritic Textbook*, by C. H. Gordon. 4th ed. Rome: Pontifical Biblical Institute, 1910.† |
| v., vv. | verse, verses. |
| Vulg. | Vulgate, Jerome's Latin translation (cited from *Biblia Sacra iuxta Vulgatam versionem*, ed. R. Weber. Rev. ed. Stuttgart: Württembergische Bibelanstalt, 1975. |
| Wellhausen | Wellhausen 1871.* |
| *I Samuel* | McCarter 1980a.* |
| (1), (2), etc. | first occurrence, second occurrence, etc. |
| $4QSam^{a,c}$ | Samuel manuscripts from Qumran Cave IV. |
| [ ] | Words or phrases enclosed in brackets in the translation do not appear in the reconstructed Hebrew text. In most cases a pronoun has been replaced by a proper noun or a proper noun by a pronoun for the sake of the English translation. |

† Ugaritic passages are cited by the *CTCA* number followed, in parentheses, by the corresponding *$UT^4$* number.

* For the full citation see the Bibliography.

# INTRODUCTION

# I. TEXT AND VERSIONS

The characteristics of the principal witnesses to the text of Samuel are described in the introduction to *I Samuel* (pp. 8–11). The description given there applies to II Samuel as well as to I Samuel except in one important detail. Throughout I Samuel the Codex Vaticanus (LXX$^{B}$) escaped the revisions to which other Greek manuscripts were subjected and therefore provides a reliable witness to the Old Greek translation. The same can be said of LXX$^{B}$ in the first nine chapters of II Samuel, but beginning in II Samuel 10 the character of LXX$^{B}$ changes. This was first recognized by Thackeray (1907; cf. 1921: 9–28), who noted the presence of two translations, "early" and "late," in the major uncial manuscripts of I–IV Reigns (= I Samuel–II Kings). He assigned the following sigla to the various sections:

| | | |
|---|---|---|
| EARLY: | *α* | I Samuel |
| | *ββ* | II Sam 1:1–11:1 |
| | *γγ* | I Kings 2:12–21:29 |
| LATE: | *βγ* | II Sam 11:2–I Kings 2:11 |
| | *γδ* | I Kings 22:1–II Kings 25:30. |

Thus, whereas LXX$^{B}$ preserves the Old Greek in the first chapters of II Samuel (*ββ*), it does not in the later chapters (*βγ*). Thackeray's late "translation" was subsequently identified by Barthélemy (1953) as a revision of the Old Greek towards an early forerunner of the Masoretic Text (MT). This recension, called *kaige* by Barthélemy because of its characteristic habit of translating Hebrew *wĕgam* by Greek *kai ge,* can be identified in a number of other biblical books. Its distinctive features have been defined most fully by Shenkel (1969:11–18), who sets the limits in III Reigns (= II Samuel) as follows:

| | |
|---|---|
| *ββ* | II Sam 1:1–9:13 |
| *βγ* | II Sam 10:1–I Kings 2:11. |

As a whole, the *kaige* recension represents "an early Jewish attempt to revise the standard Septuagint into conformity with a Proto-Massoretic Hebrew text" (Cross 1964:283). This is significant for our purposes because it means that the rich variety of textual witnesses available in I Samuel 1–II Samuel 9 for use in the reconstruction of an eclectic text is diminished in II Samuel 10–24. In these chapters, where the Old Greek is no longer directly accessible through LXX$^{B}$, we shall have to rely more heavily than usual upon the always suggestive but often perplexing "Lucianic" manuscripts (LXX$^{L}$), which offer the best witness to the Old Greek in section *βγ*.

# II. LITERARY HISTORY

As explained in the introduction to *I Samuel* (pp. 12–14), the modern study of the literary history of Samuel can be dated from a break with the theories of the earlier literary critics who posited the existence of narrative strands comparable or identical to the Yahwistic (J) and Elohistic (E) sources of the Tetrateuch running parallel through the Samuel material. There appeared in place of those theories a preference for viewing the larger Samuel narrative as a combination of several longer and shorter units of material enclosed side by side in an editorial framework. The new theories that arose, insofar as they pertain to II Samuel in particular, are presented and reviewed in the NOTES and COMMENTS of this book. The preliminary sketch that follows here is intended to acquaint the reader with the general directions recent research has taken. Two studies are fundamental: that of Rost (1926), who programmatically defined the character of the original narrative sources, and that of Noth (1981 [1943]), who provided the first full description of the editorial framework.

## THE EDITORIAL FRAMEWORK

### *Noth's Hypothesis*

According to Noth (1981 [1943]) Deuteronomy–II Kings is the work of a single writer working in the exilic period. This writer organized the various old units and complexes of material available to him into a continuous history of Israel, from the entry into the land until the beginning of the exile. Among his sources was the collection of Deuteronomic law we have today in Deut 4:44–30:20; this he incorporated into his history as the first large complex of traditions (1981:16–17). He evaluated the subsequent materials that made up his narrative according to the requirements of this law, making his evaluation known at every point throughout the history through characteristically worded editorial passages, which, along with chronological notices, represent his own contribution to the composition. This writer, then, viewed the Deuteronomic law as "a norm for the relationship between God and people and as a yardstick by which to judge human conduct" (1981:80). From his perspective in the time of the exile, he judged the past according to a legalistic conception of history, which "considered the whole of past history in relation to this law, concluded that the prescriptions of the law should have been observed at all times (2 Kings 22:13,17), and thus reached an unfavorable judgment on the history of Israel, seeing it as a period of disobedience to the will of God" (1981:80–81).

The Deuteronomistic historian, says Noth (1981:54–57), had extensive sources for the reign of David and intervened with his own comments in this part of the history only rarely, in contrast to his treatment of the period of the judges or the age of the independent kingdoms of Israel and Judah. He was "at one with the whole Old Testament tradition in seeing the figure of David, despite his weaknesses, as a model against which to judge the later Judaean kings" (1981:54); cf. I Kings 11:4; 15:3–5; etc. The Davidic ideal was subsequently realized in the time of Josiah, when the king exercised his proper role as a protector of the law (cf. 1981:82). But this offered no larger hope: For Noth's Deuteronomistic historian the reigns of David and Josiah merely illustrated the ideal that other periods failed to maintain. The spirit of optimism that pervades the early materials about David, most clearly expressed in the dynastic promise of II Samuel 7, is, therefore, pre-Deuteronomistic. The Deuteronomistic historian's own contribution in II Samuel is, according to Noth, limited to the following:

1) formulaic introductions to the reigns of Ishbaal and David: 2:10a,11; 5:4–5. These were inserted in their proper place near the end of the older story of David's rise to power (I Sam 16:14–II Sam 5:10[25]), which was incorporated as a whole into the larger history (cf. 1981:125 n. 2).

2) rearrangement of the end of the story of David's rise: chap. 5. Originally vv. 17–25 followed vv. 1–3 (1981:125–26 n. 3), and the conclusion of the old story was in v. 10. The historian's purpose was to focus attention on the capture of Jerusalem (vv. 6–10), because it made possible the recovery of the ark.

3) additions to the report of Nathan's prophecy: 7:1b,7a,11a,12b–13a,22–24. The original passage, with its negative view of the temple and its positive view of the monarchy, was not in the spirit of the Deuteronomistic history. The effect of the insertion of v. 13a, with its introduction in v. 12b (1981:126 n. 20), was to make the temple prohibition temporary. Verses 22–24, though positive in tone, refer to the past (from the Deuteronomistic historian's perspective) rather than the future.

4) introduction and conclusion to the catalogue of David's wars: 8:1a$\alpha$,14b. The catalogue in 8:1–14 was inserted (with other materials in chaps. 5–7) between the story of David's rise and the succession narrative to provide a record of David's military successes.

5) insertion of the two lists of David's officers: 8:15–18; 20:23–26. The

historian had two lists at his disposal. He assigned one to the beginning and one to the end of David's reign.

*II Samuel 7 and Deuteronomistic Theology*

Noth's work remains fundamental for the investigation of the redactional history of Deuteronomy–II Kings. Nevertheless, subsequent studies have modified his conclusions in two important ways. First, there is a widespread belief that Noth gave insufficient stress to the positive aspects of Deuteronomistic theology, especially as regards the dynastic promise to David. Second, a number of scholars have questioned the unity of the strictly Deuteronomistic component of the history.

According to von Rad (1962:vol. I:339), the Deuteronomistic historian viewed the dynasty of David as a concrete historical power as real as the Mosaic law. His negative judgment on the history of Israel was mitigated, therefore, by his confidence in the promise made to David in the prophecy of Nathan (p. 343). His purpose was not simply to pass judgment on the past: On the basis of the dynastic promise he held out a hope for the future that was, in a word, messianic. Largely in consequence of von Rad's influence, then, there is now widespread agreement that the theology of the Deuteronomistic history stands somewhere between that of the Deuteronomic law code, on the one hand, and that of the court circles in Jerusalem, on the other. Some scholars would agree with Nicholson (1967:107–18) in stressing the subordination of specifically Jerusalem traditions to a predominantly Deuteronomic outlook in the history, but few would deny the thematic importance of the dynastic promise to David for Deuteronomistic theology as a whole.

The importance of this development for us is the emphasis it places on II Samuel 7, which thus emerges as a key chapter not only in Samuel but in Deuteronomy–II Kings as a whole. It is unnecessary at this point to raise questions of interpretation to be treated in their proper context in §§ XV and XVI. We may note in advance, however, the central place accorded II Samuel 7 in the Deuteronomistic history in studies by McCarthy (1965), Cross (1973: 241–64, 274–89), Veijola (1975:72–78), Mettinger (1976:48–63), and others.

*The Case Against Editorial Unity*

Consideration of this positive side of the Deuteronomistic history moved Cross (1973:278–85) to place the primary edition of the history in the pre-exilic period, specifically in the time of Josiah, whose reform, says Cross, it was compiled to support. A pre-exilic date has also been defended by Fohrer (1968:236), Gray (1970:6–9), and others. All of these scholars, including Cross, reached this conclusion primarily on the basis of an examination of Kings. Passages in Kings in which the exile is unambiguously in view (II Kings 21:10–15; 23:26–27; etc.) derive from the hand of a later redactor living shortly after the emancipation of Jehoiachin (ca. 560 B.C.; cf. II Kings 24:27–30). Thus we may, with Cross, speak of primary (Dtr[1]) and secondary (Dtr[2]) "editions" of the Deuteronomistic history.

Another important group of investigators discern *two* subsequent redactional phases through which the primary Deuteronomistic history passed. The programmatic studies in this regard are those of Smend (1971) and Dietrich (1972). Upon examination of selected passages in Joshua and Judges, Smend observed a critical and "systematic reworking of the Deuteronomistic history . . . the chief motif of which is the law" (1971:509); he assigned to this "nomistic" redaction the siglum DtrN. Dietrich's monograph is a study of the prophetic passages by which Kings is organized according to a recurrent pattern of oracle and fulfilment (cf. von Rad 1953:74–91). In these passages he identified a redaction of the Deuteronomistic history with formal and linguistic features linking it with classical prophecy but with, at the same time, an affinity for Deuteronomistic thought. To this "prophetic" redaction he assigned the siglum DtrP. Thus Dietrich summarizes the redactional history of Deuteronomy–II Kings as follows (1972:139–48): The Deuteronomistic history (DtrG) was composed shortly after the fall of Jerusalem, ca. 580 B.C.; the nomistic redaction (DtrN) is to be dated ca. 560 B.C.; and the prophetic redaction (DtrP) falls somewhere between these dates.

Most important for our purposes is the 1975 monograph of Veijola, where, in the course of an investigation of the Deuteronomistic presentation of the Davidic dynasty, he offers a full analysis of II Samuel according to Dietrich's scheme. The attitude of the primary historian, DtrG, proves to be wholly favorable towards the monarchy, but DtrP qualifies this positive tone in categories drawn from classical prophecy, and DtrN passes a negative judgment on the monarchy based on narrow, legalistic (nomistic) grounds of Yahwistic orthodoxy. Veijola's results are listed in the following table:

| | | |
|---|---|---|
| DtrG | II Sam | 3:9–10,17–19,28–29,38–39; 4:2b–4; 5:1–2,4–5,11,12a, 17a; 6:*21; 7:8b,11b,13,16,18–21,25–29; 8:1a,14b–15; 9:1,*7,*10,11b,13aβ; (14:9); 15:25–26; 16:11–12; 19:22–23,29; 21:2b,7; 24:1,19b,23b,25bα |
| DtrP | II Sam | 12:*7b–10,13–14; 24:3–4a,10–14,15aβ,17,21bβ,25bβ |
| DtrN | II Sam | 5:12b; 7:1b,6,11a,22–24; 22:1,22–25,51. |

### *The Pre-Deuteronomistic Prophetic Edition*

In my opinion Veijola has uncovered the lineaments of the Deuteronomistic redaction of II Samuel fairly clearly, but I would disagree with his analysis in several details. First, in view of the positive attitude towards the Davidic monarchy in II Samuel and, more especially, the confidence expressed in its perpetual continuation, it seems preferable to assign a pre-exilic date to the primary edition of the Deuteronomistic history. The history offers not messianic solace but hope in a reigning son of David. Second, I think Dietrich and Veijola have misdated the prophetic component of the story. The prophetic redaction of Samuel and Kings is, as Dietrich himself observes (1972:134–39), very well integrated into the fabric of the larger story. It is an organic part of the whole, presenting a pattern of prophetic interpretation that does not sit awkwardly atop the Deuteronomistic organization of the whole but seems rather to underlie it. As argued in detail in *I Samuel*, I think this is because much of the material about the monarchy taken up by the Deuteronomistic historian already existed in prophetically edited form. It is widely agreed that the *legal* materials upon which the Deuteronomistic history was based were northern in origin and reserved in their attitude towards kingship. Examination of the stories of Saul and Samuel and of David and Nathan suggests that the *narrative* sources of the history were also influenced by attitudes alien to those of the court in Jerusalem. These stories are surcharged with a prophetic perspective, which does not reject kingship out of hand—as we might expect in an antimonarchical, *exilic* redaction of the sort identified by Dietrich and Veijola in DtrP and DtrN—but which cautiously accepts the monarchy as an unwelcome but inevitable reality. The prophetic viewpoint in Samuel clearly regards kingship as a corrupt institution, but, notably, it does not envision a future without kings. For these reasons I prefer to assign certain portions of II Samuel identified by Veijola as DtrP to a pre-Deuteronomistic stage in the development of the text. In fact, the basic arrangement of chaps. 1–5 and 9–20 seems to be pre-Deuteronomistic, although these chapters are touched at several points by an editor's hand. I agree with Noth that the miscellany in 5:11–8:18 was compiled by the Deuteronomistic historian, but even here he drew upon a variety of very ancient sources, as we shall see. There was certainly an exilic retouching of the Deuteronomistic history, but I am inclined, with Cross (1973:285–89), to think it is limited in scope except in the final chapters of Kings, where an attempt has been made to bring the pre-exilic history up to date and to explain the disaster the first "edition" of the history had not foreseen. In II Samuel there is nothing that must necessarily be assigned to this second edition of the history, though a few short passages, listed below, might be considered. (The Deuteronomistic influence on chap. 22 was, I assume, prior to its insertion in the miscellany in chaps. 21–24 and thus independent of the process that led to the Deuteronomistic history; see p. 475.) The following table illustrates the conclusions reached in the NOTES and COMMENTS about the redactional history of II Samuel (the sigla are those of Cross):

| | | |
|---|---|---|
| prophetic | II Sam | 7:4–9a,15b,20–21; 11:2–12:24; 24:10–14,16a,17–19. |
| Dtr$^{1}$ | II Sam | 2:10a(?),11(?); 3:9–10,17–18a(?),18b,28–29; 5:1–2,4–5(?),12; 6:21; 7:1b,9b–11a,13a,16,22b–24(?), 25–26,29b$\alpha$; 8:14b–15(?); 14:9; 15:*24a$\beta$(?); 21:7(?). |
| Dtr$^{2}$ | II Sam | 7:22b–24(?); 15:*24a$\beta$(?). |

## Narrative Sources

Once the extent of Deuteronomistic editing has been determined and delineated, it is possible to look behind the editorial structure and examine the older narrative sources. To be sure, the instructive study of Carlson (1964) presents the story of David entirely within a Deuteronomistic perspective. Although he assumes the existence of a pre-Deuteronomic David epic, Carlson is generally skeptical about our ability to penetrate the final, edited form of the material and grapple with this epic in its earlier forms. To this extent he is faithful to the Uppsala circle of scholarship to which he belongs (cf. Knight 1973: 327–38), but his approach is quite different from the one followed in this commentary. Therefore, although I shall frequently have recourse to Carlson's many acute observations on the text and to the insights gained from his bifurcation of the traditions into those that present "David under the Blessing" (II Samuel 2–7) and those that present "David under the Curse" (II Samuel 9–24), I cannot attempt to engage his position on the early development of the story directly or in detail. Parallels to known categories of ancient Near Eastern literature suggest themselves often enough to the reader of II Samuel to persuade me that ancient *written* documents lie behind many parts of the book. These documents are identified and discussed in the COMMENTS to follow. A preliminary list of the most important would include the following: (1) the story of David's rise to power (I Sam 16:14–II Sam 5:10); (2) the account of the transfer of the ark to Jerusalem (II Sam 6:1–13,17–19); (3) the account of David's Ammonite war (II Sam 10:1–19 + 8:3–8 + 11:1 + 12:25–31); (4) the story of Abishalom's revolt (II Samuel 13–20); (5) the story of the Gibeonites' revenge and David's patronage of Meribbaal (II Sam 21: 1–14 + 9:1–13); (6) the report of the census plague (II Samuel 24). All of these materials in their original forms, along with various archival battle reports and lists, probably derive from the time of David, as we shall see.

*The Succession Narrative Hypothesis*

Of these materials the dominant composition from a narrative point of view is the story of Abishalom's revolt. Chaps. 13–20 contain a tightly knit account of this revolt and its aftermath. According to the highly influential study of Rost (1926), however, this narrative extends beyond chap. 20 to include I Kings 1–2, where the accession of Solomon is described, and it begins before chap. 13—in chap. 9 and, in fact, even earlier, the original beginning having been interwoven into chaps. 6 and 7. This old narrative (II Sam [6–7]9–20 +

I Kings 1–2) was composed in the time of Solomon by a supporter of the king. His theme was the succession to David's throne. Holding in tension the rejection of the house of Saul (cf. II Sam 6:16,20–23) and the election of the house of David (cf. II Sam 7:11b,16), he set out to answer the question, "Who will sit on the throne of David?" (cf. I Kings 1:20,27). A crucial episode in his account is David's adultery with Bathsheba (II Sam 11:2–4), because this sin is repeated, in turn, by David's elder sons Aminon (II Sam 13:8–14), Abishalom (II Sam 16:22), and Adonijah (I Kings 2:13–17), each thereby proving himself an unworthy heir. At the end Solomon emerges as a suitable heir, restoring the stability jeopardized by the behavior of his rivals, all of whom have now been eliminated.

Rost's hypothesis has been most influential in the form in which it was adopted and interpreted by von Rad (1944). Von Rad praises the succession narrative as an epoch-making historiographical achievement by a writer who succeeds in conveying his message about the throne succession even though his most notable characteristic is "his habitual restraint" (1966:194). Despite "the immense restraint which the writer practices" (p. 195), the succession narrative is neither neutral nor impersonal. It shows clearly if subtly the working out of David's guilt, and it flows over a strong theological undercurrent. This undercurrent is not obtrusive, rising to the surface in only three key passages (II Sam 11:27; 12:24; and 17:14), which nevertheless suffice to convey the writer's perspective. Thus, in contrast with other examples of biblical historiography, a theological interpretation is successfully introduced into the narrative without compromising the remarkable secularity of plot and character that distinguishes the whole. The result, says von Rad (p. 204), is "a wholly new conception of the nature of God's activity in history."

The characterization by von Rad and others of the succession narrative as "history writing" has been much discussed. Whybray, for example, while adopting the Rost/von Rad analysis in basic outline, argues that "the Succession Narrative, although its theme is a historical one and makes use of historical facts, is not a work of history either in intention or in fact" (1968:19). Stressing the high literary quality of the composition, Whybray calls it a "novel" (p. 47) and, following Rost, also points to its function as political propaganda supportive of Solomon's claim to the throne. Whybray's chief interest, however, is in the influence of wisdom literature on the succession narrative, and after noting a series of points of contact with Proverbs he concludes (p. 95) that "there is a sufficiently close resemblance between Proverbs and the incidents and situations of the Succession Narrative to show that the author of the latter was not merely a man who shared the general outlook of the wisdom teachers, but was himself a wisdom teacher in the sense that he set out deliberately to illustrate specific proverbial teaching for the benefit of the pupils and ex-pupils of the schools." Here, however, Whybray seems to have gone too far. Apart from generalized thematic parallels, there is nothing in the succession narrative of a stylistic or ideological nature to link it peculiarly to wisdom (cf. Crenshaw 1969:137–40). The points of contact with Proverbs noted by Whybray are most useful in defining the cultural and intellectual horizons of the author, and in this respect we should note the more modest claims of Hermisson (1971), who speaks of wisdom as one factor, among others, that comes into play in the conception of history found in the succession narrative.

On the other hand, Whybray's analysis of the succession narrative as political propaganda—though it, too, has been criticized (Gunn 1978:21–26)—aligns him with a number of other scholars (Rost, Vriezen, Thornton, etc.). Pointing to I Kings 1:37, Whybray notes the possibility that "the story of the succession to the throne has been told in order to justify Solomon's claim to be the true king of Israel, and to strengthen the régime against its critics" (1968:51–52). The occasion for committing the story to writing was surely a time of crisis or danger, when the stability of Solomon's throne was threatened, and this time was very probably the early years of his reign (cf. Vriezen 1948). Thus Whybray concludes (p. 55) that the succession narrative "is primarily a political document intended to support the régime by demonstrating its legitimacy and justifying its policies."

The propagandistic character of the succession narrative is brought into clearest focus by Thornton (1968). Again the point of departure is Rost's analysis, but Thornton shows (p. 160) that the question the narrative seeks to answer is not "Who will succeed David on the throne?" (Rost) but "Why was it Solomon who succeeded David on the throne?" Thornton confirms the conclusion of Vriezen and Whybray that it was the peculiar circumstances of the accession of Solomon that necessitated the composition of an apologetic account of the throne succession. Solomon was one of the younger sons, and Adonijah was the heir apparent. Shortly after David's death, however, Solomon was on the throne, Adonijah was dead, and his chief supporters had been executed (Joab) or exiled (Abiathar). "An unexpected candidate had succeeded to the throne," says Thornton (1968:161), "and his reign had started with a minor bloodbath. What justification could there be for all this?"

*The Solomonic Apology*

In my opinion (cf. McCarter 1981) Rost, Whybray, Thornton, and others have successfully shown that the succession narrative is best characterized as a work of court apologetic. It does not follow from this, however, that they are correct in thinking of it as the original and unified composition of a Solomonic writer. Interpreters before Rost—especially Caspari and Gressmann—viewed the materials in chaps. 9ff. as a series of independent compositions *(Novellen)* joined together by a common temporal nexus. Recent interpreters such as Blenkinsopp (1966) and especially Flanagan (1972) have sought to distinguish the themes of "the legitimisation of David's own claim, and the struggle for the succession to his throne" (Blenkinsopp 1966:47), thus implying the existence of Davidic materials underlying the Solomonic succession narrative. Flanagan follows Rost in seeing a "Succession Document" in the present form of II Samuel 9–20 + I Kings 1–2, but he distinguishes from this an underlying "Court History." The purpose of the older composition was "to show how David maintained legitimate control over the kingdoms of Judah and Israel" (Flanagan 1972:181). It was incorporated into the Solomonic "Succession Document" by the addition of II Sam 11:2–12:25 and I Kings 1–2, the only portions of Rost's succession narrative in which Solomon has a part.

The identification by Vriezen, Whybray, and Thornton of the time of the accession of Solomon as the occasion for the composition of the succession narrative, together with the arguments of Flanagan for distinguishing Davidic and Solomonic issues, focuses attention squarely on I Kings 1–2. Solomon is the central figure in these two chapters, a situation that contrasts sharply with that of II Samuel 9–20, where the central figure is David and Solomon appears only in 12:24–25 as a newborn baby. What, then, is the relationship of I Kings 1–2 to the Samuel materials? The purpose of I Kings 1–2 is quite clearly to defend the legitimacy of Solomon's accession. Adonijah was the eldest surviving son of David (I Kings 1:6) and the heir apparent. He had the support of Joab, commander of David's army, and the priest Abiathar (1:7). Solomon, a younger son of David, was supported by Benaiah and the priest Zadok, among others (1:8). At David's death there was a struggle within the palace, and from it Solomon, not Adonijah, emerged as king. Adonijah was executed at Solomon's command (2:25), as was Joab (2:34), and Abiathar was exiled (2:27). Benaiah took Joab's place, and Zadok took Abiathar's (2:35). This much was public knowledge—it could not be and was not denied by the narrator of I Kings 1–2—and it cast grave suspicion on Solomon. The apologetic account we have, however, is designed to exonerate Solomon. It shows that, despite Adonijah's seniority, Solomon had a right to the throne because he was David's personal choice (1:30). It also shows that Adonijah was given a chance to save his life (1:52) but forfeited it. The account, moreover, shows—and here we come to the point—that the executions of Adonijah and Joab were warranted by the events of David's reign. In Joab's case the argument is simple: He had murdered David's two commanding officers, Abiner (II Sam 3:27) and Amasa (II Sam 20:10), thus involving David in bloodguilt (cf. I Kings 2:5). David, moreover, had instructed Solomon to punish Joab (I Kings 2:5–6). He could not be permitted to live. In Adonijah's case, the argument is indirect and guilt is imputed by association (cf. McCarter 1981:364–65). The description of Adonijah in I Kings 1:5–6 very pointedly associates him with David's other miscreant sons, Aminon and especially Abishalom. Like Abishalom (II Sam 14:25) he was very handsome. Like Abishalom (II Sam 15:1) he procured a chariot with horses and fifty runners. Like Abishalom (II Sam 15:10) he declared himself king. Against this background his request for Abishag, David's concubine (I Kings 2:17), inevitably reminds us of Abishalom's usurpation of David's harem (II Sam 16:22), thus justifying Solomon's interpretation of the request as treason (I Kings 2:22). It is clear, then, that although the accession of Solomon lies entirely outside the horizon of the Samuel materials, which are concerned with issues of David's reign, the author of the Solomonic apology composed his argument *with reference to* the earlier stories. He took up these stories and combined them with his own composition (I Kings 1–2).

*Sources from the Reign of David*

This suggests that the various narratives of II Samuel must be viewed not only as parts of the Solomonic succession document but also as discrete compositions pertinent to issues in the time of David. I have attempted a classification of these Davidic materials elsewhere (McCarter 1981:361–64), and each composition is considered in detail in the COMMENTS of the present volume. Thus, it will suffice here to identify these materials briefly:

1) the story of David's rise to power: I Sam 16:14–II Sam 5:10. See the discussion in McCarter 1980b and *I Samuel*, pp. 27–30. Events of David's own accession are alluded to in I Kings 2:5. For the view that II Sam 2:8–4:12 should be separated from the story of David's rise and grouped instead with subsequent materials in II Samuel, see Segal (1964–65:323–24), Schulte (1972: 138–44), Gunn (1978:66–68), VanderKam (1980:522), and Van Seters (1981: 159–64).

2) the story of Abishalom's revolt: II Samuel 13–20. The self-contained character of this unit has been discussed by Conroy (1978:97–105). The account shows the private issues that precipitated the public events of the revolt. The narrator's purpose is to elicit sympathy for David in the aftermath of the crisis, especially among those who had followed Abishalom. David, we are shown, was not the sort of man who would have his son put to death to further his own purposes. On the contrary, David was, if anything, too lenient and loving as a father, and Abishalom was executed against David's explicit orders.

3) the story of the Gibeonites' revenge and David's patronage of Meribbaal: II Sam 21:1–14 + 9:1–13. David's execution of the Saulides is shown not to have been motivated by a desire to consolidate his kingdom against the claims of the house of Saul, as it must have seemed to the public. The execution was necessary if the famine was to be ended. Indeed, David is presented as the benefactor of the Saulides, having arranged for their honorable burial and having welcomed the lone survivor into the palace.

*For or Against Solomon?*

Thus, the position taken in this commentary is that the Solomon succession narrative properly includes only I Kings 1–2, a *pro*-Solomonic account of his accession composed with specific reference to at least three compositions from the time of David, all of which were *pro-*Davidic accounts of important events of David's reign. An important series of recent studies by European scholars, however, suggests that the succession narrative, broadly conceived, was originally *anti-*Solomonic and *anti-*Davidic in character. The seminal study in this regard was that of Delekat (1967). In view of David's reprehensible behavior in II Samuel 10–12 and the bloodbath for which Solomon is responsible in I Kings 1–2, Delekat concluded that the slant of the succession narrative is hostile to David and Solomon. It was composed during the reign of Solomon by a writer who was opposed to Solomon's kingship and promulgated in circles unfriendly to the crown. This view has been adopted with various modifications by Würthwein, Veijola, and Langlamet, all of whom speak of an original anti-Davidic/anti-Solomonic composition that underwent an extensive pro-Davidic/pro-Solomonic redaction. Thus according to Würthwein (1974:49–59) the primitive succession narrative was not theological historiography of the sort envisioned by von Rad but rather political propaganda hostile to the excesses of David and Solomon. It was composed by contemporaries of Solomon, adversaries of absolute monarchy, which was presented as incompatible with traditional ethical values. This hostile narrative, however, has undergone a redaction described by Würthwein (1974:11–18) as apologetic. Secondarily inserted passages permit a favorable reading of the story. The behavior of David and Solomon is excused, often at the expense of another figure in the story (Ahithophel, Joab). Expansions in chaps. 10–20 (Würthwein does not regard chap. 9 as part of the succession narrative [1974:58 n. 97]) include 11:27b–12:15a; 12:24bβ; 14:2–22; 15:24–26,29,31; 16:5–13,21–23; 17:5–14,15b,23; 18:2b–4a,10–14; 20:8–13.

Veijola (1975) also concludes that the succession narrative, originally hostile to Solomon, received a pro-Davidic/pro-Solomonic redaction. In contrast to Würthwein, however, Veijola characterizes this redaction as Deuteronomistic. The details of his analysis are given above.

Langlamet, in a series of studies (1976a, 1976b, 1977, 1978, 1979–81, 1981), has endorsed Würthwein's hypothesis of a primitive, anti-Solomonic succession narrative. He sees this document ($S_2$), however, as a redaction of earlier literature from late in the reign of David ($S_1$), including a basic "Absalom history." Like Würthwein and Veijola, he believes that the Solomonic succession narrative ($S_2$) received a later redaction favorable to David and Solomon. This final redaction ($S_3$) was not Deuteronomistic, as Veijola supposes. Langlamet describes it as "theological-sapiential" and believes it to predate the Deuteronomistic history. Specific results of Langlamet's research are listed in the NOTES and COMMENTS to this commentary.

The studies of Würthwein, Veijola, Langlamet, and others (e.g., Bickert 1979) raise a fundamental issue of interpretation. They begin with a shared observation, viz. that the stories about David and Solomon found in the succession narrative present both kings as perpetrators of serious crimes. At the same time, however, the crimes are excused or glossed over by certain details of the text as it has come down to us. The hypothesis that this suggests to these scholars is that the favorable details are secondary, elements of a redactional project designed to exonerate David and Solomon. When this redactional veneer is identified and removed, therefore, the earlier, unfavorable narrative is visible.

A critique of this position must begin with two acknowledgments. First, there is no doubt that the tension these scholars have observed in the text is real. As we shall see, David is often weak and indecisive and his behavior is occasionally seriously harmful, yet there are usually details of the narrative that tend to excuse him. Second, the literary analysis upon which the redactional hypothesis rests does not rely on presumed thematic tensions alone. It draws on the customary criteria of literary and redactional criticism expertly applied. It follows that an alternative hypothesis must first explain the tension in the narrative in some other way and then address the specific critical decisions defended by the proponents of the redactional hypothesis. Both of these tasks are undertaken in the NOTES and COMMENTS. It may be helpful, however, to offer some preliminary observations on the narrative tension in the succession narrative.

The position taken in this commentary is, as noted above, that the story of Abishalom's revolt was favorable to David in its original formulation. The materials isolated by Würthwein and Langlamet as redactional belong, for the most part, to the original narrative. The narrative tension is an original element of the story. It arises from the apologetic character of the primitive account. As I have noted elsewhere (1980a:495–99; 1981:357–58; cf. *I Samuel*, pp. 29–30), royal apology, a category to which Hoffner (1975) has called attention in Hittite literature, seems to have been an important component of the literature of the Davidic court. David—because he was a Judahite and not an Israelite, because of his past career as an outlaw and a Philistine mercenary, and because of the suspicious circumstances in which he assumed the throne of Israel—found his position as king of Israel to be constantly in need of defense and justification, as the events of the Shimei incident (16:5–13) and Sheba's revolt (chap. 20) might independently suggest. The surviving literature from the time of David reflects this defensive posture. It is the nature of apologetic literature to maintain a narrative tension between apparently unfavorable or suspicious circumstances, on the one hand, and the favorable interpretation the writer wants to offer, on the other. David's behavior in the story of Abishalom's revolt is not impeccable. But this is not because the narrator was hostile to him; it is because the things he did were publicly known and could not be baldly denied. The narrative details that cast a favorable light on David's behavior are not secondary. On the contrary, they are the essential stuff of the original story, the apologetic explanation for what David did. As

I have explained elsewhere (1981:360 n. 12), "Apologetic writing presents unfavorable circumstances forthrightly in order to cast a favorable light on them by a variety of literary means. By its very nature, then, it holds conflicting ideas in literary tension. The elimination of the literary blandishments of the author by appeal to higher critical or other considerations, therefore, will inevitably produce a recital of unfavorable circumstances, but it will also distort the writer's intended product beyond recovery. It is a mistake to rely heavily on the criterion of narrative tension for identifying redactional material in these stories, when such tension is the very essence of the writer's technique."

*Literary Considerations*

We ought, finally, to take note of a growing number of scholars who are investigating the narratives of II Samuel from a more strictly literary point of view. The high literary qualities of the stories in this book have been remarked by virtually all interpreters. Studies like those of Jackson (1965) and Long (1981) attempt to take these qualities into account in the interpretation of the story. The monograph of Conroy (1978) has done this with excellent results in the case of the story of Abishalom's revolt, and Gunn's study of the larger story of David (1978) succeeds in gaining for the succession narrative, in his words (p. 9), "a fuller appreciation of its nature as a *story.*" The insights of Conroy, Gunn, and others are drawn on frequently in the NOTES and COMMENTS of this volume.

## THE END OF THE BOOK

In the received Hebrew text II Samuel ends with a conglomeration of material (20:23–24:25) that is not in sequence with the narrative that precedes or follows it. Some portions of this material may have received Deuteronomistic editing (22:1,21–25,51c), and others (21:1–14) seem to have been originally connected to passages in the succession narrative. As a whole, however, 20:23–24:25 is neither part of the Deuteronomistic history nor related to the earlier literature it embraced. It is a miscellany, a repository of diverse materials pertinent to the reign of David. We must, therefore, ask two questions about this miscellany. First, why was it placed here after the story of Sheba's rebellion? Second, what, if any, is the logic to its arrangement?

*The Position of the Miscellany*

According to Noth (1981:124–25 n. 3), "2 Sam. 21–24 is full of additions, which gradually accumulated *after* Dtr.'s history had been divided into separate books." Thus, we might conclude that the miscellany was put where it is as an appendix, at what was perceived to be the end of the book. Standing in the way of this conclusion is the fact that the witnesses to the text of Samuel and Kings preserve *two* traditions about the division between II Samuel and I Kings. According to the received Hebrew text (MT) and a majority of the versions, I Kings begins after II Samuel 21–24. According to the so-called "Lucianic" manuscripts of the Septuagint ($LXX^L$), however, III Reigns (= I Kings) begins with the verse designated I Kings 2:12 in MT, and Josephus begins book 8 of the *Antiquities* at the same point. By this arrangement II Samuel ends with David's death, just as I Kings ends with Ahab's, I Samuel with Saul's, Joshua with Joshua's, Deuteronomy with Moses', and Genesis with Jacob's and Joseph's. The criterion of consistency with other books, therefore, might be urged in favor of the conclusion that the $LXX^L$ division —between I Kings 2:11 and 2:12—is the "correct" one, as Thackeray supposed (1907:264–66; contrast Rahlfs 1904–11:vol. III:186–88). On the other hand, we must keep in mind that all divisions between books in the Deuteronomistic history belong to a late stage in the growth of the literature, and although the divisions may correspond in some cases to the separation of major epochs as understood by the historian, they have no *necessary* correlation to his original scheme. The scribes were obliged to find appropriate places to divide the literature into portions that could be accommodated on individual scrolls, and it was finally for this reason that Samuel-Kings was separated into four books of almost equal length (in *BHS*, assuming the division at I Kings 2:11–12, approximately 59, 58, 56, and 56 pages).

Returning to the original question, however, we do learn from the existence of two traditions about the end of the book that the present position of the miscellany in 20:23–24:25 is not to be explained on the assumption that it accumulated at the end of a book. The two traditions agree on the position of the miscellany, which must therefore have been determined *before* the division of the material into books (*pace* Noth). Nevertheless, the $LXX^L$ tradition provides a clue inasmuch as it calls our attention to passages recording the deaths of other major figures in the history. Comparison with the miscellany in Deuteronomy 31–33 reveals the true state of affairs. There, as Noth himself has explained (1981:35), miscellaneous materials accumulated at a point immediately before the account of the hero's death. Thus the two poems in Deuteronomy 32 (with the introduction in 31:16–22 + 30) and 33, both attributed to Moses, were inserted before the account of Moses' death in Deuteronomy 34. The position of Gen 49:1–27, a poem attributed to Jacob and inserted before the account of Jacob's death, provides another example. This suggests that the miscellany in II Sam 20:23–24:25 was inserted before the account of David's death in I Kings 1:1–2:11 at some time before the division of the history into books. To the objection that, in this case, it might have been placed immediately before I Kings 2:1–11 we can only reply that David's death is already in view in I Kings 1:1 and, moreover, that the editor(s) responsible for the insertion may have wanted to avoid breaking the narrative continuity of I Kings 1–2.

*The Arrangement of the Miscellany*

There is a curious pattern to the arrangement of II Samuel 21–24, illustrated by the following diagram:

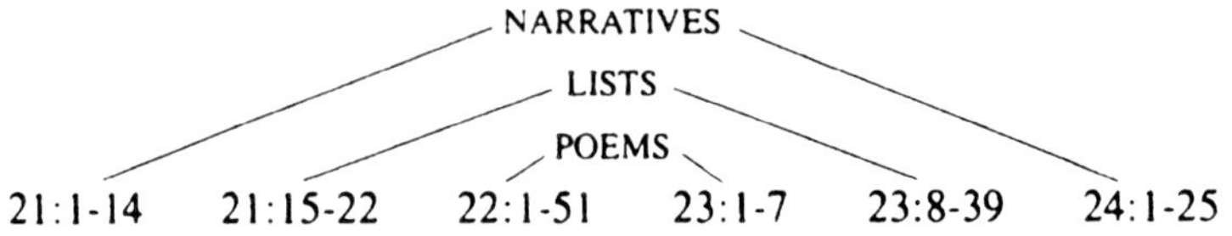


At the center of the miscellany are two poems attributed to David. On either side of these are lists of heroes and their deeds. The two endpieces are narratives about public disasters. The usual explanation of this strangely symmetrical arrangement is that given by, among others, Budde (cf. Noth 1981:124–25 n. 3). Noting the connection to 21:1–14 implied in 24:1, he concluded that the two narratives were placed here first. The continuity of these was then broken by the insertion of the hero list, 21:15–22 + 23:8–39. Finally, the hero list was split by the insertion of the poems.

This explanation seems generally correct, though it needs certain modifications. As pointed out in the COMMENTS on §§ XIX and XXXV, 21:1–14 was probably moved to the end of the story of Abishalom's revolt from an original position before 9:1–13 by a Deuteronomistic editor who wanted to relate David's question in 9:1 directly to I Sam 20.11–17. The duplication of 8:15–18 and 20:23–26 arose as a result of this relocation (cf. the COMMENT on § XXXIV). Thus 20:23–21:14 probably reached its present position before the rest of the miscellany began to accumulate. The story of the census plague (chap. 24) was inserted next. As explained in the NOTE on "again" in 24:1, the assumption that 24:1–25 was originally connected somehow to 21:1–14 is not warranted; but when the account of the census plague was added after the story of the Gibeonites' revenge, the language of 24:1 was revised slightly to relate the story to its new context. Because it accounts for the erection of the altar traditionally believed to be the holocaust altar of Solomon's temple, the story of the census plague was given a position at the end of the David materials, immediately before the account of his death and thus as close as possible to the report of the building of the temple, to which it was believed to look forward. For this reason, too, the census plague story was left at the end of the miscellany as other materials accumulated (Hertzberg). As Budde supposes, 21:15–22 and 23:8–39 (perhaps already with its own addition in vv. 13–17a) may have been introduced next. We should note, however, that there is no *literary* connection between these two units: 23:8–39 has its own clear beginning. They may have been derived from a common archival source, where the deeds of heroes were recorded, and inserted here together. If so, however, it is difficult to guess why they were separated again when the poems were inserted, unless it was because David is rescued in 21:17, and 21:15–22 therefore was seen as a fitting prologue to the psalm of deliverance in chap. 22. Otherwise we must assume that the four units in 21:15–23:39 accumulated in random fashion after all. In any case, the two poems in 22:1–51 and 23.1–7, both of which were traditionally attributed to David, were added so that David, like Moses, might end his life with a hymn of vindication (cf. Deut 32:1–43) and a testimony (cf. Deuteronomy 33).

# BIBLIOGRAPHY


Abramsky, S. 1980 The Woman Who Looked Out the Window [Hebrew]. *Beth Mikra* 25:114–24.

Ackroyd, P. R. 1977 *The Second Book of Samuel.* Cambridge Bible Commentary. London: Cambridge. Cited as Ackroyd.

1981 The Succession Narrative (so-called). *Interpretation* 35:383–96.

Aharoni, Y. 1959 The Province-List of Judah. *Vetus Testamentum* 9:225–46.

1967 Beth-haccherem. Pp. 171–84 in Winton Thomas 1967.

1981 *Arad Inscriptions.* Trans. J. Ben-Or from Hebrew 1975. Judean Desert Studies. Jerusalem: Israel Exploration Society.

Ahlström, G. W. 1959 *Psalm 89: Eine Liturgie aus dem Rituel des leidenden Königs.* Lund: Gleerups.

1960 Profeten Natan och tempelbygget. *Svensk Exegetisk Årsbok* 25:5–22.

1961 Der Prophet Nathan und der Tempelbau. *Vetus Testamentum* 11:113–27.

1978 *krkr* and *ṭpd*. *Vetus Testamentum* 28:100–2.

Albright, W. F. 1922 The *Sinnôr* in the Story of David's Capture of Jerusalem. *Journal of the Palestine Oriental Society* 2.286–90.

1925 The Administrative Divisions of Israel and Judah. *Journal of the Palestine Oriental Society* 5:20–25.

1927–28 The Name of Bildad the Shuhite. *American Journal of Semitic Languages* 44:31–36.

1930–31 Mitannian *maryannu* "Chariot-Warrior" and the Canaanite and Egyptian Equivalents. *Archiv für Orientforschung* 6:217–21.

1932a "The Seal of Eliakim and the Latest Pre-exilic History of Judah" with Some Observations on Ezekiel. *Journal of Biblical Literature* 51:77–106.

1932b Recent Works on the Topography and Archaeology of Jerusalem. *Jewish Quarterly Review* 22:409–16.

1934 *The Vocalization of the Egyptian Syllabic Orthography.* American Oriental Series 5. New Haven: American Oriental Society.

1938 What Were the Cherubim? *Biblical Archaeologist* 1:1–3 = Wright and Freedman 1961:95–97.

1943 Two Little Understood Amarna Letters from the Middle Jordan Valley. *Bulletin of the American Schools of Oriental Research* 89:7–17.

1944 The Oracles of Balaam. *Journal of Biblical Literature* 63:207–33.

1957 The High Place in Ancient Palestine. Pp. 242–58 in *Volume du Congrès. Strasbourg 1956.* Supplements to Vetus Testamentum 4. Leiden: Brill.

1961 *Samuel and the Beginnings of the Prophetic Movement.* Cincinnati: Hebrew Union College.

1966 Syria, the Philistines, and Phoenicia = *CAH* II/2, chap. 36, pp. 507–36.

1969a *Archaeology and the Religion of Israel.* 5th ed. Anchor Books. Garden City, N.Y.: Doubleday.

1969b *Yahweh and the Gods of Canaan.* Anchor Books. Garden City, N.Y.: Doubleday.

Allegro, J. M. 1956 Further Messianic References in Qumran Literature. *Journal of Biblical Literature* 75:174–87.

1958 Fragments of a Qumran Scroll of Eschatological *Midrāšîm. Journal of Biblical Literature* 77:350–54.

Alonso Schökel, L. 1973 *Samuel.* Los Libros Sagrados III, 3. Madrid: Ediciones Cristiandad.

1976 David y la mujer de Tecua: 2 Sm 14 como modelo hermenéutico. *Biblica* 57:192–205.

Alt, A. 1936 Zu II Samuel 8,1. *Zeitschrift für die alttestamentliche Wissenschaft* 13[54]:149–52.

1953 *Kleine Schriften zur Geschichte des Volkes Israel.* 2 vols. München: Beck.

1968 *Essays on Old Testament History and Religion.* Trans. R. A. Wilson Anchor Books. Garden City, N Y.: Doubleday.

Altschüller, M. A. 1886 Einige textkritische Bemerkungen zum Alten Testament. *Zeitschrift für die alttestamentliche Wissenschaft* 6:211–13.

Anbar [Bernstein], M. 1979 Un euphémisme "biblique" dans une lettre de Mari. *Orientalia* 48:109–11.

Andersen, F. I., and D. N. Freedman 1980 *Hosea. A New Translation with Introduction and Commentary.* Anchor Bible 24. Garden City, N.Y.: Doubleday.

Ap-Thomas, D. R. 1943 A Numerical Poser. *Journal of Near Eastern Studies* 2: 198–200.

al-'Ārif, 'Ārif 1974 *Bedouin Love, Law, and Legend.* Trans. H. W. Tilley from Arabic 1933. Jerusalem: Cosmos. Reprint of 1944 ed.

Armerding, C. E. 1975 Were David's Sons Really Priests? Pp. 75–86 in *Current Issues in Biblical and Patristic Interpretation. Studies in Honor of Merrill C. Tenney . . . ,* ed. G F Hawthorne. Grand Rapids, Mich.: Eerdmans.

Arnold, W. R 1911–12 The Meaning of *btrwn. American Journal of Semitic Languages* 28:274–83.

1917 *Ephod and Ark: A Study in the Records and Religion of the Ancient Hebrews.* Harvard Theological Studies 3. Cambridge, Mass.: Harvard.

Arpali, B. 1968–69 Caution, a Biblical Story! Comments on the Story of David and Bathsheba and on the Problems of the Biblical Narrative [Hebrew]. *Hasifrut* 1:580–97.

Avigad, N. 1966 Two Phoenician Votive Seals. *Israel Exploration Journal* 16. 243–51.

1976 New Light on the Na'ar Seals Pp. 294–300 in Cross, Lemke, and Miller 1976

1980 The Chief of the Corvée. *Israel Exploration Journal* 30:170–73.

Avishur, Y 1976 *Krkr* in Biblical Hebrew and Ugaritic. *Vetus Testamentum* 26: 257–61

Baker, D. W. 1980 Further Examples of the *wāw explicativum. Vetus Testamentum* 30:129–36.

Ball, E. 1977 The Co-regency of David and Solomon (1 Kings i). *Vetus Testamentum* 27:268–79.

Baltzer, K. 1971 *The Covenant Formulary in Old Testament, Jewish, and Early Christian Writings.* Trans. D. A. Green from German 1964. Philadelphia: Fortress.

Bardtke, H. 1969 Psalmi = *BHS,* pp. 1087–1226.

1973 Erwägungen zur Rolle Judas im Aufstand des Absalom. Pp. 1–8 in *Wort und Geschichte. Festschrift für Karl Elliger . . . ,* ed. H. Gese and H. P. Rüger. Alter Orient und Altes Testament. Kevelaer: Butzon und Bercker.

Barnes, W. E. 1914 David's "Capture" and the Jebusite "Citadel" of Zion (2 Sam. v. 6–9). *The Expositor* (Series 8) 7:29–39.

Barthélemy, D. 1953 Redécouverte d'un chaînon manquant de l'histoire de la Septante. *Revue biblique* 60:18–29 = Cross and Talmon 1975:127–39.

1963 *Les Devanciers d'Aquila.* Supplements to Vetus Testamentum 10. Leiden: Brill.

1972 A Reexamination of the Textual Problems in 2 Sam 11:2–1 Kings 2:11 in the Light of Certain Criticisms of *Les Devanciers d'Aquila.* Pp. 16–89 in *1972 Proceedings: IOSCS and Pseudepigrapha,* ed. R. A. Kraft. Missoula, Mont.: Scholars.

1980 La Qualité du Texte Massorétique de Samuel. Pp. 1–44 in Tov 1980.

Bartlett, J. R. 1970 Sihon and Og, Kings of the Amorites. *Vetus Testamentum* 20:257–77.

Batten, L. W. 1906 Helkath Hazzurim. *Zeitschrift für die alttestamentliche Wissenschaft* 26:90.

Baumann, E. 1945–48 Struktur-Untersuchungen im Psalter I. *Zeitschrift für die alttestamentliche Wissenschaft* 61:114–76.

Begrich, J. 1940–41 Sôfēr and Mazkîr. *Zeitschrift für die alttestamentliche Wissenschaft* 58:1–29.

Ben-Barak, Z. 1979 The Legal Background to the Restoration of Michal to David. Pp. 15–29 in Emerton 1979.

1981 Meribaal and the System of Land Grants in Ancient Israel. *Biblica* 62:73–91.

Bennett, W. H. 1937 I and II. Samuel. Pp. 273–93 in *A Commentary on the Bible,* ed. A. S. Peake. New ed. London: Nelson.

Benz, F. L. 1972 *Personal Names in the Phoenician and Punic Inscriptions.* Studia Pohl 8. Rome: Biblical Institute.

Bernhardt, K.-H. 1961 *Das Problem der altorientalischen Königsideologie im Alten Testament.* Supplements to Vetus Testamentum 8. Leiden: Brill.

Bernstein, M. *See* Anbar, M.

Bewer, J. A. 1942 Notes on 1 Sam 13 21; 2 Sam 23 1; Psalm 48 8. *Journal of Biblical Literature* 61:45–48.

Bickert, R. 1979 Die List Joabs und der Sinneswandel Davids. Pp. 30–51 in Emerton 1979.

Blenkinsopp, J. 1966 Theme and Motif in the Succession History (2 Sam. xi 2ff.) and the Yahwist Corpus. Pp. 44–57 in *Volume du Congrès. Genève 1965.* Supplements to Vetus Testamentum 15. Leiden: Brill.

1969a Kiriath-jearim and the Ark. *Journal of Biblical Literature* 88:143–56.

1969b 1 and 2 Samuel. Pp. 305–27 in *A New Catholic Commentary on Holy Scripture,* ed. R. C. Fuller, L. Johnston, and C. Kearns. London: Nelson.

1972 *Gibeon and Israel. The Role of Gibeon and the Gibeonites in the Political and Religious History of Early Israel.* Society for Old Testament Studies, Monograph Series 2. Cambridge, Eng.: Cambridge.

Boccali, G. M. 1975 *I libri di Samuele.* 2d ed. Nuovissima versione della Bibbia dai testi originali 8. Rome: Edizioni Paoline.

Boecker, H. J. 1961 Erwägungen zum Amt des Mazkir. *Theologische Zeitschrift* 17.212–16.

1969 *Die Beurteilung der Anfänge des Königtums in den deuteronomistischen Abschnitten des I. Samuelbuches.* Wissenschaftliche Monographien zum Alten und Neuen Testament. Neukirchen-Vluyn: Neukirchener Verlag des Erziehungs-vereins.

de Boer, P. A. H. 1955 "Vive le roi!" *Vetus Testamentum* 5:225–31.

1957 Texte et traduction des paroles attribuées à David en 2 S xxiii 1–7. Pp. 47–56 in *Volume du Congrès. Strasbourg 1956.* Supplements to Vetus Testamentum 4. Leiden: Brill.

1962 *Gedenken und Gedächtnis in der Welt des Alten Testaments.* [Franz Delitzsch Lectures 1960] Stuttgart: Kohlhammer.

1966 2 Sam 12,25. Pp. 25–29 in *Studia Biblica et Semitica. Theodoro Christiano Vriezen. . . .* Wageningen: Veenman.

1974 The Perfect with *waw* in 2 Samuel 6:16. Pp. 43–52 in *On Language, Culture, and Religion: In Honor of Eugene A. Nida,* ed. M. Black and W. A. Smalley. The Hague: Mouton.

1976 Samuel I II = *BHS,* pp. 443–56.

Boling, R G. 1975 *Judges. A New Translation with Introduction and Commentary.* Anchor Bible 6A. Garden City, N.Y.: Doubleday.

Borger, R. 1956 *Die Inschriften Asarhaddons, Königs von Assyrien.* Archiv für Orientforschung, Beiheft 9. Graz: Wediener.

1969 Weitere ugaritologische Kleinigkeiten. *Ugarit-Forschungen* 1.1–4.

1972 Die Waffenträger des Königs Darius. Ein Beitrag zur alttestamentlichen Exegese und zur semitischen Lexikographie. *Vetus Testamentum* 22:385–98.

van den Born, A. 1954 Étude sur quelques toponymes bibliques. *Oudtestamentische Studiën* 10:197–214.

1956 *Samuel.* De Boeker van het Oude Testament IV/1. Roermond en Maaseik. Cited as van den Born.

Böttcher, J. F. 1863 *Neue exegetische-kritische Ährenlese zum Alten Testament.* Vol. 1. Leipzig: Barth.

Bressan, G. 1944 L'espugnazione di Sion in 2 Sam 5,6–8 || 1 Chron 11,4–6 e il problema del *ṣinnôr. Biblica* 25:346–81.

1954 *Samuele.* Bibbia di Garofalo. Turin: Marietti. Cited as Bressan.

*See also* Fernandez, A.

Briggs, C. A. 1906 *A Critical and Exegetical Commentary on the Book of Psalms.* 3 vols. The International Critical Commentary. New York: Charles Scribner's Sons.

Bright, J. 1972 *A History of Israel.* 2d ed. Philadelphia: Westminster.

1976 The Organization and Administration of the Israelite Empire. Pp. 193–208 in Cross, Lemke, and Miller 1976.

Brinker, R. 1946 *The Influence of Sanctuaries in Early Israel.* Publications of the University of Manchester 298. Manchester: Manchester.

Brock, S. P. 1973 An Unrecognized Occurrence of the Month Name Ziv (2 Sam. xxi 9). *Vetus Testamentum* 23:100–103.

Brockington, L. H. 1962 I and II Samuel. Pp. 318–37 in *Peake's Commentary on the Bible,* rev. ed., ed. M. Black and H. H. Rowley. New York: Nelson. Cited as Brockington.

Brown, R. E. 1966 *The Gospel According to John (I–XII). Introduction, Translation, and Notes.* Anchor Bible 29. Garden City, N.Y.: Doubleday.

1977 *The Birth of the Messiah. A Commentary on the Infancy Narratives in Matthew and Luke.* Garden City, N.Y.: Doubleday.

Brueggemann, W. 1968 David and His Theologian. *Catholic Biblical Quarterly* 30:156–81.

1969 The Trusted Creature. *Catholic Biblical Quarterly* 31:484–98.

1971 Kingship and Chaos (A Study in Tenth Century Theology). *Catholic Biblical Quarterly* 33:317–32.

1972a Life and Death in Tenth Century Israel. *Journal of the American Academy of Religion* 40:96–109.

1972b On Trust and Freedom. A Study of Faith in the Succession Narrative. *Interpretation* 26:3–19.

1974 On Coping with Curse: A Study of 2 Sam 16:5–14. *Catholic Biblical Quarterly* 36:175–92.

Brunet, G. 1979a Les Aveugles et boiteux jébusites. Pp. 65–72 in Emerton 1979.

1979b David et le *ṣinnôr.* Pp. 73–86 in Emerton 1979.

Brunner, H. 1958 Gerechtigkeit als Fundament des Thrones. *Vetus Testamentum* 8:426–28.

Bruno, A. 1923 *Gibeon.* Leipzig: Deichert.

Buccellati, G. 1959 Da Saul a Davide. *Bibbia e Oriente* 1:99–128.

Budde, K. 1902 *Die Bücher Samuel erklärt.* Kurzer Hand-Commentar zum Alten Testament 8. Tübingen and Leipzig: Mohr. Cited as Budde.

1934 Die Herkunft Ṣadoks. *Zeitschrift für die alttestamentliche Wissenschaft* 52: 43–50.

van den Bussche, H. 1948 Le texte de la prophétie de Nathan sur la dynastie davidique. *Ephemerides Theologicae Lovanienses* 24:354–94.

Caird, G. B. 1953 The First and Second Books of Samuel. Pp. 853–1176 in *The Interpreter's Bible.* Vol. II. New York and Nashville: Abingdon. Cited as Caird.

Calderone, P. J. 1966 *Dynastic Oracle and Suzerainty Treaty. 2 Samuel 7,8–16.* Logos 1 (Ateneo University Publications). Manila: Loyola House of Studies.

1967 Oraculum dynasticum et foedus regale, 2 Sam 7. *Verbum Domini* 45:91–96.

Campbell, A. F. 1975 *The Ark Narrative (1 Sam 4–6; 2 Sam 6). A Form-critical and Traditio-historical Study.* Society of Biblical Literature, Dissertation Series 16. Missoula, Mont.: Scholars.

Campbell, E. F., Jr., and D. N. Freedman, eds. 1970 *The Biblical Archaeologist Reader 3.* Anchor Books. Garden City, N.Y.: Doubleday.

Caquot, A. 1963 La Prophétie de Nathan et ses échos lyriques. Pp. 213–24 in *Congress Volume. Bonn 1962.* Supplements to Vetus Testamentum 9. Leiden: Brill.

Carlson, R. A. 1964 *David, the Chosen King. A Traditio-Historical Approach to the Second Book of Samuel.* Stockholm: Almqvist och Wiksell.

Caspari, W. 1909 Literarische Art und historische Wert von 2 Sam. 15–20 *Theologische Studien und Kritiken* 82:317–48.

1911 Der Stil des Eingangs der israelitischen Novelle. *Zeitschrift für wissenschaftliche Theologie* 53:218–53.

1926 *Die Samuelbücher.* Kommentar zum Alten Testament 7. Leipzig: Deichter. Cited as Caspari.

Cassuto, U. 1939 Daniel et son fils dans la tablette IID de Ras Shamra. *Revue des études juives* 105[N.S. 5]:125–31.

Cazelles, H. 1955a À propos d'une phrase de H. H. Rowley. Pp. 26–32 in *Wisdom in Israel and in the Ancient Near East. Presented to H. H. Rowley,* ed. M. Noth and D. Winton Thomas. Supplements to Vetus Testamentum 3. Leiden. Brill.

1955b David's Monarchy and the Gibeonite Claim. *Palestine Exploration Quarterly* 87 165–75.

1956 La Titulature du roi David. Pp. 131–36 in *Mélanges bibliques rédigés en l'honneur de André Robert.* Travaux de l'Institut Catholique de Paris 4. Paris: Bloud et Gay.

1958 Review of *PRU* IV. *Vetus Testamentum* 8 103–6

Clements, R. E. 1975 *Prophecy and Tradition.* Atlanta: John Knox.

Coats, G. W. 1981 Parable, Fable, and Anecdote. Storytelling in the Succession Narrative. *Interpretation* 35:368–82.

Cody, A. 1965 Le Titre égyptien et le nom propre du scribe de David. *Revue biblique* 72:381–93.

1969 *A History of the Old Testament Priesthood.* Rome· Pontifical Biblical Institute.

Cogan, M. 1974 *Imperialism and Religion: Assyria, Judah, and Israel in the Eighth and Seventh Centuries B.C.E.* Missoula, Mont.: Society of Biblical Literature and Scholars Press.

Cohen, H H. 1965 David and Bathsheba. *Journal of Bible and Religion* 33:142–48.

Cohen, M. A. 1971 The Rebellions During the Reigns of David: An Inquiry into Social Dynamics in Ancient Israel. Pp. 91–112 in *Studies in Jewish Bibliography, History, and Literature in Honor of I. Edward Kiev,* ed. C. Berlin. New York. Ktav.

Condamin, A. 1898 Notes critiques sur le texte biblique: David cruel par la faute d'un copiste. *Revue biblique* 7·253–61.

Conroy, C. C. 1978 *Absalom Absalom! Narrative and Language in 2 Sam 13–20.* Analecta Biblica 81. Rome· Pontifical Biblical Institute.

Cook, S. A. 1899–1900 Notes on the Composition of 2 Samuel. *American Journal of Semitic Languages* 16 145–77.

Cooke, G. 1961 The Israelite King as Son of God. *Zeitschrift für die alttestamentliche Wissenschaft* 73:202–25.

Coppens, J. 1968a Le Messianisme royal dynastique La prophétie de Nathan, II Sam VII 1–16 *Nouvelle revue théologique* 90:227–33.

1968b L'Union du trône et du temple d'après l'oracle de Nathan. (Miscellanées bibliques 48.) *Ephemerides Theologicae Lovanienses* 44:489–91.

Cornill, C. H. 1886 *Das Buch des Propheten Ezechiel.* Leipzig: Hinrichs.
1891 *Einleitung in die kanonischen Bücher des Alten Testaments.* Freiburg: Mohr (7th ed., 1913).
Couroyer, B. 1965 L'Arc d'airain. *Revue biblique* 72:508–14.
1981 *NḤT:* "Encorder un arc"(?). *Revue biblique* 68:6–12.
Cowley, A., ed. 1923 *Aramaic Papyri of the Fifth Century B.C.* Oxford: Clarendon.
Coxon, W. 1981 A Note on "Bathsheba" in 2 Samuel 12,1–6. *Biblica* 62.247–50.
Crenshaw, J. L. 1969 Method in Determining Wisdom Influence upon "Historical" Literature. *Journal of Biblical Literature* 88:129–42.
Cross, F. M. 1947 The Priestly Tabernacle. *The Biblical Archaeologist* 10:45–68 = Wright and Freedman 1961:201–28.
1961 *The Ancient Library of Qumran.* 2d ed. Garden City, N.Y.: Doubleday.
1964 The History of the Biblical Text in the Light of Discoveries in the Judaean Desert. *Harvard Theological Review* 57:281–99 = Cross and Talmon 1975:177–95.
1966 An Aramaic Inscription from Daskyleion. *Bulletin of the American Schools of Oriental Research* 184:7–10.
1972a An Interpretation of the Nora Stone. *Bulletin of the American Schools of Oriental Research* 208:13–19.
1972b The Stele Dedicated to Melcarth by Ben-hadad of Damascus. *Bulletin of the American Schools of Oriental Research* 205:36–42.
1973 *Canaanite Myth and Hebrew Epic.* Cambridge, Mass.: Harvard.
———, and D. N. Freedman 1950 Studies in Ancient Yahwistic Poetry. Ph.D. dissertation, the Johns Hopkins University. Baltimore = Cross and Freedman 1975.
1952 *Early Hebrew Orthography. A Study of the Epigraphic Evidence.* American Oriental Series 36. New Haven: American Oriental Society.
1953 A Royal Song of Thanksgiving: 2 Samuel 22 = Psalm 18. *Journal of Biblical Literature* 72:15–34 = Cross and Freedman 1950:244–338 = Cross and Freedman 1975:125–58.
1955 The Song of Miriam. *Journal of Near Eastern Studies* 14:237–50 = Cross and Freedman 1950:83–127 = Cross and Freedman 1975:45–65.
1964 The Name of Ashdod. *Bulletin of the American Schools of Oriental Research* 175:48–50.
1975 *Studies in Ancient Yahwistic Poetry.* Society of Biblical Literature, Dissertation Series 21. Missoula, Mont.: Scholars Press = Cross and Freedman 1950.
———, W. Lemke, and P. D Miller, Jr., eds. 1976 *Magnalia Dei. The Mighty Acts of God. Essays on the Bible and Archaeology in Memory of G. Ernest Wright.* Garden City, N.Y.: Doubleday.
———, and S. Talmon, eds. 1975 *Qumran and the History of the Biblical Text.* Cambridge, Mass.: Harvard.
Crossan, J. D. 1975 *The Dark Interval: Towards a Theology of Story.* Niles, Ill.: Argus.
Crüsemann, F. 1980 Zwei alttestamentliche Witze. I Sam 21 11-15 und II Sam 6 16.20–23. *Zeitschrift für die alttestamentliche Wissenschaft* 92:215–27.
Cutler, B., and J. MacDonald 1976 Identification of the *Na'ar* in the Ugaritic Texts. *Ugarit-Forschungen* 8:27–35.

Dahood, M. J. 1952 Canaanite-Phoenician Influence in Qoheleth. *Biblica* 30:30–52, 191–221.

1954 Ugaritic DRKT and Biblical DEREK. *Theological Studies* 15:627–31

1959 The Value of Ugaritic for Textual Criticism. *Biblica* 40:160–70.

1962 Qoheleth and Northwest Semitic Philology. *Biblica* 43:349–65.

1963 *Proverbs and Northwest Semitic Philology.* Scripta Pontificii Instituti Biblici 113. Rome: Pontifical Biblical Institute.

1965a *Ugaritic-Hebrew Philology.* Rome: Pontifical Biblical Institute.

1965b *Psalms I.* Anchor Bible 16. Garden City, N.Y.: Doubleday.

1968 *Psalms II.* Anchor Bible 17. Garden City, N.Y.: Doubleday.

1969 Comparative Philology Yesterday and Today. *Biblica* 50:70–79.

1970 *Psalms III.* Anchor Bible 17A. Garden City, N.Y.: Doubleday

1972 Hebrew-Ugaritic Lexicography X. *Biblica* 53:386–403.

———, et al. 1980 Instrumental *lamedh* in II Samuel 3,34. *Biblica* 61:261.

Dalman, G. 1960 *Grammatik des jüdish-palästinischen Aramäisch.* Darmstadt: Wissenschaftliche Buchgesellschaft.

Daube, D. 1947 *Studies in Biblical Law.* Cambridge. Reprinted 1969. New York: Ktav.

Davidson, A. B. 1902 *Hebrew Syntax.* 3d ed. Edinburgh: Clark. Cited by section (§).

Delcor, M. 1967 Two Special Meanings of the Word *yd* in Biblical Hebrew *Journal of Semitic Studies* 12.230–40.

1978 Les Kéréthim et les Cretois. *Vetus Testamentum* 28:409–22 = Delcor 1979: 314–27.

1979 *Études bibliques et orientales de religions comparées.* Leiden: Brill.

Delekat, L. 1967 Tendenz und Theologie der David-Salomo-Erzählung. Pp. 22–36 in Maass 1967.

Demsky, A. 1973 Geba, Gibeah, and Gibeon—an Historico-Geographical Riddle. *Bulletin of the American Schools of Oriental Research* 212:26–31.

Dhorme, E. P 1910 *Les Livres de Samuel.* Études bibliques. Paris: Gabalda. Cited as Dhorme.

Dietrich, W. 1972 *Prophetie und Geschichte. Eine redaktionsgeschichtliche Untersuchung zum deuteronomistischen Geschichtswerk.* Forschungen zur Religion und Literatur des Alten und Neuen Testaments 108. Göttingen: Vandenhoeck und Ruprecht.

1977 David in Überlieferung und Geschichte. *Verkündigung und Forschung* 22: 44–64.

Donner, H. 1961 Der "Freund des Königs." *Zeitschrift für die alttestamentliche Wissenschaft* 73:269–77.

Driver, G. R. 1930 Corrections. *Journal of Theological Studies* 31:283–84.

1934 Hebrew Notes. *Zeitschrift für die alttestamentliche Wissenschaft* 52:51–56.

1936 Textual and Linguistic Problems of the Book of Psalms. *Harvard Theological Review* 29:171–95.

1938 Hebrew *'al* as a Divine Title. *Expository Times* 50:92–93.

1950 Problems of the Hebrew Text and Language. Pp. 46–61 in *Alttestamentliche Studien, Friedrich Nötscher . . . ,* ed. H. Junker and J. Botterweck. Bonner biblische Beiträge 1. Bonn: Hanstein.

1951 Hebrew Notes. *Vetus Testamentum* 1:241–50.
1957 Glosses in the Hebrew Text of the Old Testament. Pp. 123–61 in *L'Ancien Testament et l'Orient*. Orientalia et Biblica Lovaniensia 1. Louvain: Publications Universitaires/Instituut voor Oriëntalisme.
1962 Plurima Mortis Imago. Pp. 128–43 in *Studies and Essays in Honor of Abraham A. Neuman*, ed. M. Ben-Horin, B. D. Weinryb, and S. Zeitlin. Leiden: Brill.
Driver, S. R. 1890 *Notes on the Hebrew Text of the Books of Samuel*. Oxford: Clarendon. Cited as Driver.
1895 *A Critical and Exegetical Commentary on Deuteronomy*. International Critical Commentary. Edinburgh: Clark.
Duhm, B. 1899 *Die Psalmen*. Kurzer Hand-Commentar zum Alten Testament 14. Freiburg in Breisgau, Leipzig, and Tübingen: Mohr.
Duncan, G. 1924 Millo and the City of David. *Zeitschrift für die alttestamentliche Wissenschaft* 42:222–44.
Dus, J. 1960 Gibeon—eine Kultstätte des Šmš und die Stadt des Benjaminitischen Schicksals. *Vetus Testamentum* 10:353–74.
1961 Der Brauch der Ladewanderung im alten Israel. *Theologische Zeitschrift* 17:1–16.
Edzard, D. O. 1959 Altbabylonisch *nawûm*. *Zeitschrift für Assyriologie* 19:168–73.
Ehrlich, A. B. 1910 *Randglossen zur hebräischen Bibel*. Vol. 3. Leipzig: Hinrichs. Reprinted 1968. Hildesheim: Olms.
Eichhorn, J. G. 1803 *Einleitung in das Alte Testament*. 3d ed. 3 vols. Leipzig: Weidmann.
Eichrodt, W. 1961 *Theology of the Old Testament*. 2 vols. Trans. J. A. Baker from German 1960. The Old Testament Library. Philadelphia: Westminster.
Eissfeldt, O. 1931 *Die Komposition der Samuelisbücher*. Leipzig: Hinrichs.
1943 Israelitisch-philistäische Grenzverschiebungen von David bis auf die Assyrerzeit. *Zeitschrift des Deutschen Palästina-Vereins* 66:115–28 = Eissfeldt 1962–79:vol. II:453–63.
1950 Jahwe Zebaoth. Pp. 128–50 in *Miscellanea Academica Berolinensia*. Berlin: Akademie = Eissfeldt 1962–79:vol. III:103–23.
1951 Ein gescheiterter Versuch der Wiedervereinigung Israels (2 Sam 2:12–3:1). *La Nouvelle Clio* 3:110–27.
1952 Noch einmal: Ein gescheiterter Versuch der Wiedervereinigung Israels. *La Nouvelle Clio* 4:55–59.
1955 Zwei verkannte militär-technische Termini im Alten Testament. *Vetus Testamentum* 6:232–35.
1957 Silo und Jerusalem. Pp. 138–47 in *Volume du Congrès. Strasbourg 1956*. Supplements to Vetus Testamentum 4. Leiden: Brill = Eissfeldt 1962–79:vol. III:417–25.
1960 Review of Bright 1972 [1st ed., 1959]. *Journal of Biblical Literature* 79: 369–72.
1962–79 *Kleine Schriften*, ed. R. Sellheim and F. Maass. 6 vols. Tübingen: Mohr.
1965 *The Old Testament. An Introduction*. Trans. P. R. Ackroyd from German 1964. New York: Harper & Row.

1973 "Das Gesetz des Menschen" in 2. Sam 7,19 = Eissfeldt 1962–79:vol. V: 143–51. Not published elsewhere.

Elliger, K. 1935 Die dreissig Helden Davids. *Palästinajahrbuch* 31:29–75 = Elliger 1966:72–118.

1936 Die Nordgrenze des Reiches Davids. *Palästinajahrbuch* 32:34–73.

1955 Das Gesetz Leviticus 18. *Zeitschrift für die alttestamentliche Wissenschaft* 67:1–25 = Elliger 1966:232–59.

1966 *Kleine Schriften zum Alten Testament*, ed. H. Gese and O. Kaiser. Theologische Bücherei 32. Munich: Kaiser.

Emerton, J. A., ed. 1979 *Studies in the Historical Books of the Old Testament*. Supplements to Vetus Testamentum 30. Leiden: Brill.

Englert, D. M. C. 1949 *The Peshitto of Second Samuel*. Journal of Biblical Literature, Monograph Series 3. Philadelphia: Society of Biblical Literature and Exegesis.

Engnell, I. 1967 *Studies in Divine Kingship in the Ancient Near East*. 2d ed. Oxford Blackwell.

Erman, A., and H. Grapow 1971 *Wörterbuch der aegyptischen Sprache*. 7 vols. Berlin: Akademie.

Euler, K. F. 1938 Königtum und Götterwelt in den altaramäischen Inschriften Nordsyriens. Eine Untersuchung zur Formsprache der altaramäischen Inschriften und des Alten Testaments. *Zeitschrift für die alttestamentliche Wissenschaft* 56. 272–313.

Ewald, H 1878 *The History of Israel*. Vol 3. *The Rise and Splendour of the Hebrew Monarchy*, ed. and trans. from German [1866] by J. E. Carpenter. London: Longmans, Green, & Co.

Falk, Z. W. 1966 Ruler and Judge [Hebrew]. *Lĕšonénu* 30:243–47.

Feigin, S. I. 1950 The Heavenly Sieve. *Journal of Near Eastern Studies* 9:40–43.

Fensham, F. C. 1960 A Few Aspects of Legal Practices in Samuel in Comparison with Legal Material from the Ancient Near East. Pp. 18–27 in Ou Testamentiese Werkgemeenskap 1960.

1964 The Treaty between Israel and the Gibeonites. *The Biblical Archaeologist* 27:96–100 = Campbell and Freedman 1970:121–26.

1969 The Treaty between the Israelites and the Tyrians. Pp. 71–87 in *Congress Volume. Rome 1968*. Supplements to Vetus Testamentum 17. Leiden: Brill.

1970 The Battle between the Men of Joab and Abner as a Possible Ordeal by Battle? *Vetus Testamentum* 20:356–57.

Fenton, T. L. 1979 Comparative Evidence in Textual Study: M. Dahood on 2 Sam. i 21 and CTA 19(1 Aqht),I,44–45. *Vetus Testamentum* 29:162–70

Fernandez, A., and G. Bressan 1954 El Ṣinnor (2 Sam. 5,6–8). *Biblica* 35:217–24.

Fisher, L. R., ed. 1972 *Ras Shamra Parallels I*. Analecta Orientalia 49 Rome. Pontifical Biblical Institute.

1975 *Ras Shamra Parallels II*. Analecta Orientalia 50. Rome: Pontifical Biblical Institute.

Flanagan, J. W. 1972 Court History or Succession Document? A Study of 2 Sam 9–20 and 1 Kings 1–2. *Journal of Biblical Literature* 91 172–81.

1975 Judah in All Israel. Pp. 101–16 in *No Famine in the Land: Studies in Honor of John L. McKenzie*, ed. J. W. Flanagan and A. W. Robinson. Missoula, Mont.: Scholars Press for the Institute for Antiquity and Christianity—Claremont.

1979 The Relocation of the Davidic Capital. *Journal of the American Academy of Religion* 47:223–44.

Fleet, W. F. 1931 Psalm XVIII, 30. *Expository Times* 42:526.

Fohrer, G. 1959 Der Vertrag zwischen König und Volk in Israel. *Zeitschrift für die alttestamentliche Wissenschaft* 71:1–22.

1968 *Introduction to the Old Testament.* Initiated by E. Sellin. Trans. D. A. Green from German 1965. Nashville, Tenn.: Abingdon.

Fokkelman, J. P. 1979 *śdy trwmt* in II Sam $1_{21}$—a non-existent crux. *Zeitschrift für die alttestamentliche Wissenschaft* 91:290–92.

Forrer, E. 1920 *Die Provinzeinteilung des assyrischen Reiches.* Leipzig: Hinrichs.

Forshey, H. O. 1975 The Construct Chain *naḥᵃlat YHWH/ʾᵉlōhîm*. *Bulletin of the American Schools of Oriental Research* 220:51–54.

Freedman, D. N. 1960 Archaic Forms in Early Hebrew Poetry. *Zeitschrift für die alttestamentliche Wissenschaft* 72:101–7.

1962 The Massoretic Text and the Qumran Scrolls: A Study in Orthography. *Textus* 2:87–102 = Cross and Talmon 1975:196–211.

1971 II Samuel 23:4. *Journal of Biblical Literature* 9:329–30.

1972 The Refrain in David's Lament over Saul and Jonathan. Pp. 115–26 in vol. 1 of *Ex Orbe Religionum. Studia Geo Widengren oblata*, ed. C. J. Becker, S. G. F. Brandon, and M. Simon. Supplements to Numen/Studies in the History of Religions 21–22. Leiden: Brill.

1976 Divine Names and Titles in Early Hebrew Poetry. Pp. 55–107 in Cross, Lemke, and Miller 1976.

forthcoming On the Death of Abiner. Marvin Pope Festschrift.

*See also* Andersen, F. I.

*See also* Campbell, E. F., Jr.

*See also* Cross, F. M.

*See also* Wright, G. E.

———, and E. F. Campbell, Jr. 1964 *The Biblical Archaeologist Reader 2.* Anchor Books. Garden City, N.Y.. Doubleday.

Fretheim, T. E. 1967 Psalm 132: A Form Critical Study. *Journal of Biblical Literature* 86:289–300.

Frey, J.-B. 1952 *Corpus Inscriptionum Iudaicarum.* Vol. II. Asie-Afrique. Rome: Pontificio Instituto di Archeologia Cristiana.

Friedrich, J., and W. Röllig 1970 *Phönizisch-Punische Grammatik.* Analecta Orientalia 46. Rome: Pontifical Biblical Institute.

Fuss, W. 1962 II Samuel 24. *Zeitschrift für die alttestamentliche Wissenschaft* 74: 145–64.

Galling, K. 1956 Die Ausrufung des Namens als Rechtsakt in Israel. *Theologische Literaturzeitung* 81, cols. 65–70.

1962 Altar = *IDB* 1:96–100.

García de la Fuente, O. 1968 David buscó el rostro de Yahweh. *Augustinianum* 8:477–540.

García Trapiello, J. 1969 La profecía de Natan (2 Sam 7,1–29). *Cultura bíblica* 26:3–42.

Garsiel, M. 1972 The Character and Aim of the Story of David and Bathsheba [Hebrew]. *Beth Mikra* 49:162–82.

1973 A Review of Recent Interpretations of the Story of David and Bathsheba, II Samuel 11. *Immanuel* 2:18–20.

Gaster, T. H. 1936–37 Notes on "The Song of the Sea." *Expository Times* 48:45.

Geiger, A. 1857 *Urschrift und Uebersetzungen der Bibel in ihrer Abhängigkeit von der innern Entwicklung des Judenthums.* Breslau: Hainauer. 2d ed., 1928.

Gelb, I. J., P. M. Purves, and A. A. McRae 1943 *Nuzi Personal Names.* Oriental Institute Publications 57. Chicago: University of Chicago.

Gelston, A. 1972 A Note on II Samuel 7[10]. *Zeitschrift für die alttestamentliche Wissenschaft* 84:92–94.

Gerleman, G. 1973 Die Wurzel *šlm.* *Zeitschrift für die alttestamentliche Wissenschaft* 85:1–14.

1974 Der Nicht-Mensch. Erwägungen zur hebräischen Wurzel *NBL.* *Vetus Testamentum* 24:147–58.

1977 Schuld und Sühne: Erwägungen zu 2 Sam 12. Pp. 132–39 in *Beiträge zur alttestamentlichen Theologie. Festschrift für Walther Zimmerli . . . ,* ed. H. Donner, R. Hanhart, and R. Smend. Göttingen: Vandenhoeck und Ruprecht.

Gese, H. 1964 Der Davidsbund und die Zionserwählung. *Zeitschrift für Theologie und Kirche* 61:10–26.

Gevaryahu, C. 1969 The Return of the Exile to God's Estate in the Parable of the Wise Woman of Tekoa [Hebrew]. *Beth Mikra* 36:10–33.

Gevirtz, S. 1963 David's Lament over Saul and Jonathan. Pp. 72–96 in *Patterns in the Early Poetry of Israel.* The Oriental Institute of the University of Chicago. Studies in Ancient Oriental Civilization 32. Chicago: University of Chicago.

Ginsberg, H. L. 1938 A Ugaritic Parallel to 2 Sam 1:21. *Journal of Biblical Literature* 57:209–13.

Giveon, R. 1964 "The Cities of Our God" (II Sam 10 12). *Journal of Biblical Literature* 83:415–16.

1971 *Les Bédouins Shosou des documents égyptiens.* Documenta et Monumenta Orientis Antiqui 18. Leiden: Brill.

Glück, J. J. 1964 Reviling and Monomachy as Battle-Preludes in Ancient Warfare. *Acta Classica* 7:25–31.

1965 Merab or Michal? *Zeitschrift für die alttestamentliche Wissenschaft* 77:72–81.

1966 The Conquest of Jerusalem in the Account of 2 Sam 5,6a–8 with Special Reference to "the Blind and the Lame" and the Phrase "*wᵉyiggaʿ baṣṣinor.*" Pp. 98–105 in Ou Testamentiese Werkgemeenskap 1960.

Goldman, S. 1951 *Samuel.* Soncino Books of the Bible. London: Soncino. Cited as Goldman.

Goldstein, J. A. 1976 *I Maccabees. A New Translation with Introduction and Commentary.* Anchor Bible 41. Garden City, N.Y.: Doubleday.

Gordis, R. 1940 The Biblical Root *šdy-šd:* Notes on 2 Sam. i. 21; Jer. xviii. 14; Ps xci. 6; Job v. 21. *Journal of Theological Studies* 41:34–43 = Gordis 1976:323–31.

1976 *The Word and the Book.* New York: Ktav.

Gordon, C. H. 1935 Fratriarchy in the Old Testament. *Journal of Biblical Literature* 54:223–31.
1950 Belt-Wrestling in the Bible World. *Hebrew Union College Annual* 23:131–36.
1960 David the Dancer. Pp. 46–49 in *Studies in Bible and Jewish Religion Dedicated to Y. Kaufmann . . .*, ed. M. Haran. Jerusalem: Magnes.
1965 *Ugaritic Textbook.* Analecta Orientalia 38. Rome: Pontifical Biblical Institute. Cited by section (§). Also cited as *UT*‘.
Görg, M. 1975 *Gott-König-Reden in Israel und Ägypten.* Beiträge zur Wissenschaft vom Alten und Neuen Testament 105. Stuttgart: Kohlhammer.
Gorgulho, L. B. 1962 A profecía de Natan en 2 Sam 7,1–7. *Revista de cultura bíblica* 6,21:59–70.
Goslinga, C. J. 1950 Davids Klaaglied over Saul en Jonathan. *Gereformeerd Theologisch Tijdschrift* 50:53–70.
1956 Waneer is David koning geworden over geheel Israël? *Gereformeerd Theologisch Tijdschrift* 56:11–16.
1959 Spreekt 2 Sam 12,31 inderdaad van wrede terechtstelling der Ammonieten? *Gereformeerd Theologisch Tijdschrift* 59:138–48.
1961 De parallele teksten in de boeken Samuël en Kronieken. *Gereformeerd Theologisch Tijdschrift* 61:108–16.
1962 *Het tweede boek Samuël.* Commentar op het Oude Testament. Kampen: Kok. Cited as Goslinga.
Graetz, H. H. 1874 *Geschichte der Juden von den ältesten Zeiten bis auf die Gegenwart.* Vol. 1. Leipzig: Leiner.
Grapow, H. *See* Erman, A.
Gray, J. 1970 *I and II Kings. A Commentary.* 2d ed. The Old Testament Library. Philadelphia: Westminster.
Gressmann, H. 1921 *Die älteste Geschichtsschreibung und Prophetie Israels.* Die Schriften des Alten Testament II/1. 2d ed. Göttingen: Vandenhoeck und Ruprecht. Cited as Gressmann.
Grønbaek, J. H. 1971 *Die Geschichte vom Aufstieg Davids (1. Sam. 15–2. Sam. 5). Tradition und Komposition.* Copenhagen: Prostant apud Munksgaard.
Gröndahl, F. 1967 *Die Personennamen der Texte aus Ugarit.* Studia Pohl 1. Rome: Pontifical Biblical Institute.
de Groot, J. 1935 *II. Samuël.* Tekst en Uitleg. Groningen: Wolters. Cited as de Groot.
1936 Zwei Fragen aus der Geschichte des alten Jerusalems. Pp. 191–97 in *Werden und Wesen des Alten Testaments,* ed. P. Volz, F. Stummer, and J. Hempel. Beihefte zur Zeitschrift für die alttestamentliche Wissenschaft 66. Berlin: Töpelmann.
Gros Louis, K. R. R. 1977 The Difficulty of Ruling Well: King David of Israel. *Semeia* 8:15–33.
Gross, W. 1974 Die Herausführungsformel—zum Verhältnis von Formel und Syntax. *Zeitschrift für die alttestamentliche Wissenschaft* 86:425–53.
Grottanelli, G. 1975 Horatius, i Curiatee e 2 Sam 2,12–18. *Annali dell'Istituto Orientale di Napoli* 35:547–54.
Guillaume, A. 1962 A Note on the √*bl*‘. *Journal of Theological Studies* 13:320–22.

Gunkel, H. 1921 *Das Märchen im Alten Testament.* Religionsgeschichtliche Volksbücher 2. Tübingen: Mohr.

1926 *Die Psalmen.* 4th ed. Handkommentar zum Alten Testament 2/2. Göttingen: Vandenhoeck und Ruprecht.

Gunn, D. M. 1974 Narrative Patterns and Oral Tradition in Judges and Samuel. *Vetus Testamentum* 24:286–317.

1975 David and the Gift of the Kingdom. *Semeia* 3:14–45.

1976 Traditional Composition in the "Succession Narrative." *Vetus Testamentum* 26:214–29.

1978 *The Story of King David. Genre and Interpretation.* Journal for the Study of the Old Testament Supplement 6. Sheffield: JSOT.

Gunneweg, A. H. J. 1965 *Leviten und Priester.* Forschungen zur Religion und Literatur des Alten und Neuen Testaments. Göttingen: Vandenhoeck und Ruprecht.

Gutbrod, K. 1958 *Das Buch vom Reich: Das zweite Buch Samuel.* Die Botschaft des Alten Testaments 11/2. Stuttgart: Calwer. Cited as Gutbrod.

Guttmann, J. 1964 The Ewe Lamb [Hebrew]. *Beth Mikra* 18/19:1–11.

Haag, H. 1970 Gad und Nathan. Pp. 135–43 in *Archäologie und Altes Testament. Festschrift für Kurt Galling . . . ,* ed. A. Kuschke and E. Kutsch. Tübingen: Mohr.

Hagan, H. 1979 Deception as Motif and Theme in 2 Sm 9–20; 1 Kgs 1–2. *Biblica* 60:301–26.

Halpern, B. *See* Levenson, J. D.

Hanson, P. D. 1968 The Song of Heshbon and David's *NÎR. Harvard Theological Review* 61:297–320.

Hartmann, B. 1961 Es gibt keinen Gott ausser Jahwe. Zur generellen Verneinung im Hebräischen. *Zeitschrift der Deutschen Morgenländischen Gesellschaft* 110: 229–35.

Hauer, C. E., Jr. 1963 Who Was Zadok? *Journal of Biblical Literature* 82:89–94.

1970 Jerusalem, the Stronghold and Rephaim. *Catholic Biblical Quarterly* 32: 571–78.

Haupt, P. 1926 "Deal gently with the young man." *Journal of Biblical Literature* 45:357.

Held, M. 1959 *mḫṣ/mḫš* in Ugaritic and Other Semitic Languages. A Study in Comparative Lexicography. *Journal of the American Oriental Society* 79:169–76.

Heller, J. 1965 David und die Krüppel (2. Sam. 5.6–8). *Communio Viatorum* 8: 251–58.

1966 Die schweigende Sonne. *Communio Viatorum* 9:73–79.

1970 Die Symbolik des Fettes im Alten Testament. *Vetus Testamentum* 20:106–8.

Hermann, A. 1938 *Die ägyptische Königsnovelle.* Leipziger ägyptologische Studien 10. Glückstadt: Augustin.

Hermisson, H.-J. 1971 Weisheit und Geschichte. Pp. 136–54 in Wolff 1971.

Herrmann, S. 1953–54 Die Königsnovelle in Ägypten und in Israel. *Wissenschaftliche Zeitschrift der Karl-Marx-Universität, Leipzig* 3. *Gesellschafts- und sprachwissenschaftliche Reihe* 1:51–62.

1967 Der Name JHWꜣ in den Inschriften von Soleb. Prinzipielle Erwägungen. Pp. 213–16 in *Fourth World Congress of Jewish Studies, Papers.* Vol. 1. Jerusalem: World Union of Jewish Studies.

1981 *A History of Israel in Old Testament Times.* Trans. J. Bowden from German 1973, 1980. Philadelphia: Fortress.

Hertzberg, H. W. 1929 Mizpa. *Zeitschrift für die alttestamentliche Wissenschaft* 47:161–96.

1964 *I and II Samuel. A Commentary.* Old Testament Library. Trans. J. S. Bowden from German 1960. Philadelphia: Westminster. Cited as Hertzberg.

Hillers, D. R. 1964 A Note on Some Treaty Terminology in the Old Testament. *Bulletin of the American Schools of Oriental Research* 176:46–47.

1968 Ritual Procession of the Ark and Ps 132. *Catholic Biblical Quarterly* 30: 48–55.

Hitzig, F. 1863–65 *Die Psalmen.* Leipzig: Winter.

Hodges, Z. C. 1962 Conflicts in the Biblical Accounts of the Ammonite-Syrian War. *Bibliotheca Sacra* 119:238–43.

Hoffmann, A. 1973 *David. Namensdeutung zur Wesensdeutung.* Beiträge zur Wissenschaft vom Alten und Neuen Testament 5/20. Stuttgart: Kohlhammer.

Hoffmann, G. 1882 Lexikalisches. *Zeitschrift für die alttestamentliche Wissenschaft* 2:53–72.

Hoffner, H. A., Jr. 1975 Propaganda and Political Justification in Hittite Historiography. Pp. 49–62 in *Unity and Diversity. Essays in the History, Literature, and Religion of the Ancient Near East,* ed. H. Goedicke and J. J. M. Roberts. Baltimore and London: Johns Hopkins.

Hoftijzer, J. 1965 Review of Schottroff 1964. *Vetus Testamentum* 15:540–48.

1970a Absalom and Tamar: A Case of Fratriarchy? Pp. 54–61 in *Schrift en Uitleg. Studies . . . aangeboden aan Prof. Dr. W. H. Gispen.* Kampen: Kok.

1970b David and the Tekoite Woman. *Vetus Testamentum* 20:419–44.

1971 A Peculiar Question: A Note on 2 Sam. xv 27. *Vetus Testamentum* 21:606–9.

Holladay, W. L. 1970 Form and Word-Play in David's Lament over Saul and Jonathan. *Vetus Testamentum* 20:153–89.

Holm-Nielsen, S. 1976 Shiloh = *IDB Suppl* 822–23.

Honeyman, A. M. 1948 The Evidence for Regnal Names among the Hebrews. *Journal of Biblical Literature* 67:13–25.

Horn, S. H. 1973 The Crown of the King of the Ammonites. *Andrews University Seminary Studies* 11:170–80.

Huffmon, H. B. 1965 *Amorite Personal Names in the Mari Texts: A Structural and Lexical Study.* Baltimore: Johns Hopkins.

Hull, E. 1933 David and the Well of Bethlehem: An Irish Parallel. *Folk-Lore* 44:214–18.

Hummel, H. D. 1957 Enclitic *Mem* in Early Northwest Semitic, especially Hebrew. *Journal of Biblical Literature* 76:85–107.

Hylander, I. 1932 *Der literarische Samuel-Saul-Komplex (I. Sam. 1–15) traditionsgeschichtlich untersucht.* Uppsala: Almqvist och Wiksell.

Ishida, T. 1977 *The Royal Dynasties in Ancient Israel. A Study on the Formation and Development of Royal-Dynastic Ideology.* Beihefte zur Zeitschrift für die alttestamentliche Wissenschaft 142. Berlin: de Gruyter.

Jackson, J. J. 1965 David's Throne: Patterns in the Succession Story. *Canadian Journal of Theology* 11:183–95.

Jacob, B. 1912 Erklärung einiger Hiob-Stellen. *Zeitschrift für die alttestamentliche Wissenschaft* 32:278–87.

Jacobsen, T. 1976 *The Treasures of Darkness. A History of Mesopotamian Religion.* New Haven and London: Yale.

Jeremias, A. 1930 *Das Alte Testament im Lichte des alten Orients.* 4th ed. Leipzig: Hinrichs.

Jirku, A. 1950 Der "Mann von Ṭob" (II Sam 10 6.8). *Zeitschrift für die alttestamentliche Wissenschaft* 62:319.

1965 Rapa'u, der Fürst der Rapa'uma—Rephaim. *Zeitschrift für die alttestamentliche Wissenschaft* 77:82–83.

Johnson, A. R. 1967 *Sacral Kingship in Ancient Israel.* Cardiff: University of Wales.

Johnson, M. D. 1969 *The Purpose of the Biblical Genealogies with Special Reference to the Setting of the Genealogies of Jesus.* New Testament Studies Monograph Series 8. Cambridge: Cambridge.

Joüon, P. 1928 Notes philologiques sur le texte hébreu de 2 Samuel. *Biblica* 9: 302–15.

Kapelrud, A. S. 1955 King and Fertility. A Discussion of II Sam 21:1–14. *Norsk Teologisk Tidsskrift* 56 (= *Interpretationes ad Vetus Testamentum pertinentes Sigmundo Mowinckel . . . missae.* Oslo: Land og Kirke):113–22.

1959 King David and the Sons of Saul. Pp. 294–301 in *La regalità sacra. Contributi al tema dell' VIII Congresso Internazionale di Storia delle Religioni* [Rome, April 1955]. Leiden: Brill.

1963 Temple Building, a Task for Gods and Kings. *Orientalia* 32:56–62 = Kapelrud 1979:184–90.

1979 *God and His Friends in the Old Testament.* Oslo: Universitetforlaget.

Keil, C. F. 1875 *Die Bücher Samuel.* Biblischer Commentar über das Alte Testament III/2. 2d ed. Leipzig: Dörffling und Franke. Cited as Keil.

Kennedy, A. R. S. 1905 *Samuel.* New Century Bible. New York: Frowde. Cited as Kennedy.

Kenyon, K. M. 1974 *Digging Up Jerusalem.* London: Benn.

Ketter, P. 1940 *Die Samuelbücher.* Herders Bibelkommentar III/1. Freiburg im Breisgau: Herder. Cited as Ketter.

Kirkpatrick, A. F. 1881 *The Second Book of Samuel.* Cambridge Bible for Schools and Colleges. Cambridge: Cambridge. Cited as Kirkpatrick.

Klostermann, A. 1887 *Die Bücher Samuelis und der Könige.* Kurzgefasster Kommentar zu den heiligen Schriften des Alten und Neuen Testamentes. Nördlingen: Beck. Cited as Klostermann.

Knight, D. A. 1973 *Rediscovering the Traditions of Israel. The Development of the Traditio-Historical Research of the Old Testament, with Special Consideration of Scandinavian Contributions.* Society of Biblical Literature, Dissertation Series 9. Missoula, Mont.: Scholars.

Koehler, L. 1922 Archäologisches—17: Ein Fachwort der Graupebereitung? *Zeitschrift für die alttestamentliche Wissenschaft* 40:17–20.

1948a Äschpār Dattelkuchen. *Theologische Zeitschrift* 4:397–98.

1948b Loch- und Ringbrot. *Theologische Zeitschrift* 4:154–55.

Korošec, V. 1963 Warfare of the Hittites—from the Legal Point of View. *Iraq* 25:159–66.

Kraeling, E. G. 1928 The Real Religion of Ancient Israel. *Journal of Biblical Literature* 47:133–59.

Kraus, H.-J. 1951 *Die Königsherrschaft Gottes im Alten Testament.* Beiträge zur historischen Theologie 13. Tübingen: Mohr.

1963 *Psalmen.* 2 vols. 2d ed. Biblischer Kommentar 15:1–2. Neukirchen-Vluyn: Neukirchener Verlag des Erziehungsvereins.

1966 *Worship in Israel. A Cultic History of the Old Testament.* Trans. G. Buswell from German 1962. Richmond, Va.: John Knox.

Kuenen, A. 1890 *Historisch-kritische Einleitung in die Bücher des Alten Testaments.* Vol. 1, pt. 2: *Die historischen Bücher des Alten Testaments.* German translation from Dutch by T. Weber. Leipzig: Reisland.

Kupper, J. R. 1950 Le Recensement dans les textes de Mari. Pp. 99–110 in *Studia Mariana,* ed. A. Parrot. Documenta et Monumenta Orientis Antiqui 4. Leiden: Brill.

1957 *Les Nomades en Mésopotamie au temps des rois de Mari.* Bibliothèque de la Faculté de Philosophie et Lettres de l'Université de Liège 142. Paris: Les Belles Lettres.

Kutsch, E. 1961 Die Dynastie von Gottes Gnaden. Probleme der Nathanweissagung in 2. Sam 7. *Zeitschrift für Theologie und Kirche* 58:137–53.

1979 Wie David König wurde. Beobachtungen zu 2. Sam 2,4a und 5,3. Pp. 75–93 in *Textgemäss. Aufsätze und Beiträge zur Hermeneutik des Alten Testaments. Festschrift für Ernst Wurthwein . . . ,* ed. A. H. J. Gunneweg and O. Kaiser. Göttingen: Vandenhoeck und Ruprecht.

Labuschagne, C. J. 1960 Some Remarks on the Prayer of David in 2 Sam 7. Pp. 28–35 in Ou Testamentiese Werkgemeenskap 1960.

Lammens, H. 1920 Le Culte des bétyles et les processions religieuses chez les Arabes préislamites. *Bulletin de l'institut francais d'archéologie orientale* 17:39–101. Reprinted in *L'Arabie occidentale avant l'hégire* (Beirut: Imprimerie Catholique, 1928), pp. 100–81.

Langdon, S. 1912 *Die neubabylonischen Königsinschriften.* Vorderasiatische Bibliothek 4. Leipzig: Hinrichs.

Langlamet, F. 1976a Review of Würthwein 1974 and Veijola 1975. *Revue biblique* 83:114–37.

1976b Pour ou contre Salomon? La rédaction prosalomonienne de 1 Rois, I–II. *Revue biblique* 83:321–79,481–529.

1977 Absalom et les concubines de son père. Recherches sur II Sam., XVI, 21–22. *Revue biblique* 84:161–209.

1978 Ahitofel et Houshaï. Rédaction prosalomonienne en 2 S 15–17? Pp. 57–90 in *Studies in Bible and the Ancient Near East Presented to Samuel E. Loewenstamm . . . ,* ed. Y. Avishur and J. Blau. Jerusalem: Rubinstein.

1979–81 David et la maison de Saül. *Revue biblique* 86:194–213,385–436,481–513; 87:161–210; 88:321–32.

1981 Affinités sacerdotales, deutéronomiques, élohistes dans l'histoire de la succession (2 S 9–20; 1 R 1–2). Pp. 233–46 in *Mélanges bibliques et orientaux en l'honneur de M. Henri Cazelles*, ed. A. Caquot and M. Delcor. Alter Orient und Altes Testament 212. Kevelaer: Butzon & Becker. Neukirchen-Vluyn: Neukirchener.

Laridon, V. 1946 De prophetia Nathan. *Collationes Brugenses* 42:281–89,315–21.

Laroche, E. 1966 *Les Noms des Hittites.* Études linguistiques 4. Paris: Klincksieck.

Leibel, D. 1958–59 *ḥdšh. Lĕšonénu* 23:124–25.

1967 Mount Rephaim—the Wood of Ephraim [Hebrew]. *Yediot* 31:136–39.

Leimbach, K. A. 1936 *Die Bücher Samuel.* Die heilige Schrift des Alten Testamentes III/1. Bonn: Hanstein. Cited as Leimbach.

Lemaire, A. 1973 L'Ostracon "Ramat-Negeb" et la topographie du Negeb. *Semitica* 23:11–26.

Lemche, N. P. 1978 David's Rise. *Journal for the Study of the Old Testament* 10:2–25.

Lemke, W. *See* Cross, F. M.

Levenson, J. D. 1978 1 Samuel 25 as Literature and History. *Catholic Biblical Quarterly* 40:11–28.

———, and B. Halpern 1980 The Political Import of David's Marriages. *Journal of Biblical Literature* 99:507–18.

Levin, S. 1978 *The Father of Joshua/Jesus.* Binghamton, N.Y.: State University of New York.

Levine, E. 1975 On "Air" in the Bible [Hebrew]. *Beth Mikra* 61:288–91,306.

1976 Distinguishing "Air" from "Heaven" in the Bible. *Zeitschrift für die alttestamentliche Wissenschaft* 88:97–99.

L'Heureux, C. 1974 The Ugaritic and Biblical Rephaim. *Harvard Theological Review* 67:265–74.

1976 The *yᵉlîdê hārāpā'*—a Cultic Association of Warriors. *Bulletin of the American Schools of Oriental Research* 221 (*In Memoriam. G. Ernest Wright*, ed. R. G. Boling and E. F. Campbell, Jr.):83–85.

1979 *Rank among the Canaanite Gods: El, Baal, and the Repha'im.* Harvard Semitic Monographs 21. Missoula, Mont.: Scholars.

Lipiński, E. 1965 *La Royauté de Yahwé dans la poésie et le culte de l'ancien Israël.* Verhandelingen van de koninklijke Vlaamse Academie voor Weltenschappen . . . van België. Klasse der Letteren 27/55. Brussels: Paleis der Academiën.

1967a Peninna, Iti'el et l'athlète. *Vetus Testamentum* 17:68–75.

1967b *Le Poème royal du Psaume LXXXIX 1–5.20–38.* Cahiers de la Revue biblique 6. Paris: Gabalda.

Liver, J. 1953 The Chronology of Tyre at the Beginning of the First Millennium B.C. *Israel Exploration Journal* 3:113–20.

Liverani, M. 1962 Antecedenti dell'onomastica aramaica antica. *Rivista degli studi orientali* 37:65–76.

von Loewenclau, I. 1980 Der Prophet Nathan im Zwielicht von theologischer Deutung und Historie. Pp. 202–15 in *Werden und Wirken des Alten Testaments. Festschrift für Claus Westermann . . .*, ed. R. Albertz et al. Göttingen: Vandenhoeck und Ruprecht.

Long, B. O. 1981 Wounded Beginnings: David and Two Sons. Pp. 26–34 in *Images of Man and God: Old Testament Short Stories in Literary Focus*, ed. B. O. Long. Bible and Literature Series. Sheffield: Almond.

Loretz, O. 1961 The *Perfectum copulativum* in 2 Sm 7,9–11. *Catholic Biblical Quarterly* 23:294–96.

Luckenbill, D. D. 1926–27 *Ancient Records of Assyria and Babylonia*. 2 vols. Chicago: University of Chicago. Cited by section (§).

Maass, F. 1956 Zu den Qumran-Varianten der Bücher Samuel. *Theologische Literaturzeitung* 81:337–40.

———, ed. 1967 *Das ferne und nahe Wort. Festschrift Leonhard Rost . . . gewidmet.* Beihefte zur Zeitschrift für die alttestamentliche Wissenschaft 105. Berlin: Töpelmann.

Mabee, C. 1980 David's Judicial Exoneration. *Zeitschrift für die alttestamentliche Wissenschaft* 92:89–107.

MacDonald, J. 1976 The Status and Role of the Na'ar in Israelite Society. *Journal of Near Eastern Studies* 35:147–70. *See also* Cutler, B.

Macholz, G. C. 1972 Die Stellung des Königs in der israelitischen Gerichtsverfassung. *Zeitschrift für die alttestamentliche Wissenschaft* 84:157–82.

Maisler, B. *See* Mazar, B.

Malamat, A. 1955 Doctrines of Causality in Biblical and Hittite Historiography. A Parallel. *Vetus Testamentum* 5:1–12.

1958 The Kingdom of David and Solomon in its Contact with Egypt and Aram Naharaim. *Biblical Archaeologist* 21:96–102 = Freedman and Campbell 1964: 89–98.

1962 Mari and the Bible: Some Patterns of Tribal Organization and Institutions. *Journal of the American Oriental Society* 82:143–50.

1963 Aspects of the Foreign Policies of David and Solomon. *Journal of Near Eastern Studies* 22:1–17.

1965 Organs of Statecraft in the Israelite Monarchy. *Biblical Archaeologist* 28: 34–65 = Campbell and Freedman 1970:163–98.

1966 Prophetic Revelations in New Documents from Mari and the Bible. Pp. 207–27 in *Volume du Congrès. Genève 1965.* Supplements to Vetus Testamentum 15. Leiden: Brill.

1971 Mari. *Biblical Archaeologist* 34:2–22.

1979 UMMATUM in Old Babylonian Texts and Its Ugaritic and Biblical Counterparts. *Ugarit-Forschungen* 11:527–36.

Mann, T. W. 1977 *Divine Presence and Guidance in Israelite Traditions: The Typology of Exaltation.* Johns Hopkins Near Eastern Studies. Baltimore: Johns Hopkins.

Marget, A. W. 1920 *gwrn nkwn* in 2 Sam. 6 6. *Journal of Biblical Literature* 39:70–76.

Matthes, J. C. 1903 Miscellen. *Zeitschrift für die alttestamentliche Wissenschaft* 23:120–27.

Mauchline, J. 1971 *1 and 2 Samuel.* New Century Bible. London: Oliphants. Cited as Mauchline.

Maurin, L. 1962 Himilcon le Magonide. Crises et mutations à Carthage au début du IV<sup>e</sup> siècle avant J.-C. *Semitica* 12:5–43.

May, H. G. 1955 Some Cosmic Connotations of *Mayim Rabbîm*, "Many Waters." *Journal of Biblical Literature* 74:9–21.

Mazar, A. 1981 Giloh: An Early Israelite Settlement Site near Jerusalem. *Israel Exploration Journal* 31:1–36.

Mazar [Maisler], B. 1946–47 The Scribe of King David and the Problem of the High Officials in the Ancient Kingdom of Israel [Hebrew]. *Bulletin of the Jewish Palestine Exploration Society* 13:105–14.

1960 The Cities of the Territory of Dan. *Israel Exploration Journal* 10:65–77.

1961 Geshur and Maacah. *Journal of Biblical Literature* 80:16–28.

1962 The Aramean Empire and Its Relations with Israel. *Biblical Archaeologist* 25:98–120 = Freedman and Campbell 1964:127–51.

1963a David's Reign in Hebron and the Conquest of Jerusalem. Pp. 235–44 in *In the Time of Harvest. Essays in Honor of Abba Hillel Silver . . .*, ed. D. J. Silver. New York: Macmillan.

1963b The Military Elite of King David. *Vetus Testamentum* 13:310–20.

1976 Jerusalem in the Biblical Period. Pp. 1–8 in *Jerusalem Revealed. Archaeology in the Holy City 1968–1974*, ed. Y. Yadin. New Haven and London: Yale and the Israel Exploration Society.

McBride, S. D. 1969 The Deuteronomic Name Theology. Ph.D. dissertation, Harvard.

McCarter, P. K., Jr. 1973 The River Ordeal in Israelite Literature. *Harvard Theological Review* 66:403–12.

1980a *I Samuel*. Anchor Bible 8. Garden City, N.Y.: Doubleday. Cited as *I Samuel*.

1980b The Apology of David. *Journal of Biblical Literature* 99:489–504.

1981 "Plots, True or False." The Succession Narrative as Court Apologetic. *Interpretation* 35:355–67.

McCarthy, D. J. 1965 II Samuel 7 and the Structure of the Deuteronomic History. *Journal of Biblical Literature* 84:131–38.

McKane, W. 1963 *I and II Samuel: The Way to the Throne*. Torch Bible Paperback. London: SCM. Cited as McKane.

1970 *Proverbs: A New Approach*. Old Testament Library. Philadelphia: Westminster.

McKenzie, J. L. 1947 The Dynastic Oracle: II Samuel 7. *Theological Studies* 8: 187–218.

1959 The Elders in the Old Testament. *Biblica* 40:522–40.

McRae, A. A. *See* Gelb, I. J.

Mendenhall, G. E. 1958 The Census Lists of Numbers 1 and 26. *Journal of Biblical Literature* 77:52–66.

1973 *The Tenth Generation. The Origins of the Biblical Tradition*. Baltimore/London: Johns Hopkins.

Merli, D. 1967 L'immolazione dei Saulidi (*2 Sam* 21,1–14). *Bibbia e Oriente* 9: 245–51.

Meshel, Z. 1979 Did Yahweh Have a Consort? *Biblical Archaeology Review* 5: 24–35.

Mettinger, T. N. D. 1971 *Solomonic State Officials*. Coniectanea Biblica Old Testament Series 5. Lund: CWK Gleerup.

1976 *King and Messiah. The Civil and Sacral Legitimation of the Israelite Kings.* Coniectanea Biblica Old Testament Series 8. Lund: CWK Gleerup.

1976–77 "The Last Words of David." A Study of Structure and Meaning in II Samuel 23:1–7. *Svensk Exegetisk Årsbok* 41/42:147–56.

Meyer, R. 1959 Auffallender Erzählungsstil in einem angeblichen Auszug aus der "Chronik der Könige von Juda." Pp. 114–23 in *Festschrift Friederich Baumgärtel . . . ,* ed. J. Herrmann and L. Rost. Erlanger Forschungen A10. Erlangen: Universitäts-bibliothek.

Michel, D. 1960 *Tempora und Satzstellung in den Psalmen.* Abhandlungen zur evangelischen Theologie 1. Bonn: Bouvier.

Milgrom, J. 1976a Atonement in the OT = *IDB Suppl* 78–82.

1976b Sacrifices and Offerings, OT = *IDB Suppl* 763–71.

Millard, A. R. 1978 Saul's Shield Not Anointed with Oil. *Bulletin of the American Schools of Oriental Research* 230:70.

Miller, P. D., Jr. 1971 Animal Names as Designations in Ugaritic and Hebrew. *Ugarit-Forschungen* 2:177–86.

*See also* Cross, F. M.

———, and J. J. M. Roberts 1977 *The Hand of the Lord. A Reassessment of the "Ark Narrative" of 1 Samuel.* Johns Hopkins Near Eastern Studies. Baltimore/London: Johns Hopkins.

Moran, W. L. 1954 Review of de Vaux 1961a [1953]. *Catholic Biblical Quarterly* 16:236–38.

1963a The Ancient Near Eastern Background of the Love of God in Deuteronomy. *Catholic Biblical Quarterly* 25:77–87.

1963b A Note on the Treaty Terminology of the Sefîre Stelas. *Journal of Near Eastern Studies* 22:173–76.

Morenz, S. 1954 Ägyptische und davidische Königstitulatur. *Zeitschrift für ägyptische Sprache und Altertumskunde* 79:73–74.

1973 *Egyptian Religion.* Trans. A. E. Keep from German 1960. Ithaca, N.Y.: Cornell.

Morgenstern, J. 1918 *nkwn. Journal of Biblical Literature* 37:144–48.

1942 The Ark, the Ephod and the Tent. *Hebrew Union College Annual* 17:153–265.

Morris, M. K. 1967 *Elohim* Again: A Note on 2 Sam 14,14. *Trivium* 2:147–49.

Mowinckel, S. 1927 "Die letzten Worte Davids" II Sam 23 1-7. *Zeitschrift für die alttestamentliche Wissenschaft* 45:30–58.

1947 Natansforjettelsen 2 Sam. kap. 7. *Svensk Exegetisk Årsbok* 12:220–29.

[1956] *He That Cometh.* Trans. G. W. Anderson from Norwegian 1951. New York: Abingdon.

1967 *The Psalms in Israel's Worship.* 2 vols. Trans. D. R. Ap-Thomas from Norwegian 1951. New York: Abingdon.

Muilenburg, J. 1959 The Form and Structure of Covenant Formulations. *Vetus Testamentum* 9:347–65.

Mulder, E. S. 1960 The Prophecy of Nathan in 2 Sam 7. Pp. 36–42 in Ou Testamentiese Werkgemeenskap 1960.

Mulder, M. J. 1968 Un euphémisme dans 2 Sam. XII 14? *Vetus Testamentum* 18:108–14.

Muntingh, L. M. 1960 The Kerethites and the Pelethites—a Historical and Sociological Discussion. Pp. 43–53 in Ou Testamentiese Werkgemeenskap 1960.

Murtonen, A. 1959 The Use and Meaning of the Words *l*[e]*bårek* and *b*[e]*råkå*[h] in the Old Testament. *Vetus Testamentum* 9:158–77.

Nestle, E. 1896 Miscellen. *Zeitschrift für die alttestamentliche Wissenschaft* 16:324.

Nicholson, E. W. 1967 *Deuteronomy and Tradition.* Philadelphia: Fortress.

von Nordheim, E. 1977 König und Tempel. Der Hintergrund des Tempelbauverbotes in 2 Samuel vii. *Vetus Testamentum* 27:434–53.

North, R. 1953 Review of Simons 1952. *Biblica* 34:224–35.

Noth, M. 1928 *Die israelitischen Personennamen im Rahmen der gemeinsemitischen Namengebung.* Beiträge zur Wissenschaft vom Alten und Neuen Testament 3/10. Stuttgart: Kohlhammer. Reprinted 1966. Hildesheim: Olms.

1943 *Überlieferungsgeschichtliche Studien. Die sammelnden und bearbeitenden Geschichtswerke im Alten Testament.* Tübingen: Niemeyer. 2d ed. (unrevised), 1957. 3d ed. (unrevised), 1967 = Noth 1981.

1956 Remarks on the Sixth Volume of Mari Texts. *Journal of Semitic Studies* 1:322–33.

1960 *The History of Israel.* Trans. P. R. Ackroyd from German 1960. New York: Harper & Row.

1966 Das Deutsche Evangelische Institut für Altertumskunde des Heiligen Landes im Jahre 1965. *Zeitschrift des Deutschen Palästina-Vereins* 82:255–73.

1967 David and Israel in II Samuel VII. Pp. 250–59 in *The Laws in the Pentateuch and Other Studies.* Trans. D. R. Ap-Thomas. Philadelphia: Fortress = David und Israel in 2. Samuel 7. Pp. 122–30 in *Mélanges bibliques rédigés en l'honneur de André Robert.* Travaux de l'Institut Catholique de Paris 4. Paris: Bloud et Gay, [1957].

1981 *The Deuteronomistic History.* Trans. J. Doull et al. from German 1967. Journal for the Study of the Old Testament Supplement Series 15. Sheffield: JSOT = Noth 1943.

Nowack, W. 1902 *Richter, Ruth und Bücher Samuelis übersetzt und erklärt.* Handkommentar zum Alten Testament I/4. Göttingen: Vandenhoeck und Ruprecht. Cited as Nowack.

Nyberg, H. S. 1938 Studien zum Religionskampf im Alten Testament. *Archiv für Religionswissenschaft* 35:329–87.

O'Callaghan, R. T. 1954 Echoes of Canaanite Literature in the Psalms. *Vetus Testamentum* 4:164–76.

O'Ceallaigh, G. C. 1962 "And *so* David did to *all the cities* of Ammon." *Vetus Testamentum* 12:179–89.

Offner, G. 1962 Jeux corporels en Sumer. *Revue d'assyriologie* 56:31–38.

Oppenheim, A. L. 1949 The Golden Garments of the Gods. *Journal of Near Eastern Studies* 8:172–93.

Orlinsky, H. M. 1939 Review of Rehm 1937. *Journal of Biblical Literature* 58: 397–99.

1946 *Hā-rōqḏīm* for *hā-rēqīm* in II Samuel 6 20. *Journal of Biblical Literature* 65:25–35.

Ota, M. 1974 A Note on 2 Samuel 7. Pp. 403–8 in *A Light unto My Path. Old Testament Studies in Honor of Jacob M. Myers,* ed. H. N. Bream et al. Gettysburg Theological Studies 4. Philadelphia: Temple.

Ou Testamentiese Werkgemeenskap 1960 *Studies on the Books of Samuel.* Papers

Read at the Third Meeting of the Ou Testamentiese Werkgemeenskap in Suid-Afrika. Pretoria.

von Pákozdy, L. M. 1956 'Elḥânân—der frühere Name Davids? *Zeitschrift für die alttestamentliche Wissenschaft* 68:257–59.

Parker, S. B. 1971 Exod XV 2 Again. *Vetus Testamentum* 21:373–79.

1972 The Ugaritic Deity Rāpi'u. *Ugarit-Forschungen* 4:97–104.

Patton, J. H. 1944 *Canaanite Parallels in the Book of Psalms.* Baltimore: Johns Hopkins.

Payne, D. F. 1970 1 and 2 Samuel. Pp. 284–319 in *The New Bible Commentary: Revised,* ed. D. Guthrie and J. A. Motyer. Grand Rapids, Mich.: Eerdmans.

Pedersen, J. P. E. 1940 *Israel.* 4 vols. London: Oxford.

Perlitt, L. 1969 *Bundestheologie im Alten Testament.* Wissenschaftliche Monographien zum Alten und Neuen Testament 36. Neukirchen-Vluyn: Neukirchener Verlag.

Perry, M., and M. Sternberg 1968–69a The King through Ironic Eyes: The Narrator's Devices in the Biblical Story of David and Bathsheba and Two Exercises on the Theory of Narrative Text [Hebrew]. *Hasifrut* 1:263–92.

1968–69b Caution, a Literary Text! Problems in the Poetics and Interpretation of Biblical Narrative [Hebrew]. *Hasifrut* 1:608–63.

Pfeiffer, R. H. 1948 *Introduction to the Old Testament.* Rev. ed. New York: Harper & Bros.

———, and W. G. Pollard 1957 *The Hebrew Iliad. The History of the Rise of Israel under Saul and David.* New York: Harper.

Phillips, A. 1966 The Interpretation of 2 Samuel xii 5–6. *Vetus Testamentum* 16: 243–45.

1969 David's Linen Ephod. *Vetus Testamentum* 19:485–87.

1975 *NEBALAH*—a Term for Serious Disorderly and Unruly Conduct. *Vetus Testamentum* 25:237–41.

van der Ploeg, J. P. M. 1961 Les Anciens dans l'Ancien Testament. Pp. 175–91 in *Lex tua veritas. Festschrift für Hubert Junker . . . ,* ed. H. Gross and F. Mussner. Trier: Paulinus.

———, and A. S. van der Woude 1971 *Le Targum de Job de la Grotte XI de Qumrân.* Koninklijke Nederlandse Akademie van Wetenschappen. Leiden: Brill.

Poels, H. A. 1894 *Le Sanctuaire de Kiriath-jearim. Étude sur le lieu du culte chez les Israélites au temps de Samuel.* Louvain: Istas.

1897 *Examen critique de l'histoire du sanctuaire de l'arche.* Louvain: Van Linthout.

Pohl, A. 1959 Personalnachrichten. *Orientalia* 28:296–300.

Pollard, W. G. *See* Pfeiffer, R. H.

Polzin, R. 1969 HWQY' and Covenantal Institutions in Israel. *Harvard Theological Review* 62:227–40.

Pope, M. H. 1955 *EL in the Ugaritic Texts.* Supplements to Vetus Testamentum 2. Leiden: Brill.

1973 *Job. A New Translation with Introduction and Commentary.* 3d ed. Anchor Bible 15. Garden City, N.Y.: Doubleday.

1977 *Song of Songs. A New Translation with Introduction and Commentary.* Anchor Bible 7C. Garden City, N.Y.: Doubleday.

Porter, J. R. 1954 The Interpretation of 2 Samuel vi and Psalm cxxxii. *Journal of Theological Studies* 5:161–73.

Porporato, S. 1949 Il "trono eterno" promesso a Davide nel suo avveramento (2 Sam 7:1). *Civiltà Cattolica* 100:130–39.

Poulssen, N. 1967 *König und Tempel im Glaubenszeugnis des Alten Testamentes.* Stuttgarter biblische Monographien 3. Stuttgart: Katholisches Bibelwerk.

1978 De Mikalscène, 2 Sam 6, 16.20–23. *Bijdragen: Tijdschrift voor Filosofie en Theologie* 39:32–58.

Prado, J. 1954 El exterminio de la familia de Saul (2 Sam 21,1–14). *Sefarad* 14: 43–57.

Preuss, H. D. 1968 ". . . ich will mit dir sein!" *Zeitschrift für die alttestamentliche Wissenschaft* 80:139–73.

Pritchard, J. B. 1956 The Water System at Gibeon. *Biblical Archaeologist* 19:66–75.

1960 Gibeon's History in the Light of Excavation. Pp. 1–12 in *Congress Volume. Oxford 1959.* Supplements to Vetus Testamentum 7. Leiden: Brill.

1961 *The Water System of Gibeon.* University of Pennsylvania Museum Monographs. Philadelphia: University of Pennsylvania.

1962 *Gibeon, Where the Sun Stood Still.* Princeton, N.J.: Princeton.

Procksch, O. 1913 Die letzten Worte Davids. Pp. 112–25 in *Alttestamentliche Studien, Rudolf Kittel. . . .* Beiträge zur Wissenschaft vom Alten Testament 13. Leipzig: Hinrichs.

Purves, P. M. *See* Gelb, I. J.

von Rad, G. 1944 Der Anfang der Geschichtsschreibung im alten Israel. *Archiv für Kulturgeschichte* 32:1–42 = von Rad 1966:166–204.

1953 *Studies in Déuteronomy.* Trans. D. Stalker from German 1948. London: SCM.

1962 *Old Testament Theology.* 2 vols. Trans. D. M. G. Stalker from German 1957. New York: Harper & Row.

1966 *The Problem of the Hexateuch and Other Essays.* Trans. E. W. Trueman Dicken from German 1958. New York: McGraw-Hill.

Rahlfs, A., ed. 1904–11 *Septuaginta-Studien.* 3 vols. Göttingen: Vandenhoeck und Ruprecht.

Rainey, A. F. 1965a The Military Personnel of Ugarit. *Journal of Near Eastern Studies* 24:17–27.

1965b Royal Weights and Measures. *Bulletin of the American Schools of Oriental Research* 179:34–36.

1967a *The Social Structure of Ugarit* [Hebrew]. Jerusalem: Bialik Institute.

1967b The Samaria Ostraca in Light of Fresh Evidence. *Palestine Exploration Quarterly* 99:32–41.

1970 Semantic Parallels to the Samaria Ostraca. *Palestine Exploration Quarterly* 102:45–51.

1975 A Problem in Source Analysis for Historical Geography. *Eretz Israel* 12: *63–*76 [* = English section].

1979 The *Sitz im Leben* of the Samaria Ostraca. *Tel Aviv* 6:91–94.

Randellini, L. 1961 Il significato del vaticinio di Natan. *Bibbia e Oriente* 3:130–35.

Ravenna, A. 1956 Osservazioni sul testo di Samuele. *Rivista biblica italiana* 4: 143–44.

Rehm, M. 1937 *Textkritische Untersuchungen zu den Parallelstellen der Samuel-Königsbücher und der Chronik.* Alttestamentliche Abhandlungen 13/3. Münster: Aschendorff.

1956 *Die Bücher Samuel.* 2d ed. Die heilige Schrift in deutschen Übersetzung. Echter-Bibel 7/1. Würzburg: Echter. Cited as Rehm.

Reid, P. V. 1975 *šbṭy* in 2 Samuel 7:7. *Catholic Biblical Quarterly* 37:17–20.

Reider, J. 1952 Etymological Studies in Biblical Hebrew. *Vetus Testamentum* 2: 113–30.

Rendtorff, R. 1971 Beobachtungen zur altisraelitischen Geschichtsschreibung anhand der Geschichte vom Aufstieg Davids. Pp. 428–39 in Wolff 1971.

Reventlow, H. G. 1959 Das Amt des Mazkir. *Theologische Zeitschrift* 15:161–75.

Richardson, H. N. 1971 The Last Words of David. Some Notes on II Sam 23:1–7. *Journal of Biblical Literature* 90:257–66.

Richter, W. 1967 Beobachtungen zur theologischen Systembildung in der alttestamentlichen Literatur anhand des "kleines geschichtlichen Credo." Pp. 175–212 in vol. I of *Wahrheit und Verkündigung. Michael Schmaus . . .*, ed. L. Scheffczyk et al. Munich: Schöningh.

Ridout, G. P. 1971 Prose Compositional Techniques in the Succession Narrative (2 Sam. 7,9–10; 1 Kings 1–2). Ph.D. dissertation, Graduate Theological Union.

1974 The Rape of Tamar. Pp. 75–84 in *Rhetorical Criticism. Essays in Honor of James Muilenburg*, ed. J. J. Jackson and M. Kessler. Pittsburgh: Pickwick.

Rinaldi, G. 1959 L'ascesa a Gerusalemme. *Bibbia e Oriente* 1:129–32.

de Robert, P. 1971 Juges ou tribus en 2 Samuel vii 7? *Vetus Testamentum* 21: 116–18.

Roberts, J. J. M. 1971 The Hand of Yahweh. *Vetus Testamentum* 21:244–52. *See also* Miller, P. D., Jr.

Robertson, D. A. 1972 *Linguistic Evidence in Dating Early Hebrew Poetry.* Society of Biblical Literature, Dissertation Series 3. Missoula, Mont.: Scholars.

Robertson Smith, W. 1966 *Kinship and Marriage in Early Arabia.* 2d ed. [1907]. Oosterhout: Anthropological Publications reprint.

1969 *Lectures on the Religion of the Semites.* 3d ed. [1927]. [New York]: Ktav reprint.

Röllig, W. *See* Friedrich, J.

Rosén, H. B. 1955 Arawna—nom hittite? *Vetus Testamentum* 5:318–20.

Rosmarin, T. W. 1932 The Terms for "Air" in the Bible. *Journal of Biblical Literature* 51:71–72.

1933 Note on II Sam. 14 27. *Journal of Biblical Literature* 52:261–62.

Rost, L. 1926 *Die Überlieferung von der Thronnachfolge Davids.* Beiträge zur Wissenschaft vom Alten und Neuen Testament 3/6. Stuttgart: Kohlhammer = Rost 1965:119–253.

1965 *Das kleine Credo und andere Studien zum Alten Testament.* Heidelberg: Quelle und Meyer.

Roth, W. M. W. 1960 *NBL. Vetus Testamentum* 10:394–409.

1977 You Are the Man! Structural Interaction in 2 Samuel 10–12. *Semeia* 8:1–13.

Rothstein, J. W. 1913 Die Klagelieder Davids. Pp. 154–67 in *Alttestamentliche Studien, Rudolf Kittel . . . dargebracht.* Beiträge zur Wissenschaft vom Alten Testament 13. Leipzig: Hinrichs.

Rowley, H. H. 1939 Zadok and Nehushtan. *Journal of Biblical Literature* 58: 113–41.

1967 *Worship in Ancient Israel. Its Forms and Meanings.* Philadelphia: Fortress.

Rupprecht, K. 1977 *Der Tempel von Jerusalem. Gründung Salomos oder jebusitisches Erbe?* Beihefte zur Zeitschrift für die alttestamentliche Wissenschaft 144. Berlin: de Gruyter.

Sakenfeld, K. D. 1978 *The Meaning of Hesed in the Hebrew Bible: A New Inquiry.* Harvard Semitic Monographs 17. Missoula, Mont.: Scholars.

Sanders, J. A. 1962 Census = *IDB* 1:547.

1965 *The Psalms Scroll of Qumran Cave 11 (11 QPs[a]).* Discoveries in the Judaean Desert of Jordan 4. Oxford: Clarendon.

Sarna, N. M. 1963 Psalm 89: A Study in Inner Biblical Exegesis. *Texts and Studies* [P. W. Lown Institute, Brandeis University] 1:29–46.

Schicklberger, F. 1973 *Die Ladeerzählungen der ersten Samuel-Buches. Eine literaturwissenschaftliche und theologiegeschichtliche Untersuchung.* Forschung zur Bibel 7. Würzburg: Echter.

Schildenberger, J. B. 1951 Zur Einleitung in die Samuelbücher. Pp. 130–68 in *Miscellanea Biblica et Orientalia R. P. Athanasio Miller . . . oblata,* ed. A. Metzinger. Studia Anselmiana 27–28. Rome: Herder.

Schill, S. 1891 Zu 2 Sam. 12,6. *Zeitschrift für die alttestamentliche Wissenschaft* 11:318.

von Schlatter, A. 1893 *Zur Topographie und Geschichte Palästinas.* Calw: Verlag der Vereinsbuchhandlung.

Schlisske, W. 1973 *Gottessöhne und Gottesohn im Alten Testament.* Beiträge zur Wissenschaft vom Alten und Neuen Testament 17/97. Stuttgart: Kohlhammer.

Schmid, H. 1955 Jahwe und die Kulttradition von Jerusalem. *Zeitschrift für die alttestamentliche Wissenschaft* 67:168–97.

1970 Der Tempelbau Salomos in religionsgeschichtlicher Sicht. Pp. 241–50 in *Archäologie und Altes Testament. Festschrift für Kurt Galling . . .,* ed. A. Kuschke and E. Kutsch. Tübingen: Mohr.

Schmidt, H. 1933 *Die heilige Fels in Jerusalem. Eine archäologische und religionsgeschichtliche Studie.* Tübingen: Mohr.

1934 *Die Psalmen.* Handbuch zum Alten Testament 1/15. Tübingen: Mohr.

Schmidt, L. 1970 *Menschlicher Erfolg und Jahwes Initiative. Studien zu Tradition, Interpretation und Historie in Überlieferungen von Gideon, Saul, und David.* Wissenschaftliche Monographien zum Alten und Neuen Testament 38. Neukirchen-Vluyn: Neukirchener Verlag.

Schmidt, W. H. 1971 Kritik am Königtum. Pp. 440–61 in Wolff 1971.

Schmuttermayr, G. 1971 *Psalm 18 und 2 Samuel 22. Studien zu einem Doppeltext.* Studien zum Alten und Neuen Testament 25. Munich: Kösel.

Schottroff, W. 1964 *"Gedenken" im Alten Orient und im Alten Testament.* Wissenschaftliche Monographien zum Alten und Neuen Testament 15. Neukirchen-Vluyn: Neukirchener Verlag.

Schreiner, J. 1963 *Sion-Jerusalem, Jahwes Königssitz.* Studien zum Alten und Neuen Testament 7. Munich: Kösel.

Schult, H. 1965 Ein inschriftlicher Beleg für "Plethi"? *Zeitschrift des Deutschen Palästina-Vereins* 81:74–79.

Schulte, H. 1972 *Die Entstehung der Geschichtsschreibung im alten Israel.* Beihefte zur Zeitschrift für die alttestamentliche Wissenschaft 128. Berlin: de Gruyter.

Schulthess, F. 1905 *rîpôt* 2 Sam 17,19, *ripôt* Prov 27,22. *Zeitschrift für die alttestamentliche Wissenschaft* 25:357–59.

Schulz, A. 1920 *Das zweite Buch Samuel.* Exegetisches Handbuch zum Alten Testament 8/2. Münster: Aschendorff. Cited as Schulz.

Schunck, K.-D. 1961 Ophra, Ephron und Ephraim. *Vetus Testamentum* 11:188–200.

1963a *Benjamin.* Beihefte zur Zeitschrift für die alttestamentliche Wissenschaft 86. Berlin: Töpelmann.

1963b Erwägungen zur Geschichte und Bedeutung von Mahanaim. *Zeitschrift der Deutschen Morgenländischen Gesellschaft* 113:34–40.

Schwally, F. 1892 Zur Quellenkritik der historischen Bücher. *Zeitschrift für die alttestamentliche Wissenschaft* 12:153–61.

Scott, R. B. Y. 1959 Weights and Measures of the Bible. *Biblical Archaeologist* 22:22–40 = Campbell and Freedman 1970:345–58.

Seebass, H. 1964 Ephraim in 2 Sam. XIII 23. *Vetus Testamentum* 14:497–500.

1974 Nathan und David in II Sam 12. *Zeitschrift für die alttestamentliche Wissenschaft* 86:203–11.

Segal, M. H. 1914–15 Studies in the Books of Samuel. I. David's Three Poems. *Jewish Quarterly Review* 5:201–31.

1915–16 Studies in the Books of Samuel. II. The Composition of the Book. *Jewish Quarterly Review* 6:267–302,555–87.

1917–18 Studies in the Books of Samuel. II. The Composition of the Book (continued). *Jewish Quarterly Review* 8:75–100.

1918–19 Studies in the Books of Samuel. II. The Composition of the Book (concluded). *Jewish Quarterly Review* 9:43–70.

1964–65 The Composition of the Books of Samuel. *Jewish Quarterly Review* 55:318–39.

1965–66 The Composition of the Books of Samuel (continued). *Jewish Quarterly Review* 56:32–50,137–57.

Segert, S. 1976 *A Grammar of Phoenician and Punic.* Munich: Beck.

van Selms, A. 1957 The Origin of the Title "The King's Friend." *Journal of Near Eastern Studies* 16:118–23.

1960 The Armed Forces in Israel under Saul and David. Pp. 55–66 in Ou Testamentiese Werkgemeenskap 1960.

Seybold, K. 1972 *Das davidische Königtum im Zeugnis der Propheten.* Forschungen zur Religion und Literatur des Alten und Neuen Testaments 107. Göttingen: Vandenhoeck und Ruprecht.

Shea, W. H. 1976 David's Lament. *Bulletin of the American Schools of Oriental Research* 221:141–44.

Shenkel, J. D. 1969 A Comparative Study of the Synoptic Parallels in I Paraleipomena and I–II Reigns. *Harvard Theological Review* 62:63–85.

Simon, M. 1952 La Prophétie de Nathan et le Temple (Remarques sur II *Sam.* 7). *Revue d'histoire et de philosophie religieuses* 32:41–58.

Simon, U. 1967 The Poor Man's Ewe-Lamb. An Example of a Juridical Parable. *Biblica* 48:207–42.

1968–69 An Ironic Approach to a Bible Story: On the Interpretation of the Story of David and Bathsheba [Hebrew]. *Hasifrut* 1:598–607.

Simons, J. 1952 *Jerusalem in the Old Testament. Research and Theories.* Studia Francisci Scholten memoriae dicata 1. Leiden: Brill.

Simōta, P. N. 1965 To Chōrion B' Basileiōn 24,15 kata to Keimenon tōn O'. *Theologia* 36:580–86.

Skehan, P. W. 1969 Joab's Census: How Far North (2 Sm 24,6)? *Catholic Biblical Quarterly* 31:42–49.

Smend, R. 1971 Das Gesetz und die Völker. Ein Beitrag zur deuteronomistischen Redaktionsgeschichte. Pp. 494–509 in Wolff 1971.

Smith, H. P. 1899 *A Critical and Exegetical Commentary on the Books of Samuel.* International Critical Commentary. Edinburgh: Clark. Cited as Smith.

Smith, M. 1951 The So-called "Biography of David" in the Books of Samuel and Kings. *Harvard Theological Review* 44:167–69.

Snaith, N. H. 1945 *Notes on the Hebrew Text of 2 Samuel XVI–XIX.* Study Notes on Bible Books. London: Epworth.

Soggin, J. A. 1964 "Wacholderholz" 2 Sam VI 5a gleich "Schlaghölzer", "Klappern"? *Vetus Testamentum* 14:374–77.

1966 Die offiziell geforderte Synkretismus in Israel während des 10. Jahrhunderts. *Zeitschrift für die alttestamentliche Wissenschaft* 78:179–203.

1967 *Das Königtum in Israel. Ursprünge, Spannungen, Entwicklung.* Beihefte zur Zeitschrift für die alttestamentliche Wissenschaft 104. Berlin: Töpelmann.

1975 The Reign of 'Ešba'al, Son of Saul. Pp. 31–49 in *Old Testament and Oriental Studies.* Biblica et Orientalia 29. Rome: Pontifical Biblical Institute = Il regno di Ešba'al, figlio di Saul. *Rivista degli studi orientali* 40 (1965):89–106.

Speiser, E. A. 1950 An Analog to 2 Sam 1:21: Aqht 1:44f. *Journal of Biblical Literature* 69:377–78.

1958 Census and Ritual Expiation in Mari and Israel. *Bulletin of the American Schools of Oriental Research* 149:17–25 = Speiser 1967:171–76.

1960 "People" and "Nation" of Israel. *Journal of Biblical Literature* 79:157–63 = Speiser 1967:160–70.

1964 *Genesis. A New Translation with Introduction and Commentary.* Anchor Bible 1. Garden City, N.Y.: Doubleday.

1967 *Oriental and Biblical Studies.* Ed. J. J. Finkelstein and M. Greenberg. Philadelphia: University of Pennsylvania.

Spoer, H. H. 1907 Versuch einer Erklärung von Psalm 18. *Zeitschrift für die alttestamentliche Wissenschaft* 27:145–61.

Stähli, H.-P. 1978 *Knabe-Jüngling-Knecht. Untersuchungen zum Begriff* n'r *im Alten Testament.* Beiträge zur biblischen Exegese und Theologie 7. Frankfurt am Maim/Bern/Las Vegas: Lang.

Stamm, J. J. 1940 *Erlösen und Vergeben im Alten Testament. Eine Begriffsgeschichtliche Untersuchung.* Bern: Francke.

1960a Der Name des Königs Salomo. *Theologische Zeitschrift* 16:285–97.

1960b Der Name des Königs David. Pp. 165–83 in *Congress Volume. Oxford 1959.* Supplements to Vetus Testamentum 7. Leiden: Brill.

1965 Hebräische Ersatznamen. Pp. 413–24 in *Studies in Honor of Benno Landsberger . . .* Assyriological Studies of the Oriental Institute of the University of Chicago 16. Chicago: University of Chicago.

Sternberg, M. *See* Perry, M.

Steuernagel, C. 1912 *Lehrbuch der Einleitung in das Alte Testament, mit einem Anhang über die Apokryphen und Pseudepigraphen.* Tübingen: Mohr.

Stoebe, H. J. 1957 Die Einnahme Jerusalems. *Zeitschrift des Deutschen Palästina-Vereins* 73:73–99.

1967 Gedanken zur Heldensage in den Samuelbüchern. Pp. 208–18 in Maass 1967.

1977 David und der Ammonitkrieg. *Zeitschrift des Deutschen Palästina-Vereins* 93:236–46.

Streck, M. 1916 *Assurbanipal und die letzten assyrischen Könige bis zum Untergange Nineveh's.* 3 vols. Vorderasiatische Bibliothek 7. Leipzig: Hinrichs.

Stuart, D. K. 1976 *Studies in Early Hebrew Meter.* Harvard Semitic Monographs 13. Missoula, Mont.: Scholars.

Sukenik, E. L. 1928 The Account of David's Capture of Jerusalem. *Journal of the Palestine Oriental Society* 8:12–16.

Sukenik, Y. *See* Yadin, Y.

Swetnam, J. 1965 Some Observations on the Background of *ṣdyq* in Jeremias 23,5a. *Biblica* 46:29–40.

Szikszai, S. 1962 Samuel, I and II = *IDB* 4:202–9.

Tadmor, H. 1958 Historical Implications of the Correct Reading of Akkadian *dâku. Journal of Near Eastern Studies* 17:129–41.

Talmon, S. 1960 Double Readings in the Massoretic Text. Pp. 144–84 in *Textus. Annual of the Hebrew University Bible Project* I. Jerusalem: Magnes.

1975 The Textual Study of the Bible—A New Outlook. Pp. 321–400 in Cross and Talmon 1975.

*See also* Cross, F. M.

Thackeray, H. St. J. 1907 The Greek Translators of the Four Books of Kings. *Journal of Theological Studies* 8:262–78.

1921 *The Septuagint and Jewish Worship, a Study in Origins.* Schweich Lectures 1920. London: Milford for the British Academy.

Thenius, O. 1842 *Die Bücher Samuels.* Kurzgefasstes exegetisches Handbuch zum Alten Testament 4. Leipzig: Weidmann. 2d ed., 1864. 3d ed. (Max Löhr), 1898.

Thornton, T. C. G. 1968 Solomonic Apologetic in Samuel and Kings. *Church Quarterly Review* 169:159–66.

Thureau-Dangin, F. 1922 Nouvelles lettres d'El-Amarna. *Revue d'assyriologie et d'archéologie orientale* 19:91–108.

Tidwell, N. L. 1974 The Linen Ephod. *Vetus Testamentum* 24:505–7.

1979 The Philistine Incursions into the Valley of Rephaim (2 Sam. v 17ff.). Pp. 190–212 in Emerton 1979.

Tiktin, H. 1922 *Kritische Untersuchungen zu den Büchern Samuelis.* Forschungen zur Religion und Literatur des Alten und Neuen Testaments 16. Göttingen: Vandenhoeck und Ruprecht.

Tomback, R. S. 1978 *A Comparative Semitic Lexicon of the Phoenician and Punic Languages.* Society of Biblical Literature Dissertation Series 32. Missoula, Mont.: Scholars.

Tournay, R. 1956 En marge d'une traduction des Psaumes. *Revue biblique* 63: 161–81.

1964 Review of Gevirtz 1963. *Revue biblique* 71:283–86.

Tov, E., ed. 1980 *The Hebrew and Greek Texts of Samuel.* 1980 Proceedings IOSCS —Vienna. Jerusalem: Academon.

Tromp, N. J. 1969 *Primitive Conceptions of Death and the Nether World in the Old Testament.* Rome: Pontifical Biblical Institute.

Tsevat, M. 1958a Alalakhiana. *Hebrew Union College Annual* 29:109–34.

1958b Marriage and Monarchical Legitimacy in Ugarit and Israel. *Journal of Semitic Studies* 3:237–43.

1963 Studies in the Book of Samuel. III. The Steadfast House: What Was David Promised in II Sam. 7:13b–16? *Hebrew Union College Annual* 34:71–82.

1965 The House of David in Nathan's Prophecy. *Biblica* 46:353–56.

1975 Ishbosheth and Congeners: The Names and Their Study. *Hebrew Union College Annual* 46:71–87.

1976 Samuel, I and II = *IDB Suppl* 777–81.

Tsumura, D. T. 1976 Ugaritic Contributions to Hebrew Lexicography [Japanese]. *Studies in Language and Literature* [Institute of Literature and Linguistics, University of Tsukuba] 1:83–115.

Turro, J. C. 1968 1–2 Samuel. Pp. 164–78 in *The Jerome Biblical Commentary,* ed. R. E. Brown, J. A. Fitzmyer, and R. E. Murphy. Vol. I: *The Old Testament.* Englewood Cliffs, N.J.: Prentice-Hall.

Tur-Sinai, N. H. 1951 The Ark of God at Beit Shemesh (1 Sam. vi) and Pereṣ Uzza (2 Sam. vi; 1 Chron. xiii). *Vetus Testamentum* 1:275–86.

Ulrich, E. C., Jr. 1978 *The Qumran Text of Samuel and Josephus.* Harvard Semitic Monographs 19. Missoula, Mont.: Scholars.

1979 4QSam$^c$: A Fragmentary Manuscript of 2 Samuel 14–15 from the Scribe of the *Serek Hay-yaḥad. Bulletin of the American Schools of Oriental Research* 235: 1–25 = Tob 1980:166–88.

1980 The Old Latin Translation of the LXX and the Hebrew Scrolls from Qumran. Pp. 123–65 in Tov 1980.

VanderKam, J. C. 1980 Davidic Complicity in the Deaths of Abner and Eshbaal: A Historical and Redactional Study. *Journal of Biblical Literature* 99: 521–39.

Vannutelli, P., ed. 1931 *Libri synoptici Veteris Testamenti; seu, librorum Regum et Chronicorum loci paralleli. . . .* Rome: Pontifical Biblical Institute.

Van Seters, J. 1976a Oral Patterns or Literary Conventions in Biblical Narrative. *Semeia* 5:139–54.

1976b Problems in the Literary Analysis of the Court History of David. *Journal for the Study of the Old Testament* 1:22–29.

1981 Histories and Historians of the Ancient Near East: The Israelites. *Orientalia* 50:137–95.

Vaughn, P. H. 1974 *The Meaning of "bāmâ" in the Old Testament.* Society for Old Testament Study, Monograph Series 3. London: Cambridge.

de Vaux, R. 1939 Titres et fonctionnaires égyptiens à la cour de David et de Salomon. *Revue biblique* 48:394–405.

1961a *Les Livres de Samuel.* 2d ed. Paris: Les Editions du Cerf. Cited as de Vaux.

1961b *Ancient Israel.* Vol. 1: *Social Institutions.* Vol. 2: *Religious Institutions.* Trans. J. McHugh from French 1958, 1960. New York: McGraw-Hill.

1966 Jérusalem et les prophètes. *Revue biblique* 73:481–509.

1967 "Le lieu que Yahvé a choisi pour y établir son nom." Pp. 219–38 in Maass 1967.

1971 *The Bible and the Ancient Near East.* Trans. D. McHugh from French 1967. Garden City, N.Y.: Doubleday.

1978 *The Early History of Israel.* Trans. D. Smith from French 1971, 1973. Philadelphia: Westminster.

Veijola, T. 1975 *Die ewige Dynastie. David und die Entstehung seiner Dynastie nach der deuteronomistischen Darstellung.* Annales Academiae Scientiarum Fennicae B 193. Helsinki: Suomalainen Tiedeakatemia.

1977 *Das Königtum in der Beurteilung der deuteronomistischen Historiographie. Eine redaktionsgeschichtliche Untersuchung.* Annales Academiae Scientiarum Fennicae B 198. Helsinki: Suomalainen Tiedeakatemia.

1978 David und Meribaal. *Revue biblique* 85:338–61.

1979 Salomo—der Erstgeborene Bathsebas. Pp. 230–50 in Emerton 1979.

Vetter, D. 1971 *Jahwes Mit-Sein; ein Ausdruck des Segens.* Arbeiten zur Theologie 45. Stuttgart: Calwer.

Vincent, L. H. 1924 Le Ṣinnor dans la prise de Jérusalem (II Sam. V 8). *Revue biblique* 33:357–70.

Vogt, E. 1959 *'El haššᵉlōšā lō'-bā'.* *Biblica* 40:1062–63.

Voigt, E. E. 1923 The Site of Nob. *Journal of the Palestine Exploration Society* 3:79–87.

Vriezen, T. C. 1948 De Compositie van de Samuël-Boeken. Pp. 167–89 in *Orientalia Neerlandica. A Volume of Oriental Studies,* ed. Netherlands Oriental Society. Leiden: Sijthoff.

Walvoord, J. F. 1953 The Kingdom Promises to David. *Bibliotheca Sacra* 110: 97–110.

de Ward, E. F. 1972 Mourning Customs in 1, 2 Samuel. *Journal of Jewish Studies* 23:1–27,145–66.

Ward, R. L. 1967 The Story of David's Rise: A Traditio-Historical Study of I Samuel xvi 14–II Samuel v. Ph.D. dissertation, Vanderbilt.

Watson, W. G. E. 1970 David Ousts the City Ruler of Jebus. *Vetus Testamentum* 20:501–2.

Weill, J. 1929 II Samuel, XIX, 25. *Revue des études juives* 87:212.

Weinfeld, M. 1970 The Covenant of Grant in the Old Testament and in the Ancient Near East. *Journal of the American Oriental Society* 90:184–203.

1972 *Deuteronomy and the Deuteronomic School.* Oxford: Clarendon.

1976 Covenant, Davidic = *IDB Suppl* 188–92.

Weingreen, J. 1969 The Rebellion of Absalom. *Vetus Testamentum* 19:263–66.

Weiser, A. 1962 *The Psalms. A Commentary.* Trans. H. Hartwell from German 1959. Old Testament Library. Philadelphia: Westminster.

1965 Die Tempelbaukrise unter David. *Zeitschrift für die alttestamentliche Wissenschaft* 77:153–68.

1966 Die Legitimation des Königs David. Zur Eigenart und Entstehung der sogen. Geschichte des Davids Aufstieg. *Vetus Testamentum* 16:325–54.

Wellhausen, J. 1871 *Der Text der Bücher Samuelis untersucht.* Göttingen: Vandenhoeck und Ruprecht. Cited as Wellhausen.

1899 *Die Composition des Hexateuchs und der historischen Bücher des Alten Testaments.* 3d ed. Berlin: Reimer.

1957 *Prolegomena to the History of Ancient Israel.* Trans. Menzies and Black from German 1878. Cleveland: World.

Wenham, G. J. 1972 *Bᵉtûlāh* "A Girl of Marriageable Age." *Vetus Testamentum* 22:326–48.

1975 Were David's Sons Priests? *Zeitschrift für die alttestamentliche Wissenschaft* 87:79–82.

Westermann, C. 1967 *Basic Forms of Prophetic Speech.* Trans. H. C. White from German 1960. Philadelphia: Westminster.

Wetzstein, J. G. 1883 Briefliche Bemerkungen. *Zeitschrift fur die alttestamentliche Wissenschaft* 3:273–79.

Wevers, J. W. 1953 A Study of the Exegetical Principles of the Translator of II Sam. xi:2 = I Kings ii:11. *Catholic Biblical Quarterly* 15:30–45.

Whitley, C. F. 1972 The Positive Force of the Hebrew Particle *bl.* *Zeitschrift für die alttestamentliche Wissenschaft* 84:213–19.

Whybray, R. N. 1968 *The Succession Narrative. A Study of II Sam. 9–20 and I Kings 1 and 2.* Studies in Biblical Theology, second series 9. Naperville, Ill.: Allenson.

Wifall, W. 1975 Son of Man—a Pre-Davidic Social Class? *Catholic Biblical Quarterly* 37:331–40.

Willesen, F. 1958a The Philistine Corps of the Scimitar from Gath. *Journal of Semitic Studies* 3:327–35.

1958b The Yālīd in Hebrew Society. *Studia Theologica* 12:192–210.

Willis, J. T. 1971 An Anti-Elide Narrative Tradition from a Prophetic Circle at the Ramah Sanctuary. *Journal of Biblical Literature* 90:288–308.

Wilson, R. R. 1980 *Prophecy and Society in Ancient Israel.* Philadelphia: Fortress.

Winckler, H. 1895–1900 *Geschichte Israels in Einzeldarstellung.* 2 vols. Völker und Staaten des alten Orients 2–3. Leipzig: Pfeiffer.

Winton Thomas, D. 1960 *Kelebh* 'Dog': Its Origin and Some Usages of It in the Old Testament. *Vetus Testamentum* 10:410–27.

1963 *Bĕlîya'al* in the Old Testament. Pp. 11–19 in *Biblical and Patristic Studies in Memory of Robert Pierce Casey,* ed. J. N. Birdsall and R. W. Thomson. Freiburg/New York: Herder.

———, ed. 1967 *Archaeology and Old Testament Study.* Jubilee Volume for the Society for Old Testament Study 1917–1967. Oxford: Clarendon.

Wolff, H. W. 1964 *Amos' geistige Heimat.* Wissenschaftliche Monographien zum Alten und Neuen Testament 18. Neukirchen-Vluyn: Neukirchener Verlag.

———, ed. 1971 *Probleme biblischer Theologie. Gerhard von Rad. . . .* Munich: Kaiser.

van der Woude, A. S. *See* van der Ploeg, J. P. M.

Wright, G. E. 1966 Fresh Evidence for the Philistine Story. *Biblical Archaeologist* 29:70–86.

———, and D. N. Freedman 1961 *The Biblical Archaeologist Reader 1.* Anchor Books. Garden City, N.Y.: Doubleday.

Würthwein, E. 1974 *Die Erzählung von der Thronfolge Davids—theologische oder politische Geschichtsschreibung?* Theologische Studien 115. Zurich: Theologischer Verlag.

Wutz, F. X. 1925 *Die Psalmen. Textkritisch untersucht. . . .* Munich: Kösel und Pustet.

Yadin [Sukenik], Y. 1948 "Let the Young Men, I Pray Thee, Arise and Play before Us." *Journal of Palestine Oriental Studies* 21:110–16.

1955 Some Aspects of the Strategy of Ahab and David. *Biblica* 36:332–51.

1959 A Midrash on 2 Sam. vii and Ps. i–ii (4Q Florilegium). *Israel Exploration Journal* 9:95–98.

1963 *The Art of Warfare in Biblical Lands.* 2 vols. New York: McGraw-Hill.

Yaron, R. 1959 The Coptos Decree and 2 S XII 14. *Vetus Testamentum* 9:89–91.

Yeivin, S. 1964 The Military Campaigns of David. Pp. 151–59 in *The Military History of the Land of Israel in Biblical Times* [Hebrew], ed. J. Liver. [Tel Aviv]: Israel Defense Forces.

1971 The Benjaminite Settlement in the Western Part of Their Territory. *Israel Exploration Journal* 21:141–54.

Zadok, R. 1977 On Five Biblical Names. *Zeitschrift für die alttestamentliche Wissenschaft* 89:266–68.

Zenger, E. 1969 Funktion und Sinn in der ältesten Herausfuhrungsformel. Pp. 334–42 in *Deutscher Orientalistentag . . . 1968 in Würzburg. Vorträge 1,* ed. W. Voigt. Zeitschrift der Deutschen Morgendländischen Gesellschaft, Supplementa 1. Wiesbaden: Steiner.

Zeron, A. 1978 Der Platz Benajahus in der Heldenliste Davids (II Sam 23 20–23). *Zeitschrift für die alttestamentliche Wissenschaft* 90:20–28.

1979 The Seal of "M-B-N" and the List of David's Heroes. *Tel Aviv* 6:156–57.

Zobel, H.-J. 1975 Beiträge zur Geschichte Gross-Judas in früh- und vordavidischer Zeit. Pp. 253–77 in *Congress Volume. Edinburgh 1974,* ed. G. W. Anderson. Supplements to Vetus Testamentum 28. Leiden: Brill.

Zorell, F. 1928 Zu Ps. 18,27 (= 2 Sm. 22,27). *Biblica* 9:224.

# II SAMUEL

Translation
Textual Notes
Notes
&
Comments

# I. THE REPORT OF SAUL'S DEATH
# (1:1–16)

1 [1]After the death of Saul, David, having returned from defeating the
Amalekites, remained in Ziklag two days. [2]On the third day a man
arrived from Saul's camp with his clothes torn and dirt on his head.
When he came to David he fell down on the ground and prostrated
himself.

[3]"Where do you come from?" David asked him.

"I escaped from the Israelite camp," he told him.

[4]"What was the situation?" David asked him. "Tell me!"

"The army fled from the battle," he said, "and many of the army fell
and died. Also Saul and his son Jonathan are dead."

[5]Then David asked the soldier who was making the report to him,
"How do you know that Saul and his son Jonathan are dead?"

[6]"I chanced to be on Mount Gilboa," said the soldier, "and there
was Saul leaning on his spear, the chariotry and cavalry officers having overtaken him. [7]When he turned around and saw me, he called to
me.

" 'Here I am,' I replied.

[8]" 'Who are you?' he asked me.

" 'I am an Amalekite,' I said.

[9]" 'Stand beside me,' he told me, 'and dispatch me! For dizziness has
taken hold of me, yet there is life in me still.' [10]So, knowing that he
would not live after he had fallen, I stood beside him and dispatched
him. I took the diadem from his head and the bracelet from his arm
and brought them here to my lord."

[11]Then David took hold of his clothes and tore them, as did all the
men who were with him. [12]They mourned, weeping and fasting until
sundown over Saul and his son Jonathan and over the army of Yahweh
and the house of Israel, because they had fallen by the sword.

[13]Then David asked the soldier who was making the report to him,
"Where are you from?"

"I am the son of a sojourner," he said, "an Amalekite."

[14]"How is it," David said to him, "that you were not afraid to extend your hand to do violence to Yahweh's anointed?" [15]Then, summoning one of his soldiers, [he] said, "Go, fall upon him!" And he struck him down, and he died. [16]"Your blood is upon your own head," David said to him, "for your own mouth has testified against you, saying, 'I dispatched Yahweh's anointed.' "

## *TEXTUAL NOTES*

**1** 1. *the Amalekites* Reading *h'mlqy* with Syr. and 6 MSS of MT (Smith). We could also accept *'mlq*, "Amalek," but not *h'mlq* (so MT).

2. *from Saul's camp* That is, *min-hammaḥăneh mē'im šā'ûl*, lit. "from the camp, from with Saul" (so MT). $LXX^B$ interprets the same consonantal text as "from the camp, from *the army of* [*ek tou laou = mē'am*]." $LXX^L$ and Syr. combine the two interpretations.

*he fell down* $LXX^{AL}$ (cf. Syr.) add formulaically *epi prosōpon (autou)* = *l'pyw* (cf. I Sam 20:41; etc.), "on his face." Omit with MT, $LXX^B$.

3. *I* The *Vorlage* of $LXX^B$ seems to have made the subject emphatic: *egō* = *'nky*. We omit the pronoun with MT, $LXX^L$.

4. *"What was the situation?"* So MT: *mh hyh hdbr*, exactly as in I Sam 4:16. LXX reflects *mh hyh hdbr hzh*, "What was *this* situation?", i.e., "What was the situation there?"

*The army fled . . .* The speech is introduced by *'ăšer* (see the NOTE), as witnessed by MT, $LXX^B$. The translation of $LXX^L$ does not represent *'ăšer*, but we cannot be sure that it reflects a shorter Hebrew text. Note also that $LXX^A$, without apparent motive, omits the first several words of the speech ("The army . . . and").

*from the battle* $LXX^L$ adds "from the camp" (cf. vv. 2–3), combining variants of which the former is obviously superior.

*and died* We read *wymt*, the singular verb (cf. *npl*). The plural of MT, *wymtw*, probably arose by dittography of the *w* of the following *wgm*, encouraged by uncertainty about the number of *hā'ām*, "the army." $LXX^B$ combines plural and singular renderings, *kai apethanon kai apethanen*, associating the latter (most awkwardly) with what follows (*kai apethanen kai*, "And also [?] Saul died"). $LXX^A$, which has *kai apethanen* alone, and $LXX^L$, which omits the verb altogether (cf. Syr.), are shorter, probably in consequence of further corruption in a text identical to that of $LXX^B$, $LXX^A$ having lost *kai apethanon* before *kai apethanen* and $LXX^L$ having suffered haplography from the *kai* preceding *apethanon* to the *kai* following *apethanen*.

*Also* MT *wgm*, omitted in $LXX^A$, which like $LXX^B$ (see above) construes "and died" with "Saul."

*are dead* So MT (cf. $LXX^L$): *mtw*. Those Greek MSS that understand "Saul" as the subject of the preceding verb (see above) have a singular verb here (cf. v. 6).

6. *the soldier* Reminiscence of v. 5 has attracted "who was making the report to

him" into the text of v. 6 in most of the major witnesses. We may omit it with Syr. and a few Greek MSS.

*cavalry officers* MT *bʿly hpršym* is unparalleled, and many critics (Wellhausen, Driver, Budde) prefer to omit *bʿly* and read *hpršym*, "cavalry," alone. But LXX *hoi hipparchai/oi* evidently reflects the longer designation, *pršym* alone being rendered elsewhere by *hippeis*, and the shorter reading is without support. See also the first *Textual Note* at 1:18.

7. *me* (1) Omitted by LXX$^B$, perhaps reflecting a primitive reading.

8. *me* Omitted by LXX$^A$.

*I said* So MT *qĕrê* (cf. LXX). The *kĕtîb* is *wyʾmr*, "*he* said." MT, LXX$^{AL}$ add "to him"; omit with LXX$^B$.

9. *dizziness* See the NOTE.

*yet there is life in me still* The evidence seems to point to variant readings, viz. *ky kl npšy by* (cf. LXX$^{BA}$), "yet *all* my life is within me," and *ky ʿwd npšy by* (cf. LXX$^L$), "yet *still* my life is within me." The variants are combined in the text of MT *(ky kl ʿwd npšy by)*, in which, therefore, *kl* must be read adverbially: "yet still my life is wholly within me" (cf. GK$^2$ §128e). Our translation reflects the second variant.

10. *and the bracelet* Reading *whṣʿdh*, as in Isa 30:20 (cf. II Kings 11:12 [BDB]), in preference to MT *wʾṣʿdh*, which is an attested noun (Num 31:50) but lacks the article required by the grammatical context (Wellhausen, Driver). MT's initial *w'*- arose in a sequence of first-person verbs *(wʾʿmd . . . wʾmtthw . . . wʾqḥ . . . wʾbyʾm)*.

11. *as did . . . with him* That is, *wgm kl hʾnšym ʾšr ʾtw*, lit. "and also all the men who were with him," to which LXX$^B$ adds "tore their clothes" (omit with MT, LXX$^{AL}$).

12. *weeping and fasting* So MT, LXX$^{AL}$. The order is reversed in LXX$^B$.

*the army of Yahweh* So MT. LXX substitutes "Judah" for "Yahweh" under the influence of the traditional pairing of "Judah" and "Israel."

15. *and he died* So MT *(wymt)*, LXX$^B$ *(kai apethanen)*. LXX$^L$ diverges: *kai ebalon auton epi tēn gēn*, "and threw him on the ground."

16. *saying* So MT, LXX$^L$. LXX$^B$: "saying *that.*"

## NOTES

**1** 1. *After the death of Saul.* The book begins in the same way as Joshua ("After the death of Moses . . .") and Judges ("After the death of Joshua . . ."). It has been asked if this might be a Deuteronomistic editorial device (Carlson 1964:41–42), but there is nothing distinctively Deuteronomistic about it (*wayhî ʾaḥărê môt* PN, an unremarkable transitional formula [Gen 25:11; etc.]), and the common beginning of these books probably indicates less about the structural techniques of the writers who composed them than about the criteria by which much later generations divided them. Samuel, originally one overlong book (cf. *I Samuel*, pp. 3–4), was divided after the death of a central figure, Saul, in conformity to the pattern of previous books. I see no reason, however, to conclude, as Hertzberg seems to, that the beginning of the present passage was reformulated for the sake of this conformity. Kings, too, was one book originally, and it was also divided after the death of a major figure (Ahab); but there was no adjustment of II Kings 1:1 to the particular phraseology of Josh 1:1 and Judg 1:1.

*from defeating the Amalekites.* Amalek (*'ămālēq*) was the name of a nomadic tribe, native to the desert south of Judah and best known in biblical tradition as a company of enemies and plunderers. Israel harbored an ancient grievance against the Amalekites (see *I Samuel*, the third NOTE at 15:2), and we may assume that they were feared and despised in the time of David. The reference here is to David's pursuit and massacre of a band of Amalekite brigands who had burned and looted Ziklag (I Sam 30:1–31).

*Ziklag.* The city granted David in return for military service by Achish, the Philistine king of Gath (see I Samuel 27, especially vv. 5–6 and the NOTE there in *I Samuel*). It was later incorporated into the Negeb province of Judah (Josh 15:31). The currently preferred identification of the site seems to be Tell esh-Sherî'ah, ca. fifteen miles southeast of Gaza (cf. *I Samuel*, the NOTE at 27:6). See Map 1.

2–4. The account of the Amalekite's arrival and questioning by David is strikingly similar in narrative pattern to that of the messenger's report to Eli of the Philistine victory at Ebenezer in I Sam 4:12–17. See the NOTE there in *I Samuel*, where I attribute the similarity to "the common use of a literary motif by different writers, who drew upon . . . a shared repertoire of conventional narrative situations." For a fuller treatment in the same vein, see the discussion of Gunn (1974:290–92), who concludes from his study of this and other passages with similar patterning (where, in his judgment, direct literary assimilation can be excluded) that "the stereotyped aspect of the passages is part of the narrator's stock-in-trade, a conventional, probably traditional, tool of composition" (p. 311). It would be inappropriate in this context to attempt a full evaluation of Gunn's further contention (pp. 311–16) that such patterning is best understood on the assumption of *oral* traditional composition, a thesis to which Van Seters (1976a, 1976b) has taken exception. Even if the patterns in question reflect the requirements of oral composition ultimately, it does not follow that the present narrative derives, even in part, from a time prior to the transition to written composition, which in its early stages would be expected to preserve many of the formulaic features of the older, oral composition. It may also be pertinent to recall, in this context, that both I Sam 4:12–17 and II Sam 1:2–4 belong to larger compositions that correspond in type to known categories of ancient Near Eastern *written* literature (Miller and Roberts 1977:9–16; McCarter 1980a).

2. *with his clothes torn and dirt on his head.* Conventional signs of grief (cf. 15:32 as well as I Sam 4:12); see de Ward 1972:6–10. If the man's story is a lie, as suggested in the COMMENT, his torn clothes and disheveled condition may be contrived to lend dramatic weight to his story. The ruse of the Gibeonites in Josh 9:3–15 comes to mind (Freedman).

3–4. The Amalekite reports the disastrous outcome of the battle fought with the Philistines on Mount Gilboa; see I Sam 31:1–2.

4. *"The army fled . . ."* The quotation is introduced by *'ăšer*, which replaces the more common *kî* often before object clauses and occasionally even before direct quotations, as here and in I Sam 15:20. See GK[2] §157c; Driver 1890:97.

*Saul and his son Jonathan are dead.* According to I Sam 31:2 the dead include two other sons of Saul, viz. Abinadab and Malchishua. The names and number of Saul's sons are in doubt (cf. *I Samuel,* the NOTE at 14:49), but we know that one, Ishbaal, still lives and has an important role to play in the ensuing events (see 2:8; etc.).

5. *the soldier.* As explained in the NOTE on "some soldiers" at 2:14, Hebrew *na'ar,* which means "young man, youth," seems commonly to refer to a (young) fighting man in particular. In light of this fact, we can no longer accept the judgment of the older literary critics that the identification of the Amalekite as *'îš,* "a man," in v. 2 and *hanna'ar,* "the young man," in v. 6 is evidence for two different literary sources underlying the present narrative; the first designation is generic, the second professional. See the COMMENT.

6–10. The sharp contradiction between this account of the manner of Saul's death and that given in I Sam 31:3–5 is discussed below in the COMMENT, where the explanation is accepted that the Amalekite is lying, exaggerating his own role in the affair in an attempt to curry favor with David. We are probably to assume that the man happened upon the body of the dead king, stripped it of the crown and bracelet, and later conceived the idea that these treasures might be most valuable if used to ingratiate himself to David.

6. *Mount Gilboa.* The scene of the battle (cf. the NOTE at vv. 3–4 above). The scarp of Gilboa was the eastern wall of the Valley of Jezreel at the northern limit of the central hill country.

*leaning on his spear.* That is, wounded and supporting himself with his weapon. J. P. Hyatt (*apud* Ward 1967:129) suggests that Saul may have been trying to commit suicide, but *niš'ān 'al,* "leaning on," seems unlikely to imply more than support; for the sense supposed by Hyatt we should expect *nōpēl 'al* (cf. I Sam 31:4; I Chron 10:4,5).

*chariotry.* The chariot was perhaps the most important of the Philistine weapons, devastating in open country against an enemy (like Saul's army) that did not possess it. It was ineffective, however, in mountainous terrain (cf. Judg 1:19), and accordingly the older literary critics (Nowack; cf. Grønbaek 1971:271 and n. 134), arguing that the use of chariotry in mountain warfare developed later (I Kings 22:38; etc.), found in the present reference warrant for considering the II Samuel 1 account of Saul's death to be later than and secondary to that in I Samuel 31, where chariotry is not mentioned (see the COMMENT). This argument is excessively subtle and difficult to accept. I doubt that the Philistines left their chariots at home when a battle seemed likely to involve fighting in the mountains. We are told in I Sam 13:5, for example, that they had mustered chariotry and cavalry units in addition to "an army like the sand on the seashore in number" in preparation for the battle of Michmash pass "in the hill country of Bethel" (I Sam 13:2). Moreover, the battle in which Saul died probably began on the plains of Jezreel between the Philistine camp at Shunem on the slope of the hill of Moreh and the Israelite camp pitched opposite it on Gilboa (I Sam 28:4); it was the Israelite retreat that drew the scene of action up onto the slopes of Gilboa (I Sam 31:1–2), where Saul was overtaken by the Philistines, chariots and all.

8. *"I am an Amalekite."* The messenger turns out to be an Amalekite! See the COMMENT, where the significance of this fact is discussed.

9. *and dispatch me!* Hebrew *ûmōtětēnî.* The *Polel* of *mwt,* "die," refers to dispatching or "finishing off" someone already wounded and near death. Cf. Judg 9:54; I Sam 14:13; 17:51.

*dizziness.* The meaning of Hebrew *haššābāṣ* is uncertain. The verb *šbṣ* seems to have meant "mix" (Biblical Hebrew *šibbēṣ*, "interweave"; Syr. *šĕbaṣ*, "mix, confuse"), and the meaning of the noun was possibly "confusion, dizziness." This, at least, was the opinion of some of the ancient translators. Syr. has *ṣawrānā'*, "dizziness, giddiness," corresponding probably to Greek *skotodinos*, "dizziness," which is to be restored from LXX *skotos deinon*, "a dreadful darkness" (see Smith). I assume the Amalekite means that Saul was saying he is too giddy from his wounds to dispatch himself (cf. the interpretation of Josephus, *Ant.* 7.3).

10. *the diadem . . . and . . . the bracelet.* These are royal insignia. The diadem *(hannēzer)* was given to the king at the time of his investiture (II Kings 11:12; cf. Jer 13:18; Ezek 21:31 [21:26]; Pss 89:40 [89:39]; 132:18). Its precise nature is not known. Though often translated, somewhat misleadingly, as "crown" (RSV), it is more likely to have been an emblem worn on the forehead, comparable in some ways to the uraeus worn on the forehead by the kings of Egypt. See especially the discussion of Mettinger (1976:287–88), who points to the identification in Lev 8:9 and elsewhere of the priestly insignia *ṣîṣ hazzāhāb*, "the golden plate(?)," and *nēzer haqqōdeš*, "the holy headpiece." (I am less inclined to interpret the priestly *ṣîṣ* in light of *ṣîṣ*, "flower" [Mettinger], than of *ṣîṣīt*, "forelock" [Ezek 8:3], "tassel" [Num 15:38–39], an indication of the place it was worn but not of its appearance.) The bracelet *(haṣṣĕ'ādâ;* see the *Textual Note)* is not mentioned elsewhere (unless it is to be restored in II Kings 11:12 with Wellhausen 1899:292–93 and n. 2; but cf. von Rad 1966:225–29). In the present context the importance of the two objects is that they are insignia emblematic of the kingship of Israel. As such they were worn by Saul. Now they are handed over to David. The significance of this is considered in the COMMENT below.

11. Rending one's garments was a traditional sign of grief and mourning (cf. 3:31; etc.); see, in general, de Ward 1972:8–10 and the bibliography there. It may have been, as de Ward (p. 8) supposes, "a palliative of self-mutilation," which was also practiced (Jer 41:5; 48:37; cf. *CTCA* 5[= *UT*' 67].6.17–22; 6[= *UT*' 62].1.2–5).

12. *fasting.* On fasting as a mourning rite, see de Ward 1972:159–61.

13. *a sojourner.* The sojourner *(gēr)* was neither a native nor a foreigner in legal status, but he had some of the privileges and responsibilities of each. He was a resident alien, accepted and protected by the community among whom he lived more or less permanently but by whom he was regarded finally as a foreigner. See, for example, de Vaux 1961b:vol. I:74–76. Pertinent here is the fact that a sojourner, even in cultic and ceremonial matters, was not exempt from the laws of the community or to the penalties prescribed by them (Lev 24:22; cf. 20:2; 24:16; etc.). It may be that like Doeg the Edomite, who alone among the servants of Saul was willing to carry out the execution of the priests of Nob (I Sam 22:17–19), this Amalekite was less scrupulous than a native-born Israelite might have been about the peculiar sanctity of the life he took; even so, he can derive no excuse for his behavior from his Amalekite parentage, for legally he is a sojourner in Israel and subject in this case to the same law as the native.

14. *to do violence to Yahweh's anointed.* Hebrew *lĕšaḥēt 'et-mĕšîaḥ yahweh.* Saul, as "Yahweh's anointed," was a sacrosanct individual; his person was not to be violated. See *I Samuel*, the NOTE at 26:9, where it is argued that the verbs *šiḥēt* and *hišḥît* refer especially to the defilement of the sanctified body of the king. David's indignation here is consistent with his past behavior; he has always been, according to our narrator, fastidious on this point (I Sam 26:9; cf. 24:7). See further the COMMENT.

## COMMENT

The story of David's rise to power that extends from I Samuel 16 to II Samuel 7—in its earliest form, I Sam 16:14–II Sam 5:10 (cf. *I Samuel,* p. 30)—can be divided into three major sections. The first tells of the days David spent at the court of Saul (I Samuel 16–20), the second of the period of estrangement between the two men (I Samuel 21–31), and the third of the consolidation of David's rule over Judah and Israel after Saul's death (II Samuel 1–7). The present passage begins the third section. It follows the account of the death of Saul on Mount Gilboa in I Samuel 31. That account brought to an end the description of the long period of estrangement between Saul and David, during which David lived as a fugitive and outlaw, constantly pursued by Saul, and finally as an expatriot, reluctantly serving a Philistine king. During this last phase, the time of David's stint as a Philistine mercenary, all contact between him and Saul was broken, and in this regard it is useful to think of the present episode as restoring the former connection (cf. Grønbaek 1971:219). To be sure, Saul is dead now and David will not see him again, but at last it is possible for the younger man to reassert his loyalty, if only by expressions of grief. He no longer needs to fear the vindictiveness with which the old king, driven by suspicions arising from his own delusive imagination, pursued him, and he will now be able to return safely to his native Judah (2:1) and renew his old relationship with other parts of Saul's kingdom (2:4b–7). The episode, in other words, reestablishes David's connection with the people of Saul's kingdom, if not with the slain king himself, and gives a fresh expression to his true allegiance.

This episode, however, though chiefly concerned with reaction to past events and the renewal of former ties, is not entirely retrospective. It also looks ahead toward David's own kingship, the way to which is now beginning to clear. The death of Saul and three of his sons (I Sam 31:2; cf. the second NOTE at v. 4 above) has raised the question of succession. One son of Saul, as we are about to learn, remains alive and must be regarded as a candidate for the throne. But the reader will not have forgotten the special loyalty and affection the people of Israel conceived for David when he served as a commander in Saul's army (see *I Samuel,* § XXV, the COMMENT and especially the NOTE at I Sam 18:16; cf. also II Sam 5:1–2). David, too, must be considered a candidate. And it is to him, though under unusual circumstances, that the diadem and bracelet of Saul, objects emblematic of the kingship of Israel (see the NOTE at v. 10), are brought in the present episode.

*The Unity of the Account*

In I Sam 31:3–5 we were told that Saul took his own life. "The battle raged on against Saul," said the narrator. "The archers found him with their bows, and he was wounded in the belly. So [he] said to his weapon-bearer, 'Draw your sword and run me though with it, lest these uncircumcised come and have their way with me!' But his weapon-bearer was unwilling, for he was greatly afraid; so Saul took the sword himself and fell upon it. When his weapon-bearer saw that Saul was dead, he too fell upon his sword and died with him." The testimony of the Amalekite in the present episode contradicts this account. Saul died, we are told, not by his own hand but by that of the man now making the report to David (v. 10). And there are differences in detail. It is not "the archers" who have overtaken Saul, but "the chariotry and cavalry officers" (v. 6). There is no mention at all of a weapon-bearer. Of the sons of Saul only Jonathan is said to have died (v. 5; cf. v. 12), whereas in the previous account three sons are listed among the slain (I Sam 31:2,6,8).

Some scholars have concluded from all this that the accounts of Saul's death in I Samuel 31 and II Samuel 1 derive from two distinct narrative sources, a position that has continued to find adherents until fairly recently (de Vaux) but one more at home among the older literary critics. Smith's conclusion about II Sam 1:1–16, for example, was that "we have here a document differing from the one just preceding"; he notes that the excision of I Samuel 31 would not disrupt the narrative thread running from David's return to Ziklag at the end of I Samuel 30 into the present episode.

On the other hand, we must remember that the incompatibility of the two accounts arises primarily from the clash of the details each gives about the manner of Saul's death, and that with regard to the other major issues—the defeat of Israel, the death of Saul and his son(s)—there is substantial agreement (cf. Grønbaek 1971:217). Accordingly, a larger number of scholars, even among older adherents of the documentary analysis of the material, have preferred a more modest interpretation of the evidence. These (Budde, Nowack, etc.) find the present account to be a continuation of the material in I Samuel 31; the contradictions, they argue, reflect a combination of literary strands within II Sam 1:1–16. From an older source, which continues I Samuel 31, they derive II Sam 1:1–4 and 11–12. According to this more ancient account, then, David and his men received the news of the defeat of Israel and the death of Saul from a messenger whose identity was not mentioned (i.e., he was not said to be an Amalekite), and they wept bitterly. The materials in vv. (5,)6–10 and 13–16 were drawn from a later document, which reflects the development of an alternative version of the story according to which David peremptorily put the carrier of bad news to death (cf. 4:10), a detail softened somewhat in further development by the identification of the messenger as an Amalekite. By the time this version had arisen, the use of chariots in mountainous terrain, a tactic unknown in the time of David, had become common, and the identification of Saul's assailants was changed from "archers" to "chariotry and cavalry officers" (Nowack; cf. the NOTE at v. 6 above). This is a position that continues to find adherents, though there is now, under the influence of the insights of tradition-historical analysis, a tendency to think not of a combination of *documents* in II Sam 1:1–16 but of the existence of two independent *traditions* underlying a substantially unified narrative (cf. especially Grønbaek 1971:217–18). Ackroyd, for example, speaks of Saul's death at the hands of an Amalekite as "an alternative tradition" (to that in I Samuel 31) used by "the compiler . . . no doubt because he sees it as an apt pointer to divine judgment on Saul" in light of Saul's failure to carry out his instructions in the campaign against the Amalekites described in I Samuel 15.

It has not gone unnoticed, however, that all these problems evaporate if we assume that the Amalekite is lying. According to this hypothesis, the assertion that he "chanced to be on Mount Gilboa" (v. 6) can be accepted as true, but every other detail he gives of his encounter with Saul is to be taken as fabrication. He did not find Saul alive, as he alleges, but already dead, having taken his own life in the manner described in I Sam 31:4. With an Amalekite's greed for plunder, he stripped the king's body of its regalia and, perhaps subsequently, conceived the plan of conveying them to David, hoping thereby to procure the favor of the most powerful man in Judah (see the NOTE at vv. 6–10). In the expectation that it would lend further support to his scheme, he decided to represent himself as the slayer of Saul, but in this respect he, like the men who subsequently would assassinate Ishbaal (see § VII), fatally misjudged David. Whether David was deceived or not we cannot tell; his reaction ("your own mouth has testified against you," v. 16) is appropriate in either case.

This solution has found increasing acceptance among the last generation or two of scholars (Pfeiffer 1948:350–51; Hertzberg; Caird; Ward 1967:128–29; cf. Grønbaek 1971:218–19), but it was generally rejected by earlier commentators (Smith, Kennedy), who recognized its advantages but found no support for it in the text. Smith, for example, writes: "The easiest hypothesis is that the Amalekite fabricated his story. But the whole narrative seems against this. David has no inkling that the man is not truthful, nor does the author suggest it." On the other hand, we must not expect too much of the text. Nowhere is it stated explicitly that the messenger has not called upon David in good faith with no other purpose in mind than dutifully to report the tidings of war, and yet it would be a very naive interpreter who did not recognize the man as the opportunist that he is. Nor are we told here that the messenger thinks his sorrowful report will give David secret joy; yet we assume so, and we shall learn in 4:10 that David assumed so, too. These things can be guessed from the one important clue the text does give, viz. the identification of the messenger as an Amalekite. "Amalekites remain Amalekites," as Hertzberg puts it, "even if they are sojourning in Israel." As soon as the ancient audience learned the messenger's identity (v. 8), it would have begun to suspect him of treachery, for treachery was what it had come to expect of Amalekites (cf. the second NOTE at v. 1), and its cynicism had just been reinforced by the story of the rape of Ziklag in I Sam 30:1–3. And if we can conclude, on this basis, that the messenger is an opportunist and a miscreant, as virtually all expositors seem to do, then why, in view of the failure of his report to jibe with what we were told in I Samuel 31, can we not also conclude that he is a liar? Naturally we hesitate to dismiss the conclusions of source-critical analysis in favor of what might be a harmonizing interpretation of the facts, but the testimony of the same analysis when applied to adjacent materials, where there is very little evidence of composite authorship (cf., for example, Eissfeldt 1965:275), favors a presumption of unity here. Accordingly, I feel safe in accepting what seems to have become the majority position, viz. that II Sam 1:1–16 is a unified composition, substantially from the hand of the original author of the story of David's rise to power, who is also the author of the contradictory account in I Samuel 31, and that the contradiction is deliberate, a result of the writer's self-conscious portrayal of the Amalekite messenger as a liar.

### *Apologetic Themes*

The chief purpose of the original author of the story of David's rise to power was to demonstrate the legitimacy of David's claim to the throne of Israel and, in particular, to exonerate him of any suspicion of blame in the events that led to his accession (see McCarter 1980b:499–502). The present passage furthers the apologetic claims of the larger narrative, which is especially concerned at this point with the question of David's involvement in the death of Saul and his sons. In the writer's time—probably the reign of David (McCarter 1980b:494–95)—much circumstantial evidence seemed to condemn David. The principle of *cui bono* was against him: He was the chief beneficiary of the fall of the house of Saul. He had been a mercenary in the Philistine army at the time Saul died fighting against the Philistines. Indeed, the forces of Achish of Gath, David's Philistine overlord, were known to have been involved in the battle (cf. I Sam 29:1–2). Moreover, after the battle and the death of Saul and his sons, the diadem and bracelet of the slain king turned up in the possession of David! We can hardly doubt that all of these things were publicly known in the reign of David and that, taken collectively, they cast a shadow over his kingship.

It was specifically to these issues that the writer addressed himself. He meant to dispel the shadow by filling in the details that were *not* publicly known, details of things that happened privately and, when brought to the attention of the public, would, he hoped, exculpate David. Such, indeed, is the force of the account he produced, in the course of which each of the implied charges is contradicted. We have already been shown, in the description of Achish's dismissal of David in I Sam 29:1–11, that David was not involved in the battle on Mount Gilboa in any way but had returned to Ziklag before the Philistines encountered the Israelite force. Indeed, he was fighting Amalekites in the south while the battle raged in the north and was using the booty he collected to enrich the cities of Judah (I Samuel 30). As for Saul's regalia, the present narrative shows that David came by it innocently and by an agent acting on his own initiative. So there is no genuine reason, we are to believe, to suspect David of any wrongdoing in the matter of Saul's death. On the contrary, the present passage devotes considerable space to fresh demonstration of a theme that runs throughout the story of David's rise, viz. that David looked upon Saul with loyalty and affection. When he learns of the king's death he is deeply moved, expressing his grief openly and elaborately (vv. 11–12). Moreover, he has always been careful to respect the sanctity of the person of the anointed king (cf. the NOTE at v. 14), at least once refusing an opportunity to take Saul's life with ease (I Samuel 26; cf. I Sam 24:2–23), and he displays the same conscientiousness here as he expresses outrage at the Amalekite's avowal. Thus, as stressed by Mabee (1980:89–98), the condemnation of the Amalekite in vv. 13–16, which constitute a brief legal proceeding, gives formal expression to David's exoneration. "In essence, then, the judicial narrative militates against any charge that David was involved in a military coup d'etat in the midst of Saul's demise" (p. 98).

We might ask, finally, why this episode was a necessary part of the apology. Once David's absence from the battle on Mount Gilboa was established, why did the narrator need to go further? The answer is surely that David's possession of the diadem and bracelet required explanation. The narrator shows that these were conveyed to David by an Amalekite. Where, then, was this Amalekite who might have corroborated the story? He was executed by David for regicide. It is true that Saul took his own life, but David did not know this when he listened to and believed the Amalekite's lie (Freedman).

To be sure, David will benefit from Saul's death in the end, but it does not follow that he contrived it or deliberately exploited it. Instead, we are to understand, all these events were under the control of a higher will. On the eve of the fatal battle Saul was warned of the disaster by Yahweh himself, speaking through the agent of a ghost (cf. *I Samuel*, the COMMENT on § XLIII): "And tomorrow you are going to fall along with your sons—indeed Yahweh will deliver the camp of Israel into the hand of the Philistines!" (I Sam 28:19). Similarly, the events that follow will conform to the inexorable working out of the divine will as understood by our narrator. "David continued to grow greater and greater," he will assert in conclusion, "because Yahweh Sabaoth was with him" (5:10).

## II. THE ELEGY FOR SAUL AND JONATHAN (1:17–27)

1 [17]David sang this elegy for Saul and his son Jonathan [18]and said it
should be taught to the people of Judah. It is recorded in the Book of
Jashar.

[19]Alas, prince of Israel, slain standing erect!
How the warriors are fallen!

[20]Don't tell it in Gath,
don't spread the news in the streets of Ashkelon,
lest the daughters of the Philistines rejoice,
lest the daughters of the uncircumcised exult!

[21]O mountains in Gilboa,
let there be no dew or rain upon you
    or flowing of the deeps!
For there is begrimed the shield of the warrior,
the shield of Saul is not rubbed with oil.

[22]From the gore of the slain, from the warriors' fat
the bow of Jonathan did not retreat,
the sword of Saul did not draw back empty.

[23]Saul and Jonathan! Beloved and charming!
They were not parted in life,
and in death they were not separated.
They were swifter than eagles!
They were stronger than lions!

[24]O daughters of Israel, weep for Saul,
who dressed you in luxurious crimson,
who set golden jewelry on your gowns!

25 How the warriors are fallen
    amid the battle!
Jonathan, slain standing erect!
26 I grieve for you, my brother,
    you were so dear to me.
Your love was wonderful to me,
    more than the love of women.

27 How the warriors are fallen
and the weapons of war lost!

## *TEXTUAL NOTES*

1 18. A much discussed verse. MT reads *wy'mr llmd bny yhwdh qšt hnh ktwbh 'l spr hyšr,* lit. "And he said to teach the sons of Judah *a bow.* It is recorded in the Book of Jashar." This text has exercised translators considerably because of the enigmatic reference to "a bow." For *qšt,* "a bow," Targ. has *mgd bqšt',* "the drawing of the bow," and, accordingly, some interpreters (e.g., Eissfeldt 1955:234) have agreed with Isaaki (as cited by Smith) that "David said, now that the mighty men of Israel have fallen, it is necessary that the Children of Judah learn war and draw the bow." Thus AV renders, "Also he bade them teach . . . *the use of* the bow." Others have supposed "A Bow" to be the title of a song, perhaps of David's elegy itself—thus, "and said The Song of the Bow should be taught . . ." (cf. RV, NJV). In the *Textual Note* on "and said it should be taught" below, I express the opinion that the problem vanishes when it is recognized that *qšt,* "a bow," is intrusive and can be struck from the text, a solution supported by the major witnesses to the Greek tradition. When rid of this troublesome word, the verse has a plain meaning. David, having sung his lament, commands that it be learned by his countrymen as a memorial to Saul and Jonathan. When the narrator has explained this, he cites his source for the poem, the Book of Jashar.

Certain modern expositors, however, have preferred to retain *qšt,* interpreted in one way or another. Segal (1914/15:207), for example, takes *llmd bny yhwdh qšt* to be "a later musical superscription" of the sort known from the Psalms. Others attempt to make sense of the verse by conjectural emendation. For all of these the common starting point is Klostermann's opinion, based on comparison with the beginning of David's lament over Abiner in 3:33, that everything after *wayyō'mer* must originally have been part of the poem. Accordingly they expect to discover elegiac poetry even in the present verse. One notable effort along these lines is that of Gevirtz (1963:73–76). His starting point is provided by Smith, who proposes an emendation of *bny yhwdh,* "the sons of Judah," to *bky yhwdh,* "Weep, O Judah!" To this Gevirtz finds a suitable parallel in *spr hyšr,* "the Book of Jashar," emended to *spd yśr'l,* "Mourn, O Israel!" The problematic *qšt*, "a bow," he takes as a form of the adjective *qāšeh*, "hard, severe" (cf. Klostermann, Budde). Other emendations lead finally to a restored bicolon:

*yll mr bky yhwdh*
*qšt nhy spd yśr'l*
(With) a bitter wailing, weep O Judah!
(With) a grievous lament, mourn O Israel!
(Gevirtz's translation)

Gevirtz's treatment is accepted by Holladay (1970:162–68), with the exception of the emendation of *hyšr* to *yśr'l*, to which Holladay (p. 164) prefers retention of *yšr*, or rather *l(?)-yšr*, interpreting *spd l(?)-yšr* as "Lament for the upright!"

*and said it should be taught* Reading *wy'mr llmd*, lit. "and said to teach (it)," with LXX[BL]. Later in the verse MT (cf. LXX[AO]) adds *qšt*, "a bow," evidently construed as an object of *llmd*—thus, "and said to teach . . . a bow(?). . . ." The shorter text of LXX[BL] shows the word to be intrusive in those witnesses that have it. It probably found its way into the text of MT at this point after arising as a marginal gloss to some nearby passage, such as 1:22 (Ackroyd) or, more likely, 1:6, where *b'ly pršym*, "cavalry officers," may have been glossed to read *b'ly qšt*, "archers," in view of I Sam 31:3 (Wellhausen). Most interpreters have tried to understand the verse with *qšt* in place (see the preceding *Textual Note*), but its retention spoils a shorter and problem-free text.

*Judah* So MT, LXX[B]. LXX[A] has "Israel," and LXX[L] combines the two readings ("Israel and Judah").

At the end of the verse LXX[L], OL, and a few other witnesses add "And he said" as an introduction to the poem that follows.

19. *Alas, prince of Israel* This interpretation of *hṣby yśr'l* is discussed in the NOTE. In MT *h-* is understood as the article—thus, *haṣṣĕbî yiśrā'ēl*, "The prince (lit. 'gazelle'), O Israel." For *hṣby* LXX[N] has *stēlōson*, reflecting *hṣb* understood as *haṣṣeb*, "Erect (a monument)!"; but there is no evidence that the *Hip'il* of *nṣb* can imply its own object, as this understanding seems to assume. The translation of LXX[LM], *akribasai* (cf. OL[MSS] *considera, cura te*), points to a passive or reflexive form of *nṣb*, probably *hṣb* again but understood as *hoṣṣab*, the *Hop'al* imperative (a rare form, which, where it does occur, has reflexive force [cf. GK[2] §46a N]), perhaps to be translated "Take your stand!" From this Holladay (1970:162–68) reconstructs *hnṣb(w)*, the *Nip'al* imperative, which he regards as original; but the loss of the *n* in the principal witnesses would be hard to explain. I assume that *hṣby* was the primitive reading, misread in the tradition ancestral to LXX as *hṣbw* and subsequently altered to *hṣb*. Targ. preserves the intermediate form: *'t'tdwn* = *hṣbw*.

*slain standing erect* This interpretation of *'l bmwtyk ḥll*, the reading of MT, is explained in the NOTE. LXX[L] has *peri tōn tethnēkotōn sou traumatiōn*, reflecting *'l mtyk ḥll(ym)*, "over your dead (who were) slain." This was the OG reading; it is combined with that of MT in the text of LXX[B], and the MT reading seems also to have been introduced marginally in the text of LXX[L], finding its way erroneously into v. 21 (see the *Textual Note* on "upon you").

20. *Don't tell it* So MT, LXX[BL], etc. LXX[A]: "Tell it. . . ."

*in Gath* The witnesses to the text are unanimous in reading *bgt*. Cross and Freedman (1950:46,48), Gevirtz (1963:82–84), and Stuart (1976:188,193), troubled by the absence of a term corresponding to *ḥwṣt,* "the streets of," in the next line, conjecture that the original here was *brḥb(w)t gt,* "in *the plazas of* Gath."

*don't* So MT. LXX, Syr.: "*And* don't. . . ." Cf. Dahood in Fisher 1972:109.

*lest* (2) So MT and $LXX^{BA}$. $LXX^{L}$ and Syr. have "*And* lest. . . ."

21. *O mountains in Gilboa* Hebrew *hārê baggilbōaʿ.* The unusual construction (see the NOTE) is attested by MT and most Greek MSS. $LXX^{L}$ seems to reflect a Hebrew text in which the construct relationship was normalized by omission of the preposition.

*let there be no dew* MT *ʾl ṭl,* expanded in LXX to read *ʾl yrd ṭl,* "Let dew not descend . . . ," as reflected variously in $LXX^{BAMN}$. $LXX^{L}$ reflects *ʾl ypl ʿlykm wʾl ṭl,* "Let it/him(?) not fall upon you, and let there be no dew. . . ." The versions felt the need for a verb here, but wrongly so, as it seems in light of the Ugaritic parallel cited in the *Textual Note* on "upon you . . . the deeps" below. Among modern interpreters Smith would read *ʾl yrd ṭl* with LXX, and Holladay (1970:171–72) prefers *ʾl ṭl ypl,* "Let dew not fall," citing $LXX^{L}$ in support. See also the following *Textual Note.*

*or rain* That is, *wʾl mṭr,* "and let there be no rain. . . ." $LXX^{A}$ *mēde huetos pesoi* suggests *wʾl mṭr ypl* (cf. $GK^{2}$ §152h), "and let rain not fall . . . ," evidence which Hertzberg might have cited in support of his restoration after *mṭr* of *yplw,* which he construes with both preceding nouns—thus, "let no dew or rain fall on you."

*upon you . . . the deeps* MT (cf. $LXX^{BA}$) has *ʿlykm wśdy trwmt,* which seems to mean, "upon you, nor fields of offerings" (AV). This reading has been taken by those who retain it "to mean that David lays a curse on the hills of Gilboa that there be no field bearing fine fruits, worthy of being set aside for sacred imposts" (so Gordis [1940: 35], who goes on to say, "That this is far-fetched and unsatisfactory is obvious . . ."). $LXX^{L}$ *epi ta hypsē sou orē thanatou* suggests a different reading, viz. *ʿl bmwtyk hry mwt,* "on your ridges, O mountains of death." This reading is intelligible in the context, and a case might be made for its originality (cf. Tournay 1964:285); but the first part of it, *ʿl bmwtyk,* which corresponds to MT *ʿlykm wśdy,* is evidently an intrusion from the opening line of the poem, which may have been introduced marginally to correct the reading of $LXX^{L}$ at v. 19, *peri tōn tethnēkotōn sou* = *ʿl mtyk,* to the reading of MT (see the *Textual Note* on "slain standing erect" at v. 19) but found its way into the text at this point. Surely, then, *ʿlykm wśdy* is to be preferred to *ʿl bmwtyk* here, and it follows that we must reject the rest of the $LXX^{L}$ reading as well, inasmuch as it makes little sense after *wśdy* ("and the fields of the mountains of death" [?]). We are obliged, it seems, to make sense of *wśdy trwmt* by reinterpretation or emendation.

The most cogent case for retention of the received reading is based on comparison with *mĕrômê śādeh,* "the heights of the field" (RSV), in Judg 5:18, a text that seems first to have been elicited in explanation of the present passage by Graetz (cf. Smith) and that recently has been pointed to again, independently of Graetz, by Freedman (1972:121–22; cf. Dahood 1972:398–99) and Fokkelman (1979). Freedman and Dahood are especially eager to preserve against emendation the parallelism they find between *hārê baggilbōaʿ,* "O mountains in Gilboa," and *ûśĕdê tĕrûmōt.* They argue that *tĕrûmâ* means "height" and take "the *waw* before *śdy* as an emphatic particle, here with vocative force" (Freedman 1972:122; cf. Dahood 1968:204). Thus Freedman translates " 'Even you lofty fields,' i.e., 'fields of the heights,' the plateau in the Gilboa range where the battle actually took place," comparing *mĕrômê śādeh* of Judg 5:18, "usually rendered 'heights of the field' but clearly referring to an elevated plain, or plateau" (122). Freedman's solution is accepted by Shea (1976:140–41), who, however, doubts the expression has vocative force and translates "or the fields of heights." I am sympathetic to Shea's caution about the vocative use of the conjunction, a grammatical feature of which other examples have been proposed (e.g., Dahood 1968:204) without, in my opinion, successfully demonstrating its existence. But Shea's own interpretation, which, if I understand him correctly, assumes a distinction between the mountains of Gilboa (the scarp itself) and "the fields of heights" (the western slope of the Gilboa watershed)—thus, "upon you or the fields of heights"—seems excessively precise and, in any case, would be more naturally expressed by *wʿl śdy*, etc.—thus, "upon you or *upon* the fields of heights." Nor, finally, is it clear to me that the parallel vocatives sought by Freedman and Dahood are desirable after all. Driver, for example, contends that "a *second* vocative . . . after *hry bglbʿ* spoils the rhythm."

If we concede that no satisfactory interpretation of the received text has been achieved, we must turn to emendation. A number of proposals were made by the older critics, but none achieved any widespread acceptance. Smith, for example, suggested *śdwt hmwt*, "O fields of death!" (cf. LXX$^{L}$). Klostermann's conjecture—*śdwt rmyh*, "O fields of deceit!"—was revived by Schulz in a form that departs in no important way from MT, viz. *w(?)śdy trmt (= tarmīt)*, adopted by de Vaux and Hertzberg, who render it as "you false fields!" A well-received modern solution, first put forward by Ginsberg (1938), finds its clue in verses from a Ugaritic poem (*CTCA* 19.1[=*UT*ʿ 1 Aqht].44–45). The passage in question, which contains an imprecation uttered by the poem's protagonist after the death of his son, reads: *bl ṭl bl rbb bl šrʿ thmtm*, "Let there be no dew, no rain, no upsurging(?) of the double deep!" A number of scholars have found the parallel sufficiently striking to accept Ginsberg's emendation of *wśdy trwmt* in the present passage to *wšrʿ thmt* (for bibliography see Schoors in Fisher 1972:56–58, to which add Speiser 1950 and Fenton 1979, where Ginsberg's solution is defended against the objections of Freedman and Dahood) and translate the restored text "nor upsurgings of the deep" (RSV) or the like. This proposal, however, is not without its difficulties. Such an emendation must be able to demonstrate a high potential for graphic confusion in the texts it proposes to relate, especially when the product of the supposed corruption is a reading at least as obscure as the reconstructed original. In this case, then, we must compare *wšrʿ thmt* and *wśdy trwmt* in the scripts in which our texts were transmitted. The second word presents no problem: The confusion of *h* for *rw* was easy in scripts of the Hasmonean and Herodian periods. The first word is more difficult: *wš* and *wś* were, of course, identical and *r* and *d* almost identical in scripts of every period; but confusion of ʿ for *y*, while not impossible (both were small letters written high on the line), was not easy at any period. Proponents of this emendation, then, must assume it likely that the error was made in copying a damaged original. There are, moreover, lexical difficulties in Ginsberg's proposal. Ugaritic *šrʿ* is itself obscure—Ginsberg's comparison of Arabic *srʿ*, "hasten," a verb not known to have been used of bodies of water, is not very helpful (cf. Gordis 1940:35; Speiser 1950:378)—and, in any case, no Hebrew cognate is attested (*śārûaʿ* in Lev 21:18; 22:23 is not demonstrably related). It is difficult, in short, to maintain Ginsberg's proposal in its original form.

The parallel between the Ugaritic and Hebrew passages remains impressive, however. Each involves a mournful cursing of the ground in response to the death of a hero. More specifically, each involves a wish for the failure of the sources of fresh water. In the Ugaritic passage this includes not only the sources of water from above—*ṭl*, "dew," and *rbb*, "rain"—but also the sources of water from below—*thmtm*, "the double deep," and biblical and extrabiblical materials can be cited to show this duality to have been conventional in blessings and curses (see the NOTE on "dew . . . rain . . . flowing of the deeps"). In the present passage we have the former—*ṭl*, "dew," and *mṭr*, "rain" —and we expect the latter—*thmwt*, "the deeps." It would be a mistake, therefore, not to follow Ginsberg's lead; but we require a variation of his solution with modifications addressed to the paleographical and lexical problems. This has already been provided, in my opinion, by Gordis (1940:35–36), who suggests the reading *wšdy*, based on the Aramaic verb *šdy*, "pour, flow, empty out." This suggestion eliminates the paleographical difficulties we encountered with *wšrʿ*, and it is lexically unobjectionable, based on a well-known Northwest Semitic verb. We read, therefore, with Gordis: *wšdy thmwt*, "or flowing of the deeps."

*shield* (bis) Reading *māgēn* each time with MT and the versions. Freedman (1972: 122–23), comparing Punic *magon*, a title equivalent to Latin *imperator*, "commander," or *dux*, "leader" (cf. Maurin 1962), and shown by Dahood to occur in Biblical Hebrew (cf. especially Pss 84:10[84:9]; 89:19[89:18]), renders the word "chieftain" in both places ("the warrior chieftain . . . Saul the chieftain"). If Freedman is correct, we should emend *māgēn* to *māgān*, the Hebrew equivalent of Phoenician-Punic *magon*. A case against such a change is made by Shea (1976:142 n. 5).

*of the warrior* For MT *gbwrym*, "of the warriors," we read *gbr-m*, the singular, as suggested by the parallel, *mgn šʾwl*, "the shield of Saul," augmented by the enclitic *-m* particle, an archaic feature of Hebrew poetry that has been studied systematically by Hummel (1957). I take "the warrior" as a reference to Saul.

*is not rubbed with oil* Reading MT *(qĕrê) bĕlî māšûaḥ* (see below) *baššāmen*. Some interpreters relate this expression to Saul, as required by MT *(kĕtîb) mšyḥ*, "anointed," others to the shield, as allowed though not required by MT *(qĕrê) māšûaḥ*. Our translation conforms to the latter understanding (see the NOTE). The former seems to founder upon the fact that Saul *was* anointed with oil (cf. 1:14,16). Indeed, the versions that relate the expression unambiguously to Saul either omit the negative particle, *bĕlî* (Syr., Targ.), or paraphrase epexegetically (Vulg. *quasi non unctus;* cf. AV "*as though he had* not *been* anointed"). Freedman (1972:123) addresses this difficulty by arguing "that we have here an instance of the asseverative use of *bl/bly* instead of the negative use" and translates "*duly* anointed with oil" (cf. Whitley 1972). Note, finally, that a few scholars have accepted Graetz's (see Smith) emendation of *bly*, "not," to *kly*, "a weapon"—thus, "the weapon rubbed with oil" or, perhaps, "the weapon of the one who was anointed with oil" (cf. Holladay 1970:174).

22. *From* OL, Syr.: "*But* from . . ."

*the slain . . . warriors'* MT *ḥllym . . . gbwrym*. The order is reversed in LXX[L]. Gevirtz (1963:88–90), on the basis of the parallelism of *gibbôrîm* and *ḥayil*, "valor," elsewhere, emends *ḥălālîm*, "the slain," to *ḥayyālîm*, "the valiant," an otherwise unknown word (cf. Holladay 1970:176–77).

*from* LXX[L] and certain other MSS have "*and* from."

*did not retreat* So MT: *lʾ nśwg ʾḥwr* for *lʾ nswg ʾḥwr* (cf. Ps 129:5 and the treatment of both passages by LXX), as many MSS of MT actually read *(BHS)*. In anticipation of the following line LXX reads "did not retreat *empty*." Because *qšt*, "bow," is feminine, Budde (followed by Holladay 1970:176) emends *nśwg* to *tśwg*, but *nāśôg*, if it is not to be understood as an infinitive absolute (GK[2] §113ff.), may be said to be masculine by attraction to "Jonathan."

23. *Beloved . . . not separated* In MT v. 23 reads *hn'hbym whn'ymm bḥyyhm wbmwtm l' nprdw*, "Beloved and charming in their life, and in their death they were not separated." A number of critics have sensed an imbalance in the parallelism here. Gevirtz, for example, is inclined to introduce a verb, *dbqw* or *htlkdw*, after *bḥyyhm* to correspond to *l' nprdw*—thus, in his translation, "The beloved and the pleasant! / In their lives they were joined / And in their death they were not divided" (1963: 91–92). A close look at the text of LXX, however, suggests that the problem can be solved without conjectural emendation. LXX[BA] read *hoi ēgapēmenoi kai hōraioi ou diakechōrismenoi euprepeis en tē zōē autōn kai en tō thanatō autōn ou diechōristhēsan*, "The beloved and lovely, not separated. Lovely in their life, and in their death they were not separated." *Euprepeis* is a duplicate of *hōraioi*, which was the OG translation of *n'ymym*, as the translation of *n'mt* by *hōraiōthēs* in v. 26 shows (cf. Wellhausen). Moreover, LXX[LMN] omit *euprepeis*, suggesting that it was introduced late as a correction toward the reading (*n'ymm bḥyyhm*, etc.) of MT. At first glance *ou diakechōrismenoi* seems to be another duplicate, in this case of *ou diechōristhēsan;* but certain facts weigh against such a conclusion. First, it is present in all MSS of LXX, and its presence is probably not, therefore, related to the introduction of *euprepeis*. Second, its position between *hōraioi* = *n'ymym* and (excluding *euprepeis*) *en tē zōē autōn* = *bmwtm* corresponds to nothing in the text of MT, a fact that indicates it did not arise recensionally. Third, it is grammatically at variance with *ou diechōristhēsan* = *l' nprdw;* specifically, it has the form of a participle, not a finite verb. In short, *ou diakechōrismenoi* seems to be an original part of the text of LXX, and we must conclude that another word, quite likely a negated participle, stood here in the Hebrew *Vorlage* of LXX. Now another form of *nprd* would seem to be aesthetically objectionable (cf. Wellhausen). I suggest, therefore, that the translator of LXX used two forms of the same Greek word to render different Hebrew originals here. Tentatively we may retroject *ou diakechōrismenoi* as *l' nbdlym*, "not parted, divided." With LXX, then, we may restore *(h)n'hbym wn'ymym l' nbdlym bḥyyhm wbmwtm l' nprdw*. Here we have the balance sought by Gevirtz—with chiasm as a bonus. MT, we can conclude, originally shared the longer reading of LXX, but *l' nbdlym* was lost by haplography, a scribe's eye skipping from *-(y)m* at the end of *wn'ymym* to *-ym* at the end of *nbdlym*.

*They* (3) So MT, LXX[L]. LXX[BAMN], Syr.: "*And* they. . . ."

24. *weep* The text of LXX[L] suggests that this preceded "for Saul," but evidently the original word order was *'l š'wl bkynh*, as shown by MT, LXX[BAM]. In LXX[B] *klausate* = *bkynh* is repeated, probably by dittography.

*for* Reading *'l*, for which MT has *'l* as frequently in this material (2:9; etc.). Cf. LXX *(epi)*, Syr. *('l)*, Targ. *('l)*.

*who dressed you* We read *hmlbškm* with MT. In view of the frequent use of masculine pronouns to refer to feminine antecedents (GK[2] §135o), emendation to *hmlbškn* would be hypercorrect (cf. Holladay 1970:180).

*luxurious crimson* MT *šny 'm 'dnym*, lit. "crimson with luxuries." It is not certain, however, that *'dnym* can mean "luxuries"; in Jer 51:24 it seems to refer to food—thus "dainties, delicacies," like *m'dnym*—and Targ. expands interpretively to "who dressed you in crimson *and fed you* (*wmwkyl;* other MSS have *wmwbyl,* "and brought you") delicacies *(tpnwqyn).*" The basic meaning of *'dn* seems to be "provide (richly)": compare line 4 of the unpublished Aramaic-Akkadian bilingual inscription from Tell el-Fakariyeh, where *m'dn* corresponds to *muṭaḫḫidu,* "providing (richly)." Emendation of *'dnym* to *sdnym,* i.e., *sĕdînîm,* "fine linen," found support among earlier critics (Graetz, Klostermann, Smith) and remains attractive (cf. Ackroyd) despite the absence of textual corroboration. LXX *kosmou hymōn* reflects *'dykm* (on the gender of the suffix, see the preceding and succeeding *Textual Notes*), "your jewelry," which, though preferred by Gevirtz (1963:93–94), is to be rejected as an anticipation of *'dy,* "jewelry," below.

*golden jewelry* That is, *'dy zhb,* lit. "jewelry of gold" (MT, LXX$^{BAMN}$, etc.). LXX$^{L}$ = *'dy wzhb,* "jewelry *and* gold."

*your gowns* Reading *lbwšykm* for MT *lbwškn,* "your (fem.) gown." In the older orthography, in which vowels were not represented, the number of the noun was ambiguous *(lbškm),* a situation that led to the confusion in MT; but the required plural is reflected by LXX$^{BAMN}$, Syr. The "masculine" form of the suffix has MS support *(BHS)* and probably ought to be read as *lectio difficilior* (see the *Textual Note* on "who dressed you" above).

25. *slain standing erect* MT *'l bmwtyk ḥll,* as in v. 19. LXX$^{BA}$ follow MT, but LXX$^{LMN}$ offer a different reading, viz. *eis thanaton etraumatisthēs* = *lmwt ḥllt,* lit. "unto death you were slain," that is, "you were mortally wounded." At the end of the verse LXX$^{L}$ adds *emoi* = *ly,* "for me, to me," in anticipation of the three occurrences of *ly* in the next verse.

26. *for you, my brother* MT and LXX$^{BA}$ have "for you, my brother *Jonathan,*" an explicative addition that echoes v. 25. The name appears in the MSS of LXX$^{L}$ as well, but its varying position shows it to have been added secondarily to correct the text toward the MT tradition—thus, $bc_2$: *epi soi iōnathan adelphe,* "for you, Jonathan, (my) brother"; o: *epi soi adelphe mou iōnathan,* "for you, my brother Jonathan"; $e_2$: *iōnathan epi soi adelphe,* "Jonathan, for you, (my) brother." The *Vorlage* of OG had *'lyk 'ḥy,* "for you, my brother," evidently the primitive reading.

*was wonderful* Instead of the expected form, *npl'h* or perhaps *npl't* (cf. Ps 118:23), MT has *npl'th.* The anomaly leads Freedman (1972:123; cf. Cross and Freedman 1950:47,50) to read two words, *npl' 'th,* "you were extraordinary" (rendering the rest of v. 26b as "Loving you, for me, was better than loving women"). I prefer to explain the anomaly by reference to the pattern of the final-*he* verbs, a category from which final-*'alep* verbs frequently borrowed forms (Driver; cf. GK$^{2}$ §75oo). Thus *npl'th* is formed on the analogy of *nglth,* etc. (cf. *hḥb'th* for the expected *hḥb'h,* "she hid," in Josh 6:17). Corresponding to *npl'th* is *epepesen* = *nplh,* "fell," in LXX$^{L}$, which is different throughout v. 26b: *epepesen ep' eme hē agapēsis sou hōs hē agapēsis tōn gynaikōn* = *nplh 'ly 'hbtk k'hbt hnšym,* "Your love fell upon me like the love of (the) women."

27. *the weapons of war* MT *kly mlḥmh,* for which LXX$^{L}$ *skeuē epithymēta* reflects *kly mḥmd,* "the precious vessels." The expression *kĕlê maḥmad* or *kĕlê ḥemdâ* is often used in reference to treasures of state (II Chron 32:27) or temple (II Chron 36:10,19), especially when carried off as booty by an enemy (Hos 13:15; Nah 2:10 [2:9]). Thus the LXX reading would be entirely appropriate in the present context. But Freedman

has convinced me of the probability that this concluding refrain refers to the weapons mentioned along with the warriors in the body of the poem (vv. 21,22) and of the improbability that it introduces an entirely new element, viz. the loss of sacred objects to the enemy.

## NOTES

1 18. *the Book of Jashar.* A lost anthology of poetry. It included the present elegy, the verses to the sun and moon in Josh 10:12–13, and Solomon's little poem on the dedication of the temple in I Kings 8:12–13 (cf. 8:53+ [LXX]). The significance of the title, *sēper hayyāšār,* is unknown. It seems to mean "the Book of the Upright," but what this might signify is hard to say. In the Greek text of I Kings 8:53+ it is called *bibli[os] tēs ōdēs,* as if *sēper haššîr* (i.e., *šyr* for *yšr*), "the Book of (the) Song," an entirely appropriate title.

19. *Alas, prince of Israel.* Following Cross (1973:122 n. 34) and Stuart (1976:188,193; cf. Ackroyd), I understand *hṣby yśr'l* as *hō ṣĕbî yiśrā'ēl.* The particle *hō,* "Alas!", is found in Amos 5:16 *(hô),* where it is used of mourners. It occurs also in II Sam 3:33, where the archaic spelling *(h-)* has again caused confusion. The literal meaning of *ṣĕbî* is "gazelle" (Syr. *ṭby'*), an example of the common use of animal names as designations for heroes and other notable persons in Northwest Semitic literature (cf. Miller 1971). It is used here to refer to Saul (according to Freedman 1972:119–20, Jonathan) as Israel's "gazelle," that is, "commander" or "prince" (Dahood 1959: 161–62; Miller 1971:185); cf. the use of Ugaritic *ẓby* in *CTCA* 15 [= *UT*[4] 128].4.7,18.

*slain standing erect.* Hebrew *'al-bāmôtêkā ḥālāl* has in the past been interpreted in one of two ways. (1) Taking *hṣby,* understood as "the gazelle" or "the glory," as the subject of *ḥll,* and *yśr'l,* "Israel," as the antecedent of the pronoun *-k,* "your," many read "The gazelle (= Saul), O Israel, upon your heights is slain!" (2) A different interpretation is suggested by lines of poetry from the Qumran "Scroll of the War of the Sons of Light Against the Sons of Darkness" (1QM 12.10):

*tn ydkh b'wrp 'wybykh*
*wrglkh 'l bmwty ḥll*
Set your hand on the neck of your enemies
and your foot on the backs of the slain.

To the first line compare Gen 49:8; the second contains the sequence that concerns us, *'l bmwty ḥll,* "on the backs of the slain." This suggests an interpretation of our passage similar to that of Gevirtz (1963:77–82; see p. 79 n. 25 for earlier bibliography). Taking *hṣb( )* as a verb (see above) and "Israel" as the antecedent of *-k,* "your," we might read, "Erect (a monument), O Israel, over your backs of slain!", that is, "over the bodies of your slain!"

There are, in my opinion, two decisive objections to both of these interpretations. (1) In both cases "Israel" is the antecedent of the pronoun "your." In v. 25, however, the expression *'l bmwtyk ḥll* occurs again, but there "Israel" is not available as an antecedent. (2) Neither of these understandings of *bāmôt* (the "heights" of the mountains, the "backs" of the enemies) yields an acceptable meaning when applied to *'l bmwty* in 22:34 (cf. Hab 3:19), which seems to contain a form of the same expression. We seek an explanation of *'l bmwtyk ḥll* that makes sense of both its occurrences in the present poem and, by extension, of *'l bmwty* in 22:34.

A systematic treatment of Hebrew *bāmâ* and its cognates by Vaughn (1974) suggests that in its most primitive sense the word refers to the swell of the rib cage of a human being or animal and that other meanings, both anatomical ("back, flank") and topological ("high place, ridge, hill-flank"), arose from this. Now in II Sam 1:19,25 it is not Israel's *bāmôt*, "heights," that are intended, as we have seen. In v. 25 it can only be Jonathan's *bāmôt* that are referred to, and thus in v. 19 it must be the *bāmôt* of Saul ("prince of Israel"). Evidently, then, the reference is to Saul's "back"—or, rather, "backs," since *bmwtyk* is plural or dual. Thus, David says of Saul that he was upon his "backs" when he was slain. To be or stand (22:34) upon one's "backs" is evidently an idiom; but what does it mean? Ugaritic *bmt* also means "back," and Akkadian *bantu* (< **bamtu)* refers to the torso, specifically the area between the thighs and ribs. As a dual, then, Hebrew *bāmôt* probably refers specifically to the haunches or hips and loins. With this in mind, II Sam 22:34 becomes especially instructive. The passage describes Yahweh's preparation of the psalmist for battle. According to the imagery, as we shall see, Yahweh is actually manufacturing a powerful fighting man. After planting his legs firmly in place as a foundation (v. 34a), he causes him to stand upon his *bāmôt* (v. 34b), i.e., erect(!). To be or stand upon one's "backs" is evidently an idiom meaning to stand upright or erect. Thus, in the present passage David praises Saul for having died in battle. He was fatally wounded *(ḥālāl)* while standing bravely erect (upon your "backs"), i.e., not cowering before his enemies. The same is said of Jonathan in v. 25. The praise in v. 22, then, is in the same vein.

20. *Gath . . . Ashkelon.* Major Philistine cities. Modern 'Asqalân is situated on the coast, ca. twelve miles north of Gaza, and Tell eṣ-Ṣâfī, which seems now to be the leading candidate for the disputed site of ancient Gath (Rainey 1975; cf. Wright 1966:78–86), is some fifteen miles farther on to the east-northeast.

21. *O mountains in Gilboa.* Hebrew *hārê baggilbōa'*, a rarity of poetic grammar in which a noun preceding a prepositional phrase to which it stands in close relation is in the construct state (cf. Isa 9:2; etc.). See GK² §130a. For Gilboa, see the NOTE at 1:6.

*dew . . . rain . . . flowing of the deeps.* See the *Textual Note* on "upon you . . . the deeps." These are the fresh waters, both celestial—the dew and rain, which fall from the sky—and subterranean—the deeps, which "go forth in valley and mountain" (Deut 8:7) to water the ground. They have a conventional place in blessings:

> Blessings of the sky above!
> Blessings of the deep that lies below!
> (Gen 49:25; cf. Deut 33:13)

And they have a place in curses as well. A Ugaritic imprecation (discussed in the *Textual Note* on "upon you . . . the deeps") reads:

> Let there be no dew, no rain,
> no surging(?) of the double deep!

In an Old Babylonian myth (*Atrahasis* 2:11–13; cf. *ANET*[3], p. 104) the earth is cursed as follows:

> Above let Adad withhold his rain!
> Below let the flood not flow,
> let it not rise from its source!

The evil David invokes upon Gilboa, then, is in the tradition of these even more ancient curses. As Speiser puts it (1950:378), "what is involved . . . is the total failure of the normal sources of life-giving water, in the form of rains from above and springs from below."

*begrimed . . . not rubbed with oil.* These two expressions, both often misunderstood, stand in parallelism, and each helps to clarify the other. Hebrew *nig'al* is unique, *g'l* occurring nowhere else in *Nip'al* in the Bible. The meaning is shown by Rabbinic Hebrew, in which it means "be soiled" in *Nitpa'el,* and Aramaic, in which it means "be polluted, soiled" in *Hitpe'el* (cf. Jastrow, p. 261). Driver doubts this, regarding this sense of the verb as Aramaic and preferring a translation like "rejected with loathing." He is supported by the *Qal* meaning of Biblical Hebrew *g'l,* viz. "reject," and by Aquila's translation (*apeblēthē,* "was rejected"). But the parallel, *bĕlî māšûah baššāmen,* "not rubbed with oil," decisively favors a rendering like "is soiled, begrimed" for *nig'al.* The meaning of "not rubbed with oil" is elucidated by Isa 21:5, where *mišḥû māgēn,* "Rub the shield (with oil)!" implies "Prepare for battle!" (Driver). Shields were made of leather and were oiled to keep them ready for use. Millard (1978) has assembled ample material from Mesopotamian sources, including references in cuneiform texts to leather shields and makers of leather shields, to illustrate this point; most illuminating is a reference to "oil to rub shield(s)," in which "Sumerian *šéš* is equivalent to Akkadian *pašāšu,* a verb used like Hebrew *māšaḥ* for 'anointing' in both secular and sacred senses." The point of the present bicolon, then, is that Saul's shield is not oiled and ready for action, as befits a hero's shield; rather, it lies neglected and covered with grime on Mount Gilboa.

22. *the warriors' fat.* We are not to think of the Philistines slain by Jonathan and Saul as paunchy and soft. On the contrary, fat seems to have been thought of as the seat of power and strength, or, as Heller puts it, "Im Fett ist die Kraft" (1970:107).

23. *not parted in life.* An instance of elegiac generosity. To be sure, Jonathan lived with and fought alongside his father to the end; he was no Abishalom. But the relationship between the two men was, at least at times, a highly strained one. According to our sources, the cause of the tension was their differing attitudes toward David. See especially I Sam 20:24b–34.

24. *luxurious crimson.* Hebrew *šānî 'im-'ădānîm* (see the *Textual Note*). Clothing dyed with the brilliant red called *šānî* was regarded as a sign of prosperity (Prov 31:21). The source of the dyestuff was the dried bodies of the various kermes insects (Arabic *qirmiz;* cf. English "crimson").

25. Talmon (1975:364–65) has shown the relationship of this verse to v. 19 to be an important structural component of the lament. The two verses are linked by "distant inverted parallelism." The repetition of the refrain "How the warriors are fallen!" creates an inclusion that rounds off the main body of the poem. V. 25b ("Jonathan . . .") answers to v. 19a ("Alas, prince of Israel . . .") and thus effectually connects the Jonathan "afterthought," as Talmon describes it, to the main body of the poem.

26. On the close relationship between David and Jonathan, a major feature of the stories of David's days at the court of Saul, see I Sam 18:1–5; 19:1–7; 20:1–21:1, and 23:14–18. In the ancient Near East "love" terminology belonged to the language of political discourse, and many of the statements made about Jonathan's love for David are charged with political overtones (cf. *I Samuel,* the NOTE on 20:17). But as the present passage illustrates well, there was also warm personal intimacy in the relationship between the two men.

27. *and the weapons of war lost.* The verb *(w)y'bdw* might mean "perished" as well as "lost" (thus RSV, "and the weapons of war perished"). Gevirtz (1963:95) concludes that "Saul and Jonathan are themselves the perished instruments of war" (so Thenius, Keil, Driver, Smith, etc.). Freedman (1972:123–24), taking *gbwrym,* "heroes," as the subject of *y'bdw,* "perished," as well as *nplw,* "are fallen," relegates *kly mlḥmh* to ablative force—thus "with (their) weapons" or "by the instruments of war."

## COMMENT

Our narrator quotes the lyrics of David's lament verbatim, citing the Book of Jashar as his source (see the NOTE at v. 18). He also tells us that the people of Judah were instructed by David to learn the song. David's fellow southerners, in other words, were to elegize the fallen king of Israel. If there was at that time in Judah a mood of resentment toward Saul, then David did not share or encourage it. Instead, it was his conviction, as demonstrated by the command to teach the song, that Judah owed respect to Saul's throne. In this way the details of v. 18a contribute to the general impression made by the inclusion of the elegy itself in the narrative that David's loyalty to Saul persisted to the last, that he remembered Saul with honor and affection, and that the news of Saul's death inspired in him a deep sense of public loss joined with no more selfish private emotion than grief.

### *The Argument of the Elegy*

At the beginning of the poem, v. 19, Saul ("prince of Israel") is invoked (v. 19a), the refrain—"How the warriors are fallen!"—is sounded for the first time (v. 19b), and the lament is begun.

In v. 20 the wish is expressed that the report of Israel's affliction be kept from reaching the homeland of the enemy. The Philistine women, if they learn the news, will have an opportunity to make merry at Israel's expense. Next, in v. 21, the Gilboa ridge, the site of the tragedy, is cursed. Saul's shield ought to be put safely away in the Israelite battle camp, its leather surface cleaned and treated with oil in anticipation of future battles, but instead it lies on the mountain's slope encrusted with the grime of combat. In consequence an imprecation is uttered against the mountain itself. The fresh waters that sustain life are forbidden to nourish Gilboa from above or below.

In vv. 22–23 the heroism of Jonathan and Saul is eulogized. Though they lost their lives, we are told in v. 22, they did not shrink from combat, inflicting heavy casualties on the enemy. They are remembered together in v. 23 as popular and winning leaders. Father and son, they were joined in life by the natural ties of kinship, and death, too, was a thing they shared (v. 23a). Finally (v. 23b), their prowess is remarked upon again.

In v. 24 the song turns to Saul alone. The women of Israel are called upon to mourn him in memory of the prosperity his rule brought them.

After a repetition of the refrain (v. 25aα) attention is shifted to Jonathan alone in vv. 25–26. The grief expressed here is the poem's most personal and poignant.

The elegy returns at its conclusion, v. 27, to the refrain, lamenting again the fall of the warriors, whose once proud weapons (cf. vv. 21,22) now lie useless and still.

### *Authorship*

Here and there in the major prose narratives of the Bible a poem appears. In most cases the subject of the poem is generally appropriate to the context; often the poem is explicitly attributed to a major figure in the story. Occasionally, however, there are details in the verses of such a poem that seem incompatible with its context, and rather frequently there are good reasons to doubt the poem's attribution to its purported author. The last major poem in the larger narrative before David's elegy is a case in point. Hannah's song in I Sam 2:1–10 is a pious lyric of thanksgiving, generally suited to the context in which it stands, where a child has been born in response to a barren woman's prayer; yet the blessing invoked for the king at the end of the poem shows that it, in fact, originated in monarchical times and that its attribution to Hannah is pseudonymous (cf. *I Samuel*, especially pp. 74–76). Similarly, we shall find reason to qualify the claims of high antiquity and Davidic authorship made on behalf of the poem in chap. 22.

What, then, can we conclude about the origin of the present poem? Was it, too, composed in some later age? Probably not. The evidence in this case points in the other direction. The subject matter of our poem is specifically—not merely generally—pertinent to the narrative context. The composition of an elegy for Saul and Jonathan generations after their death would be pointless. It is difficult, then, to think of the origin of the present poem at a date long after the events described in the surrounding narrative. But is the attribution to David spurious? Again, probably not. The sentiments expressed in the lament correspond to those that David held—at least according to the author of the account of his rise to power; that is, the sentiments are those David wanted the people of Israel and Judah to ascribe to him. The highly personal declaration of grief over Jonathan's death in vv. 25–26, moreover, would be out of place on any lips but David's. Nor must we even assume that the elegy was written *for* David by a singer in his retinue, for our oldest tradition about David's youth remembers him as a musician (I Sam 16:14–23). It is reasonable to assume, in short, that the narrator's claims about the authorship of our poem and the occasion of its composition are sound.

# III. DAVID BECOMES KING OF JUDAH
# (2:1–11)

**2** [1]Afterwards David inquired of Yahweh: "Shall I go up into one of
the cities of Judah?"
"Yes," Yahweh told him.
"Where shall I go?" asked David.
"To Hebron," he said.
[2]So David went up along with his two wives, Ahinoam of Jezreel and
Abigail, the widow of Nabal of Carmel, [3]and the men who were with
him, each with his family. They took up residence in Hebron.
[4]Then the men of Judah came and anointed David king over the
house of Judah.

### *An Overture to the Lords of Jabesh*

When David was informed that the men of Jabesh-gilead had buried
Saul, [5][he] sent messengers to the lords of Jabesh-gilead. "May you be
blessed by Yahweh!" he said to them. "You acted loyally towards your
lord, Saul, by burying him. [6]Now may Yahweh act loyally and constantly towards you! And I too shall establish such a friendship with
you, since you did this thing! [7]Now let your hands be steady and be
stalwart! For your lord, Saul, is dead, and it is I whom the house of
Judah have anointed over them as king."

### *Ishbaal Becomes King of Israel*

[8]Now Abiner son of Ner, the commander of Saul's army, had taken
Saul's son Ishbaal and conducted him to Mahanaim, [9]where he made
him king over Gilead, the Geshurites, Jezreel, Ephraim, Benjamin, and
Israel in its entirety— [10](Ishbaal son of Saul was forty years old when
he began to rule over Israel, and he ruled for two years.) But the house
of Judah followed David. [11](The time David ruled in Hebron over the
house of Judah was seven years and six months.)

## *TEXTUAL NOTES*

2 2. *So David went up* All witnesses are expansive. MT, LXX$^{A}$: "So David went up *there.*" LXX$^{L}$: "So David went up *to Hebron.*" LXX$^{BMN}$: "So David went up *there to Hebron.*"

3. *and the men* So LXX$^{BMN}$. MT, LXX$^{AL}$: "And *his* men." Syr.: "And *David* and his men."

*who were with him* At this point MT (cf. LXX$^{AO}$) adds "David brought up," understanding v. 3a as a new sentence; cf. Wellhausen. Syr. adds *slqw* = *'lw,* "(they) went up."

*each with his family* MT (cf. LXX) *'yš wbytw.* Syr.: *w'nšy byth* = *w'nšy bytw,* "and the men of his house." Targ.: *gbr w'nš bytyh* = MT(?).

*in Hebron* With Syr. we omit *'ry,* "the cities of," found in the other witnesses, an echo of "the cities of Judah" in v. 1. The puzzling statement that David and his men took up residence "in *the cities of* Hebron" has prompted considerable discussion; cf., most recently, Grønbaek 1971:223.

4. *anointed David* All witnesses add "there." MT, LXX$^{A}$: "anointed *there* David"; LXX$^{B}$: "anointed David *there.*" The variety of location suggests that the adverb is secondary. Cf. the *Textual Note* at 2:2.

*king* That is, *lĕmelek* (so MT). Most MSS of LXX, Syr., and Targ. interpret the same consonantal text as *limlōk,* "to rule." See also the second *Textual Note* at 2:7.

*that* The clause that follows is introduced by *lē'mōr* and is to be understood as direct speech (thus MT, lit. "And they informed David, saying, 'The men of Jabesh-gilead . . .' "), though here rendered indirectly for the sake of the English. At the same time, however, the clause is introduced by *'ăšer,* as is sometimes the case in direct speech (so 1:4 above and also I Sam 15:20; cf. GK$^{2}$ §157c). This *'ăšer* has been displaced in MT (cf. LXX$^{L}$) to follow "Jabesh-gilead" (as if "[It was] the men of Jabesh-gilead *who* buried Saul"), but it is reflected by LXX$^{B}$ *hoti* in its original position.

5–11. Substantial portions of these verses, including all of vv. 6 and 11, are missing from LXX$^{B}$, our most direct witness to the text of OG. For this reason witnesses normally of secondary consequence, such as Syr. and LXX$^{A}$, take on special significance here.

5. *the lords of* Reading *b'ly* on the basis of LXX$^{B}$ *hēgoumenous* (cf. Judg 9:51 [LXX$^{A}$]) in preference to MT *'nšy,* "the men," which is reminiscent of the preceding verse. For *b'ly ybyš gl'd,* see MT's text of 21:12, where, in a reversal of the present situation, it is LXX that shows substitution of the more common, inferior reading; see the *Textual Note* there.

*You acted loyally* Reading *'śytm ḥsd* on the basis of LXX$^{L}$ *pepoiēkate eleon.* Other witnesses are expansive. MT (cf. LXX$^{MN}$) has *'śytm hḥsd hzh*—thus, "you did this loyal deed." LXX$^{B}$ is missing at this point, but LXX$^{A}$ has *to eleos tou theou* = *ḥsd h'lhym,* "the loyalty of God"; note *'lyhm,* "to them," earlier in the verse, which may have stood immediately above *ḥsd* in some MSS. Space considerations suggest that 4QSam[a] combined the readings represented by MT and LXX[A]: *[ḥsd h'lhym hz]h.*

*towards* MT (cf. Syr.) *'im.* LXX *epi* and 4QSam[a] *'l* point to *'al,* otherwise attested with *ḥesed* in MT only in I Sam 20:8, where the versions reflect *'im.* The expected preposition is *'im,* and *'al* might be preferred here and in I Sam 20:8 as *lectio difficilior.*

*Saul* MT *('m)* and LXX[LMN] *(epi = 'l)* repeat "towards," which, though conforming to good Hebrew idiom, is to be omitted with LXX[A]. The versions show further expansion after "Saul"—thus LXX[MN], "*towards* Saul, *the anointed of Yahweh*"; Syr., "*towards* Saul, *the anointed of Yahweh, and towards Jonathan, his son.*" Space considerations suggest that 4QSam[a] read *'l š'wl* with LXX[L] but lacked the subsequent expansions of the other versions.

*him* So MT, LXX[A]. Syr.: "*them*" (see the preceding *Textual Note*). LXX[M] is again expansive: "him *and Jonathan, his son.*"

7. *your lord, Saul* So MT, LXX[BAM]. LXX[LN], Syr.: "Saul, your lord."

*over them as king* So 4QSam[a]: *'lyhm l[mlk]* (cf. LXX[BM]). MT, LXX[A]: "as king over them." There is no basis for preference between these arrangements. Note that, as in the case of 2:4, some witnesses (Syr., Targ.) understand *lmlk* as *limlōk,* "to rule," rather than *lĕmelek,* "as king."

8. *Abiner* The correct pronunciation of the name is shown to have been *'ăbînēr* by its first occurrence in MT in I Sam 14:50 and by its usual LXX transcription, *abennēr.* Elsewhere in MT, including the present passage, it appears as *'abnēr,* "Abner." See *I Samuel,* p. 256.

*the commander of Saul's army* Evidently the original reading was *śr ṣb' š'wl* (i.e., *śar ṣĕbā' šā'ûl;* cf. 10:16; etc.) as suggested by LXX *archistratēgos (tou) saoul.* In 4QSam[a] this has become *śr hṣb'* '[*šr lš'wl*], "the commander of the army whom Saul had," or rather, "Saul's commander of the army." MT preserves an intermediate stage, viz. *śr ṣb' 'šr lš'wl.*

*had taken* MT *lqḥ.* LXX[L] *kai elaben* reflects *wyqḥ,* showing a different understanding of the first part of this verse: "Now Abiner son of Ner was commander of Saul's army, and he took. . . ."

*Ishbaal* That is, *'îš ba'al,* "Man of Baal" (see the NOTE). The original is reflected by one MS of LXX[L] ($e_2$), which reads *eisbaal* (but $boc_2$ [cf. LXX[N], Syr.] have *memphibosthe,* "Mephibosheth," on which see the first *Textual Note* at 4:1), sustained by OL and the Greek texts of Aquila, Symmachus, and Theodotion *(BHS).* MT (cf. LXX[BAM]) has *'yš bšt,* that is, *'îš bōšet,* "Man of Shame," a euphemism shared by Josephus (*Ant.* 7.9) and 4QSam[a] in 2:10 below ([*'yš b*]*št;* the scroll is not extant in the present passage).

*Mahanaim* MT *mḥnym,* rendered twice by LXX[B] (cf. Josephus, *Ant.* 7.10) as *ek tēs parembolēs,* "from (cf. 2:12) the camp," and *eis manaem,* a transcription (omitted by LXX[ALN]). 4QSam[a] has *mḥn*[*ym*].

9. *over* The preposition is repeated for each of the six parts of Ishbaal's dominion. In each case we read *'l* with LXX *epi.* In the first three cases MT has *'l;* cf. the second *Textual Note* at 1:24.

*Gilead* So MT: *gl'd.* LXX reflects *hgl'dy,* "the Gileadite(s)," under the influence of the name that follows in the list.

*the Geshurites* The witnesses offer conflicting testimony. MT *h'šwry,* "the Ashurites, Assyrians" (?), suggests *hā'ăšērî*, "the Asherites" (cf. Judg 1:32), supported by Targ. *dbyt 'šr* and perhaps by LXX[L] *ton esrei* (so $e_2$; $boc_2$ have *ton ezrei*). LXX does not sustain this, nor does it suggest a suitable alternative (*ton thaseirei* = *ht'šyry* [?]; cf. Wellhausen). Syr. *gšwr* and Vulg. *gesuri* point to *hgšwry*, "the Geshurites," a reading geographically suited to this position in the list (between Gilead and Jezreel; see the NOTE and Map 2) and preferable for that reason to *h'šwry*. Contrast Soggin 1975:41. The gentilic form is preserved in most witnesses and is probably original despite the divergence of Syr. *(gšwr)* and LXX[A] *(ton thasour)*, in which the nongentilic pattern of the rest of the names in the list has been adopted.

*Israel in its entirety* So MT: *yśr'l klh* (cf. LXX[A]). LXX[BMN] *panta israēl* points to *kl yśr'l*, "all Israel."

10. *Ishbaal* Represented in the major witnesses exactly as in 2:8; see the *Textual Note* there.

*forty* One MS of OL has "thirty."

*ruled* LXX[N] adds "over Israel."

11. *The time . . . was* That is, *wyhyw hymym*, lit. "The days were . . ." (cf. LXX[AM]). MT (cf. LXX[LN]) has *wyhy mspr hymym*, "The number of days was. . . ."

*David ruled* Reading *mlk* (i.e., *mālak*) *dwd* on the basis of LXX[LN] *ebasileusen daueid*. MT has *hyh dwd mlk (melek)*, "David *was king*."

## NOTES

2 1. The narrator wants his audience to understand that David's return to Judah was intended by Yahweh. The move is fraught with political implications, and there is no explicit attempt in the account to deny this. But the ultimate motivating force is shown to have been Yahweh's will, not David's ambition. See the COMMENT.

*David inquired of Yahweh.* Presumably the divine will is discovered by agency of the sacred lots (cf. *I Samuel*, the NOTE at 14:40–42) administered by Abiathar, David's priest, as previously in the narrative (I Sam 23:1,4,9–12; 30:7–8). See further 5:19,23–24 and the NOTE on "David inquired of Yahweh" at 5:19.

*Hebron.* The city lay ca. nineteen miles south-southwest of Jerusalem at the center of the territory of Judah (see Map 1); it was probably the most powerful city of the region. As Flanagan explains (1979:236–39), it was "a place for which there was lingering nostalgia and allegiance" (p. 236). Thus Abishalom will begin his rebellion in Hebron (15:10), his birthplace (2:3). David, too, has close ties with Hebron: His two wives come from villages south of the city, and he can claim to be a benefactor of the Hebronites. The people of Hebron were among those he ingratiated with gifts from the spoils brought back from his pursuit of the Amalekite plunderers of Ziklag (I Sam 30:31).

2–3. *his two wives . . . and the men who were with him.* David is accompanied by his family and his entire retinue. Perhaps the narrator's purpose in mentioning this is to indicate, as Hertzberg suggests, that the change of address is a permanent one ("They took up residence . . ."; cf. I Sam 27:3).

2. *Ahinoam of Jezreel and Abigail . . . of Carmel.* David's two wives (cf. I Sam 25:43) went with him to Ziklag (I Sam 27:3), where they were almost lost to Amalekite brigands (I Sam 30:5,18), and now they accompany him to Hebron. For both this is a homecoming. Ahinoam is from Jezreel, a village listed in Josh 15:56 among the Judahite hill towns south of Hebron (cf. *I Samuel,* the NOTE at 25:43), which also included Carmel, Abigail's home (Josh 15:55). The site of the latter is Tell el-Kirmil, ca. seven miles south of modern Hebron. See Map 1. (For the story of David's first meeting with Abigail and his dealings with her churlish first husband, Nabal, see I Sam 25:2–42.) As Ackroyd and others have observed, "These marriages represented useful alliances for David in the southern area"; cf. Levenson's more emphatic statement of this point (1978:25–28) and the more detailed discussion of Levenson and Halpern (1980:508–13).

4a. *the men of Judah.* Comparison of 19:12 to 19:15 suggests that these "men of Judah" are identical to the "elders of Judah" of I Sam 30:26–31, to whom David distributed gifts from the spoils of his punitive mission against the Amalekite plunderers of Ziklag (cf. Mettinger 1976:118,141–42,198). That is, they are the leading citizens of the towns of Judah and are empowered, it seems, to act officially on behalf of the people of Judah, who constitute, we must assume, some kind of organized and at least partially independent political body (cf. especially Zobel 1975).

*anointed.* That is, consecrated to office by smearing the head with sweet-smelling oil. According to the prophetic framework in which our narrative is now set (see the Introduction, pp. 7–8) David has already been anointed king over all Israel, presumably including Judah, by Samuel (I Sam 16:13). Indeed, it was an essential principle of the prophetic theory of political leadership that kings must be designated and anointed by the agency of a prophet. But here in the older narrative David is anointed king without reference to a prophet (or, for that matter, a priest [cf. I Kings 1:34,41], though we may suspect one was involved), and the basis for his election is popular initiative rather than prophetically mediated divine designation, as also in 5:3, where David is anointed by the elders of Israel. See Mettinger 1976:185–232, especially 198–201; Kutsch 1979.

4b–7. This section must be read in light of the account of Saul's victory over Nahash the Ammonite in I Samuel 11, where the basis for the allegiance of Jabesh to Saul is to be found, and of the report of Saul's death in I Samuel 31, where we learn of the act of loyalty referred to here by David.

4b. *Jabesh-gilead.* Jabesh was one of the principal cities of Gilead, Transjordanian Israel. The modern site is probably Tell Abū Kharaz on the east bank of the Jordan. See Map 2. Cf., for further discussion, *I Samuel,* the fifth NOTE at 10:27b.

5. *You acted loyally.* Hebrew *ʿăśîtem ḥesed* (see the *Textual Note*), "You did *ḥesed.*" An act of *ḥesed,* generally speaking, involved "a responsible keeping of faith with another with whom one is in a relationship" (Sakenfeld 1978:233). The Jabeshites' retrieval and burial of Saul's remains (I Sam 31:11–13) amounted to such an act not only because of the fealty they owed Saul as king ("your lord, Saul") but also because of Saul's rescue of Jabesh from the Ammonite siege in the days before he became king (I Samuel 11). See also Sakenfeld 1978:40–42.

6. *Now may Yahweh act loyally . . . towards you!* Having done *ḥesed* for Saul (see the previous NOTE), the Jabeshites deserve to be beneficiaries of Yahweh's *ḥesed.* But Sakenfeld (1978:107–11) has shown by comparison to other such benedictory refer-

ences to *ḥesed* (II Sam 15:20; Ruth 1:8) that there is a further implication here. Yahweh's *hesed* is invoked on the Jabeshites because Saul is dead and cannot return their loyalty, just as it is invoked on Ittai and the Gittites in 15:20 because David expects to be unable to reward them for their allegiance, and on Ruth and Orpah in Ruth 1:8 because Naomi intends to leave them behind where she cannot repay their previous *ḥesed* toward her. It follows, says Sakenfeld (p. 111), that "David in using the phrase 'may Yahweh do *ḥesed*' is apparently suggesting that the Jabesh Gileadites' political relationship was to Saul and that with his death that relationship is now ended. They are now free to establish a new formal relationship with David (rather than with Saul's descendants), which David offers and suggests that they do." We might press this one step further. By their act of *ḥesed* towards Saul, the Jabeshites, says David, have *discharged* their responsibility to the house of Saul and are now free to establish a new relationship with whomever they choose.

*And I too shall establish such a friendship with you.* David proposes a renewal of the relationship that existed between Saul and the Jabeshites, but now with himself as lord. Hillers (1964) has shown that Hebrew *'āśâ ṭôbâ,* like Akkadian *ṭābūta epēšu* (cf. Moran 1963b; Mettinger 1976:147 and nn. 32,33), may refer to the establishment of friendship, i.e., diplomatic amity, by treaty. Hillers explains (p. 47) that "David is seeking to maintain the same relation"—i.e., "such a friendship" *(haṭṭôbâ hazzō't)*—"that prevailed in the days of Saul. . . . Since treaties did not automatically continue in force when a new king took the throne, it was necessary for David actively to seek a renewal of the pact." We might add to this the observation that if the relationship *had* continued in force after Saul's death, the loyalty of Jabesh would probably have been transferred to Ishbaal, not David, and David's overture would have been "necessary" in any case. So it is not that the end of the relationship between Saul and Jabesh makes this overture *necessary* but that it makes it *possible* (cf. the preceding NOTE).

7. *Now let your hands be steady and be stalwart!* David calls the men of Jabesh into his service. The expression *teḥězaqnâ yĕdêkem,* "let your hands be steady" (not "let your hands be *strong*"), means, in effect, "take courage" or "be confident," as in 16:21 (also Judg 7:11; Ezek 22:14; Zech 8:9,13). "Stalwart men" *(bĕnê ḥayil)* are those who may be depended upon for loyal service, as in 13:28 (cf., further, *I Samuel,* the NOTE at 10:26,27a). Cazelles (1958:104) compares David's words to the language of a letter from the Hittite king Shuppiluliumash to his vassal Niqmaddu II, the king of Ugarit (RS 17.132 [*PRU* vol. IV:35]), counseling courage and loyalty.

8. *Abiner.* Abiner *('ăbînēr;* cf. the *Textual Note)* was, as here indicated, Saul's chief military officer and his first cousin, the son of his uncle, Ner (according, at least, to one interpretation of I Sam 14:50,51; see the NOTE there in *I Samuel*). The language used in this and the following verse makes it clear that he, not the figurehead Ishbaal, wields real power in Israel now that Saul and Jonathan are dead.

*Ishbaal.* Both the form and the interpretation of the name are disputed. In the received Hebrew text of Samuel it appears consistently as *'îš bōšet,* apparently "Man of Shame" (see below), whereas Chronicles calls the same man *'ešba'al* (I Chron 8:33; 9:39). Scholars have long assumed that *bōšet,* "shame," is a euphemistic substitution for *ba'al,* understood as the name of the Canaanite god Baal. This assumption has recently been issued a thoroughgoing challenge by Tsevat (1975), who prefers an interpretation of *bōšet* based on the Akkadian onomastic element *bāštu,* which means "dignity, pride, vigor" and thus "guardian angel, protective spirit" (p. 76); the Hebrew element does not have quite the force of the Akkadian, he argues, but is rather to be understood as "a divine-feature-turned-epithet" (p. 77). Tsevat doubts what he calls "the hypothesis of dysphemism" (p. 71), i.e., the invidious substitution of *bōšet* for *ba'al*. "In postbiblical times such tendencies were operative and effective," he admits (p. 85), "but this is questionable for biblical times. . . ." But Tsevat's argument is seriously impaired, it seems to me, by his failure to treat those passages where *bōšet* has been substituted for *ba'al* in contexts exclusive of proper names. In particular we may cite I Kings 18:19,25, where the received Hebrew text reads *ba'al*, "Baal," but the Greek has *tēs aischynēs*, reflecting *bōšet*, "shame," unambiguously, and Jer 11:13, where the reverse situation prevails, viz. *labbōšet*, "to shame," in the Hebrew and *tē baal*=*lĕba'al*, "to Baal," in the Greek. Such examples eliminate any question that euphemistic substitutions were made in our text, and it is difficult in their light to accept Tsevat's interpretation of *bōšet* as a word not otherwise attested in Hebrew or any other Northwest Semitic language. (For Tsevat's discussion of related names in Samuel, see the *Textual Notes* on "Meribbaal" at 4:4, "Jerubbaal" at 11:21, and "Yeshbaal" at 23:8.)

With regard to the first element in the name, we must consider three possible interpretations:

1. The original may have been *'îš*, "man." This interpretation is supported by the received Hebrew reading, *'îš*, by the Qumran reading, *'yš*, in v. 15 (cf. v. 10), and probably by the reading *eis-* in certain Greek manuscripts. It has been preferred by a number of modern interpreters, including Noth (1928:138; 1956:324) and recently Tsevat (1975:77–79). Accordingly, the name would be *'îš ba'al*, "Man of Baal" or "Man of the Lord" (see below), a familiar type in the ancient Semitic onomasticon.

2. The original may have been *'iš* or perhaps *'eš*, a verbal element corresponding to the more common *yēš*, "(he) exists," but attested in the form *'iš* in II Sam 14:19 and Mic 6:10. This interpretation seems favored by the Chronicler's form, *'eš-*, and perhaps by the enigmatic name *yiš(wî)*, identified as a son of Saul in I Sam 14:49 (cf. *I Samuel*, the *Textual Note* on "Ishvi" at 14:49). It was supported most vigorously by Albright (1969a:110 and n. 62; cf. Lipiński 1967a:72 and n. 11), who compared *'ešba'al*, "Baal exists," to the Ugaritic verses " 'Al'iyan Baal lives! The Prince, Lord of Earth, exists (*'iṯ*)!" (*CTCA* 6[= *UT*[4] 49].3.8–9). The equivalent name occurs in Ugaritic Akkadian (RS 12.34 + 12.43.25; cf. *PRU III*, pl. IX and p. 193) as *i-ši-*[d]*Ba'al* (Moran 1954). (Cf. "Jeshbaal" in 23:8.)

3. The original may have been *'āš*, "(he) has given," or some other form of verb or noun derived from *'wš*, "give" (on this verb, see especially Cross 1966:8–9 n. 17). Compare the Ugaritic name *'išb'l* (*PRU V*, 69.8; 117.2.35 = *UT* 2069.8; 2117.35), which cannot mean "Baal exists" at Ugarit, where the verb "exist" is *'iṯ*, and is difficult to understand as "Man of Baal" owing to the apparent lack of **'îš*, "man," in the Ugaritic lexicon. In support of this interpretation, according to which the name might be taken to mean "Baal has given" or "Gift of Baal," are Dahood (1965a:52 n. 42) and Schoors (in Fisher 1972:8–9).

The evidence will not, in my judgment, permit a confident choice among these three possibilities. Provisionally I prefer the first.

Finally, we must ask to whom the theophorous element in this name, *ba'al*, "[the] lord," refers. While it is true that it was at times especially associated with the Canaanite god Hadad or Haddu—"Baal"—and indeed was regarded in later biblical tradition as unambiguously a title of a foreign god—hence its frequent mutilation to *bōšet*, "shame"—there is reason to suppose it was considered an acceptable epithet of Yahweh in the early days of the monarchy. In this regard Freedman reminds me of the name *bĕ'alyâ* (= *ba'alyāh*?), "Baaliah," who, according to I Chron 12:6, was one of David's warriors; this name seems to mean "Yahweh is lord." There is nothing in the biblical record to suggest that Saul, for all his troubles, was anything but a Yahwist, and he would have had little reason to name a son after a foreign god. (David, too, had at least one son whose name contained the element *ba'al;* see 5:16.) In all likelihood, then, the name *'īš ba'al,* "Ishbaal," meant "Man (= Servant) of the Lord," i.e., "Man of Yahweh." Contrast the argument of Noth (1928:120–22).

*Mahanaim.* For attempts to identify the modern site, which must lie near the Jabbok River (Nahr ez-Zerqā; see Map 2), see Bartlett 1970:264 n. 1. A city on the banks of the Jabbok would have been, in Bartlett's words, "a good point for controlling territory such as Geshur and Jezreel to the north and northwest," and Mahanaim is "presumably here thought of as capital of Gilead" (p. 264). We have already noted the close ties of the family of Saul to Gilead, or at least to the city of Jabesh (cf. the NOTES at 4b–7 and 4b above), and here is further evidence of the amicable relationship that existed between Benjamin and Transjordanian Israel. It has even been suggested that Mahanaim was a Benjaminite colony (Schunck 1963b). In any case, the transfer of the Israelite seat of government to Transjordan is understandable in light of the political situation that must have prevailed in Palestine after the Philistine victory at Gilboa. The heartland of Saul's kingdom in the Benjaminite hills was now too vulnerable to serve as the seat of the rump government that Abiner set up in Ishbaal's name, and the more remote forests of Gilead offered refuge and security to Ishbaal, just as they would to David later on (cf. 17:21–29).

9. These are the territories over which the house of Saul claimed sovereignty. For the locations, see the individual identifications below and Map 2.

*Gilead.* Though all of Transjordanian Israel was sometimes referred to in a general way as Gilead, the extent of the region *sensu stricto* corresponded to the tribal claims of Gad and Reuben, territory ruled by Saul after his victory over Nahash, king of the neighboring state of Ammon, who "had been oppressing the Gadites and Reubenites grievously" (I Sam 10:27+; cf. *I Samuel,* pp. 198–207).

*the Geshurites.* The Geshurites lived in northeastern Palestine in territory formally claimed by Israel (cf. Josh 13:13). The southern boundary of Geshur lay beyond the region known as Havvoth-jair in northern Manasseh (Deut 3:14). David had his own connections with the kingdom of Geshur: Abishalom's mother, as we shall see, was a Geshurite princess (3:3). On Geshur in general, see Mazar 1961:18–21.

*Jezreel.* The Jezreel Valley separated the Samarian hills from those of Galilee to the north, but it is difficult to imagine a serious Israelite claim to control of this entire region after the debacle at nearby Gilboa. We should probably think instead of the district surrounding the city of Jezreel, modern Zer'în, at the eastern end of the valley on the northwest slope of Mount Gilboa, the place where the Israelites gathered before the disastrous battle. The district may have corresponded roughly to the traditional tribal territory of Issachar. Cf. Alt 1968:209–10; Soggin 1975:42.

*Ephraim.* The Israelite heartland, probably "to be taken here in the wider sense, which, besides the tribe of Ephraim, includes Manasseh and therefore the whole 'House of Joseph' " (Alt 1968:210).

*Benjamin.* The tribal claim of Benjamin centered on the ridge of hills that ran between Jerusalem and Bethel. This was the homeland of the house of Saul.

*Israel in its entirety.* Hebrew *yiśrā'ēl kullōh,* the equivalent of *kol-yiśrā'ēl,* "all Israel," in 3:12 and 3:21 below (read here by the principal Greek witnesses to the text; see the *Textual Note*), which show that it refers to Ishbaal's kingdom in a general way. Flanagan has shown that "all Israel" in this context "designates a completely northern group which was the union of two separate elements, namely, Israel and Benjamin" (1975:108). In our passage, then, "Israel in its entirety" does not refer to yet another geographical area apart from Ephraim and Benjamin; it is a summary including both in its meaning.

10a,11. The parenthetical information given here is characteristic of the biblical materials about the kings of Israel and Judah. The accounts of the reigns of the kings of the divided monarchy are organized according to a framework of synchronisms based on chronological information that must have come from archival sources; cf. I Kings 14:21; 22:42; etc. This framework derives, we assume, from the Deuteronomistic compilation of the history of the kingdom (cf. Noth 1981:54–55,107 n. 26). Similar information stands in the materials about the kings of the united monarchy, Saul (I Sam 13:1), Ishbaal (II Sam 2:10a), David (II Sam 2:11; 5:4–5; I Kings 2:11), and Solomon (I Kings 11:42). It is not clear, however, that this latter information derives from archival sources or that its presence in the text can be accounted to the work of the Deuteronomistic historian. The data on Saul's reign are wanting (see *I Samuel,* pp. 222–23). The other information seems to be made up largely of estimates or outright guesses in round numbers—Ishbaal was forty years old when he began to reign (II Sam 2:10a); David was thirty (II Sam 5:4a); David reigned forty years (II Sam 5:4b; I Kings 2:11); Solomon reigned forty years (I Kings 11:42). The notices in the present verses lack the organizing force of the Deuteronomistic framework passages in Kings (I Kings 14:21; etc.) and indeed provide only limited help in coordinating the reigns of Ishbaal and David (see below). They interrupt the flow of the older narrative, v. 10b being originally the direct continuation of v. 9 (Wellhausen, etc.). Moreover, textual considerations add to our suspicion of this and similar passages. Josephus gives no chronological information at this point in his retelling of the story (*Ant.* 7.10), and his text may have lacked anything corresponding to the present vv. 10a,11. Similarly, the notices about David's reign in 5:4–5 seem to be missing from the text of the great Samuel scroll from Qumran, just as in the text of I Chronicles 11 (cf. the *Textual Note* at 5:4–5). All of these things suggest that these notices (I Sam 13:1; II Sam 2:10a,11; 5:4–5; and perhaps I Kings 2:11; 11:42) were not part of the original Deuteronomistic framework of the history of the kingdom but were instead very late additions to the text in the spirit of that framework. Many of the data thus introduced—the above-mentioned round numbers, for example—are likely to be unreliable, but some may lay at least a remote claim to reliability. In the present case the lengths of the two reigns—of Ishbaal in Mahanaim, two years; of David in Hebron, seven years and six months—can be regarded as at least plausible information. Many scholars, to be sure, have rejected the two-year figure for Ishbaal's reign, arguing that he must have been king of Israel for as long as David was king of Judah alone. But Soggin (1975:33–41) has argued forcefully for the received figures. He notes that the two reigns need not be assumed to have started simultaneously. Instead, the two years of Ishbaal's kingship corresponded to the *last* two of David's. This was preceded by an interregnum of over five years in the north, during which time Abiner was presiding over the reorganization of the country after the Gilboa disaster. For a different solution, see Mazar 1963a:239; Flanagan 1979:237–38.

## COMMENT

David's reign as king in Hebron seems to have been an important stage in the development of the bonds and institutions that eventually made possible the unification of Judah and Israel under a single ruler (cf. Mazar 1963a:238–40). Having prepared the way with gifts to the cities of Judah (I Sam 30:26–31; cf. the first NOTE at v. 4a above), David first established his kingship at Hebron, the traditional capital of the region and the seat of the powerful Calebite clan, with whom he had ties by marriage (cf. the NOTE at v. 2). He built diplomatic bridges to northern Gilead by his overture to the people of Jabesh (vv. 4b–7) and to the kingdom of Geshur in the present-day Golan Heights by marriage alliance (cf. 3:3). He thus set his own kingdom in direct conflict with that of Saul, which also laid claim to Gilead and Geshur (v. 9), and initiated a struggle with Saul's son Ishbaal, the figurehead sovereign of a rump Israelite government at Mahanaim in Transjordan, from which he would emerge victorious in the end.

From the perspective of the modern historian, then, David's activities in this period seem shrewd, calculated, and consistently effective. His success seems the result of foresight and careful deliberation. This is not, however, the perspective of our narrator, or at least it is not the view of David's actions he means his audience to take. The details he provides about the negotiations between David and the people of Hebron or the elders of Judah, about the fortunes of the Israelite state after the battle of Gilboa, and about the political climate in general in Palestine during this period seem frustratingly incomplete or cryptic to the historian (cf. Mazar 1963a:239; Grønbaek 1971:222–23). The reason for this is that the sequence of events is presented, as throughout the story of David's rise to power, not merely as an interplay between circumstances and human deeds, certainly not as a consequence of the ambitious machinations of David, but as the working out of Yahweh's will. We may think of the gifts to the cities of Judah as preparing the way for David's assumption of kingship in the south and even speak of the gesture, as Mettinger does (1976:118), as "made with the conscious aim to prepare the way for his recognition by [the elders of Judah]." But such a historical judgment, quite possibly accurate in itself, is alien to our narrative, which suggests no more self-interested motive for the gifts than, perhaps, a desire to enrich "all the places that David and his men had frequented" (I Sam 30:31) during David's days as a fugitive in the Judaean countryside. We are not told that David took up residence in Hebron seeking a base from which to prosecute his claim to the crown. We *are* told that he entered the city *at Yahweh's command* (v. 1). The overture to the lords of Jabesh is not presented to us as an act of crass ambition. The emphasis of these verses (4b–7) is plainly on the Jabeshites' loyalty to Saul and on David's desire to reward them for it, and the impact of this account of the incident, then, is, as Ward points out (1967:146–47), to give further demonstration of David's respect for Saul. There is a certain irony in this, one must admit. David's negotiations with Jabesh, which the modern historian will be inclined to see as an attempt to drive a wedge between the house of Saul and its most conspicuously allegiant domain, are set forth as evidence of David's respect for Saul! Yet this is precisely what we have here, and it illustrates the apologetic character of our story well. The narrator describes an incident that might seem to show David to be ambitious, contriving, even ruthless, in such a way as to offer the more favorable alternative interpretation of David as less self-glorifying than compliant to the intention of his god that he should have glory. He speaks to the people of Jabesh not as one who would overturn the legitimate succession to the throne of Israel but, on the contrary, as one who is becoming increasingly aware of the legitimacy of his own claim to that succession: ". . . it is I whom the house of Judah have anointed over them as king" (v. 7).

Taken as a whole, this section seems designed to prepare us for things to come. As many interpreters have stressed (Ward 1967:144; Grønbaek 1971: 223–24), David's kingship is not yet complete and will not be complete until he takes the northern crown as well in 5:1–3; the assumption of kingship in Hebron described here in vv. 1–4a is only a stage along the way. Verses 4b–11 also look ahead, preparing specifically for the account of the outbreak of war that follows immediately (cf. Eissfeldt 1951:124; Grønbaek 1971:226).

## IV. THE OUTBREAK OF WAR
## (2:12–32)

2 [12]Abiner son of Ner and the servants of Ishbaal son of Saul marched
out of Mahanaim towards Gibeon. [13]Joab son of Zeruiah and the servants of David had also marched out, and they met each other at the
pool of Gibeon, one group drawing up beside the pool on one side and
the other group beside [it] on the other.

### *The Contest at Flints' Field*

[14]Then Abiner said to Joab, "Let some soldiers take the field and play
before us!"
"Yes," replied Joab, "let them take the field!"
[15]So they took the field, squaring off by number: twelve of the Benjaminites of Ishbaal son of Saul and twelve of the servants of David.
[16]They took hold of each other's heads, their swords at each other's
sides, and fell dead together. (So the place was called Flints' Field. It
is in Gibeon.)

### *The Death of Asael*

[17]The fighting was very fierce that day, and Abiner and the men of
Israel were driven back by the onslaught of the servants of David. [18]The
three sons of Zeruiah—Joab, Abishai, and Asael—were there, and
Asael, who was as fleet of foot as one of the gazelles of the open plain,
[19]chased after Abiner, turning neither to the right nor the left as he
followed [him].
[20]Abiner turned around. "Is that you, Asael?" he said.
"Yes," he replied, "it is!"
[21]"Turn aside," Abiner told him, "to the right or the left! Catch one
of the soldiers and take his spoil!" And when Asael would not stop
following him, [22]Abiner spoke to [him] again: "Stop following me! Why
should I strike you to the ground? How could I show my face to Joab,
your brother?" [23]But he refused to stop. So Abiner struck him in the

belly with the butt of his spear, [which] came out at his back. He fell down and died there in his tracks.

Everyone came to a stop when they reached the place where Asael had fallen and died, 24 but Joab and Abishai went on after Abiner, and, as the sun was setting, came to the hill of Ammah, opposite Giah on the road to the wilderness of Gibeon. 25 The Benjaminites had gathered into a single company behind Abiner, coming to a stop on top of a certain hill.

26 Then Abiner hailed Joab. "Must the sword devour forever?" he asked. "Don't you realize that the consequences will be bitter? So how long will it be before you tell the army to turn back from the pursuit of their brothers?"

27 "As Yahweh lives!" said Joab. "If you hadn't spoken, it would have been morning before the army gave up the pursuit of their brothers!" 28 Then [he] sounded the shofar, and the whole army came to a halt. They no longer chased after Israel, and they fought no more.

29 Abiner and his men marched in the Arabah all that night; then they crossed the Jordan and, having marched all morning, came to Mahanaim. 30 Joab, when he had returned from the pursuit of Abiner, assembled the entire army. Nineteen men in addition to Asael were found missing from the servants of David, 31 [who], however, had slain three hundred and sixty of the Benjaminites, Abiner's men. 32 They took up Asael and buried him in his father's tomb in Bethlehem. Then Joab and his men marched all night, and the light dawned on them in Hebron.

## *TEXTUAL NOTES*

2 12. *Ishbaal* See the *Textual Notes* at 2:8,10.

*towards Gibeon* So MT *(gbʿwnh)* and 4QSam$^a$ *([gb]ʿ̊wnh).* LXX$^{LN}$ *(eis) bounou* suggests *gbʿh* or *gbʿth,* "towards *Gibeah.*"

13. *marched out* LXX adds "from Hebron." Omit with MT.

*the pool* (2) LXX$^B$ adds "of Gibeon"; omit with MT, LXX$^{AM}$, Syr. Note the defective state of the text of LXX$^L$ in this verse. It seems originally to have shared the longer reading of LXX$^B$ at this point, viz. *epi tēn krēnēn tēn gabaōn;* this combined with the similar or identical sequence earlier in the verse to trigger a long haplography, which subsequently was repaired only in part. In its present condition the text of LXX$^L$ reads *kai synantōsin allēlois epi tēn krēnēn gabaōn kai ekathisan houtoi enteuthen kai houtoi enteuthen epi tēn krēnēn,* as if "and they met them at the pool of Gibeon, one group drawing up on one side and the other group on the other side beside the pool." This corruption is likely to have been inner-Greek; the text of 4QSam$^a$, which might be expected to share the divergent reading of LXX$^L$, is sufficiently legible at this point to show that it conforms generally to the text of MT.

15. *twelve of the Benjaminites of Ishbaal* Reading *šnym ʿśr lbny bnymn ʾyš bʿl* on the basis of 4QSam$^a$ (*[šnym] ʿśr lbny bnymn ʾyš [bšt]*) and LXX$^L$ (cf. LXX$^N$) *dōdeka tōn hiuōn beniamein tou eisbaal* (so $e_2$; $boc_2$: *memphibosthe*). MT has lost *bny* by haplography before *bnymn* (cf. Syr.) and reads *wlʾyš bšt* instead of *ʾyš bʿl* (Syr. omits *w-*)—thus, *šnym ʿśr lbnymn wlʾyš bšt*, "twelve belonging to Benjamin and to Ishbosheth. . . ." There is confusion in the text of LXX$^B$, but it seems originally to have shared the reading of LXX$^L$. The name "Ishbaal" is represented in the major witnesses exactly as in 2:8,10,12; see the *Textual Note* at 2:8.

*of the servants* So MT (*mʿbdy*), Syr. (*mn ʿbdʾ*), and LXX$^B$ (*ek tōn paidōn*). LXX$^{LN}$ *tōn paidōn* points to *lʿbdy* (cf. *lbny* above).

16. *each other's heads* That is, *ʾyš brʾš rʿhw*, lit. "each one the head of his fellow" (so MT; cf. Syr., LXX$^N$). LXX$^{BA}$ reflect *ʾyš byd rʾš rʿhw*, "each one *with (his) hand* the head of his fellow."

*their swords* Preceded in LXX$^O$ by *(kai) enepēxan*, "*and thrust* their swords *into* each other's sides."

*Flints'* MT *haṣṣūrîm*; see the NOTE. LXX *tōn epiboulōn* and Syr. *ṣdn* (Syr.$^{MSS}$ *ṣrn*) point to *ṣōdîm*, "Plotters' " (Wellhausen; cf. I Sam 24:11). It is difficult to choose between the alternatives *ṣrm* and *ṣdm*. Budde: *haṣṣiddîm*, "Sides' " (cf. "their swords at each other's sides" above). Batten 1906: *haṣṣārîm*, "Treacherous Fellows'."

22. *to [him]* That is, *ʾl ʿśhʾl*, "to Asael" (so MT, etc.). After "Asael" Syr. adds *dnsṭʾ mn btrh wʾmr*, as if reading *lswr mʾḥryw wyʾmr*, "to stop following him, and he said." This arose in reminiscence of the end of v. 21, where "Asael" is also followed in Syr. by *dnsṭʾ mn btrh*.

*Why should I strike you to the ground?* So MT, etc. Syr.: "Why should I strike you *and lay you (wʾrmyk)* on the ground?"

*How could I . . . your brother?* MT *wʾyk ʾśʾ pny ʾl ywʾb ʾḥyk*, rendered by LXX$^{(L)}$ as *kai pōs arō to prosōpon mou pros iōab ton adelphon sou*. To this LXX adds *kai pou estin tauta epistrephe pros iōab ton adelphon sou*, which apparently reflects a corrupt duplicate of the preceding (Wellhausen), viz. *wʾyk ʾlh pnh ʾl ywʾb ʾḥyk*, "And how can these things be? Return to Joab, your brother!"

*my face to Joab* Syr.: ". . . my face *and look at (wʾḥwr)* Joab. . . ."

23. *he refused* So MT, LXX$^{BAM}$, Syr. LXX$^{LN}$: "*Asael* refused."

*in the belly* See the *Textual Note* at 3:27.

*[which]* That is, *hḥnyt*, "the spear." So MT, etc. Omitted by Syr.

*and died* So MT, etc. Omitted by Syr.

24. *but Joab and Abishai went on after* MT *wyrdpw ywʾb wʾbyšy*. Syr. has *wqm(w) ywʾb wʾbyšy wrdpw*, "but Joab and Abishai *arose and* went after. . . ."

*Ammah* See the NOTE.

*Gibeon* So MT, LXX$^{BA}$. LXX$^{LMN}$ = "Gibeah." Cf. the *Textual Note* at 2:12.

26. *that the consequences will be bitter* Reading *ky mrh thyh hʾḥrwnh* on the basis of LXX$^L$ (so Smith). MT and most other witnesses read *ky mrh thyh bʾḥrwnh*, "that there will be bitterness in the future," which is also acceptable.

*their brothers* So MT, LXX$^{L}$, Syr. LXX$^{BA}$: "*our* brothers."

27. *Yahweh* So LXX, Syr. MT: "God."

28. *They no longer chased* That is, *wl' yrdpw,* which does not mean "They did not chase," which would be *wl' rdpw* (so MT$^{MSS}$[*BHS*]). The durative nuance of the verb is reinforced (unnecessarily) in MT (cf. LXX$^{LNO}$, Syr.) by the addition of *'wd;* delete with LXX$^{BAM}$.

29. *to Mahanaim* Cf. the *Textual Note* at 2:8. Here MT has *mḥnym* and 4QSam$^{a}$ [*mḥ*]*nymh.* LXX$^{B}$ has *eis tēn parembolēn,* "to the camp," and LXX$^{L}$ combines a translation with a (corrupt) transcription, viz. *eis parembolas* (cf. Josephus, *Ant.* 7.18) *madiam* (cf. OL), "to the camps, Mahanaim." We read *mḥnym.*

30. *Nineteen men* So MT, LXX$^{BAMN}$. LXX$^{L}$ and certain other Greek MSS reflect a text in which this was prefaced by *hnplym,* "Those who had fallen."

*in addition to Asael* That is, *w'śh'l,* "and Asael" (MT). Syr. has *w'ś'yl myt,* "and Asael was dead."

*were found missing* MT *wayyippāqědû,* rendered twice by Syr. as *w'tmnyw,* "were counted (as missing)," and *w'tmḥyw,* "were stricken," the second translation being probably a corrupt duplicate of the first.

31. *of the Benjaminites* Reading *mbny bnymn* with LXX. MT has lost *bny* by haplography. In 4QSam$^{a}$ *bnymn* stands at the right margin, so that despite the loss of the end of the preceding line we can assume that the scroll shared the reading of LXX. Cf. the *Textual Note* at 2:15.

*Abiner's men* That is, *m'nšy 'bnr,* lit. "from the men of Abiner," as witnessed by 4QSam$^{a}$ *(m'nšy* [*'bnr*]*)* and LXX$^{BAMN}$ *(tōn andrōn abennēr);* cf. also Syr. LXX$^{L}$ has *ek tou laou abennēr,* as if *m'm 'bnr,* "from Abiner's *army,*" or perhaps "from (those who were) with Abiner." MT has *wb'nšy 'bnr,* "*and among*(?) the men of Abiner."

At the end of the verse MT has *mtw,* probably a corrupt and displaced duplicate of the previous *m'wt;* it is reflected in LXX$^{BAMN}$ *(par' autou)* as *m'tw.* Omit with LXX$^{L}$, Syr.

32. *in Bethlehem* MT *byt lḥm* (cf. LXX$^{A}$). LXX$^{B}$, MT$^{MSS}$: *bbyt lḥm.*

*his men* So MT, LXX$^{LMN}$, OL, Syr., and 4QSam$^{a}$. LXX$^{BA}$: "the men who were with him."

## NOTES

2 12. Abiner's expedition is probably to be seen as a direct response to David's overture to the people of Jabesh-gilead, described in vv. 4b–7 above. The material intervening between that passage and this (viz. vv. 8–11) provides circumstantial information necessary to the main narrative thread, which resumes here in v. 12. Ishbaal considered himself ruler of Gilead (cf. v. 9) and doubtless would have regarded David's gesture to Jabesh as an open challenge.

*marched out.* Hebrew *wayyēṣē';* cf. *yāṣě'û,* v. 13. The verb suggests that each group was engaged in an unambiguously military operation; cf. Eissfeldt 1951:124.

*Mahanaim.* See the NOTE at 2:8.

*Gibeon.* The modern site is el-Jīb, ca. six to eight miles north-northwest of Jerusalem (see Map 2). The location suggests that the city had considerable strategic importance in the struggle that emerged between David and Ishbaal. We know, moreover, that there was a history of ill feeling between Gibeon and the house of Saul, who, according to 21:1–9, once "put the Gibeonites to death" (v. 1), i.e., tried to exterminate them as foreigners living in the midst of Israel (vv. 3,5). It is not unlikely, then, that Joab and his troops found Gibeonite sympathy or even open support in the showdown that occurred here (cf. Fensham 1970).

13. *Joab son of Zeruiah.* Joab was the most prominent of the three sons of Zeruiah (cf. v. 18), who figure so prominently in the stories of David's reign. Here he seems already to be in command of David's army, but there is reason to believe that he assumed that position permanently only after his heroism in the siege of Jerusalem (see I Chron 11:6 and the first NOTE at 5:8 below).

*the pool of Gibeon.* The "abundant waters that are in Gibeon" (Jer 41:12) were a major landmark of the city. The "pool" has been identified with a huge round pit—thirty-seven feet around and eighty-two feet deep—cut out of rock on the north side of the site of ancient Gibeon, just within the Iron Age city wall (Pritchard 1956; 1961; 1962:159–60). This water system was accessible by a rock-cut stairway that circled the inside of the pit.

14–16. Abiner proposes a contest to settle the differences between the opposing parties. Twelve men from each side will fight to the death. Many commentators (Budde, etc.), influenced by the reference to *hannĕʿārîm*, which they understand as "the lads, young men," and the use of the verb *wîśaḥăqû*, "and (let them) play," have thought of this clash as mere sport that got out of hand and precipitated a battle (cf. especially Segal 1917/18:95). The most elaborate development of this position is represented by the argument of Batten (1906) that Ishbaal's men did not play fair in the game but, being right-handed men ("Benjaminites"!), carried concealed weapons to be drawn with their left hands after the model of Ehud, the Benjaminite hero of Judg 3:15–30. Thus, argues Batten, only David's men perished. But the text of v. 16 (unless emended conjecturally by the insertion of an explicit subject—"*The Benjaminites* took hold . . . : [cf. *BHK*[3]]) is more easily understood to mean that all twenty-four combatants "fell dead together" (v. 16). Moreover, it is not certain that the contest was intended as lighthearted competition by either side. The NOTES that follow suggest that *hannĕʿārîm* refers to trained fighting men and that the verb *śiḥēq* does not always indicate carefree play. Instead, as Eissfeldt (1951; 1952) has suggested, what we have here may be a case of battle by representative *(Vertretungskampf)*, a well-attested ancient practice, of which the most famous example is the contest between the Horatii and Curiatii of Roman legend (cf. Grottanelli 1975). This is, in other words, a completely serious fight, and the control of all Israel may be at stake (so already Thenius, Klostermann; see also Yadin [Sukenik] 1948, Buccellati 1959:118–19, Glück 1964:30–31, and de Vaux 1971:130–31; contrast Hertzberg, McKane). The general battle that ensues is necessary because the result of the contest is indecisive: All twenty-four combatants are slain. See further the COMMENT.

14. *some soldiers.* Hebrew *hannĕʿārîm* (the function of the article is that described in GK[2] §126q–s). The meaning of the noun *naʿar* in the Hebrew Bible is manifold and somewhat complicated. It may imply no more than "(male) child, boy," as in 12:16,

or "young man," as apparently in 18:5, where David is laying stress on Abishalom's youth. Or it may imply "servant, attendant," though as the study of seals and seal impressions bearing the legend $PN_1$ *na'ar* $PN_2$ has shown, such a *na'ar* might hold an important office in the retinue of a powerful citizen (Albright 1932; Avigad 1976); cf. the NOTE on "Saul's steward" at 9:9. But *na'ar* also has a military use (cf. Albright 1930/31). This seems clear from references to "young men = soldiers" in the present passage, as well as 1:15; 16:2; and 20:11—to mention only examples from the present book. Similarly, Ugaritic *n'rm* occurs frequently in lists of fighting men as a category of soldier, and in Egyptian texts of the New Kingdom *n'rn* refers to skilled warriors in or from Canaan. According to Rainey (in Fisher 1975:99), "there can be no doubt that the term *n'r*, 'youth,' in Ugaritic and Hebrew, could be applied to first-class fighting men"; see further Rainey 1965a; 1967a:76,147 and nn. 203–11; MacDonald 1976; Stähli 1978.

*and play before us.* Hebrew *wîśaḥăqû lĕpānênû.* The verb *śiḥēq* means "play" but may, in a context like this, imply gladiatorial play. Such is probably the case, for example, in Judg 16:25–27, where Samson is required to play for the entertainment of his Philistine captors. And it is also the case here. See Eissfeldt 1951:118–21; Yadin [Sukenik] 1948; Gordon 1950.

16. Each man tries to gain an advantage over his opponent by seizing his head with one hand, leaving the sword hand free to plunge the weapon into his side. A relief from Tell Ḥalāf, biblical Gozan, which derives from a time almost contemporary with the events described here, provides a striking illustration of soldiers in just such a posture (Yadin [Sukenik] 1948; Eissfeldt 1952; Yadin [Sukenik] 1963:267).

*Flints' Field.* Hebrew *ḥelqat haṣṣūrîm;* see the *Textual Note.* We must assume that the weapons used in the contest are here understood as flint swords or knives, i.e., *ḥarbôt ṣūrîm* (Josh 5:2,3), unless *haṣṣūrîm* can refer to the flintlike *edges* of the (metal) sword blades (cf. Ps 89:44 [89:43]; so Driver). Verse 16b is an annotation to the story, which probably arose secondarily, identifying a well-known place in Gibeon as the site of the contest on the basis of a rather fanciful etymology. It is much less likely, I think, that the story in vv. 14–16 itself grew up as an etiological tradition explaining the place-name (so, for example, Grønbaek 1971:230).

18. *The three sons of Zeruiah.* Zeruiah was David's sister (I Chron 2:16), and it is presumably for this reason that Joab, Abishai, and Asael are identified by their mother's name rather than their father's. The matronymic, however, is used with consistency—we never learn their father's name—and this suggests that more might be involved than a narrative reminder of the link with David. I doubt Van Seters is correct in supposing (1976b:25) that Zeruiah was actually the father after all. It is possible that Zeruiah's marriage was of a special kind and that her husband was not a member of her household. Compare the discussion in the NOTES at 17:25 of the marriage of Amasa's parents, which was probably of this kind. In such a case it would not seem unusual for the children to be called by the mother's name, especially if she was a member of the royal family. In the case of Amasa's family, however, the father's name is given, so that it must be said that the comparison is as damaging to the possibility that such an arrangement existed in Zeruiah's case as it is supportive of it.

*Joab.* See the NOTE at v. 13 above.

*Abishai.* Joab's older brother and the eldest of the three sons of Zeruiah (I Chron

2:16). We first heard of Abishai as David's companion on his secret visit to Saul's camp in I Sam 26:6–12. He will become a prominent figure at David's court, sharing military leadership with Joab. The stories present him as heroic and fiercely loyal (cf. II Sam 21:16–17) but rash and rather cold-blooded in dealing with enemies, often requiring restraint (I Sam 26:8–11; II Sam 16:9–12; 19:21–22). These qualities, which he shares with both Joab and Asael, will prove to be of major importance in the unfolding of events (cf. 3:39 and the COMMENT on 3:6–39).

*Asael.* The youngest of the sons of Zeruiah, though he held important positions in the early organization of David's army (II Sam 23:24 = I Chron 11:26; I Chron 27:7), is remembered in the Bible for no deed other than those described in the present passage.

*as fleet . . . the open plain.* A similar metaphor appears in I Chron 12:9 [12:8].

24. *the hill of Ammah, opposite Giah.* The spot is not mentioned elsewhere. Hebrew *'ammâ* probably means "water channel" (cf. Rabbinic Hebrew *'ammâ,* "canal, sewer"; Syr. *'amā',* "conduit, pool"; thus a few Greek MSS render *'mh* as *hydrogōgos*—hence Vulg. *aquae ductus*) and *gîaḥ,* "spring" (cf. the verb *gyḥ,* "gush" [Job 40:23; etc.], and the river name *gîḥôn* [Gen 2:13; I Kings 1:33; etc.]). Presumably, though, the scene of action is now too far from Gibeon for us to think of identifying "Ammah" with the water shaft that extended fifty-two meters from the city to a spring, "Giah," below (cf. Pritchard 1961:5).

28. *shofar.* See the NOTE at 6:15.

29. *the Arabah.* A depression extending south from the Sea of Galilee to the Gulf of Aqabah, embracing the Ghor or Jordan Valley north of the Dead Sea and the Wadi el-'Arabah south of it. Abiner's troops are marching north along the Jordan.

*all morning.* Hebrew *kol-habbitrôn,* the translation of which is uncertain. It used to be assumed that *bitrôn* was a place-name—thus AV: "through all Bithron"—perhaps meaning "cleft, ravine" (BDB). Our translation follows the suggestion of Arnold (1911/12) that it means "part of, half of (the day)," that is, "forenoon, morning."

## COMMENT

In the present episode the confrontation of the new kings in Hebron and Mahanaim erupts into open warfare. The precipitating factor was probably David's attempt to treat with the lords of Jabesh-gilead, a gesture that Ishbaal must have regarded as a direct challenge to his authority (cf. the first NOTE at v. 12). In response an armed force marches south out of Mahanaim and encounters a Judahite host at the city of Gibeon. The commanders of the two armies agree upon a contest, evidently a kind of gladiatorial competition intended to settle the issue in lieu of an open battle (cf. the NOTES at vv. 14–16); but each contingent is slain to the last man, and general fighting breaks out after all. A count of the slain when the day is ended (v. 30) shows a decisive advantage in favor of David.

The account has two foci. The first is the contest at Flints' Field. The second is the death of Asael. The whole, however, is a well-unified narrative, as even the older literary critics acknowledged (Budde; cf. Eissfeldt 1965:275). To be sure, recent tradition-historical analyses have concluded that originally independent traditions underlie the account before and after v. 17, which serves to bind them together (e.g., Grønbaek 1971:230 and n. 28). But except for the etiological annotation in v. 16b (see the NOTE on "Flints' Field," v. 16), the entire passage is, I think, an original part of the old story of David's rise to power and can be seen to serve the apologetic purposes of that composition by the particular details of each of the two narrative foci just identified.

With respect to the clash at Flints' Field, it is important to keep in mind the fact that such contests were believed to be decided not only by the relative strength and skill of the competitors but also, and more importantly, by the divine will. In the account of David's monomachy with the Philistine champion, for example, David calls upon Yahweh for help (I Sam 17:45–47), while his adversary curses him by his own god (I Sam 17:43); the account leaves no doubt that the outcome is divinely determined. Fensham (1970), citing the work of Korošec (1963:164), has compared the present passage to accounts of ordeals by battle among the Hittites in which the victor was believed to be determined by the will of the gods. He cites, in particular, a passage in the so-called apology of Hattushilish III, which we have reviewed in connection with the story of David's rise as a whole (McCarter 1980b:496–99), wherein the thirteenth-century Hittite king claims to have settled the dispute between himself and his predecessor by a formally declared ordeal by warfare, a divinely sanctioned test of right, the outcome of which was decided, he says, by the favor of the gods and of the goddess Ishtar in particular. Fensham argues plausibly that the same issues—those of the divine will and the legitimation of kingship—are implicitly present in the account of the conflict at Gibeon. The formal competition in vv. 14–16 is inconclusive, but the general battle that results goes decisively to David's advantage. Nowhere in the present passage is this explicitly said to be consequential of Yahweh's favor for David, but as we have seen time and again (I Sam 16:18; 18:14,28; cf. II Sam 5:10), "Yahweh is with him (David)" is the overriding theological theme of the larger composition (cf. McCarter 1980a:502–4), and Fensham is justified in taking its applicability here for granted.

In consideration of the second focus, the death of Asael, we must look ahead. The enmity between the surviving sons of Zeruiah and Abiner, their brother's killer, will be a major factor in the future course of events. In particular, the rancor of David's brooding, willful general, Joab, will finally cost Abiner his life and throw Ishbaal's kingdom into confusion. These events will be described to us in considerable detail, and the factors leading up to them will be presented with particular care. The reason for this is not difficult to surmise. Our narrator is intent that we understand Abiner's death to have been the consequence of a blood feud between him and Joab's family, and that Joab, therefore, was acting privately rather than officially when he contrived Abiner's assassination (3:22–27). Here and elsewhere the sons of Zeruiah—Abishai and Asael as well as Joab—are shown to be rash, precipitate men who prefer violent, swift action to reason and restraint. Abishai has already been presented this way (I Sam 26:8–11; see the NOTE at v. 18 above). Asael appears in the present story as one so headstrong that he will not listen to reason even to save his own life, as he relentlessly pursues the much stronger Abiner, who finally has no recourse but to slay him (vv. 18–23a). The audience is being prepared for the contrast that David himself will make in 3:39, where he describes himself as "gentle" *(rak)* in contrast to the sons of Zeruiah, who, he says, "are rougher *(qāšîm)* than I am." David is king of Judah, but he cannot control these hard soldiers from Bethlehem. There need be no ambiguity, then, about the responsibility for the harsh deed described in the materials that follow in 3:6–39.

# V. THE SONS OF DAVID
## (3:1–5)

**3** [1]The fighting between the house of Saul and the house of David dragged out, with David growing stronger and stronger and the house of Saul growing weaker and weaker.

[2]Sons were born to David in Hebron. His firstborn was Aminon by Ahinoam of Jezreel, [3]and his second was Daluiah by Abigail of Carmel. The third was Abishalom, the son of Maacah, daughter of Talmai, king of Geshur; [4]the fourth was Adonijah, the son of Haggith; the fifth was Shephatiah by Abital; [5]and the sixth was Ithream by David's wife Eglah. These were born to him in Hebron.

### *TEXTUAL NOTES*

**3** 1. *The fighting* Cf. MT, $LXX^B$, etc. $LXX^L$ suggests a text in which the article was lacking: "Fighting . . . dragged out," or rather, "And there was protracted fighting. . . ."

*dragged out* MT *'rkh ('ărukkâ;* cf. Symmachus' translation, *makros).* LXX *epi polu,* OL *magna* seem to point to *hrbh* (*harbēh;* cf. Driver), "(the fighting) was great," perhaps from *hrkh,* a defectively written representation of *h'rykh (he'ĕrîkâ,* the verbal equivalent of *'ărukkâ).* The word is omitted altogether in Syr.

*David* (2) LXX has "*the house of* David" in reminiscence of the preceding (cf. Wellhausen). Omit "the house of" with MT, Syr., OL, $4QSam^a$, and one MS of $LXX^L$.

*growing weaker and weaker* The witnesses interpret the subject, "the house of Saul," variously as singular ($4QSam^a$ *hwlk* [*wdl*]; cf. LXX) and plural (MT *hlkym wdlym;* cf. Syr.).

2–5. In $4QSam^a$, as in MT and $LXX^B$, this section is set off from what precedes and follows it by paragraphing.

2. *Sons . . . in Hebron* So MT, $LXX^B$, Syr., and $4QSam^a$. $LXX^L$ (cf. $LXX^M$): ". . . in Hebron *six* sons" (cf. Josephus, *Ant.* 7.21). See I Chron 3:4.

*were born* MT*(kĕtîb): wyldw* = *wayyullĕdû,* i.e., *Pu'al* as in 3:5. MT*(qĕrê): wayyiwwālĕdû,* i.e., *Nip'al* (cf. Syr. *w'tldw;* Targ. *w'tylydw*). $4QSam^a$ has *wywld,* probably also *Nip'al,* but singular (cf. I Chron 3:1; etc.).

*Aminon* See the *Textual Note* at 13:20.

3. *Daluiah* The correct reading seems to be *dlwyh*, as shown by LXX *dalouia* and 4QSam[a] *dl*[ ]. MT has *kl'b* (so Targ.; cf. Syr. *klb*), which is evidently corrupt; note the repetition of the sequence *l'b* at the beginning of the next word and the ease with which *d* and *k* could be confused, especially in a MS in which the lower part of the letter was damaged. Josephus (*Ant.* 7.21) has *danielos*, to which compare I Chron 3:1, where MT has *dny'l* (LXX[B] *damniēl*) but LXX[AL] *dalouia*. See further the NOTE.

*by Abigail of Carmel* Reading *l'bygyl hkrmlyt* with LXX, OL, and 4QSam[a] (*l'bygyl h*[ ]); cf. I Chron 3:1. MT (cf. Syr.) has *l'bygl 'št nbl hkrmly*, "by Abigail, *the widow of Nabal* of Carmel," which is reminiscent of 2:2.

*Abishalom* That the correct vocalization of MT *'bšlwm* is *'ăbîšālôm* is shown by LXX *abessalōm*. The old, defective spelling of the name, *'bšlm*, gave rise to the traditional mispronunciation *'abšālōm*, "Absalom," reflected in MT. Cf. the *Textual Notes* on "Abiner" at 2:8 and "Aminon" at 13:20.

*Talmai* MT, 4QSam[a] *tlmy*. LXX[B] *thommei* represents an inner-Greek corruption of *tholmei* (so LXX[AMN]), which, combined with Syr. *twlmy*, favors a vocalization **tolmay*. But to my knowledge only MT *talmay* corresponds to a known onomastic element, viz. Hurrian *tal(a)mi*, "great," in names such as *talmi-tešub*, "Teshub is great" (cf. Gröndahl 1967:259–60; Gelb, Purves, and McRae 1943:242); cf. Mazar 1961:23 n. 26; Blenkinsopp 1972:61,125 n. 35.

4. *Adonijah* MT *'dnyh* (cf. Josephus, *Ant.* 7.21). LXX[B] *orneil* arose by confusion of the Greek majuscules *alpha* and *lambda* from *orneia* (so LXX[MN]), which reflects a Hebrew text that had *'rnyh* in consequence of confusion of *d* and *r*.

*Haggith* MT *ḥgyt*; LXX[LMN] *aggeith*. LXX[B] (cf. LXX[A]) has *pheggeith*, the initial *phi* having arisen from a marginal annotation to the next name, "Shephatiah," which appears in LXX[B] as *sabateia* and which a scribe meant to correct to *saphateia* (cf. LXX[ALMN]; Josephus, *Ant.* 7.21) by the marginal *phi*, which, however, found its way into the text at this earlier point.

*Shephatiah* Cf. the preceding *Textual Note*.

*by* So 4QSam[a] (cf. LXX), the style used with regard to the first, second, and sixth sons. MT, Syr. have "the son of," the style used with regard to the third and fourth sons. It is impossible to determine which reading is original.

5. *to him* MT, LXX[BAMN] have "to David." LXX[L] has "to him, to David." The less explicit reading will have been original, though it survives only in LXX[L] and is there combined with "to David," which has been leveled through the other witnesses to make the reading explicit and in reminiscence of v. 2.

## NOTES

**3** 1. This verse belongs to the original narrative. It leads directly into the story in 3:6ff. The insertion of the list of David's sons that follows interrupted the continuity and made necessary the expansion of v. 6 in resumption of the narrative line. See the COMMENT below and the first NOTE at 3:6 in § VI.

2. *Aminon.* The fate of David's eldest son is the subject of chap. 13.

*Ahinoam of Jezreel.* See the NOTE at 2:2.

3. *Daluiah.* David's second son is not mentioned again in the story, and we must assume that he, like the first and third sons, Aminon and Abishalom, was dead before Adonijah, the fourth, began to press his claim to David's throne (see below, the NOTE on "Adonijah," v. 4).

*Abigail of Carmel.* The heroine of I Samuel 25. See the NOTE at 2:2.

*Abishalom.* For this form of the name, see the *Textual Note.* David's third son is the central figure of chaps. 13–19.

*Maacah, daughter of Talmai, king of Geshur.* In 13:37 Abishalom will find it necessary to seek asylum in the kingdom of his maternal grandfather. For Geshur, see the NOTE at 2:9, where we are told that Ishbaal claimed sovereignty over the Geshurites. David's connection by marriage to the local royal family was, therefore, a political advantage to him and a threat to Ishbaal's claims.

4. *Adonijah.* David's fourth son will be his oldest surviving heir at the time of his death. I Kings 1–2 describes Adonijah's unsuccessful efforts to assume the throne and his death at the hand of his rival, Solomon.

*Shephatiah.* Mentioned only here and in the synoptic list in I Chron 3:3.

5. *Ithream.* Mentioned only here and in I Chron 3:3.

## COMMENT

The insertion of vv. 2–5, containing information about David's family, interrupts the flow of the narrative from 3:1 to 3:6 (see the NOTE at 3:1 and the first NOTE at 3:6). This is a list of David's sons who were born in Hebron. The list of those born in Jerusalem appears in 5:13–16 (§ X). The data are combined in the Chronicler's synoptic passage, I Chron 3:1–9. The present list may be a contribution of the Deuteronomistic historian or, as Noth supposes (1943:63 n. 3), an earlier editor. In either case it must have been attracted to this position by the reference to the waxing of the house of David in 3:1 (contrast Grønbaek 1971:234–35).

# VI. THE DEATH OF ABINER
# (3:6–39)

3 [6]As the war between the house of Saul and the house of David
continued, Abiner was gaining power in the house of Saul.

### *Abiner's Quarrel with Ishbaal*

[7]Saul had had a concubine, Rizpah daughter of Aia, and Ishbaal son
of Saul said to Abiner, "Why have you been sleeping with my father's
concubine?"
[8]Abiner was enraged by the thing Ishbaal had said. "Am I a dog's
head?" he said. "Is it for myself that I've been doing all these things,
dealing loyally with the house of Saul, your father, on behalf of his
kinsmen and associates? I kept you from falling into David's hands, and
now you've found fault with me over an offense involving a woman!
[9]May God do thus to me and thus again—what Yahweh has sworn
concerning David I'll accomplish for him! [10][I'll] transfer the kingship
from the house of Saul and raise up David's throne over Israel as well
as Judah, from Dan to Beersheba!" [11]Ishbaal was unable to say anything
else to Abiner, because he was so afraid of him.

### *Abiner's Parley with David*

[12]Abiner sent messengers to David as his representatives to say,
"Make a pact with me, and my influence will be on your side, bringing
all Israel over to you."
[13]"Very well," said [David], "I'll make a pact with you. But there is
one thing I'll require of you: You won't see me unless you bring along
Michal daughter of Saul when you come to see me."
[14]David sent messengers to Ishbaal son of Saul to say, "Hand over
my wife Michal, whom I betrothed for a hundred Philistine foreskins!"
[15]So Ishbaal had her taken from her husband, Paltiel son of Laish,
[16][who] went with her, weeping behind her, as far as Bahurim, where
Abiner told him to turn back, and he did so.

[17]Meanwhile Abiner's message had reached the elders of Israel: "Not long ago you were eager for David to be king over you. [18]Now then, act! For Yahweh has said of David, 'It is by the hand of my servant David that I am going to save Israel from the Philistines and all their [other] enemies.' " [19]Abiner spoke personally with the Benjaminites, and then [he] went to Hebron to speak personally with David about everything Israel and the whole house of Benjamin thought good [to do].

[20]When Abiner came to David in Hebron along with twenty men, David prepared a banquet for [him] and the men with him.

[21]"I must go now," Abiner said later to David, "and gather all Israel to my lord the king, so that they may make a pact with you, and you may rule over all that you desire." So David dismissed Abiner, and he went in peace.

### *The Assassination*

[22]Now David's servants, including Joab, had just come in from a raid bringing plunder with them. Abiner was not in Hebron with David, for he had dismissed him, and he had gone in peace. [23]So when Joab and the rest of his army arrived, it was reported to [him] that Abiner son of Ner had come to David and that he had dismissed him and he had gone in peace.

[24]Joab went to the king. "What have you done?" he said. "If Abiner came to you, why did you dismiss him and let him go? [25]Don't you know the treachery of Abiner son of Ner? It was to dupe you that he came, to learn your going out and your coming in and to learn everything else you do."

[26]When Joab had left David, he sent emissaries after Abiner, and they brought him back from Bor-hassirah. David did not know [of this]. [27]When Abiner got back to Hebron, Joab drew him aside beside the gate to speak with him in private, and there he struck him in the belly and he died for the blood of Asael, [Joab's] brother.

[28]Sometime later, when David heard, he said, "I and my kingship are innocent before Yahweh now and forever! And may the blood of Abiner son of Ner [29]devolve upon the head of Joab and all his father's house! And Joab's house shall not be without someone who has a discharge or a skin disease or clings to a crutch or falls by the sword or is in need of food!" [30](Now Joab and his brother Abishai had been laying for Abiner because he killed their brother Asael in the battle at Gibeon.)

*The Funeral*

[31]Then David said to Joab and all the people who were with him, "Tear your clothes, put on sackcloth, and wail in Abiner's path!" King David himself followed behind the bier, [32]and when they buried Abiner in Hebron, the king raised his voice and wept beside his grave, and all the people wept, too.

[33]David sang an elegy for Abiner. He said:

> Alas, as an outcast dies, Abiner died!
> [34]Your hands were bound—though not by manacles!
> Your feet—though not by fetters—were confined!
> As a criminal falls, you fell!

And all the people continued to weep over him.

[35]All the people came to give David bread to eat while the day lasted, but David swore an oath. "May God do thus and so to me and thus again!" he said. "Before the sun sets I will taste no bread or anything else!" [36]Now all the people took note of this, and everything the king did in [their] sight seemed good to them. [37]So all the people and all Israel knew at that time that it was not the king's will to kill Abiner son of Ner.

[38]Then the king said to his servants, "You know, don't you, that a commander and a nobleman has fallen today in Israel. [39]And I, though anointed king, am still a gentle man; but these men, the sons of Zeruiah, are rougher than I am."

## *TEXTUAL NOTES*

3 7. *Rizpah* MT, LXX$^{L}$ preface this with "and her name (was)," but the shorter text of 4QSam$^{a}$, LXX$^{BAM}$ is to be preferred.

*Aia* MT *'yh*. LXX$^{B}$ *ial* probably arose from *ail*, a corruption of *aia*, which is read by a few Greek MSS, by confusion of the majuscules *alpha* and *lambda;* note that elsewhere (21:8; etc.) LXX$^{B}$ has *aia*. Syr. *'n'* is the result of inner-Syriac confusion of *y* and *n* (Englert 1949:16). More difficult to explain is LXX$^{LM}$ *s(e)iba* (cf. *sibatou* in Josephus, *Ant.* 7.23), which seems to point to *ṣyb'*, "Ziba," who has an important part in later events (9:2; etc.); perhaps Ziba's close association with Mephibosheth (Merib-baal) had something to do with attracting his name into the text in this context, where Mephibosheth's name also appears in LXX (see below). In 21:8,10,11 LXX$^{LM}$ have *aia* corresponding to MT *'yh*.

At this point LXX$^{L}$ adds *kai elaben autēn abennēr*, "and Abiner took her," and another Greek MS *kai eisēlthen pros autēn abennēr*, "and Abiner went in to her." A few critics (Smith, etc.) have regarded some such addition as necessary preparation for Ishbaal's accusation of Abiner, but the textual evidence suggests that the writer deliberately left the case ambiguous (see the second NOTE to v. 7). The additions cited are probably epexegetical expansions having no counterpart in MT, $LXX^{BAMN}$, or (as space considerations indicate) $4QSam^a$.

*Ishbaal son of Saul* Cf. v. 11 below and 4:1,2. $LXX^{BL}$ here have "Mephibosheth son of Saul," a reading originally shared by MT, where, however, it has been suppressed as obviously in error (so Targ.). $LXX^{AMN}$ (cf. OL; Josephus, *Ant.* 7.23; Syr.) have "Ishbosheth son of Saul." The name appeared in $4QSam^a$, but the relevant part of the scroll is lost; in view of the evidence of $4QSam^a$ at 4:1,2 (see the *Textual Note* there), we can reconstruct the present reading as [*mpybšt bn*] *š'wl.* See further Ulrich 1978:55. The source of the confusion may be 21:18, where there is a son of Saul called *mpybšt* and where Rizpah is also involved (21:10).

8. *by the thing Ishbaal had said* Cf. $LXX^{BAM}$. $LXX^{LN}$: "by *this* thing. . . ." MT: "by the things. . . ." The name appears in the major witnesses in the same distribution as in the preceding verse, except that *'yš bšt* appears here in MT.

*a dog's head* That is, *rō'š keleb* (see the NOTE), but evidently understood as *rō'š kālēb,* "the chief of Caleb," in the tradition behind MT, where it is glossed *'šr lyhwdh,* "which belongs to Judah," perhaps in the sense of "one who is on the side of Judah." The addition arose, in other words, from the pen of a glossator who was puzzled by *r'š klb,* analyzed it as meaning "the chief of Caleb," the tribe that controlled the Hebron area (cf. the NOTE at 2:2), and, therefore, glossed it *'šr lyhwdh* based on his conclusion that Abiner is objecting to being treated like an enemy. We omit the gloss with LXX.

*he said* So MT. LXX and $4QSam^a$ add "to him (Ishbaal)." LXX and Syr. make the subject explicit: "*Abiner* said."

*Is it for myself . . . dealing loyally* Among the major witnesses the original text is best reflected at this point by $LXX^L$ and OL. The former reads *emautō sēmeron epoiēsa panta tauta kai epoiēsa eleon,* from which we reconstruct *hly hywm "śh 't kl 'lh w"śh ḥsd,* "Is it for myself that today I've been doing all these things, acting loyally. . . ." In all other witnesses *hly* has been lost after the preceding *'nky,* and the repetition of *"śh* has triggered haplography. Thus MT (cf. $LXX^B$) reads *hywm "śh ḥsd,* "Today I've been acting loyally. . . ." The word "today," which is represented in different places in MT, $LXX^B$, and $LXX^L$, can be omitted with OL.

*on behalf of his kinsmen and associates* We read *'l 'ḥyw w'l mr'hw,* which is essentially the text of MT except that MT substitutes *'l* for *'l* as frequently in Samuel (cf. LXX *peri . . . peri*). The versions (LXX, Syr., OL) introduce this with the conjunction: "*and* on behalf of," etc. OL *et cum fratribus tuis et cum amicis patris tui,* "and *with your* kinsmen and *with* the associates *of your father,*" reflects the influence of the preceding "*with* the house of Saul, *your father.*"

*I kept you . . . David's hands* So MT: *wl' hmṣytk byd dwd.* LXX is different: *kai ouk ēutomolēsa eis ton oikon daueid,* which may reflect *wl' hšlmty bbyt dwd,* "I didn't make peace with the house of David" (Thenius, Wellhausen), or, more likely, *wl' hšlmty 'l byt dwd,* "I didn't sue the house of David for peace," as in Josh 11:19.

*you've found fault with me over an offense* Reading *wtpqd 'ly 'l 'wn* on the basis of $LXX^{BA}$ *kai epizēteis ep' eme hyper adikias.* MT has lost *'l* (thus, "you've accused me of an offense"), and in $LXX^L$ *'th* is reflected in place of *'ly* (thus, "you [emphatic] have found fault over an offense").

*involving a woman* That is, *'šh;* cf. LXX. MT, Syr.: *h'šh,* "(involving) *the* woman."

9. *May God . . . again* Reading *kh y'śh ly h'lhym wkh ysyp* on the basis of LXX$^{L}$ *tade poiēsai moi ho theos kai tade prostheiē.* MT (cf. LXX$^{B}$) has *kh y'śh 'lhym l'bnr wkh ysyp lw,* "May God do thus *to Abiner* and thus again *to him.*"

*for him* At this point LXX$^{BL}$ add *en tē hēmera tautē* = *bywm hzh,* "on this very day," but there is no apparent motive for its loss if original, and we must prefer the shorter text of MT, LXX$^{A}$, Syr.

11. *Ishbaal* Again MT, which like LXX$^{BAL}$ had "Mephibosheth," has suppressed the name in preference to perpetuating an obvious error. See the *Textual Note* at 3:7.

12. *as his representatives to say* That is, *tḥtw l'mr,* lit. "in his stead to say. . . ." So MT and LXX *parachrēma* (understanding *tḥtw* as "on the spot, right away"; cf. Job 40:12) *legōn.* Grønbaek (1971:237 n. 53): "Abner first sends messengers, representatives, 'in his place,' later [v. 20] he arrives in person." But there is another phrase in the text of most witnesses here. In MT it follows *tḥtw l'mr* and reads *lmy 'rṣ l'mr,* "To whom does (the) land belong? saying. . . ." The repetition of *l'mr* is suspicious, and *lmy 'rṣ* cannot be read as if it were *lmy h'rṣ.* The words appear in a different position in the text of LXX, adding to the suspicion that they are intrusive here. Preceding *tḥtw l'mr (parachrēma legōn)* LXX$^{A}$ (cf. LXX$^{BMN}$) has *eis thēlamou gēn,* a representation by transliteration and translation of *tḥtw* (*eis the-/thai-* [LXX$^{B}$]) *lmw 'rṣ (-lamou gēn).* LXX$^{L}$ *eis chebrōn legōn* apparently reflects the shorter, original text with *tḥtw* understood in reference to David ("where he was") and rendered interpretively as "in Hebron." The source of the intrusive *lmy/w 'rṣ (l'mr)* is as difficult to surmise as its meaning.

*a pact* Cf. LXX$^{L}$. MT, LXX$^{B}$, Syr.: "*your* pact."

*all Israel* So MT, LXX$^{LMN}$. LXX$^{BA}$: "all *the house of* Israel."

13. *said [David]* Reading *wy'mr* with MT. LXX, Syr. make the subject explicit.

*unless you bring along* Reading *ky 'm hby't* on the basis of LXX *ean mē agagēs* and Syr. *'l' 'n tyt'.* MT *ky 'm lpny hby'k* is the result of conflation of variants, viz. *ky 'm hby't* and *lpny hby'k,* "before (= until) you bring along."

*Michal* MT *mîkal.* LXX (cf. Syr.; Josephus, *Ant.* 7.26) *melchol.*

*daughter of Saul* LXX$^{L}$ adds "with you," an expansion that Syr. has earlier, after "you bring along."

*when you come to see me* Omitted by Syr.

14. *Ishbaal* MT, LXX$^{MN}$: "Ishbosheth." LXX$^{BA}$: "Mephibosheth."

*Hand over* LXX, Syr. add *ly,* "to me." Omit with MT, which, however, has the same expansion below, after "I betrothed." See the *Textual Note* there.

*Michal* Omitted by Syr.

*I betrothed* MT *'rśty,* the expected Greek equivalent of which would be *emnēsteusamēn* (cf. Deut 20:7; etc.). LXX *elabon* points to a replacement of the distinctive reading of MT with *lqḥty,* "I acquired." The verb is followed in some witnesses by *ly,* "for myself" (so MT, Syr., LXX$^{A}$), an expansion to be omitted here with LXX$^{BL}$, which place it earlier, after "Hand over" (see above). It is original in neither position.

15. *Ishbaal* MT, LXX$^{LMN}$: "Ishbosheth." LXX$^{BA}$: "Mephibosheth."

*her husband* Unaccountably, MT omits the suffix: *'yš,* "a man." Read *'yšh* with LXX *andros autēs,* Vulg. *a viro suo,* Syr. *b'lh,* Targ. *b'lh.* At this point most witnesses repeat "from" (MT *m'm;* LXX$^{B}$ *para;* Syr. *mn lwt*); omit with LXX$^{L}$ and two Hebrew MSS *(BHS).*

*Laish* That is, *layiš* (so MT *qĕrê*, Syr., LXX$^{A}$; cf. I Sam 25:44). MT *kĕtîb: lwš*. Several MSS of Syr. add *dmn glym* = *'šr mglym*, "who was from Gallim" (cf. I Sam 25:44), and this may be a clue to the corruption of "Laish" in LXX$^{LN}$ (cf. LXX$^{BM}$) to *sellei/em*.

16. [*who*] That is, *'îšāh*, lit. "her husband."

*with her* Omitted by Syr.

*weeping* Cf. LXX$^{BAMN}$. MT (cf. LXX$^{L}$, Syr.): *hlwk wbkh*, "weeping *as he went.*"

*Bahurim* Doubtful. We read *baḥūrîm* with MT, but LXX, though not troubled by this name elsewhere (16:5; 17:18; 19:17 [LXX 19:16]), is different, reading *barakei* (LXX$^{B}$) or *barakein* (LXX$^{LM}$); among the major witnesses to LXX only LXX$^{A}$ has the expected *baoureim*. (Syr. has *byt ḥwrym*, to which compare LXX$^{B}$ *baathoureim* in I Kings 2:8.) Perhaps we should posit an otherwise unknown place-name, *brqy*.

17. *Meanwhile Abiner's message had reached* So MT (cf. LXX$^{L}$): *wdbr 'bnr hyh 'm . . . l'mr (wy'mr)*, lit. "And the word of Abiner was with . . . saying (and he said). . . ." LXX$^{BAMN}$ reflect *wy'mr 'bnr 'l . . . l'mr*, "And Abiner said to . . . saying . . ." (cf. v. 16b).

*to be king* MT: *lĕmelek*. LXX = *limlōk*.

18. *by the hand . . . save* Reading *byd 'bdy dwd 'wšy'* with LXX$^{BLMN}$ (cf. LXX$^{A}$, Syr.). MT *byd dwd 'bdy hwšy'*, "by the hand of David, my servant, he has saved . . .," is impossible. Schmidt (1970:135–36) expresses doubt about this solution, which has been adopted by almost all critics, arguing instead that *hwšy'* was original and altered tendentiously to *'wšy'* in order to stress Yahweh's involvement in the deliverance of Israel. Accordingly, he proposes to strike *byd*, "by the hand of," and read v. 18b as "For Yahweh has said to David: 'David my servant will save my people Israel,' " etc. Even if we overlook the lack of textual support for the omission of *byd*, however, Schmidt's proposal does not seem to work. How can *hwšy' (hôšîa')* be translated "will save" ("wird . . . retten")? Schmidt compares Judg 6:14 and I Sam 9:16, but in each of these passages the verb stands after the conjunction in the *converted* perfect, *wĕhôšîa'*, properly "and he will save."

*Israel* So LXX$^{BAMN}$. MT, LXX$^{L}$: "*my people*, Israel."

19. *the Benjaminites* Reading *bny bnymyn* with LXX$^{L}$ and Syr. In the other major witnesses *bny* has been lost by haplography.

*the whole house of Benjamin* So MT, etc. LXX$^{L}$ reflects *bny bnymyn*, which is reminiscent of the reading discussed in the preceding *Textual Note*.

20. *a banquet* So MT. Syr.: "a *great* banquet."

21. *all Israel* So MT, LXX$^{B}$, etc. LXX$^{L}$: "all *the people of* Israel" (cf. Josephus, *Ant.* 7.30).

*so that they may make* MT (cf. Syr.) *wykrtw* (cf. 5:3). LXX has *kai diathēsomai* = *w'krth*, "so that *I* may make," after the pattern of the three preceding verbs.

*with you* So MT. LXX: "with *him*" (i.e., with the king or, perhaps, the people).

*dismissed* MT *wayyĕšallaḥ*, in contradiction of GK$^{2}$ §20m. De Boer *(BHS)* notes that this is the reading of the Leningrad Codex, which *BHS* follows, whereas a number of other MSS omit the *dāgēš* from the *yod*.

22. *had . . . come in* That is, *bā'û* or perhaps *bā'îm*, the *-m* having fallen out before the *m-* of the following word (Wellhausen, Driver); cf. LXX, Syr., Targ. MT has the singular, *bā'*, by attraction to "Joab" (cf. GK$^{2}$ §146e).

*plunder* So LXX$^{L}$. LXX$^{BAMN}$, MT: "*much* plunder."

23. *his army* Cf. LXX$^{B}$. MT, LXX$^{L}$, Syr.: "the army that was with him" (cf. v. 31).

*arrived* MT (cf. LXX$^{MN}$, Syr., etc.) *b'w*. LXX$^{BA}$ reflect *hby'w*, "brought (the plunder)," perhaps in reminiscence of *hby'w* in v. 22. LXX$^{L}$ *ēkousan* reflects *šm'w*, "heard."

*it was reported* LXX$^{B}$ (cf. Syr.) *apēngelē* = *wayyuggad*. MT has *wayyaggīdû*, "they reported." LXX$^{L}$ *apēngeilan* = *wayyuggĕdû*, "they were informed."

*David* So LXX, 4QSam$^{a}$ (cf. Josephus, *Ant.* 7.31). MT substitutes "the king" in anticipation of v. 24, and the two readings are combined in Syr. here and in v. 24 *(mlk' dwyd)*. Cf. Ulrich 1978:82.

24. *he said* LXX$^{L}$, Syr. add "to him." Omit with MT, LXX$^{BAM}$.

*Abiner* LXX$^{L}$ adds "son of Ner." Omit with MT, LXX$^{B}$, 4QSam$^{a}$.

*and let him go* That is, *wayyēlek*, lit. "and he has gone." In reminiscence of vv. 21, 22, and 23 LXX adds "in peace," which Thenius and Wellhausen suppose to have been original. Syr. *mn lwtk* reflects *m'mk*, "from (being) with you," another expansion.

25. *Don't you know* Reading *hlw' yd't* with LXX$^{BLMN}$ (cf. LXX$^{A}$, Syr.). Instead of *hlw'*, MT reads *hlwk*, construed with the verb at the end of the preceding verse—thus, *wylk hlwk*, "for he has indeed gone." Contrast Driver.

*the treachery of Abiner* So LXX: *tēn kakian abennēr* = *'t r't 'bnr*. MT, Syr. have *'t 'bnr*, "Abiner." The latter might be retained as *lectio brevior*, but I assume with Steven L. McKenzie (private communication) that *'t r't* fell out of MT after the preceding *yd't*.

*son of Ner* Omitted from a few Hebrew MSS and 4QSam$^{a}$ *(['])bnr)*. I assume that in these witnesses *bn nr* was lost haplographically after *'bnr*, but it might be expansive where it does occur (MT, LXX).

*It was to dupe you* MT (cf. LXX) *ky lpttk*, lit. "that it was to dupe you. . . ." 4QSam$^{a}$ has *ky hlptwtk*, which ought to mean "for was it to dupe you . . . ?" Ulrich (1978:131) cites I Kings 8:27 = II Chron 6:18 as another example of the interrogative *hă-* following *kî*. But the reading of the scroll is very strange. While *hă-* may introduce a question expecting a negative answer *(num?)*, as in the case of the passage cited by Ulrich ("But can a god really dwell with men on earth?"), it does not normally introduce a question expecting a positive answer *(nonne?)*, as this one must be ("Was it to dupe you that he came?").

27. *When Abiner got back* MT *wyšb (wayyāšob) 'bnr*, interpreted by LXX$^{(B)}$ as *wayyāšeb ('et-)'ăbînēr*, "When he (Joab?) brought Abiner back. . . ." LXX$^{L}$ and Josephus (*Ant.* 7.34) share the interpretation of MT.

*to Hebron* MT: *ḥbrwn*. LXX: *eis chebrōn* = *ḥbrwnh* or *bḥbrwn* or *'l ḥbrwn*. 4QSam$^{a}$: *[ḥbr]wnh*.

*drew him aside* MT *wyṭhw*. Syr. has *wṭšyh* for *wsṭyh* (Englert 1949:17).

*beside* MT *'l twk*, "into the midst of," is a corruption of *'l(= 'l) yrk*, as reflected by LXX *ek plagiōn* (cf. Lev 1:11; Num 3:29,35). Contrast Barthélemy 1980:20.

*in private* MT, 4QSam$^{a}$ *bšly* (cf. *I Samuel*, the *Textual Note* on "privately" at 1:9), apparently rendered twice by LXX$^{L}$ as *enedreuōn* (cf. LXX$^{B}$), "by lying in ambush," and *en paralogismō*, "in deception, on false pretenses."

*in the belly* MT has simply *hḥmš* (cf. GK$^{2}$ §117ll), but elsewhere the preposition *'l* is affixed; cf. 2:23; 4:6; 20:10 (where 4QSam$^{a}$ has *'l*). Here LXX$^{B}$ *eis tēn psoan* reflects *'l hḥmš*, and LXX$^{MN}$ *epi tēn psoan* reflects *'l hḥmš*. 4QSam$^{a}$ has *'d hḥmš*. Because of the presence of the preposition elsewhere in the narrative and the frequent substitution of *'l* for *'l* in MT, I am inclined to think *'l hḥmš* original here and in the other passages cited. See also Ulrich 1978:55–56.

*[Joab's] brother* Reading *'ḥyw*, "his brother," with MT, LXX[L], and 4QSam[a] *('ḥyhw)*. Other MSS of LXX make the name explicit, and this is also necessary in English.

28. *now and forever* So LXX[LMN]: *apo (tou) nyn kai heōs (tou) aiōnos* = *m'th w'd 'wlm*. In LXX[B] *(kai heōs aiōnos* = *w'd 'wlm)*, *m'th* has been lost after the preceding word, *yhwh*. In MT and 4QSam[a] *('d 'wlm)* the same loss has occurred, and *w-* has been deleted to "correct" the curious sequence *m'm yhwh w'd 'wlm*, "from Yahweh and forever," which thereby arose.

*And . . . the blood* Reading *wdm* with 4QSam[a] (cf. LXX[L]). MT (cf. LXX[B], etc.) has *mdmy*, "*of* the blood," which may be the result of dittography after *'wlm*.

29. *devolve* Reading *yḥl (yāḥōl)* with 4QSam[a] *([yḥ]wl)*. MT (cf. LXX[BAMN]) has *yḥlw*. Omitted by LXX[L] (thus, "may the blood . . . *be* upon," etc.).

*and all* That is, *w'l kl*; so 4QSam[a] and MT[MSS]. MT has *w'l kl*. Syr. has *w'l ryš klh*, "and *the head of* all."

*his father's house* So MT, LXX. 4QSam[a] has *byt yw'b*, "the house of Joab," in anticipation of the same reading later in the verse. Contrast Ulrich 1978:126–27.

*And Joab's house shall not be without* So 4QSam[a], which has *wlẇ' ykrt mbyṫ [yw'b]*, as recognized by Ulrich (1978:131), who compares 17:12 and I Sam 14:36 (cf. GK[2] §§107o, 109d). The reading of MT (cf. LXX) is *w'l ykrt mbyt yw'b*, "And let Joab's house not be without," the more usual form of imprecation, which is (therefore) less distinctive and less likely to have been original here.

30. *had been laying for* MT has *hrgw l-*, "had slain" (cf. Syr., Targ. *qṭlw*), but the construction of *hrg* with *l-* is found otherwise only in relatively late passages (Job 5:2; Ps 135:11 = 136:9,10) where Aramaic influence on the language may have taken place (cf. GK[2] §117n), and in any case LXX[LMN] (cf. LXX[B]) *diaparetērounto* points to a more distinctive reading. Ewald (1878:117 n. 1) and Klostermann supposed this to be *'rbw l-*, "had been laying for," but the reading of 4QSam[a], *[ ]ṗnw l-*, suggests that the original was instead a synonymous expression, viz. *ṣpnw l-* (cf. Prov 1:11,18), which is adopted here. The verse amounts to a retrospective parenthesis reflecting on the entire incident and reminding the reader of the background events in 2:12–32. See the NOTE.

31. *King David himself* Syr. adds *wkwlh 'm'*, "and all the people."

*behind* So MT *('ḥry)*, LXX[BAMN] *(opisō)*, Syr. *(btr)*, and 4QSam[a] *('ḥr[y])*. LXX[LMmg] *emprosthen* reflects *lpny*, "in front of," a reminiscence of the previous *lpny*, "in front of (Abiner), in (Abiner's) path."

32. *his grave* So LXX[BAMN]. MT, LXX[L], Syr., and 4QSam[a] have "*Abiner's* grave." Cf. the following *Textual Note*.

*the people wept, too* LXX[BAMN] add "over Abiner." Omit with MT, LXX[L], Syr., and 4QSam[a]. Cf. the preceding *Textual Note*.

33. *Alas* See the NOTE on "Alas, prince of Israel" in 1:19. Here again a lament begins with *hō*, "alas," written archaically as *h-*. MT takes this as the interrogative particle.

34. *Your hands were bound . . . not by manacles* So 4QSam[a]: '*[swrwt ydyk l']* *bzqym*. MT (cf. LXX) has a shorter reading: *ydk* (= *ydyk) l' 'srwt*, "Your hands were not bound!" There is no apparent mechanism for the loss of *bzqym*, and a case might be made for the shorter text of MT. Freedman, however, has convinced me of the original-

ity of *bzqym,* "by manacles," a distinctive phrase providing an excellent parallel to *bnḥštym,* "by fetters." The two do not occur in parallel elsewhere, however, so that it is not likely that *bzqym* arose here by scribal expansion.

*Your feet* Reading *rglyk* with LXX^(B) for MT, 4QSam^a *wrglyk,* "*and* your feet."

*not* The position of the negative particle *l'* varies. In MT it precedes "by fetters." In 4QSam^a, which we follow, it follows "by fetters." In LXX it seems to be represented in both positions.

*by fetters* Reading *bnḥštym* with 4QSam^a *(bnḥš[ty]m)* in preference to MT *lnḥštym.* But if Dahood (1980) is correct in interpreting *l-* as instrumental, we should probably give preference to MT.

*confined* Reading *huggāšû* (cf. BDB 621; *BHS huggāšû*), lit. "brought near," i.e., shackled together *by* fetters, not brought near *to* (= thrust into) fetters (cf. the following *Textual Note*). 4QSam^a has *hgš* (= *higgîš* or *hoggēš* [cf. GK² §113z]?). Dahood (1980), comparing Job 3:18, suggests *huggāšû,* which he translates "tortured."

*As a criminal falls* MT has *knpwl lpny bny ʿwlh,* "like a falling before criminals." Many follow Klostermann in reading *kĕnōpēl,* "like one who falls," for *kinpôl.* LXX *hos nabal,* "like Nabal," suggests *kĕnābāl,* "like an outcast," an error probably shared by 4QSam^a *(knb[l]).* In order to recover the original sense of the poetic line, suggested by symmetry with the first line of the lament, we should probably strike *lpny* as a corrupt duplicate of *-l bny* and, with Ehrlich (1910:281), read *bn* for *bny.* Thus we read *knpwl bn ʿwlh.*

*all the people* So MT and all versions: *kl hʿm.* 4QSam^a reads *kl,* "everyone" (?); but this is not good Hebrew, and we must assume that a scribe simply omitted *hʿm.* (The note in *BHS* indicating that the scroll also omits *kl* is incorrect.)

*continued* Reading *wyspw* with MT *(wayyōsîpû)* and 4QSam^a *([w]yspw).* LXX^BL reflect *wysp,* understood as *wy'sp* (cf. 6:1 MT)—thus LXX^B *kai synēchthē* = *wayye'ĕsōp,* "And he (David) gathered all the people," etc., and LXX^L *kai synēlthen* = *wayyē'āsēp,* "And all the people gathered," etc.

35. *came* So MT, LXX, 4QSam^a. Syr.: *w'mrw* ("All the people *said* David should be given bread to eat," etc.).

*to give . . . to eat* So MT: *lhbrwt,* for which MT^MSS have *lhkrwt,* a variant commented on in Sanhedrin 20a.

*or anything else* So MT: *'w kl m'wmh.* 4QSam^a combines the first two words *'wkl m['wmh],* "*eating* anything else." LXX^B: *ē apo pantos tinos* = *'w mkl m'wmh,* "or *any of* anything else." LXX^L: *oude pantos tinos* = *wl' kl m'wmh,* "*nor* anything else."

36. *and everything . . . to them* Reading *wyyṭb bʿynyhm kl 'šr ʿšh hmlk bʿyny hʿm* on the basis of LXX^B *kai ēresen enōpion autōn panta hosa epoiēsen ho basileus enōpion tou laou* and 4QSam^a *[wyyṭb] bʿynyhm [kl 'šr ʿ]šh h[mlk bʿyny hʿ]m* (LXX^L reflects *kl hʿm,* and perhaps we should restore this in the scroll also). MT marks *bʿynyhm* with the *'atnāḥ,* thus dividing the verse differently, and adds another predicate at the end (cf. LXX^AO)—thus, *wyyṭb bʿynyhm kkl 'šr ʿšh hmlk bʿyny kl hʿm ṭwb,* "and it seemed good to them, just as (?) everything the king did was good in the eyes of (seemed good to) the people."

38. *to his servants* Omitted by Syr. by haplography *(lʿbdwh l').*

39. *And I . . . am still a gentle man* So MT: *w'nky hywm rk,* lit. "And I today am gentle." LXX^LMN (cf. OL) have *kai hoti sēmeron syngenēs* = *wky hywm dd,* "and that

he (viz. Abiner) was today a kinsman." The confusion of *rk* and *dd* was graphically possible in the scripts of many periods. The balance between the elements of this statement—*w'nky* . . . *rk*, "And I . . . am . . . gentle"—and those of the one that follows —*wh'nšym h'lh* . . . *qšym*, "but these men . . . are . . . rougher," strongly favors the reading of MT (Thenius, Wellhausen); see the NOTE.

*though anointed king* So MT: *wmšwḥ mlk*. LXX[B] *kai kathestamenos hypo basileōs* probably reflects the same text interpreted in reference to Abiner: "and one anointed (= appointed) by a king." Wellhausen doubts that *rk wmšwḥ mlk* can mean "gentle though anointed king," arguing on linguistic grounds that the attributes should harmonize. He rejects the treatment of Ewald (1878:118), "Truly now I live in palaces and am anointed king . . . ," because of its disregard for the contrast between *rk*, "gentle," and *qšym*, "rough." Associating *mšḥ* with *šḥḥ*, "be low(ly)," and changing *mlk* to *mmlk*, he suggests "too weak and lowly for a king."

At this point MT adds *yšlm yhwh l'śh hr'h kr'tw*, "May Yahweh repay the evildoer according to his evil!" The versions also reflect this addition, and Josephus bases his understanding of David's speech on it (see the NOTE); but it is lacking in 4QSam[a], enough of which is extant at this point to show that the *vacat* before the "paragraph" that begins in 4:1 must have begun immediately after the end of v. 39a. The half-verse probably arose from the pious addition of a scribe.

## NOTES

3 6. *As the war . . . continued.* This half-verse echoes the language of 3:1 explicitly, resuming the narrative thread after the interruption of vv. 2–5. See the NOTE at 3:1 and the COMMENT on the last section.

*was gaining power in.* Hebrew *mitḥazzēq bĕ-*, which here, as in I Chron 11:10 and II Chron 12:13, refers to the securing or strengthening of someone's position within a certain context. A few interpreters take the expression to mean instead that Abiner was supporting the house of Saul energetically, that he "was exerting himself in connexion with the house of Saul, for the purpose of maintaining it" (Driver), and it is true that this is the role Abiner himself claims in v. 8 to have been playing (McKane; cf. Grønbaek 1971:235 n. 44). But such an interpretation is not supported by the other occurrences of the expression. The point here is that Abiner is gathering more and more power to himself as the war drags on. For this reason, we may assume, Ishbaal is becoming increasingly wary, and the accusation in the next verse is to be viewed against this background.

7. *Rizpah daughter of Aia.* Rizpah figures prominently in the story of the Gibeonites' revenge in 21:1–14. She was a "concubine," a slave woman attached to the house of Saul, but the fact that she had borne two sons to the king (21:8) made her an important figure in the royal household, as the present incident attests.

"*Why have you been sleeping with my father's concubine?*" A serious charge. Adonijah will be put to death merely for asking for Solomon's father's concubine (I Kings 2:13–25). A violation of the royal harem was not only an act of *lèse majesté* (Bennett

1937:287); it was tantamount to a public declaration of pretension to the throne (cf. Tsevat 1958b). Thus Abishalom, when he has forced David into exile and occupied Jerusalem, will visit his father's harem openly in public demonstration of the transfer of the crown (16:20–22). Here, as in the case of Adonijah and Solomon, a rival challenges a new king's authority by claiming for himself a woman from the harem of the late king. Or so the offended kings, Ishbaal and Solomon, would have us believe. In the case of Adonijah, we might take the narrator's meaning to be that since David's relationship with Abishag had not been consummated (I Kings 1:4), Adonijah did not regard her as his father's wife or concubine and asked for her without the ulterior motive that Solomon, who was seeking an excuse to eliminate the threat to his throne that a living older brother posed, chose to impute to him. The present case is also shrouded with uncertainty. Are we meant to believe that Abiner has actually been sleeping with Rizpah, as Ishbaal claims? The text, except where expanded by ancient hands to resolve the uncertainty (see the *Textual Note*), does not say. Perhaps Ishbaal is slandering Abiner in the hope of exposing him to public censure and thereby checking his growing power (cf. v. 6b). Although it is impossible to be certain (cf. Soggin 1975:45 n. 22), I assume that we are intended to suppose that Abiner did in fact take Rizpah for himself as a gesture of contempt for Ishbaal designed to display publicly the relationship that actually existed between himself and the king of whose domains he was the *de facto* ruler.

8. *a dog's head.* This expression, *rōʾš keleb,* is otherwise unknown and its signification is uncertain. Freedman suggests plausibly that it "is a euphemism: to be a 'dog' was a term of opprobrium, and to be the rear end of a dog was obviously worse; this is a polite substitute for the latter." Another interesting interpretation, developed by Winton Thomas (1960:417–23) on the basis of the ingenious suggestion of G. Margoliouth, is that it means "dog-headed or dog-faced *baboon.*" Symmachus' translation, *kynokephalos,* brings to mind the genus *Cynocephalus,* the dog-faced baboons of Africa and Arabia, of which at least *C. hamadryas,* the sacred baboon of Egypt, must have been known to the Israelites. If this interpretation is correct, Abiner is complaining that he is being treated like an ape. If it is not correct, we must suppose that "a dog's head" belongs in some undetermined way to the wider use of references to dogs in expressions of reproach and self-abasement (see the NOTE on "a dead dog like me" in 9:8).

*dealing loyally.* See the NOTE at 2:5 and, on the use of *ḥesed,* "loyalty (to a relationship)," in the present passage, the discussion in Sakenfeld 1978:27–31.

9–10. These words are rather surprising on Abiner's lips (cf. Ackroyd). The vow assumes knowledge of Yahweh's condemnation of Saul and promise to transfer his kingship to another (I Sam 13:13–14; 15:26–28), and of the choice of David as the successor (I Sam 15:35–16:13), all key episodes in the prophetic presentation of the stories of Saul and David (see *I Samuel,* pp. 18–23). The present verses are probably secondarily interpolated, then, perhaps by the prophetic hand that fashioned the larger story or by a still later Deuteronomistic editor. Budde, to be sure, supposed Abiner's words to refer to material within what we have taken as the original body of the narrative of David's rise to power, viz. the oracle referred to cryptically in I Sam 22:10 (cf. also Eissfeldt 1931:27); but such a supposition is difficult to adopt with confidence when we are totally ignorant of the content of the oracle in question. More persuasive, therefore, are the recent interpreters who regard these verses as Deuteronomistic in origin (e.g., Schmidt 1970:126–31; Veijola 1975:59–60; contrast Mettinger 1976:44), looking ahead to Yahweh's promise to David in II Sam 7:5–17, and comparable, then, to other passages in the story of David's rise that we have taken to be Deuteronomistic expansion (especially I Sam 25:28b–31; cf. below the NOTES at 3:18 and 5:1–2 and the Introduction, pp. 4–8).

9. *May God . . . again.* Hebrew *kōh ya'ăśeh lî hā'ĕlōhîm wĕkōh yōsîp* (see the *Textual Note*), a standard oath formula (I Sam 3:17; etc.), here followed by *kî,* as in I Sam 14:44; 20:13; etc. (cf. Driver and GK[2] §149d). See *I Samuel,* the NOTES on 3:17 and 14:44.

10. *from Dan to Beersheba.* A conventional way of describing the full extent of the united kingdom of Israel. Dan (Tell el-Qâḍī on the southern slope of the Hermon) and Beersheba (Tell es-Seba', ca. twenty-three miles southwest of Hebron) lay at the traditional northern and southern extremes of the land.

12. *all Israel.* That is, the territories ruled by Ishbaal, as listed in 2:9. See the NOTE there on "Israel in its entirety" and Flanagan 1975:107–8.

13. *You won't see me.* Hebrew *lō'-tir'eh 'et-pānay,* lit. "You will not see my face." Those who were privileged to "see the face" of a king on a regular basis were the members of his inner circle of personal advisers (cf. II Kings 25:19 = Jer 52:25; Esth 1:14). It was a sign of favor and privilege to be granted an interview with a king or other person of high rank, and expressed exclusion from "seeing the face" of the king was, conversely, a form of disgrace (cf. David's treatment of Abishalom in 14:24ff.). See also the following NOTE.

*Michal daughter of Saul.* The story of David's marriage to Michal was told in I Sam 18:20–27. After David's estrangement from Saul and flight—with Michal's help (I Sam 19:11–17)—from the Israelite court, Saul remarried his daughter "to Palti, the son of Laish, who was from Gallim" (I Sam 25:44). We may suspect with Caird and most other commentators that "the request for the return of Michal was a political move to reinforce the claims of David to the kingship," but our narrator, according to whom any such ambition was alien to David's personality (see the COMMENT), puts forward a different reason. David requires Abiner to arrange the return as proof of his good faith. Only on this condition will he grant the Benjaminite general the privilege of an interview. Compare Gen 43:3,5, where Joseph requires his brothers to bring Benjamin as a sign of their truthfulness. "You won't see me," says Joseph in language identical to that of David in the present passage, "unless your brother is with you."

14–16. It is surprising to find Ishbaal involved in these proceedings, especially in view of the fact that the negotiations between David and Abiner are aimed at his elimination. Accordingly, Noth (1960:184 n. 1) followed earlier critics in challenging the integrity of these verses. The claim that Michal became David's wife during Saul's lifetime was, in Noth's opinion, made only late in the development of the tradition, and the relevant portions of I Samuel 18–19 reflect this later tradition. In the present passage, then, v. 14 would seem to be secondary—an adjustment of the older story, in which Michal became David's wife here for the first time—to the tradition in I Samuel 18–19, and v. 15 would have to be corrected to read "Abiner" instead of "Ishbaal" as the subject of the verb. But Grønbaek (1971:237–38), while sharing Noth's doubt of the historicity of an early marriage between David and Michal, has emphasized an essential element of the passage not taken into account by Noth. The involvement of Ishbaal, son of Saul and brother of Michal, serves the author's apologetic purpose of giving further legitimation to David's union with Michal, which might otherwise seem to have been illicitly arranged. These verses, in other words, contribute directly to what we have taken to be the major purpose of the larger composition. They are best regarded, therefore, as a necessary part of the narrative, not a product of revision of the sort imagined by Noth or, indeed, a scrap of "an alternative account" (Ackroyd). We are told that Ishbaal cooperated in the return of Michal, which might otherwise have been condemned as a consequence of the treachery of a treasonous member of Ishbaal's court but which instead, by virtue of the king's own involvement, had the character of an officially sanctioned act of state.

But if we assume that the story of David and Michal, with all its components, belongs to the oldest version of this story and is likely, therefore, to correspond somehow to historical reality, we are obliged to offer an explanation of the rather strange behavior of the principals in the present episode. On what basis does David make the demand for the return of Michal? Why does Ishbaal cooperate at the cost of giving credibility to David's right to the northern throne? How can our narrator, whose purpose is to present David's behavior in the best possible light, expect his audience to overlook an apparent violation of marriage law (e.g., Deut 24:1–4)? None of this makes sense unless we assume there are special legalities involved to which all parties are acting responsibly. In a recent study (1979) Ben-Barak, on the basis of Mesopotamian materials drawn from a variety of periods, has shown that such legalities existed, at least in Mesopotamia, and may have been applicable in the present case. Biblical prohibitions against remarrying one's former wife after she has become a second man's wife apply specifically to cases where the first husband has divorced the woman willingly (Deut 24:1; cf. Jer 3:1), but no stipulation is made about cases in which the first husband is forcibly removed from his wife. The Mesopotamian laws cited by Ben-Barak apply specifically to cases of the latter kind. If a husband is forced to leave the country and give up his wife, she becomes legally a widow after a certain period of time and may remarry. If, however, the first husband subsequently returns, he may reclaim her and she must return to him. Ben-Barak concludes plausibly that David's claims are made on some such basis as this and that Ishbaal, whatever he might have preferred to do, was not in a strong enough position to flout an established legal practice. Certainly it seems to be the case that David, by citing the "bride-price" he paid for Michal (see the following NOTE), means to state a legal basis for his demand.

14. *whom I betrothed for a hundred Philistine foreskins.* An allusion to the story in I Sam 18:20–27. Saul himself had set this unusual *mōhar* or "bride-price" (on which see *I Samuel,* the NOTE at 18:22b–25) in the hope and expectation that David would lose his life trying to acquire it (v. 25). But Saul's scheme backfired (as usual), and David, with Yahweh's help (cf. v. 28), met the requirement and won a royal bride (v. 27).

15. *Paltiel son of Laish.* Cf. I Sam 25:44, where Michal's second husband is called by a shorter form of his name, "Palti." His home is said there to be Gallim, a Benjaminite town north of Jerusalem (cf. Isa 10:30).

16. *Bahurim.* Cf. the *Textual Note.* The modern site is Râs eṭ-Ṭmîm, just east of Mount Scopus, Jerusalem; see Maps 3 and 7. Ancient Bahurim was a Benjaminite village, the home of Shimei, David's accuser in later life (16:5; 19:17; II Kings 2:8), and Azmaveth, one of David's heroes (cf. 23:31 and the *Textual Note* there on "the

Bahurimite"). It seems to have been a kind of border town, guarding one of the main roads connecting Israel with Judah and Jerusalem.

17. The reference to the Israelites' eagerness to have David as king is perhaps an allusion to the days when David was a general in Saul's army, when he "went out and came in before" the Israelites (I Sam 18:16). At that time, we know, "all Israel and Judah loved him," that is, paid him the loyalty that might have seemed properly due to Saul (see *I Samuel,* the NOTE to 18:16).

*the elders of Israel.* Senior tribesmen who exercised jurisdiction on behalf of the people of Ishbaal's kingdom. See McKenzie 1959; van der Ploeg 1961; Malamat 1965; and, for the present passage, Mettinger 1976:109,114–15.

18. *For Yahweh . . . enemies.* I agree with a majority of commentators that part of vv. 17–18—at least 18b—is secondary, probably Deuteronomistic, expansion (cf. Veijola 1975:60–63). The language of v. 18b in particular is reminiscent of statements made about Saul in the prophetic account of his anointing (I Sam 9:16; 10:1). As Schmidt (1970:136–38) has pointed out, the effect of this is to stress the continuity between the reigns of Saul and David, on the one hand, and, especially with the emphasis placed on the military role of the king in these passages (pp. 133–34), the continuity of the reigns of both kings with the period of the judges, on the other. All of this serves the editorial purposes of the Deuteronomistic writer who shaped the larger history. Note also how v. 18b looks ahead to the subsequent Deuteronomistic passages in its allusion to an oracle of Yahweh about David, which has no discernible referent apart from II Samuel 7 (cf. the NOTE on vv. 9–10 above), as well as its use of the epithet "my servant" in reference to David and its anticipation of David's subjugation of Israel's enemies, on both of which see the NOTES that follow.

*my servant David.* Elsewhere especially (though not exclusively) in Deuteronomistic contexts; see Cross 1973:251 n. 140,253; Veijola 1975:127–28. Cf. the NOTE at 7:5.

*the Philistines and all their [other] enemies.* This looks ahead to David's victories over the Philistines recorded in 5:17–25 (Veijola 1975:103; Mettinger 1976:42),21:15–22, and 23:8–39; but, more specifically, it points to the Deuteronomistically compiled catalogue of David's successes against the Philistines and Israel's other enemies in chap. 8.

19. *Abiner spoke personally with the Benjaminites.* The expression *dibbēr bĕʾoznê PN,* lit. "speak in the ears of PN," suggests a personal audience with someone, just as to hear something with one's own ears (7:22; cf. 18:12) is to learn it directly, not secondhand. The use of the expression in the present verse, therefore, points to a distinction between Abiner's communication to the elders of Israel in general (v. 17), which was accomplished, we may assume, through messengers, and his negotiations with the Benjaminites in particular, which he undertook in person. There must have been at least two reasons for the special treatment of Benjamin. First, Abiner was himself a Benjaminite and must have had considerable influence among his fellow tribesmen. Second, Benjamin was the tribe of the house of Saul, and its cooperation would be crucial to the success of Abiner's plan. This nuance of wording, moreover, has yet another implication. To speak in someone's ear is to give him formal notice and, in effect, enlist him as a witness in the future (Deut 5:1; etc.). The narrator, whose larger apologetic argument is aimed especially at the Israelite, non-Jerusalemite component of David's kingdom, who may have doubted the legitimacy of the succession, is reminding the

Benjaminites in his audience that they themselves know that what is here related about Abiner is true. You yourselves know, says the writer to any Benjaminite skeptical about David's innocence in the death of Abiner, that before he died Abiner was negotiating a transfer of the allegiance of the Israelites from the house of Saul to the house of David. So why would David have wanted Abiner dead? See further the COMMENT.

*good.* That which seemed "good" *(ṭôb)* to the Israelites was what David would be obliged to do to establish a covenantal relationship with them. On this use of *ṭôb* as treaty terminology, see Malamat 1965:63–64 and, for general background, Moran 1963b.

21. *all Israel.* See the NOTE at v. 12 above.

*and he went in peace.* Hebrew *wayyēlek bĕšālôm,* with which this and each of the next two verses conclude. It hardly requires a subtle exposition of the text to show that this detail, which is repeated three times within the compass of a few words, was regarded as important by the narrator. Abiner is about to be killed. It must be understood clearly, therefore, that he parted from David on good terms.

22. Joab returns. His absence on routine duty during Abiner's visit seems almost suspiciously convenient, and many commentators (e.g., Caird) have supposed it to have been arranged deliberately by David to avoid the conflict he knew would otherwise arise.

25. *your going out and your coming in.* That is, your military maneuvers. The expression *yāṣā' ûbā',* "go out and come in," most often refers to marching to and from battle; cf. I Sam 18:13,16; 29:6; and elsewhere, Josh 14:11; etc. Joab, in other words, is claiming that Abiner, though visiting under the pretext of a parley, in fact came to acquire intelligence about David's military activities in the hope of gaining an advantage for the house of Saul in the ongoing war (vv. 1,6).

26. *Bor-hassirah.* That is, *bôr-hassīrâ,* an oasis *(bôr)* that lay, according to Josephus (*Ant.* 7.34), twenty stades, i.e., about two and a half miles, north of Hebron. This would place it near modern Ṣîret el-Bella'. See Map 1.

*David did not know [of this].* The remark may seem superfluous, but the writer wants to leave no ambiguity on this point. See the COMMENT.

27–30. Note that v. 30 in its present position seems isolated and out of place (cf. Caird). It would, however, follow quite naturally upon v. 27: "and he died for the blood of Asael, [Joab's] brother, for Joab and Abishai had been laying for [him] because," etc. This calls attention to the material that intervenes, vv. 28–29, which might be suspected of having arisen secondarily. There is internal evidence to support such a suspicion. David's explicit avowal of his innocence clashes with the narrator's style of argument in the rest of his account of this episode, which exonerates David not by open assertion but by a careful recounting of events. The harsh and apparently public denunciation of Joab is incompatible with what we are told of David's subsequent dealings with his chief general, who, indeed, is instructed to lead the funeral procession in the passage that follows immediately. The statement in v. 39a is not nearly so strong. I suspect, therefore, that those scholars who, like Veijola (1975:30–31) and Mettinger (1976:40 n. 36), regard vv. 28–29 as of Deuteronomistic origin are correct. Seen in this light certain other details become more clear, as the following NOTES show. (On v. 30, see further the NOTE there.)

27. *for the blood of Asael, [Joab's] brother.* This phrase, *bĕdam 'ăśâ-'ēl 'āḥîw,* is

appended to remind us of the events of 2:17–28 and to emphasize the point that Abiner's death was the result of a personal quarrel between him and the sons of Zeruiah, a matter in which David was not involved. Joab has exercised his duty as Asael's kinsman and avenger. He is "the redeemer of blood" (*gō'ēl haddām*, Num 35:19; etc.), whose "most solemn responsibility . . . was to enforce blood-vengeance, and here we encounter [a] law of the desert, the *ṯâr* of the Arabs" (de Vaux 1961b:vol. I:11). Biblical law sanctions the system of blood vengeance but controls it by establishment of the so-called cities of refuge; see Num 35:9–34; Deut 4:41–43; 19:1–13; Joshua 20. See also the preceding NOTE.

28. *I and my kingship.* David is portrayed as concerned not only for himself but also for his kingship, to which compare 7:12 and especially 7:16. The use of *mamlākâ*, "kingship," in such a context raises the question of dynasty (cf. *I Samuel*, the NOTE to 13:13 and the COMMENT on 13:2–5). This is nowhere a concern of the story of David's rise in its original form, but it is a characteristically Deuteronomistic interest.

28–29. *may the blood . . . devolve upon the head of Joab.* Hebrew *wĕdam . . . yāḥōl 'al-rō'š yô'āb* (see the *Textual Notes*). Interpretation of the verb by reference to Jer 23:19 = 30:23 (Driver, Ackroyd), where there is mention of a "storm of Yahweh" *(sa'ărat yahweh)* that "will whirl *(yāḥûl)* about the heads of the wicked," may be misleading. Rabbinic Hebrew (Jastrow 432) shows that *ḥāl 'al* could refer to hovering over or revolving about the head in the sense of "alight upon" as a duty or obligation. The sense here is that responsibility for the death of Abiner is to rest upon Joab and his family as a permanent liability.

Looking far ahead, we see that Joab will die by command of Solomon (I Kings 2:28–34). The language in that passage recalls the present events explicitly, and the statement David makes here is echoed in particular in I Kings 2:33: "And the blood [of Abiner] shall come back upon the head of Joab and upon the heads of his descendants forever, but for David and his descendants and his house and his throne there will be peace forever before Yahweh!" These two parts of the larger history are thus linked by two insertions (II Sam 3:28–29 and I Kings 2:33) from a Deuteronomistic hand.

*clings to a crutch.* Hebrew *maḥăzîq bappelek*, understood by Driver to mean a man who holds a distaff (*pelek*, Prov 31:19), i.e., an effeminate; cf. Akkadian *pilakku* (< Sumerian *bila*[*k*], against Driver's etymology) and Ugaritic *plk*, both "spindle." But Phoenician *plkm* means "crutches" in the Karatepe inscription (*KAI* 26 A II.6), and this sense seems better to me here.

*falls by the sword.* McKane compares I Sam 31:4 and concludes that here as there the meaning is "falls *upon* the sword," i.e., commits suicide. But this is incorrect. To fall *by (bĕ-)* the sword is to die in battle (cf. 1:12, where the reference is not only to Saul but also to Jonathan and all the Israelite soldiers who fell in the debacle on Gilboa), and this, *nāpal bĕ-*, is the expression used here, not *nāpal 'al*, "fall *upon*," as in I Sam 31:4.

30. I suggested above that this verse originally followed immediately upon v. 27. In that position it seems immune to the criticisms of those scholars who would strike it as misplaced and disruptive (Caird; cf. Ackroyd). But those commentators who follow the received Hebrew text, which says that "Joab and his brother Abishai *killed (hārĕgû lĕ-)* Abiner," are further troubled by the contradiction to the description of the

deed in v. 27, where Abishai is not mentioned. The introduction of Abishai, they argue, is "unexpected" (Ackroyd), "inaccurate" (Caird), "almost certainly incorrect" (Hertzberg). Hebrew *hārĕgû lĕ-*, moreover, is a "solecism of the later period" (GK² §117n), *hārag* taking the accusative in the classical phase of the language. These difficulties are relieved, however, by the restoration of the primitive text, made possible by the assistance of Greek and Qumran evidence (see the *Textual Note*). Joab and Abiner, we are told, "had been laying for" *(ṣāpĕnû lĕ-)* Abiner ever since the death of Asael. To the possible objection that the statement, however interpreted and wherever located, is superfluous to the narrative, we should reply that here, as in the threefold repetition of the detail that Abiner left David "in peace" (vv. 21,22,23) and in the certification of David's ignorance of Abiner's recall (v. 26), there is extreme care being taken to avoid any ambiguity about the human motives that gave rise to the events being recounted. Joab and Abishai, the surviving sons of Zeruiah, have continued to prosecute their blood feud against Abiner since the death of their brother. The narrator invites his audience to contemplate these things one last time at the end of his account of the slaying of Abiner and prior to his description of the funeral rites.

31. Abiner's funeral procession, as here described, was led by his assassin, Joab, accompanied by Joab's army. (Was this extraordinary arrangement necessitated by security reasons?) Then came the bier, followed by the king.

*Tear your clothes.* See the NOTE at 1:11.

*put on sackcloth.* Another sign of mourning. Hebrew *śaq* (whence Greek *sakkos*, Latin *saccus*, and, by way of an early Germanic borrowing, English "sack") referred both to sackcloth and to an ordinary kind of household bag used, for example, for carrying grain (cf. Gen 42:25; etc.), and it is probable that it was material from such bags that was worn in mourning. For the practice in general, see de Ward 1972:10–15.

32. *Hebron.* No attempt is made to return the body to Benjamin for burial. See also 4:12.

33. *an outcast.* For this translation of *nābāl*, traditionally "fool," see the NOTE at 13:13. A *nābāl* is one who has committed an act of *nĕbālâ*, "sacrilege" (13:12), thus severing himself from his place in society. The sense of David's lament is that Abiner, "a commander and a nobleman" (v. 38), has suffered the death of an "outcast" or "criminal" (*ben 'awlā'*, v. 34). Though he was not a convicted outlaw, a prisoner shackled in chains, he died like one, executed in secret by Joab and the palace guard and thus denied the dignified death that would have befitted his rank and character.

35. *May God . . . again!* See the NOTE at v. 9. The oath formula is the same, but here *kî* is followed by *'im* (cf. I Sam 25:34). See Driver and GK² §149d.

*I will taste no bread.* Cf. 1:12 and the NOTE there on "fasting."

36–37. David's behavior impresses the people favorably. The narrator makes a point of explaining that "at that time"—i.e., at the time of the funeral, when the events could still be remembered clearly—everyone, including "all Israel"—i.e., Abiner's own countrymen (see the NOTE at v. 12 above)—acknowledged David's innocence in the matter. They knew, he says, that Abiner's death "was not the king's will" (*lō' hāyĕtâ mēhammelek*, lit. "it was not from the king") or, in other words, the king had not instigated it (cf. Judg 14:4).

38–39. Veijola (1975:31–32) considers these verses, like vv. 28–29, to be secondary and Deuteronomistic, but in this case I cannot agree. The strongly moralizing half-verse

39b is shown by the evidence of the scroll to be the pious comment of a scribe (see the third *Textual Note* at v. 39), and the rest displays no formal or thematic characteristic necessarily requiring us to bracket it as secondary.

38. *a nobleman.* Hebrew *gādôl,* lit. "a great one," to which Wifall (1975) has compared Amarna Akkadian *awīlu,* lit. "man," and Egyptian *wr,* lit. "great one." All of these, he says, signify membership in the ruling aristocratic class in the semifeudal social structure the early Israelite monarchy shared with other states.

39. David says that although he has been anointed king over Judah (2:4), he is still (lit. "today") a gentle man, an assertion that highlights his innocence of complicity in the violent death of Abiner. The foil to his gentleness is the brutality of his kinsmen, the sons of Zeruiah. The syntax accentuates the contrast: *wĕʾānōkî . . . rak . . . wĕhāʾănāšîm hāʾēlleh . . . qāšîm,* "And I . . . am . . . gentle . . . but these men . . . are rougher." Everything we have been told so far about the sons of Zeruiah bears this out; they are seasoned warriors, fiercely loyal, and callous, cruel, and precipitate; see the COMMENT.

## COMMENT

Some time has passed—we do not know how much—since Abiner slew Asael in the aftermath of the contest at Flints' Field (see § IV). The war between Israel and Judah has "dragged out" (3:1). It is the narrator's wish, however, that the former events should be fresh in our minds for what we are about to hear, and he has joined his account of them directly to the present episode. Despite the later insertion of a list of the sons born to David in Hebron (3:2–5), the original collocation of materials achieves its purpose. As we read the account of Abiner's negotiations with David, we are mindful of the feud he reluctantly ignited in the field outside Gibeon (2:17–28). We know that Joab and Abishai are seeking revenge for their brother's blood, that they are "laying for" Abiner (cf. v. 30). We find nothing incredible or even surprising, therefore, about Joab's behavior when he returns to Hebron to chide his lord for treating with Abiner (vv. 22–25) and lays a trap for the Benjaminite general (vv. 26–27).

It is the chief goal of this part of the story of David's rise to demonstrate the new king's innocence of the two assassinations (viz. of Abiner and Ishbaal) that opened the way to his kingship in the north (cf. McCarter 1980b:501–2). The narrator, therefore, wants to leave no ambiguity about the slaying of Abiner. David benefited from the deed inasmuch as it removed the sturdiest obstacle from his path to the throne of Israel. Abiner, moreover, was received by David in Hebron shortly before his death, and he was slain by David's ranking officer and kinsman. These things the narrator does not attempt to deny. Nevertheless, he says, David was not responsible for the assassination.

His negotiations with Abiner were frank and harmonious. Abiner, in fact, pledged his support to David and when he died he was in the midst of negotiations intended to establish David's rule in the north. This last point, we are told, can be attested by the Benjaminites themselves, the group who might seem most clearly to have grievances against David and to whom the old story of David's rise was probably principally addressed, for Abiner discussed the matter "personally" with them (cf. the NOTE at v. 19). After the parley described in vv. 20–21, Abiner left David's court "in peace"—our narrator is not satisfied until he has made this point three times (vv. 21,22,23) —and David had no reason to believe that he did not also return home in peace. As it happened, he was recalled to Hebron by Joab, but, as we are explicitly told, "David did not know [of this]" (v. 26). So the killing, when it came, was not David's responsibility. It was, as we have said, the result of a blood feud, a personal matter, related only indirectly to the larger political issues.

Nowhere is the story of David's rise more insistent in its apologetic tone than here in its controversion of David's involvement in Abiner's death. The care with which the acquitting facts are presented is itself a clue that this suspicion, more than others, was a problem in the time of the composition of the narrative. The rabbis perceived these circumstances clearly, commenting (Sanhedrin 20a) that David's purpose in following the bier was to appease the people and convince them of his innocence. In this, concluded the rabbis, David succeeded. In fact, the favorable response of the people is given special stress in the story. It is the narrator's testimony that those who witnessed the events in person were entirely persuaded of David's innocence by the sincerity with which he mourned the fallen Israelite leader: ". . . everything the king did in [their] sight seemed good to them" (v. 36). The point being made, it seems, is that only in retrospect, only in the present (i.e., the time of the composition of the story) is suspicion possible, for "all the people and all Israel knew *at that time* that it was not the king's will to kill Abiner son of Ner" (v. 37). Nevertheless, the suspicion arose—perhaps in retrospect, perhaps without justification, but it was there—and it lingered on throughout David's reign, as attested by the Shimei incident in 16:5–14 and indeed by the persistently defensive tone of the present account itself.

If David was not murderous and ambitious and Abiner did not fall prey to David's ambition, then why did all this take place? What factor or factors moved these events forward? From the perspective of the larger narrative, the motivating force was Yahweh's will and his special favor for David, but the working out of the divine plan remains implicit in the present episode, becoming explicit only where a later hand has touched the original version and drawn it out (vv. 9–10,18b,28–29; see the NOTES). Instead, these events are described as the consequences of the interplay of four human personalities, and, indeed, the entire episode stands as a testimony to the peril of human recklessness and vindictiveness. Two of the key personalities—ironically enough, the two kings—are essentially passive. *Ishbaal* is presented as weak, indecisive, and cowardly, a thoroughly unkingly invertebrate, unable to control or even coexist with the masterful and mercurial Abiner. *David* is depicted as passive, too "gentle" to harness the "rougher" (v. 39) sons of Zeruiah; but there is no suggestion that his passivity is a serious defect of character, and he has the affection and trust of his people. He is not ambitious—the negotiations concerning kingship in the north are initiated by Abiner, the demand for Michal is only (we are told) a test of Abiner's good faith, and, all in all, David's passive attitude toward this part of his destiny is consistent with his behavior as presented elsewhere in the larger story. Yet he seems firmly in control of his own kingdom, and he is quick and resolute in denouncing injustice when it appears. In short, he is a new king not yet in possession of his full powers but as well suited for kingship as Ishbaal is ill suited. The other two personalities are much more forceful; they play the decisive roles. *Abiner* is presented as a strong and able man, a great warrior, and a clever politician. But he seems easily to find himself embroiled in a quarrel, whether with friend or foe. He is a thoroughly unpredictable and controversial fellow, and he is fatally careless. *Joab* is depicted as powerful and fiercely loyal but also ruthless, vindictive and, as we have noted, "rougher" than David (v. 39). It may be that he was also ambitious and jealous of his position. Josephus (*Ant.* 7.31,36, cf. 37–38) took this to be the real reason for his rancor against Abiner, a potential rival for the leadership of David's armies, and many modern commentators (Caird, Ackroyd, etc.; cf. Noth 1960:185; Soggin 1975:46) have suspected the same thing. But as the story is told here, the whole affair is a matter of blood revenge, and Joab is a cold-blooded and skillful avenger. He and Abishai share the rash impetuosity of their slain brother, Asael (cf. 2:17–23), and it is the recklessness of these sons of Zeruiah, together with their vindictiveness and treachery, that finally emerges as the most important of all these factors leading to the death of Abiner.

With Abiner dead, the one remaining obstacle in David's path to the kingship of Israel is Ishbaal, the withering scion of the house of Saul. The removal of this last obstacle is the subject of the next section.

## VII. THE DEATH OF ISHBAAL
## (4:1–12)

4 [1]When Ishbaal son of Saul heard that Abiner had died in Hebron,
his courage flagged, and all Israel was dismayed.

### *The Murder of Ishbaal*

[2]Now there were two men, commanders of raiding bands of Ishbaal
son of Saul: The name of the first was Baanah, and the name of the
second was Rechab; they were sons of Rimmon the Beerothite, a Benjaminite (for Beeroth is reckoned to the Benjaminites—[3]the Beerothites
fled to Gittaim and have lived there as sojourners to this day).
[4]Jonathan son of Saul had a lame son, who was five years old. When
the news about Saul and Jonathan came from Jezreel, his nurse picked
him up and fled. In her hurry to flee she dropped him, and he was
crippled. His name was Meribbaal.
[5]The sons of Rimmon the Beerothite, Rechab and Baanah, set out
and, when the day was growing hot, came to the house of Ishbaal as
he was taking his midday rest. [6]The portress of the house had been
gathering wheat; she had nodded and fallen asleep. So Rechab and
Baanah, his brother, slipped by [7]and went into the house, where [Ish-
baal] was lying upon a couch in his bedchamber. They struck him and
killed him and, cutting off his head, took it and travelled the Arabah
road all night.

### *David and the Sons of Rimmon*

[8]They brought Ishbaal's head to David in Hebron. "The head of
Ishbaal son of Saul, your enemy, who sought your life!" they said to
the king. "Yahweh has granted my lord the king vengeance today on
Saul and his descendants!"
[9]Then David answered Rechab and his brother, Baanah, the sons of
Rimmon the Beerothite. "As Yahweh lives, who has saved my life

from every danger," he said to them, [10]"the man who brought me word that Saul was dead, who thought of himself as a bearer of good news—I seized him and put him to death in Ziklag—a man to whom it would have been suitable for me to give a reward! [11]All the more so then when guilty men have slain an innocent man in his own house on his own bed! Therefore I shall hold you responsible for his blood and purge you from the land!" [12]So David gave instructions to his soldiers, and they put them to death, cut off their hands and feet, and hung them beside the pool in Hebron. But they buried Ishbaal's head in Abiner's grave.

## *TEXTUAL NOTES*

**4** 1. *Ishbaal son of Saul* Cf. the *Textual Note* at 3:17. Here LXX$^{\mathrm{BAL}}$ and 4QSam$^{a}$ *(mpẏb[št bn š'wl])* have "Mephibosheth son of Saul," a mistake for "Ishbosheth son of Saul" (cf. Syr., LXX$^{\mathrm{MN}}$). In MT, which once shared the erroneous reading, the name was recognized as an obvious mistake, but the scribes preferred to suppress rather than correct it; thus MT now has "the son of Saul" alone. See Cross 1961:191 n. 45; Ulrich 1978:42–45.

*and all Israel* So MT and 4QSam$^{a}$ *([wk]l yṡ[r'l])*. LXX has "and all *the men of* Israel."

2. *of Ishbaal* 4QSam$^{a}$ has *lmpybšt* for *l'yšbšt,* as in the preceding verse, and the reading of the scroll was shared by the *Vorlage* of LXX$^{\mathrm{BA}}$. Again the name (along with the preposition) has been suppressed in MT. Note also that MT, followed by Syr., Targ., makes the verb explicit, reading *hyw,* "were"; omit with 4QSam$^{a}$ and probably LXX.

*the Beerothite* MT *hb'rty,* written defectively in 4QSam$^{a}$: *hbrty.*

*for Beeroth* Cf. LXX$^{\mathrm{B}}$. MT *(ky gm b'rwt)* and 4QSam$^{a}$ *(k̇ẏ gm [brwt]):* "for Beeroth, too."

*to the Benjaminites* Reading *lbny bnymn* on the basis of LXX *tois huiois beniamein* and Syr. *'m bny bnymyn.* In MT *bny* has been lost—thus, *'l bnymn,* "to Benjamin." 4QSam$^{a}$ has *lbnymy[n]* or possibly *'̇l bnymy[n]*; see Ulrich 1978:145.

3. *the Beerothites* MT: *hb'rtym.* 4QSam$^{a}$: *hbrtym.*

4. *When the news . . . came* Reading *wyhy bb' šm't* with 4QSam$^{a}$ *(wyhy ḃ[b]' šṁ['t]).* Instead of *wyhy,* MT has *hyh* (thus, ". . . who was five years old when the news came . . ."), and LXX *kai houtos* reflects *whw'* (thus, "And as for him, when the news came . . .").

*Meribbaal* Throughout Samuel the name of Jonathan's crippled son is given in MT as *mĕpîbōšet* (once as *mĕpībōšet,* in 19:25, where he is called "son of Saul"; see the *Textual Note* there), "Mephibosheth." In general, the same reading is reflected by LXX (e.g., LXX$^{\mathrm{B}}$ *memphibosthe*) and the other versions, except for LXX$^{\mathrm{L}}$, which has *memph(e)ibaal,* and OL (e.g., in 9:6), which has *memphibaal.* The latter reflect the original form of the name, probably **mippî ba'al,* "Mippibaal" (see the NOTE at 21:8), the change from *ba'al* to *bōšet* being euphemistic, as explained in the NOTE on "Ishbaal" at 2:8. But whose name is this? In 21:8 it is the name of a son of Saul by his concubine Rizpah (3:7). Throughout Samuel, as just noted, it is the name of Jonathan's crippled son. But he—Jonathan's son—is called "Meri(b)baal" by the Chronicler (MT *mĕrî-ba'al* in I Chron 9:40, *mĕrîb ba'al* in I Chron 8:34[*bis*] and 9:40; LXX *meribaal;* see below). Which of these names, Mephibosheth/Mippibaal or Meri(b)baal, belongs to Jonathan's son? Most commentators, mindful of the alteration of *ba'al* to *bōšet,* have attempted to explain Mephibosheth as a euphemism for Meri(b)baal—thus Driver, ". . . the change to *mrybbšt* (or *mrybšt*) appears not to have been thought sufficient; and the name was further disguised by being altered to *mpybšt,* which was probably taken to mean 'One who *scatters* or *disperses* (cf. Dt. 32,26 *'p'yhm*) Shame.' " But there are problems with this explanation. In the first place, the Lucianic reading *memphibaal* points to an original name, *mpyb'l,* which cannot be "an intermediate form," as described by Driver, whose explanation supposes an intermediate form *mrybšt,* which is nowhere attested, not *mpyb'l,* which, if we follow Driver's argument, would have to mean "One who scatters or disperses Baal" (!). Once the substitution of *bōšet* for *ba'al* has been made, moreover, it is difficult to imagine why it would be thought necessary for the name to be "further disguised." It seems necessary to suppose, therefore, that Mephibosheth/Mippibaal and Meri(b)baal are distinct names (to this extent I agree with Tsevat 1975:81–82). Then do both refer to the same man (cf. Tsevat 1975:81)? This is possible, but I prefer to reason differently. The confusion between Ishbosheth/Ishbaal and Mephibosheth/Mippibaal in 3:8 and subsequent verses provides a clue. It is noteworthy that this confusion begins in the primary witnesses (MT, $LXX^{B}$) in 3:8 and not before, though Ishbosheth/Ishbaal is mentioned as early as 2:8. The probable source of the confusion is 21:8, where Rizpah is involved (21:10), as she is at the beginning of chap. 3 (v. 7), and where alone there is a son of Saul named Mephibosheth/Mippibaal (cf. the *Textual Note* on "Ishbaal son of Saul" at 3:8). The confusion next crops up at the beginning of chap. 4 (vv. 1,2). At this point the name Mephibosheth/Mippibaal is shuffled onto a son of Jonathan with a similar sounding name, Meri(b)baal; perhaps this was the reason for the displacement of v. 4 from chap. 9 (see the NOTE on v. 4). The confusion is thereby resolved (cf. 4:5), and Meri(b)baal is consistently referred to as Mephibosheth/Mippibaal hereafter. I assume, therefore, that Mephibosheth/Mippibaal was the name of the son of Saul mentioned in 21:8, and that Meri(b)baal was, as the Chronicler maintains, the crippled son of Jonathan. For the interpretation of the name Meri(b)baal, see the NOTE.

5. *Baanah* $LXX^{L}$ adds "his brother."

*Ishbaal* Here MT has (correctly) "Ishbosheth" (cf. $LXX^{MN}$, Syr.). $LXX^{BAL}$ continue with "Mephibosheth."

6. *The portress . . . asleep* Our translation is based on LXX, which here reads *kai idou hē thyrōros tou oikou ekathairen pyrous kai enystaxen kai ekatheuden,* which reflects *whnh (wehinnēh) šw'rt hbyt lqṭh(?) ḥṭym wtnm wtyšn.* The retroversion of *ekathairen* as *lqṭh* is problematic; it was proposed by Thenius and rejected somewhat superciliously by Wellhausen. The Greek verb means "cleaned, cleared, purged"; it is used by Philo in reference to clearing or pruning vines (*De agricultura* 10) and in LXX to threshing (Isa 28:27). Here it seems to refer to gleaning. In any case, *lqṭh*

(i.e., *lōqĕṭâ,* understood by LXX as *lāqĕṭâ*) is graphically closer to *lqḥy,* the corrupt correspondent in MT (see below), than other possibilities, such as *sqlh* (Wellhausen), which is also objectionable on the grounds that (1) a *Pi'el* form *(msqlh)* would seem to be required for the meaning "clean of stones" (cf. BDB 709) and (2) use of *sql* with reference to the stoning of grain is not otherwise attested. MT is corrupt at this point. It seems likely that a damaged text led to a graphic confusion in the first words of the verse *(whnh šw'rt hbyt > whnh b'w 'd t<wk> hbyt)* and the corruption then spread throughout the first half of the verse. It now reads, in redundant anticipation of subsequent material: *whnh (wĕhēnnâ) b'w 'd twk hbyt lqḥy ḥṭym wykhw 'l hḥmš,* "And they (feminine!) went inside the house fetching wheat and struck him in the stomach."

*his brother* So MT, LXX^L^. LXX^B^: "the brothers."

7. [*Ishbaal*] The primitive reading is that of MT: *hw',* "he." Many Greek MSS make the subject explicit—thus LXX^BA^ (incorrectly), "Mephibosheth"; LXX^MN^ (correctly), "Ishbosheth"—and this is also necessary in English.

*his bedchamber* LXX^L^ adds *to mesēmbrinon* = *hṣhrym,* "at midday," in reminiscence of v. 5.

*They . . . took it* Reading *wyqḥw* with LXX^L^. MT, LXX^B^ repeat "his head." Note that while Syr. and Vulg. omit the previous clause (*wysyrw 't r'šw,* lit. "and they took off his head," here rendered "and, cutting off his head"), it is doubtful that these witnesses alone, which show consistent adjustment toward MT, can be assumed to point to a primitive reading; they probably arose from haplography in a text identical to that of MT, LXX^B^.

8. *Ishbaal's . . . Ishbaal* In each occurrence MT, LXX^MN^, Syr. correctly have "Ishbosheth." LXX^BAL^ continue with "Mephibosheth."

*vengeance* So MT, LXX^LMN^, Syr. LXX^B^ adds "on his enemies."

*today* MT *hywm hzh.* LXX *hōs hē hēmera autē* reflects *kywm hzh,* "as on this day." Thus the LXX understanding of v. 8b is "Yahweh has granted my lord the king vengeance *on his enemies* (see the preceding *Textual Note*) *as on this day,* on Saul, *your enemy* (see the following *Textual Note*), and on his descendants!" This reflects a Hebrew text that might instead be taken to mean, "May Yahweh grant my lord the king vengeance on his (other) enemies, as (he has) on this day on your enemy Saul and on his descendants!"

*Saul* (2) LXX, in reminiscence of the first part of the verse, adds "your enemy."

10. *who thought of himself* So MT: *whw' . . . b'ynyw,* lit. "and he was in his own eyes." LXX, Syr. reflect *whw' . . . b'yny,* "and he was in *my* eyes."

11. *an innocent man* Syr. omits "innocent." MT, understanding the following phrases, "in his house on his own bed," as restrictive and *'îš-ṣaddîq,* therefore, as determined, affixes *'et-* (for a different explanation see GK[2] §117d). I prefer to omit *'et-,* which is not reflected in LXX or, according to spacing considerations, 4QSam^a^.

*Therefore I shall hold you responsible for his blood* Reading *w'th 'bqš 't dmw mydkm,* lit. "And now I shall seek his blood from your hand . . . ," with LXX, Syr. MT: *w'th hlw',* etc.: "Therefore shall I not hold you responsible for his blood . . . ?"

12. *his soldiers* Reading *n'ryw* with LXX. MT and 4QSam^a^ (*[h]n'rym*) have *hn'rym,* "*the* soldiers." There is no basis for choosing between these alternatives.

*they buried* Reading *qbrw* on the basis of LXX^BALM^ *ethapsan.* MT has *lqḥw wyqbrw,* "they *took and* buried." 4QSam$^a$ has *lqḥ w[yqbr]*, "*he* took and buried" (cf. LXX$^N$ *ethapsen* = *qbr*, "he buried").

*Ishbaal's head* MT, LXX$^{MN}$, OL, Syr. read correctly "Ishbosheth's head." LXX$^{BAL}$ and 4QSam$^a$ (*[r']š mpybšt)* have "Mephibosheth's head."

*in Abiner's grave* Though all witnesses display longer readings, we read *bqbr 'bnr*. LXX$^{BA}$ add *huiou nēr* = *bn nr*—thus, "in the grave of Abiner *son of Ner*"—and it is possible that this reading was original, *bn nr* having fallen out of some MSS after *'bnr*. MT (cf. LXX$^N$) adds *bḥbrwn*—thus, "in Abiner's grave *in Hebron.*" A combination of these expansions—*bqbr 'bnr bn nr bḥbrwn*, "in the grave of Abiner son of Ner in Hebron"—is reflected by LXX$^{LM}$, OL, and, as space considerations require, 4QSam$^a$ (*[bqbr 'bnr bn ]nr bḥ[brwn]*).

# NOTES

4 1. *his courage flagged.* Hebrew *wayyirpû yādāyw*, lit. "(and) his hands hung loose." Steady hands meant confidence, as explained in the NOTE to 2:7. The apparently masculine verb, *wayyirpû*, construed with a feminine dual subject, *yādāyw*, has been explained "from a dislike of using the 3rd plur. fem. imperf." (GK$^2$ §145p). But in the six biblical occurrences of the expression in the imperfect, *yadayim*, "hands," is construed with *yirpû* four times (II Sam 4:1; Zeph 3:16; Neh 6:9; II Chron 15:7) and with *tirpênâ*, the expected feminine plural, only twice. The "masculine" form, in other words, is the rule, not the exception, and we must reckon it possible that it is not masculine at all but common in gender and dual in number. The common dual imperfect in Hebrew seems to have had the form *y/tqṭl(n)*, as also in Ugaritic (cf. *UT*$^4$ §9.15); see *I Samuel*, the NOTE on "went straight ahead" in 6:12.

*all Israel.* That is, the territories ruled by Ishbaal, including Ephraim and Benjamin along with adjoining Gilead and Jezreel, but not Judah. See 2:9 and the NOTE there on "Israel in its entirety."

2–3. *(for Beeroth . . . to this day).* This parenthesis may have been inserted by a later hand. It explains why Rimmon the Beerothite is called a Benjaminite. Beeroth's indigenous population was not, according to biblical tradition, eliminated during the Israelite conquest. The city was part of a tetrapolis, led by Gibeon, that made a treaty with Israel and so survived (Joshua 9; cf. especially v. 17). Thus it is somewhat surprising to find a Beerothite called a Benjaminite, unless the designation is merely formal, based on the official assignment of Beeroth to Benjamin in Josh 18:25. The parenthesis explains that the original population had fled previously and, presumably, were replaced by Benjaminites. We are not told the reason for the flight. Most scholars assume that they left to escape Saul, whose hostility to Gibeon (cf. 21:2) may have extended to all the members of the Gibeonite federation and not alone to Gibeon proper. But the present narrative seems to regard this history as beside the point. According to the story as we have it, the sons of Rimmon are not acting out of some long-standing political resentment against the house of Saul (as supposed, for example, by Noth 1960:186; Blenkinsopp 1972:36; Soggin 1975:47). On the contrary, they are themselves Benjaminites, *not* indigenous Beerothites at all, and are officers in Ishbaal's army. Their treachery is born not of revenge but of crass opportunism and the hope of a reward from David.

2. *Beeroth.* The name *bĕʼērôt* means "Wells" and is identical in form to that of the well-known Phoenician city of Beirut. The best evidence seems now to point to Khirbet el-Burj, four to five miles northwest of Jerusalem and a couple of miles south of el-Jīb, ancient Gibeon, as the site of Beeroth; the ancient name is preserved in that of nearby Khirbet el-Biyâr. See Yeivin 1971:142–44.

3. *Gittaim.* The name, which means "the Double Gath or Winepress," is mentioned elsewhere only in Neh 11:33 as one of the cities repopulated by Benjaminites after the Exile. An identification with the Gath of I Chron 7:21 and 8:13, which does not seem to be the well-known Philistine city of 1:20 (see the NOTE) and elsewhere, has been suggested. For bibliography, see Blenkinsopp 1972:8–9 and 110 nn. 35–37.

4. The introduction of Meribbaal at this point seems purposeless, unless it is intended to make us aware that the line of Saul will not be brought to an end by the assassination that is about to take place. Perhaps this intrusion, which interrupts the flow of the narrative unnecessarily, arose in connection with the confusion over the identity of the "son of Saul" in vv. 1,2 and elsewhere in this passage (cf. the *Textual Note* on "Meribbaal" in v. 4). Josephus, whose text seems to have escaped this confusion, says nothing of Meribbaal at this point (*Ant.* 7.46–47) but reports the information given here at a place in his narrative corresponding to 9:3 (*Ant.* 7.113). It is quite possible that the present verse originally stood there as a part of Ziba's speech (Budde; cf. Carlson 1964:51–52 n. 3). But contrast Wellhausen: "The statement is too distinctive [*eigenthümlich*] to be a gloss, nor is it to be dispensed with as a connective to chap. 9. It has the purpose here to show that after the death of Ishbaal no one of royal descent remained among the tribes of Israel to whom they could offer the kingship, and thus it provides a prerequisite for 5:1."

*Meribbaal.* See the *Textual Note.* The name is either *mĕrîb baʻal* (cf. I Chron 8:34; 9:40) or, perhaps, *mĕrî baʻal* (cf. I Chron 9:40). The former would mean "The lord is advocate," the latter "The lord is my master" (cf. Aramaic *mar,* "master, lord"). In either case I assume that *baʻal,* "(the) lord," refers to Yahweh, as explained in the NOTE on "Ishbaal" in 2:8. The Masoretic vocalizations of the name, *mĕrîb baʻal* (I Chron 8:34 *bis;* 9:40) and *mĕrî baʻal* (I Chron 9:40), seem intended euphemistically as "One who contends with Baal" (cf. Judg 6:32) and "Rebelliousness of Baal," respectively.

7. *the Arabah road.* Also II Kings 25:4 = Jer 52:7; Jer 39:4. This is the way to and from Mahanaim, Ishbaal's capital; cf. 2:29 and the NOTE there on "the Arabah."

10. David refers to the incident described in 1:2–16.

*a man . . . a reward.* Hebrew *ʼăšer lĕtittî-lô bĕśōrâ.* The use of the infinitive is that described in GK[2] §114l. Cf. Driver, who explains, "The clause can hardly express *David's* view of the transaction: he could not think that the Amaleqite really deserved a reward for his tidings: it must express what David ought to have done in the judgment of the Amaleqite himself, or of men in general unable to appreciate David's regard for Saul."

11. *an innocent man.* Compare 1:14–16. In contrast to Saul, Ishbaal is not described as Yahweh's anointed or even as a king. His kingship is not recognized by David, and thus, as Mabee says (1980:104), "the crime is *not* regicide." Our narrator presents David as Saul's successor in Israel, not Ishbaal's (cf. Grønbaek 1971:243).

## COMMENT

After Abiner's death Ishbaal's comes almost as an anticlimax. Abiner was the effective ruler in Israel (2:8–9; 3:6), and it was his death that signaled disaster for the rump government he had set up in Gilead. When the news reached Ishbaal, we are told, "his courage flagged, and all Israel was dismayed" (v. 1). The mood in Mahanaim must have been one of confusion and apprehension. The chance was now negligible that the house of Saul could prevail in its struggle with David for control of central Palestine.

Nevertheless Ishbaal, not Abiner, was king of Israel. While he lived the leaders of the northern tribes had an alternative to accepting David as king. Though it was unlikely that another Abiner would arise soon to reestablish the northern state as a serious military rival to Judah, it would be very awkward politically for David to move toward the throne of Israel while a living son of Saul was sitting upon it. This was especially true if David was, as our narrator insists, reluctant to press his own interests at the expense of the house of Saul, for whom he continued to carry respect and loyalty. So we must think of this last obstacle in the way of David's kingship as an important one.

The extreme defensiveness of the previous section is lacking here—the public circumstances are not as damning to David as in the case of Abiner's assassination—but the tone is apologetic nonetheless. *Cui bono?* It was David who stood to gain most from Ishbaal's death. Did he suborn the sons of Rimmon to commit their treachery? Our narrator controverts any such charge by an account of the events that shows the assassins to have acted on their own initiative. In expecting gratitude from David (cf. v. 8) they misjudged him completely. His true character, as the narrator means us to understand it, is revealed by his outraged response. The crime of the sons of Rimmon, says David, is worse than that of the Amalekite who administered the coup de grace to Saul, for they are "guilty men [who] have slain an innocent man in his own house in his own bed" (v. 11). He has them put to death and their bodies, as the narrator is careful to remind his audience, are publicly displayed. Who could suspect David of collusion after this? Thus the "narrative intentionality" of the account, to use Mabee's phrase, is "effectually to disassociate David from the action of those who have slain his royal counterpart" (Mabee 1980: 107).

At this point there is no king in Israel. The way is now open for David to step into the breach left by the deaths of Saul and Ishbaal. In the next section David will become king of "all Israel" (5:5) as the story of his rise to power nears its end.

# VIII. DAVID BECOMES KING OF ISRAEL
# (5:1–5)

**5** [1]All the staff-bearers of Israel came to David at Hebron to say, "We
are your bone and your flesh! [2]Even formerly, when Saul was king over
us, it was you who led Israel in and out, and it was you to whom
Yahweh said, 'You will shepherd my people, Israel, and you will become prince over Israel.' "

[3]All the elders of Israel came to the king at Hebron. King David
made a pact with them at Hebron before Yahweh, and they anointed
David king over Israel.

[4]David was thirty years old when he became king, and he ruled for
forty years. [5]In Hebron he ruled over Judah for seven years and six
months, and in Jerusalem he ruled for thirty-three years over all Israel
and Judah.

## *TEXTUAL NOTES*

**5** 1. *staff-bearers* See the NOTE. In revocalizing MT *šibṭê*, "tribes," as *šōbĕṭê* we follow Reid 1975:20; see the *Textual Note* at 7:7.

*of Israel* Syr.: "of *the house of* Israel."

*to say* So 4QSam[a], OL, and LXX[MN] (cf. I Chron 11:1): *l'mr.* MT has *wy'mrw l'mr,* "and said, saying," and LXX[BA], Syr. reflect *wy'mrw lw,* "and said to him."

2. *it was you who led . . . in and out* The consonantal text of MT is wrongly divided: *'th hyyth mwṣy' whby.* We read *'th hyyt hmwṣy' whmby(')* with MT *(qĕrê)* and the Masorah (cf. LXX, Syr.). On the omission of the final *'alep* of *whmby,* see Driver and the other examples he cites in which final *'alep* is omitted before a word beginning with *'alep,* as in this case. Note also the shorter, more primitive text of I Chron 11:2 (MT): *'th hmwṣy' whmby'.*

*and it was you to whom Yahweh said* Reading *wlk 'mr yhwh* on the basis of LXX[L] *soi eipen ho kyrios.* Other witnesses reflect the less distinctive *wy'mr yhwh lk,* "and Yahweh said to you."

3. *over Israel* So MT. LXX: "over *all* Israel" (cf. v. 5).

4–5. 4QSam[a] is badly damaged at this point, and only a few scraps of vv. 2–6 survive on the leather. There is enough material extant, however, to show that the scroll lacked anything corresponding to vv. 4 and 5 in MT. This is also the case in OL, which here probably preserves the OG reading (cf. Barthélemy 1980:18). In this regard, then, 4QSam$^a$ and OG share the pattern of I Chronicles 11, the text of which proceeds directly from its equivalent of II Sam 5:3 (I Chron 11:3) to its equivalent of II Sam 5:6 (I Chron 11:4). It is possible, as Barthélemy (1980:17–18) supposes, that vv. 4–5 were suppressed in one textual tradition because of the inexact correspondence of the years of David's reign given in vv. 4 (40) and 5 (7½ + 33). But the chronological notices for the entire period of the united monarchy are suspect; see further the NOTE and Ulrich 1978:60–62.

4. *and* The conjunction, *w-*, has been omitted from MT after *bmlkw*, "when he became king," but it should probably be restored with MT$^{MSS}$ *(BHS)* and LXX, Syr., and Vulg.

5. The translation represents the order of the elements of the verse as it appears in MT, to which LXX$^A$ has been conformed (cf. LXX$^L$). In LXX$^B$ the order is different: "For seven years and six months he ruled in Hebron over Judah, and for thirty-three years he ruled over all Israel and Judah in Jerusalem."

## NOTES

**5** Despite harmonizing attempts to interpret vv. 1–2, on the one hand, and v. 3, on the other, as descriptions of separate, successive interviews between David and differing representative bodies of Israelites (e.g., Hertzberg), most commentators have preferred to see in these verses independent accounts of a single event, redactionally combined. A few have regarded vv. 1–2 as the earlier version (e.g., Budde), but most have considered v. 3 to be older (Nowack, Caird, Ackroyd, etc.). There are several concrete reasons to bracket vv. 1–2 as a secondary addition to the older narrative, of which v. 3 was a part (see Schmidt 1970:124–26; Veijola 1975: 63–66; 1977:70; Kutsch 1979:78). Note, first, the word-for-word duplication of vv. 1a and 3a. Second, there is the anachronism in the Israelites' description of themselves to David as "your bone and your flesh," on which see the NOTE at v. 1 below. Third, and most important, is the contact with chap. 7, the Deuteronomistic capstone of the story of David's rise to power, in the reference to Yahweh's promise in v. 2, as explained in detail in the NOTE there. These two verses, then, belong in the list of Deuteronomistic expansions of the older narrative in anticipation of the oracle of Nathan in chap. 7. This list includes I Sam 25:28b–31; II Sam 3:9–10,18b,28–29; 5:1–2,12; 6:21; and 7 *passim*.

1. *the staff-bearers of Israel.* Hebrew *šōbĕṭê yiśrāʾēl* (see the *Textual Note*), as in 7:7 and 19:10. As pointed out in the NOTE at 7:7, a staff-bearer (**šōbēṭ*) was probably a person who exercised authority over a tribe *(šēbeṭ)*. Here, therefore, "staff-bearers" stands parallel to "elders" (v. 3), on whom see the NOTE at 3:17.

*"We are your bone and your flesh!"* This expression asserts blood kinship (Gen 29:14), which might be cited as a basis for political loyalty (Judg 9:2). From the perspective of our oldest materials, however, Judahite parentage would not qualify a

man as a kinsman of the Israelites, as shown by a passage later in our story (19:13) where David himself addresses the elders of Judah as "my bone and my flesh" in specific *contrast* to "all Israel." This is another indication, therefore, of the insertion of vv. 1 and 2 by a Deuteronomistic writer, from whose much later perspective the kinship of a native of Judah to "all the tribes of Israel" would hardly seem questionable.

2. *it was you who led Israel in and out.* Hebrew *'attâ hāyîtā hammôṣî' wĕhammēbî' 'et-yiśrā'ēl* (see the *Textual Note*). The expression *yāṣā' ûbā',* "go out and in" (I Sam 18:13; 29:6; cf. II Sam 5:24 below), refers to the activity of a soldier in battle (cf. Josh 14:11; etc.). To this, *hôṣî' wĕhēbî',* the causative of the same expression, adds a specific connotation of leadership (cf. Num 27:11), and this is the sense here. The Israelites are saying that even when Saul was king, it was David who exercised the military leadership appropriate to the royal office. The reference is generally to the situation described in I Sam 18:9–16, according to which Saul, his pathological jealousy and suspicion of David growing every day, sent the younger man away from court, giving him a military command "so that he went out and came in before the army" (v. 13). According to vv. 14–16, "David was successful in all his undertakings, for Yahweh was with him; and although Saul, seeing how successful he was, lived in fear of him, all Israel and Judah loved him, since it was he who went out and came in before them."

*it was you to whom Yahweh said. . . .* We know of no previous oracle with such a message. Budde and Eissfeldt (1931:27) assume that this was part of the content of the lost oracle of Ahimelech, the priest of Nob, referred to in I Sam 23:10 (cf. v. 13), but it seems more likely that this statement is an indicator of the Deuteronomistic origin of these two verses (see the NOTE on vv. 1–2 above). As the following NOTES show, the words of the oracle have specific verbal contacts with the Deuteronomistically revised words of Nathan in chap. 7.

*You will shepherd my people.* Cf. 7:7. Schmidt (1970:124) points out that only in these two passages is the verb *ra'â,* "shepherd," used in the sense of "rule" in Samuel-Kings.

*you will become prince.* Hebrew *'attâ tihyeh lĕnāgîd,* to which compare 7:8. Schmidt (1970:124–25) notes that the expression *hāyâ lĕnāgîd,* "become prince," occurs only in these two passages and I Kings 1:35 (where, however, it is preceded by the verb *ṣiwwâ,* "command"); elsewhere the expressions used are "anoint as prince" (*māšaḥ lĕnāgîd,* I Sam 9:16; 10:1 [*bis*]), "command to be prince" (*ṣiwwâ lĕnāgîd,* I Sam 13:14; 25:30), or "appoint as prince" (*nātan nāgîd,* I Kings 14:7; 16:2). For *nāgîd,* "prince, king-designate," see *I Samuel,* pp. 178–79 (the NOTE on "prince" at 9:16) and the NOTE at 7:8 in the present volume.

3. *the elders of Israel.* On this group see the NOTE at 3:17, where we learned of Abiner's efforts, apparently futile at the time, to bring the present moment to pass.

*King David made a pact with them.* The evident meaning is that David bound himself formally to certain contractual obligations toward the Israelites. See Fohrer 1959 and Mettinger 1976:114–15,137–41.

*they anointed David king.* See the NOTE on "anointed" at 2:4a, where "the men of Judah," who must be the southern equivalent of "the elders of Israel" in the present passage (Mettinger 1976:198), make David king of Judah. Here there seems to be a certain reciprocity between the covenant David makes, with its contractual promises to the elders (see the preceding NOTE), and their anointing him king (so Mettinger 1976:139).

4–5. To these chronological data compare 2:10a and 11, the notices on the independent reigns of Ishbaal and David. The present passage exhibits the stereotyped pattern of the Deuteronomistic notices on the accessions of the kings of Israel and Judah (I Kings 14:21; 22:42; etc.); it is, in contrast to 2:11, "the formulaic introduction to the reign of David" (Noth 1981:55). But see the NOTE on 2:10a,11, where the possibility is raised that the present notice (missing from the texts of OG, 4QSam$^a$, and I Chronicles 11; cf. the *Textual Note*) and others like it pertaining to the period of the united monarchy were not original parts of the Deuteronomistic framework of Samuel-Kings but were instead very late additions to the text in the spirit of the authentically Deuteronomistic notices that pertain to the reigns of the kings of the divided monarchy.

4. *thirty years . . . forty years.* Round numbers not likely to be accurate. Forty years is an admirably long time to reign, and it must have seemed fitting to some ancient chronographer that David (cf. I Kings 2:11) and Solomon (I Kings 11:42) each ruled precisely that long. Similarly, we note that the years of David's life were seventy—the standard "threescore years and ten" of the psalmist (Ps 90:10 [AV]). The modern reader cannot be accused of unreasonable skepticism if he raises an eyebrow at such figures.

5. *Jerusalem.* The account of the capture and rebuilding of David's new capital city follows immediately.

## COMMENT

The original narrative is represented by only a couple of sentences. Verses 1 and 2 are Deuteronomistic expansion, looking ahead to Nathan's oracle in chap. 7 and to 7:7–8 in particular (see the NOTES on vv. 1–2 above). Verses 4 and 5 are also secondary, providing chronological data on the reign of David (cf. the NOTE on vv. 4–5). Only v. 3 was a part of our oldest account of David's rise to power. Brief as it is, however, it is highly significant, for here is the climax to which the story has been building since its beginning, when David came to Saul's court as a musician and royal weapon-bearer (I Sam 16:14–23). David is king of Israel now, and with a final repetition of its central theological claim (5:10; see § IX) the narrative, its argument complete, can draw to a close.

The report of David's anointment seems almost laconic in its brevity. The attention to detail that characterized the account of the assassination of Abiner or, to a lesser degree, that of the death of Ishbaal is missing here. But it is not our narrator's purpose to celebrate David's kingship. Instead he wants, as we have seen, to absolve David from any suspicion of wrongdoing in the course of his ascent to the royal office. To this end he has presented David throughout as a man innocent of overweening ambition, whose extraordinary successes result less often from self-interested undertakings of his own than from the willing deeds of others—the men of Judah (2:4), Achish of Gath (I Sam 27:5;

cf. 29:6), Jonathan (I Sam 19:4; 20:9; 23:16; etc.), Michal (I Sam 19:11–17), Saul himself (I Sam 16:21–22), and still others—whose affection and loyalty he seems to command naturally—or rather supernaturally, by the will of Yahweh. The present episode is not an exception to this pattern. There is nothing here to suggest that David has made any prior contact with the elders of Israel asserting his claims to the throne. Abiner's negotiations described in 3:17–18a might be supposed to have laid the groundwork for the Israelite leaders' acceptance of a Judahite king, but the narrative leaves us no warrant for believing that David owed his kingship to Abiner, who died before his schemes could bear fruit (cf. Grønbaek 1971:240), and in any case we were shown that Abiner was not acting at David's instigation. As our narrator presents it, then, the initiative for the anointing of David is on the side of the elders of Israel. They come to Hebron and offer the kingship freely, and David passively accepts.

# IX. THE CAPTURE OF JERUSALEM (5:6–10)

5 ⁶Then the king and his men went to Jerusalem, to the Jebusites, the inhabitants of the region; but they told David, "You shall not come in here!" (For the blind and the lame had incited them, saying, "David shall not come in here!") ⁷So David seized the stronghold of Zion, which is now the City of David, ⁸and [he] said at that time, "Whoever smites a Jebusite, let him strike at the windpipe, for David hates the lame and the blind!" (This is the reason it is said, "No one who is blind or lame shall come into the temple.")

⁹David occupied the stronghold and called it the City of David. He built a city around it from the Millo inward.

¹⁰David continued to grow greater and greater, because Yahweh Sabaoth was with him.

## *TEXTUAL NOTES*

5 6. *the king* So MT, $LXX^{L}$, OL. $LXX^{B}$ (cf. I Chron 11:4 [MT]): "David"; Syr.: "King David."

*and his men* So MT, $LXX^{BA}$, $4QSam^{a}$. $LXX^{LMN}$, OL: "and *all* his men."

*but they told* Reading *wy'mr* with MT, LXX. The translation is plural because the implicit subject is the collective *haybûsî*, "the Jebusites," of the earlier part of the verse—thus I Chron 11:5, *wayyō'mĕrû yōšĕbê yĕbûs*, "But *the inhabitants of Jebus* said. . . ." In the present passage OL, Syr., and $Targ.^{MSS}$ represent the verb as plural. Watson (1970), rejecting the collective interpretation, takes *haybûsî* as the Jebusite ruler *(yōšēb)* of the city and renders *wayyō'mer* "and he said."

*For* Reading *ky* with $4QSam^{a}$ and LXX *(hoti)*. MT has *ky 'm*, "but, on the contrary" ($GK^{2}$ §163a) or "except that, unless" ($GK^{2}$ §163c). See the following *Textual Note.*

*had incited them* An old crux on which $4QSam^{a}$ sheds new light. MT reads *hĕsîrĕkā*, as if the clause might be taken as part of the speech of the Jebusites and understood to mean "except that/on the contrary (see the preceding *Textual Note*) the blind and the lame will turn you away." But there are problems of number and tense with this interpretation. A singular verb with "the blind and the lame" as subject is most awkward, and we should expect an imperfect. Accordingly, Wellhausen proposed an emendation to *yĕsîrūkā*. An alternative interpretation (Klostermann) takes the clause to mean "except thou take away the blind and the lame" (AV). But again there are problems. We expect a finite verb rather than an infinitive after *kî 'im* (Driver), and "the blind and the lame" is not marked as accusative (Smith). LXX has *antestēsan*, "stood in opposition," pointing to a text that understood the clause as not belonging to the speech of the Jebusites—thus, "for the blind and the lame stood in opposition" —but what Hebrew original this might correspond to has proved elusive (cf. Smith). 4QSam[a] seems to preserve the primitive reading and (probably) the original of LXX *antestēsan*. The scroll reads *hsyt*[*w*], showing that the clause is not to be understood as part of the Jebusites' speech but rather as explanatory of it: "for the blind and the lame had incited them" (the object is understood) or, colloquially, "had put them up to it." See also the NOTE on vv. 6–8 and the second NOTE at v. 6. MT *hsyrk* is probably to be explained as the result of graphic confusion of *-t(w)* and *-rk*.

8. *at the windpipe* MT *baṣṣinnôr;* see the NOTE. LXX[(B)] *en paraxiphidi*, "with a dagger," may point to *bṣwr* understood as *baṣṣôr* in light of the noun *ṣōr*, "(flint) knife" (Exod 4:25; cf. II Sam 2:16 and the *Textual Note* at 2:16 on "Flints' "). Syr. *bskr'* reflects *bṣnh*, "on the shield." Unfortunately 4QSam[a] is damaged at this point (*b*[ ]).

*for David hates the lame and the blind* We read *w't hpsḥym w't h'wrym śn'h npš dwd*. In some witnesses (LXX[MN], Syr., 4QSam[a]) the order of the objects is reversed (cf. 5:6 and, below, v. 8b); see Ulrich 1978:128–29. Most attempt to construe the objects with *(w)yg'*, "then let him strike" (cf. the preceding *Textual Note*), and some, accordingly, omit the initial conjunction (e.g., Syr.). Similarly, in many witnesses *śn'h*, which is preserved in 4QSam[a] (cf. Syr., Targ.), has become *śn'y* (= *śĕnū'ê;* so MT [*qĕrê*]), "those hated by," or *hśn'y* (= *haśśōnĕ'ê*, as reflected by LXX *tous misountas*), "those who hate"—thus, "then let him strike . . . the lame and the blind, *those hated by/those who hate* David."

*the temple* So MT: *hbyt*, "the house." LXX makes it explicit that "the house" thus referred to is the temple, reading "the house *of Yahweh*."

9. *He built a city* The primitive reading is preserved in 4QSam[a]: *w*[*y*]*bnh 'yr*. This was read also by LXX (LXX[L] reflects *wybn h'yr* [so I Chron 11:8], in consequence of a misdivision of the words), which interpreted *wybnh* as *wayyibnāh*, "He built *it* (viz. the City of David)"; but *wybnh* (*pace* Wellhausen) is to be read *wayyibneh*, a rare but well-attested (Josh 19:50; I Kings 18:32; II Chron 26:6) long form of the much more common *wayyiben*, which MT reads here. For *'yr* MT has, by graphic confusion, *dwd* —thus, "*David* built."

*from the Millo* Omitted by Syr.

*inward* That is, *wābáyitāh*. LXX reads the same consonantal text as *ûbêtô*, "and his house" (cf. v. 11 below).

10. *Yahweh Sabaoth* Reading *yhwh ṣb'wt* with LXX[(B)] and 4QSam[a]. MT (cf. LXX[A]) has *yhwh 'lhy ṣb'wt*, "Yahweh, *the god of* armies."

## NOTES

5 6–8. These very difficult verses contain obscure references that have exercised the ingenuity of interpreters since ancient times. Among the modern literature we should mention especially the studies of Bressan (1944), Stoebe (1957), Glück (1966), and Brunet (1979a, 1979b), in addition to others cited below. In my opinion the problems here were compounded when an old account, which had become obscure to a later audience, was enlarged epexegetically. Specifically, a brief description of the siege of Jerusalem has been expanded twice. The original account is found in vv. 6abα + 7–8a. The expansions in 6bβ and 8b appear here in parentheses. The first of these (6bβ) arose because of confusion over the meaning of the word *ṣinnôr* in v. 8. The meaning intended was "windpipe" or "gullet, throat" (see below), but this was forgotten in later times, as the witnesses to the text demonstrate (see the *Textual Note* on "at the windpipe" in v. 8). With the loss of the meaning of *ṣinnôr* David's command to "strike at the windpipe" became obscure; it may have been reinterpreted as "strike at the water channel," an understanding reflected in some of the ancient witnesses and the studies of many modern commentators (see the NOTE on "the windpipe" in v. 8). But at this point the clause "for David hates the lame and the blind," originally an explanation of the command to deliver only fatal blows ("strike at the windpipe"), seemed inexplicable. What did David have against the lame and the blind? Verse 6bβ represents an ancient attempt at a solution to the problem. David hated the lame and the blind because it was they who had incited (*hēsîtû;* cf. the *Textual Note* on "had incited them," v. 6) the Jebusites against him. Thus v. 6bβ arose as an epexegetical annotation and was retained in the textual tradition of MT; it is missing in I Chron 11:5, which in this case represents the primitive situation. The second expansion of this passage (v. 8b) is recognized as such by nearly all modern commentators. It interprets a practice current in the time of the annotation in light of the incident described in the passage (see below).

6. *the king and his men.* Contrast the Chronicler's idealized version: "David and all Israel" (so MT at I Chron 11:4, where LXX preserves the primitive reading found in MT in II Sam 5:6). Herrmann (1981:154–55): "David did not take possession of the city with the help of the armies of either Judah or Israel, but with his own mercenaries alone. . . . He won the city for himself by his own means, which on the one hand guaranteed him military success and on the other excluded the claims and privileges of others, from wherever these might be sought."

*the Jebusites.* The name, according to biblical tradition, of the pre-Israelite inhabitants of Jerusalem. They are regarded as a people of Canaanite origin (Gen 10:16; cf. Josephus, *Ant.* 7.61), most closely associated with the Amorites (Josh 10:5; cf. Num 13:29). When the Israelites conquered Canaan, we are told, the Jebusites were not driven out (Josh 15:63; Judg 1:21); they maintained their control of Jerusalem until the time of David (cf. Judg 19:10–12). The notion that the city itself was once called Jebus (Judg 19:10,11; I Chron 11:4,5) is not supported by extrabiblical evidence, in which the name Jerusalem is attested in the third and throughout the second millennia B.C. (cf. Josh 10:5).

*(For . . . "David shall not come in here!").* The parenthesis is secondary. As explained in the NOTE on vv. 6–8, it is an attempt to supply a motive for David's aversion to the lame and the blind, the mention of which in v. 8 seemed pointless after it was forgotten that *ṣinnôr* meant "windpipe" and thus that David was commanding his men to deliver only fatal blows. As A. Finklestein has pointed out to me, the Jewish exegetes of the Middle Ages came to the conclusion that "the lame and the blind" were two idols, deprecating images of Jacob (cf. Gen 32:31) and Isaac (cf. Gen 27:1) placed on the walls by the Jebusites to remind the Israelites of a covenant they allegedly had broken (cf. Pirke Rabbi Eliezer 36). In Gersonides' commentary on our passage these idols became fearsome fighting robots that were hydraulically operated and could therefore be rendered useless by an attack on the water supply (*ṣinnôr,* v. 8). Those modern scholars who take v. 6b$\beta$ as an original part of the story, eliminated secondarily from I Chron 11:5, have proposed a variety of interpretations of its significance. These proposals, all of which are based on the received Hebrew text (*kî 'im hĕsîrĕkā,* etc.; see the *Textual Notes* on "For" and "had incited them"), include the following:

1) It is an arrogant boast by the Jebusites, who tell David that he cannot enter: "On the contrary, the blind and the lame will turn you away." That is, the city is so strong that its blind and lame citizens will suffice to drive off David. This was the interpretation of Josephus (*Ant.* 7.61) and Kimchi, and it has found a number of modern adherents (Caird, McKane, Hertzberg, and Ravenna 1956; cf. Ackroyd).

2) It refers to an attempt to protect the city by magic and sorcery. Heller (1965) suggests that the lame are taboo cultic personnel of the Jebusite shrine. They are stationed on the wall on the assumption that the Israelites will respect the taboo and thus be barred from storming the stronghold, but David, being "gottlos" as far as Canaanite ritual rules are concerned, is not deterred. Somewhat differently, Yadin (1963:267–70) compares the role of the infirm in a Hittite ritual oath taken by soldiers before battle as described in a tablet found at Boghazkoy (*ANET*[3] 353–54). After an oath of loyalty to the king and queen has been sworn, a number of objects and people, including a blind woman and a deaf man, are paraded before the troops to conjure blindness, deafness, and other afflictions on any man who might break his oath. In the present case, then, the blind and the lame are instruments of a ritual defense of the city. They provide incentive to the Jebusites who defend the city and intimidation to the attackers. In an elaboration of this interpretation Brunet (1979a) supposes that a prior alliance between David and the Jebusites existed involving an oath of nonaggression of which the blind and the lame are instruments or at least reminders of the sanctions to be imposed if David violates the oath and enters the city. Brunet (pp. 70–71) paraphrases the Jebusites' warning to David in v. 6b: "You shall not enter our premises by force, for you cannot put aside the guarantees and instruments of the oaths you have taken. These guarantees, these powerful instruments, they are there. Your men cannot enter the city without clashing with them, and the first one who touches them will become blind or lame!"

3) It refers to those among David's own troops who are like blind and lame men in the presence of the impregnable fortress. These must be "put aside," say the taunting Jebusites, before David can hope to conquer the city. This is the proposal of Stoebe (1957; criticized by Hertzberg).

7. *the stronghold of Zion . . . the City of David.* The pre-Israelite city lay at the southeast corner of later Jerusalem, occupying the crest of a single hill overlooking the Kidron Valley and the Spring Gihon, the only perennial source of fresh water in the area, to the east. The hill was well fortified; archeology has exposed the east wall of the Jebusite city and shown it to have remained in use from the Middle Bronze Age to the eighth century B.C. (see Kenyon 1974:83–97; Mazar 1976:1–2). This hilltop, then, was "the stronghold of Zion" or "the City of David" in the strict sense (cf. I Kings 8:1; II Chron 5:2); but as the city was extended, first north beyond the Ophel to include the temple mount (the present-day Ḥarām esh-Sherîf) and then west, the names "Zion" and "City of David" came to be used more broadly. On David's renaming of the city, see the NOTE at v. 9 below.

8. At this point in the account of the Chronicler, who has nothing to say about the lame and the blind, another incident is reported. "David said, 'Whoever smites a Jebusite first shall become commander-in-chief *(lĕrōʾš ûlĕśār)*'; and Joab son of Zeruiah went up first and became chief" (I Chron 11:6). Compare Judg 10:18; 11:11. We learn elsewhere that Joab was "in charge of the army" *(ʿal-haṣṣābāʾ)* in David's administration (II Sam 18:16; 20:23; I Chron 18:15); that is, he was David's "commander of the army" (*śar-ṣābāʾ*: II Sam 19:14; I Chron 27:34; cf. II Sam 24:2 MT). This passage seems to explain how he attained his position. Many historians regard it as a scrap of accurate information (contrast Ward 1967:178–79), though some are troubled by the fact that Joab seems already to have been in charge of David's armies at an earlier time (cf. 2:13; etc.), a detail that causes Mazar (1963a:241) to suppose that the capture of Jerusalem actually took place much earlier, before David's war with Ishbaal.

*the windpipe.* Hebrew *ṣinnôr.* In Rabbinic Hebrew the word meant "(water) pipe, spout, duct" (Jastrow 1291), and many modern commentators, following Vincent (1924), have assumed that its meaning here is the same or nearly the same. Specifically, they identify the *ṣinnôr* with a vertical shaft discovered by Charles Warren in 1867; it was cut by the Jebusites in the Late Bronze Age to provide access to the Spring Gihon (see the preceding NOTE) from within the city. Thus we might read, "Whoever would smite the Jebusites, let him get up the water shaft . . ." (RSV), or, better, since there is nothing in the text corresponding to "get up," "Whoever would smite the Jebusites, let him strike at the water shaft!" The meaning would be that the *ṣinnôr* was the single vulnerable point in the city's defenses, either because it offered access to the city from the outside or possibly, as Brunet (1979b) argues, because it could be attacked at its lower stage, at the "overflow" (as Brunet [p. 80] understands *ṣinnôr*) of the spring, which could be diverted in such a way as to drain the city's water source. The assumption that *ṣinnôr* refers to Warren's shaft, therefore, is entirely plausible in itself. As we have seen, however, it leaves the succeeding reference to the lame and the blind meaningless. The same difficulty besets the explanation of the passage that interprets *ṣinnôr* as some kind of tool or weapon in light of Aramaic *ṣinnôrāʾ*, "hook." Sukenik's view (1928), taken up also in his son's work (Yadin [Sukenik] 1963:268), was that *ṣinnôr* refers to a particular weapon, specifically a trident, to be used in the siege. Others have thought of a siege instrument, perhaps a grapnel—thus NEB reads, "Everyone who would kill a Jebusite, let him use his grappling-iron. . . ." Still other scholars have thought it likely that *ṣinnôr* refers to a body part. Wellhausen demonstrated the possibility that it means "throat," the interpretation upon which my understanding of the passage is also based (see below). Budde argued for "neck" on the basis of an emended text (reading *ṣwrw*, "his own neck"); he assumed that David's words are a warning intended to *protect* the Jebusites ("Anyone who smites a Jebusite risks [lit. 'strikes at'] his own neck!"). Albright concluded in 1922 that *ṣinnôr* means "joint"—thus, ". . . let him strike a joint!"; David, according to Albright, intends every Jebusite to be lamed. Glück (1966) has argued ingeniously that *ṣinnôr* means "phallus" and thus that David is placing his soldiers under an oath made by touching the genitals ("let him touch the phallus") as in Gen 24:2 and 47:29. The correct solution, in my opinion, is precisely opposite to that attempted by Albright. David wants *no* Jebusite lamed or blinded, for the lame and the blind are loathsome to him. Whoever strikes a Jebusite, therefore, must strike at the windpipe or throat and, therefore, deliver a fatal blow. As Wellhausen points out, "throat" is a natural semantic extension of a word meaning "pipe, spout, duct." In tenth-century B.C. Hebrew the range of meaning of *ṣinnôr* must have included "(wind)pipe, gullet," and thus "throat." The force of David's command, then, is that the Jebusites who are struck down are to be slain, not mutilated and left alive. See further the NOTE that follows.

*David hates the lame and the blind.* This is the reason for the command to strike only lethal blows. David does not wish to take control of a city filled with crippled and blinded men. Note the syntax of this clause, which reads literally, "but the lame and the blind the soul of David hates." "The lame and the blind" stands in the emphatic first position, offering a contrast to what precedes. We may paraphrase David's words as follows: "Whoever strikes down a Jebusite must deal a fatal blow, for otherwise the city will be filled with mutilated men whom we have wounded but not slain, and I find such men intolerable." David's aversion to "the lame and the blind" is not, we may assume, simply a matter of personal sensibility, still less of callous convenience or a lack of charity. Instead, the remark is probably intended to reflect religious scruples against the mutilation of living human beings, a violation of the sanctity of the body to which David finds killing preferable. To this extent, therefore, the annotator responsible for the parenthesis that follows was justified in associating David's remarks with the exclusion of the disfigured from the temple (see the following NOTE). We should also remember that Jerusalem, being a Palestinian city, was subject to the ban *(ḥērem)*, at least according to its rules as they were later formulated (Deut 20:10–18), so that its people were supposed to be put to death when the city was captured by Israelites. It may be that the ban in some form is operative here and David's words refer to its imposition.

*(This . . . the temple.).* Verse 8b is a secondary parenthesis offering an explanation of a practice current in the time of its author on the basis of the events described here. Priests with bodily defects were disqualified from service at the altar (Lev 21:16–23), and at least in certain cases a mutilated person was excluded from public worship altogether (cf. Deut 23:2 [23:1]). Such regulations had their origin in the complex of Israelite beliefs regarding purity and holiness, not in some historical precedent involving a hero of the past, as supposed by the author of this annotation.

9. *the City of David.* Several examples of the renaming of a city in one's own honor, especially a captured and/or capital city, are known from the ancient Near East. Sargon II (721–705 B.C.), for example, the scion of the Sargonid branch of the Assyrian royal family, under whose kings the Neo-Assyrian empire reached its greatest extent, founded a new capital at modern Khorsabad, which he called *dūr šarru-kīn*, "Sargons-

burg." Mazar (1963a:238 n. 7) mentions "Tukulti-Ninurta City," the new capital of another Assyrian monarch, Tukulti-Ninurta I (ca. 1244–1208); and still other examples could be listed.

*the Millo.* Hebrew *hammillô',* that is, "the Fill." This must refer to a major earthwork of some kind, a rampart perhaps or a platform produced by filling in a ravine (cf. Simons 1952:131–37). Kenyon (1974:100–3) identifies the Millo with the Jebusite terracing she found on the eastern slope of the stronghold of Zion. These were stamped-earth structures added to support houses on the downward slope of the city as part of a general expansion of building in the Late Bronze Age (Kenyon 1974:94–95). If this identification is correct, we need not regard the present reference to the Millo as anachronistic (so Hertzberg and others); the description of Solomon's building activities may be understood to refer to a *re*building of the Millo (I Kings 9:15,24), or perhaps to an expansion of its extent in the time of his father (I Kings 11:27).

At this point the Chronicler supplies a further detail: "And Joab salvaged (*yĕḥayyeh;* cf. Neh 3:34[4:2]) the rest of the city" (I Chron 11:8).

10. A final reiteration of the theological leitmotiv of the story of David's rise. See the COMMENT.

## COMMENT

David, having united Israel and Judah under his rule, leads an armed expedition to Jerusalem, a city located between the two states but belonging to neither. The Jebusites, Jerusalem's indigenous inhabitants, forbid entry to David, but he captures the citadel, the stronghold of Zion, and renames it the City of David. Those Jebusites who resist are put to death (v. 8), and the city is occupied and rebuilt as the new capital of David's kingdom.

Historians have duly pointed out the advantages Jerusalem offered as a capital city. It was centrally located and therefore could be hoped to be acceptable to both Judah and Israel. "Hebron," writes Bright (1972:195; cf. Noth 1960:189–90), "located far to the south and on Judahite soil, could not have been permanently acceptable as a capital to the northern tribes. But a capital in the north would have been doubly unacceptable to Judah. Jerusalem, centrally located between the sections and within the territory of none of the tribes, offered an excellent compromise." For the same reasons the new capital would be a place from which the united territories could be ruled with relatively little interference from northern or southern factions, especially since the city had been captured by "the king and his men," i.e., David's personal militia, apparently without the help of troops conscripted from Judah or Israel (see the first NOTE at v. 6 above). In such a location the new government might take root and grow strong, extending the royal authority to the most distant of David's dominions while maintaining a single, autonomous center of power.

Such considerations as these must have been in David's mind when he determined to eliminate the old Jebusite enclave from the midst of his newly united kingdom, but the narrator of our account of the siege has nothing to say on this subject. His purpose is to report with a minimum of detail only that Jerusalem *was* captured by David as the final episode in the long story of his ascent to the throne of Israel. The climax of this story has already been reached (5:3), and the writer does not want the conclusion to be long delayed.

### *The End of the Story of David's Rise*

This brings us to a consideration of v. 10. "David continued to grow greater and greater," we read there, "because Yahweh Sabaoth was with him." The finality in this statement is unmistakable. It encapsulates subsequent events in a single, propitious remark while offering a final reiteration of the theological leitmotiv that runs through the story, "Yahweh was with [David]" (I Sam 16:18; 18:14,28; cf. McCarter 1980b:503–4). Rost, in his programmatic description of the story of David's rise (1926), argued that the original narrative ended in chap. 5, and subsequent opinion has tended to agree, most often identifying v. 10 itself as the precise end point (Grønbaek 1971:29–35; etc.). Those who differ (e.g., Mettinger 1976:41–45) generally do so on the basis of an analysis of the material that includes in the original narrative several passages (I Sam 25:28b–31; II Sam 3:9–10,18b [cf. 3:28–29]; 5:1–2; cf. Mettinger 1976:35–38,44–45) that look ahead to the promises made David in II Samuel 7, which might therefore be regarded as the conclusion to the story of David's rise. However, our analysis suggests that II Samuel 7 and the passages that anticipate it belong to the framework of the larger Deuteronomistic history and that Nathan's oracle, although it probably incorporates older material, includes nothing that was part of the original story of David's rise as we have described it (see the COMMENT on 7:1–29). It is true that from the perspective of the text in its present, Deuteronomistically edited form chap. 7 can be considered the conclusion, indeed the capstone, of the story of David's rise. But the original, much older narrative said nothing of an eternal kingship or a dynastic promise, the central themes of Nathan's oracle; it attempted nothing more than to demonstrate the legitimacy of David's succession of Saul and, more especially, David's innocence of any wrongdoing in the course of his ascent to the throne (cf. *I Samuel*, pp. 27–30, and McCarter 1980b *passim*).

Nor can any of the various other materials collected in chaps. 5–8 be regarded with confidence as an original part of this old apologetic document. The notice about Hiram's benefaction in 5:11–12 seems to be an isolated fragment attracted to a position following the statement that David rebuilt the Millo (5:9b) because of its own reference to building in Jerusalem (see the COMMENT on § X). The information inserted at 5:13–16 and 8:15–18 is clearly annalistic data of the sort found also in 3:2–5. The rest of chap. 8 (vv. 1–14) is a miscellany on the subject of David's victories, presented for the most part in summary form (see further the COMMENT on § XVII). All of this (5:11–16; 8:1–18) was gathered by an editor, most probably the Deuteronomistic historian himself, and inserted in its present position following the notice of David's accession. So there remain only the report of David's Philistine wars in 5:17–25 and the account of the transfer of the ark to Jerusalem in chap. 6 to be accounted for. These materials do, in fact, display points of contact with the story of David's rise in its original form. The use of the oracle in 5:19, for example, is strongly reminiscent of the events of 2:1 or, more especially, I Sam 23:2 (cf. vv. 9–12) and 30:7–8. The appearance of Michal in 6:20–23 harks back to 3:13–16 and beyond (I Sam 18:20–27; 19:11–17). But our discussion of §§ XII–XV will suggest reasons to regard 5:17–6:23 as old but independent material. The report of the battle at Baal-perazim (5:17–21) might possibly have belonged at one time to the story of David's rise, but even if it did it has been dislodged from its original location (see the COMMENT on § XII). It now stands together with 5:22–25 as a necessary introduction to the account of the transfer of the ark from Kiriath-jearim in chap. 6, which was not possible before the Philistines had been driven back "from Geba to Gezer" (5:25), and this account, 6:1–19, is itself an example of a known ancient Near Eastern category of literature, viz. "the historical chronicles that record the return of despoiled images by victorious monarchs" (cf. Miller and Roberts 1977:23), not a part of the royal apology of I Sam 16:14–II Sam 5:10 (see the COMMENT on § XIV).

It seems possible, therefore, to sustain the old opinion that the auspicious phrases of II Sam 5:10 represent the conclusion to the original account of David's rise to power. The narrator has completed his task, having traced the tortuous route from the pastures of Bethlehem to the stronghold of Zion by way of Gibeah, the wilderness of Judah, Ziklag, and Hebron, and having—at least to his own satisfaction—exonerated David from any suspicion of wrongdoing along the way. What follows does not come from this writer's hand. We enter now upon a collection of materials of various kinds, all dealing with the reign of David.

# X. HIRAM'S MISSION
## (5:11–12)

5 [11]Hiram king of Tyre sent messengers to David with cedar, carpenters, and builders, and they built a house for David. [12]Then David knew that Yahweh had established him as king over Israel and had exalted his kingship for the sake of his people Israel.

## *TEXTUAL NOTES*

5 11. *and builders* That is, *wḥršy qyr,* lit. "and craftsmen of wall(s)." "Wall" is read by 4QSam[a] *(qyṙ),* $LXX^{L}$ ($oc_2e_2$ *toichou,* but b *toichou lithōn*) and OL *(parietum);* cf. also I Chron 14:1 and Josephus, *Ant.* 7.66. $LXX^{BMN}$ offer an alternative, viz. *lithōn* = *'bn(ym),* "stone(s)"—thus, "and stoneworkers, masons." These variants are combined in the texts of MT *('bn qyr),* Syr. *(dk'p' d'st'),* and $LXX^{A}$ *(lithōn toichou).* See further Talmon 1960:167; Cross 1964:293; Ulrich 1978:99–100.

12. *had exalted his kingship* So MT: *niśśē' mamlaktô.* The versions (LXX *epērthē hē basileia autou,* Syr. *'ttrymt mlkwth,* Targ. *mnṭl' mlkwtyh*) share the reading of I Chron 14:2, *niśśē't . . . malkûtô,* "his kingship was exalted" (i.e., *nś't mlktw* for *nś' mmlktw;* cf. Wellhausen).

*for the sake of his people Israel* OL: "over *(supra* = *'l)* the land of Israel, his people."

## NOTES

5 11. *Hiram.* Apart from the biblical references to Hiram, we are dependent for information about the early kings of Tyre on Josephus' citations of Menander of Ephesus in *Contra Ap.* 1.116–26 and *Ant.* 8.144–46. There Hiram's reign is described as long and successful, a time of building, especially of temple precincts, and foreign conquest. In the Bible he appears as a contemporary of Solomon as well as David. In I Kings 5:15–26 [5:1–12]—a passage cast in Deuteronomistic terminology (Noth 1981: 58) but probably based on ancient material (cf. Fensham 1969:75–76)—we are told that

it was on the basis of Tyre's prior amity with Davidic Israel ("Hiram had always loved David," v. 15 [1]) that Hiram provided Solomon with the craftsmen and materials for the temple (vv. 15–24 [1–10]) in return for annual supplies of food (v. 25 [11]), and the two made a formal treaty (v. 26 [12]). For the chronological questions raised by the present position of vv. 11–12, see the COMMENT. On the chronology of Tyre early in the Iron Age, see Liver 1953; also Cross 1972a:17 n. 11 and bibliography cited there.

*Tyre.* The Iron Age capital of the Phoenicians—or, as they were called by the earlier biblical writers (I Kings 5:20 [5:6]), by Homer (Iliad 23.743) and by themselves (*KAI* 31.1), the Sidonians. The modern town of Ṣûr lies on the Lebanese coast less than fifty miles south of Beirut.

*cedar.* Phoenician cedar was prized all over the ancient world. Mesopotamian kings were carrying it home to panel their temples as early as the third millennium B.C., and the people of Byblos were exporting it to Egypt as early as the fourth. By the time of Hiram and David the Lebanon was largely deforested, so that the gift was all the more precious. The reference here to the building of David's cedar house prepares us for 7:2 (see the COMMENT).

12. *established him as king . . . exalted his kingship.* The language (*hĕkînô*, "established him"; *mamlaktô*, "his kingship") anticipates that of chap. 7, especially v. 12, where Yahweh promises to "raise up [David's] offspring . . . and establish his kingship" (*wahăkînōtî 'et-mamlaktô);* cf. Carlson 1964:57,119. This is dynastic language (cf. I Sam 13:13–14) and, accordingly, has no place in the oldest account of David's rise to power (Grønbaek 1971:33,257–58); the entire verse (5:12) may be Deuteronomistic in origin. See the COMMENT.

*Israel.* In a Deuteronomistic verse like this "Israel" refers to united Israel, i.e., Israel and Judah, as in v. 2 above, not to the northern tribes alone, as in the oldest materials, such as v. 3 above (cf. Noth 1981:126 n. 14).

## COMMENT

At the time Solomon began to build the temple, in the fourth year of his reign (I Kings 6:1), Hiram of Tyre was, according to Josephus, in his eleventh (*Ant.* 8.62) or twelfth (*Contra Ap.* 1.126) year of rule. It follows from this that he began to reign only seven years before Solomon's accession. If the traditional assignment of a forty-year reign to David (5:4; I Kings 2:11) is even approximately correct, the events described in the present passage belong late, not early, in David's reign (cf. Bright 1972:199 and n. 49). Accordingly some scholars would follow Thenius in identifying the present king of Tyre as Abibaal, who, according to the evidence of Menander of Ephesus as cited by Josephus (*Ant.* 8.144; *Contra Ap.* 1.116), was Hiram's father; the name of the father was displaced by that of the son, well known because of his role in the construction of the temple (I Kings 5:15–26 [5:1–12]) and his fabled relationship with Solomon (Josephus, *Ant.* 8.141–43).

It is now generally acknowledged, however, that vv. 11–12 are chronologically out of place at this point in the narrative. They share the spirit of the miscellaneous catalogue of David's successes found in 8:1–14 (cf. Noth 1960: 197 n.2) and, specifically, of the report of the mission of Tou of Hamath in 8:9–11 (Noth 1981:56). Chapter 8 is probably a Deuteronomistic compilation (see the COMMENT on § XVII), and it seems likely that a Deuteronomistic hand was also responsible for the present location of 5:11–12. The insertion was motivated not only by "the proximate mention of the king's building plan in Jerusalem" (Hertzberg) but serves the purposes of the larger history by providing a transition from the old narrative that concludes in v. 10 to the Deuteronomistically formulated materials that follow. The general reference to David's taking up residence in Jerusalem in v. 9 is qualified by the specific mention of a cedar house in v. 11 in preparation for 7:2 (Grønbaek 1971:257). To the theme of David's continuing success in v. 10 is added that of an exalted dynasty in v. 12 in anticipation of 7:12 (see the NOTE at v. 12). The history of Tyre's relations with Davidic Israel, therefore, must be reconstructed independently of the present arrangement of these materials (see in general Fensham 1969:71–87, especially 73–76).

# XI. MORE SONS OF DAVID
# (5:13–16)

5 13 David took other concubines and wives from Jerusalem after he came from Hebron, and more sons and daughters were born to [him]. 14 These are the names of those born to him in Jerusalem: Shammua, Shobab, Nathan, Solomon, 15 Ibhar, Elishua, Nepheg, Japhia, 16 Elishama, Baaliada, and Eliphelet.

## *TEXTUAL NOTES*

5 13. *concubines and wives* So MT, LXX$^{A}$, and 4QSam$^{a}$ *(pyl[g]šym w[nšym])*. LXX$^{(B)}$ has "wives and concubines." I Chron 14:3 has "wives" alone. Ulrich (1978: 163,182) explains that the reading of MT is original, the order having been reversed in LXX "perhaps for protocol" (p. 163) and "concubines" having been deleted from I Chron 14:3 "to insure the legitimacy of the sons' pedigree" (p. 182).

*from Jerusalem* LXX$^{N}$ and a few other Greek MSS share the reading of I Chron 14:3, "*in* Jerusalem." Wellhausen supposes the latter to have been original, but note "in Jerusalem" immediately below in v. 14.

*from Hebron* So MT, LXX$^{ALMN}$, OL, etc. LXX$^{B}$: "*to* Hebron."

*more . . . to [him]* MT (cf. LXX$^{A}$, OL, Syr., Targ.): *ʿwd ldwd.* 4QSam$^{a}$ (cf. LXX$^{BLMN}$, Syr.$^{MSS}$): *ldwyd ʿwd* (cf. I Chron 14:3). See Ulrich 1978:83,160–61.

14–16. The evidence for the names listed in these verses is copious. In addition to MT and the versions in the present passage, where LXX$^{B}$ provides a double list (LXX$^{B_1}$ and LXX$^{B_2}$), are copies of the list in I Chron 14:4–7, I Chron 3:5–8, and Josephus, *Ant.* 7.70. In MT and LXX$^{B_1AMN}$ we find eleven names; in LXX$^{B_2L}$ and both Chronicles lists there are thirteen (see below, the second *Textual Note* at v. 15).

14. *those born* So MT, LXX$^{B}$, etc. Syr.: "*the sons* who were born"; LXX$^{L}$: "*his* sons who were born"; OL: "his *seventeen* sons who were born." Space considerations suggest that 4QSam$^{a}$ shared the insertion of *bnyw,* "his sons," at this point.

*in Jerusalem* LXX$^{L}$ adds *tekna daueid deka tria,* "thirteen children of David."

*Shammua* That is, *šammûaʿ*. So MT and I Chron 14:4; cf. LXX$^{B_1}$ *sammous.* I Chron 3:5 has *šimʿāʾ,* to which compare LXX$^{B_2}$ *samae,* LXX$^{L}$ *samaa* and OL *samaet.*

*Shobab* MT *šôbāb* (so I Chron 3:5 and 14:4, LXX$^{B_1}$ [*sōbab*], and Syr. [*šbwb*]). LXX$^{B_2}$ has *iesseibath* (cf. OL *asebath*) and LXX$^{L}$ *iesseban* (cf. Josephus *seban*); the initial syllable may have arisen by confusion of *waw* and *yod* from initial *w-*, "and," in a list that did not consistently join the names with conjunctions (cf. the irregular use of conjunctions in I Chron 3:4–7, their total absence in LXX$^{B_2}$, etc.).

15. *Elishua* I Chron 3:6 has "Elishama" in anticipation of that name later in the list.

At this point one group of witnesses (LXX$^{B_2L}$; I Chron 3:6–7; 14:5–6) inserts two names not found in the other group. These are "Eliphelet" (I Chron 3:6 *'ĕlîpāleṭ;* I Chron 14:5 *'elpāleṭ;* LXX$^{B_2}$ *elphalat*) and "Nogah" (*nōgah;* cf. LXX$^{L}$ *nageth*, LXX$^{B_2}$ *naged).* Space considerations suggest that 4QSam$^{a}$ shared the additional names, and Josephus' *eliēn phalnageēn*, which stands between *iebarē* and *naphēn*, his correspondents of "Ibhar" and "Nepheg," is apparently a corrupt combination of these two names with the preceding "Elishua"—thus, **elisoue- eliphalat nage-* > **eli- phal(at) nage-* (homoioarkton) > *eliēn phalnageēn*. Since "Eliphelet" is a duplicate of the last name in the list, we might surmise that it is a vestige of a long haplography (a scribe's eye having skipped from the *'ayin* at the end of *'lyšw'* to the *'ayin* at the end of *b'lyd'*), which was subsequently corrected by reintroduction of the last five names on the list. "Nogah" seems likely to have arisen independently as a variant of "Nepheg."

16. *Baaliada* I Chron 14:7 has *b'lyd'*, vocalized *bĕ'elyādā'*, probably to suggest *'elyādā'*, "Eliada," the reading of I Chron 3:8 and MT in the present passage (cf. LXX$^{AM}$ *elidae*). The correct vocalization is *ba'alyādā'*, as indicated by LXX$^{B_2}$ *baaleimath (< *baaleidaa-)* and LXX$^{L}$ *baaleidath* (so $e_2$; $boc_2$ differ slightly). See further the NOTE.

## NOTES

5 13. *concubines.* Slave women who belonged to wealthy households and bore children but did not share all the legal privileges of wives.

14. According to I Chron 3:5 the four sons listed in this verse were the children of Bathsheba (there called "Bathshua daughter of Ammiel"; cf. the first two *Textual Notes* at 11:3).

*Nathan.* Not to be confused with the prophet (7:2; etc.) or the hero's father (23:36) of the same name. In Luke's genealogy of Jesus, by the way, the descent from David is traced through Nathan (Luke 3:31), not Solomon, as in Matthew's version (Matt 1:6); "this may reflect a popular Jewish uneasiness about the taint attached to Solomon's scandalous life" (Brown 1977:85 n. 53; cf. Johnson 1969:135–36).

16. *Baaliada.* The name *ba'alyādā'* (see the *Textual Note*) means "The lord knows." The theophorous element *ba'al*, "lord," also appeared in the names of the sons of Saul, as we have seen. It probably referred to Yahweh (see the NOTE on "Ishbaal" at 2:8), but because of its common association with the Canaanite god Haddu it was later eschewed in Yahwistic names—hence the Masoretic reading, *'elyādā'*, "God knows," in the present passage and I Chron 3:8.

*Eliphelet.* Not to be confused with the hero listed in 23:34.

## COMMENT

This list continues that in 3:2–5. The sons born to David in Hebron are named there, his Jerusalemite sons here. This passage is repeated in I Chron 14:3–4, and the two lists are combined and amplified in I Chron 3:1–9.

# XII. TWO VICTORIES OVER THE PHILISTINES (5:17–25)

5 [17]When the Philistines heard that David had been anointed king
over Israel, [they] came up in search of [him], but when David heard
of this, he went down to the stronghold.

### *The Battle of Baal-perazim*

[18]When the Philistines had arrived and spread out in the lowlands of
Rephaim, [19]David inquired of Yahweh.

"Shall I go up against the Philistines? Will you hand them over to me?"

"Go up!" Yahweh told [him]. "For I shall indeed hand them over to you!"

[20]So David entered Baal-perazim and defeated them there. (Then he
said, "Yahweh has burst through my enemies before me like an outburst of water!" So he named that place Baal-perazim.) [21]They left their
gods there, and David and his men carried them off.

### *Another Victory*

[22]Again the Philistines came up and spread out in the lowlands of
Rephaim. [23]So David inquired of Yahweh.

"You must not go up!" said [Yahweh]. "Circle around them and
approach them in front of Bachaim. [24]Then, when you hear the sound
of the wind in the asherahs of Bachaim, look sharp, for Yahweh will
have marched out ahead of you to attack the Philistine camp!"

[25]David did as Yahweh had instructed him, and he defeated the
Philistines from Gibeon to Gezer.

## *TEXTUAL NOTES*

5 17. *David had been anointed* Reading *nmšḥ dwd* on the basis of LXX *kechristai daueid;* this reading also appears in I Chron 14:8. In the present passage MT has *mšḥw 't dwd,* "they had anointed David."

*king* That is, *lĕmelek.* Syr., Targ.[MS] understand the same consonantal text as *limlōk,* "to rule." Cf. 2:4,7.

[*they*] That is, "the Philistines." MT, LXX[B], etc., have "*all* the Philistines"; we omit "all" on authority of LXX[L].

18. *spread out* Reading *wynṭšw* with MT. The meaning is discussed in the NOTE. LXX *kai synepesan* seems to reflect *wypšṭw,* "were making raids," as in I Chron 14:9. But elsewhere in Samuel *pšṭ* with this meaning takes the preposition *'l* (I Sam 23:27; 27:8 [MT *'l* = *'l;* cf. LXX]; 27:10 [cf. *I Samuel,* the *Textual Note* on "Against whom"]; 30:1 [MT *'l* = *'l;* cf. LXX]; 30:14 [insert *'l* with LXX]); *pšṭ b-* is the language of the Chronicler (II Chron 25:13; 28:18). It seems likely that *wypšṭw* arose in the tradition shared by LXX and Chronicles because of graphic confusion of *nun* and *pe* and transposition of *šin* and *ṭet* (cf. Tidwell 1979:197 n.27).

19. *them* (2) So LXX[L], Syr. (cf. I Chron 14:10). MT, LXX[B], etc., make the object explicit: "the Philistines."

20. *So David entered Baal-perazim* MT *wyb' dwd bb'l prṣym.* LXX *kai ēlthen daueid ek tōn epanō diakopōn* (cf. OL) suggests *wyb' dwd mm'l (l)prṣym,* "So David entered over breaches," which sounds more appropriate to the siege of a city than a battle in open country. See also the *Textual Note* on "Baal-perazim" below.

*and defeated them there* So OL, Syr. MT, LXX[L]: "and *David* defeated them there." LXX[B]: "and defeated *the Philistines* there."

*Then he said* So MT. LXX, Syr. (cf. I Chron 14:11): "Then *David* said."

*my enemies* So MT, LXX[LMN], OL. LXX[B]: "the Philistine enemies."

*Baal-perazim* See the *Textual Note* on "So David entered Baal-perazim" above. Here again LXX, OL seem to reflect *mm'l (l)prṣym* for *b'l prṣym.*

21. *They* LXX[L] makes the subject explicit: "The Philistines."

*their gods* Reading *'t 'lhyhm* as in I Chron 14:12 on the basis of LXX *tous theous autōn.* MT has *'t 'ṣbyhm,* "their *idols.*"

*his men* So MT, LXX[LM], OL. LXX[BAN]: "his men *who were with him.*"

In place of "and David and his men carried them off" I Chron 14:12 has *wy'mr dwyd wyśrpw b'š,* "and David gave instructions and they burned (them) with fire," and in the present passage some Greek MSS append something close to this at the end. LXX[M]: + *kai eipen katakausai autous en pyri* = *wy'mr lśrpm b'š,* "and he said to burn them with fire." LXX[L]: + *kai legei daueid katakausate autous en pyri* = *wy'mr dwd śrpwm b'š,* "and David said, 'Burn them with fire!' "

22. *spread out* See the *Textual Note* at v. 18. Again we read *wynṭšw* with MT in preference to *wypšṭw* as reflected by LXX *kai synepesan* (cf. I Chron 14:13).

23. *David inquired of Yahweh* LXX[M] and a few other MSS, in reminiscence of v.

18, add *legōn ei anabō pros tous allophylous kai paradōseis autous eis tas cheiras mou* = *l'mr h'lh 'l hplštym wttnm bydy,* "(saying) 'Shall I go up against the Philistines, and will you hand them over to me?' "

*"You must not go up!"* So MT. LXX adds *eis synantēsin autōn* = *lqr'tm,* "to meet them, opposite them."

*said* [*Yahweh*] Reading *wy'mr,* lit. "and he said," with MT. LXX$^{B}$ reflects *wy'mr yhwh,* "and *Yahweh* said," and LXX$^{L}$, Syr. reflect *wy'mr lw yhwh,* "and Yahweh said *to him*" (cf. I Chron 14:14).

*Circle around them* Reading *hsb mhm* with LXX (*apostrephou ap' autōn*). For *mhm* MT has *'l 'ḥryhm,* and Syr. has *mn bstrhwn* = *m'ḥryhm,* which appears in a few MSS of MT (*BHS*)—thus, "Circle around *to their rear*" or "Circle around *behind them.*"

*Bachaim* See the NOTE.

24. *the wind* MT has *hṣ'dh,* "marching," both here (so MT$^{MSS}$; MT: *ṣ'dh*) and in I Chron 14:14. Syr. agrees: *(d)hlkth* = *hṣ'dh.* Targ. *ṣwḥt'* reflects *hṣ'qh,* "an outcry," evidently a mistake for *hṣ'dh.* LXX$^{LMN}$, on the other hand, have *tou synseismou,* "the commotion" = *hs'rh,* "the wind" (cf. Thenius), of which LXX$^{B}$ *tou synkleismou,* "the confinement(?)," is probably an inner-Greek corruption. In I Chron 14:14 LXX has the same reading (*tou sysseismou*), and it is clear that Josephus' text had this as well from his statement (*Ant.* 7.76; cf. 77) that David was told to wait "until the grove was shaken (*saleuesthai*)." We must choose, therefore, between *hṣ'dh,* "marching," and *hs'rh,* "the wind." Each is a good, distinctive reading, appropriate to its context. "Marching" is precisely the issue here: ". . . Yahweh will have marched out (*yāṣā'*) ahead of you. . . ." The (storm)wind is a conventional medium of theophany (see the NOTE). Tentatively I should read *hs'rh* with LXX, which, without question, has the better reading of the word that follows.

*in the asherahs* MT has *br'šy,* "in the tops of"—thus, "the sound of marching *in the tops of* the *bākā'*-trees(?)." But this is a corruption by transposition of *b'šry* (cf. LXX$^{L}$ *tōn alsōn*) or *m'šry,* as reflected by OL$^{MS}$ *de silvis* (cf. LXX$^{B}$ *apo tou alsous* and OL$^{MS}$ *de silva* = *m'šrt*). Our translation agrees with the interpretation by LXX of *b'šry/m'šry* as "in/from the (sacred) groves," that is, "in/from the asherahs." See the NOTE.

*look sharp* So MT: *tḥrṣ.* LXX$^{BAMN}$: *katabēsei pros autous* = *trd 'lyhm,* "go down to (against) them." LXX$^{L}$ (cf. OL): *katabēsei eis ton polemon* = *trd bmlḥmh,* "go down into battle" (cf. I Chron 14:15 *tṣ' bmlḥmh,* "go forth into battle").

*camp* So MT: *mḥnh.* LXX reflects *mlḥmh,* "battle, war" (thus ". . . to make a strike in the Philistine war"). The two words were frequently confused.

25. *as* Reading *k'šr,* to which MT, LXX$^{L}$ and certain other witnesses prefix *kn,* "thus, so." Omit *kn* with MT$^{MSS}$, LXX$^{BAMN}$, Vulg. (cf. I Chron 14:16).

*Gibeon* So LXX and I Chron 14:16. MT has "Geba." Thenius, Wellhausen, and most subsequent commentators have preferred Gibeon, modern el-Jīb, ca. six to eight miles north-northwest of Jerusalem, as more consistent with the geography of the passage than Geba, modern Jeba', ca. six miles north-northeast of Jerusalem; the clash at Bachaim took place somewhere north or northwest of the city (see the NOTE on "Bachaim," v. 23). See also Isa 28:21. Demsky (1973) has argued that in the old cycle of stories about Saul in I Samuel the narrator consistently refers to Gibeon as *geba';*

if Demsky is correct and the same practice is in effect here, then we should judge MT's reading to be primitive, correctly updated by the Chronicler.

*to Gezer* So LXX[L] (cf. I Chron 14:16): *heōs gazēra* = *'d gzrh*. LXX[B] *heōs tēs gēs gazēra* suggests "as far as *the land of* Gezer," but *gēs* may be a corrupt duplicate of *gazēra*. MT: *'d b'k gzr*, "as far as the approach to Gezer" (cf. I Sam 17:52).

## NOTES

5 17. *the stronghold.* According to the present arrangement of the materials in chap. 5, *hammĕṣûdâ*, "the stronghold," seems to refer to "the stronghold of Zion" *(mĕṣûdat ṣiyyôn)*, as in vv. 7,9. But considerations discussed in the COMMENT suggest that 5:17–25 was originally an independent unit or pair of units and that the stronghold of Zion was not originally intended here. Elsewhere in the oldest materials about David's early career (I Sam 22:1,4; 24:23) and in other stories of the Philistine invasion of the lowlands of Rephaim (II Sam 23:13,14 = I Chron 11:15,16) "the stronghold" refers to David's fastness at "the stronghold of Adullam" *(mĕṣūdat 'ădullām)*, a fortress in the Shephelah, ca. sixteen miles southwest of Jerusalem, modern Tell esh-Sheikh Madhkûr (Josh 15:34; II Chron 11:7); see Map 3. The Israelite military maneuvers about to be described suggest an external base of operations (see Hauer 1970:575–76; Yeivin 1964:152–56), and we should probably think of Adullam, not Jerusalem, as David's headquarters in this section.

18. *and spread out.* Hebrew *wayyinnāṭĕšû*. Tidwell (1979:195–96) has called attention to the use of this verb here, an important detail overlooked by earlier investigators. The verb is incompatible with the notion that the Philistines are preparing for a pitched battle, still less the siege of a city (see the COMMENT). It suggests instead a dispersal of troops for some purpose. Tidwell goes too far, however, in arguing that this purpose must be plunder (so BDB 644). The one other occurrence of *nṭš* in *Nip'al* in a military context is Judg 15:9, and there the Philistines state their purpose explicitly: They have come to capture Samson (v. 10), just as in the present episode they have come "in search of" David (v. 17).

*the lowlands of Rephaim.* The Philistines have come up from their home on the coastal plain, probably by way of the Valley of Sorek (Wâdī eṣ-Ṣarâr), and deployed in the plain or lowland region *('ēmeq)* known as Rephaim, which was cut at its northern end by the deep Valley of Hinnom on the boundary of Judahite and Benjaminite territory (Josh 15:8; 18:16); see Map 3. (This region is usually identified with the plain southwest of Jerusalem known today as el Baqa', but this is not absolutely certain [cf. Hauer 1970:573 n.10].) The Philistine strategy evidently is to sever the lines of contact between David's newly united dominions (see the COMMENT).

19. *David inquired of Yahweh.* David seeks an oracle before undertaking any action against the Philistines. Cf., in addition to 2:1, I Sam 23:9–12 and 30:7–8, where the oracle is administered by a priest (Abiathar) with an ephod, a sacerdotal garment containing within it (presumably) the Urim and Thummim of I Sam 14:41 and elsewhere; these were "cast" (I Sam 14:42) to obtain the answer to a question asked of the

oracle. Because the oracle could only provide answers to questions involving a choice between alternatives (Urim and Thummim), queries directed to it were restricted to the "yes or no" type. In the present case, therefore, David asks two such questions—"Shall I go up against the Philistines?" and "Will you hand them over to me?"—and receives affirmative replies to each. Cf. v. 24 and the NOTE there.

*"Shall I go up . . . ?"* That is, "Shall I attack?" Some commentators treat this as a question of tactics, as if it meant "Shall I make a frontal assault?" a tempting interpretation in view of v. 23, where the answer to the same question is, in effect, "No, circle around and approach from the rear!" But a survey of the use of *ʿālâ (ʿal),* "go up (against)," in military contexts will show that it is a general expression for attacking, engaging in battle; it need not refer to a frontal assault. Indeed a frontal assault in pitched battle against the larger Philistine force would have been foolhardy if not suicidal (cf. Tidwell 1979:209) for "David and his men," that is, David and his personal militia (see the NOTE at v. 21). As a matter of fact, v. 20 suggests the actual, limited scope of the operation. David won his victory in Baal-perazim, a place where he would have encountered some, but certainly not all, of the Philistines, who were "spread out in the lowlands of Rephaim" (v. 18). See also the NOTE on v. 23 below.

20. *Baal-perazim.* "The lord of Perazim" (see the NOTE that follows), a sanctuary on or near Mount Perazim (Isa 28:21). David is marching north from "the stronghold" (i.e., Adullam, as explained in the NOTE, v. 17), so that this encounter with the Philistines must have taken place on the southern or western border of the lowlands of Rephaim. The precise spot, however, is unknown, and none of the several modern proposals has found general acceptance.

*(Then he said . . . Baal-perazim.).* This parenthesis, which is probably secondary and late, plays on the sanctuary name Baal-perazim, properly "the lord of Perazim," in reference to the deity (a local manifestation of Yahweh?) who was worshiped in the sanctuary and whose domain Mount Perazim was believed to be. The wordplay hinges on the verb *pāraṣ,* "burst upon," and the noun *pereṣ,* "outburst." Thus David is depicted as saying, "Yahweh has burst through *(pāraṣ)* my enemies before me like an outburst *(pereṣ)* of water!" and (therefore) as naming the place *baʿal pĕrāṣîm,* "the lord of outbursts." The referent of this playful etiology is evidently to a breach in a wall or fence caused by some violent rush of water, perhaps a flash flood (cf. Hertzberg). David is saying, in other words, that by granting him a victory in this particular spot Yahweh has opened a gap in the Philistine wall of resistance. The etiology, therefore, is consistent with the limited scope of David's operation against the larger Philistine force in this first battle (cf. the NOTE on "Shall I go up . . . ?" v. 19). See also Tidwell 1979:209.

21. *their gods.* Sacred images brought into battle to ensure divine assistance and, therefore, success. It was customary for a victorious army to carry off the "gods" of the enemy as a sign of the superiority of its own divine help (see Miller and Roberts 1977:9–16 and bibliography in nn. 69–72, p. 91). The ark of Yahweh was the Israelite equivalent of the images of the Philistines and others. It was brought into the great battle at Ebenezer (see I Sam 4:1–11, where the Philistines speak of the arrival of the "gods" of the Hebrews [vv. 7,8]) and suffered the fate of the Philistine images in the present episode (I Sam 4:11).

*David and his men.* Cf. I Sam 23:5,24,26; 24:3,4,23; 25:20; 27:8; 29:2,11; 30:1,3; etc. The Israelite force here is David's personal militia, recruited during his days as a fugitive from Saul's court (cf. I Sam 22:2). The size of such an army seems to have been fixed at about six hundred men (I Sam 23:13; 27:2; 30:9; cf. 25:13; 30:10), a convention based, according to Mazar (1963b:314), on ancient tradition (cf. Judg 18:11; I Sam 13:15; II Sam 15:18). The same force was used for the capture of Jerusalem (5:6).

*carried them off.* The synoptic passage in Chronicles reflects a post-Deuteronomistic sense of religious propriety in its assertion that David ordered the Philistine idols burned (Deut 7:5,25; etc.). Cf. the last *Textual Note* to v. 21.

22. *Again the Philistines came up.* Verses 22–25 contain a second, independent battle account sharing with the first the common terrain of the lowlands of Rephaim, also the location of the incident described in 23:13–17 and, for all we know, a number of other similar events the accounts of which have not survived. In the COMMENT the case is made that the two accounts found in 5:17–25, both deriving from ancient archives, were selected and placed in their present position to serve the editorial purposes of the Deuteronomistic compiler of 5:11–8:18. Some scholars, however, have doubted the antiquity of the second account. Arnold (1917:41) suspects that the report in vv. 22–25 was inauthentic because of an absence of details about the occasion and circumstances of the battle, and Caird shares this suspicion on the grounds of the anomalous detail that the oracle in vv. 23–24 gives more than a "yes or no" answer (see the NOTE at vv. 23–24). Ackroyd asks if the two units, so noticeably similar in form, might not represent varying traditions about a single battle. Tidwell, however, has been able to demonstrate that the similarity in form is simply a reflection of the conventionalized nature of battle reports (1979:193–95,206). His own analysis suggests that vv. 17–25 combine the report of a relatively insignificant Israelite success (vv. 18–21) with that of a decisive victory (vv. 22–25), and to this extent his conclusions are compatible with our own.

23–24. David again consults the oracle; see the first NOTE at v. 19. In this case the oracle gives a "no" answer; he is not to attack right away. Instead he is to take up a new position and follow Yahweh's lead (see below). The latter information, especially the content of v. 24, is not conveyed in the "yes or no" form of reply to which the oracle was confined. This situation, if it does not lead us to question the authenticity of vv. 22–25 (cf. the previous NOTE), at least provokes us to ask if some other means of divination is being used here. Yet it is possible to see behind vv. 23b–24 a number of "yes" and "no" answers reported in combination by the narrator (cf. Ackroyd); indeed, we must assume that David's oracular priest (Abiathar?) had some latitude in interpreting the verdict of the lots.

23. *Bachaim.* Does Hebrew *běkā'îm* refer to a group of trees (cf. Yeivin 1964:154–55 and fig. 28)? Its treatment in some of the versions shows that the belief that it does is fairly ancient. The Targum, for example, reads *'ylny'*, "trees," and the Septuagint of I Chron 14:14,15 has *tōn apiōn*, "pear trees" (cf. Aquila and the Vulgate), probably in light of Rabbinic Hebrew *běkāy*, a species of pear (Jastrow 169). The rabbis supposed the word to refer to mulberry trees, and modern commentators have argued for balsams, mastic terebinths, and still others. But the evidence will not sustain any of these specific proposals, and the cautious contemporary judgment seems to favor no more precise interpretation than "*bākā'*-bush" or the like (cf. KB[3] and, already, Thenius). It is by no means clear, however, that *běkā'îm* refers to trees or plants. Josephus' mention of trees here (*Ant.* 7.76–77) derives from the Septuagint's understanding of the

previous word as "(sacred) groves" (see the *Textual Note* on "in the asherahs," v. 24), and this may have had something to do with the presence of trees in other ancient interpretations. On the other hand, the Septuagint *(tou klauthmōnos)*, which Josephus follows, and the Peshiṭta *(bwkyn)* seem to understand *bk(')ym* in light of the place name *bôkîm*, "Bochim," in Judg 2:1–5. Whatever the merit of such an identification might be, it does seem likely that *bĕkā'îm* in the present passage, which stands here in v. 23 without the article (contrast I Chron 14:14), is intended as a place-name. We might compare *'ēmeq habbākā'*, "the plain of Bacha," in Ps 84:7 [84:6]. The latter is a dry place on the way to Jerusalem, where, according to the psalm, fountains and pools are to appear miraculously; in interpretation of this Gunkel (1926:371) and others have cited Arabic *baka'a*, "have little water or milk." Perhaps the present reference is to the same place or another place with the same name—*bĕkā'îm*, a plural of "local extension" (GK[2] §124b). The meaning would be something like "The Parched Place." It would serve no purpose to attempt to identify a precise location for Bachaim. David's attack in vv. 17–21 was from the south or west of the plain of Rephaim (see the NOTE on "Baal-perazim," v. 20). Here he is told to "Circle around [the Philistines]," and we may suppose the clash takes place somewhere to the north. We conclude that Bachaim was a town or region—the presence of asherahs suggests a shrine of some kind—north or northwest of Jerusalem on the edge of the lowlands of Rephaim.

24. *the sound of the wind in the asherahs.* An asherah *('ăšērâ)* was a wooden cult object, part of a shrine or sanctuary. It is not clear whether an asherah was a tree or a pole; perhaps it was either. Asherahs *('ăšērîm* or *'ăšērôt)* were strictly forbidden by Deuteronomic law (Deut 16:21; etc.), and, probably at least in part because of this prohibition, the Bible provides little information about them. Modern scholarship offers a variety of interpretations of the asherah and its relationship to the Canaanite goddess Asherah. In lieu of a fuller discussion, which would be out of place here, there follows a brief statement of my own understanding. Etymologically *'ăšērâ* derives from the verb **'ṯr*, the most basic meaning of which seems to have been "walk in the steps of, track." An asherah is the "track" or "trace" of a deity, and the expression *'ăšērat DN* refers to the cultic presence or availability of a deity, which, at least in Israel, was invested specifically in an upright wooden object erected near a shrine to that deity. It is to be compared to a group of similar expressions in Northwest Semitic religious terminology, such as Phoenician-Punic *šim DN*, "name of DN," and *panê DN*, "presence of DN," Aramaic *'ešem DN*, "name of DN," etc. Especially instructive is *'anat DN*, "sign of (the active presence of) DN" (cf. Albright 1969a:168 and 192–93 n. 14). All of these referred in one way or another to the cultic availability of a male deity, and all were subject to hypostasis and personification as female deities in their own right. In the two cases of *'ăšērat DN* and *'anat DN*, there were major Canaanite goddesses, Asherah and Anat, who originated as hypostases of gods—Asherah of Yamm, the Sea (cf. Ugaritic *rabbatu 'aṯiratu yammi*, "the lady [who is] the asherah of Sea"), and Anat perhaps of Baal—but attained to the status of independent divine beings. In Israel Yahweh's asherah was revered as a goddess, as shown by votive inscriptions from the Sinaitic outpost of Kuntillet 'Ajrūd "to Yahweh of GN and to his asherah" *(lyhwh GN wl'šrth)*, adjacent in one case to a drawing of a divine couple in human-bovine form (see provisionally Meshel 1979). In the present passage we have not the goddess but the cult object—or rather objects, since there is more than one—standing near Ba-

chaim, evidently a place where Yahweh was worshiped. David is to wait until he hears a wind blowing in these asherahs. The (storm)wind *(sa'ārâ)* is a standard vehicle for theophany in the Bible (Ezek 1:4; Job 38:1; 40:6; etc.), especially characteristic of passages in which Yahweh appears as a warrior marching forth to battle (cf. Jer 23:19; 30:23; Zech 9:14). Here the sound of the wind is to be an audible token of the divine warrior's involvement. That it will be blowing "in the asherahs" is consistent with our understanding of their significance as signs of Yahweh's presence.

25. *from Gibeon to Gezer.* We have seen that Gibeon lay ca. six to eight miles northwest of Jerusalem (the NOTE at 2:12). Gezer is modern Tell Jezer, ca. fifteen miles east of el-Jīb (Gibeon) in the direction of the Philistine plain; it lay roughly on the unofficial border between Israel and Philistia. David has succeeded, in other words, in driving the Philistines out of the Israelite territory they have occupied since the battle of Ebenezer (I Samuel 4).

## COMMENT

The Philistines respond to the news of David's anointment with an invasion of the plain of Rephaim, near Jerusalem, but David, relying on the oracle of Yahweh for strategic advice, defeats them in two pitched battles. The second engagement is decisive, and the enemy is driven back to the border city of Gezer.

The present arrangement of materials in our text presents both battles as having taken place after David's capture of Jerusalem. There are several reasons, however, to doubt the historicity of this arrangement. Though the Philistines encamp in the vicinity of Jerusalem, nothing is said to suggest that they are preparing a siege. At most we might suppose that they hope to draw David out of the city into a pitched battle (cf. Hauer 1970:575 n. 20), but the language of the passage does not support this conclusion either. The Philistines, we are told, have come "in search of" *(lĕbaqqēš)* David, an expression strongly reminiscent of Saul's pursuit of David during the time the latter was a fugitive in the Wilderness of Judah (cf. I Sam 23:14,25; 24:3; 26:2; 27:1,4; etc.). In the single instance in which David's flight took him inside a walled city, the language used of Saul's pursuit was different: "Saul summoned the entire army to war, to go down to Keilah and *besiege (lāṣûr)* David and his men" (I Sam 23:8). Note, further, that when in the present episode the Philistines reach the plain of Rephaim, they "spread out" (vv. 18,22). The narrator uses a term of deployment appropriate to the dispersal of troops for some purpose, such as gathering plunder or (as in this case) searching out a particular enemy, but inappropriate to preparation for a pitched battle or a siege (see the NOTE on "and spread out," v. 18).

Apparently, then, David was not yet ensconced in Jerusalem when the

Philistines arrived. He "went down," we are told, "to the stronghold" (v. 17). The present sequence of materials requires the assumption that this refers to "the stronghold of Zion" (cf. vv. 7,9), but the statement that David went *down* to the stronghold belies this assumption, not only because the verb implies movement and David (according to the present arrangement of the text) was already in Zion (Wellhausen) but also because in the Bible one always goes *up*, never *down*, to the eminence of Zion (Driver and most commentators; contrast Caird). In David's fugitive days, moreover, "the stronghold," even without further specification, was the stronghold of Adullam (I Sam 22:1,4; 24:23), and David will use this same base of operations, the stronghold of Adullam, against the Philistines during the incident described in II Sam 23: 13–17 (cf. vv. 13,14), which may belong to the present context (see the COMMENT on 23:8–39). In all probability, then, David was operating out of Adullam at the time of the two victories described here.

Note that according to the account itself it was David's accession to the throne of Israel, not his capture of Jerusalem, that provoked the Philistine show of force. The invasion was intended, in the opinion of most historians (Noth 1960:188; Bright 1972:194; etc.), to prevent the united kingdom that David's anointment implied from becoming a political reality. The lowlands of Rephaim, lying southwest of Jerusalem and thus directly between David and the northern territories that had recently acknowledged his sovereignty, were chosen as the target of the invasion with the purpose of driving a wedge between David's two constituencies (Herrmann 1981:154). It might be useful to mention in passing that the Philistines' alarm over the developments in Hebron was well founded. After the unification of Israel and Judah and the battles described here, the balance of power in Palestine shifted in favor of the Israelites, and the Philistines were increasingly confined to the coastal plain (cf. 5:25; 8:1).

If, therefore, these two battle accounts are chronologically out of place at this point, belonging instead between the report of David's accession to the northern throne in 5:1–3 and the description of the capture of Jerusalem in 5:6–10 (so already Wellhausen 1899:256), we must ask why they stand here and not there. Grønbaek (1971:250–55,271) considers 5:17–25 to have been an original part of the old story of David's rise to power that ends in 5:10. This unit, he says, was displaced to its present position by a Deuteronomistic editor in support of the reference to Jerusalem in the accession formula he inserted at 5:4–5, which would now be followed immediately by the account of the capture of the city, and in the interest of the continuing narrative that followed in his larger history, the transition to which would be smoothed by diluting, to some extent, the climactic finality of the beginning of chap. 5. This proposal is a plausible one—certainly 5:17–25 has the flavor of the old narrative, especially in its use of the oracle motif in vv. 19,23–24 (cf. I Sam 23:9–12; 30:7–8; see Grønbaek 1971:254; Mettinger 1976:42)—but it does not seem to me to be a necessary one. We need not assume that all the early literature handled by the Deuteronomistic editor of these chapters came from a single composition. Nor is Grønbaek's discussion of the factors motivating the displacement convincing. I prefer to follow Alt (1936) and others in thinking of 5:17–25 as an ancient fragment—or pair of fragments (see below)—about David's Philistine wars, probably drawn from a larger archive of such material (of which 21:15–22 and 23:8–39 may be further examples), which had no literary relationship to the other materials in chap. 5 before their Deuteronomistic compilation into their present form. The reason this unit, 5:17–25, was placed here rather than included in the miscellany in chap. 8, or the one at the end of the book (like 21:15–22; 23:8–39), or omitted altogether seems clear. In Abiner's prophecy in 3:18, a Deuteronomistic addition to the story of David's rise (see the NOTE at 3:18), we were told that "Yahweh has said of David, 'It is by the hand of my servant David that I am going to save Israel from the Philistines and all their [other] enemies." At the conclusion of the story of David's rise, therefore, we should not be surprised to find Deuteronomistically collated materials (5:17–25 + 8:1–14) that demonstrate the fulfilment of this prophecy (cf. Veijola 1975:102–5; 1977:78). These two battle accounts were put here to serve this function (so also Ward 1967:183 and Mettinger 1976:42, both of whom, however, regard both prophecy and fulfilment as original parts of the story of David's rise) and, therefore, to emphasize David's role in the enactment of Yahweh's will.

The two fragments included here (5:17–21 and 22–25) make the last point especially well since both show David acting in accordance with the oracle of Yahweh (vv. 19 and 23–24). This was a principal reason, we must assume, for the selection and combination of these particular anecdotes from among the many tales of David's Philistine wars that may have been available. The first of the two (vv. 17–21) may have been chosen specifically because of the reference to the capture of the Philistine "gods" in v. 21 (see the NOTE). This amounts to a reversal of the Philistines' capture of the ark of Yahweh in I Sam 4:11 (contrast Tidwell 1979:210–11, who questions the reference to "gods" or "idols" in the present passage) and, accordingly, prepares us for the entry of the ark into Jerusalem in the section that follows. The second episode (vv. 22–25) carries this reversal theme further with the expulsion of the Philistines from the territory occupied in their previous victories (cf. especially v. 25 and the NOTE there). As explained in the COMMENT on § XIII, it is the judgment of modern historians that this shift in political ascendancy (cf. Bright 1972:194) made possible the restoration of the ark of Yahweh to a central position in Israelite religious life. Access to the ark, in fact, in the Gibeonite city of Kiriath-jearim, where it currently resided (I Sam 7:1), may have been impossible before the expulsion of the Philistines "from Gibeon to Gezer" (v. 25; see the remarks of Blenkinsopp cited in the NOTE on "Baalah" in 6:2). The compiler of 5:10–8:18 understood these developments as reflections of the will of Yahweh and, therefore, positioned this old story—the account of a decisive victory over the Philistines led by David with the guidance of Yahweh's oracle—immediately before the description of the "bringing up" of the ark, which stands in the section that follows.

# XIII. THE TRANSFER OF THE ARK TO JERUSALEM (6:1–19)

6 1 David assembled all the elite troops of Israel—thirty thousands—
2 and [he] and the entire army that was with him went to Baalah to bring
up from there the holy ark over which the name of Yahweh Seated-
upon-the-Cherubim is called. 3 He mounted the ark of Yahweh upon a
new cart and carried it away from the house of Abinadab on the Hill.
Uzza and Ahio, sons of Abinadab, were guiding the cart 4 with the ark,
Uzza walking alongside the ark and Ahio walking in front of [it].
5 David and the Israelites were reveling before Yahweh with sonorous
instruments and songs—with lyres, harps, tambourines, sistrums, and
cymbals.

### *The Incident at Uzza's Breach*

6 When they came to the threshing floor of Nodan, Uzza put his
hand on the holy ark to steady it, for the oxen had let it slip. 7 Yahweh
became angry at Uzza and struck him down, and he died there before
God.

8 David became angry (the reason being that Yahweh had made a
breach in Uzza—that place is called Uzza's Breach to this day) 9 and
fearful of Yahweh at that time. "How," he said to himself, "can the
holy ark come with me?" So when Yahweh's ark arrived, 10 David,
unwilling to take [it] with him into the City of David, redirected it to
the house of Obed-edom the Gittite.

11 Yahweh's ark remained in the house of Obed-edom the Gittite for
three months, and Yahweh blessed Obed-edom and all his house.

### *The Ark's Arrival in the City of David*

12 When King David was told that Yahweh had blessed the house of
Obed-edom and all he had because of the holy ark, [he] said to himself,
"I'll bring the blessing back to my own house!" So [he] went and
brought Yahweh's ark up from the house of Obed-edom to the City of

David with festivity; [13]whenever the ark bearers advanced six paces, he would sacrifice a fatted bull.

[14]David, clad in a linen ephod, was strumming on a sonorous instrument before Yahweh, [15]as [he] and all Israel brought Yahweh's ark up amid shouting and the sound of the shofar. [16]As the ark entered the City of David, Michal daughter of Saul was watching through a window, and when she saw King David leaping and strumming before Yahweh, she felt contempt for him.

[17]They brought Yahweh's ark in and set it up inside the tent David had pitched for it, and David offered holocausts before Yahweh. [18]When he finished offering the holocausts and communion offerings, he blessed the people by the name of Yahweh [19]and doled out to all of them—the whole multitude of Israel, both men and women—a ring of bread, a date-cake, and a raisin-cake each. Then all the people went to their own homes.

## TEXTUAL NOTES

6 1. *assembled* MT *wysp* is a defective spelling of *wy'sp (wayye'ěsōp),* but it is vocalized *wayyōsep,* "(and he) added, did again," and this has attracted *'wd,* "again," which frequently follows this verb (cf. v. 22 above), into the text (Wellhausen).

*of Israel* So MT$^{MSS}$, Syr., Targ. MT: "*in* Israel." LXX: "*from* Israel" (cf. I Sam 24:3).

*thirty* So MT. LXX$^{L}$: "seventy." LXX$^{BAMN}$, OL: "*about* seventy."

2. *to Baalah* Reading *b'lh* alone. 4QSam$^{a}$ has *b'lh hy' qr[yt y'rym 'šr] lyhwdh* (the *d* of *lyhwdh* was omitted and restored supralinearly), "to Baalah, that is, Kiriath-jearim, which belongs to Judah" (cf. Josh 15:9), and I Chron 13:6 displays a similar gloss, *b'lth 'l qryt y'rym 'šr lyhwdh,* "to Baalah, to Kiriath-jearim, which belongs to Judah." MT has *mb'ly yhwdh,* as if "(all the people who were with him) from the lords of Judah"; but this is probably a corrupt remnant of a reading like that of 4QSam$^{a}$. We hear of "the lords of Judah" nowhere else, and the reading leaves the subsequent *miššām,* "from there," without antecedent, unless it refers back to "from Gibeon to Gezer" in 5:25 (cf. Blenkinsopp 1969a:152) or, assuming an original connection with the ark narrative of I Samuel (see the COMMENT), to "the house of Abinadab on the Hill" in I Sam 7:1 or "Kiriath-jearim" in 7:2 (Campbell 1975:169–71). LXX$^{(B)}$ *apo tōn archontōn iouda en anabasei* reflects *mb'ly yhwdh b'lh,* understanding *b'lh,* properly "to Baalah," as "in going up"; here the corrupt reading of MT was inserted recensionally into a text which preserved the short, primitive reading. See Ulrich (1978:198–99), who, however, argues that the original text must also have included

"Judah." LXX[L] diverges from other Greek MSS in representing *en anabasei* as *en te anabasei tou bounou,* reflecting *b'lh hgb'h,* "in going up *the hill,*" or rather "to Baalah, to the Hill," i.e., the place in Baalah called the Hill where Abinadab lived (see v. 3 and the NOTE there).

*over which the name . . . is called* That is, *'šr nqr' šm . . . 'lyw.* This is the reading of MT except that in MT *šm* is repeated, evidently by dittography. We delete *šm* (2) with LXX. 4QSam[a] has *'t 'sr n[qr' šm . . . 'lyw].* A case can be made for retaining MT *šm šm* and reading the first as *šām,* "there (i.e., in Baalah)," with Syr. and MT[MSS] (so Carlson 1964:63).

*Yahweh Seated-upon-the-Cherubim* MT has *yhwh ṣb'wt yšb hkrwbym,* "Yahweh *Sabaoth* Seated-upon-the-Cherubim," but space requirements show that 4QSam[a] had a shorter text: *[yhwh y]šb hkrwb[ym].* Cf. Ulrich 1978:201.

3. *He mounted . . . and carried* We read the singular verbs of LXX[B] in preference to the plurals of MT and certain other MSS.

*the ark of Yahweh* So LXX[BAMN]. MT, LXX[L] have *'rwn h'lhym,* "the ark *of God,*" that is, "the holy ark," as in v. 2.

*upon* Reading *'l* with 4QSam[a] and LXX *eph'.* MT has *'l* for *'l,* as frequently in Samuel.

*from* So MT, LXX[LMN], 4QSam[a]. LXX[BA] have "to," erroneously (cf. I Sam 7:1).

*Ahio* The proper name *'ḥyw* (MT *'aḥyô*) is understood by LXX as "his brothers." Wellhausen, Budde, Caird, and Campbell (1975:129,171) prefer reading it as "his brother" (singular), to which Budde (1934:49), followed by Caird, would prefix *ṣdwq,* "Zadok"; contrast Driver, Smith, and Carlson 1964:63.

*the cart* Followed in MT by *ḥdšh wyś'hw mbyt 'byndb 'šr bgb'h,* a long dittography from the first part of the verse. Delete with LXX, 4QSam[a].

4. *the ark* So LXX[BAMN]. MT, LXX[L]: "the ark *of God,*" that is, "the holy ark," as in v. 2 and v. 3 (MT, LXX[L]).

*Uzza walking alongside the ark* That is, *w'z' hlk l'mt h'rwn,* which was lost after the previous *h'rwn* (homoioteleuton). It has been partially restored in the text of LXX[L], which reads the last part of the verse as *kai oza kai hoi adelphoi autou aporeuonto emprosthen kai ek plagiōn tēs kibōtou,* "*Uzza* and his brothers [= Ahio] walking in front of *and alongside* the ark," a combination of the lost *w'z' hlk l'mt h'rwn* and the final words of the verse, *w'ḥyw hlk lpny h'rwn.*

*Ahio* Again read as "his brothers" by LXX. See the *Textual Note* in the preceding verse.

5. *and the Israelites* So LXX[BAMN]: *kai hoi huioi israēl* = *wbny yśr'l.* 4QSam[a]: *[wkl] bny yśr[']l,* "and *all* the Israelites" (cf. LXX[L]). MT: *wkl byt yśr'l,* "and all *the house of* Israel."

*with sonorous instruments* That is, *bkly 'z,* lit. "with instruments of might," as in v. 14 below (see the *Textual Note* there) and II Chron 30:21. Here and in v. 14 this is rendered *en organois hērmosmenois,* "with tuned instruments," by LXX, and it is prefixed in the present passage with *en ischui* = *b'z,* a vestige of a second rendering. In v. 14 MT has *bkl 'z,* "with all (his) strength," and I Chron 13:8, the Chronicles correspondent to the present verse, supports the same reading here; but *bkl 'z* is to be rejected in both cases as a clear case of *lectio facilior.* For the reading of MT, see the *Textual Note* that follows.

*and songs* Reading *wbšyrym* with LXX *kai en ōdais* and 4QSam[a] [*w*]*bšyrym* (cf. I Chron 13:8). For *bkly ʿz wbšyrym,* "with sonorous instruments and songs" (cf. the preceding *Textual Note*), MT has *bkl ʿṣy brwšym,* "with every sort of cypress wood." This seems to be an obvious error, but its originality is vigorously maintained by Soggin (1964), who would render it "and with all clappers of juniper" or (reading *kly* for *kl* with LXX, Vulg.) "with instruments of juniper."

*sistrums* MT *wbmnʿnʿym,* for which LXX *(kai en kymbalois)* and 4QSam[a] *(wbṁ[ṣl]ṫym)* have *wbmṣltym,* "(and with) cymbals" (cf. I Chron 13:8). It is impossible to choose between these variants.

*and cymbals* MT *wbṣlṣlym,* for which LXX *(kai en aulois)* has *wbḥlylym,* "and (with) clarinets"; 4QSam[a] is not extant at this point. Again, there is no basis for choosing between the variants.

6. *Nodan* So 4QSam[a]: *nwdn.* LXX[B] *nōdab* is probably a corruption of **nōdan,* and Josephus' form, *cheidōn(os)* (*Ant.* 7.81), reflects *kydn* (so I Chron 13:9), which, though preferred by Rehm, is surely a corruption of *nwdn.* MT *nkwn,* which also arose from *nwdn* (> **nwkn*), has been interpreted in a variety of ways (see Carlson 1964:77–79): (1) as a proper name, "Nacon"; (2) as a *Nipʿal* participle, "a *certain* threshing floor" (Morgenstern 1918), "a *secure* threshing floor" (Arnold 1917:62), "a *permanent* threshing floor (Marget 1920), "a *prepared* threshing floor" (cf. Syr. *taqnāʾ*); (3) a common noun (cf. Job 12:5), "the threshing floor of the *stroke*" (Tur-Sinai 1951:279). LXX[L] has *orna tou iebousaiou* = *ʾrwnh hybwsy,* "Araunah the Jebusite," whose threshing floor is involved in 24:18–25.

*his hand* Reading *ʾt ydw* with 4QSam[a] *(*[*ʾt*]*ydw),* LXX, Syr., Targ., and Vulg. MT, which reads *ʾl* for the following *ʿl* as in v. 3 above and frequently, has lost *ʾt ydw* by haplography (homoioarkton). Alternatively, we might defend the shorter reading of MT as elliptical (cf. GK[2] §117g), as in the poetry of 22:17.

*on* That is, *ʿl* (LXX[B] *epi,* Syr. *ʿl*), for which MT, as noted in the previous *Textual Note,* has *ʾl* (so 4QSam[a] and LXX[L] [*pros*]).

*to steady it* Two readings compete for attention here. MT has *wyʾḥz bw,* "and steadied it." The OG reading was *(tou) kataschein autēn* = *lʾḥz bw* or *lʾḥzw,* "to steady it" (so LXX[MN]; cf. Josephus, *Ant.* 7.81; I Chron 13:9). In LXX[BAL] the MT reading has been added to the text, producing a doublet: *kataschein auten kai ekratēsen* (LXX[L] *ekrataiōsen*) *autēn,* and LXX[BA] add *tou kataschein autēn* yet again at the end of the verse. Our choice of *lʾḥz bw* is arbitrary. See, further, Ulrich 1978:199–201.

*had let it slip* Read *šĕmāṭô* with LXX *periespasen autēn* (LXX[B] *auton*) and probably Targ. *mrgwhy* = *mgrwhy* (cf. Targ. *wmgrwhʾ* for MT *wyšmṭwh* in II Kings 9:33); the form is probably dual (< **šĕmāṭāhū*). MT has *šĕmāṭû,* "had let (it) slip" (plural); there is no Biblical Hebrew evidence for an intransitive meaning of this verb in *Qal* (*pace* RSV, NEB "stumbled").

7. *Yahweh* So LXX[BA]. MT, followed by LXX[LMN] and 4QSam[a], has "the wrath of Yahweh."

*and struck him down* That is, *wykhw,* to which all witnesses to the Samuel text add *šm hʾlhym,* understood as "and *God* struck him down *there.*" Probably, however, *šm* (which, if taken to mean "there," is oddly repetitious before *šm,* "there," a few words later) is to be read *šēm*, "name"—thus, "and *the name of God* struck him down"—the hypostasis having been introduced in accordance with the Deuteronomic and post-Deuteronomic notion that it was Yahweh's name, not the god himself, that was cultically available in the ark (compare, e.g., the Deuteronomic formulation in 7:13 with the older statement in 7:6). Thus I Chron 13:10, which lacks *šm h'lhym*, exhibits the primitive form of the text here.

After *šm h'lhym* there is another plus in many witnesses. MT has *'l hšl*, which is taken by those Greek MSS that represent it (LXX$^{AL}$) to mean *epi tē propeteia*, "on account of (his) rashness," and similarly by Targ. as *'l d'štly*, "because he had erred" (cf. Sotah 35a). But, in fact, *'l hšl* is a remnant of a longer addition, viz. *'l 'šr šlḥ ydw 'l h'rwn*, which appears in I Chron 13:10 and 4QSam$^a$ (*['l 'šr šlḥ 't ydw ']l [h]'rwn*) and was probably in the Greek text used by Josephus (cf. *Ant.* 7.81); cf. also Syr.

*before God* Reading *lpny (h)'lhym*, as in I Chron 13:10, on the basis of LXX *enōpion tou theou*, which, however, is preceded by *para tēn kibōton (tou) kyriou*. The latter reflects *'m 'rwn yhwh*, corresponding to MT *'m 'rwn h'lhym*, "with the holy ark." Of these variants, that shared by OG and Chronicles is preferable; the reading of MT is reminiscent of v. 4.

8. *David became angry* That is, *wyḥr ldwd;* so MT and 4QSam$^a$ (*[w]yḥr ld[wyd]*). The LXX translation, *kai ēthymēsen daueid*, "(and) David was disheartened," in place of the expected *kai ethymōthē daueid* (cf. v. 7), is euphemistic. Cf. I Sam 15:11 and Sotah 35a.

*is called* LXX interprets *wyqr'* as *wĕyiqqārē'* and renders it *(kai) eklēthē*, "is called"; MT reads it as *wayyiqrā'*, "he (David) called." A third possibility is *wĕyiqrā'*, "one calls."

9. *and fearful of* That is, *wayyīrā' dāwīd*, lit. "and *David was* fearful of."

*he said to himself* MT: *wy'mr*. 4QSam$^a$: *l'mwr* (so LXX and I Chron 13:12).

*"can . . . with me?" So . . . arrived* Reading *wybw' 'ly 'rwn h'lhym wyb' 'rwn yhwh* on the basis of LXX$^L$ *eiseleusetai pros me hē kibōtos tou theou kai ēlthen he kibōtos kyriou*. This reading might be taken as the result of a combination of variants, viz. *ybw' 'ly 'rwn h'lhym* and *ybw' 'ly 'rwn yhwh;* but it would be strange to find such a long doublet preserved when the variation involved only a single word. I assume, then, that LXX$^L$ reflects the primitive text, shortened by haplography in all other witnesses to *ybw' 'ly 'rwn yhwh*, ". . . can Yahweh's ark come with me?"

10. *[it]* Reading *'rwn yhwh*, "the ark of Yahweh," with MT. LXX reflects *'rwn bryt yhwh*, "the ark *of the covenant* of Yahweh."

*the Gittite* LXX$^L$ adds *mēnas treis*, "for three months," the remnant of a long haplography from "the house of Obed-edom the Gittite" in v. 10 to "the house of Obed-edom the Gittite" in v. 11, which has been repaired (the restored material standing under the Hexaplaric asterisk in $e_2$).

11. *Obed-edom and all his house* So MT, LXX$^A$. LXX$^L$ (cf. LXX$^{BMN}$), in anticipation of v. 12, reads "the house of Obed-edom and everything he had."

12. *[he] said to himself, "I'll . . . house!"* This reading survives only in the texts of LXX$^L$ *(kai eipen daueid epistrepsō tēn eulogian eis ton oikon mou)* and OL *(et dixit david revocabo benedictionem in domum meam): wy'mr dwd 'šyb 't hbrkh 'l byty*, lit. "and David said, 'I shall bring back the blessing to my house.' " This was lost in MT when a scribe's eye skipped from *wy'mr dwd* to *wylk dwd* at the beginning of the next

sentence (Freedman). In view of the light it casts on David's motives, it can hardly be an expansion, though it might have been deleted in MT by a scribe who wanted to protect David (cf. Smith).

*Yahweh's ark* So LXX, Syr., and Targ. MT has "the ark of God," that is, "the holy ark."

13. *whenever . . . six paces* This is substantially the text of MT: *whyh* (see the NOTE to this verse) *ky ṣ'dw nś'y h'rwn ššh ṣ'dym* (deleting *yhwh* after *'rwn* with LXX$^{B}$). The divergence of LXX is difficult to understand. LXX$^{B}$ reads *kai ēsan met' autōn airontes tēn kibōton hepta choroi,* "and with them were seven dancing troops carrying the ark"; and OL diverges further, reading "with David" and omitting "carrying the ark"; cf. also Josephus, *Ant.* 7.85.

*he would sacrifice* LXX *kai thyma* reflects *wzbḥ,* which we read as a verb (see the NOTE to this verse). MT has *wyzbḥ,* "he sacrificed," also discussed in the NOTE. Syr. has "*David* sacrificed."

*a fatted bull* So MT: *šwr wmry'* (cf. LXX), lit. "a bull and a fatling," which is probably, as Freedman points out to me, a case of hendiadys. Compare Syr., which has *twr' mpṭm',* "a fattened bull," for *twr' wmpṭm',* "a bull and a fatling." Enough of 4QSam$^{a}$ survives at this point to show that it diverges from all other witnesses to the text of Samuel and sides with I Chron 15:26: [ ]*šb*[*'h*] *pṙ*[*y*]*ṁ wšb'*[*h 'ylym*], "seven bullocks and seven rams."

14. *clad* We read *whw' ḥgwr,* lit. "and he was clad," with LXX$^{L}$. Other Greek MSS share the reading of MT and 4QSam$^{a}$, which has [*wdw*]*yd ḥgwr,* "and *David* was clad."

*strumming* That is, *mkrkr* (so MT), rendered *anakroueto* = *krkr* by LXX. For the meaning of the verb, see the NOTE on "strumming on a sonorous instrument."

*on a sonorous instrument* LXX *en organois hērmosmenois* reflects *bkly 'z,* which is superior to MT's *lectio facilior, bkl 'z,* "with all (his) might" (see the *Textual Note* on "with sonorous instruments," v. 5). We read *bkly* as singular *(biklî),* rather than plural (LXX *en organois* = *biklê*).

15. *all Israel* So LXX$^{L}$, Syr., MT$^{MSS}$ (cf. I Chron 15:28). MT, LXX$^{BAMN}$: "all *the house of* Israel."

16. *As the ark entered the City of David* So LXX$^{B}$: *kai egeneto tēs kibōtou paraginomenēs heōs poleōs daueid* = *wyhy h'rwn b' 'd 'yr dwd.* MT differs in three ways:

1) For *wyhy* MT has *whyh,* to which LXX *kai egeneto* and 4QSam$^{a}$ *wyhy* (cf. I Chron 15:29) seem preferable. However, de Boer (1974) notes the several instances in Samuel where *whyh* stands in MT for an expected *wyhy* (I Sam 1:12; 10:9; 17:48; 25:20) and challenges their routine emendation (cf. GK$^{2}$ §112uu). He asks, with justification, why a good, smooth reading, *wyhy,* was changed to one that does not seem to make sense, *whyh.* Building on the earlier work of Davidson (1902 §54), de Boer argues that there was "a special meaning of perfect with *waw:* an attempt to express a brief resumption of an event described in detail previously . . ." (1974:46). Specifically, he concludes that in the construction introduced by *whyh* at the beginning of the present verse we have "a brief statement of the situation, resuming the event of the bringing up of the ark previously described in detail" (p. 48). "2 Sam. 6:16a," he says (p. 50), "seems to preserve an intentional construction, a perfect with *waw* followed by two participles, expressing the condition by picturing the situation and introducing the verbal clause —she despised him. 'Well, thus it was, the ark of the Lord coming into David's city,

and Michal, Saul's daughter, looking down through the window. . . ." (See also Campbell 1975:130–31).

2) MT expands *h'rwn*, "the ark," preserved by LXX^BMN^, to *'rwn yhwh*, "the ark *of Yahweh*" (so LXX^AL^, Syr.).

3) MT omits *'d* before *'yr*, against LXX and I Chron 15:29. Note also that for *b' 'd 'yr dwd*, Syr. has *bbyth ddwyd*, as if reflecting *bbyt dwd*—thus, "When the ark of Yahweh *was in the house of* David. . . ."

*leaping and strumming* MT *mpzz wmkrkr*. So (?) LXX^B^: *orchoumenon kai anakrouomenon* = *mpzz (mrqd?) wmkrkr*. LXX^L^ prefixes the reading of LXX^B^ with *paizonta kai* = *mśḥq w-* —thus, "*reveling and* leaping and strumming." The reading of I Chron 15:29 is *mrqd wmśḥq*, "skipping and reveling."

17. *and set it up* MT, LXX add "in its place," an expansion to be omitted with Syr. and, as space considerations indicate, 4QSam^a^. Josephus' text seems also to have had the shorter reading (*Ant.* 7.86), and I Chron 16:1 also displays the primitive situation. The source of the expansion may be I Kings 8:6, where it is said that during the dedication of Solomon's temple the ark was brought "*to its place*—the sanctum of the temple, the holy of holies—beneath the cherubim." Note that the syntax of the Kings passage shows that here "in its place" in the present passage is to be read in apposition to "in the tent"—thus, "*in its place*—the tent David had pitched for it." Thus, even if "in its place" were primitive here, it could not be used as evidence for a separate chamber (a *dĕbîr* or holy of holies) within the Davidic tent (*pace* Cross 1947:64). The textually secondary character of this reading also vitiates Rupprecht's comparison of II Sam 6:17 and I Kings 8:6 (1977:59–61), from which he concludes that "in its place," assumed to be primitive, received nearer definition as "in the tent," etc., secondarily because of its present literary context (cf. 7:1–7); this is putting the matter precisely backwards.

*and David offered* So MT, LXX^ALMN^, and 4QSam^a^. LXX^B^: "and *he* offered *for it (autē = lô).*"

*holocausts before Yahweh* MT, LXX: "holocausts before Yahweh *and communion offerings.*" Syr. (cf. I Chron 16:1): "holocausts *and communion offerings* before Yahweh." Its varying position suggests that "and communion offerings" *(wšlmym)* is secondary, an anticipation of the following verse.

18. *the holocausts* Cf. LXX. MT: "the holocaust" (singular).

*Yahweh* All extant witnesses to the text of Samuel add "Sabaoth," but I Chron 16:2 omits it. In light of v. 2 above (cf. the *Textual Note* on "Yahweh Seated-upon-the-Cherubim") we may assume that the OG reading here was "Yahweh," to which "Sabaoth" was added recensionally in LXX^B^ *(tōn dynameōn)* as well as LXX^L^ *(sabaōth)*, and that 4QSam^a^, which is not extant at this point, shared the shorter, primitive reading. Cf. Ulrich 1978:201–2.

19. *to . . . the whole multitude of Israel* Preceded in LXX^L^ by "from Dan to Beersheba."

*a* (tris) So LXX (cf. I Chron 16:3). MT: one . . . one . . . one.

*a ring of bread* MT: *ḥlt*. LXX: *kollyrida* = *lbbt* (cf. 13:6,8,10). I Chron 16:3 has *kkr*.

*a raisin-cake* MT, I Chron 16:3: *'šyšh*. LXX: *laganon apo tēganou* = *rqq mḥbt* (?), "a griddle cake."

# NOTES

6 1. *thirty thousands.* That is, thirty units. The *'elep,* "thousand," was a military contingent of an unknown size, perhaps about 5 to 14 troops (see *I Samuel,* the NOTE on "thirty thousands of the infantry" at 4:10, and Mendenhall 1958:63). According to these figures, David was accompanied by 150 to 420 men.

2. *Baalah.* See Map 3. The city is also called *ba'ălâ* in the description of the northern border of Judah in Josh 15:9,10. Elsewhere it is called *qiryat ba'al,* "Kiriath-baal (the City of Baal)" (Josh 15:60; 18:14; cf. LXX, v. 15), or *qiryat yĕ'ārîm,* "Kiriath-jearim (the City of Forests")," as in the material that forms the background to the present episode (see I Sam 6:21; 7:1,2). The identification of these two is made explicit in Josh 15:9; I Chron 13:5; and a Qumran text of the present passage (see the *Textual Note*). But all scholars do not regard it as certain (see the discussion in Schicklberger 1973: 133–40). The modern site of Kiriath-jearim is Tell el-'Azhar, near Qaryet el-'Enab, ca. fourteen miles northwest of Jerusalem. It was one of the four Gibeonite cities, a point stressed in connection with 5:25 above by Blenkinsopp (1972:134 n. 4; cf. pp. 53,79), who understands the position of the present episode immediately after the account of David's victories in 5:17–25 to suggest "that the ark could be moved only after the Philistines had been driven from the Gibeonite region." Cf. Carlson 1964:58–60.

*the holy ark.* Hebrew *'ărôn hā'ĕlōhîm.* The ark, a portable box or chest venerated as the visible sign of the presence of Yahweh (see the NOTE on "Yahweh Seated-upon-the-Cherubim" below and the discussion in *I Samuel,* pp. 108–9), has resided at Baalah (Kiriath-jearim) since shortly after its return from the territory of the Philistines, who captured it in the battle of Ebenezer (I Sam 4:1–11); see I Sam 7:1,2, where we are told that its sojourn in Kiriath-jearim lasted twenty years.

*over which the name of Yahweh . . . is called.* That is, where Yahweh can be invoked. A person, place, or thing over which someone's name is called *(niqrā' šēm 'al)* is specially identified with him (cf. the NOTE on "and my name will be called there" in 12:28), and in cultic use the expression identifies something associated with a deity, especially the temple of Yahweh (I Kings 8:43 = II Chron 6:33; Jer 7:10,11,14,30; 32:34; 34:15). In the present passage we are told that the sacred object in question is a "holy ark" *('ărôn hā'ĕlōhîm)* and that in particular it is associated with Yahweh—it is Yahweh's ark. Thus, calling Yahweh's name over the ark implies his having or taking possession of it (BDB 1027–28; cf. Schreiner 1963:41; Carlson 1964:74), but this does not entitle us to suppose it formerly belonged to another god (cf. Galling 1956).

*Yahweh Seated-upon-the-Cherubim.* Hebrew *yahweh yōšēb hakkĕrūbîm,* a liturgical epithet of the god of Israel that envisions him as an enthroned monarch flanked by a pair of the sphinxlike mythological creatures known as cherubim (see *I Samuel,* the NOTE at 4:4). The ark was thought of as a portable cherub-throne or palanquin (cf. Exod 25:10–21; 37:1–9), which could be carried about by the deity's human subjects. In theophanic poetry Yahweh was said to fly in a cloud-chariot on cherub wings (see 22:11 and the NOTE there; Eissfeldt [1957:144] also cites Ps 104:3). The purpose of the longer title is specification: Yahweh Seated-upon-the-Cherubim is distinguished from other manifestations of Yahweh. It was, presumably, to the Yahweh of Shiloh *(yahweh ṣĕbā'ôt bĕšīlōh,* I Sam 1:3; *yahweh šīlô,* I Sam 1:25) that this particular epithet pointed (cf. Eissfeldt 1950:139–46). Biblical tradition suggests that in the late pre-monarchical period Shiloh was an Israelite shrine of considerable importance, the authority of which David may deliberately have attempted to transfer to Jerusalem by the adoption of the cherub-throne iconography and other features of the Shilonite cult of Yahweh (cf. Eissfeldt 1957:143–45).

3. *a new cart.* Cf. I Sam 6:7. The requirement that the vehicle of transference be new has to do, presumably, with ritual purity. The cart must not have been polluted by previous secular use.

*the house of Abinadab on the Hill.* Where the ark was deposited in I Sam 7:1. Abinadab was the father of the priests Uzza and Ahio as well as Eleazar (I Sam 7:1; but see the following NOTE), and he bears a name that Budde would compare to that of Nadab, Aaron's eldest son (Exod 6:23; etc.). The Hill *(haggib'â)* is, presumably, a district of Kiriath-jearim (Baalah). Aharoni (1959:228–29), reading *gb't kryt* <*y'rym*>, "the Hill of Kiriath-jearim," in Josh 18:28 on the assumption of a loss of *y'rym* before the following *'rym,* supposes the Hill to have been the older, Benjaminite district of this border town, as distinct from the later Judahite settlement. I am not convinced by the evidence assembled by Blenkinsopp (1972:79–83) that the Hill refers to Gibeon.

*Uzza and Ahio.* (Or possibly "Uzza and his brother[s]"; see the *Textual Note* on "Ahio".) In I Sam 7:1 neither Uzza nor Ahio is mentioned. Instead we read of the consecration of "[Abinadab's] son Eleazar." Perhaps these are three brothers. We must allow the possibility, however, that Uzza (*'uzzā'* or *'uzzâ,* as his name is sometimes spelled [cf. vv. 7,8 MT]) is identical to Eleazar *('el'āzār);* for the alternation of the *'z* and *'zr* elements compare the (priestly) musician's name given as Uzziel *('uzzî'ēl)* in I Chron 25:4 (where LXX$^B$ has *azaraēl*) and as Azarel *('ăzar'ēl)* in I Chron 25:18, and especially the name of King Uzziah (*'uzzīyāhû* in II Kings 15:32; etc.; *'uzzīyâ* in II Kings 15:13; etc.), who is called Azariah elsewhere (*'ăzaryāhû* in II Kings 15:6; etc.; *'ăzaryâ* in II Kings 14:21; etc.).

5. *lyres, harps, tambourines, sistrums, and cymbals.* Instruments of revelry and celebration. The lyre *(kinnôr)* and harp *(nēbel)* were the most common stringed instruments. David himself was a skilled lyrist (I Sam 16:16). The tambourine was a small, double-membraned drum, carried and beaten with the hand. The **mĕna'ănēa'* is mentioned nowhere else in the Bible; the translation of *mĕna'ăn'îm* in the present passage as "sistrums" is based on etymology (cf. Rabbinic Hebrew *n'n',* "shake") and the Vulgate's rendering, *sistra.* The term used here for cymbals, *ṣelṣĕlîm,* was apparently a less common synonym of *mĕṣiltayim,* which appears (earlier) in the present list in the Qumran scroll and in I Chron 13:8 (see the *Textual Note* on "sistrums").

6–7. The incident described in these verses recalls the wave of plague and death that coincided with the ark's sojourn in Philistine territory (I Samuel 5) and more particularly the slaying of the Beth-shemeshites in I Sam 6:19. Tur-Sinai (1951:282–85) even argued that the story of the smiting of the men of Beth-shemesh in I Samuel 6 and that of the smiting of Uzza in II Samuel 6 are two versions of a single etiological legend, and Kraeling (1928:156 n. 81) supposed that the ark was removed to the house of Obed-*edom* to placate the god of plague, Resheph, with whom the deity Edom was associated (cf. the NOTE on "the house of Obed-edom the Gittite," v. 10). But it seems sufficient to point out that the ark, being a very holy object, was also, therefore, a very dangerous one. The ancient Israelite understood that all sacred things were to be approached with great care and that the manipulation of sacred objects was an activity necessarily insulated by ritual precautions and taboos. The transference of the ark from one place to another, therefore, was not a task to be taken lightly; it amounted to a sacred rite. Any defect in preparation for or error in the performance of such a rite might provoke a harmful response from a potentially beneficial power. Because it was believed that the stronger the power was, the greater the care required in coping with it, the two incidents in I Samuel 6 and II Samuel 6 could be understood as instances of the awesome power of Yahweh's ark.

8. *(the reason being . . . to this day).* The spot where the incident reported in vv. 6–7 was remembered as having taken place was called *pereṣ 'uzzâ,* "Uzza's Breach." The parenthesis in the present verse was added by the writer or, more likely, a later editor. It introduces a fanciful explanation of the place-name, and by calling the contemporary site and its name to the attention of the reader (". . . to this day") it offers confirmation of the veracity of the larger account. The place got its name, we are told, because it was there that Yahweh "made a breach *(pāraṣ . . . pereṣ)* in Uzza," i.e., caused an interruption in the descent of his family line (cf. Judg 21:15). This explanation is likely to be historically accurate in part. Uzza's Breach probably did take its name from Uzza son of Abinadab, who was remembered as having died there. But *pereṣ,* "breach," must have been a geographical term designating a breach or gap in the fortifications of Jerusalem, which served as an entrance through which David had intended to convey the ark.

10. *the City of David.* See the NOTES at 5:7,9. The name is used here in its strict sense, designating the fortified hilltop called "the stronghold of Zion" in 5:7 and renamed after its capture by David (cf. 5:9). This, then, is not a reference to Jerusalem as a whole, and it is safe to suppose that "the house of Obed-edom" was located somewhere in the larger city (see Simons 1952:245).

*the house of Obed-edom the Gittite.* The man is a foreigner from Gath, almost certainly the Philistine Gath, in the army of whose king David once served (I Samuel 27). In 15:18 we learn of six units ("hundreds") of Gittite soldiers "who had followed [David] from Gath"; they were led by a certain Ittai (15:19), a zealously loyal vassal of David (cf. 15:21), who seems to have occupied a position of considerable authority in David's personal militia (cf. 18:2,5,12). Obed-edom is probably another partisan whose loyalty dates to David's days in Gath and Ziklag, a man upon whom David can rely. Later tradition, perhaps troubled by the consignment of the ark to the care of a foreigner, ascribed to Obed-edom a Levitical genealogy and remembered him as a musician (I Chron 15:21; 16:5, cf. v. 38) and gatekeeper (I Chron 15:18,24). In I Chron 26:4–8 we are told that he was the father of eight sons—"because God had blessed him" (v. 5; cf. v. 11 in the present passage)—whose special responsibility was the south gate of the temple and care of the storehouse (*bêt hā'ăsūpîm;* I Chron 26:15). But it is highly unlikely that Obed-edom was a Levite. Indeed, his name, *'ōbēd-'ĕdôm,* seems to be non-Yahwistic, meaning "servant of (the deity) Edom," identified by Albright with *'a-tu-m,* the consort of the chthonic deity Resheph according to Egyptian magical papyri (cf. Albright 1969b:140 and bibliography cited in n. 76).

13. Our interpretation follows that of Arnold (1917:41) and Miller and Roberts (1977:17 and 96, n. 157) against Hertzberg (". . . the passage does not, of course, mean 'after each sixth step' . . ."). As Driver points out, however, this requires that the verbs read *whyh . . . wzbḥ*. There is support for *wzbḥ* in the Greek text, which is widely divergent in the first clause. The sense of the received Hebrew text (*wyhy . . . wyzbḥ*, "when the ark bearers advanced six paces, he sacrificed," etc.) apparently is that after the first six paces of the journey, which showed David that Yahweh would now allow the ark to be brought into the City of David, sacrifices were made in gratitude (cf. I Chron 15:26). But the evidence collected by Miller and Roberts provides for repeated sacrifices along the way in processions accompanying the transfer and installation of "gods." One can hardly object that the number of sacrificial animals seems excessive here in view of the statistics given for the ceremony accompanying Solomon's installation of the ark in the temple in I Kings 8:5,63—twenty-two thousand victims from the herds and one hundred twenty thousand from the flocks!

14. *a linen ephod.* See Tidwell 1974. In contrast to the ornate garment of the high priest (cf. Exodus 28; 39), the ephod referred to here is a simple linen loincloth like that worn by the child Samuel (I Sam 2:18). The common assumption that it was special priestly clothing has been questioned by Phillips (1969), who argues that it is simply a child's garment, inappropriate for an adult (p. 487). It is clear, in any case, that David is scantily clad and that at least one spectator, Michal, finds this offensive (v. 15; cf. v. 20).

*strumming on a sonorous instrument.* Hebrew *mĕkarkēr biklî ʿōz* (see the *Textual Notes*). The basic meaning of the verb *krr* seems to have been "hop, jump" or the like, and in the present passage *mkrkr* has usually been understood to refer to David's hopping about, i.e., dancing. Recently, however, *mkrkr* has received further study in light of the Ugaritic verb *krkr*, which Avishur (1976) considers to stand in parallel with *ṣḥq*, "laugh," in *CTCA* 4(= *UT*⁴ 51).4.26 = 30, but which Ahlström (1978) has shown to be parallel rather to *ṯpd*, "stamp (the foot)." Both of these scholars believe *mkrkr* in II Sam 6:14,16 refers specifically to an activity of the fingers, as it does in the Ugaritic passage cited. Avishur (1976:261) thinks it means David is playing with his hands or fingers. Ahlström (1978:101) takes *mkrkr* "as a 'pars pro toto' reference to David's dancing gyrations," meaning that David's fingers are "snapping, wiggling, turning, twisting, fidgeting (or whatever)," the counterpart of the dancing of his feet. Neither Avishur nor Ahlström mentions the Septuagint's treatment of the phrase that follows *mkrkr*, from which we derive the translation "on a sonorous instrument" (see the *Textual Note*). Combining this evidence with the understanding of *mkrkr* as referring specifically to an activity of the fingers, we arrive at the possibility that we should render *mĕkarkēr biklî ʿōz* as "fingering—i.e., strumming on—a sonorous instrument." Note, further, that the Greek verb corresponding to *mkrkr* in the Septuagint here *(anakroueto)* and in v. 16 *(anakrouomenon)* is *anakrouesthai*, which refers specifically to the playing of musical instruments (see also Josephus, *Ant.* 7.85). To be sure, David is dancing, but *mĕpazzēz*, "leaping," which is introduced in v. 16 when David's dancing becomes the issue, conveys this fact adequately alone. Nor should we be surprised in such a context to find David, who first entered public life as a lyrist (I Sam 16:14–23), "strumming on a sonorous instrument."

15. *the shofar.* A common ram's horn instrument ordinarily used for signaling (Josh

6:4; etc.) rather than music making (but cf. Ps 150:3). The shofar is probably sounded here, therefore, to assemble the people and announce the arrival of the procession rather than as a part of the ceremonial music mentioned in v. 5 above.

16. *Michal daughter of Saul.* See the NOTE at 3:13. Michal has been in David's household since the conclusion of the negotiations described in 3:12–16.

*watching through a window.* The literary motif of "the woman at the window" occurs also in Judg 5:28; II Kings 9:30; Prov 7:6 (LXX); and Cant 2:9. It corresponds to a sculptural motif known from ivory plaques from Samaria, Arslan Tash, Nimrud, and Khorsabad (cf. Aharoni 1967:180–81). It has been associated with the cult of the Babylonian goddess Kililu, who was called *šarratu ša apāti,* "the queen of windows," and *mušīrtum ša apāti,* "she who leans out windows" (*CAD* 10, pt. II:271), or that of the Cypriote goddess called *aphroditē parakyptousa,* "Aphrodite Peeping-Out(-a-Window)" (see Dahood 1952:214–15; McKane 1970:334–36). Porter (1954:166), in support of his attempt to explain the Michal episode in the present chapter by appeal to a sacred marriage ritual (see the COMMENT on § XIV), has suggested that the use of the motif here has a cultic implication, Michal being depicted as a hierodule. We cannot assume, however, that the motif of the woman at the window, which became a narrative convention in Hebrew literature (cf. Abramsky 1980), retained any cultic associations after being taken up by the biblical writers. Moreover, there are two sides to the motif corresponding to the two sides of the character of goddesses like Kililu and the Cypriote Aphrodite, who were invoked in connection with fertility but also with death and destruction. The woman in the window is the bride or paramour (Prov 7:6 [LXX]; cf. II Kings 9:30) watching for her lover's arrival, but she is also the bride or mother watching anxiously for her beloved's return from battle or danger, as in Judg 5:28:

> Through the window she gazed,
> Sisera's mother cried through the lattice:
> "Why is his chariot so slow in coming?
> Why do the hoofbeats of his rig lag behind?"

Thus the motif belongs with the joyous side of the tradition of ancient Near Eastern love poetry, in which the bride-sister stands waiting in her chamber for her lover's entrance (Cant 2:9), but also with the anxious or grievous side of the same tradition (Cant 3:1–3), in which the bride or mother stands waiting, sometimes in vain, for a young man who has disappeared or perished (cf., for example, the texts treated by Jacobsen 1976:25–73). As for the present passage, it seems to me at least as likely that the dark side of this tradition suggested the use of the woman-in-the-window motif to the writer as that the light side did, as Porter supposes. After all, David is returning home from an important expedition, which, at least according to the present shape of our text, involved two major battles (5:17–25). Michal, therefore, is depicted in the conventional way, as the woman in the window awaiting her husband's return from war. Thus she has more in common with Sisera's poor mother than with the harlot of Prov 7:6 (LXX) or the painted queen of II Kings 9:30.

17. *the tent David had pitched for it.* The ark customarily resided in a tent, a detail that will become a central issue in chap. 7 (see the NOTE at 7:6). David's preparation of a tent for the ark's arrival, a gesture of respect for custom and precedent, is often cited as an example of his political sagacity. Public acceptance of the relocation of the ark was more likely if sacred tradition was preserved as much as possible. Cross

(1947:61–65) has suggested that David's tent was not identical to the tent-shrine of the pre-monarchical period but incorporated features from contemporary Canaanite temple architecture; thus, he believes, "the tent of David" or "an idealized reconstruction based on historical traditions of David's shrine" (1973:322) was the prototype of the Priestly tabernacle, which was at once a tent-shrine and, in effect, a portable temple (cf. the NOTE at 7:6). Rupprecht (1977), who believes that there was a temple in Davidic Jerusalem (cf. 12:20 and the NOTE there), argues that the present reference to a tent is secondary, a deliberately formulated assertion concerning the structural nature of the ark's abode before its transfer to Solomon's temple, motivated by 7:1–7 (p. 62); see the *Textual Note* on "and set it up."

*holocausts.* Whole burnt offerings *(ʿōlôt);* cf. Leviticus 1.

18. *communion offerings.* Hebrew *šělāmîm,* sacrifices offered to the deity and eaten by the worshipers near the altar (cf. Deut 27:7). Our translation assumes that this meal was thought of as a feast shared with the deity. But this has been doubted; see Milgrom 1976b:769, where other interpretations are listed.

19. *a ring of bread.* Hebrew *ḥallat leḥem,* forerunner of the Jewish bread challah. For the meaning of *ḥallâ,* "ring-shaped loaf," see Koehler 1948b.

*a date-cake.* Hebrew *ʾešpār,* which occurs only here and in the synoptic passage in I Chron 16:3. The meaning is uncertain. The rabbis understood an eshpar to be a choice cut of meat (cf. Biblical Hebrew *špr,* "be beautiful, pleasing," and Rabbinic Aramaic *šûpěrâ,* "beauty; best portion [of meat]"), according to Pesahim 36b one sixth of a bullock (as if *šiššît happār*); cf. Jastrow 130 and 154. But the treatment of the word by the Septuagint (*escharitēn,* "an ash-baked cake" [= *ʾšpt* or *ʾškr?*]) and by Aquila and Symmachus (*amyritēn* = *amylitēn* [?], "a hand-ground cake") suggests a kind of bread. In the present translation we follow Koehler (1948a).

## COMMENT

Yahweh's ark—a sacred object in the form of a cherub throne upon which the Israelites believed their god to be present—in earlier days was kept at Shiloh (I Sam 3:3); but when a Philistine army came up to Aphek and encamped on the threshold of the Ephraimite hills, the ark was brought to the battlefield by the anxious Israelites (I Sam 4:1–4), and in the battle that ensued it was captured (I Sam 4:11). It remained in enemy hands for seven months (I Sam 6:1), and all the while Yahweh afflicted the Philistine cities with a plague. Finally the Philistines, chastened now and fearful of the ark, returned it to Israelite territory with a compensatory offering of gold (cf. I Sam 6:1ff.). It came to rest at last in Kiriath-jearim (I Sam 7:1), and there it has remained, as far as we know (cf. *I Samuel,* the *Textual Note* at 14:18), until the beginning of the present episode.

Now David organizes an expedition to Kiriath-jearim, here called Baalah (see the NOTE, v. 2), to get the ark and conduct it to Jerusalem. The procession is an elaborate one: We are told of "reveling" and "songs," and there is a long catalogue of musical instruments (v. 5). One incident mars the transfer of the ark. As the party approaches Jerusalem, the officiating priest is struck down by Yahweh in consequence of a ritual accident (vv. 6–7), and David, at once annoyed and frightened, suspends his plan to bring the ark into the citadel. The same series of events, however, serves to remind the king of the potential benefits of the ark's presence, as the household to which it is diverted and lodged acquires Yahweh's blessing. After an interruption of three months, therefore, the procession is resumed (vv. 11–12). Amid great festivity and with numerous sacrifices (vv. 13,17–18) the ark of Yahweh enters the City of David and takes its place in a tent that David had prepared for it.

### *The Place of 6:1–19 in the Larger History*

In the larger sequence of events this episode follows immediately upon two victories in battle (5:17–25), in the second of which David succeeded in expelling the Philistines from Israelite territory (5:25), and it precedes the delivery of Nathan's oracle concerning the temple and Davidic dynasty to come (7: 1–7). This arrangement reflects the interpretation of these events made by the Deuteronomistic compiler of 5:11–8:18, whose overarching concern was a demonstration of Yahweh's choice of David and Jerusalem (cf. the Introduction, pp. 4–6). In the events described in 5:17–25 he saw the fulfilment of the divine promise that David would liberate Israel from Philistine control (3:18; cf. the COMMENT on § XII). In Nathan's prophecy he found—or rather, he articulated, since, as we shall see, chap. 7 shows considerable Deuteronomistic expansion—the definitive expression of Yahweh's exaltation of David and his house. In the transfer of the ark to Jerusalem he saw the climax of a long sequence of events that began in the wilderness of Transjordan when Moses first promised the people of Israel "rest from [their] enemies all around" (Deut 12:10) and spoke to them of "the place that Yahweh your god will choose . . . to put his name" (Deut 12:5), and which will find its denouement in Solomon's long speech in dedication of the temple in Jerusalem (I Kings 8) after Yahweh "has given rest to his people Israel" (I Kings 8:56); see, further, the COMMENT on § XV ("The Place of Nathan's Oracle in the Deuteronomistic History"). In this larger sequence of events the fortunes of the ark, where Yahweh's "name"—his cultically available power—is peculiarly present (cf. vv. 2,18), are given special attention as the holy object moves, in Deuteronomistic understanding, inexorably toward Jerusalem. Its departure from Shiloh was, according to the Deuteronomistically confected oracle in I Sam 2:27–36, a consequence of Yahweh's rejection of Shilonite (and all non-Jerusalemite!) priests in favor of the priestly house of Zadok of Jerusalem, whose dynasty is foretold in v. 35 in terms strikingly similar to those used of David's house in chap. 7 below (see *I Samuel,* the first NOTE at 2:35 and, more generally, the

COMMENT on § IV). The ark's arrival in Jerusalem, therefore, is a critical moment in this larger design: Yahweh's "name" is in its place and Israel is soon to have the promised "rest from all their enemies" (7:11). See, further, the COMMENT on § XV ("The Place of Nathan's Oracle in the Deuteronomistic History").

### *Historical Considerations*

As in the case of the relationship between the passages describing David's capture of Jerusalem (5:6–10) and his victories over the Philistines (5:17–25), therefore, the editorial concerns governing the position of the present passage are not chronological but thematic (cf. the COMMENT on § XII). We may not assume out of hand that the transfer of the ark succeeded the battles recounted in the preceding section. In this case, however, the judgment of most modern historians vindicates the received arrangement. "The final compiler," as Hertzberg puts it, "[is] right in connecting the bringing up of the ark with ch. 5; only after the victory over the Philistines will the possibility of bringing the ark and making it once again a national shrine have arisen. It could hardly have been done in the days of Saul. He never obtained the freedom from the Philistines that would have enabled him to take such a step." We should probably reconstruct the relative chronology of the period as follows:

1. After Ishbaal's death David became king of Israel (5:1–5), thereby uniting Judah and Israel under a single leader, at least in principle.
2. The Philistines, recognizing the danger this new situation represents for them (cf. p. 158 above), came up "in search of" David (5:17), doubtless in the hope that by laying hold of the new king they could prevent the unification of Judah and Israel from becoming a reality.
3. David engaged the Philistines in battle and enjoyed a series of successes (described in 5:17–25 as well as 23:13–17 and probably other stories that have not survived; cf. 8:1), the last of which (5:22–25) rendered Israelite territory altogether free of Philistines.
4. David moved against Jerusalem, the one remaining non-Israelite dominion in central Palestine, and captured it (5:6–10). He called the citadel the City of David and made it the capital of his newly united kingdom.
5. David retrieved the ark of Yahweh from Kiriath-jearim and set it up in the City of David (6:1–19), thereby transferring to his new capital city the venerable position once occupied by Shiloh as the seat of worship of Yahweh Seated-upon-the-Cherubim (cf. the NOTE at v. 2).

It is obvious that David must have emerged from this sequence of events in a very strong position. He was now king of Israel as well as Judah. His kingdom's enemies had been eliminated or neutralized. He had a new capital city that could serve him as a personal base of power inasmuch as he had conquered it with his private militia (see the NOTE on "the king and his men" at 5:6), and that could make a claim on the spiritual allegiance of the Israelites inasmuch as it was now the place where Yahweh's ark was venerated.

### *Psalm 132 and II Samuel 6*

In Ps 132:1–10 we read:

[1]Remember, O Yahweh, of David
        all his hardships,
[2]When he swore to Yahweh,
        vowed to Jacob's bull:
[3]"I will not enter the shelter of my house,
I will not lie on the mattress of my bed,
[4]I will not let my eyes have sleep,
        or my eyelids slumber,
[5]until I find a place for Yahweh,
        a camping place for Jacob's bull!"
[6]Lo, we heard of it in Ephrathah!
We found it in the territory of Jaar!
[7]Let us go to his camping place!
Let us prostrate ourselves at his footstool!
[8]Arise, O Yahweh, at your resting place,
        you and your mighty ark!
[9]Let your priests be clothed with vindication!
Let your faithful shout for joy!
[10](Arise) for the sake of your servant David!
Do not rebuff your anointed one!

Although it has not been admitted by all interpreters (cf. the survey in Fretheim 1967:294), this psalm makes reference to the events recounted in II Samuel 6. This is clear from the mention of Ephrathah and the territory of Jaar *(śĕdê yắʿar)* in v. 6 of the poem. That the territory of Jaar is Kiriath-jearim = Baalah has seldom been doubted. But it is often supposed that Ephrathah refers to the Bethlehem region, as elsewhere (Ruth 4:11; Mic 5:1[5:2]; I Chron 4:4), David's home district. In addition to Ephrathah of Judah, however, there was an Ephrathah of Benjamin (cf. *I Samuel,* the NOTE on "Rachel's Tomb" at 10:2, and especially Blenkinsopp 1969a:154–56), as shown by the Chronicler's genealogies, according to which Hur, the firstborn of Caleb's second wife, Ephrathah (I Chron 2:19), was the father of "Shobal, the father of Kiriath-jearim" (I Chron 2:50) as well as "Salma, the father of Bethlehem" (I Chron 2:51; 4:4). The parallelism in Ps 132:6 shows that the northern Ephrathah is intended here (cf. also Cross 1973:94–95 n. 16, and his references to the earlier work of F. Delitzsch). The thing found at Kiriath-jearim turns out to be Yahweh's ark (cf. v. 8), here referred to as "his footstool," as in Ps

99:5 and I Chron 28:2 (cf. Isa 66:1). So there can be little doubt that the events described in II Samuel 6 are referred to in Ps 132:6.

The psalm begins (v. 1) with a petition on behalf of David *(lĕdāwîd)* that Yahweh be mindful of the hardships *('unnôtô)* David endured in fulfiling the vow cited in vv. 3–5 (so correctly Fretheim 1967:291; cf. Weinfeld 1970:187). In the vow, we are told, David forswore the comforts of his own house (i.e., shelter and rest) until he could provide a dwelling place for Yahweh. Specifically, he spoke of a "place"—i.e., a shrine (cf. the NOTE at 7:10), a place *(māqôm)* where a deity may "arise" (*qûm;* cf. v. 8), a place for theophany—and a "camping place" (cf. Ps 78:28)—probably a tent-shrine or tabernacle (*miškānôt;* cf. Cross 1973:95 and n. 17, 244 and n. 107). At this point (v. 6) we have the announcement of the discovery of the ark at Kiriath-jearim and a summons (v. 7) to worship at Yahweh's "camping place." The latter must be a tent provided for the ark ("his footstool") in Kiriath-jearim, though this is mentioned nowhere else (see below); presumably it is not the "camping place" (in Jerusalem) anticipated in David's vow earlier in the psalm. The correct interpretation of the verses that follow (vv. 8–10) is made possible by Hillers' recognition that *limnûḥātékā* in v. 8 is to be translated "from"—not "to"—"your resting place," a detail of interpretation for which his arguments are incontrovertible (1968:49–50). Yahweh is entreated to "arise" from the place where he has been inactive; the verb used *(qûmâ)* is a common one in the biblical terminology of theophany, ordinarily referring to vigorous action of the deity on someone's behalf (Hillers 1968:50). In v. 10 we learn that the action in this case is to be on David's behalf, a point reinforced by the structure of the poem itself, in which vv. 1 and 10 correspond in a kind of semantic envelope (cf. Fretheim 1967:291–92). That is, Yahweh is petitioned to remember what David did (v. 1) and *therefore* to "arise" on David's behalf (v. 10), i.e., to stir himself from his inactivity "for the sake of . . . David." The conclusion of the psalm (vv. 11–18) shows the petition to have been successful. "Yahweh has chosen Zion" (v. 13), the City of David, as his dwelling place *(môšāb),* of which he says (v. 14), "This will be my resting place [cf. v. 8] from now on." Yahweh's ark, "his footstool" (v. 7), will go to the new "camping place" anticipated in David's vow (v. 5). Yahweh is pleased to act on behalf of David, whose descendants, he has promised, "from now on will sit upon your throne" (v. 12). The juxtapositions of Ephrathah in v. 6 and Zion in v. 13, of the references to the old "resting place" in v. 8 and the new one in v. 14, and of the petitions on behalf of the priests and faithful and David in vv. 9–10 and the divine promises regarding them in vv. 16–17—all these show that the psalm thematically and structurally centers "upon the transition from the old sanctuary to the new" (Cross 1973:96).

Cross (1973:94–97) stresses the differences between the account of David's transfer of the ark in II Samuel 6 and the allusions to the same story in Psalm 132. He speaks of a conflict between the accounts and argues that the underlying traditions are "wholly independent" (p. 97). There are differences, to be sure. We hear nothing of David's vow in II Samuel 6, for example, and the "camping place" of Ps 132:7, presumably a tent-shrine at Kiriath-jearim, is not mentioned in the Samuel narratives. But it does not follow that these things were not mentioned in a longer narrative from which II Samuel 6 was drawn. We must keep the character of 5:11–8:18 in mind: It is a compilation of narrative fragments joined and filled out editorially (see pp. 142–43, and *passim* in the COMMENTS on §§ X–XVII). There is no reason to suppose that David's vow, for example, was not reported in material preceding chap. 6 in its original context but not included here. The vow, in fact, belongs considerably earlier, before the capture of Jerusalem, since the "place" looked forward to in v. 5 of the psalm is obviously in Jerusalem and David has not yet been able to "find" it (cf. Fretheim 1967:294–96). It is possible, in other words, that Psalm 132 is based on material in a more nearly complete form of the story of the transfer of the ark in the very version from which II Samuel 6 is drawn, and we need not assume, in any case, that it reflects a substantially divergent version. It is true that the psalm makes no mention of the Obed-edom episode (Cross 1973:96–97) or, for that matter, the Michal incident; but these things are extraneous to the concerns of the psalmist, who had no reason to include them, and the Michal material is probably of discrete origin in any case (see the COMMENT on § XIV).

I think it is safe to suppose, therefore, that the impression given by the opening verses of II Samuel 6 that "the place of the Ark [is] well known and the Ark in effect in storage awaiting its transfer to a genuine national sanctuary" (Cross 1973:96) is historically erroneous. We are misled by the eclectic editing of the compiler of 5:11–8:18. The situation was more complex. The location of the ark had, in fact, been forgotten or at least had become inaccessible. David had vowed to provide Yahweh with a shrine, and the fulfilment of the vow required two things: the acquisition of a suitable site and the recovery of the sacred object in connection with which Yahweh made his presence felt. It was David's expulsion of the Philistines from Israelite territory that led to the satisfaction of both of these requirements (cf. the COMMENT on 5:17–25), the first by the capture of Jerusalem (5:6–10) and the second by the discovery (Ps 132:6) and transfer (II Samuel 6) of the ark.

### *Background in Ritual*

The recitation in a psalm of events connected with the transfer of the ark from Kiriath-jearim to Jerusalem raises the question of a cultic function of the story. As pointed out by Hillers (1968:48), it is widely supposed that in the Jerusalem cult of the monarchical period "the ark was carried in recurring cultic processions, into Jerusalem and into the temple (cf. Mowinckel 1967:vol. I:174ff., but also Cross 1973:91–111 *passim*), a supposition for which Psalm

132 is the critical bit of evidence (cf. Mowinckel 1967:vol. I:132). This psalm, in Mowinckel's words (1967:vol. I:174–75), is "the 'text' of a dramatic procession . . . [that] is here looked upon as a repetition of Yahweh's first entry into Jerusalem, when David laid the foundation of the cult of Yahweh there and introduced the holy ark as the centre of the cult. . . ." Note, however, that Hillers' successful challenge to the traditional rendering of Ps 132:8a as a pregnant construction meaning "Arise, O Yahweh, (and go) *to* your resting place!" (see above) eliminates any clear reference in the psalm to a *procession*, even though it remains the case that the theme of the poem is the passage of the ark from one place to another. Moreover, we must ask if it is fair to assume that a psalm thematically centered on an event of this kind necessarily served as the text for a periodic cultic reenactment of the event. A judgment on this question is beyond the scope of our present inquiry, but raising the question prepares us for consideration of the cultic background of II Sam 6:1–19, in connection with which the same question must be asked and answered.

There is no doubt that there is a cultic procession in II Samuel 6. Indeed, there are two processions, the first of which is prematurely terminated by the incident at Uzza's Breach (vv. 6–11). Involved are David and his entire elite corps of thirty military contingents (vv. 1–2), as well as the priests charged with the care of the ark (vv. 4–5), and (presumably) these are joined by civilians and laity when the party reaches Jerusalem (cf. "all Israel," v. 15). There is music (vv. 5,14,16), dancing (v. 16), "and the sound of the shophar" (v. 15). Animals are sacrificed every six paces (cf. the NOTE at v. 13) along the way.

The cultic event in II Samuel 6, therefore, is present and plain to see. How, then, are we to analyze it? It is widely held that the ritual details of this passage reflect practices of the Jerusalem cult of the monarchical period. According to Mowinckel, the festival of the kingship of Yahweh, an annual ceremony he reconstructs from various psalms (1967:vol. I:106–92), has influenced the composition of II Samuel 6. The ceremony, he says, reenacted David's transfer of the ark, but memory of the historical events involved was absorbed into the celebration of the greater mythic event of Yahweh's enthronement at the beginning of the cultic year; "the festival of the institution of Temple and cult in Jerusalem was identical with the new year festival, the enthronement festival of Yahweh" (1967:vol. I:175). Kraus (1951:27–35; 1966:183–85), while agreeing with Mowinckel that the rites of a later festival have shaped II Samuel 6, believes that the festival commemorated purely historical events, viz. the choice of Zion and election of David, the events of II Samuel 6 and 7. Porter (1954) attempts to mediate between these positions, reasoning, like Kraus, that the festival celebrated "the installation of David as king in Jerusalem" but arguing, on the basis of his study of II Samuel 6, that "David became king of Jerusalem by means of a Canaanite coronation rite" in which the enthronement of the king "was inseparable from the victory and enthronement of the god . . ." (see his summary, pp. 172–73; Porter's views in some ways anticipate the more broadly ranging discussion in Cross 1973:79–111, which, however, does not touch on the question of the cultic background of II Samuel 6). These studies, for all their differences, have in common the assumption that the festival described in II Samuel 6 was celebrated annually in the cult, an assumption that has led many scholars to conclude further that, as Mowinckel puts it (1967:vol. I:175), the author of the account "had no contemporary reports about the festival from the time of David, so he described it on the model of the celebration of his own day."

The picture changes, however, when one examines the (non-Israelite) ancient Near Eastern parallels to the cultic event in II Samuel 6. Note first the data brought forward by Miller and Roberts (1977). In the historical accounts (especially Mesopotamian) of the capture and return of divine images, of which the ark is the Israelite equivalent, Miller and Roberts have found numerous instructive parallels to the so-called "ark narrative" of I Samuel (cf. *I Samuel*, pp. 24–26 and 77–139 *passim*). As a by-product of their investigation they note that "one must now question the widespread tendency to regard 2 Samuel 6 as the reflex of a regular temple liturgy. Such an interpretation runs counter to the parallels, where the similar historical return of an image to its sanctuary is accompanied by ritual practices analogous to those mentioned in [the account of David's transfer of the ark to Jerusalem]" (1977:16). In particular, Miller and Roberts point to texts from the annals of Esarhaddon (Borger 1956:15–25) and Assurbanipal (Streck 1916:vol. II:265–69) in which the Assyrian kings describe the return of Marduk, the god of Babylon, to his city and temple after eleven years of exile in Assur. The parallels between Assurbanipal's account of the ceremony accompanying Marduk's return (English translation in Luckenbill 1926/27: vol. II:§§988–89) and the biblical account of the transfer of the ark are striking. "Just as Assurbanipal's army participated in the return of Marduk to his new sanctuary, so David's army participated in the return of the ark of Yahweh. Just as Marduk's journey was accompanied by music and rejoicing, so was the ark's. Moreover, just as the Assyrians offered sacrifices every double mile from the quay of Assur to the quay of Babylon, so David offered an ox and a fatling after every six steps" (Miller and Roberts 1977:16–17).

Illuminating as the parallels drawn by Miller and Roberts are, they are not as precise as one could wish. They contain excellent examples of the kind of ceremony that might accompany the escort of a god into a city—and to this extent they seem especially instructive here—but the restoration of a god to his temple, the subject of them all, is not, after all, the subject of II Samuel 6. The ark, though neglected and perhaps even inaccessible, has already been returned from captivity (I Sam 6:1–7:1; cf. Mann 1977:215), and there is as yet no temple of Yahweh in Jerusalem. There is, however, a royal palace—a new one (5:11)—and, indeed, a new royal city. II Sam 6:1–19 is an account of the introduction of Yahweh, present in his holy ark, to the City of David.

It can be compared, therefore, to other ancient Near Eastern accounts of the introduction of a national god to a new royal city. The several Assyrian examples exhibit a similar and more or less fixed pattern. In monumental or annalistic descriptions of newly founded or refounded royal cities and palaces, the introduction of Assur, the national god, with accompanying ceremonies is regularly reported. The inscriptions of Sargon II (721–705), for example, record his construction of a new royal city, which he called "Sargonsburg" (*dūr šarrukīn*, modern Khorsabad). After completion of the city and erection of the palaces, we are told (Luckenbill 1926/27:vol. II:§§94,98,101), Assur and the other great gods of Assyria were "invited into them" and honored by sacrifices; there followed a banquet and "a feast of music" (§98). The records of Sargon's son and successor, Sennacherib (704–681), describe the dedication of Nineveh, his new royal city, in similar terms (Luckenbill 1926/27:vol. II:§§370,403,416). When the royal palace was completed, Assur and the gods and goddesses of Assyria were invited in and offered sacrifices. Then, says Sennacherib (§§403,416), "I drenched the foreheads of my people with wine, with mead I sprinkled their hearts." Still later Esarhaddon (680–669), when he restored the palace at Nineveh, observed almost identical ceremonies. The invitation to Assur and the other gods was followed by sacrifices and "feasts and banquets of choice dishes" for all the people of the land (Luckenbill 1926/27:vol. II:§§699,700). This pattern—ceremonial invitation of the national god into a royal city, the presentation of sacrifices, and the preparation of a feast for the people of the land—finds its most lavish known example in the dedication of the palace of Assurnasirpal II (884–860) in his new royal city of Calah (modern Nimrud). He invited in Assur and the other great gods of the country and bestowed on them an extraordinarily long list of sacrifices, after which he provided food and drink for 69,574 (!) guests from Assyria and abroad (*ANET*[3], pp. 558–60). Note that later, when Sargon restored Assurnasirpal's palace at Calah (Luckenbill 1926/27:vol. II:138), not then the national capital, he invited in not Assur, the national god, but Nergal, Adad, and the other gods to whom Calah was traditionally sacred. Still, the ceremonial pattern was the same: A sacrifice of oxen, lambs, fowl, and so on, was followed by "a feast of music" for the people.

This ceremonial pattern is comparable to what we have in II Sam 6:17–19a. Yahweh, represented by his ark, is brought into David's new royal city and offered sacrifices. A banquet of breads and cakes is then distributed to the people. The mood is one of festivity, with music and feasting. Note especially David's desire for the blessing of his house (v. 12; cf. 7:29). A similar wish motivated the Assyrian kings mentioned above, whose texts invoke the favor of Assur for their palaces, their cities, themselves, and their dynasties (Luckenbill 1926/27:vol. II:§§94,101; etc.). The same was true of a certain Azitawadda, an eighth-century ruler calling himself king of the Danunians, who left a series of bilingual Hittite and Phoenician inscriptions (see *ANET*[3], pp. 653–

54) dedicating a city he built in Anatolia (modern Karatepe in southern Turkey) and named for himself. "When I had built this city," he says (*KAI* 26:II:17–III:1), "and given it the name Azitawaddiya, I caused (the god) Baal-*krntryš* to take up residence in it and caused a sacrifice to be brought for all the molten images. . . ." There follows in the text (III:3–11; cf. III:16–IV:12) an invocation of blessing on Azitawadda himself and on the city and its people. As explained in the COMMENT on § XVI, the emphasis on the blessing of the king and his house in such texts is suggestive for the interpretation of the relationship between the present account and the ancient materials underlying chap. 7.

Whether or not Mowinckel and the others are correct in postulating an annual procession involving the ark, therefore, they seem to be mistaken in reading the account of the transfer of the ark as a reflex of such a ceremony. The parallels suggest that II Samuel 6 preserves the details of a historically unique cultic event of a well-known type; there is no reason to suppose that it has been reshaped by any practice dating to post-Davidic times.

Note, finally, that in the non-Israelite examples of the introduction of a national god to a new royal city cited above, and in the reports of the restoration of a god to his sanctuary cited by Miller and Roberts, special emphasis is placed on the role in the proceedings played by the king, whose pious service to the deity in question is thus stressed. These accounts are, in the final analysis, testimonies to the special thing the king has done for the god and his people. They are frequently accompanied by professions of the high regard in which the deity holds the king and, as noted, prayers for divine favor uttered by the king. In this context we note the role played by David in the story in II Samuel 6. He shares the center of interest only with the ark itself; he is the principal celebrant in the rites and the supervisor of the procession. He appears unambiguously as the patron and founder of the cult of Yahweh in Jerusalem.

### *II Samuel 6 and the Ark Narrative*

Because it relates the return of the ark of Yahweh to a major Israelite sanctuary after its exile in Philistia and its sojourn at Kiriath-jearim, this section can be said to continue the story of the ark begun with its capture in I Samuel 4 and suspended after its deposit in the house of Abinadab in I Sam 7:1. Those numerous scholars who have accepted and refined Rost's analysis of the old narrative sources of Samuel (1926) regard all or parts of II Samuel 6 as belonging to an originally independent "ark narrative" comprising (generally speaking) I Sam 4:1b–7:1 + II Samuel 6 (see, most recently, Campbell 1975:126–43,169–74, and *passim*). The authors of several recent studies of the ark narrative, however, have preferred to exclude II Samuel 6 from its original boundaries (Schunck 1963a:97–101; Schicklberger 1973:129–49; Miller and Roberts 1977:22–26). These studies enter into extensive detail, which will not be rehearsed here. They identify many discrepancies in vocabulary and style between I Samuel 4–6 and II Samuel 6. Especially damaging to the assumption that these chapters originally belonged to a single composition are the changes of the name of the town from Kiriath-jearim (I Sam 6:21; 7:1,2) to Baalah (II Sam 6:2) and the name of the officiating priest from Eleazar (I Sam 7:1) to Uzza (II Sam 6:3; etc.), it being far from certain in the latter case that the same individual is intended by the two names (cf. the NOTE on "Uzza and Ahio," v. 3). In my judgment, however, the most compelling evidence for the original independence of II Samuel 6 from the ark narrative is the fact that these two compositions correspond in detail to distinct categories of surviving ancient Near Eastern literature. As shown by Miller and Roberts (1977:9–16), the ark narrative stands within a group of theological treatises on the capture in battle and return of divine images. II Samuel 6, as we have seen, belongs with a separate group of accounts of ceremonies accompanying the introduction of national gods to new royal cities. The ark narrative, like its Mesopotamian counterparts, is concerned preponderantly with the will of the deity involved, and for this reason we "seldom see any human participant rise above anonymity, for . . . the chief protagonist is no man but the ark of Yahweh itself" (*I Samuel,* p. 107). On the other hand, II Samuel 6, as we noted above, shares with *its* Mesopotamian counterparts an emphasis on the role of the king; David is indisputably the protagonist here. These fundamental generic differences weigh heavily against the theory that II Samuel 6 was once the conclusion of an independent narrative of which the body was I Samuel 4–6.

Moreover, as Miller and Roberts have shown (1977:73–75), the climate of military and political turmoil following the disastrous battle of Ebenezer (I Sam 4:1b–11), which evoked the searching questions addressed by the ark narrative, cannot have persisted beyond David's victories over the Philistines described in II Sam 5:17–25. "Why has Yahweh routed us today before the Philistines?" ask the elders of Israel in I Sam 4:3. How can the ark, the presence of which was supposed to guarantee victory, have itself been captured by the enemy? The ark narrative addresses these questions squarely and offers answers that reassure the audience of the power of Yahweh and attempt to explain his hidden purposes (see *I Samuel,* the NOTES and COMMENTS on §§ III, VI, VIII, and IX). It follows that this narrative must have been "formulated before David's victories removed the theological problem that created the need for it" (Miller and Roberts 1977:75). On the other hand, we have found historical reasons to doubt that the recovery of the ark could have taken place until after the expulsion of the Philistines "from Gibeon to Gezer" (5:25; see "Historical Considerations" above). Indeed it may have been the victories described in chap. 5 that made the capture of Jerusalem possible (see the COMMENT on § XII). If these historical judgments are correct, it is obvious that the story of the transfer of the ark must have been written sometime after the decisive battle reported in 5:21–25. In short, the ark narrative of I Samuel, which must have been composed *before* this battle, and the story in II Samuel 6, which must have been composed *after* it, can hardly have been original components of the same composition.

II Samuel 6, as I understand it, is based on an account of the transfer of the ark of Davidic date. Perhaps it was drawn from David's annals, as suggested by the annalistic character of some of the comparable Mesopotamian documents cited above. In any case, it is likely to have belonged to a larger composition or collection (known to the author of Psalm 132), which mentioned David's vow to find a "place" for Yahweh (Ps 132:3–5), described the capture of Jerusalem (cf. II Sam 5:6–10), and reported the discovery of the ark "in the territory of Jaar" (Ps 132:6). At this point the account of David's expedition to Baalah and the transfer of the ark followed. This must have included the basis of II Sam 6:1–13,17–19. As explained in the COMMENT on § XIV, the Michal materials in vv. 14–16,20–23 were probably secondary. Instead there followed, as in comparable ancient accounts of the foundation of cults, an invocation by the king for divine blessing on his house (cf. 6:12; 7:29); see the COMMENTS on §§ XV and XVI. But in our story as it now stands, Michal, the daughter of Saul, is called to our attention as soon as the ark enters the City of David (v. 16), and she assumes a central part in the drama as the narrative continues in the section that follows.

# XIV. THE ESTRANGEMENT OF MICHAL (6:20–23)

6 [20]When David returned to greet his household, Michal daughter of Saul came out to meet [him]. She greeted him and said, "How the king of Israel distinguished himself today, flaunting himself before the eyes of his servants' wenches like some dancer!"

[21]"In Yahweh's presence I *am* a dancer!" said David to Michal. "Blessed be Yahweh, who chose me over your father and all his house to appoint prince over his people Israel! I'll revel before Yahweh, [22]behaving even more shamelessly than this, and humiliate myself before his eyes! And as for the wenches you mentioned, let them think me distinguished!"

[23]So Michal daughter of Saul was childless to the day of her death.

## *TEXTUAL NOTES*

6 20. *She greeted him* Reading *wtbrk 'tw* on the basis of LXX *kai eulogēsen autōn.* In MT *wtbrk 'tw* has fallen out before *wt'mr,* "and (she) said."

*like some dancer* That is, *khglwt nglwt 'ḥd hrqdym,* lit. "as one of the dancers flaunts himself." Nevertheless, *hglwt nglwt* is textually suspicious (GK[2] §75y; cf. Driver and especially Talmon 1960:174). For *hrqdym,* "the dancers" (LXX *tōn orchoumenōn),* MT has *hrqym (hārēqîm),* "the idle fellows" (cf. Judg 9:4; 11:3), and this is preferred by Wellhausen, who describes "the dancers" as "rather insipid" *(ziemlich nichtssagend);* but Orlinsky (1946), following Klostermann, has demonstrated the superiority of the LXX reading on a variety of grounds (contrast Carlson 1964:91).

21. The beginning of the verse is defective in MT. It can be recovered from LXX[B] *kai eipen daueid pros melchol enōpion kyriou orchēsomai eulogētos kyrios hos,* which reflects *wy'mr dwd 'l mykl lpny yhwh 'rqd brwk yhwh 'šr,* lit. "And David said to Michal, 'In Yahweh's presence I will dance! Blessed be Yahweh, who. . . .' " MT has suffered haplography, a scribe's eye skipping from the first *yhwh* to the second—thus, "And David said to Michal, 'In the presence of Yahweh, who. . . .' " (cf. Thenius, Wellhausen, Ackroyd). Corresponding to LXX[B] *eulogētos* = *brwk,* LXX[L] has *zē* = *ḥy*—thus, "As Yahweh lives, who," etc.; see Orlinsky (1946:27–28 n. 5), who makes

a strong case in favor of the LXX[B] reading on the basis of usage elsewhere in Samuel.

*to appoint* MT *lṣwt*. LXX *(tou) katastēsai* probably reflects a variant, *lśwm*.

*his people* So LXX. MT: "the people *of Yahweh*."

*I'll revel* So MT: *wśḥqty*, for which LXX reflects *wśḥqty wrqdty*, "I'll revel *and dance*," representing a conflation of variants of which the second is reminiscent of the beginning of the verse.

At this point LXX[A] omits everything from *kai paixomai* = *wśḥqty* to *kai apokalyphthēsomai* = *wnglty* by haplography—thus, "I'll revel more than this!"

22. *behaving . . . more shamelessly than this* Reading *wnqlty . . . mz't* with MT. LXX has *kai apokalyphthēsomai . . . houtōs* = *wnglty . . . kz't*, "flaunting myself (again) in this way." Either reading is acceptable, but LXX *wnglty* can be impeached as reminiscent of v. 20.

*before his eyes* Reading *b'nyw* with one MS of MT *(BHS)*. David stresses his humility before Yahweh (see the NOTE on vv. 21–22), but the ancient scribes, fearful that the statement might be taken to mean "and lower myself in his opinion," tampered with the text. MT now has *b'yny*, "in my own eyes," and LXX *(en ophthalmois sou)* and OL *(ante oculos tuos)* point to *b'ynyk*, "in your [i.e., Michal's] eyes."

*let them think me distinguished* MT *'mm 'kbdh*, lit. "let me be distinguished with (= in the opinion of) them." LXX takes the verb as part of the preceding clause, understanding the context as "and I'll be humiliated in your [see above] eyes and among the wenches among whom you said I was distinguished *(me doxasthēnai)*."

## NOTES

6 20. *to greet his household*. Hebrew *lĕbārēk 'et-bêtô*, which could also be translated "to bless his house." David has already expressed a wish for such a blessing (6:12), which conventionally followed upon a ceremony of the sort described in the preceding verses (see the COMMENT on § XIII), and he will, in fact, invoke Yahweh's blessing on his house in 7:29. But the present statement must—at least in the text as presently constituted—be taken as the ordinary language of greeting, especially in view of the fact that Michal will greet him in return *(wattĕbārēk 'ōtô* [cf. the *Textual Note*]—hardly a blessing from *her!)* in v. 21. Cf. Murtonen 1959:167, criticized by Carlson 1964:92 n. 3.

*She greeted him. . . .* Michal's greeting is ironic. She refers to David's distinguishing himself *(nikbad)* but implies the opposite, viz. that he has acted shamelessly (**nāqēl*; cf. v. 22 and, on the opposition of the verbs *kbd* and *qll* here, Crüsemann 1980:225–26). She further implies that the distinction or honor David has actually gained is not the esteem that becomes a king but the sensational acclaim of a common dancer. By "flaunting himself before the eyes of his servants' wenches," she suggests, he has earned a certain *sexual* honor (cf. Schulte 1972:146 n. 43), but not the honor appropriate to the king of Israel. As Crüsemann (1980) has shown, Michal's irony is compounded by the details of the episode. In vv. 21–22 David, alert to her tone, will respond to her implication rather than her actual words ("I'll revel before Yahweh, behaving even more shamelessly [*ûnĕqallōtî*, v. 22] than this . . ."), shameless behavior, however, being now equated with pious self-humiliation (". . . and humiliate myself before his eyes!" [cf. the NOTE at v. 22]). The final twist of irony in v. 23 will renew the sexual theme introduced here by Michal, as the episode concludes with her exclusion from David's bed.

*flaunting himself.* In 6:16 we were told that David was scantily clad in a linen ephod (see the NOTE). Thus, by his vigorous dancing he is "exposing himself" *(niglâ)*, or, as Michal perceives it, "flaunting himself."

*his servants' wenches.* Hebrew *'amhôt 'abādāyw*. Princess Michal's tone is aristocratic. As one king's daughter and another's wife she does not hesitate to refer to all the young women of Israel, whether slave or free, as the "maidservants" or "wenches" of the king's subjects; thus there is no reason to suppose that "the noblewomen of the free Israelites are excluded from the offensive remark" (Crüsemann 1980:226).

21. *Blessed be Yahweh . . . Israel!* This pious exclamation, though *textually* primitive as here restored (cf. the *Textual Note*), is probably *literarily* secondary, a contribution of the Deuteronomistic hand responsible for the final arrangement of 5:11–8:18 (Schulte 1972:134 n. 4, 146 n. 43; Veijola 1975:66–68; Crüsemann 1980:223; contrast Mettinger 1976:45 and n. 56).

22. *and humiliate myself.* Hebrew *wĕhāyîtî šāpāl*, which suggests not disgrace but rather pious modesty (cf. Prov 29:23).

23. (On the apparent contradiction in 21:8 [MT] see the *Textual Note* on "Merob" there.) Although a few critics would strike the present verse as a midrashic expansion (cf. Arnold 1917:42 n. 3), most see it as the essential point the episode is included here to make (see the COMMENT). What is not clear is whether we are to understand that Michal was childless because she was excluded from David's bed, as I assume, or because Yahweh made her barren in disapproval of her attitude toward David's dancing, as many commentators conclude (Hertzberg, etc.).

## COMMENT

Michal, Saul's daughter, became David's wife when he was a rising star at her father's court (I Sam 18:20–27). She loved him then (cf. I Sam 18:20), and when the old king's paranoid animosity forced him to flee Gibeah, she assisted the escape (I Sam 19:8–17). With David out of the way, Saul remarried Michal to a certain Paltiel (I Sam 25:44; cf. II Sam 3:15), but after Saul's death David, his own kingship now in view, negotiated her return (II Sam 3:12–16). This gesture was less sentimental than political or tactical (see the NOTE on "Michal daughter of Saul" at 3:13), and we should probably assume that whatever ties of affection once existed between David and Michal had been broken or at least attenuated by the long separation. We are not told how Michal felt about her recall—any open objection would surely have been futile and dangerous—but we must suppose that with the trail of tears Paltiel shed from

Gallim to Bahurim (3:16) were mingled a few of her own. In any case, the Michal of the present episode exhibits no vestige of the old infatuation. She appears here as a mature and haughty aristocrat, openly contemptuous of her royal husband.

The purpose of this episode, as the title we have given it implies, is to explain the estrangement and childlessness of Michal. After her quarrel with David, she was excluded from his bed (v. 23; cf. the NOTE) and thus "was childless to the day of her death." This point is important because it answers the question of the presence of Saulid blood in the Davidic line, a question that arises naturally from the early stories of David's intimate relationship to the house of Saul, especially his marriage to Michal. Note, in this regard, the position of the episode in the larger narrative. It follows a series of stories about David's rise and the advent of his kingship, which grow out of his relationship to Saul and his family. It precedes a series of stories about David's own family, which lead up to the succession of one of them as king. It stands, therefore, as an editorial junction, holding together the thematic threads running backwards and forwards in the larger story (cf. Rupprecht 1977:63; Crüsemann 1980:223). Because of its characters and content, some have thought of it as an original part of the story of David's rise to power (Weiser 1966:344). Others have taken the theme of Michal's childlessness to mean that it was a primitive component of the succession narrative, i.e., the story of *Solomon's* attainment to the throne (Rost 1926:120–27; von Rad 1966:177). In view of its editorial function, however, and its present inclusion in the Deuteronomistic assemblage of materials in 5:11–8:18 (cf. pp. 142–43), it is safest to think of it as part of an ancient document—perhaps affiliated with the original story of David's rise, perhaps not—taken up by a Deuteronomistic writer precisely because of the thematic link it provides in the larger narrative.

What was the original meaning of this episode? Crüsemann (1980:223–27) has argued that it was an off-color joke about David's honor (cf. the first NOTE at v. 20), which arose in gentle criticism of his behavior in his increasingly problematic relationships with the women in his life (Michal, Abigail, Bathsheba, Abishag). Porter (1954:164–66), in support of his theory of the influence of the liturgy of an annual cultic celebration in chap. 6 (see "Background in Ritual" in the COMMENT on § XIII), has argued that the Michal episode points to a sacred marriage rite that accompanied the ceremony. David's dancing, says Porter (p. 166), has "a fertility and orgiastic character" and is "a prelude to sacred marriage," whereas Michal's gazing out the window (v. 16) suggests a hierodule motif widespread in the ancient Near East (see the NOTE at 6:16). Here, however, the sacred marriage is consummated with Israelite bondmaids (v. 22) instead of Michal, who, as a representative "of what seems to have been the invariable reaction of [traditional] Yahwism to the fertility aspect of Canaanite religion" (p. 165), refuses to participate. In reply to Crüsemann one might suggest the plausibility of a historical basis for the present episode in preference to a traditional basis. Michal's role of critic of the ceremony accompanying the arrival of the ark in Jerusalem is not improbable in view of her association with the previous regime, during which the capital was at Gibeah and the ark was neglected (cf. I Chron 13:3). As Porter suggests, she might thus be expected to represent a style of Yahwism to which David's activities were unacceptable. Against Porter, however, we must reiterate the likelihood that, as explained in the COMMENT on § XIII, the context and details of 6:1–15,17–19 reflect not a cultic reenactment but a historical ceremony of the sort that traditionally marked the introduction of a national god into a new capital city. Sacred marriage had no part in such a ceremony, and we must prefer the conclusion of Rost (1926:107–8) and a majority of subsequent scholars that 6:16,20–23 had no original connection with the rest of chap. 6.

# XV. NATHAN'S ORACLE
# (7:1–17)

7 [1]When the king was sitting in his house, [2][he] said to Nathan the
prophet, "Here I sit in a house of cedar, while the holy ark sits amid
curtains!"
[3]"Do whatever you have in mind," Nathan told the king, "for Yahweh is with you!"
[4]That night the word of Yahweh came to Nathan: [5]"Go say to my
servant David, 'This is what Yahweh has said: "Are *you* going to build
*me* a house for me to live in? [6]I haven't lived in a house from the day I
brought up the Israelites until this very day! Instead I've gone about in a
tent [7]wherever I happened to go throughout Israel. Did I ever speak with
one of the staff bearers of Israel whom I appointed to shepherd my people
Israel and say, 'Why haven't you built me a house of cedar?' " '
[8]"And now, this is what you are to say to my servant David. 'This
is what Yahweh Sabaoth has said: "*I* took you from the sheep pasture
to be prince over my people Israel. [9]I was with you wherever you went,
clearing all your enemies from your path. And I shall make you a name
like the names of the nobility in the land. [10]I shall fix a place for my
people Israel and plant it, so that it will remain where it is and never
again be disturbed, and nefarious men will no longer abuse it as in the
past, [11]in the days when I appointed judges over my people Israel. Then
I shall give them rest from all their enemies."
" 'Also Yahweh discloses to you that, as for a house, he will build
one for you! "When [12]your life is completed and you lie down with your
fathers, I shall raise up your offspring, the issue of your own body, after
you and establish his kingship. [13]*He* will build a house for my name,
and I shall keep his throne forever stable. [14]I shall become a father to
him, and he will become a son to me. If he does wrong, I shall discipline
him with the rod men use, with the blows of human beings. [15]But I shall
not withdraw my favor from him as I withdrew it from your predecessor. [16]Your royal house will be secure forever in my care, and your
throne will be stable forever." ' "

[17]Then Nathan reported all these things to David, wholly in accord with this vision.

## *TEXTUAL NOTES*

7 1. MT adds as v. 1b *wyhwh hnyḥ lw msbyb mkl 'ybyw*, "and Yahweh had given him rest round about from all his enemies." This addition is shared by all witnesses to Samuel with slight variations. (Instead of *hnyḥ lw*, LXX$^{B}$ reflects a different interpretation of the same consonantal text, reading *kateklēronomēsen auton* = *hnḥylw*, "had given him possession [of property]." At the end of the verse LXX$^{BMN}$ have [*tōn*] *kyklō* = *sbyb*, "round about," and the earlier *msbyb* was probably missing in the *Vorlage* of OG, though all these MSS now show correction to the pattern of MT, reading *kyklō* = *sbyb* [LXX$^{B}$] or *kyklothen* = *msbyb* [LXX$^{MN}$] in the earlier position.) The synoptic passage in I Chron 17:1, however, omits any equivalent of v. 1b. Moreover, as critics have long recognized, retention of this half-verse at this point poses serious difficulties of interpretation. The catalogue of David's wars, which follows immediately in chap. 8, shows that David had anything but "rest" at this point, and, indeed, it was the understanding of the last (Deuteronomistic) editor of this material that David did *not* have "rest," as explicitly stated in I Kings 5:17–18 [5:3–4]! A related problem is that of v. 11a$\beta$, where, according to all textual witnesses, David ("you") is promised a "rest" from all his enemies. This promise of "rest" again conflicts with the view that David did not have "rest," and it is also incompatible with the present assertion that he already had "rest."

This may be one of those cases where two textual problems cast light on each other and offer a mutual solution. As explained in the *Textual Note* at v. 11, the older critics recognized that v. 11a$\beta$ should contain a promise of "rest" to Israel from its enemies *(. . . lw . . . 'ybyw)* rather than to David from his enemies *(. . . lk . . . 'ybyk)*. Quite probably, therefore, the statement in v. 1b arose as a marginal correction of v. 11a$\beta$ and later found its way into the text at the wrong point. This took place before the translation of the OG but after the composition of the Chronicler's history, which preserves the original, short form of v. 1.

2. *curtains* LXX$^{L}$ has "curtains *of Yahweh*," which may have arisen from a gloss on "God" in the next verse, where MT has "Yahweh" (cf. the *Textual Note* on "Yahweh," v. 3).

3. *Do* So MT$^{MSS}$, Syr., as in I Chron 17:2. MT, LXX: "Go (and) do."

*Yahweh* LXX$^{L}$ (cf. I Chron 17:2) has "God."

4. *Nathan* MT$^{MSS}$, LXX$^{L}$, Syr. have "Nathan *the prophet.*"

5. *to my servant David* So LXX, Syr., etc. (cf. *BHS*). MT: "to my servant, *to* David." I Chron 17:4: "to David, my servant."

*Are* you *going to build* So MT: *h'th tbnh*. LXX *(ou su oikodomēseis)* and Syr. *('nt l' tbn')* reflect *l' 'th tbnh*, "*You* must not build," as in I Chron 17:4.

*for me to live in* A few MSS of MT have "for *my name* to live in," as in v. 13 *(BHS)*.

6. *the Israelites* All extant witnesses to the text of Samuel add "from Egypt" or, in a few cases (cf. *BHS*), "from *the land of* Egypt," but the variety of positions in which it stands (before "the Israelites" in LXX$^{B}$, after "the Israelites" in MT, LXX$^{ALMN}$), together with its absence from I Chron 17:5, shows that it probably did not appear in OG, surviving Greek MSS having been corrected recensionally to the text of MT. We read the shorter text.

*in a tent* MT adds *wbmškn*, "and in a tabernacle," and the redundancy might be retained as a remnant of poetic parallelism (cf. Cross 1973:255). It seems more likely, however, that *bmškn* arose as a gloss or variant of *b'hl* as suggested by the evidence of LXX$^{L}$, which reflects *b'hl bmškn* without the conjunction, and Syr., which reads *bmškn'*, probably reflecting not *bmškn* alone (*pace* Smith) but *b'hl* alone as in 6:17.

7. *throughout Israel* Read *bkl yśr'l* with LXX, as also in I Chron 17:6. MT has *bkl bny yśr'l*, "among all the Israelites"; so Syr. (Syr.$^{MSS}$: "in all *the house of* Israel").

*Did I ever speak* The unanimously attested text is *hdbr dbrty*, which is perhaps better read as *hădabbēr dibbartî* with LXX *ei lalōn elalēsa* (cf. Vulg.) than *hădābār dibbartî*, "Did I speak a word . . . ?"

*staff bearers* Reading *šōbĕṭê* for MT *šibṭê* with Reid (1975); cf. Falk (1966). All witnesses to II Sam 7:7 attest directly or indirectly to *šbṭy* (LXX *phylēn* = *šbṭ* showing loss of *y* before *yśr'l*); but the observation of Driver and others that Yahweh did not appoint "the tribes (*šibṭê*) of Israel" to govern his people has force, and a majority of translators have adopted the reading of I Chron 17:6 (MT), *špṭy* = *šōpĕṭê*, "judges." The reading *špṭy*, however, must be regarded as *lectio facilior*, having arisen, perhaps, under the influence of v. 11 (cf. de Robert 1971:116–17). The agreement of LXX with MT in the present passage against the reading of Chronicles suggests that the Chronicler altered his text. Moreover, the antiquity of the reading *šbṭy* is attested to by the interpretive Deuteronomistic paraphrase of the present passage in I Kings 8:16: "From the day I brought my people out of Egypt I chose no city from all the tribes of Israel (*šbṭy yśr'l*) to build a house where my name might be. . . ." How, then, is *šbṭy* to be explained? It has been proposed that we read *šōbĕṭê*, "judges," a dialectal variant involving interchange of *p* and *b* (Dahood 1963:43; cf. *idem* 1962:361–62; 1969:74–75), but this seems precarious, especially in view of the occurrence of *špṭym* in v. 11 below. Reid's suggestion is better. He posits a substantive **šōbēṭ*, a denominative *Qal* participle from *šēbeṭ*, "staff," which he attempts (1975:20) to recover elsewhere in Biblical Hebrew (Deut 33:5; etc.; cf. the NOTES at 5:1; 19:10)—thus, *šōbĕṭê*, "those who hold the staff, staff bearers," in the present passage.

8. *to my servant David* So LXX, Syr., MT$^{MSS}$. MT: "to my servant, *to* David," as in I Chron 17:7.

*from the sheep pasture* Hebrew *mnwh hṣ'n*. This is the reading reflected by LXX$^{B}$ *ek tēs mandras tōn probatōn*. MT (cf. LXX$^{AO}$, I Chron 17:7) has *mn hnwh m'ḥr hṣ'n*, "from the pasture, from behind the sheep." The source of the intrusive *m'ḥr* is probably Ps 78:71 (contrast Wellhausen). For *m'ḥr hṣ'n*, LXX$^{L}$ (*ex henos poimniōn*) and OL (*ex uno grege*) read *m'ḥd hṣ'n* by graphic confusion of *r* and *d*—as if, "from the pasture, from (being?) *one of the flock* (!)."

*to be prince* So MT: *lhywt ngyd*. LXX *tou einai se eis hēgoumenon* reflects *lhywtk lngyd*, "for you to become prince."

*over my people Israel* The primitive reading was *'l 'my yśr'l*, as attested by

LXX$^{L}$, Syr., Targ.$^{MS}$, Vulg. (cf. I Chron 17:7). In MT this was expanded to *'l 'my 'l yśr'l,* "over my people, *over* Israel." In certain MSS dependent upon MT this repetition has led to haplography and the loss of *'my 'l;* thus in LXX$^{AO}$, Targ.$^{MS}$ we find a shorter, but not superior, reading, "over Israel."

9. *And I shall make* So MT: *w'śyty* (cf. I Chron 17:8). LXX *kai epoiēsa* points to *w''ś,* "and I made," which may have arisen by attraction to the preceding verbs *(w'hyh . . . w'krth).*

*a name* So LXX$^{BAMN}$ (cf. I Chron 17:8). MT, LXX$^{L}$: "a *great* name." See Cross 1973: 248 n. 122.

10. *for my people Israel* So MT$^{MSS}$, Syr., Targ.$^{MSS}$ (cf. LXX$^{LN}$), as in I Chron 17:9. MT, Targ. (cf. LXX$^{BAM}$): "for my people, *for* Israel."

*nefarious men* MT *bny 'wlh,* lit. "sons of wrongdoing." LXX *huios adikias* reflects *bn 'wlh,* "a nefarious man," read also by a midrashic text from Qumran (4QFlorilegium; cf. the *Textual Note* on "as for a house, he will build one for you," v. 11); cf. Allegro 1958:351. See also Ps 89:23 [89:22].

*will no longer abuse it* MT *wl' ysypw . . . l'ntw* (cf. LXX$^{LMN}$). LXX$^{BA}$, Syr. reflect *wl' ysyp(w) 'wd . . . l'ntw.*

11. *in* Reading *lmn* on the basis of MT$^{MSS}$ (cf. LXX$^{BA}$, Syr., Vulg.). MT has *wlmn,* "*and* in" (cf. LXX$^{LMN}$).

*the days* So LXX. MT: "the day" (sing.). Cf. I Chron 17:10.

*Then I shall give them rest from all their enemies* Emending *whnyḥty lk mkl 'ybyk* to *whnyḥty lw mkl 'ybyw* with Ewald (1878:vol. III:132) and most of the older critics (Wellhausen, Driver, Budde, Nowack). The change is without textual support, but if our interpretation of the origin of v. 1b as a marginal correction to the present verse (see the *Textual Note* at v. 1) is correct, its necessity was recognized in antiquity.

*Also Yahweh discloses to you that* Reading *whgyd lk yhwh ky* with all witnesses to the text of Samuel. The shift from first to third person has troubled some commentators, and indeed I Chron 17:10 has *w'gd lk w-,* "And I disclosed to you and. . . ." Cross (1973:256 and n. 158), noting the Chronicler's reading, would restore *w'gd lk ky,* which he translates "And I (now) make known to you that," on the assumption that the corruption of *whyh* to *yhwh* later in the verse (see the *Textual Note* on "When") led to the reformulation of *w'gd* as third person, *whgyd,* and the subsequent introduction of *yhwh* after *whgyd lk.* But the absence of *yhwh* in I Chron 17:10, where *ky* is also missing, can be explained by haplography: A scribe's eye skipped from *-k y-* (in *lk yhwh*) to *ky* in a text identical to that of II Sam 7:11, and *y* was misread as *w.* Moreover, as Cross himself observes elsewhere (1973:255 n. 156), the agreement of LXX$^{BL}$ (Samuel) with MT (Samuel) against Chronicles is a clue that the Chronicler may have revised his text. After the haplographic loss of *yhwh* just described, the reformulation of *whgyd* to first person in conformity to the other verbs in the passage would not be surprising. Thus we must prefer the text of Samuel here over that of Chronicles, which has been subjected to accident and revision: **whgyd lk y(hwh ky)* > **whgyd lk w-* > *w'gd lk w-.* The shift at this point in the oracle from first to third person, therefore, cannot be eliminated on textual grounds. Nor does it need to be, for the problem is only an apparent one. Verse 11b is to be read, I believe, as a rubric comparable to "This is what Yahweh Sabaoth has said" in v. 8 and "This is what Yahweh has said" in v. 5. Because the oracle is here being given to Nathan to be related later to David, it is equipped with a double set of introductory phrases. These include (1) instructions to Nathan ("Go say to my servant David," v. 5, and "And now, this is what you are to say to my servant David," v. 8), which, of course, will not be repeated to David, and (2) the rubrics listed above, which will be repeated to David. Verse 11b belongs to the second category. On the translation of *wĕhiggîd*, see the NOTE on "Also Yahweh discloses to you."

*as for a house, he will build one for you* We read *byt ybnh lk*, a reading preserved in 4QFlorilegium (*byt ybnh lkh;* cf. Allegro 1956:176–77), a Qumran scroll containing a collection of midrashim on certain biblical texts (Allegro 1958). MT is similar but substitutes *y'śh* for *ybnh* and understands the succeeding *yhwh*, a corruption of *whyh* (see the following *Textual Note*), as the subject of the verb—thus, *byt y'śh lk yhwh*, "as for a house, Yahweh will make one for you." The reading *ybnh* is confirmed by LXX$^{L}$ *oikodomēsei* and indirectly by LXX$^{B}$ *oikodomēseis* (= *tbnh*) and *'bnh* in v. 27 below. Cross (1973:256 n. 160) agrees that the verb *bnh* is to be preferred to *'śh*, but he restores *'bnh*, "I shall build," on the basis of v. 27. For *lk*, LXX reads *lw*. Thus LXX$^{B}$ has *oikon oikodomēseis autō* = *byt tbnh lw*, "as for a house, you will build one for him," and LXX$^{L}$ *oikon oikodomēsei heautō* = *byt ybnh lw*, "as for a house, he will build one for himself," a reading that curiously anticipates one line of modern interpretation of Nathan's oracle (see the NOTE on "Are *you* going to build me a house . . . ?" v. 5).

*When* We read *whyh* on the basis of LXX *kai estai*. MT has *yhwh*, "Yahweh," construed with v. 11 (see the preceding *Textual Notes*). I Chron 17:10–11 *(yhwh whyh)* combines the readings of MT and LXX in our passage.

12. *and establish his kingship* So MT, LXX$^{BL}$, etc. LXX$^{A}$, in anticipation of v. 13, adds "forever." 4QFlorilegium (see the *Textual Note* on "as for a house, he will make one for you," v. 11) reads "and establish *the throne of* his kingship" (cf. the *Textual Note* on "his throne," v. 13, and see I Kings 9:5); cf. Allegro 1956:176 n. 19.

13. *He* Prefixed in Syr. and a few MSS of MT and LXX by the conjunction.

*a house for my name* So MT (cf. LXX$^{AM}$): *byt lšmy*. I Chron 17:12 has *ly byt*—thus, "(*He* will build) me a house"—and LXX$^{BLN}$ combine the two readings: *moi oikon tō onomati mou* = *ly byt lšmy*. Originally, then, LXX probably agreed with I Chron 17:12 against MT. We must choose between the variants *byt lšmy* and *ly byt*. In view of the close association between vv. 5b and 13a (see the NOTES and COMMENT), we must suspect the wording of the former *(ly byt)* of having influenced the text of the present passage.

*his throne* So LXX$^{BLMN}$ (cf. I Chron 17:12). LXX$^{A}$ has "his kingship" (cf. v. 12), and MT combines the two ("the throne of his kingship").

14. *If he does wrong* We read *wbh'wtw*, to which compare Syr. *wbsklwth* (= *wb 'wtw?*) and MT *'šr bh'wtw*. LXX *kai ean elthē (hē) adikia autou* seems to reflect *wb' (bō') 'wtw*, "If his wrongdoing has come."

15. *I shall not withdraw* Reading *l' 'syr* on the basis of LXX *ouk apostēsō* and Syr. *l' "br* (cf. I Chron 17:13). MT has *l' yswr*, "(But my favor) will not withdraw."

*from your predecessor* The witnesses differ considerably at this point. We can identify three variants, of which the third (C) is probably a combination of the first two. These are: (A) *m'šr hyh lpnyk*, lit. "from him who was before you," i.e., "from your predecessor," as preserved in I Chron 17:13 and reflected in the first part of the conflate text of Syr. (*mn š'wl dhw' mn* [but omit *mn* with Syr.[MSS]] *qdmyk,* "from Saul who was before you"); (B) *m'šr hsrty mlpny,* "from him whom I removed from before me," as reflected in LXX *(aph' hōn apestēsa ek prosōpou mou)* and the second part of the conflate text of Syr. *(w"brth mn qdmy);* (C) *m'šr hsrty mlpnyk,* "from him whom I removed from before you," as represented by MT *m'm š'wl 'šr hsrty mlpnyk,* "from Saul whom," etc. Note that in MT, Syr., and a few other witnesses the identity of David's predecessor has been made explicit. As for the variants, C, as noted, is probably a combination of A and B. Of these two, most critics (Wellhausen, Smith, etc.) prefer A; the repetition of *hsrty* in B is, in Driver's words, "not an elegancy."

16. *Your royal house . . . your throne* So MT (cf. Syr.): *bêtĕkā ûmamlaktĕkā* (lit. "Your house and your kingship"—see the NOTE) . . . *kis'ăkā.* LXX has "*His* royal house . . . *his* throne" in conformity to the third-person pronouns of the preceding verse.

*in my care, and* That is, *lpny w-* (cf. LXX, Syr.), lit. "before me, and." MT has confused *waw* for final *kap* and construed the letter with the preceding word: *lpnyk,* "before *you.*" See also Seybold 1972:32 n. 48.

## NOTES

7 1. *the king was sitting in his house.* This notice provides a narrative link to 6:20a above, sets the stage for what follows below, and introduces the key word of chap. 7, "house" (cf. the NOTE on "as for a house, he will build one for you," v. 11, and the COMMENT). Note that the pattern here conforms to that suggested by the opening verses of Psalm 132, where it is said that David vowed not to enter his house until he had provided a "place," a shrine, for Yahweh (cf. the COMMENT on § XIII). The "place" has been provided, the tent-shrine mentioned in 6:17, and David has taken up residence in his house. The present notice, in short, seems to have specific literary and thematic functions in the narrative of chaps. 6 and 7. On the other hand, Herrmann interprets it as a reflection of a conventional feature of the Egyptian *Königsnovelle,* or "royal novelette," a literary genre with which he associates II Samuel 7 (see the COMMENT). The *Königsnovelle* typically begins with the king sitting in his palace, in the *d'dw,* the "hall of audience," where he appears before his subjects. But see the objections of Cross (1973: 248) and, on the *Königsnovelle* hypothesis in general, the COMMENT below.

2. *Nathan the prophet.* Nathan is mentioned here for the first time. We are not told where he came from or how he came to David's court. He will play an important role in subsequent events, in the aftermath of the Bathsheba affair (chap. 12) and in the dispute involving the succession (I Kings 1). In the latter case he appears as a supporter of Solomon's cause, and it is reasonable to suppose that he is the same Nathan whose sons held important positions in Solomon's administration. These were Azariah (MT *'ăzaryāhû,* I Kings 4:5) or possibly Adonijah (LXX *ornia,* I Kings 2:46+; 4:5), who was "in charge of the prefects" *('al hanniṣṣābîm),* and Zakor (LXX *zachour,* I Kings 2:46+; LXX[L] *za(k)chour,* I Kings 4:5) or Zabud (MT *zābûd,* I Kings 4:5), who is identified as "advisor" (LXX *ho symboulos* = *yô'ēṣ,* I Kings 2:46+) and "friend of the king" *(rē'eh hammelek,* I Kings 4:5).

In all likelihood Nathan was a seer attached to the courts of David and Solomon and loyal to the king, as his role in I Kings 1 suggests (cf. Herrmann 1981:166–67). It is true that here and especially in chap. 12 he has an adversary relationship to David, and for this reason some scholars have preferred to describe him as "the witness to and guardian of a tradition that confronted and repudiated the Canaanite institutions" (Kraus 1966:183) or, at the opposite extreme, a spokesman for "certain, probably Jebusite circles in Jerusalem [who] sought to thwart David's plan to build a temple" (Ahlström 1961:120–21; cf. Kutsch 1961:138 n. 1 and, most recently, von Loewenclau 1980) or to suppose that his apparent opposition to the temple was a sham, an accommodation to the political realities of the time (Ishida 1977:98). But we have seen that the older stories have been transmitted to us in prophetic form (see the Introduction, pp. 7–8), the principal source of II Samuel (including I Kings 1 and 2) being probably "The Chronicles of Nathan the Prophet" (I Chron 29:29; II Chron 9:29), and in such a context Nathan's role has been enlarged in a manner reminiscent of the portrayal of Samuel in I Samuel. In the present form of our story, therefore, Nathan stands, here and also in chap. 12, as the chief representative of the prophetic point of view with which the older materials have been editorially surcharged (see further the COMMENT). The stern and straightforward Nathan who opposes the building of a temple here and censures the king's conduct in chap. 12 is barely recognizable in the obsequious Nathan of I Kings 1, who, bowing and scraping before the king (v. 23), pleads Solomon's case with every courtly indirection and blandishment. The latter, we must suppose, is closer to the historical Nathan.

*a house of cedar.* On David's palace, built for him by Tyrian craftsmen with Lebanese cedar, see 5:11.

*amid curtains.* That is, in a tent; cf. 6:17.

The contrast David is making—that he sits or dwells *(yōšēb)* in a cedar house while Yahweh's ark sits or resides *(yōšēb)* in a tent—expresses a pious anxiety. As Josephus (*Ant.* 7.90) puts it, "he thought he would be doing wrong if, while he himself dwelt in a stately house built of cedar and having beautiful furnishings as well, he permitted the ark to lie (neglected) in a tent."

3. *Do whatever you have in mind.* As just noted, David's words in v. 2 must be understood as the expression of a wish to build a temple. Accordingly, Nathan's reply seems to indicate agreement and encouragement. In vv. 5–7, however, Nathan is told to transmit a divine message indicating that David will not build a temple. Evidently we are to think of v. 3 as Nathan's spontaneous and initially enthusiastic response to what seemed a good idea to him and to understand vv. 5ff. as the more circumspect opinion he reached after realizing, under the impact of divine revelation, that the time was not right (so already Thenius). This, at least, was the intent of the Deuteronomistic editor of chap. 7, from whose hand v. 13a, which shows it to be Yahweh's will that a temple be built in the future, derives (see the COMMENT). In the pre-Deuteronomistic form of the oracle, however, the negativity of vv. 5–7 was unqualified and permanent (see the NOTE there and the COMMENT), and the shift in tone from that of the present verse was, therefore, more striking. Indeed, it is difficult to think of v. 3 and vv. 5–7 as the work of a single author. It is often argued by those who regard vv. 1–7 as a unified composition hostile to temple building that Nathan's initial reply should be regarded merely as a courtly courtesy, a polite and formal response to the king not necessarily reflecting the speaker's considered opinion, and, for that matter, that the oracle in vv.

5ff. need not be taken to represent the prophet's personal views, which are not at issue in the passage (Noth 1967:257; cf. Cross 1973:241–42; etc.). It remains very difficult, nevertheless, to think of vv. 3 and 5ff. as deriving from the hand of a single writer who was fundamentally hostile to David's plan. Why would he place words in the prophet's mouth that suggest, polite formalities or not, that the king was divinely guided ("Yahweh is with you")? If, on the other hand, he wanted some reason to show that Nathan's private response was overruled by the reception of the oracle (cf. Kutsch 1961:138 n. 1), why did he not make this clear; and why is there no hint elsewhere that Nathan's personal inclinations were not in accord with his official prophetic duties? For these reasons and others we shall come to the conclusion in the COMMENT that the positive tone of v. 3 represents the attitude of the author of the oldest stratum of our passage, upon which the negativity of vv. 5–7 was subsequently imposed.

*Yahweh is with you.* A formula of blessing found widely in Deuteronomistic and pre-Deuteronomistic literature. See the first NOTE at v. 9.

4. This verse indicates the formal reception by the prophet of an oracle, "the word of Yahweh." Oracles of special importance are frequently received at night (cf. I Samuel 3; etc.).

5–7. In the opening section of the oracle David's intention to build a house for Yahweh receives a negative reply. According to the larger oracle in its present, Deuteronomistically edited form, the negativity is a consequence of a divinely ordained movement of history toward the Solomonic temple (see "The Place of Nathan's Oracle in the Deuteronomistic History" in the COMMENT). Thus the present verses are to be read in light of v. 13a, "*He* (David's offspring) will build a house for my name." As explained in the COMMENT, however, the negative verdict on a temple was originally intended as final and fundamental. The reasons for this response can be discovered by giving close attention to grammatical considerations, especially syntax. The details are given in the NOTES that follow. In anticipation of the discussion there and in the COMMENT ("Literary History") we may state at this point that a temple turns out to be unnecessary and unwanted. That David should propose such a grandiose gesture of patronage toward Yahweh—who is, as he has always been (cf. vv. 8–9a), David's patron —is taken as an affront. Yahweh has always moved about freely in a tent, never taking up residence in a temple. David's concern about the lack of a temple (v. 2) is groundless, as should be obvious from the fact that Yahweh has never chastised any of Israel's previous leaders for failing to provide one.

5. *Go say to . . . David.* The Israelite prophet understood himself as a messenger of Yahweh, and thus the characteristic literary forms of ancient message-sending are also those of prophetic speech. Here we have a double commission (*lēk wĕʾāmartā,* lit. "Go and say") of the sort frequently found in the prophetic books (Isa 6:9; Jer 1:7; etc.) and also common in ancient message literature; cf. Westermann 1967:120.

*my servant David.* Cf. v. 8. The expression "my servant PN" is characteristically Deuteronomistic (see the NOTE at 2:18) and may represent secondary expansion of the prophetic commission here and in v. 8. But we cannot be sure of this: The designation of kings as "servants" of their gods was widespread in the ancient Near East (cf. de Vaux 1971:155–56) and cannot be regarded as distinctively Deuteronomistic in Israel.

*This is what Yahweh has said.* That is, *kōh ʾāmar yahweh,* the so-called "messenger formula," a characteristic part of prophetic speech. In the ancient world it was the responsibility of a messenger to repeat verbatim the words entrusted to him. Messages, therefore, were delivered in the first person and prefaced by the naming of the sender with the formula "This is what PN has said" (cf. Gen 45:9; etc.). A prophet conceived of himself as a messenger of Yahweh and discharged his responsibility accordingly.

*Are* you *going to build* me *a house for me to live in?* Hebrew *hā'attâ tibneh-lî bayit lĕšibtî.* The sentence is distinguished by its use of emphatic pronouns. The opening *'attâ,* "you," focuses attention squarely on David; the issue, that is, is not so much what David is going to do as the fact that he, David, is going to do it. In the present form of the oracle, then, a contrast exists between David *("you"),* who *will not* build a temple, and David's offspring (emphatic "*He,*" v. 13a), who *will* build a temple. As explained in the COMMENT, however, v. 13a is part of the final, Deuteronomistic revision of the passage; thus the original force of the emphatic "*you*" must be explained differently. In this regard de Vaux and others have pointed to a contrast between David *("you")* and Yahweh ("I") revolving about the wordplay on "house" in vv. 5 and 11 —thus, "*You,* David, will not build a house (= temple) for me; rather *I,* Yahweh, will build a house (= dynasty) for you" (cf. Wellhausen 1899:257). Thus, they say, the oracle shows that Yahweh does not want a temple but that he will establish a dynasty for David. Simon (1952:50,52), followed by Gese (1964:21), Noth (1967:251), and others, also stresses the contrast between David and Yahweh, but he understands the issue to be one of religious propriety and human initiative. Ought not the impetus for building a temple come from Yahweh himself and not from any human being, even if he is the king (cf. the *Textual Note* on "as for a house, he will build one for you," v. 11)? Thus the negative is not addressed to David as David but to David as a mortal man: "Are *you,* a human being, proposing to build a house for *me,* a god?" The implication is that Yahweh does not want a house (Simon, Noth)—or, at least, that he does not want one yet (Gese)—and David has behaved presumptuously in pondering one.

This issue can be clarified by reference to a key consideration that has not figured in the discussion, viz. the presence of a second emphatic pronoun in v. 5b. The end of the sentence, *bayit lĕšibtî,* adequately expresses "a house for me to live in," and the preceding *lî,* "(for) *me,*" is unnecessary except as an emphatic reinforcement of the first-person pronoun. Thus we have a pair of emphatics: "Are *you* going to build *me* a house . . . ?" The force of this construction is to suggest that things are proceeding in the wrong direction, that David's gesture posits a reversal of the appropriate or previously known roles. This impression is reinforced by another emphatic pronoun, *'ănî,* "*I,*" at the beginning of v. 8, which resumes the stress on "*me*" in v. 5—"It was *I,*" says Yahweh, "who did all these things for you!" Thus the implication of the question "Are *you* going to build *me* a house . . . ?" is "Shall not *I* build a house for *you?*" The statement in v. 11b, then, is the point to which our gaze is being directed: "as for a house he [Yahweh] will build one for you!" (de Vaux). The issue being raised is the propriety of human initiative in the relationship between Yahweh and the king, but, as the following NOTES show, it does not follow from this that the propriety of a house for Yahweh is not also called into question (*pace* Gese). Yahweh is indignant that David should propose to build a temple that is not wanted or needed (Simon, Noth), and v. 5b expresses this indignation (cf. GK[2] §150d) by reference to the fact that Yahweh is David's patron, not the reverse.

6–7. *I haven't lived in a house... throughout Israel.* A fundamental contrast is drawn between two types of shrine, a house and a tent, a preference for the latter being implied. Alternatively, a few scholars have supposed an implied contrast between divine "living" or "dwelling" *(yāšab)* and "tabernacling" (*šākan,* cf. *miškān,* "tabernacle," at the end of v. 6 in MT) to be intended here (Schreiner 1963:89–94). Thus understood, the passage would represent an assertion of Yahweh's transcendence at the expense of his immanence: Though he may choose to "tabernacle" among the Israelites, he does not reside permanently among them. It would follow that no objection to a temple as such is intended here; the issue is rather the manner of divine manifestation whether in a temple or elsewhere. But even apart from the text-critical vulnerability of *miškān* (cf. the *Textual Note* on "in a tent"), it is difficult to find warrant in the wording of vv. 6–7 for such an interpretation, which relies on specific theological distinctions that took shape only at a relatively late date (see Cross 1973:245–46). The contrast of house and tent is ineluctable (cf. Cross 1973:244). To be sure, the theological problem of the manner in which Yahweh is present among his people is also involved, but only as a function of the house/tent distinction. It is a question of living or residing in a temple (*lō' yāšabtî bĕbayit,* "I haven't lived in a house") or moving about freely in a tent-shrine ("I've gone about in a tent wherever I happened to go"). The theological problem of the protection of the divine transcendence is simply not at stake here, and it would be misleading to compare our passage to expressions of Deuteronomistic deprecation of the notion of Yahweh's dwelling in a temple, such as I Kings 8:27 (cf. Rupprecht 1977:69–71), or the even stronger post-exilic hostility to the same notion, such as Isa 66:1. In the present passage we are dealing with alternative modes of immanence differentiated by the issue of the mobility of the place of manifestation. The passage shows that Yahweh's choice has always been a tent-shrine, in which he can move about freely, as the idiomatic language of vv. 6b–7aα indicates (see the NOTE on "wherever I happened to go," v. 7). At least implicitly, then, a temple, a fixed place of divine residence, is criticized as imposing a restriction on Yahweh's freedom of movement. See further the COMMENT.

6. *I haven't lived in a house.* But the stories of Samuel's childhood indicate that when the ark was in Shiloh it resided in a "house of Yahweh" (*bêt yahweh,* I Sam 1:7), a temple elaborate enough to have a nave (*hêkāl,* the temple proper, I Sam 1:9; 3:3), doorposts (I Sam 1:9), and a *lishka* (I Sam 1:18 [LXX]). How are we to resolve the contradiction? Hertzberg (cf. McKane) relies on the alleged distinction between *yāšab,* "dwell permanently," and *šākan* (cf. *miškān,* vs. 6 [MT]), "make a temporary stay," to assert that "even the stay at Shiloh appears to be regarded merely as an episode in a series of temporary stopping-places." But, as explained in the preceding NOTE, the presence of such a distinction in our passage cannot be maintained, and in any case the oracle specifically distinguishes between a *house* (vv. 5,7) and a *tent* (v. 6), and if there was a house at Shiloh, the contradiction noted above remains. We must suppose either that memory of the Shiloh temple was suppressed out of zeal for Jerusalem or that the references to a temple at Shiloh in I Samuel 1 and 3 are anachronistic (cf. Cross 1973:73 n. 114). The issue is difficult to decide. The reference to "the house of God" in Shiloh in Judg 18:31 lends authenticity to the tradition underlying I Samuel 1–3. Jeremiah (Jer 7:12,14; 26:6,9) seems to speak of the ruins of a temple at Shiloh (cf. Rupprecht 1977:92), yet he seems deliberately to avoid the term *bayit* when referring to Yahweh's

shrine (ambiguously *mĕqômî*, "my place" [7:12]) there in contrast to the Jerusalem temple (*habbayit hazzeh*, "this house" [26:6; etc.]). Ps 78:60 describes the holy place at Shiloh with the terms *miškān*, "tabernacle," and *'ōhel*, "tent," and Josh 18:1 and 19:51, admittedly isolated passages (Noth 1943:184), refer to "the tent of meeting" there (cf. I Sam 2:22 [MT] and *I Samuel*, p. 81). There is no clear archeological evidence of a temple of the Israelite period at Seilûn, ancient Shiloh, but the summit of the mound has been denuded by erosion and rebuilding (cf. Holm-Nielsen 1976:823).

*the day I brought up the Israelites.* That is, from Egypt (cf. the first *Textual Note* to v. 6). The reference is to the Exodus. The expression occurs in Deuteronomistic contexts elsewhere (I Sam 8:8; II Kings 21:15; etc.), and some have taken it as a sign of the touch of a Deuteronomistic hand here (Veijola 1975:77; Rupprecht 1977:76–77); but it also occurs in older contexts (Cross 1973:253; Gross 1974:440 n. 7; cf. Veijola 1977:42) and cannot in itself be taken as a mark of Deuteronomistic composition, even when concluded by the ubiquitously Deuteronomistic phrase "until this very day" (cf. Judg 19:30).

*a tent.* Israelite tradition held that in the pre-monarchical period the ark was housed in a tent. The most detailed descriptions of the tent are found in Exodus 26 and 36:8–38, Priestly materials that attained their present form no earlier than the sixth century B.C. The principal subject of these passages is the dwelling or "tabernacle" *(miškān)*, the plan of which has been determined anachronistically by the form of the Solomonic temple and perhaps the tent of David (see the NOTE at 6:17). But the memory of an authentically ancient tent-shrine may be preserved in specifications for "a tent over the tabernacle" (*'ōhel 'al-hammiškān*, Exod 26:7; 36:14) made of veils of goats' hair with a covering of red-dyed rams' skin beneath an outer layer of leather. The probability that these references point back to a cult object in use in pre-temple times is supported by the analogy of the *qubbah* of pre-Islamic Arabian tribes, a small, leather tent-shrine, sometimes mounted on camelback to be transported when a tribe struck camp; it was carried in religious processions or taken into battle (Lammens 1920; Morgenstern 1942:207–29; cf. Cross 1947:59–61; de Vaux 1971:137–39). Like the Israelite tent, the *qubbah* was attended by young women (cf. Exod 38:8 and the Masoretic plus in I Sam 2:22), it was resorted to for oracular guidance (cf. Exod 33:7), and it was made of red-dyed leather (cf. Exod 26:14; 36:19). Just as the ark was sheltered in the tent (Exod 26:33; 40:21), so the tribal idols were kept in the *qubbah*. We are justified, therefore, in thinking of the tent as a very ancient Israelite institution, which (together with the ark) was analogous to the *qubbah*.

7. *wherever I happened to go.* Compare I Sam 23:13, where it is said that David and his men, seizing an opportunity to escape from Keilah where Saul had confined them (cf. v. 7), went out "to wander where they might" *(wayyithallĕkû bă'ăšer yithallĕkû)*. In the present passage, too, the idiom expresses freedom of movement in contrast to confinement. "I've gone about (*mithallēk*, v. 6) . . . ," says Yahweh, "wherever I happened to go *(bĕkōl 'ăšer-hithallaktî)*." This expression, therefore, can be grouped with others in the Bible that share the *idem per idem* form and stress, in one way or another, the divine freedom. Among these we may list not only *'ehyeh 'ăšer 'ehyeh*, "I am who I am," in Exod 3:14, but also *wĕḥannōtî 'et-'ăšer 'āḥōn wĕriḥamtî 'et-'ăšer 'ăraḥēm*, "I show favor to him to whom I show favor and I show compassion to him to whom I show compassion," in Exod 33:19, *'ădabbēr 'ēt 'ăšer 'ădabbēr*, "I say what

I say," in Ezek 12:25, and so on. The issue in the present passage, then, is the divine freedom of movement. A temple, in contrast to a tent-shrine, is presented as a kind of sanctuary that would impose a restriction on Yahweh's freedom to move about as he chooses. To this use of the verb *hithallek*, "move about," in reference to Yahweh's presence among the Israelites, compare Lev 26:12 and, in the context of the regulations for the battle camp, Deut 23:15 [23:14].

*the staff bearers of Israel.* As explained in the *Textual Note,* we follow Falk (1966) and Reid (1975:20) in reading *šōbĕṭê yiśrā'ēl* here. The reference is to Israel's premonarchical leaders. Perhaps the term "staff bearer" (**šōbēṭ*) could be used generally for one who exercised authority over a tribe (*šēbeṭ*) without having national authority like a king; cf. 5:1, where "staff bearers" stands parallel to "elders" in 5:3. But the pastoral metaphor of the present verse may have influenced the choice of terms: Those appointed "to shepherd" (*lir'ôt*) Israel are referred to as "staff bearers," i.e., those who wield the *šēbeṭ*, the shepherd's staff (cf. Lev 27:32; etc.).

*a house of cedar.* Cf. v. 2. From remote antiquity cedar was the fabric of temples as well as palaces; see the NOTE at 5:11. The description of the nave of Solomon's temple includes the boast that "Everything was cedar; there was no stone to be seen" (I Kings 6:18). But according to vv. 5b–7 of Nathan's oracle Yahweh does not want a sumptuous, cedar-paneled house.

8–9. Verses 8aα–9a ("*I* took you . . . your path") refer to the story of David's rise to power in I Samuel 16ff., to which II Samuel 7, in the final form of the larger story, provides a culminating retrospective and conclusion (see the COMMENT and the Introduction, p. 6).

8. On the formulaic oracular rubrics in this verse, see the NOTES at v. 5.

*I took you from the sheep pasture.* The reference is to I Sam 16:1–13, the prophetic account of the call of David, who was summoned home from the pasture where he was shepherding his father's flock to be anointed by Samuel.

*prince.* Hebrew *nāgîd*, the meaning of which is literally "designee (for office)," especially used as in the present case in reference to the king-designate or crown prince (see *I Samuel,* the NOTE on "prince" at 9:16). It was characteristic of the prophetic school of thought from which this part of the oracle of Nathan probably derives (see the COMMENT) to stress Yahweh's appointment of a future king as "prince" in affirmation of the divine prerogative of making and unmaking the leaders of Israel (cf. *I Samuel,* pp. 186–87). The term *nāgîd* does not appear in I Sam 16:1–13, to which the present verse refers (see the preceding NOTE), but it is used in allusions to David's appointment as "prince" twice elsewhere, once in an oracle uttered by Samuel condemning Saul (I Sam 13:14) and once in an auspicious speech by Abigail (I Sam 25:30).

9. *I was with you.* "Yahweh was with him (David)" was the theological leitmotiv of the story of David's rise to power (see *I Samuel,* p. 30, and especially McCarter 1980b:494,503–4), occurring in I Sam 16:18; 17:37; 18:14,28; and II Sam 5:10. The present reference recalls the events of that story. The expression "Yahweh was with PN" occurs in certain key Deuteronomistic passages (Judg 2:18; etc.), and it has been cited as a part of the Deuteronomistic revision of the present passage (Cross 1973:252). But I see no reason to regard "Yahweh was with PN" as an exclusively Deuteronomistic expression. It is a common expression, widely used to indicate divine favor and help (Gen 26:3; etc.; see the list in Vetter 1971:4). There is nothing else to suggest that the

passages in which it occurs in the story of David's rise do not belong to the original composition. In I Sam 3:19, after the prophetic account of Samuel's call, it is said of Samuel that "Yahweh was with him," and in the present passage, too, it may come from the hand of a prophetic writer. See also the discussion in Preuss 1968.

*all your enemies.* In the context of the retrospective of vv. 8a$\beta$–9a (see the NOTE at vv. 8–9 above) the enemies removed by Yahweh must be understood to include Saul, Abiner, Ishbaal, and all those who stood in the way of David's kingship.

*And I shall. . . .* These verses (vv. 9b–11a) have perplexed readers and given rise to a variety of interpretations. Most of the verbs have the form *wĕqāṭal;* that is, they are perfects attached to the conjunction: *wĕʿāśītî . . . wĕśamtî . . . ûnĕṭaʿtîw wĕšākan . . . wahănîḥōtî.* Ordinarily, then, we should expect a *future* translation to be required ("I shall make . . . I shall fix . . . [and] I shall plant," etc.), and yet the predicted deeds —at least on first inspection—seem to be things already accomplished in the past. Yahweh provided a "place" for the Israelites—the Promised Land—at the time of the conquest. Accordingly, some translators would follow Rost (1926:59–60; cf. Hertzberg) in rendering these verbs in the past tense ("I made . . . I fixed . . . [and] I planted," etc.). But such a construction (i.e., of the perfect with *wĕ-* as a past tense) is common only in very late Biblical Hebrew (under Aramaic influence) and in certain passages in Kings where later interpolation is suspected (cf. GK[2] §112pp). To be sure, Meyer (1959) has defended the antiquity of the Kings passages on the basis of a few other biblical instances of apparent *wĕqāṭal* preterites and by comparison to features of the Ugaritic verb system, and Loretz (1961) has extended Meyer's argument to the present verses. Yet even if one concedes that Meyer and Loretz have established the admissibility of an occasional, exceptional past translation of this construction in classical Biblical Hebrew prose (and I should not concede that they have), it remains the rule that the expected reference of such a construction in any given passage is the future. Moreover, the rule seems especially likely to apply in the present sequence, which embraces two prefixed verbs preceded by *lōʾ (lōʾ yirgaz . . . lōʾ yōsîpû . . . lĕʿannôtô),* for which *only* an imperfect translation is possible ("[they will] be disturbed no more . . . will no longer oppress").

If we grant the probability that the verbs refer to the future, how are we to explain the reference to a "place" to be established for Israel? Some interpreters (Smith, Ackroyd, etc.) have supposed that these verses come from the hand of an exilic author whose purpose was to hold out hope for a return to the land to the people of his own day. If we prefer not to accuse the writer of such an anachronistic distortion, however, we must conclude that the "place" mentioned in v. 10 is not the Promised Land. And, indeed, the plain meaning of the passage is that the establishment of this "place" is to occur when not only the conquest but the period of the judges is already in the past (v. 11a). So what, we ask again, is this "place"?

The possibility that a *place of worship* might be intended here was raised long ago by Caspari (cf. Noth 1967:252 n. 10), and this view has been taken up again recently by Gelston (1972). Agreeing with Rost and Loretz that "the appointment of a place for Israel, and the settling of Israel there, can hardly be envisaged . . . as still lying in the future" (p. 93), but insisting that the natural referent of the passage is to the future, Gelston concludes that the "place" *(māqôm)* refers not to the land but to the temple to which the oracle of Nathan in its present form looks forward. Accordingly, *māqôm* is to be understood in its specialized sense of "(cult) place, shrine," in particular the "place" that, in Deuteronomistic thought, Yahweh chose to be worshiped (Deut 12:5; etc.), that is, the Jerusalem temple. For this interpretation Gelston (p. 94) finds support from an ancient source, 4QFlorilegium, a Qumran scroll containing a collection of midrashim on certain biblical texts (Allegro 1956, 1958). Having cited a portion of Nathan's oracle ending with "over my people Israel" in v. 11, this scroll adds exegetically, "This"—presumably the "place" referred to in the biblical passage—"is the house that [. . .] in time to come." Gelston (pp. 93–94) reasons further that the object of the verbs "plant" and "abuse" and the subject of "remain" and "be disturbed" are to be understood to be this "place" and not "my people Israel." Thus he avoids the difficulty that "plant (the people) so that they will remain where they are" suggests the settlement in the land. In support of such an interpretation we may also cite (1) the close link in Deuteronomistic thought between the promised "place" of worship and the promised "rest" for the people, the latter being an essential component of vv. 9b–11a as we have reconstructed them (see the NOTE on "I shall give them rest," v. 11), and (2) the common use of *māqôm* and its Phoenician equivalent in reference to sacred sites (see the NOTE on "a place," v. 10). See, further, the COMMENT.

*I shall make you a name.* An expression common to many ancient Near Eastern languages (on the attempt of Herrmann [1953/54:59] and Morenz [1954:73–74] to find evidence of Egyptian influence here, see Kutsch 1961:153 and Cross 1973:248–49). It refers to the establishment of some kind of memorial to keep remembrance of an individual alive in the future, "an abiding sign that will not be cut off" (Isa 55:13). Thus it may indicate the erection of a monument of some kind, like the commemorative stela set up by David in 8:13, and it is not impossible that the erection of a temple by David's offspring, forecast in v. 13a (cf. Gen 11:4), is hinted at here. A man's name, however, is also perpetuated in his progeny (cf. 14:7; 18:18), and we should probably understand this promise of a name for David primarily as an anticipation of the dynastic promise in vv. 11b–16 below.

*the nobility.* Hebrew *haggĕdōlîm*, on which see the NOTE on "a nobleman" at 3:38.

10. Note the emphasis in this verse on the fixing of a place of worship, its permanence and immobility. This is to be seen in contrast to the former lack of a fixed shrine of Yahweh indicated by vv. 6–7 ("I've gone about . . . wherever I happened to go"). Though the author of vv. 5–7 may have thought of the former situation as desirable, the Deuteronomistic author of vv. 9b–11a, who viewed these events as a stage in a continuing sequence of events leading up to the erection of the Solomonic temple, did not agree. In his opinion the lack of a central sanctuary in the time of the judges rendered the cult insecure and subject to abuse (cf. the NOTE on "nefarious men" below). See, further, the COMMENT.

*a place.* That is, a place of worship. As explained in the NOTE on "And I shall . . ." at v. 9, this interpretation is preferable to that which takes "a place" as a reference to the Promised Land. We may understand the noun *māqôm* as a place where a deity "arises" (*qûm;* cf. Num 10:35; Ps 132:8 = II Chron 6:41; etc.), i.e., where he manifests himself. It refers to a shrine or other place of epiphany often elsewhere in the Bible (cf. BDB 880), most notably in expressions of the Deuteronomistic expectation of a chosen place of worship (Deut 12:11; etc.). Here, too, it looks forward to the erection of the sanctuary in Jerusalem. Phoenician *maqūm*, commonly used in reference to temples (cf. Tomback 1978:195–96), affords a useful comparison. In two Jewish inscriptions from the beginning of the Common Era, synagogues are referred to as *mqwmwt*, "(holy) places" (Frey 1952:159–60 [nos. 973,974]).

*nefarious men.* By this reference to "nefarious men" *(bĕnê-'awĕlâ)* who abused the cult in the time of the judges the writer probably means Hophni and Phinehas, the corrupt sons of Eli the priest. Their iniquitous administration of the cult of Yahweh at Shiloh is described in detail in I Sam 2:11–26. According to I Sam 2:27–36, a passage that, like vv. 9a–11b here, derives from a Deuteronomistic hand, their behavior was the reason for the rejection of the ascendancy of the priestly house of Eli in favor of that of Zadok (cf. I Kings 2:26–27,35b). In the new sanctuary, we are assured, such corruption will not take place.

11. *I shall give them rest.* As explained in the COMMENT, "rest" is an important theme in the Deuteronomistic interpretation of Israel's experience in the land. In Deut 12:9–10 Moses reminds the people that they have not yet come "to the restful estate" *('el-hammĕnûḥâ wĕ'el-hannaḥălâ*, lit. "to the place of rest and to the estate") that Yahweh is going to give them, but he assures them that a time will come when Yahweh "gives you rest from your enemies on all sides" *(wĕhēnîaḥ lākem mikkol-'ōyĕbêkem missābîb)*. This promise of "rest" for the people is fulfilled, at least in a preliminary way, by the conquest. In preparation for the invasion of the land Joshua reminds the people of Moses' assurance that "Yahweh your god is going to give you rest" *(mēnîaḥ lākem*, Josh 1:13; cf. v. 15), and when the victory is complete the narrator reflects as follows:

> So Yahweh gave Israel all the land that he had sworn to their fathers, and they took possession of it and settled in it. Yahweh gave them rest on all sides *(way-yānaḥ yahweh lāhem missābîb)* just as he had sworn to their fathers. Of all their enemies not a man had withstood them; Yahweh had handed all their enemies over to them. Of all the good things Yahweh had promised to the house of Israel nothing had failed to happen. Everything had come true!
>
> (Josh 21:43–45; cf. 22:4; 23:1)

From the outset, however, the theme of rest for the people is tied to the prospect of a central sanctuary (see the COMMENT). Deuteronomy 12, where Moses first utters the promise of rest, is chiefly concerned with the confinement of worship in the land to the one "place Yahweh will choose" (v. 5, etc.). The themes of rest and the chosen place are brought together in vv. 10–11 of the same chapter, where the people are told, with respect to their offerings, that when Yahweh "gives you rest from your enemies on all sides . . . then the place that Yahweh will choose . . . *there* you must take all the things I command you. . . ." The final "rest" to which the people look forward, therefore, will come only with the establishment of Yahweh's chosen "place." It is this time to which the Deuteronomistic phrases of vv. 9b–11a in the present oracle refer (see the preceding NOTE), and the "rest" promised here, therefore, is that to which Solomon will allude in I Kings 8:56 when, standing before the altar of the new central sanctuary in Jerusalem, he offers a blessing in a reflection of the language of Deut 12:9 and Josh 21:45:

> Blessed be Yahweh, who has given a place of rest *(mĕnûḥâ)* to his people Israel just as he promised! Not one thing has failed to happen of all the good things he promised through his servant Moses!

*Also Yahweh discloses to you.* Hebrew *wĕhiggîd lĕkā yahweh* (see the *Textual Note*). The verb is not to be read in sequence with those preceding it within the oracle proper —thus not "*will* disclose"—but as a perfect with the force of a solemn declaration (GK[2] §106j), as recognized by Mettinger (1976:59 n. 29), whose translation reflects the sense accurately: "And hereby the Lord declares to you. . . ." In the earliest form of our passage v. 11b ("Also . . . you!") may have followed v. 3 immediately (Coppens 1968b:489–90; see "Literary History" in the COMMENT), but in the present form of the oracle it is to be read as a rubric intervening between major sections and introducing the dynastic promise in vv. 12ff.

*as for a house, he will build one for you.* Hebrew *bayit yibneh lĕkā* (see the *Textual Note*). The emphasis given the word *bayit*, "a house," by its position preceding the verb is retrospective. We are reminded that the first part of the oracle (vv. 5–7) was concerned with a house. But that house, a temple for Yahweh, was rejected. Now our attention has turned to David, and as for a *house*, we are told, one will be built for him. In this case, however, *bayit* refers not to a physical structure—David already has a palace (vv. 1–2)—but to a family. To be sure, David already has a family too —a large one (3:2–5; 5:13–16)—but the son through whom David's kingship will be passed to his descendants has not yet been born. The sense of "house" here, then, is *dynasty*.

12. *your offspring, the issue of your own body.* Hebrew *zar'ăkā . . . 'ăšer yēṣē' mimmē'êkā*. Both expressions, the second in particular (cf. 16:11; Gen 15:4), emphasize physical descent, but both are in themselves ambiguous with respect to the question of whether only the next generation or a series of generations is referred to (cf. Mettinger 1976:53). Are the third-person-singular pronouns in vv. 12–16 to be understood collectively or singularly? With v. 13a in place the answer is obvious. The reference must be to an individual, Solomon. Before the insertion of v. 13a, however, David's descendants in general were probably meant, as the use of the word *zera'*, "seed, offspring," implies. Thus we follow most previous commentators (Wellhausen, Budde, Smith, Nowack, Caird, McKane, Hertzberg, Ackroyd, etc.) and Rost (1926:65,68) in concluding that an originally collective promise of ruling offspring was narrowed by the insertion of v. 13a to refer to Solomon (see the COMMENT). This long-established conclusion has been challenged recently on the grounds that it is improbable that a dynastic promise should be narrowed in scope to an individual (Veijola 1975:69–70). Note, however, that the change from David's sons collectively to his immediate heir, though it reduces the dynastic dimension of the promise from explicit to implicit, does not in fact eliminate it. As explained in the NOTES below, the royal grant language of vv. 14–15 implies a gift of kingship with an enduring base. Moreover, v. 16, shown by its characteristic language also to be Deuteronomistic, eliminates any doubt on this point. The Deuteronomistic editor of vv. 12 + 13b–15 added v. 13a to focus the promise on the temple builder, but he also added v. 16 to ensure that the dynastic dimension of the promise should not be lost.

13. He *will build a house for my name.* David's heir is to build the temple refused in vv. 5–7. The emphatic pronoun *(hû', "He")* echoes another in v. 5 *('attâ, "you")*, and the effect achieved is one of contrast—"*You* will not build me a house . . . *he* will." As pointed out in the NOTES above and in the COMMENT, Yahweh's rejection of the temple in vv. 5–7 seems final, absolute, so that the present statement (v. 13a) comes

as a surprise—indeed, it renders the oracle incoherent (Simon 1952:50–51). It is best explained as a Deuteronomistic interpolation identifying David's "offspring," originally conceived collectively, as the temple builder (see the preceding NOTE). As explained in the COMMENT, the Deuteronomistic redaction of Nathan's oracle had as one of its chief purposes the transformation of an oracle negative toward the building of a temple into an oracle approving but postponing the building until the next generation. This purpose was accomplished by the addition of vv. 9b–11a, which place the oracle within the Deuteronomistic historiographical framework, and the present statement, which renders the negativity of vv. 5b–7 temporary. In its final form, then, with v. 13a in place, Nathan's oracle stands as a *vaticinium post eventum* explaining why David did not build the temple (cf. Cross 1973:254–55).

*my name.* As pointed out in the NOTE at v. 9 the establishment of someone's "name" assured that he would be remembered. A king might set up his "name"—a monument —in conquered territory to represent him there after his departure (cf. 8:13). Thus, a fourteenth-century ruler of Jerusalem expressed his fealty in a letter to the king of Egypt by saying that "the king has set his name *(sakān šumšu)* in the land of Jerusalem forever" (*EA* 287:60–61; cf. 288:5–7). The assertion of a king's sovereignty through his "name," a surrogate presence, assured his continuing control of a dominion in his absence (cf. de Vaux 1967). The theological counterpart of this problem of absence and presence is the problem of transcendence and immanence. A god, having once appeared in a place, might cause his "name" to be remembered there (Exod 20:24). The "name" of a god, then, was his cultically available presence, effectually protecting his transcendence. Deuteronomistic theology consistently referred to the presence of Yahweh's "name" in the temple in Jerusalem, eschewing language that suggested that Yahweh himself might dwell there (von Rad 1953:37–44). Thus the temple was the place Yahweh chose "to place" *(lāśûm)* his name or "to cause his name to dwell" *(lĕsakkēn 'et-šĕmô;* cf. *EA* 287:60, cited above); cf. Deut 12:5,11; etc. The present reference to Yahweh's name also derives from this Deuteronomistic "name theology." See, further, McBride 1969.

*and I shall keep his throne forever stable.* In the original form of Nathan's oracle, in its highly parallelistic, almost poetic, prose, this statement stood parallel to that in v. 12b:

> I shall establish his kingship,
> And keep his throne forever stable.

With the interpolation of v. 13a, however, a new parallelism was achieved:

> *He* will build a house for my name,
> And I shall keep his throne forever stable.

This juxtaposition is significant. It signals reciprocity. The security of the throne is linked to the temple. See, further, the NOTE at v. 14 and the COMMENT.

*forever.* Seybold (1972:33 n. 52) has remarked that "forever" (*'ad-'ôlām* or *lĕ'ôlām)* occurs seven times in chap. 7. A concern with permanence is everywhere. The grant of kingship made to David's heir will remain in effect in perpetuity. That is, the grant has no term. This in itself does not imply immutability (cf. Tsevat 1963:73,75–77): In I Sam 2:30, for example, there is reference to a divine promise of priesthood to the house of Eli *'ad-'ôlām* that is revoked because of the behavior of Eli's sons. The irrevocability of the present promise must therefore be guaranteed by a further provision in vv. 14b–15a (see the NOTE on "If he does wrong . . . from him" below).

14. *a father to him . . . a son to me.* Kings of Damascus in the ninth century B.C. took the name or title "Son of Hadad" (*bir hadad;* biblical *ben-hădad,* I Kings 15:18 = II Chron 16:2; etc.), and at least one king of the Syrian state of Sam'al was called "Son of Rakib" (*bir rākib;* cf. *KAI* 215.1, etc.; *ANET*[3] 655); in each case the king was identified as the son of the national or dynastic deity (see, further, Cross 1972b:41 n. 22). As the present passage shows (also Pss 2:7; 89:27–28 [89:26–27]), similar statements were made about the Israelite king, who was thought of as the son of Yahweh. It is misleading, however, to elicit parallels from Egypt, where the king was believed to be physically descended from his divine father, or to speak of the Israelite king as the divine fruit of a ceremony of "sacred marriage" *(hieros gamos),* as does, for example, Engnell (1967:77–78; cf. Pedersen 1940:vol. III/IV:84,431–33). The language used here ("I shall become a father to him, and he will become a son to me") and in Ps 2:7 ("You are my son; today I beget you") has nothing to do with physical descent or, therefore, with divine kingship. It is adoption language (Cooke 1961:209–11; de Vaux 1961b:vol. I:112–13; Schlisske 1973:109–10). Its purpose is to qualify the king for the patrimony Yahweh wishes to bestow on him. Thus in Psalm 2 the formula of adoption is continued: "Ask me, and I shall grant the nations as your estate, the ends of the earth as your domain" (v. 8). Calderone (1966:50–53) and Weinfeld (1970: 190–92; 1976:190–91) have illuminated this concept by demonstrating that the model from which the language is drawn was the grant of land and/or "house" made by a king or lord to a loyal vassal. Such grants were made patrimonial, and thus permanent, by means of the legal adoption of the vassal as the son of the lord. Here the establishment of a "house" for David is legitimated in the same way. Israel becomes, in effect, the patrimonial estate of David's family. The grant is permanent ("forever," vv. 13,16) and, in this case, inalienable (v. 15; see below). There will always be a fief (*nîr;* see Hanson 1968) in Jerusalem for David; see I Kings 11:36; 15:4; II Kings 8:19 = II Chron 21:7. In the second of these passages, I Kings 15:4, the Deuteronomistic narrator goes on to say explicitly that David was given a fief "because [he] did what Yahweh thought right, not departing from his instructions all the days of his life . . ." (v. 5). That is, the grant was made because of David's loyal service to Yahweh (see, further, Weinfeld 1970:186–88), a notion that, as Weinfeld points out (p. 187 n. 28), may be implicit in the juxtaposition of the present chapter with chap. 6, where David retrieves the ark of Yahweh and sets it up in Jerusalem. As explained in the COMMENT, however, divine grants of ruling offspring were commonly associated with the provision of temples for gods by kings, and it seems likely that in the earliest form of our passage the promise was given in response to David's expression of an intention to build a temple (v. 2).

14–15. *If he does wrong . . . from him.* It follows from their adoption as sons of Yahweh that David's heirs, if they are disobedient, will be chastened like wayward children. The language is that used in Proverbs in the context of child rearing and discipline (McKane; Weinfeld 1970:192). The meaning of "the rod men use" (*šēbeṭ 'ănāšîm,* lit. "the rod of men") and "the blows of human beings" is probably "the usual human methods of chastisement" (cf. Weinfeld 1970:193 and n. 81). The chastisement, however, will not go beyond parental correction. Verse 15 asserts that the grant of kingship will remain in effect regardless of the behavior of David's sons. Again the documents cited by Weinfeld (see the NOTE on "a father to him . . . a son to me," v. 14) provide valuable illumination. As noted, the promise of kingship to David's offspring is couched in the language of royal grants to faithful vassals in return for acts of loyalty and service. Such grants might be patrimonial, in that they were sanctioned by adoption of the vassal by the king, and—in special cases (cf. Weinfeld 1970:193)—inalienable, in that they were not conditional upon the future behavior of the descendants of the grantee. The inalienability was often expressed in terms reminiscent of the language of the present verses. In the text of a grant from a thirteenth-century Hittite king to a certain Ulmi-Tešup, for example, we read, "After you, your son and grandson will possess it, nobody will take it away from them. If one of your descendants sins . . . the king will prosecute him at his court . . . But nobody will take away from the descendant of Ulmi-Tešup either his house or his land . . ." (as cited by Weinfeld 1970:189; cf. Calderone 1966:53–57). Similarly, familial documents from Nuzi, a Mesopotamian city whose archives have yielded much information about second-millennium social customs, show a special concern to be sure that an adopted son not only, as Weinfeld puts it (1970:192–93; cf. 1976:191), "has the duties of a son (= respecting his parents) but has also the privileges of a son: he has to be treated like the son of a free citizen and not like a slave." Thus, in the present passage David's heirs must expect to be punished if they do not behave respectfully toward their adoptive parent, but that punishment will not extend beyond the ordinary kinds of discipline administered by a father of disobedient sons ("the rod men use . . . the blows of human beings"), and the sons, however chastised, will not be alienated (v. 15).

15. *my favor.* Hebrew *ḥasdî.* We have seen two examples (2:5 and 3:8) of *ḥesed* as "a responsible keeping of faith with another with whom one is in a relationship" (Sakenfeld 1978:233). The specific content of Yahweh's *ḥesed* in the present passage is, according to Sakenfeld (1978:139–45), "the supportive power by which God maintains the family line on the throne" (p. 144); thus, "The act of *ḥesed* is simply the provision for the continuance of the relationship" between Yahweh and David's son (p. 145). This relationship, as we have seen in previous NOTES, is conceived on the pattern of royal grants to loyal vassals, and Yahweh's *ḥesed,* therefore, is to be understood as the continuing divine favor that will maintain the grant of kingship in effect in perpetuity (cf. Seybold 1972:41). The term is equivalent in implication, then, to *ṭôbâ,* "good thing," in v. 28 below (see the NOTE) and *bĕrît 'ôlām,* "everlasting covenant," in 23:5 (see Weinfeld 1976).

*as I withdrew it from your predecessor.* A reference to the rejection of Saul in I Sam 13:7b–15a (cf. I Sam 15:22–28,35; etc.), which is described from a prophetic point of view making (negative) use of language that may be drawn from the present passage. See the COMMENT ("Literary History"), where the possibility that this statement (v. 15b) is a contribution of the prophetic writer responsible for vv. 4–9a is considered.

16. *Your royal house.* Expressed by hendiadys: *bêtĕkā ûmamlaktĕkā,* lit. "Your house and your kingship." Note the parallelism of "your throne."

*secure.* The theme of David's "secure house" (*bayit ne'ĕmān,* I Sam 25:28), his enduring dynasty, though hinted at before in Deuteronomistic supplementation to the story of David (I Sam 25:28–31), is given its first and full articulation in the present passage. See the COMMENT.

## COMMENT

David was introduced to us as a shepherd tending his father's flock in Bethlehem. He entered public life as a musician at the court of Saul and immediately became the king's weapon-bearer. Thereafter his rise to power was swift and direct. Neither the ill will of his enemies nor his own occasional rashness was enough, finally, to hold him down. Every development in his life seemed to turn in his favor, every event to benefit him in some way. Nevertheless, in spite of repeated successes and final victory, he was never free of hardship. From the time of his arrival at court until the present moment his life has been crowded with conflict, uncertainty, and danger. He has been unable to pause and reflect upon his attainments.

Now for the first time David is at rest (cf. v. 1[MT]). His enemies are gone or powerless. The two kingdoms of Israel and Judah are united under his rule, and the land, at least temporarily, is at peace. The new capital is secure, and Yahweh's ark, the focal point of the worship of the Israelite god, is there. As David sits in the palace built for him by Phoenician craftsmen (5:11), he thinks of the ark housed in its tent-shrine nearby (6:17). Should a nation's king have a house of cedar when its god does not?

The king confides his concern to Nathan, a prophet and ranking member of the court, who appears here for the first time. Nathan's role in the story is that of mediator between David and Yahweh. His initial reaction to David's desire to build a temple is enthusiastic (v. 3), but at night Yahweh's word is revealed to him (v. 4), presumably in a dream, and he learns that David is *not* going to build a temple (v. 5b). Moreover, Yahweh seems in something of a dudgeon over the very suggestion! He has always moved about freely in a tent and has never once complained to any of Israel's past leaders about the lack of a temple (vv. 6–7). At this point, however, after David has been reminded that it was Yahweh who established him in his present position (vv. 8–9a), the oracle goes on to indicate that a change is coming. David is going to have a great name (v. 9a). Yahweh will establish a "place," a sanctuary, for the Israelites: It will be fixed, permanent, and the moving about of vv. 6–7, together with the abuses that the old arrangement was subject to, will come to an end (v. 10). Then the people will have peace (v. 11a). As for a "house," Yahweh will build one—a dynasty—for David (v. 11b)! David's offspring will rule after him (v. 12), and *he* will build a house—a temple—for Yahweh (v. 13a).

Nathan's oracle, therefore, is an intricate (some might say "tortuous") interweaving of two oracular ideas or motifs, "house of Yahweh" and "house of David"—that is, temple and dynasty. David promises to build Yahweh a house, and Yahweh promises to build David a house. At first glance it seems that Yahweh's promise is given *in reward for* David's promise. But a second glance, focused this time on the opening words of the oracle proper, suggests that perhaps Yahweh's promise is given *in spite of* David's promise. Yet if we look a third time, we may conclude that Yahweh has had his own plan all along and that his promise is actually made *without regard to* David's! Our discussion below of the literary history of the passage will suggest that each of these three statements is an accurate interpretation of the meaning of the oracle at one stage of its growth, but at this point we can observe that, at least in the present form of the passage, the two motifs of temple and dynasty, after wandering more or less independently across the surface of the text, are finally brought together in Yahweh's proclamation concerning David's offspring in v. 13: "*He* will build a house for my name, and I shall keep his throne forever stable." It is the heir in whom the Davidic dynasty will be established who will build a temple for Yahweh. He will build Yahweh's house (v. 13a), and Yahweh will establish the kingship of his house on a lasting basis (vv. 13b,16). Thus the permanence of the Davidic dynasty, as well as the security of the people (v. 11a), is linked to the erection of a fixed and permanent "place" (v. 10) for the worship of Yahweh.

### *The Modern Interpretation of Nathan's Oracle*

Among the literary critics of the nineteenth and early twentieth centuries II Samuel 7 was generally regarded as a late insertion in the Samuel corpus. The Davidic theology it reflects was not believed to have been fully formulated before the last years of the monarchy. A few scholars thought of the chapter as a product of the Exile (e.g., Smith), but the majority favored a late pre-exilic date. Most (Budde, Nowack, Kennedy, etc.) followed Cornill (1891:115) in noting the absence of anything to suggest that the Exile and interruption of the Davidic line lay within the purview of the author of the oracle. Thus, while they generally agreed that the chapter "can scarcely have been written before Josiah" (Cornill), they found it impossible to date it long *after* Josiah. Its evocation of the divine promise to David they understood as an appeal to the long duration of the Judaean dynasty as a source of confidence in the troubled days of Josiah's reign (cf. Wellhausen 1899:254–55).

Alongside the tendency to assign a late date of composition to II Samuel 7 was a correspondingly low estimation of its literary and historical value. Arnold, for example, dismissed the chapter as "monkish drivel" (1917:42 n. 3), an appraisal that has won him a certain notoriety. But the most vehement spokesman for this point of view was probably Pfeiffer, in whose work it survived into the middle of the twentieth century. Rejecting the arguments for a pre-exilic date, he regarded II Samuel 7 as a very late, midrashic confection arising out of the piety of post-exilic scribes (1948:370–73). It is "a mire of unintelligible verbiage" (p. 372), characterized by confusion and illiteracy and a "complete misunderstanding of the religion in the period of . . . David" (p. 373). The author, whose style is "consistently wretched," is at once "prolix" and "banal" (p. 372); he "repeats himself *ad nauseam*" (p. 373).

It seems fair to say that these older critics were often misled by their inability to find a place for II Samuel 7 in the scheme by which they reconstructed the literary history of the Samuel materials. They viewed the larger corpus as a combination of two parallel narrative strands analogous or identical to the so-called "J" and "E" strata of the Pentateuch, but they found it difficult to associate chap. 7 closely with either strand—hence their assessment of it as a late interpolation. Only rarely did they consider the possibility of more ancient materials underlying the chapter (cf. Steuernagel 1912:325). In this respect the work of Rost (1926) represents a major new departure. It was Rost's opinion that the Samuel narratives were produced not by an interweaving of continuous parallel strands but by editorial arrangement of a number of shorter and longer narrative units standing side by side (see *I Samuel*, pp. 13–14). He characterized II Samuel 7 as a combination of originally distinct compositions expanded by certain editorial additions (1926:47–74). The basic source was an old, pre-Solomonic document expressing a negative attitude toward the prospect of a temple but looking forward to the Davidic dynasty. Of the dynastic promise in its present form (vv. 8–16) he attributed only vv. 11b and 16, with their references to David's everlasting "house," to the original document (p. 63); vv. 8–11a,12, and 13b–15, which display a sense of historical retrospective, he derived from another, later source (pp. 64–65). Following earlier critics (Wellhausen, Budde, Smith, etc.), he considered the prediction of Solomon's temple building in v. 13a to be a late insertion, probably Deuteronomistic in origin, made to soften the attack on the temple and conform the oracle to historical fact (pp. 65,67).

Rost's conclusions have found a wide following (cf. Noth 1981:55–56; von Rad 1962:vol. I:310 n. 4; Hertzberg; Poulssen 1967:43–55; etc.). As we shall note below, most of the particular details of his view of the growth of the oracle have been challenged at one time or another, but his more general position that II Samuel 7 is a patchwork of earlier and later pieces remains widely accepted. Subsequent scholarship has been inclined to address the exegetical difficulties presented by Nathan's oracle not by positing a "hopeless" confusion that "existed in the mind of the author" (Pfeiffer 1948:372) but by accepting a degree of thematic disharmony as resulting from a combination in the passage of disparate components. It has become the prevailing view that the oracle is composite in origin, and attempts to read it as a coherent literary unit are often dismissed as "harmonizing" (cf. Cross 1973:241–46).

There is, nevertheless, an offsetting tendency in the study of the oracle to stress its unity. Most scholars have been inclined to acknowledge that, whether or not II Samuel 7 arose from originally unrelated or even incompatible materials, it now—at least in its present form—admits of a unified interpretation. Here we must distinguish three lines of argument, only the first of which is incompatible with the general conclusions of Rost: (1) an etiological argument (Mowinckel); (2) a form-critical argument (Herrmann); and (3) an editorial argument (McCarthy).

### *The Etiological Argument*

According to Mowinckel (1947), Nathan's oracle is an etiology composed to explain why Solomon and not David built the temple. Mowinckel's study is particularly addressed to the assumption of Rost and others that v. 13a is secondary and vv. 5b–7 preserve a fundamental prohibition of temple building, which was editorially reinterpreted as temporary and applying only to David when it was incorporated into the larger passage. Rejecting this notion, Mowinckel argues instead that the oracle as a whole is to be viewed as a literary unit without editorial manipulation. It is the composition of a single author who wanted to show that David intended to build a temple and was blessed for it, but that it was Yahweh's will that he should not do so. Mowinckel's argument has attracted little following. In particular, his interpretation of vv. 5b–7 has not been accepted (cf. Simon 1952:43–45; von Nordheim 1977: 440–41), and his postulation of a single author has not fared well alongside the tendency in recent research to stress the existence of a combination of Deuteronomistic and non-Deuteronomistic language in the chapter. Most contemporary scholars prefer to understand the etiological purpose Mowinckel discerned within the larger context of the Deuteronomistic history as a whole and, indeed, to view the unity he described as editorial, not authorial, in origin.

### *The* Königsnovelle *Hypothesis*

A more widely influential argument for the unity of our passage was put forward by Herrmann in 1953–54. It is essentially a form-critical argument; that is, it is concerned principally with the analysis of literary forms or genres, and its purpose is to show that the various parts of II Samuel 7 are held together by a formal unity inherent in the literary genre to which the chapter belongs. The basis of the argument is a comparison of the chapter to a category of second- and first-millennium Egyptian historiographical literature known to Egyptologists as the *Königsnovelle,* or "royal novelette," which is characterized by a combination of the themes of temple building and royal theology. The *Königsnovelle,* we are told, traces the origin of a certain activity, institution, or structure—quite often a temple—to a divinely inspired initiative of the king, whom the text lauds for his achievement (Hermann 1938:11). Herrmann stresses the similarity between features of the narrative in II Samuel 7 and the formal elements of the *Königsnovelle.* In a typical Egyptian text the king, described as sitting in state before his retainers, devises a plan, perhaps involving the building or restoration of a temple, and imparts it to ranking members of the court, who then acclaim its wisdom. The intimacy that exists between the king and the state god, identified as the king's father, is stressed throughout. Similarly, II Samuel 7 opens with the king sitting in his house (v. 1), where he conceives a plan for building a temple and discloses it to a prominent member of his court (v. 2), who then declares his assent to the plan, noting the close relationship the king enjoys with the state god (v. 3). The influence of the Egyptian genre on this biblical passage, Herrmann concludes, is clear. He then goes on to argue that despite the presence of two principal themes II Samuel 7 could, on form-critical grounds, be declared a fundamentally unified composition, inasmuch as the particular combination of themes found here, temple building and royal theology, is characteristic of the *Königsnovelle,* to which the formal correspondences just described link the biblical chapter.

As noted, Herrmann's hypothesis has received considerable support (von Rad 1962:vol. I:48–49; de Vaux 1966:484–85; Whybray 1968:100–1; etc.). Noth (1967[1957]:257–59), for example, accepts comparison to the *Königsnovelle* as the key to understanding the formal unity of the chapter, which in his opinion derives from Davidic times, when there was much Egyptian influence on Israel (pp. 256–57 and nn. 19–21) and when, he says (pp. 258–59), the two issues of temple building and royal ideology were settled in the ways the oracle suggests, viz. by a decision not to build a temple and promulgation of a dynastic theology. Nevertheless, though persuaded by Herrmann's form-critical argument that there is a unity of content in the chapter, Noth finds it unnecessary to discard the conclusions of the earlier literary critics. On the basis of his judgment that "the rejection [in vv. 5–7] of the plan to build a temple was certainly meant as fundamental" (p. 258), he continues to regard v. 13a as a Deuteronomistic addition (p. 251). By contrast, Weiser (1965: 154–56), followed by Seybold (1972:28–29) and others, accepts Herrmann's hypothesis with retention of v. 13a. Rejecting Noth's assignment of a pre-Solomonic date (p. 159), Weiser insists that the *Königsnovelle* form required execution of the royal plan, and that the passage, therefore, must date to Solomonic times, when the temple was in fact built. Verses 5–7 are not to be read as an unconditional refusal (p. 156), and v. 13a must be primitive (p. 155). Indeed, the Solomonic age, Weiser reasons, is the time when Egyptian influence is most to be expected.

The critics of the *Königsnovelle* hypothesis (Kutsch 1961:151–53; Schreiner 1963:75–76; Cross 1973:247–49; Veijola 1975:71–72; etc.) have been as outspoken as its adherents. In addition to questioning specific details of Herrmann's case (cf. the NOTES on "The king was sitting in his house," v. 1; "I shall make you a name," v. 9; and "a father to him . . . a son to me," v. 14), they have deemed the formal correspondence between parts of II Samuel 7 and its alleged Egyptian prototype an insufficient basis for arguing the unity of the chapter as a whole. Ishida (1977:83–92) has been able to show that Mesopotamian parallels are, on the whole, much more impressive. In a recent attempt to salvage the hypothesis on a limited basis, one scholar (von Nordheim 1977:438–39) has avowed that clear evidence for the formal similarity of the chapter to Egyptian parallels is confined to the first three verses, as outlined above. The case seems to rest heavily upon the thematic and ideological parallels drawn by Herrmann. These, however, have been discounted by critics as flawed or specious. Especially troubling is the dominant role of Nathan as an intermediary between Yahweh and David in the biblical passage, a situation quite alien to the Egyptian context, in which the relationship between the king and state god was so close and direct as to be a virtual identity. The problem becomes even more acute when one notes that the king's plan is actually annulled by the prophetically mediated divine word. As one critic puts it, "the contravention of the king's proposal by a subject is unthinkable, transferred to an Egyptian court" (Cross 1973:248). Aware of this difficulty, one recent advocate of the *Königsnovelle* hypothesis (Görg 1975:178–271) has argued for the existence of an original form of vv. 1–7 in which the prophet was not mentioned and the oracle, therefore, was communicated directly to David (Görg 1975:178; cf., much earlier, Rost 1926:68–69).

In the opinion of most critics, however, the major stumbling block for Herrmann's proposal is the fact that David's plan to build a temple is not realized (Kutsch 1961:152; cf. von Nordheim 1977:438). As they have pointed out, it is essential to the *Königsnovelle* that the king's plan be carried through to completion. In II Samuel 7, however, the king's plan is not carried through. This difficulty remains even if, with Weiser (see above), one retains v. 13a, where it is said that finally a temple *will* be built, as a primitive component of the oracle; for in that case it is Yahweh's plan, not David's, that is carried through. In anticipation of this objection, Herrmann speaks of a "Copernican revolution of the *Königsnovelle* on Israelite soil" (1953/54:59), supposing a transformation of the Egyptian genre in its adaptation to the peculiarities of Israelite thought. The king is removed from the center of the story in favor of the sovereign Israelite god. This line of reasoning, however, does not succeed in obviating criticism of the hypothesis on the point in question. Many continue to think it odd that the *Königsnovelle*, the very purpose of which is to praise the king for a great accomplishment, should be appealed to in connection with a biblical passage that not only lacks any such accomplishment but is in fact designed to show that a proposed royal accomplishment will not be achieved. After all, the point of II Samuel 7, insofar as the temple question is concerned, is that David will not be the builder. Thus, the transformation proposed by Herrmann, when applied to this passage, would amount to the complete subversion of a literary genre, the *Königsnovelle* form being used to show that a king did *not* accomplish something. At this point the critics follow

Kutsch (1961:152) in asking why someone would have fashioned II Samuel 7 in a form that implied the opposite of what he wanted to show.

### *The Case for Editorial Unity*

That II Samuel 7 has received Deuteronomistic editing has been recognized since the nineteenth century, but the older literary critics, with a few exceptions (Kuenen 1890:47 n. 5; cf. Smith, Nowack), tended to minimize its extent, and it was played down emphatically by Noth (1981:55). By contrast, more recent scholars, under the influence of a surge of interest in Deuteronomistic thought and equipped with increasingly sophisticated methods of identifying its literary expressions, have been inclined to assign considerable responsibility for the present shape of the chapter to Deuteronomistic editing (McKenzie 1947; etc.) and to stress the place of Nathan's oracle in Deuteronomistic theology. With regard to the last point, McCarthy's study of "II Samuel 7 and the Structure of the Deuteronomic History" (1965) has been especially influential. Prescinding from the question of literary history, McCarthy treats the oracle in its present form as a unity of form and content with Deuteronomistic characteristics (1965:131). He associates it with a series of key passages in the larger Deuteronomistic history identified by Noth (1981:5–6). These include speeches by major figures (Joshua, Samuel, Solomon) as well as observations by the narrator himself. They reflect on the past and look ahead to the future at crucial junctures in Israel's experience: the beginning and end of the conquest (Josh 1:11–15; 23); the transition from the period of the judges to the age of the kings (I Samuel 12); the erection of the temple (I Kings 8:14–66); the fall of Samaria (II Kings 17:7–23); etc. Similarly, Nathan's oracle looks backwards to the time of the judges (vv. 7,11), the rejection of Saul (v. 15), and the rise of David (vv. 8ff.) and ahead to the accession of Solomon (v. 12) and the erection of the temple (v. 13). Its unity lies precisely in its editorial integration of these themes from the larger history.

Increasing recognition of the Deuteronomistic features and functions of II Samuel 7 has led some scholars to the conclusion that "the compositional structure of [the chapter] does not allow the drawing of definite conclusions regarding its pre-Deuteronomic form" (Carlson 1964:105; cf. Schulte 1972:139). Rupprecht, for example, prefers to speak of Nathan's oracle in terms of its editorial role. Along with the Michal episode and certain other additions to chap. 6, he says, it has "the function of holding together the originally independent stories of David's rise, his throne succession, and the ark" (1977:63). II Sam 7:1–7, with which he is especially concerned, Rupprecht finds to be a consistently late combination of elements, evidently a Deuteronomistic product (pp. 75–78; cf. Dietrich 1977:61). Nevertheless, certain other scholars, while sharing the emphasis on the Deuteronomistic character of the chapter in its present form, believe it is also possible to cast light on the underlying sources. Because our own conclusions reached below stand closest to this position, it may be useful, for purposes of comparison, to conclude with summaries of the specific views of three scholars: Cross (1973:249–60), Veijola (1975:72–78), and Mettinger (1976:51–55).

Cross follows McCarthy in arguing that "the unity of 2 Samuel 7 is a unity imposed on his sources by the mind and point of view of the Deuteronomistic historian" (1973:252). For Cross these sources included (1) the "old oracle" of Nathan underlying vv. 1–7, an originally poetic prohibition of temple building, and (2) the eternal decree of kingship to David underlying vv. 11b–16, which was also originally in poetry. Nathan's oracle attained its present form when these two ancient sources—probably dating to the days of David and Solomon, respectively—were recast in Deuteronomistic prose and fastened together by an editorial link (vv. 8–11a), which itself had absorbed older elements (pp. 254–60). In the process, says Cross (p. 255), "the proscription of the temple" contained in the old oracle of Nathan was reinterpreted as "temporary, applying only to David."

Veijola, in a study of the Deuteronomistic view of the origins of the Davidic dynasty (1975), adopts a position similar to that of Cross (pp. 72–78). He, too, sees Nathan's oracle as a Deuteronomistic combination of two older sources: (1) a proscription of the temple plan (vv. 1a,2–5,7), and (2) a promise of offspring to David (vv. 8a,9,10,12,14,15,17). The rest of the material in vv. 1–17, he says, is Deuteronomistic, including v. 13a, which was added to identify David's heir as the temple builder and thereby to join together the two sources as one oracle. In his discussion of the second source Veijola (pp. 69–70) addresses himself critically to the assumption of Rost (1926:63–65) that an ancient oracular kernel (vv. 11b,16) promising David an eternal dynasty was later narrowed to refer only to David's son. On the contrary, he concludes (p. 78), it is more reasonable to assume that the older oracle applied only to Solomon; it was the Deuteronomistic historian who inserted vv. 11b and 16, thus expanding the promise to refer to David's dynasty.

Mettinger (1976) also reaches a conclusion like that of Cross and Veijola but differing in major details. He, too, stresses the Deuteronomistic character of 7:1–17 in its present form, but he is more conservative in assigning specific materials to an editorial hand, identifying only vv. 1b and 10–11a as Deuteronomistic (pp. 51–52). With most interpreters he identifies two *skopoi,* or thematic foci, in the oracle, one (vv. 8–11,16) concerning David and his dynasty, the other (vv. 12–15) concerning Solomon and the temple (p. 52). Verses 1–7, he says (p. 53), are linked to the second *skopos,* as the connection between vv. 5 and 13 shows. Corresponding to the two *skopoi* Mettinger posits two pre-Deuteronomistic layers (p. 54). Impressed by Veijola's criticism of Rost (p. 48; see above) and on the basis of his own investigation (p. 54) he concludes that the Solomonic layer (vv. 1–7 + 12–14a) was the older, original oracle. Its point was "that David is not going to build a house for the Lord, but that Solomon is to do this"—there is no question of a fundamental and permanent prohibition for Mettinger, nor does he consider v. 13a editorial (pp. 50,56–57). The Davidic layer (vv. 8,9,11b,14b–15,16) arose when the old oracle "was later submitted to a redaction that imposed a Davidic-dynastic *skopos* on the old kernel of the text" (p. 54).

### *The Place of Nathan's Oracle in the Deuteronomistic History*

As we have seen, not all scholars agree that the unity of Nathan's oracle is a function of its Deuteronomistic redaction, but few deny that Deuteronomistic material is present in the oracle or that the oracle occupies an important position in the larger Deuteronomistic corpus. It follows that any discussion of the literary history of the oracle must begin with an assessment of its Deuteronomistic character. How extensively was it edited? To what degree was the editing a factor in determining its present form? What were the purposes of the editor? These questions must finally be answered in the context of a literary-critical analysis of the oracle itself (see below, "Literary History"), but such an analysis can be facilitated and controlled by reference to the larger Deuteronomistic history, especially to those passages in I Kings that offer retrospection on the events described in II Samuel 7 (I Kings 5:17–19 [5:3–5]; 8:17–19). For these reasons I prefer to preface consideration of the literary history of Nathan's oracle with a discussion of the place of II Samuel 7 in Deuteronomistic thought.

The two principal themes of Nathan's oracle, temple and dynasty, are also central issues in the larger Deuteronomistic history (Deuteronomy–II Kings). The prospect of a central sanctuary arises first in Deuteronomy 12, where it is linked to a promise of security for Israel in the land. Moses assures the people that one day they will be safe from their enemies—Yahweh will give them "rest" (Deut 12:9,10)—and that they will then begin to worship only at "the place Yahweh will choose" (Deut 12:5,11,14). Until that time there will be no central, unifying sanctuary; every Israelite will do "what seems right to him" (Deut 12:8). At the beginning of the conquest Joshua reminds the people of the promise of rest (Josh 1:13,15), and when the victory is won the time of fulfilment seems at hand (Josh 21:43–45; 22:4; 23:1). As in Deuteronomy, however, security is linked, finally, to the proper worship of Yahweh. The gift of "rest" requires obedience in response (Josh 22:4–5). Therefore the age that follows, the period of the judges, is a precarious and tumultuous one. When obedient, Israel lives in security; but whenever the people fail to worship Yahweh alone, they fall into the hands of an enemy (Judg 2:11ff. and *passim*). Clearly the time of "rest" envisioned in Deuteronomy 12 has not yet arrived. The land is not fully secure, and the people have not begun to worship in the one place Yahweh will choose. Instead, each of them does "what seems right to him" (Judg 17:6; 21:25). This expression, which echoes Deut 12:8, has now become a slogan for the cultic and political chaos of the time of the judges, appearing in passages concerned with private or local sanctuaries (Weinfeld 1972:170). Moreover, it now becomes linked to another saying, viz. "In those days there was no king in Israel" (Judg 17:6; 21:25; cf. 18:1; 19:1). This is our first clue that the central sanctuary theme is going to be joined in the end to the theme of kingship.

The transition from the age of judges to the age of kings is marked by the Deuteronomistic passages in Samuel's farewell address in I Samuel 12 (especially vv. 6–15), which link the security of the people in the land indissolubly to the new institution of monarchy (cf. Noth 1981:5,47–51; McCarthy 1965: 134–36; also *I Samuel,* pp. 219–21). It is now clear that the promise of "rest" will be realized with a king on the throne—but not, as we soon discover, the first king, Saul. Shortly after the young David makes his first appearance at Saul's court in I Samuel 16, we begin to hear propitious statements about his future, some cast in characteristically Deuteronomistic language, others looking ahead specifically to II Samuel 7. Yahweh is going to cut off David's enemies from the face of the earth (I Sam 20:15; cf. II Sam 7:9), and David is going to become king (I Sam 23:17; 24:21; II Sam 3:9; 5:2). Indeed, Yahweh will make David "a secure house" (I Sam 25:28; cf. II Sam 7:11,16), a dynasty, in accordance with "the good thing" he has promised him (I Sam 25:30; cf. II Sam 7:28). It is David, not Saul, whom Yahweh has appointed "to save Israel . . . from all their enemies" (II Sam 3:18). These statements have been intercalated among the succeeding episodes of the old story of David's rise to power, where they stand as incidental or even superfluous remarks on the lips of both friends and foes; but taken together they form a concatenation of auspices looking ahead to Nathan's oracle. Thus the story of David's rise, wherever it may have concluded originally (see the COMMENT on § IX), should in its present, Deuteronomistic form be thought of as embracing at least 5:11–7:29 as well. Indeed, it reaches its climax in II Samuel 7. From the Deuteronomistic perspective David's rapid ascent from sheep pasture to royal palace (cf. II Sam 7:8) was possible not only because he was divinely destined for kingship, as already implied in the oldest form of the story, but also because he was to be the primogenitor of the chosen dynasty, his "secure house," and the savior whose victories would make possible the promised "rest" for Israel (cf. McCarthy 1965:131–32).

II Samuel 7, therefore, is not only editorially retrospective, representing the culmination of David's rise to power, but also prospective, preparing for the kingship of David's offspring and the age of peace that is to ensue. Specifically, it looks forward to three things: (1) the establishment of a "place" where Israel may worship Yahweh (v. 10); (2) the provision of "rest" for the people (v. 11a); and (3) the creation of a dynasty for David (vv. 11b,16). These correspond to the two ancient promises, a fixed place of worship and a "rest" for the people, and a third, a dynasty for David, to which they have now been joined.

McCarthy (1965) has stressed the attachment of the old notion of "rest" to the dynasty of David with particular reference to II Samuel 7:11. According to this verse, he says (p. 133), David and his line are the successors to the judges, who will usher in the "rest" the judges could not achieve. This, we should add, is apparently the Deuteronomistic understanding of the significance of David's victories, which are (therefore) reviewed in an editorial catalogue placed immediately after Nathan's oracle and David's prayer, in chap. 8. It is especially through the efforts of David, then, that the land will be pacified and the promised "rest" will be realized. And along with this "rest" the worship of Yahweh in his chosen place will begin; the central sanctuary will be established. According to II Sam 7:13 David's son will build a house for Yahweh. In this verse the building of the temple ("*He* will build a house for my name . . .") is linked to the constitution of the ruling Davidic line (". . . and I shall keep his throne forever stable"). The reference to the Davidic throne looks ahead to the establishment of the kingship of David's line and specifically to the accession of Solomon in I Kings 1–2, where we find a series of statements reflecting on the accession in language pointedly reminiscent of II Samuel 7 (2:12,24,33b,45,46a [?]). The reference to Yahweh's house looks ahead to the temple pericope in I Kings 5–9, where again we find a number of specific references to Nathan's oracle (5:17–19 [5:3–5]; 6:12; 8:15–19,24–26; 9:5). Finally, then, when the hopes of v. 13 are realized, the rightfully enthroned Davidic heir (promise 3), in the peroration of his long prayer in dedication of the newly erected temple (promise 1), will utter the following benediction in reflection on Moses' ancient assurance of "rest" (promise 2):

> Blessed be Yahweh, who has provided rest for his people Israel, just as he promised. Not one thing has failed to happen of all the good things he promised through his servant Moses.
>
> (I Kings 8:56)

Now David, as primogenitor of the chosen dynasty, might have been expected to erect the temple himself. Why was this done instead by Solomon? It is usually assumed (cf. Cross 1973:254) that one of the purposes of Nathan's oracle, at least in its present form, is to answer this question. Verse 2 shows that David thought of building a temple. In v. 5b, however, Yahweh tells him that he is not going to do so, adding that he, Yahweh, has never "lived in a house," but that instead he has always "gone about in a tent" (v. 6); nor, he says, has he ever censured any previous Israelite leader on that account (v. 7). That this part of the oracle (vv. 5b–7) may represent an ancient and fundamentally negative attitude toward temple building—a matter of scholarly disagreement, as we have seen—will have to be considered below. Here, however, we are concerned only with the explanation of David's failure to build a temple that was accepted in Deuteronomistic thought, and about this, fortunately, there is little uncertainty. In I Kings 5:17–19 [5:3–5] Solomon addresses the king of Tyre in a speech replete with Deuteronomistic clichés and says:

> You are aware that my father, David, was unable to build a house for the name of Yahweh, his god, because of the warfare that surrounded him, until Yahweh put [his enemies] under the soles of his feet. But now Yahweh, my god, has given me rest all around: There is no adversary or misfortune. So I intend to build a house for the name of Yahweh, my god, in keeping with what God [cf. LXX[L]] promised my father, David, namely, "Your son, whom I shall place on your throne in your stead—he will build a house for my name!"

In this passage a Deuteronomistic editor appeals to his own periodization of history, according to which, as we have seen, David's age was a time of wars, which prepared for the fulfilment of the promise of "rest." The temple came in its time, when the land was pacified. David had all he could manage with the wars catalogued in chap. 8; he could not build a temple too. This state of affairs was a consequence of ancient promises and, finally, the will of Yahweh. No blame whatever, then, could be attached to David for his failure to carry out his plan to build a temple. On the contrary, the plan itself was enough to merit divine approbation. This point is made explicit in I Kings 8:17–19, a part of Solomon's dedicatory speech amounting to a Deuteronomistic midrash on II Sam 7:1–17 (cf. Rupprecht 1977:74):

> My father, David, had in mind [*ʿim-lēbab,* cf. II Sam 7:3] building a house for the name of Yahweh, god of Israel. But Yahweh said to David, my father, "Because you had in mind building a house for my name, you have done well, inasmuch as you had it in mind. Nevertheless *you* [emphatic *ʾattâ,* cf. II Sam 7:5] will not build the house. Rather your son, the issue of your own body [cf. II Sam 7:12]—*he* will build the house for my name [cf. II Sam 7:13]."

Finally, if we permit our gaze to range still farther ahead, we see that Nathan's oracle will remain an important theological reference point even later in the Books of Kings, where it provides the basis for a central motif in the Deuteronomistic theology of the history of the divided kingdom, viz. the preservation of Jerusalem as a seat for the ruling Davidic dynasty (cf. von Rad 1953:74–91, especially p. 85). The survival of Judah will be linked explicitly to the choice of Jerusalem and the promise to David (I Kings 11:34–36; etc.), while, conversely, the doom of the northern kingdom will be tied to "the sin of Jeroboam," i.e., his establishment of rival centers of worship at Dan and Bethel (I Kings 12:26–53; II Kings 17:20–23; etc.; see Cross 1973:278–85).

## *Literary History*

It is clear that II Samuel 7 expresses certain important Deuteronomistic ideas, for which it stands as a primary point of reference in the larger history. A perusal of the NOTES to §§ XV and XVI, moreover, will show that the present form of the text is built largely of Deuteronomistic rhetoric. One is tempted, therefore, to dismiss the entire chapter, as Cross does David's prayer in vv. 18–29 (1973:254 n. 54), as "a free Deuteronomistic composition . . . without clear evidence of the use of earlier sources." It is difficult to believe, on the other hand, that ideas as theologically central to Israelite thought as those expressed here had no early documentary basis, or that a Deuteronomistic writer passed over such material in fashioning the present account. Nevertheless, even if the presence of older material is assumed, it is by no means easy to recover it by the application of standard literary-critical methods to the text, the surface of which seems to have been touched almost everywhere by a Deuteronomistic hand. We can readily sympathize with those scholars (Carlson, Dietrich, Rupprecht, etc.) who are, to one degree or another, skeptical about the possibility of recovering a pre-Deuteronomistic form of II Samuel 7.

For these reasons any description of the literary history of Nathan's oracle must be regarded as approximate and provisional, as the variety of conclusions arrived at by the modern interpreters cited above suggests. We must rely as much on identifiable thematic inconsistencies as on more strictly literary criteria. Indeed, the chief indication of the presence of diverse materials in the oracle is its fundamental conceptual inconsistency. I refer not to the presence of the two oracular motifs of temple and dynasty, for these are in themselves entirely compatible ideas. As we shall see, the promise or gift of a dynasty is a conventional response to the erection of a temple by a king. But it is precisely in light of this convention that Nathan's oracle takes on an anomalous appearance, for here a dynasty is promised while a temple is refused. To be sure, divine rejection of a proposal to build a temple is not in itself unparalleled. Consider, for example, the text of a letter to Zimri-Lim, king of Mari, reporting a divine revelation concerning a "house," presumably a temple (*ARM* 13 no. 12; complete English translation by Moran in *ANET*[3] 623–24; see also Malamat 1966:223–24; Ishida 1977:87). The letter refers to a revelatory dream or vision in which a seer

> saw the following: "Do not rebuild this dilapidated house! If this house is rebuilt, I shall make it collapse into the river." On the day he saw this dream, he did not speak (about it) to anyone. Again, on the next day, he saw the following vision: "It was a god. 'Do not rebuild this house! If you do rebuild it, I shall make it collapse into the river.' "

Thus it was possible that a god might refuse a king's offer to build him a temple, and the ancient records indicate that this happened fairly often (see the examples cited in Ishida 1977:87). Nevertheless, it would be quite surprising to find such a refusal, which implied divine displeasure (cf. Ishida 1977:95), combined with a promise of dynasty, which implied special divine favor. Yet this is precisely what we have in Nathan's oracle!

Within the oracle proper (vv. 5–16) these two incongruous ideas—the refusal of a temple (vv. 5b–7) and the promise of a dynasty (vv. 11b–16)—are joined together in a precarious unity by v. 13a, "*He* [the scion of the dynasty] will build a house for my name. . . ." This half-verse, then, is the linchpin of the passage. When it is removed the oracle falls apart: There is no other reference in vv. 11b–16 to a temple, and there is no reference in vv. 5b–7 to David's offspring. Thus the likelihood that v. 13a is editorial is very high. Our survey of research showed that this view was held by many of the earlier literary critics and by Rost, and that it has been favored by a majority of recent scholars as well. A few, on a variety of grounds, attribute v. 13a to the oldest part of the oracle (Mowinckel 1947:223; Gese 1964:21; Weiser 1965:155; Mettinger 1976:56–57) or to a very early age of editorial expansion (cf. Tsevat 1963), but such a view seems unacceptable for at least three reasons. First, as just noted, v. 13a stands isolated by content in its present context. Verses 11b–16, apart from v. 13a, are concerned solely with the establishment of the rule of David's offspring. The identification of the royal heir as the temple builder comes as a surprise after vv. 11b–12, and the temple question is not picked up again in vv. 13b–16. Second, v. 13a clearly refers to a specific individual, whereas the references to David's offspring elsewhere in vv. 12–15 were probably intended to be understood generally or collectively (cf. the NOTE on "your offspring, the issue of your body," v. 12). Third, the statement itself is cast in distinctively Deuteronomistic language (see the NOTE on "a house for my name"). We may therefore conclude with some confidence that v. 13a is, as most modern interpreters of Nathan's oracle have believed, a Deuteronomistic plus, forging a tenuous link between the incongruous oracular motifs of temple refusal and dynastic promise.

It follows that we may envision the growth of the oracle in one of two ways. We might suppose that two originally unrelated oracles, one rejecting David's proposal to build a temple and the other promising David a dynasty, were combined by a Deuteronomistic writer into a single, composite prophecy (so, for example, McKane; Cross 1973:254; Veijola 1975:78). Alternatively, we might think of one of the oracular motifs as having been added to an older document expressing the other at a stage prior to the Deuteronomistic redaction of the passage (so, for example, Mettinger 1976:53–55). Against the first view is the negative tone of the temple oracle. It is difficult to believe that a Deuteronomistic writer would voluntarily select a source that was unenthusiastic about a temple and embarrassing to David for the construction of an oracle glorifying Solomon's temple and the dynasty of David. One cannot argue that he cited it "to explain the historical fact that David did not build a temple" (Cross 1973:255), for the accepted Deuteronomistic explanation of this fact was, as we have seen, David's preoccupation with warfare. Indeed, the Deuteronomistic passages in I Kings 5:17 [5:3], where this explanation is given, and 8:17–19, where Yahweh's warm approval of David's contemplation of a temple is stressed, seem designed, each in its own way, to nullify the criticism of David and thus the disapproval of a temple that II Sam 7:5b–7 implies. We must reckon, therefore, with the probability that the Deuteronomistic editor of Nathan's oracle found the temple refusal already in place in relation to the dynastic promise in his source. One of these oracular motifs must have been added at a relatively early (pre-Deuteronomistic) date to a still older oracle expressing the other. Because of the incompatibility of the two, we must also suppose that the addition was intended as a corrective commentary on the original.

Which of the two motifs found expression in the earliest document? Many scholars, as we have seen, have regarded the temple refusal as pre-Solomonic at base (Rost, etc.; cf. already Wellhausen 1899:254,268), and we might argue that it was original, conveyed, perhaps, in an oracle from the time of David, which was later subjected to a dynastic redaction. Against this view are both the immediate context of the oracle itself and the general pattern of literary development elsewhere in the Books of Samuel. The narrative introduction to the oracle (vv. 1–3) raises the temple issue in a wholly positive way, and the negativity of vv. 5b–7 is a surprise after the euphoria of v. 3 (see the NOTE on "Do whatever you have in mind"). In view of the conventional association of temple building and dynasty, on the other hand, the promise of a house to David seems a natural sequel to the introductory scene (see below). Moreover, it can be argued that v. 11b, where the promise is first given, was the original continuation of v. 3 by appeal to the awkward shift from first to third person in the text of the oracle as presently constituted (Coppens 1968b:489–90; cf. Rost 1926:47–74 and the *Textual Note* on "Also Yahweh discloses to you that," v. 11). Note also that David's prayer in vv. 18–29, which is a direct response to Nathan's oracle, makes no reference to a temple, a surprising situation in any case (cf. the COMMENT on § XVI) but almost inconceivable if we suppose the temple issue to have been the subject of the original version of the oracle (cf. Rost 1926:56). With regard to the larger Samuel corpus, we should keep in mind our conclusion that the old stories of Saul and the young David came into Deuteronomistic hands editorially arranged and expanded according to a point of view suspicious of dynastic kingship and its associated institutions and best described as prophetic (see *I Samuel,* pp. 18–23 and *passim*). As explained below, there are several reasons to associate the motif of temple refusal in the present passage with this pre-Deuteronomistic prophetic history of the early monarchy.

For all these reasons, therefore, we conclude that the earliest form of Nathan's oracle was a promise of dynasty to David made in connection with his declared intention to build a temple for Yahweh. This ancient document was expanded by a writer with a less favorable view towards the temple and towards David himself. The final form of the passage was the work of a Deuteronomistic editor who further amended it to express his own point of view. The discussion that follows assumes that 7:1–17 developed in these three phases, each of which expressed the relationship between the temple and dynasty in a distinctive way.

**1. "You have promised to build a house for me.
Therefore I shall build a house for you!"**

The motifs of temple and dynasty, closely associated in Nathan's oracle, are linked in Deuteronomistic thought, as we have seen; but the same combination is often encountered in non-Israelite literature from the ancient Near East as well, especially in royal annals and building inscriptions. A number of scholars, in discussing the ideas expressed in II Samuel 7, have stressed the close relationship between kings and national sanctuaries in the ancient Near East (Coppens 1968b:490; von Nordheim 1977:441–43; etc.) and, more especially, the connection between the establishment of royal sovereignty and the erection of temples to patron gods (Kapelrud 1963; Mann 1977). Kutsch (1961:147–49) and Ishida (1977:87–90) have cited a number of particularly relevant parallels to the subject matter of the present passage. Mesopotamian kings frequently made records of temple projects connecting their service to the gods (viz. the building of the temples) to an expectation of personal rewards, including prosperity and a lasting reign but often posterity and the ongoing rule of their offspring as well (cf., for example, Borger 1956:68 [cited by Kutsch]; Langdon 1912:60–62 [cited by Ishida]; and *passim* in the building inscriptions in Luckenbill 1926–27). There was, in other words, an ancient and widely understood association between a king's erection of a temple to a particular god (or gods) and the hope for divine sanction of the continuing rule of the king and his descendants. In the present case we may speak of a connection between the establishment of a royal dynasty and the provision of a temple for the dynastic god. The common factor is permanence—the perpetuity of dynastic rule and the perdurability of a monumental temple.

The association of temple and dynasty, then, is not a uniquely Deuteronomistic or even Israelite construct, and the correlation of the establishment of the Davidic dynasty with the erection of the temple in Jerusalem, therefore, is not likely to have been a Deuteronomistic innovation. Among other evidence, the testimony of pre-Deuteronomistic poetry, such as Ps 78:68–71, confirms this conclusion. A priori we should expect such a correlation to derive in Israel from Solomonic times, the time of the building of the temple and the reign of the first descendant of David. In the present passage, however (and elsewhere—I Kings 8:17; etc.), we are told that David himself wanted to build a temple, and the promise of dynasty is linked to this gesture. The notion that David intended to build a temple can hardly have been an invention of the Deuteronomistic historian, who in I Kings 5:17 [5:3] and elsewhere is anxious to excuse David for not bringing his plan to completion, as we have seen. On the other hand, we cannot be sure that it derives from the time of David himself either. It is curious that nothing is said in vv. 11bff. of David's own reign, as we should expect on the basis of the comparative literature from Mesopotamia; the promise concerns only the rule of his offspring. We know, moreover, that it was characteristic of Solomon's administration to sanction its deeds and policies by appeal to the wishes of David, real or spurious (cf. Cross 1973:231; McCarter 1981:359–61; and see the Introduction, pp. 11–13). It seems probable, then, that the association of the endurance of the Davidic dynasty with the erection of a temple in Jerusalem was first made in the reign of Solomon and projected back into the time of David. The present passage—if it had a long pre-Deuteronomistic history, as we have assumed—is likely to have arisen in its original form in this period.

We may posit a primitive document underlying 7:1–7 and including vv. 1a,2–3,11b–12, and 13b–15a. The story it told was as follows. The king, sitting in his house, expressed his intention to build a house for Yahweh (vv. 1a–2). He was encouraged by Nathan or, perhaps, an anonymous prophet (v. 3), who went on to say that Yahweh had declared his intention to build a house for David (v. 11b). The oracle proper, then, began in v. 12; it articulated the dynastic promise in language we now know also from Ps 89:20–38 [89:19–37] and elsewhere, forecasting the rule of David's offspring *collectively* (". . . I shall raise up your offspring . . . and establish *their* kingship," etc.).

The purpose of this old document, which we must suppose to derive from the court of Solomon, was to sanction the erection of a new national sanctuary, the temple in Jerusalem, by associating it and all that it implied with David. It showed the building of a temple to have been intended by David (v. 2) and approved by Yahweh (v. 3). Indeed, the establishment of the Davidic line, of which Solomon was the scion, was shown to have been predicated on the temple project (vv. 3 + 11b), in keeping with the ancient international association of temple and dynasty. Yahweh's message to David, as conceived at this earliest stage in the development of the oracle, can therefore be summarized as "You have promised to build me a house. Therefore I shall build you a house!"

**2. "You will not build me a house.
I shall build you a house!"**

A second thematic aspect of II Samuel 7 that weighs against its dismissal as a free Deuteronomistic composition is the negative attitude towards David's plan to build a temple expressed in the opening words of the oracle (vv. 5b–7). Why is David not to build a temple? According to the Deuteronomistic interpretation of the passage, the reason was apparently that the time was not yet right. When Yahweh had appointed the "place" he would be worshiped (v. 10) and had given the people "rest" (v. 11a), then David's offspring would build the temple (v. 13a). Thus understood, vv. 5b–7 can be accommodated to the notion subscribed to elsewhere (I Kings 5:17 [5:3]) by the Deuteronomistic school that David was too busy fighting wars to carry out his plan; David's wars achieved the necessary "rest." But vv. 5b–7, though some have found the mark of a Deuteronomistic hand in v. 6 (cf. the NOTE on "the day I brought up the Israelites"), cannot be Deuteronomistic as a whole. Contrast the Deuteronomistic way of referring to a temple in v. 13a (*bayit lišmî,* "a house for my name") to that in v. 5b (*bayit lěšibtî,* "a house for me to live in"). The use of the verb *yāšab,* "live, dwell," in vv. 5–6 in reference to Yahweh's presence in a temple is unthinkable in an original Deuteronomistic composition (cf. Cross 1973:255). Thus we must reckon with a pre-Deuteronomistic version of our story in which David was told he would not build a temple and the negativity of this divine reply was not mitigated by a promise that his heir would.

How is the negativity of vv. 5b–7 to be explained? According to some scholars it is primarily a question of divine indignation at the presumption of David, who, though a mere human being, has proposed to build a temple Yahweh has not requested (Simon 1952:50; Noth 1967:251). Thus the propriety of human initiative in such a project is finally at stake (cf. Gese 1964:21). Many others would explain the negativity as reflecting a religious preference for a tent-shrine on the part of the author, who therefore can be thought of as a spokesman for an old northern tent tradition (von Rad 1966:119) or, more generally, a school of thought identifying itself with the pre-temple traditions of early Israel (cf. Simon 1952:52,55; de Vaux 1961b:vol. II:329–30; Cross 1973:255; etc.). A careful reading of the verses in question supports each of these readings in a general way. Verse 5b indicates that David will not build a temple. As explained in the NOTE on "Are *you* going to build *me* a house . . . ?" close attention to the syntax is necessary for the correct interpretation of this half-verse. It is a rhetorical question, and this in itself may suggest divine indignation (cf. GK[2] §150d). Both personal pronouns are emphatic. Thus the stress is not as much on the building of a temple as such as on the fact that David has proposed to build one for Yahweh. How can David presume to become Yahweh's benefactor? The force of the second pronoun ("*me*") is resumed in v. 8 by another emphatic pronoun ("*I* took you," etc.). It is Yahweh who has been solely responsible for David's every success. Yahweh, in other words, has been and will be the benefactor. And if there is a house to be built, Yahweh will build one for David (v. 11a), not the reverse! Verse 6 indicates that Yahweh has never taken up residence in a temple but has always moved about in a tent. Again we must give careful attention to language and syntax. As explained in the NOTES, the first verb, "I haven't lived (in a house)," refers to continuous residence or presence in one place, while the verbal expression "I've gone about (in a tent) wherever I happened to go" is an idiomatic way of indicating freedom of movement. The pointed contrast is reinforced by the nouns "house" and "tent," and the overall effect is a strong implication that the proposed temple would impose a restriction on the divine freedom. Verse 7 indicates that Yahweh never found fault with any of Israel's past leaders for their failure to build him "a house of cedar." Yet again language and syntax are important. This time the rhetorical question is reinforced by an infinitive absolute (see the *Textual Note* on "Did I ever speak"). We are probably to think of the tone of the oracle as impatiently condescending or simply exasperated—"Did I *ever* speak . . . ?" Note especially that we are not told that Yahweh never *asked* for a temple. We are probably to assume that he never did, but the point being made is a different one. The particular phrasing of the question never addressed to any of Israel's leaders—"Why haven't you built me a house of cedar?"—indicates an indictment (see the NOTE). Yahweh never *censured* any of them for not building a temple. Evidently we are to understand this assertion as a direct response to David's concern, clearly implied in v. 2, that he might be at fault for not building a temple. No, David is told, you are doing no wrong; on the contrary, the tent has always been Yahweh's preference.

In short, it is the implied contention of vv. 5b–7 that a temple is unnecessary and unwanted and that David's proposal is uncalled for and presumptuous, an act of royal supererogation. This attitude towards the building of a temple is strongly reminiscent of the attitude towards another innovation, viz. the inauguration of monarchy itself, that finds expression in those sections of I Samuel dominated by the actions of the prophet Samuel—the section the older literary critics described somewhat improperly as "antimonarchical." In chaps. 7–8, for example, kingship is shown to have been a divine concession to a wanton demand of the people. It is portrayed as entirely unnecessary (cf. I Sam 7:13–17), a needless hardship (cf. I Sam 8:10–18), and the people's request is shown to have been presumptuous if not blasphemous (cf. I Sam 8:7). The portrayal of the royal temple in the present passage as another unnecessary and presumptuously conceived institution seems likely to have arisen from the same religious milieu, especially in view of what we have already said about the intimate relationship between kings and national sanctuaries. Not only was temple building the special prerogative of the king (Kapelrud 1963: 56), but a "king's sanctuary" or "temple of the realm" (*miqdaš-melek . . . bêt mamlākâ,* Amos 7:13) was ordinarily incorporated into a single architectural complex with the royal palace, and the king had final jurisdiction over the temple cult (Poulssen 1967). In the sections just referred to in I Samuel any attempt by the king to arrogate cultic functions to himself is viewed gravely (cf. I Sam 13:9–14; 15:17–23). A plan to build a royal temple, therefore, can be interpreted as an attempt to confiscate the cult itself for the personal use of the king. In our analysis of the stories of Samuel and Saul we attributed material of this kind to the hand of an editor or writer who gave the earliest narrative sources their primary editorial formulation according to a point of view best described as prophetic (see *I Samuel,* pp. 18–23 and *passim*). Despite the use of ancient documents and the presence of subsequent Deuteronomistic editing, this writer's perspective dominates the narrative in I Samuel 1–15. He also introduced the old story of David's rise to power (I Sam 16:14–II Sam 5:10) with his own account of David's anointing by Samuel (I Sam 16:1–13), and it is not surprising to find the touch of his hand here at the end of the same story.

In II Sam 7:1–17 the presence of prophetic editing is discernible in vv. 4–9a, 15b. The passage as a whole, which even in its primitive version was set apart formally from non-Israelite building inscriptions by its prophetic character (cf. Ishida 1977:90–92), is now dressed out in conventional prophetic speech forms (vv. 4–5a,8a$\alpha$), which point to the mediating role of the prophet in the relationship between Yahweh and the king. To David's proposal to build a temple we now have the reply that a temple is not needed or wanted (vv. 5b–7). David's presumption in making such a proposal is underlined by a glance at his past (vv. 8a$\beta$–9a), formulated to show that it was Yahweh ("*I* took you," etc.) who set David in his present lofty position. The retrospect is a capsule review of the story of David's rise to power, the central theological motif of which is "Yahweh was with David" (cf. the NOTE at 5:10), to which compare v. 9a$\alpha$ ("I was with you," etc.). The original version of this story probably began in I Sam 16:14 (cf. *I Samuel,* p. 30). As just noted, however, an introductory account of David's call from tending his father's flock and his anointing by Samuel (I Sam 16:1–13) was added by a prophetic writer, and, not surprisingly, this event is emphasized in the present review ("*I* took you from the sheep pasture," v. 8a$\beta$). Emphasis is also given to David's status as *nāgîd,* "prince" or "king-designate" over Israel (v. 8b). The latter term, though it does not occur in I Sam 16:1–13, was an important element in the prophetic understanding of kingship, emphasizing Yahweh's free choice in the election and rejection of Israel's leaders (cf. *I Samuel,* especially pp. 186–87). From the prophetic perspective the call of David and the rejection of Saul, himself once designated "prince" over Israel (I Sam 10:1), were two sides of a single coin. Similarly the promise of a dynasty to David had as its inevitable corollary the condemnation of Saul's own dynastic hopes. Note, in this regard, that the prophetic account of the renunciation of the kingship of Saul in I Sam 13:7b–15 uses language that is strongly reminiscent of vv. 12–13 of the present passage and may, in fact, have been modeled on the dynastic promise to David for purposes of contrast. It also seems probable that v. 15b of the present passage, in which Saul's rejection is recalled, was inserted here by a prophetic hand.

With vv. 4–9a and 15b in place, then, Nathan's oracle offers a prophetic reflection on David's rise to power, forming an inclusion with the story of the rejection of Saul and anointing of David in I Sam 15:1–16:13 as reinforced by the prophetic revision of the incident at En-dor in I Sam 28:3–25 (cf. *I Samuel,* pp. 422–23). Its purpose is to assert that David's success, already attributed to divine favor in the original account of David's rise (cf. the COMMENT on

§ IX), was brought about by Yahweh, following ineluctably from the prophet Samuel's summons of the young David from his father's pasture and designation of him as *nāgîd,* "prince," over Israel. Yahweh's freedom in electing and rejecting kings, a central theme in the prophetic version of Saul's career, is reaffirmed in the contrast drawn between the treatment of David's "offspring" and that of Saul (vv. 14–15). David is promised the abiding kingship of which Saul was deprived in I Sam 13:7b–15.

What we see here, then, is the prophetic theology of kingship coming to terms with the historical reality of the Davidic dynasty. Dynastic succession, because it seemed to interfere with the free divine appointment of the king, must have been viewed with suspicion by those circles within which the legitimacy of a ruler was believed to depend on his anointment by a prophet of Yahweh. In this regard it may seem surprising to find phrases drawn from the royal theology of Jerusalem, especially those touching on the concept of the divine sonship of the king and the unconditionality of the grant of dominion in vv. 14–15, preserved in a passage reshaped by a prophetic hand. Nevertheless, the dynasty of David was, as we have said, a fact of history, and dynastic succession therefore could not be thought of as abhorrent to Yahweh in all circumstances. Indeed the dynasty of Saul was accepted in principle—though rejected in fact—by prophetic theology (I Sam 13:13). Still, it would be uncharacteristic of our prophetic narrator, as we came to know him in I Samuel, to leave the promise of an enduring dynasty without a cautionary comment or an expression of suspicion. And, in fact, he will have his say, but in a later episode. The final prophetic verdict on the house of David is not yet in—for that we must await another oracle of Nathan (12:7–12). David will have a "house," a dynasty; but, as we shall see, Yahweh will "stir up trouble for [David] out of [his] house" when he does wrong. Because of his promise to David, Yahweh will never remove his favor *(wĕḥasdî lōʾ ʾāsîr,* 7:15; cf. the *Textual Note)* from David's "offspring," but because of David's wrongdoing the sword will never be removed *(lōʾ tāsûr ḥereb)* from his house. Just as kingship itself, from the prophetic point of view, was a divine concession to a willful demand of the people (I Samuel 8; etc.), so the Davidic dynasty was a gift to a favored servant who finally, like any king, proved corruptible. But this matter will be taken up in its proper place in the COMMENT on § XXII.

Note, finally, that the effect of the introduction of prophetic material in the present passage is to undermine the implication of the original Solomonic document that the dynastic promise in vv. 11bff. was a direct and positive response to David's expression of his plan to build a temple. The provision of a house for David is now a free and uninduced divine gift (cf. Gese 1964:21). Indeed, it has the effect of confirming and amplifying the contrast between the pointless gesture of a temple plan and Yahweh's ongoing benefaction for David. Thus the message of the oracle at this stage in its growth is: "*You* will not build a house for me. *I* shall build a house for you!"

**3. "You will not build me a house.
Your son will build me a house!"**

We have already considered the place of Nathan's oracle in Deuteronomistic thought. We saw that II Samuel 7 occupies an important position in the Deuteronomistic history, for which it provides a point of reference for the key themes of temple and dynasty. The Deuteronomistic redaction of vv. 1–17—to which we may attribute at least vv. 1b,9b–11a,13a, and 16, as well as, possibly, other touches here and there throughout the text (see the NOTES)—was intended to incorporate David's temple plan and the dynastic promise into the larger history and to soften the negativity of the opening words of the oracle.

The predictive part of the oracle in its pre-Deuteronomistic form began in v. 11b with the dynastic promise. This the editor prefaced with vv. 9b–11a. Yahweh, we are told (v. 9b), is going to make David a great "name," a prediction that looks ahead to both temple and dynasty, as explained in the NOTE. The temple issue is taken up first. Yahweh is going to establish a "place," a permanent, immovable, sacred site (see the NOTE) for the Israelites (vv. 10–11aα), who will then have "rest" (v. 11aβ). Here we recognize the lineaments of the larger structure of the Deuteronomistic history. The fulfilment of the ancient promises of "rest" and "a place Yahweh will choose" (Deut 12:10–12) have become imminent in the time of David, and the dynastic issue, which is next addressed, is to be understood in light of this development. Yahweh promises David a house not simply because of David's intention to build him a house, as in the oldest account. The promise is seen as an important and integral part of Yahweh's dealings with Israel past and future. The recipient of the promise and progenitor of the chosen dynasty is the human agent through whom Yahweh's will for his people, as expressed by Moses in Deuteronomy 12, is being mediated. With the establishment of the dynasty will come the erection of the long-awaited temple. The Deuteronomistic insertion of v. 13a makes this explicit. It also has the effect, however, of identifying David's "offspring" (v. 12), understood collectively in the older oracle (see above), as an individual, viz. Solomon, and it may have been for this reason that the dynastic promise was expanded by the addition of the prediction about David's "royal house" in v. 16, recognizable as secondary by the shift of focus from David's offspring to David himself and by its characteristic Deuteronomistic clichés (see the NOTE). Thus the fact that David is promised a dynasty, not merely a ruling heir, is reinforced, and the continuing divine sanction of the Davidic line ("secure forever in my care") is certified. In any case, v. 13a serves to associate the ancient promise of a chosen sanctuary unambiguously with the temple built by Solomon in Jerusalem. This particular temple, we are to understand, was the target of that vector in history. The negativity of the initial words of Yahweh's response to David's own temple proposal, therefore, is to be read in this light. David will not build a temple because the time is not yet right. Verses 5b–7, then, represent a refusal, but only a temporary one. David's son *will* build a temple. To secure this point the editor exploited the emphatic pronoun at the beginning of v. 5b by means of a contrasting pronoun of his own—not you but *he* will build a temple. Thus understood, the force of the oracle may now be paraphrased as: "You will not build me a house. Your son will build me a house!"

(On the relationship between the materials in chap. 7 and the story of the ark's arrival in Jerusalem [6:1–19] see the COMMENT on § XVI.)

# XVI. DAVID'S PRAYER
## (7:18–29)

7 [18]King David went in and remained before Yahweh. "Who am
I, my lord Yahweh, and what is my house," he said, "that you
have brought me to this place? [19]Yet this seems a trifle to you, my
lord, for you have spoken of your servant's house at a distant time
and shown me the generation to come, my lord Yahweh! [20]What
can David do for you that you should honor your servant? You,
Yahweh, know your servant. [21]For the sake of your servant and as
it pleased you, you have done all this, this great thing, informing your
servant.
[22]"Therefore, my lord Yahweh, you are great! Yes, there is none
like you—no god apart from you—according to everything we have
heard with our own ears. [23]And what other nation is there on earth
whom, like your people Israel, a god led along to ransom as a people
of his own, making a name for himself, doing great and fearful deeds,
driving out before his people, whom he ransomed as his own from
Egypt, both a nation and its gods? [24]For when you established your
people Israel as your own people forever, you, Yahweh, became their
god.
[25]"Now then, my lord, as for the thing you promised concerning your
servant and his house, let it be confirmed for all times! Do as you
promised, [26]and your name will be great forever—Yahweh Sabaoth, god
over Israel—and the house of your servant David will be established
in your care!
[27]"It was because you, Yahweh Sabaoth, god of Israel, permitted
your servant to hear you say, 'I shall build you a house,' that your
servant found the courage to offer this prayer to you. [28]So now, my lord
Yahweh, since you are God and your words are true, and since you
have said this good thing about your servant, [29]please bless your servant's house that it might be forever under your care; for you, my lord
Yahweh, have spoken. And by your blessing may your servant's house
be blessed forever!"

## TEXTUAL NOTES

7 18. *you have brought me* So MT: *hby'tny.* LXX has *ēgapēkas* (*ēgapēsas* LXX[LN]) *me,* "you have loved me." The reading of MT is better before *'d hlm,* "hither, to this place," but it is difficult to decide whether the error in LXX was inner-Greek (*ēgapēsas* < *ēgages* [so Aquila, Symmachus]) or derived from a defective Hebrew *Vorlage* (*'hbtny* < *hb'tny*).

19. *Yet this seems a trifle to you* We read *wtqṭn z't b'ynyk,* to which cf. LXX, OL, Syr., and I Chron 17:17. MT has *wtqṭn 'wd z't b'nyk,* "Yet this *still* seems a trifle to you."

*my lord* So LXX[BA]. MT (*kětîb*), LXX[LMN]: "my lord Yahweh." MT (*qěrê*): "my lord God."

*of your servant's house* MT inserts *gam*—thus, "*also* of your servant's house." Omit with LXX, Syr., and MT[MSS].

*and shown me the generation* MT has *wz't twrt h'dm,* "and this is the law of mankind," which critics from Gesenius (cf. BDB 436) to Eissfeldt (1973) have attempted to explain without success. The versions add nothing substantially different. Ewald (1878:vol. III:132) was the first to recognize that the solution to the puzzle lies in the text of I Chron 17:17, which reads *wr'ytny ktwr h'dm* in MT and *kai epeides me hōs horasis anthrōpou* = *wtr'ny ktwr* (= *kt'r*) *h'dm* in LXX. From this Ewald reconstructed *whr'tny btwr h'dm,* "and you have let me look upon the ranks of men." Because of the requirements of the verbal sequence, we should follow Wellhausen's modification of Ewald's text and read *wtr'ny* with LXX (I Chron 17:17), vocalized *wattar'ēnî.* On the other hand, Wellhausen was probably mistaken in rejecting *twr* in favor of *dwrt,* "generations," which he thinks is favored by "the final *taw* in *twrt* and the meaning." But the final *-t* is missing in I Chron 17:17 and at least one witness to II Sam 7:19 (Targ. *hzy',* "vision," which points to *twr* understood as *tō'ar,* "appearance," with quiescent *'alep*). *Twr,* moreover, can be interpreted in either of two ways: (1) as *tôr* (< **tō'ar*), "appearance" (Targ.; cf. LXX [I Chron 17:17] *horasis*)—thus, *twr h'dm,* "the appearance of mankind," i.e., "a human form" (cf. Klostermann); or (2) as *tôr,* "turn (in a succession)." The latter meaning, as Ewald recognized, is especially suitable. It occurs in Esth 2:12,15 in the sense of a scheduled turn in a succession and in Rabbinic Hebrew (Jastrow 1656) with a similar meaning. Thus *twr h'dm hm'lh* (cf. the following *Textual Note*) will mean literally "the turn of mankind to come," that is, "the generation to come."

*to come* There is nothing in the text of Samuel at this point. I Chron 17:17 has *hm'lh,* which Wellhausen and others would emend to *lm'lh* and insert here. Symmetry with *lmrḥq,* "at a distant time," favors the restoration of something here, and I should tentatively read *hm'lh,* assuming that as it stands it can have adverbial force equivalent to *lm'lh,* lit. "onwards, upwards" and thus "(in time) to come" (cf. Wellhausen).

20. *What . . . your servant?* Cf. I Chron 17:18: *mh ywsp 'wd dwd 'lyk lkbd* (LXX

*tou doxasai;* MT has *lkbwd) 't 'bdk,* lit. "What more can David add to you (i.e., that you do not already have) to honor your servant?" In II Sam 7:20 MT has *wmh ywsp dwd 'wd ldbr 'lyk,* "And what more can David say to you?" The loss of *lkbd 't 'bdk* can be explained by homoioteleuton, the intrusive *ldbr* having probably arisen subsequently in clarification of the defective text.

*Yahweh* See LXX$^{B}$ (cf. I Chron 17:19). MT *(kětîb)* has "my lord Yahweh" (cf. LXX$^{MSS}$). MT *(qěrê)* has "my lord God" (cf. MT$^{MSS}$, Syr., Targ., Vulg.).

21. *your servant* So LXX$^{B}$ (*'bdk* [cf. I Chron 17:19]), adding *pepoiēkas* = *'śyt,* "you did, acted," in anticipation of the next clause. MT (cf. LXX$^{A}$, Syr.) has "your *word*" *(dbrk).* LXX$^{L}$ combines the readings of MT and LXX$^{B}$.

*and as it pleased you* That is, *ûkělibběkā,* lit. "and according to your heart." Tur-Sinai (1950/51:415–16) has suggested reinterpreting the same consonantal text as *wěkalběkā,* "and your dog." Thus he would read the beginning of v. 21 as "For the sake of your servant and your dog," citing II Kings 8:13 and ancient Near Eastern courtly language in general (cf. II Sam 16:9). Tur-Sinai's suggestion has been adopted by the Jerusalem Bible: "For your servant's sake, this dog of yours," etc.

22. *Therefore . . . you are great!* MT *'l kn gdlt.* LXX *heneken megaly(thē)nai se* reflects *b'bwr gdlk,* "for the sake of your being great," that is, "in order to magnify yourself."

*my lord Yahweh* So MT *(kětîb);* cf. LXX$^{LMN}$. MT *(qěrê)* and MT$^{MSS}$ have "my lord God" as in Chronicles throughout (cf. Wellhausen); cf. Syr., Targ., Vulg.

*according to everything* Reading *kkl* with Targ., MT$^{MSS}$. MT, LXX: *bkl,* "*among* all (those of whom)."

23. On the text of this verse in general see Geiger 1857:288.

*other nation* So LXX: *ethnos allo* = *gwy 'ḥr.* MT: *gwy 'ḥd,* "one nation"—thus, "And who is like . . . Israel, one nation on earth. . . ."

*Israel* So LXX, Syr., Targ., MT$^{MSS}$. MT: "*like* Israel." See Altschüller 1886:212.

*a god* MT *'lhym,* which might mean "a god," "gods," or "God." LXX has *ho theos* = *h'lhym,* as in I Chron 17:21, unambiguously "God."

*led along* We follow LXX$^{BAMN}$ *(hōdēgēsen auton)* in interpreting *hlkw* as *hôlîkô,* "led (him) along," rather than *hālěkû,* "(gods) went." LXX$^{L}$ *(hōdēgēsas auton)* reflects *hlktw,* "you led him along, (O God!)." I Chron 17:21 has *hlk,* "went" (sing.), adopted by Geiger (cf. Wellhausen, Driver).

*of his own* LXX$^{L}$: "of *your* own" (cf. the preceding *Textual Note*).

*making* Cf. LXX and I Chron 17:21. MT: "*and* making."

*for himself* So MT. LXX (cf. I Chron 17:21): "for *your*self."

*doing* So LXX and 4QSam$^{a}$ *([l']śwt ġ[ ]).* MT, Syr., Targ.: "*and* doing *for you* (pl.)."

*great and fearful deeds* The original was probably *gdlwt wnr'wt* (cf. I Chron 17:21). LXX seems to read *gdwlh wnr'h,* "a great and fearful deed," and MT mixes the numbers awkwardly, *hgdwlh wnr'wt,* "the great deed and fearful deeds."

*driving out* Reading *lgrš* (cf. LXX), as in I Chron 17:21. MT has *l'rṣk,* "in (?) your land."

*his people, whom he ransomed as his own* Here the chief witnesses, following the tendency elsewhere in the passage, read "your people, whom *you* redeemed as *your* own." The question, addressed rhetorically to Yahweh, alludes to what Yahweh himself has done, and so the second person naturally arises (e.g., LXX[L] "whom . . . *you,* O God, led along to redeem as a people of *your* own"; LXX, I Chron 17:21 "making a name for *yourself*"; etc.); but properly the question asks what *other* god has done this, and the third person is to be retained or restored throughout (cf. Driver).

*a nation* So LXX: *ethnē* = *gwy* (cf. OL). MT: *gwym,* "nations" (pl.), "as not one nation merely but several were driven out before Israel" (A. Geiger *apud* Driver). The originality of *gwy* is assured by the singular suffix remaining on *'lhyw,* "its gods."

*and its gods* So MT: *'lhyw.* 4QSam[a] has *w'hlym,* "and *tents*" (!), an obvious error shared by LXX (*kai skēnōmata;* cf. OL).

24. *your people Israel as your own people* That is, *lk 't 'mk yśr'l l'm* (cf. LXX, Vulg.). MT inserts another *lk* after *yśr'l.*

25. *my lord* So LXX[BA], OL[MS]. As in MT[MSS] in vv. 28,29 below, MT here (cf. OL, Syr.) has "my lord (= Yahweh) God," an instance of the *qĕrê* (cf. vv. 19,20,22) intruding into the text. LXX[LMN] have "my lord Yahweh."

*and his house* So MT, LXX[BAMN]. LXX[L] has "and *concerning* his house" as in I Chron 17:23.

*let it be confirmed* So LXX[L] (cf. LXX[BAMN]): *pistōthētō* = *yē'āmēn,* as in I Chron 17:23. MT has *hāqēm,* "cause it to stand."

*for all times* Followed in LXX[B] by *kyrie pantokratōr thee tou israēl* = *yhwh ṣb'wt 'lhy yśr'l.* Omit with MT, LXX[ALMN]. The LXX[B] plus is the remnant of a misplaced correction of that MS's long haplography in vv. 26–27 (see below).

*Do* So MT: *w'śh.* LXX[O], along with Aquila and Symmachus (cf. LXX[L]), correct LXX *kai nyn* = *w'th,* "And now, now then," to the reading of MT (*kai poiēson* = *w'śh);* note the error in *BHS.*

26–27. LXX[B] has suffered a long haplography, corrected in LXX[ALMN], from "Yahweh Sabaoth, god over Israel" in v. 26 to "Yahweh Sabaoth, god of Israel" in v. 27.

26. *forever* MT, LXX[LMN] add *l'mr.* Delete with LXX[BA].

*in your care* Syr., MT[MS], Targ.[MS] add "forever."

27. *god of Israel* LXX[A] and certain other MSS here repeat parts of vv. 25–26: ". . . god of Israel. And now, as you promised, 'Let your name be great forever!' said Yahweh Sabaoth, god of Israel. . . ."

*found the courage* That is, *mṣ' . . . 't lbw,* lit. "found his heart." LXX[L]: "found his heart *in God.*"

28. *my lord Yahweh* So MT (*kĕtîb);* cf. LXX. In MT[MSS] the *qĕrê,* "my lord God" (thus *yhwh 'lhym*), has intruded into the text (cf. Syr., Targ.) as in MT in v. 25 and MT[MSS] in v. 29. LXX[A] "my lord" probably does not reflect an original, shorter text (but cf. I Chron 17:26, "Yahweh").

*about* Cf. LXX, Syr., Targ.[MSS]. MT has "to," as if ". . . you have said . . . to your servant"; but this is a case of the frequent substitution of *'l* for *'l* in the text of Samuel (1:24; 2:9; etc.).

29. *please bless* So MT: *hw'l wbrk.* 4QSam[a] confirms *hw'l (h*[*w*]*'l),* for which LXX *arxai* and Syr. *šr'* reflect *hḥl,* "begin (to bless)."

*my lord Yahweh* So MT (*kĕtîb);* cf. LXX. In MT[MSS] the *qĕrê,* "my lord God," has intruded into the text (cf. Syr., Targ.) as *yhwh 'lhym,* as in vv. 25 (MT) and 28 (MT[MSS]) above.

## NOTES

7 18. *went in.* That is, into the tent-shrine of the ark (6:17; 7:2).

*remained before Yahweh.* That is, before the ark where Yahweh was believed to be present. The verb, *wayyēšeb,* suggests lingering after others have departed (cf. I Sam 1:22). At a primitive stage in the growth of the larger narrative David may have remained before the ark after the conclusion of the ceremony described in chap. 6 (see the COMMENT). According to the present form of the text, however, *wayyēšeb* must be understood to indicate that David remained for some time after entering the tent, perhaps because of the earnestness of his prayer (cf. I Sam 1:16), or that David *sat* before Yahweh. Prayer in such a posture, however, is not otherwise known in the Bible, and, as Smith says, "the unusual attitude has occasioned prolix discussion on the part of the commentators." Caird's comment is typical: "What is probably meant is a kneeling position in which the worshiper sat back on his heels with his head erect—one of the postures used by the Mohammedan in prayer." The rabbinic notion that only the Davidic kings were permitted to sit down in the temple court (Yoma 25a) probably arose from this verse (cf. Thenius).

*Who am I . . . what is my house . . . ?* Echoed in another prayer of David in I Chron 29:14, this is the appropriately humble response to divine (Judg 6:15; I Sam 9:21) or royal (I Sam 18:18) favor.

20–21. As explained in the COMMENT on § XV ("Literary History"), parts of Nathan's oracle derive from prophetic circles hostile to the idea that the dynastic promise to David might be regarded as a divine response to David's plans to build a temple, or, indeed, to any grandiose gesture of patronage towards Yahweh by David. As the NOTES that follow show, the present verses (20–21) seem designed to introduce a similar point of view into David's prayer.

20. *What . . . your servant?* Hebrew *mâ yôsîp dāwīd ʿôd ʾelêkā lĕkabbēd ʾet-ʿabdĕkā,* lit. "What more can David add to you to honor your servant?"; see the *Textual Notes.* David can give Yahweh nothing he does not already have (cf. 7:5, "Are *you* going to build *me* a house . . . ?"). Thus Yahweh's decision to glorify David is a free, unmotivated act of divine favor.

21. *as it pleased you.* Hebrew *kĕlibbĕkā,* lit. "according to your heart," used also in another prophetic context (I Sam 13:14) to stress the divine freedom, in that case involving the selection of the king (cf. *I Samuel,* the NOTE on "a man of his own choosing" at 13:14).

*this great thing.* Hebrew *haggĕdullâ hazzōʾt,* an act of divine largess, a *magnalium dei.* Driver and others have found "the meaning of the expression 'done *all this greatness*' " to be "obscure," but it is evidently the purpose of the following infinitive construct phrase (*lĕhôdîaʿ ʾet-ʿabdĕkā,* "informing your servant") to provide the more exact definition needed. Thus the "great thing" here referred to is not the dynastic promise, as Driver evidently assumes, but its revelation.

*informing your servant.* See the preceding NOTE. The phrase could also mean "to make your servant known" (cf. NEB). If our interpretation is correct, the allusion is to the revelation mentioned in v. 19. The absence of a second object specifying what David was informed has troubled some commentators (Smith, etc.), but the usage is paralleled (Jer 11:18).

22–26. In these verses the horizon of David's praise broadens from the previous theme of Yahweh's benefaction towards him and his house to encompass Yahweh's great deeds on behalf of Israel as a whole. Such a shift of focus suggests Deuteronomistic expansion, as in vv. 9b–11a above. The association of the welfare of the people with the welfare of the Davidic dynasty suggested by the juxtaposition of ideas found here is a characteristic Deuteronomistic theme (cf. McCarthy 1965:132). The Deuteronomistic character of vv. 22–24 was recognized by Rost (1926:49,53–54,72). Noth believed they contain "deuteronomistic extensions" (1967:252 n. 8; cf. 1981:55), and most subsequent scholars have agreed (contrast Hertzberg; Seybold 1972:38). Mettinger (1976:51) has argued persuasively that the full extent of the insertion is vv. 22b–26 on the grounds that Deuteronomistic expressions occur in v. 25 as well as vv. 22–24 and that the *kî-* clause beginning v. 27 was probably the original continuation of v. 22a (now continued by the *kî-* clause in v. 22b). The Deuteronomistic character of vv. 22b–26 is demonstrated by the presence of the following characteristic themes and clichés (cf. especially Weinfeld 1972:37–38 and n. 4):

1) *'yn kmwk,* "there is none like you," to which compare I Kings 8:22. Cf. Jer 10:6,7.

2) *'mk yśr'l,* "your people Israel," as in Deut 21:8; 26:15; and I Kings 8:33,34, 38,43,52. Cf. Jer 32:21.

3) *lpdwt . . . pdh,* "to ransom . . . he ransomed" (cf. Driver 1895:101; Stamm 1940:21). Used of Yahweh's ransom of Israel from bondage in Egypt in Deut 7:8; 9:26; 13:6; 15:15; 21:8; and 24:18.

4) *lw l'm,* "as a people of his own," to which compare Deut 4:20; 7:6; 14:2; 26:18; 28:9; 29:12 [29:13]; and I Sam 12:22. Cf. Jer 7:23; etc.

5) *hgdwlwt whnwr'wt,* "great and fearful deeds," exactly as in Deut 10:21.

6) *wtkwnn lk . . . l'm,* "when you established . . . as your own people." Similarly, Deut 28:9; 29:12; and I Sam 12:22. See also no. 4 above.

7) *w'th . . . hyyt lhm l'lhym,* "you . . . became their god" (cf. Baltzer 1971:102). See Deut 26:17; 29:12. Cf. Jer 7:23; etc.

8) *hdbr 'šr dbrt . . . y'mn,* "the thing you promised . . . let it be confirmed," exactly as in I Kings 8:26. Similar expressions with forms of the verb *qwm,* "be established," which occurs here in MT, are common in Deuteronomic and Deuteronomistic passages (Deut 9:5; I Sam 3:12; I Kings 2:4; 6:12; 8:20; 12:15; cf. Jer 29:10; 33:14; in pre-Deuteronomistic literature: Num 23:19; I Sam 1:23); see Weinfeld 1972:350; Veijola 1975:75; Mettinger 1976:51 and n. 9.

9) *dbrt,* "you promised" *(bis).* Cross (1973:254 [no. 21]) has called attention to the use of *dibbēr,* "speak," in reference to divine promises in Deuteronomic (Deut 1:11; 6:3; 9:3; and very often) and Deuteronomistic (Josh 13:14,33; 22:4; 23:5,10; etc.; cf. the passages listed in no. 8 above) literature.

10) *wygdl šmk,* "let your name be great." Cf. the references to Yahweh's "great name" in I Sam 12:22; I Kings 8:42; Jer 10:6; 44:26. See also the NOTE on "your name" below.

*according to everything we have heard.* The "we" language is another indication of the intrusiveness of vv. 22ff. (cf. Mettinger 1976:51). Deuteronimistic theology constantly emphasizes the people's own witness to Yahweh's greatness. When referring to his deeds it is what they have *seen with their own eyes* that is stressed (Deut 4:9; 7:19; 10:21; 11:7; 29:1 [29:2]; Josh 23:3; 24:7; etc.). Here where Yahweh himself—not his deeds—has just been praised, the Deuteronomistic writer prefers to speak of what the people have *heard with their own ears* (cf. Deut 4:33 and see Weinfeld 1972:38,207–8).

23. As noted in the COMMENT on § XV, Pfeiffer's opinion of II Samuel 7 was very low. He regarded the present verse, with its overtly confessional rhetoric and its troubled text (cf. the *Textual Notes*), as "the worst instance of illiterate inanity" in the passage (1948:372). In fairness to the Deuteronomistic author of vv. 22–26 we ought to point out that while his theology is hardly subtle or gracefully expressed, the text he produced (and our *Textual Notes* attempt to reproduce) was not the perplexing clutter that Pfeiffer found in the received Hebrew text.

*what other nation.* Cf. Deut 4:7,8, and vv. 32–40, especially v. 34, which reads: "Or has another god ever tried to go take a nation for himself from the midst of another nation by ordeals, signs, wonders, and warfare, by a strong hand and an extended arm, and by great terrors, as Yahweh your god did with you in Egypt before your very eyes?" Cf. Weinfeld 1972:38 n. 1.

24. The covenantal language of this verse (cf. Deut 29:9–12 [29:10–13]: "Today you all stand before Yahweh your god . . . to enter into a covenant . . . in order that he may establish you today as his people and he himself may become your god . . .") is formally comparable to that used in v. 14 above to describe Yahweh's adoption of David's offspring: "I shall become a father to him, and he will become a son to me." Similarly, the use of "forever" here recalls the emphasis on the permanence of the dynastic promise (cf. the NOTE on "forever" at 7:13). As stressed by McCarthy (1965: 132–33), it is axiomatic to Deuteronomistic thought that finally "the people's position depends on that of the king and his line" (cf. I Sam 12:13–15). Noth (1967:253–54) and Hertzberg, though they do not regard vv. 22b–26 as Deuteronomistic expansion throughout, offer a similar interpretation of the juxtaposition of king and people. Hertzberg says, "The promise that the house of David will be 'for ever' corresponds to the choice of Israel to be the people of God 'for ever' . . . The house of David and the people of God are thus bound together eternally by the promise of Nathan."

26. *your name.* The greatness of Yahweh's name is linked to the establishment of the Davidic dynasty. McCarthy (1965:135–36) sees in this a further link between the welfare of the kings and that of the people in view of the fact that it was "on account of his great name" that Yahweh did not abandon his people when they first demanded a human king (I Sam 12:22), providing instead that his name should be magnified through a chosen dynasty.

27. See v. 11 above.

28. *this good thing.* According to II Kings 25:28, when Amel-Marduk, king of Babylon, freed Jehoiachin from prison and gave him a position at court, he "said good things" *(waydabbēr . . . ṭōbôt)* to him and "set his throne above the thrones of the other kings with him in Babylon." In I Kings 12:7 Rehoboam is advised to "speak good words" *(wĕdibbartā . . . dĕbārîm ṭôbîm)* to the Israelites so that they would "become [his] servants always." To "say a good thing" *(dibbēr ṭôbâ),* said of a suzerain, is to enter into a covenantal relationship with a vassal according to usage that can be

illuminated by reference to covenantal terminology from non-Israelite sources (see *I Samuel*, pp. 322,399, and bibliography cited there). In the present passage Yahweh, by saying "this good thing" *(haṭṭôbâ hazzō't)* to David—that is, by promising him a "house . . . forever under [Yahweh's] care" (cf. v. 29)—has brought David and his dynasty into a covenantal relationship with himself (cf. Malamat 1965:64). On the absence of the word *bĕrît*, "covenant," here, see, in addition to Malamat, Cross 1973: 260,270.

## COMMENT

David enters the tent he pitched for the ark (6:17) and offers a long prayer in response to the oracle reported by Nathan (7:5–16). After an opening expression of his own insignificance (v. 18) and Yahweh's graciousness in revealing his plan for David's house (vv. 19–21), the king extols Yahweh's uniqueness (v. 22) and his beneficent acts on behalf of Israel (vv. 23–24). There then follows a series of petitions imploring Yahweh to keep his promise and establish the rule of the Davidic dynasty (vv. 25–29). In particular, David invokes Yahweh's blessing on his house for all time to come (v. 29).

In the COMMENT on § XIII ("Background in Ritual") we noted the features the description of the ark's arrival in Jerusalem in 6:1–19 shares with other ancient Near Eastern accounts of the introduction of national gods into new capital cities. As pointed out there, these accounts conventionally included an invocation of blessing on the kings and their people. The kings would say, as Sargon did after the construction of Sargonsburg *(dūr šarrukīn*, modern Khorsabad), "The gods who dwell in that city,—may every work of my hand be acceptable to them. That they will dwell in their shrines, and that my rule (dynasty) may be secure,—may this be their command to all eternity" (Luckenbill 1926/27:vol. II:§94). In II Samuel 6 David, too, is motivated by a desire to secure divine blessing. The temporary interruption of the ark's progression into the City of David and its sojourn in the house of Obed-edom (6:10–11) provide an occasion for this desire to be stated explicitly: "When King David was told that Yahweh had blessed the house of Obed-edom and all he had because of the holy ark, [he] said to himself, 'I'll bring the blessing back to my own house!' " (6:12). When the ark finally comes to rest (6:17), David offers sacrifices, prepares a feast for the people, and invokes a blessing on them (6:18), but nothing is said of a blessing on David's house (cf. the first NOTE at 6:20) before v. 29 of the present passage.

The pertinence of the invocation of blessing in v. 29 to the events of chap. 6 is part of the larger question of the original relationship between chaps. 6 and 7—or, rather, between the story of the transfer of the ark in 6:1–19 and the reports of Nathan's oracle in 7:1–17 and David's prayer in 7:18–29. As we have seen, 6:1–19 is a document of Davidic date describing the introduction of Yahweh's ark into Jerusalem. At the core of 7:1–17 is a Solomonic document linking David's plan to build a temple to a divine promise of abiding dynasty. In its present form, 7:18–29 is a response to the dynastic promise. Oddly enough, however, it makes no reference to a temple (cf. Mettinger 1976:54–55). To this fact, moreover, we may add another oddity, viz. that the major thrust of David's prayer is a request for something he has already been promised (cf. Tsevat 1965:355). We must not overstress this point. In vv. 25–29, as they now stand, David is praying for the fulfilment of a promise (". . . as for the thing you promised . . . let it be confirmed . . ." etc.), the promise is explicitly referred to in v. 27, and in any case, as Cross (1973:247 n. 118) puts it in criticism of Tsevat, "A traditionally pious man prays daily that the divine promise . . . be fulfilled." Nevertheless, the primary thrust of the prayer towards the blessing of David's house, combined with the total absence of the temple theme, suggests that David's prayer in its primitive form was associated with the ark ceremony in chap. 6 rather than the dynastic promise in chap. 7.

The pre-Deuteronomistic portions of 7:18–29, apart from the prophetic insertion in vv. 20–21 (see the NOTE), include vv. 18–19, 22a + 27–29. Of this vv. 18 and 29, (29a + b$\beta$; "for you, my lord, Yahweh, have spoken" [29b$\alpha$] is intrusive) can be reckoned to the conclusion of the ark ceremony. David, having blessed, feasted, and dismissed the people, remained (cf. the NOTE at v. 18) to ask for a blessing on his house. In this request a Solomonic writer, from whose hand come vv. 19,22a + 27–28 (29b$\alpha$), found an occasion to attach his account of Nathan's oracle to the older document describing the ark's arrival in Jerusalem. His purpose was to show that David's request for a dynasty was buttressed by a divine promise, and that the erection of the temple was an outgrowth of the arrival of the ark in Jerusalem. That is, he sought to associate his own twin themes of dynastic promise and royal temple with events in the time of David.

In its final form David's prayer has another focus, viz. praise of the uniqueness of Yahweh (v. 22b) and his ransom of Israel from Egypt (vv. 23–24). This is characteristic of the editorially expanded prayers and litanies of the Deuteronomistic history (see Weinfeld 1972:36–40). The shift of attention from the house of David to the people in general in v. 23, the presence of a long series of Deuteronomistic clichés in vv. 22b–26, and other factors mentioned in the NOTES indicate that at least this section (vv. 22b–26) is late and thus that David's prayer has undergone substantial revision. Indeed, a few scholars doubt our ability to penetrate beyond the Deuteronomistic veneer of 7:18–29 (Carlson 1964:128; Cross 1973:254 n. 154; Veijola 1975:74–77), but it seems clear that some attempt to recover the conclusion of the Davidic-Solomonic documents in chaps. 6 and 7 is called for, and that a minimal view of the extent of their revision should be taken (cf. Mettinger 1976:51–52).

Nevertheless, it is helpful to keep in mind the probability that the final arrangement of the materials found throughout the larger section of text with which we are now concerned (5:11–8:18) is the work of a Deuteronomistic editor. From his point of view the events described here are of signal importance. As explained in the COMMENT on § XV, Deuteronomistic thought viewed the reign of David as an age of promise and preparation looking ahead to the establishment of the chosen dynasty and the erection of the temple. The reign of Solomon would be the age of fulfilment—but only if it was an age of peace: Solomon must have "rest" to build the temple (cf. I Kings 5:18 [5:4]. It fell to David, therefore, not only to receive the promises and pray for their fulfilment ("Do as you promised . . . !" v. 25) but also to *prepare* for their fulfilment by pacifying the land. In keeping with this view, our editor has placed a catalogue of David's victories in the passage that follows.

# XVII. THE WARS OF DAVID
## (8:1–14)

### *The Philistines*

8 [1]After this David defeated the Philistines and subjugated them,
taking the common land out of Philistine control.

### *The Moabites*

[2]He also defeated the Moabites and, making them lie down on the
ground, measured them off by line—two lines were to be put to death
and one full line was to be spared. So the Moabites became tribute-
bearing servants of David.

### *The Arameans*

[3]On his way to leave his stela at the River David defeated Hadadezer
son of Rehob, the king of Zobah, [4]capturing from him a thousand of
chariots, seven thousands of cavalrymen, and twenty thousands of foot
soldiers. [He] hamstrung all the chariot horses, saving a hundred of
them. [5]When the Arameans of Damascus came to support Hadadezer,
king of Zobah, David slew twenty-two thousands of [them]. [6][He]
stationed a prefect in Aram Damascus, and the Arameans became
tribute-bearing servants of David. (Yahweh gave David victory wherever he went.) [7]David took the golden bow cases carried by the servants
of Hadadezer and brought them to Jerusalem. [8]Also, from Tebah and
Berothai, Hadadezer's cities, King David took a very large amount of
bronze.
[9]When Toi, the king of Hamath, heard that David had defeated all
the forces of Hadadezer, [10]he sent Joram, his son, to greet him and
congratulate him for having fought against Hadadezer and defeated
him, for he himself was involved in hostilities with Hadadezer. [Joram]
had with him articles of silver, gold, and bronze, [11]and these King
[David] sanctified to Yahweh in addition to the silver and gold he had

sanctified from all the nations he had subdued—[12]Edom, Moab, the Ammonites, the Philistines, and Amalek—as well as that from the spoil of Hadadezer son of Rehob, king of Zobah. [13]David built a monument when he returned from his defeat of the Arameans.

## *Edom*

Also, Abishai son of Zeruiah defeated the Edomites in the Valley of Salt—eighteen thousands. [14][David] stationed a prefect in Edom, and all the Edomites became servants of the king. Yahweh gave David victory wherever he went.

## *TEXTUAL NOTES*

**8** 1. *taking* We read lit. "And David took," the unanimous reading of the witnesses to the text of Samuel. I Chron 18:1 preserves a shorter text, "And *he* took."

*the common land* MT has *mtg h'mh*, which ought to mean "the bridle of the water channel" (cf. Rabbinic Hebrew *'ammâ*, "canal, sewer") or "the reins of the forearm" (cf. Hertzberg). Some older commentators took it to mean "control of the mother city" (cf. 20:19 and Phoenician *'m*, "metropolis"). The recent tendency is to leave it untranslated and treat it as a proper noun, "Metheg-ammah" (so AV, RSV, NJV; cf. NEB). I Chron 18:1 reads *gt wbntyh*, "Gath and its daughter villages." Perhaps the original was *mgt h'mh/h'mth*, that is, *miggat hā'ammâ* or *hā'ammātâ*, "from Gath to Ammah," i.e., the place in the vicinity of Gibeon near which the action takes place in 2:24. But this seems forced. Provisionally I prefer to follow LXX *tēn aphorismenēn* (cf. OL *dilectionem*) and read *hmgrš* (Wellhausen: *mtgršh*).

2. *were to be put to death* Reading *wyhyw . . . lhmyt* on the basis of LXX *kai egeneto . . . tou thanatōsai*. MT has *wymdd . . . lhmyt*, "*he measured off* to be put to death."

*and one full line* MT *wml' hḥbl*, lit. "and the fulness of a line" (so LXX$^{MN}$; cf. LXX$^{L}$, OL, "the fulness of the *third* line"). LXX$^{BA}$: "and two lines."

*became* MT: *wthy*. 4QSam$^{a}$: *wy*[ ]. I Chron 18:2: *wyhyw*.

*to be spared* So MT, OL. LXX: "he (LXX$^{A}$ "they") spared."

*servants of David* MT *ldwd l'bdym*, the first part of which *(ldwd)* has been lost in LXX$^{A}$ and another Greek MS by homoioarkton.

3. *to leave* That is, *lĕhōšîb*, "to cause to remain, leave; put." MT reads the same consonantal text as *lĕhāšîb*, "to restore, replace," and I Chron 18:3 substitutes for it a synonym, *lĕhaṣṣîb*. It is impossible to tell whether LXX *epistēsai* reflects *lĕhaṣṣîb* or, as I suspect, *lĕhōšîb*.

*the River* Glossed (correctly) by MT *(qĕrê)*, MT$^{MSS}$, LXX, and I Chron 18:3 as "the River *Euphrates*." Omit *prt* with MT *(kĕtîb)*. Cf. Nedarim 37b.

4. *capturing* Lit. "and David captured."

*from him* Omitted at this point by 4QSam[a]; but we cannot be certain that the scroll did not read *mmnw* elsewhere in the clause (cf. Ulrich 1978:57).

*a thousand of chariots, seven thousands of cavalrymen* We read *'lp rkb wšb't 'lp pršym* on the basis of LXX *chilia harmata kai hepta chiliadas hippeōn* (cf. OL), 4QSam[a] *'lp r*[ ], and I Chron 18:4 *'lp rkb wšb't 'lpym pršym* (cf. Josephus, *Ant.* 7.99). MT has *'lp wšb' m'wt pršym,* "a thousand and seven hundreds of cavalrymen." I assume that MT lost *rkb wšb't 'lp* by haplography and that the present text arose from an imperfect attempt to correct the damage. See also Ap-Thomas (1943), who concludes from a comparison of the Hebrew and Greek texts of the various passages where these statistics are given (II Sam 8:4; 10:18; I Chron 18:4; 19:18; cf. Josephus, *Ant.* 7.99) that the original figures were one thousand chariots, seven hundred cavalrymen, and twenty thousand foot soldiers.

*of them* So MT, Syr. LXX[B]: "for himself." LXX[ALMN]: "of them for himself."

6. *a prefect* So LXX[BAL]. MT, LXX[MN], Josephus (*Ant.* 7.104): "prefects."

7. *carried by* Lit. "that were upon," reading *'l* (LXX *epi;* Syr., Targ. *'l*) for MT *'l,* which, as Driver observes, cannot indicate possession; see the *Textual Note* on "about" in 7:28. LXX[B] has "that *he had made* upon" (cf. I Kings 14:26 [MT, LXX[B]], "the golden shields that Solomon had made")—hence the tradition that the *šilṭê hazzāhāb* were golden yokes or collars (OL[MS]: *torques;* Aquila to II Sam 8:7 and LXX to I Chron 18:7: *tous kloious*). See the NOTE on "the golden bow cases."

*Hadadezer* So MT. LXX adds "king of Zobah."

At this point LXX[L] adds *kai panta ta hopla ta chrysa kai ta dorata,* "and all the gold shields *(hopla = mgny)* and the large shields [*dorata* = *ṣnh*(!), cf. I Kings 10:16]." The source of this plus is the text of LXX[(B)] at I Kings 14:26, where we read of "the large gold shields [*dorata* = *ṣnh*(!)] that David took from the hand of Hadadezer, king of Zobah, and brought to Jerusalem—everything that he took, the gold shields [*hopla* = *mgny*]." In I Kings 14:26 both MT and LXX are corrupt; there is confusion between the golden objects David took from Hadadezer in the present passage and the golden shields *(ṣinnâ* and *māginnîm)* made by Solomon in I Kings 10:16–17. See, further, the *Textual Note* that follows.

*to Jerusalem* Here LXX, OL, 4QSam[a], and Josephus (*Ant.* 7.105) all exhibit another long plus not found in MT or I Chronicles 18. LXX has *kai elaben auta sousakeim basileus aigyptou en tō anabēnai auton eis ierousalēm en hēmerais roboam* (so LXX[ALN]; LXX[B] has *ieroboam) huiou solomōntos,* reflecting *wyqḥ 'tm šwšq mlk mṣrym b'ltw 'l yrwšlm bymy rḥb'm bn šlmh,* "and Shoshenq, king of Egypt, took them when he came up to Jerusalem in the days of Rehoboam, son of Solomon." The text of the scroll is fragmentary, but it can be reconstructed with the help of LXX and OL. It reads *gm 'wtm l*[*qḥ 'ḥr šwšq* (cf. OL *et haec accepit postea susac*) *mlk mṣrym b*]*'lwtw 'l y*[*rwšlym*] *bymy rḥb'm bn šlw*[*mh*], "These, too, Shoshenq, king of Egypt, later took," etc.; for this word order see v. 11. Though it is possible to think of ways in which this notice might have been lost from MT (e.g., by haplography from *yrwšlm*[*h*] at the end of the verse to *šlmh* at the end of the plus or, in a text arranged at the end like OL [*in diebus roboam filii salomonis cum ascendisset in ierusalem* = *bymy rḥb'm bn šlmh b'ltw 'l yrwšlm*], from *yrwšlm* to *yrwšlm*), it is probable that the short text of MT stands closer to the primitive situation. There is considerable evidence of a tendency towards conflation of the present passage and I Kings 14:26. Cf. also Barthélemy 1980:15.

8. *Tebah* So Syr. *(ṭbḥ)*, LXX$^{L}$ *([ma]tebak)*, etc.; cf. I Chron 18:8 *(ṭbḥt)*. MT has *bṭḥ*. See the NOTE.

*Berothai* MT *brty*. LXX *tōn eklektōn* reflects *bḥry*, "the young men of." I Chron 18:8 has *kwn*. See the NOTE.

*King . . . bronze* Syr. has this clause before "and brought it . . ." in v. 7.

*King David took* We read the word order of MT, 4QSam$^{a}$, LXX$^{ALMN}$, etc. LXX$^{B}$ reads these words between the names of the two cities (setting aside the conjunction) —thus, "Also, from Tebah King David took from the young men (cf. the *Textual Note* on "Berothai" above) of Hadadezer's cities," etc.—and OL omits them altogether.

*a very large amount of bronze* MT: *nḥšt hrbh m'd*. 4QSam$^{a}$, I Chron 18:8: *nḥšt rbh m'd*.

At this point LXX, OL, Josephus (*Ant.* 7.106), and I Chron 18:8 have another long plus (the scroll is not extant after *m['d]*). LXX: *en autō epoiēsen salōmōn tēn thalassan tēn chalkēn kai tous stylous kai tous loutēras kai panta ta skeuē* (LXX$^{L}$ adds *ta chalka*) = *bh 'śh šlmh 't ym hnḥšt w't h'mwdym w't hkyrwt w't kl hklym (kly hnḥšt)*, "With it Solomon made the bronze sea and the pillars and the basin and all the utensils (bronze utensils)." I Chron 18:8: "With it Solomon made the bronze sea and the pillars and bronze utensils *(w't kly hnḥšt)*. OL: ". . . from which *(de quo)* Solomon made all the bronze utensils in the temple *(omnia vasa aerea in templo)* and the pillars and the altar *(et altare = w't hmzbḥ)*." Cf. I Kings 7:13–47 and Barthélemy 1980:16.

9. *Toi* MT *tō'ī*. LXX$^{BMN}$ *(tho[u]ou)* and OL *(thou)* reflect *tô'û*, "Tou" (so I Chron 18:9). LXX$^{L}$ has *eleiab* = *'ly'b*, "Eliab."

10. *Joram* See the NOTE. MT has *yôrām*. In I Chron 18:10 we find *hădôrām*, "Hadoram" (cf. Josephus, *Ant.* 7.107: *adōramos*). In the present passage LXX has *ieddouran*, evidently a corrupt mixture (cf. Malamat 1963:6 n. 23).

*having fought* So MT, LXX$^{LMN}$. LXX$^{B}$: "having defeated."

*for he . . . Hadadezer* MT and I Chron 18:10 have *ky 'yš mlḥmwt t'y/w hyh hdd'zr*, "for Hadadezer was a man-of-wars-of (i.e., often at war with) Toi." LXX reflects a shorter and divergent text: *hoti (anti)keimenos ēn tō adraazar* = *ky mtḥrh hyh bhdd'zr*, which I have adopted. For *(anti)keimenos* we expect something graphically closer to *'yš mlḥmwt* than, for example, *śṭn*, "adversary" (cf. I Kings 11:14,25), but hardly *'yš mlḥmwt* itself, as frequently assumed, for which we should expect a more literal rendering. In Isa 41:11 *antikeimenoi soi* corresponds to *hnḥrym bk*, "those hostile to you," in precisely the sense required here, and *nḥrh* or (for graphic reasons more likely) *mtḥrh* seems a likely retroversion for *(anti)keimenos* here. Alternatively, read *mṣh* (i.e., *maṣṣeh*, "engaged in a struggle with"); cf. *'nšy mṣwtk* parallel to *'nšy mlḥmh* in Isa 41:12 and *bhṣwtw* in Ps 60:2.

11. *King [David]* So LXX$^{B}$. MT, LXX$^{ALMN}$, Syr., I Chron 18:11: "King David."

*nations* So MT, I Chron 18:10. LXX: "cities" (cf. v. 8).

12. *Edom* So LXX, Syr., as in I Chron 18:12. MT has *'rm*, "Aram."

*Moab* So MT, Syr., LXX$^{ALMN}$. LXX$^{B}$ has "*the land of* Moab."

*from the spoil* So MT: *mšll*. Syr. *mn šwlṭnh*, "from the *authority*," is probably an inner-Syriac error for *mšll* under the influence of v. 7.

13. *David built a monument* So MT, LXX: *wy'ś dwd šm* (for *šēm*, "name," in the sense of "monument," see the NOTE). The rather curious reading of Targ.—*wknš dwyd mšrym*, "David gathered troops"—is shown by I Sam 14:48, where Targ. *wknš mšrym*

corresponds to MT *wy'ś ḥyl,* to reflect a variant, viz. *wy'ś dwd ḥyl,* "David acquired power" (for this translation, see *I Samuel,* the NOTE at 14:48); cf. also Syr.

*when he returned . . . the Edomites* The chief witnesses display considerable divergence here. MT has *bšbw mhkwt 't 'rm,* "when he returned from his defeat of the Arameans," a reading shared by Syr., which, however, has *'dwm,* "Edom, the Edomites," for *'rm.* LXX has *kai en tō anakamptein auton epataxen ten idoumaian,* which reflects *wbšbw hkh 't 'dwm,* "and when he returned, he defeated the Edomites." I Chron 18:12 has *w'bšy bn ṣrwyh hkh 't 'dwm,* "and Abishai son of Zeruiah defeated the Edomites," to which compare Josephus, *Ant.* 7.109. A comprehensive solution to the several problems here is possible, I think, if we assume the original text to have read as follows: *bšbw mhkwt 't 'rm w'bšy bn ṣrwyh hkh 't 'dm.* MT is to be explained on the assumption of haplography caused by homoioteleuton, a scribe's eye having skipped from *'t 'rm* to *'t 'dm,* leaving *bšbw mhkwt 't 'dm,* the text reflected by Syr., $MT^{MSS}$; in MT *'rm* arose subsequently from *'dm* at the beginning of v. 12. In LXX and I Chron 18:12, the haplography involved the similar sequences *(w)bšbw* and *w'bšy.* In Chronicles *(w)bšbw mhkwt 't 'rm* was left out, leaving the text as it now stands (see above). In LXX *mhkwt 't 'rm w'bsy* was left out, leaving **(w)bšbw bn ṣrwyh hkh 't 'dm.* This intermediate stage in the development of the text of LXX is corroborated by the superscription of Psalm 60, where, in a reference to David's Aramean wars, we are told (v. 2) that "Joab (!) returned and defeated the Edomites in the Valley of Salt." Clearly, the author of this superscription knew a text of our passage that read *wbšbw bn ṣrwyh hkh 't 'dm,* "and when he returned, the son of Zeruiah defeated the Edomites"; he quite naturally identified *bn ṣrwyh* as the most prominent of Zeruiah's sons, Joab, whose exploits in Edom are on record elsewhere (I Kings 11:15,16). In the text of LXX, "the son of Zeruiah" was subsequently omitted, probably by recensional adjustment to MT, leaving the Greek reading that we now have (see above).

*in the Valley of Salt* So MT: *bgy' mlḥ.* $LXX^{L}$ (cf. OL): *kai en gemelex* = *wbgy' mlḥ,* "*and* in the Valley of Salt." $LXX^{BM}$ (cf. OL): *en gebelen* = *bgblm,* "in *their territory.*"

*eighteen thousands* So MT, I Chron 18:12. LXX: "*as much as (eis* = *'d)* eighteen thousands." Syr.: "*he slaughtered (ḥrb)* eighteen thousands." $OL^{MS}$: "as much as *twenty-three* thousands." Ps 60:2: "*twelve (šnym* for *šmwnh)* thousands."

14. *[David] stationed a prefect in Edom* MT is conflate: *wyśm b'dwm nṣbym bkl 'dwm śm nṣbym,* "And he stationed in Edom prefects, in all Edom he stationed prefects" (cf. $LXX^{ALO}$). Perhaps the variants were (A) *wyśm b'dwm nṣyb* (sing., with $LXX^{N}$, Syr.), "And he stationed in Edom a prefect," and (B) *wbkl 'dwm śm nṣbym,* "And throughout Edom he stationed prefects." We read variant A. I Chron 18:13 has *wyśm b'dwm nṣbym,* perhaps in consequence of haplography in a text identical to that of MT. See also Talmon 1960:177.

*[David]* The subject is made explicit in a few witnesses ($LXX^{L}$, Syr., etc.) and is necessary in English. In the Hebrew original, however, the syntax alone allowed such an interpretation (*pace* Wellhausen), the statement about Abishai being couched in the syntax of a circumstantial clause *(w'bšy . . . hkh . . . ,* not *wyk 'bšy)*—thus, ". . . David built a monument . . . and, Abishai son of Zeruiah having defeated the Edomites in the Valley of Salt, he (i.e., David) appointed," etc.

*and all the Edomites became* MT: *wyhy kl 'dwm l-,* lit. "and all Edom became . . . ," probably the primitive reading. LXX *kai egenonto pantes hoi idoumaioi* and Syr. *whww klhwn 'dwmy'* (cf. Targ.) reflect *wyhyw kl h'dwmym,* lit. "and all the Edomites were. . . ." LXX$^{L}$: "and all in Edom *(pantes en tē idoumaia = kl b'dwm)* were. . . ." I Chron 18:13: *wyhyw kl 'dwm,* "and all Edom were. . . ."

*of the king* So LXX$^{B}$. MT, Syr., LXX$^{LMN}$, I Chron 18:13: "of *David.*"

## NOTES

Map 4 shows the location of the various states conquered by David according to this chapter.

8 1. Alt (1936) has argued that this verse is an epitome of 5:6–26, written by an editor who inserted chaps. 6 and 7 into a series of battle accounts. Thus it concerns the capture of the city-state of Jerusalem (*h'mh,* "the mother city"?; cf. the *Textual Note* on "the common land") from Philistine control (cf. de Groot 1936:192). It may, however, refer to a subsequent victory or series of victories.

*the common land.* The reading is uncertain (see the *Textual Note*). In the time of Saul (cf. I Samuel 13–14) the Philistines occupied the rural territory adjacent to the Israelite cities (*hammigrāš,* "the common land"). Despite occasional Israelite victories (I Sam 17:52; II Sam 5:20,25) the Philistine presence seems to have persisted (cf. I Sam 14:52; 31:1; II Sam 5:17,22) until the final expulsion mentioned here. See further the COMMENT.

2. Saul, too, fought successfully against Moab (I Sam 14:47). David, before he became king, had cordial relations with the Moabites according to I Sam 22:3–5, where we are told that he sequestered his parents in Mizpeh of Moab to protect them during his days as a fugitive from Saul's court, and biblical tradition even asserts that there was Moabite blood in David's family (Ruth 4:13–22). Whatever friendship once existed between David and the king of Moab (cf. I Sam 22:3), however, seems to have vanished when David became king of Israel.

*measured them off by line.* This method of selecting prisoners of war for execution is not mentioned elsewhere.

3. *On his way . . . the River.* This phrase stands at the end of the verse in the Hebrew text, and it is commonly supposed that it is Hadadezer who was marching to the Euphrates (cf. Malamat 1963:3). But, if so, he would hardly have encountered David on the way since Israel was south of Zobah and the Euphrates north. Surely it was David, in the flush of recent victories, who was marching to the Euphrates to leave a monument to himself. It is quite possible, moreover, that the occasion for David's march was his victory at Helam over the Aramean coalition (10:15–19), which may thus have preceded the events of vv. 3ff. in the present chapter (cf. Elliger 1936; Bright 1972:197 n. 41). This victory cost Hadadezer his allies, including forces from beyond the Euphrates (10:16), and left him vulnerable to a final blow. David was now at Helam with new allies to the north and east (10:19) and, therefore, with his way open to the Euphrates. The events of 8:3ff. fit neatly at this point (viz. between 10:19 and 11:1).

*his stela.* Hebrew *yādô,* lit. "his hand," which here means "stela, monument" (cf.

18:18 and I Sam 15:12), as recognized by some recent translators (NEB, NJV); cf. Delcor 1967:230–34. The interpretation that David (or Hadadezer; cf. the preceding NOTE) went to the Euphrates ("the River"; see below) to "restore his power" (RSV; cf. the *Textual Note* on "to leave") is also possible, but we must keep in mind the fact that the Euphrates was a boundary to which western kings aspired to march and leave a monument. Thus, for example, the Egyptian king Thutmosis III boasts in the records of his eighth campaign that he erected a stela on the bank of the Euphrates near Carchemish beside another stela erected by Thutmosis I a generation earlier (*ANET*[3] 239; cf. 240).

*the River.* The Euphrates, called in the Bible *nĕhar pĕrāt,* "the River Euphrates," *hannāhār haggādôl,* "the Great River," and, most often, simply *hannāhār,* "the River," as in this case (cf. the *Textual Note*). According to de Groot and van den Born, however, the river here is the Yarmuk, and others have taken it to be the Jordan.

*Hadadezer son of Rehob.* The leader of the coalition of mercenaries that opposed David in the conflict described in chap. 10, which chronologically may have preceded the present events (see above). Hadadezer's patronymic, "son of Rehob," has been taken as evidence that Zobah at this time was ruled by a dynasty from Beth-rehob, another Aramean state and an ally according to 10:6. Malamat (1963:2–3), noting the fact that the armies of Beth-rehob and Zobah are mentioned as a single contingent in 10:6 (cf. I Sam 14:47 [LXX]), argues that Hadadezer ruled first in Beth-rehob, with which he later combined Zobah in a personal union analogous to David's rule of Judah and Israel. Hadadezer's role in chap. 10, where he appears as the leader of a large coalition of states, suggests that he wielded considerable power, his influence extending beyond the Euphrates into northwest Mesopotamia (10:15) and as far southeast as Ammon (10:6); see Malamat 1963:1–2 and bibliography in n. 4. He is not mentioned by name in contemporary extrabiblical sources, but he has been provisionally identified with an unnamed Aramean king mentioned in Assyrian annals as having conquered certain territories on the upper Euphrates south of Carchemish in the time of the Assyrian monarch Ashurrabi II, a contemporary of David (Malamat 1958:101–2; Albright in *CAH*[3] II/2:534; cf. Luckenbill 1926/27:vol. I:§603). Josephus (*Ant.* 7.101–3) cites the Roman period historian Nicolas of Damascus as recording that Hadadezer, whom he calls Hadad *(adados),* "having become very powerful, ruled over Damascus and the rest of Syria except Phoenicia. He waged war against David, the king of Judah, and having been tested in many battles—the last being beside the Euphrates, where he was defeated—he came to be thought of as the strongest and manliest of kings. . . . After his own death his descendants ruled for ten generations, each taking up both the sovereignty and the name of his father, like the Ptolemies in Egypt." Nicolas was probably mistaken in concluding that the Ben-hadads of Damascus were descended from Hadad(ezer) of Zobah: The king who established the Damascene dynasty is more likely to have been Rezon son of Eliada, a onetime vassal but not a descendant of Hadadezer (cf. the NOTE on "Damascus," v. 5), and the throne name *bir hadad,* "Son of Hadad," is probably to be explained differently (see the NOTE at 7:14).

*Zobah.* The leading Aramean state in the time of David and before the rise of Damascus, Zobah was centered on the eastern slope of the Anti-Lebanon mountain range and may have included parts of Coele-Syria as well (cf. the NOTES on "Tebah" and "Berothai," v. 8); see Forrer 1920:62; Malamat 1963:4 n. 13. Zobah survived until at least the seventh century B.C., when "the district of Zobah (Assyrian *subatu* [*subutu, subite*])" was the name of an Assyrian province (cf. *ANET*³ 298; Forrer 1920:62,69).

4. *thousand(s) . . . hundred.* The size of these military units is uncertain. An *'elep* ("thousand") of infantry may have had about a dozen men. Cf. *I Samuel*, the NOTE at 4:10.

*hamstrung all the chariot horses.* Hebrew *way'aqqēr . . . 'et-kol-hārekeb.* The verb *'iqqēr* means "uproot, tear loose, mutilate" (cf. Jastrow 1108) and specifically "hamstring" in Josh 11:6–9, where we are told that Joshua, having defeated a coalition of kings hired to defend the Canaanite stronghold Hazor, "hamstrung their horses and burned their chariots" (v. 9). Presumably, then, this is its meaning here, *hārekeb*, lit. "the chariotry," being used metonymically for "the chariot horses," though one might also consider some such translation as "stripped down all the chariots." Assuming the correctness of our translation, we must ask why David would waste a horde of valuable animals by hamstringing them. Was this because "Israelite armies in the past had not used the chariot, and they still fought mainly on foot" (Bright 1972:199)? Or, if David's troops did use chariots, was it because they already had an almost full complement of horses and, having taken the few they could use ("a hundred"), destroyed the rest as a precaution against their falling into enemy hands (cf. Yadin 1963:vol. II:285)? It is possible that some such practical motivation lay behind David's action, but comparison with Josh 11:6–9 suggests another kind of explanation. In both passages the hamstrung horses are captured from *mercenary* enemies. It may be that a special code of punishment applied in such cases, as in the case, for example, of covenant violations. The fact that in the Joshua passage the hamstringing of the horses is divinely commanded (v. 6) reinforces the possibility that some special code, ritually sanctioned, is being applied. " 'Don't be afraid of them,' said Yahweh to Joshua, 'because at this time tomorrow I'm going to present them all to Israel as ritually profane [*ḥălālîm*]: Their horses you will hamstring and their chariots you will burn.' "

5. *Damascus.* The city became the capital of an Aramean state after the collapse of the Hittite empire ca. 1200 B.C. In the time of David, Aram Damascus was evidently one of several small Aramean states overshadowed by the power of Aram Zobah. After the events described here and in chap. 10 these became tributaries of Israel. But late in the reign of Solomon it was Damascus, not Zobah, that was able to cast off the Israelite yoke and take the lead in what soon would become a substantial Aramean empire (cf. Mazar 1962:104–6). The author of the Damascene rise was a certain Rezon son of Eliada, who had once been a vassal of Hadadezer. A notice in the received Hebrew text of I Kings 11:24 suggests that Rezon's desertion from the army of Hadadezer took place "when David slew them," i.e., at the time of the present events (cf. 10:19); but we cannot be certain of this: The notice, which is lacking in the Septuagint ($LXX^{BL}$), is secondary, having arisen as a marginal note to v. 23 (cf. Gray 1970:286).

6. *a prefect.* Hebrew *nĕṣîb* (*niṣṣāb?;* cf. I Kings 4:7,19), which might also mean "garrison." In either case the establishment of a formal Israelite presence, probably including an army of occupation, is indicated. Cf. I Sam (10:5) 13:3,4, where the presence of a Philistine prefect in Gibeah, Saul's capital, is mentioned.

*(Yahweh gave David victory wherever he went.).* See v. 14. The notice is premature at this point. It may have arisen from a textual accident, later repaired, when a scribe,

misled by the similarity of vv. 6a and 14a, omitted everything in between. As the *Textual Notes* show, the names "Aram" and "Edom" were especially liable to confusion.

7. *the golden bow cases.* Hebrew *šilṭê hazzāhāb.* Borger (1972) has clarified this previously obscure term. A **šeleṭ* was a bow case that might be carried ceremonially by a royal official. The tomb of a certain Aspathines, a dignitary of the Persian King Darius I, bears a relief showing Aspathines carrying Darius' bow case, described in an accompanying inscription by the Babylonian term *šalṭu* (written with the logogram for wooden objects). Babylonian *šalṭu* is an Aramaic loanword meaning "quiver" (*AHw* 1147). In a MS from Qumran (11QtgJob) Aramaic *šlṭ* is used to translate Hebrew *'šph,* "quiver" (van der Ploeg and van der Woude 1971:76). Thus, in the present passage the translation of *šlṭy* by *pharetras,* "quivers," found only in Symmachus (cf. Josephus, *Ant.* 7.104), is correct. Evidently, however, a further distinction is to be made between **šeleṭ,* "bow case," and *'ašpâ,* "quiver" (Borger 1972:393).

8. *Tebah.* Hebrew *ṭebaḥ* (cf. the *Textual Note*), which according to Gen 22:24 was the name of a son of Abraham's brother Nahor by a concubine and thus the eponymous ancestor of a collateral Aramean tribe. It was a city in the Biq'ā (Coele-Syria) south of modern Homs, mentioned in the Amarna archive *(ṭu-bi-ḫi),* Thutmosis III's list of conquered Asian cities *(du-bi-ḫi),* and the Papyrus Anastasi (*ANET*[3] 477); see Albright 1934:40 (VI.C.19) and 66 (XXI.C.4).

*Berothai.* Hebrew *bērōtay,* probably identical to *bêrōtâ* of Ezek 47:16. The modern site is thought to be Bereitan, a few miles south of Râs Ba'albek in the Lebanon Valley. Râs Ba'albek is the site of Cun (*Ku-nú* of Ramesses III's list; cf. Albright 1934:60 [XVII.C.7]), which appears in the synoptic parallel to the present passage in I Chron 18:8. We should probably think of all three—Tebah, Berothai, and Cun—as principal cities of the kingdom of Zobah.

9. *Toi, the king of Hamath.* The city of Hamath, which lay on the middle Orontes (modern Ḥamā), was the capital of a Neo-Hittite state that bordered Zobah on the north (cf. I Chron 18:3). The king's name given here, *tōʻî,* is probably a hypocoristic form of a longer name (*tʻy*-DN) containing the common Hurrian element **taǵi-* or **teǵi-,* known from syllabic *(taḫi-, teḫi-)* and alphabetic *(tǵ-)* cuneiform texts. See Liverani 1962:70 and, for the Ugaritic examples, Gröndahl 1967:263. His son's name, however, is Semitic (see below).

10. Joram's mission establishes an alliance between Israel and Hamath, in which Israel was evidently the senior partner. As Malamat (1958:101; 1963:6) puts it, "The fact that the embassy was headed by . . . the son of the king of Hamath, and that it brought David expensive gifts, seems to imply that it was not simply a show of courtesy nor even an act for concluding a parity treaty."

*Joram.* It is surprising that Toi's son has an Israelite name (*yôrām* < **yāhū-rām,* "Yahweh is exalted"). In I Chron 18:10 he is called *hădôrām* (= **haddu-rām,* "Haddu/Hadad is exalted"), "Hadoram," and many commentators would restore this name here. As Malamat (1963:6–7) has argued, however, we should probably assume that this prince, whose Aramean name was in fact Hadoram, took a second name indicative of his fealty to David.

11. *sanctified to Yahweh.* David has the booty ritually purified for cultic use. It will eventually become part of Solomon's treasure (I Kings 7:51).

12. *Amalek.* The only campaign of David against the Amalekites recorded in the Bible took place before he became king (I Samuel 30), and the plunder was not sanctified but distributed among the cities of Judah (30:26–31).

13. *a monument.* Hebrew *šēm,* lit. "a name," which here means a memorial or monument; cf. Isa 55:13, where *šēm* stands in parallel to *'ôt 'ôlām lō' yikkārēt,* "an abiding sign never cut off." Thus *šēm* here is equivalent to *yad,* "hand," in v. 3 (see the NOTE on "his stela"); cf. Isa 56:5. The question we cannot answer is whether the "name" David makes is a victory monument like the "hand" of v. 3 or a cult object of some kind, perhaps even an idol, made from portions of the sanctified booty (cf. Exod 32:2–4; Judg 8:24–27).

*Abishai son of Zeruiah.* See the NOTE at 3:18.

*the Valley of Salt.* The location is unknown, but the battle must have taken place in Edomite territory. The name *(gê'-melaḥ)* would suit any of several places south and east of the Dead Sea, and the common identification with the Wâdī el-Milḥ, south of Beersheba, has little to recommend it.

## COMMENT

Although a rough attempt was made to place the events of this chapter into a sequential relationship with the preceding materials ("After this . . ." v. 1), it is clear that the organizing principle here is theme, not chronology. This is a catalogue of victories. Fragments of the records of David's successes against the Philistines, the various inhabitants of Transjordan, and the Arameans to the north have been assembled to show what David did "to save Israel . . . from all their enemies" (3:18) and to illustrate "the warfare that surrounded him, until Yahweh put [his enemies] under the soles of his feet" (I Kings 5:17 [5:3]). In the larger story, therefore, the catalogue serves to show the pacification of the land and extension of its boundaries under David. The repeated refrain, "Yahweh gave David victory wherever he went" (vv. 6,14), attributes the success to divine favor.

As explained in the COMMENT on § XV, Deuteronomistic thought understood the time of David as an age of glorious preparation for the fulfilment of the ancient promises of "rest" for the people and a chosen place of worship (Deut 12:10–11). The catalogue of victories in the present chapter shows how David's exploits made the time of "rest" possible. It is probably a Deuteronomistic compilation of ancient fragments organized about the theme of victory and placed immediately after Nathan's oracle of temple and dynasty, which was to be fulfilled when the Israelites had "rest from all their enemies" (7:10–11).

Viewed as a historical resource, this catalogue—along with the materials in 5:6–10,17–25; 10:1–11:1 + 26–31; and 21:15–22—provides a cogent picture of the political significance of David's wars. As Alt pointed out some time ago (1968[1930]:225–27; 1953:vol. II:68–69; cf. Malamat 1958:100), the Philistines can be regarded as the heirs, at the beginning of the Iron Age, to the Egyptian empire in Palestine. The Israelites were at first one of the peoples under the sway of the Philistines, as the biblical narratives of the reign of Saul, who achieved no lasting victory over them, illustrate well. The Philistines failed, however, in their attempt to check the unification of Judah and Israel by David (see the COMMENT on § XII), who was able to confine them permanently to the coastal plain (cf. 5:25) and free the Palestinian countryside ("the common land"?; see the NOTE) from occupation.

By establishing its ascendancy in central Palestine, therefore, Davidic Israel supplanted Philistia as heir to Egyptian suzerainty there. This brought Israel into direct conflict with Aram Zobah in the north (Malamat 1958:100). This state had grown in power in a fashion comparable to Israel itself, and under Hadadezer it had expanded its dominion eastward from a base in Coele-Syria until it exercised some jurisdiction in districts from Transeuphrates south to Transjordan (see the NOTE on "Hadadezer son of Rehob," v. 3). Thus, in the clash between these two fledgling powers, Israel and Zobah, nothing less was at stake than "the political hegemony over the area between Mesopotamia and Egypt" (Malamat 1958:101). The issue was resolved in a series of three battles, of which the final and decisive one was that described here in 8:3–5 (on the chronological priority of 10:1–19 to 8:3–5, see the first NOTE at v. 3). In the aftermath of this victory David conquered the Ammonite capital (11:1 + 26–31) and received gifts of fealty from the king of Hamath (cf. the NOTES to v. 10). With other conquests in Moab (v. 2) and Edom (vv. 13b–14), of which the chronological position relative to the Philistine and Aramean campaigns is unknown, David established a small empire extending from the Orontes to the River of Egypt.

# XVIII. DAVID'S CABINET (I)
# (8:15–18)

8 15 So David ruled over Israel, exercising justice and equity for all his
people. 16 Joab son of Zeruiah was in charge of the army. Jehoshaphat
son of Ahilud was remembrancer. 17 Zadok son of Ahitub and Abiathar
son of Ahimelech were priests. Shausha was scribe. 18 Benaiah son of
Jehoiada was in charge of the Cherethites and the Pelethites. The sons
of David were priests.

## *TEXTUAL NOTES*

8 15. *Israel* So LXX$^{B}$. MT, LXX$^{MN}$: "*all* Israel."
*exercising* That is, *wyhy ʿśh,* lit. "and he did." So LXX$^{B}$. MT, LXX$^{AIMN}$: "and *David* was doing."

16. *Ahilud* MT *ʾḥylwd* (cf. LXX$^{MN}$, OL, Josephus [*Ant.* 7.110], I Chron 18:5), as in 20:24 and I Kings 4:3. LXX$^{B}$: *acheia* = *ʾḥyh,* "Ahijah." LXX$^{A}$: *achimelech* = *ʾḥymlk,* "Ahimelech." LXX$^{L}$: *acheinaab* for *acheinadab* (?) = *ʾḥyndb,* "Ahinadab," or *acheinaam* = *ʾḥynʿm,* "Ahinoam."
*remembrancer* So MT: *mzkyr.* MT$^{MSS}$: *hmzkyr,* "*the* remembrancer." LXX: *epi tōn hypomnēmatōn* = *ʿl hzkrnwt,* "in charge of the records" (cf. OL).

17. *Abiathar son of Ahimelech* Only in Syr. and Eth., and probably in these witnesses by secondary correction. All others, including I Chron 18:16, have the name and patronymic in reverse order; that this is erroneous can be shown by reference to 20:25, where it is said that Zadok and Abiathar (not Ahimelech) were David's priests, and I Sam 22:20; 23:6; 30:7, where Abiathar's father is identified as Ahimelech. Wellhausen, assuming that Ahitub was the grandson of Eli mentioned in I Sam 14:3, argued that Zadok could not be his son, since no Elid but Abiathar escaped the massacre at Nob (I Sam 22:20). Noting a tendency to subordinate Abiathar to Zadok elsewhere (II Sam 15:24–29), Wellhausen concluded that the original reading of the present passage was the reverse of the received reading: "Abiathar son of Ahimelek son of Ahitub and Zadok." Wellhausen has been widely followed in this proposal (cf. Gunneweg [1965:99, 104–5], who explains MT as an attempt to provide Zadok with a Levitical genealogy), but Cross (1973:212–14) has discovered a mechanical solution to the problem. Criticizing Wellhausen's assumption that the Ahitub mentioned here must be the descendant

of Eli, Cross proposes that haplography occurred, perhaps in a text that (like LXX$^{MSS}$, I Chron 18:16; cf. LXX$^{B}$ at I Sam 21:2,9; etc.) had *'bymlk* for *'ḥymlk.* Thus *wṣdwq bn 'ḥyṭwb w'bytr bn 'bymlk,* "Zadok son of Ahitub and Abiathar son of Abimelech," became *wṣdwq bn 'ḥyṭwb w'bymlk,* "Zadok son of Ahitub and Abimelech." This reading, in turn, says Cross (p. 214), "was further corrupted from a marginal note reading *'bytr,* inserted in the wrong place and filled out with *bn.*"

*Shausha* The name is uncertain. Evidence favoring *šawšā',* "Shausha," includes LXX$^{BMN}$ *(s)asa* here and LXX *sousa* in II Sam 20:25 (LXX$^{MN}$, cf. OL) and I Chron 18:16 (cf. LXX$^{B}$ *iēsous* at II Sam 20:25 and *sousan* in Josephus, *Ant.* 7.293) as well as MT *šawšā'* in I Chron 18:16 and MT *(qĕrê) šĕwā'* in II Sam 20:25. There is some support for *šîšā',* "Shisha," which stands in MT in I Kings 4:3 and the Targ. *(šyš')* to I Chron 18:16; note also Josephus' reading (*Ant.* 7.110), *seisan.* MT here has *śĕrāyâ,* "Seraiah," in which it is followed by LXX$^{AL}$ *saraias* and Syr. *sry'* in I Chron 18:16 (but here Syr. has *šry'* = *šĕrāyâ,* "Sheraiah").

Mettinger (1971:25–30) follows Cody (1965) in an ingenious but unconvincing interpretation of the evidence. They take Seraiah to be the man's name and *šyš'* or the like to be a corrupt approximation of the Egyptian scribal title *sš š'.t.* See, further, the *Textual Note* on "Shausha" at 20:25.

18. *in charge of . . . and* The original reading was probably *'l . . . w-,* as in I Chron 18:17. In the present passage Syr., Targ., Vulg. reflect *'l . . . w'l,* "in charge of . . . and in charge of," as in MT in 20:23. Here MT has *w- . . . w-* (as if, "Benaiah son of Jehoiada and the Cherethites and the Pelethites and the sons of David," etc.), but we know that Benaiah was put in charge of David's Cherethite-Pelethite bodyguard (cf. 23:23; I Kings 1:38). LXX *symboulos kai . . . kai* points to *yw'ṣ w- . . . w-,* "counselor and . . . and." The divergence of MT and LXX from the indisputably correct sense must be explained by appeal to other passages, the influence of which may be felt here. For MT see I Kings 1:38, where "Benaiah son of Jehoiada and the Cherethites and the Pelethites" is correct. For LXX compare I Chron 27:33–34, where we read, "Ahithophel was counselor to the king . . . and after Ahithophel was Jehoiada son of Benaiah [*sic*]"; apparently a son of Benaiah who shared Benaiah's father's name succeeded Ahithophel as royal counselor, a fact that led a confused scribe to identify the grandfather with the grandson in the present passage by inserting *yw'ṣ,* "counselor," as a gloss after "Jehoiada."

*were priests* So MT: *khnym hyw.* This reading is grammatically odd—*hyw* is superfluous at best—and textually uncertain, finding support from the versions only in the texts of Vulg. *(sacerdotes erant)* and Aquila *(hiereis ēsan).* In place of *khnym,* "priests," Syr. has *rwrbyn* and Targ. *rbrbyn,* both "great men" (= *gdwlym*?), and LXX has *aularchai,* "princes of the court, courtiers" (cf. OL *in principes . . . domus regis,* "princes in the house of the king"). The reading of I Chron 18:17 is *wbny dwd hr'šnym lyd hmlk,* "And the sons of David were foremost, next to the king," or perhaps, "And the elder sons of David (cf. Josephus, *Ant.* 7.110) were next to the king"; for *lyd hmlk,* LXX in I Chron 18:17 has *didoxoi tou basileōs,* perhaps *mšny hmlk,* "second to the king." In light of this evidence Wenham (1975:80–82) has recently proposed an original *sknym,* "administrators (of the royal estates)," comparing nouns of office in Ugaritic *(skn)* and Neo-Assyrian *(šaknu)* texts; cf. Shebna in Isa 22:15. The reading *sknym* was already suggested by Hitzig (1865:318), and Cody (1969:103–5) mentions it too, though as a tendentious corruption of *khnym*. In support of his proposal Wenham might have noted the proximity of *khnym* in v. 17, which in many MSS (as in *BHS*) must have stood immediately above the reading in question in v. 18. It is difficult, however, to think of the surprising designation of David's sons as priests as having arisen by corruption from an uncontroversial text. Almost all critics, therefore, have agreed that the readings of I Chron 18:17 and the versions in II Sam 8:18 are interpretive paraphrases of the reading of MT by scribes who considered it impossible that there should be non-Levitical priests. Tentatively, we follow this majority opinion.

## NOTES

8 16. *Joab son of Zeruiah.* See the NOTE at 2:13. Joab's formal command of the army dates from his heroism in the siege of Jerusalem (I Chron 11:6; cf. the NOTE at 5:8). Except for a brief period during which he is displaced (17:25; 19:13), he will remain in command throughout David's reign.

*Jehoshaphat son of Ahilud.* According to I Kings 4:3, Jehoshaphat remained in office under Solomon.

*remembrancer.* Hebrew *mazkîr.* The title might be taken to suggest that this was the official in charge of public records, the recorder (RSV). It has been compared, however, to the Egyptian office of *whmw*, "speaker," whose duty it was to make reports to the king and transmit royal decrees (Erman and Grapow 1971:vol. I:344); see de Vaux (1939), Begrich (1940/41), Mettinger (1971:52–62), and Bright (1976:202–3), and contrast Reventlow (1959), who is criticized by Boecker (1961). The suitability of appealing to Egyptian sources for the elucidation of the obscure titles "remembrancer" and "scribe" (see below) depends on the likely assumption of Egyptian influence on the Davidic court either directly or indirectly by way of the highly Egyptianized Canaanite and Phoenician courts. If the office of *mazkîr* arose by analogy to that of *whmw*, then it may have "united the functions of a master of the ceremonies and foreign minister and other duties also" (Eissfeldt in *CAH*³ II/2:585).

17. *Zadok.* Zadok shared the high priesthood with Abiathar until David's death, when his colleague and rival was banished (I Kings 2:26) and he took full title to the office (cf. I Kings 2:35). Deuteronomistic tradition saw in this the fulfilment of a divine decree of priesthood analogous to the divine decree of kingship found in chap. 7 (see the oracle in I Sam 2:27–36 and the notice of its fulfilment in I Kings 2:27). It offered a justification for the exclusion of non-Jerusalemite priests from temple service that the cultic centralization of the Deuteronomic reform produced. Eventually only those priests who traced their descent to Zadok were regarded as eligible for temple duties (Ezek 40:46; etc.). According to I Chron 5:29–34 [6:3–8], Zadok was a descendant of Aaron's son Eleazar, but it has been widely believed since the time of Wellhausen (1957[1878]:121–40) that this genealogy is a sacerdotal fiction. Wellhausen regarded the Zadokites as parvenus without authentic Levitical genealogy. Recently, however, Cross (1973:207–15) has defended the authenticity of the Aaronid lineage of Zadok, tentatively identifying him with an aide-de-camp of the same name who, according to

I Chron 12:28, was part of a contingent of Aaronid troops who joined David in Hebron (contrast Hauer 1963). See also Cross's acute criticism of the so-called "Jebusite hypothesis" of Rowley (1939) and others, according to which Zadok was the priest of the Canaanite temple in pre-Davidic Jerusalem.

*son of Ahitub.* As in I Chron 5:33–34 [6:7–8]. This Ahitub can hardly be Saul's chaplain, the Ahitub of I Sam 14:3, who was Eli's grandson and Abiathar's grandfather (cf. I Sam 22:20); see Cross 1973:214.

*Abiathar son of Ahimelech.* See the *Textual Note.* A descendant of Eli, the priest of Shiloh in I Samuel 1–4 (see the preceding NOTE), Abiathar is the only survivor of Saul's massacre of the priesthood at Nob (I Sam 22:6–23), after which he came under David's protection and served as his personal priest (cf. I Sam 23:6–13; 30:7–8). He will share the office of high priest with Zadok throughout David's reign until, having sided against the succession of Solomon (cf. I Kings 1:7; etc.), he is banished from court after David's death (I Kings 2:26). For the Deuteronomistic interpretation of this, see the NOTE on "Zadok" above and *I Samuel,* pp. 92–93,366.

*Shausha.* See the *Textual Note.* The name *šawšā'* is non-Semitic, possibly Egyptian (de Vaux 1939:398–99) or Hurrian (Mazar [Maisler] 1946/47:110–12). According to I Kings 4:3, his sons succeeded him in office.

*scribe.* Hebrew *sōpēr.* As in the case of "remembrancer" (see the NOTE above), the office may have existed by analogy to the Egyptian office of scribe *(sš),* who was "the personal secretary of the pharaoh and his *chef de bureau*" (Eissfeldt in *CAH*[3] II/2:585). See also Mettinger 1971:35–51.

18. ***Benaiah son of Jehoiada.*** See 23:20–23. Benaiah will supplant Joab as commander of the army under Solomon (cf. I Kings 2:35). The position he holds now, captain of the bodyguard (cf. 23:23), is the one David himself once held under Saul (cf. I Sam 22:14).

*the Cherethites and the Pelethites.* The royal bodyguard (cf. 23:23). David probably raised this private mercenary army while living in Ziklag (I Samuel 27–31), near which was "the Negeb of the Cherethites" (I Sam 30:14), presumably the homeland of the first of the two groups. Like the Philistines, the Cherethites and Pelethites probably came to Palestine with the migrations of the Peoples of the Sea. The Cherethites have been plausibly identified as Cretans; the origin of the Pelethites is totally obscure (see, in general, Muntingh 1960; Delcor 1978). The name *happĕlētî* may have become distorted after the pattern of *hakkĕrētî,* "the Cherethites," but it is not likely that they were, as often supposed (cf. Hertzberg, etc.), *happĕlištî,* "the Philistines" themselves. We should probably seek another Aegean or Anatolian place-name; cf. Schult (1965), who cites a Punic votive inscription from Constantine, Algeria, in which a certain Hannibal son of Baalhanun is called *hplty.*

*The sons of David were priests.* The statement is surprising because it implies that in the time of David "the priesthood was not yet regarded as hereditary or as limited to the tribe of Levi" (Rowley 1967:95–96). The versions suggest that *kōhănîm* might mean something other than "priests" (see the *Textual Note*); according to Kimchi they were simply high-ranking officers; and Grotius (cited by Thenius) assumed that although a *kōhēn* of God was a priest, a *kōhēn* of a king was a minister of state. But there is no evidence to warrant assigning a special meaning to *kōhănîm* here. We must assume, with most interpreters (most recently Armerding 1975), that in the time of

David and Solomon (1) there were special priests assigned to the royal household, like Ira the Jairite (II Sam 20:26) and possibly Zabud son of Nathan (I Kings 4:5 [but cf. Gray 1970:131]), and (2) members of the royal family might serve in this capacity.

## COMMENT

This roster of David's cabinet may be compared to that in 20:23–26, which has a different arrangement of the names found here and adds those of Ira the Jairite, a priest, and Adoniram, the master of the *corvée.* The latter also served under Solomon (I Kings 4:6) and seems to have still been in office at the beginning of Rehoboam's reign (I Kings 12:18 [LXX]). It has been argued that Adoniram cannot have been appointed until late in David's reign and, therefore, that the present list, in which he does not appear, is earlier than the one in chap. 20, in which he does (Begrich 1940/41:5–6). I agree with Ackroyd, however, who thinks it likely that the two lists are "simply variants, rather than reflections of different periods of David's reign" (cf. I Kings 4:2–6 and 2:46 + [46h]). The variants probably arose in the course of the final arrangement of the book, when 21:1–14 was removed from its original position preceding chap. 9 (see the COMMENTS on §§ XIX and XXXV and the Introduction, pp. 18–19) to its present location. The last portion of chap. 8 was reproduced in both places, producing the doublet we now have.

# XIX. MERIBBAAL
## (9:1–13)

**9** 1"Is anyone still left of the house of Saul," asked David, "whom I
may treat loyally for Jonathan's sake?"
2Now there was a servant of the house of Saul named Ziba, and he
was summoned to David.
"Are you Ziba?" the king asked him.
"Your servant," he said.
3"Is there now no one of the house of Saul whom I may treat with
the loyalty of God?" asked the king.
"There is still a son of Jonathan," Ziba told the king, "a cripple."
4"Where is he?" asked the king.
"He is in the house of Machir son of Ammiel," Ziba told the king,
"in Lo-debar." 5So the king had him brought from the house of Machir
son of Ammiel in Lo-debar.
6When Meribbaal son of Jonathan son of Saul came to David, he fell
on his face and groveled.
"Meribbaal," said David.
"Your servant," he said.
7"Don't be afraid," David told him, "for what I'm going to do is treat
you loyally for the sake of your father, Jonathan! I'm going to return
to you all the property of your grandfather, Saul, and as for you, you're
going to eat your food at my table from now on!"
8"What is your servant," he said, groveling, "that you should pay
attention to a dead dog like me?"
9Then the king summoned Ziba, Saul's steward. "I have given everything that belonged to Saul and all his house to your master's son," he
told him. 10"You are to work the land for him—you and your sons and
your servants. You will bring food into your master's house for them
to eat. But Meribbaal, your master's son, will eat his food at my table
from now on." (Ziba had fifteen sons and twenty servants.)
11"Just as my lord the king instructs his servant," said Ziba to the
king, "your servant will do."
So Meribbaal ate at David's table like one of the king's sons. 12Merib-

baal had a small son named Micah. All who lived in the house of Ziba were Meribbaal's servants. [13]Meribbaal himself lived in Jerusalem, for he always ate at the king's table. He was crippled in both legs.

## TEXTUAL NOTES

**9** 2. *Ziba* (2) So MT, LXX$^{BAMN}$. LXX$^{L}$: "Ziba the steward" (cf. v. 9).

*"Your servant"* So MT, LXX$^{L}$. LXX$^{BAMN}$, Syr., Vulg.: "*I am* your servant."

3. *asked the king* Reading *wy'mr hmlk,* lit., "and the king said," with MT, LXX. Syr. adds "to him."

4. *asked the king* Reading *wy'mr hmlk,* lit., "and the king said," with LXX$^{BAMN}$. MT, LXX$^{L}$, Syr. add "to him."

*in Lo-debar* So MT. MT$^{MSS}$, LXX, Syr.: "*from* Lo-debar," as in v. 5 and 17:27.

5. *the king* So Syr. MT, LXX: "King David."

6. *Meribbaal* See the *Textual Note* at 4:4.

*groveled* LXX adds "to him." Omit with MT.

*said David* LXX, Syr. add "to him." Omit with MT.

7. *your grandfather* So LXX$^{BMN}$ = *'by 'byk* (contrast Ehrlich 1910:292). MT (cf. Syr., LXX$^{AL}$) has lost *'by* by haplography—thus, "your father."

8. *he said, groveling* So MT, Syr., LXX$^{L}$. LXX$^{BAMN}$ make the subject explicit.

9. *the king* So MT, LXX$^{BAMN}$. LXX$^{L}$: "King David."

*Saul's steward* Omitted by Syr.

10. *You will bring food into your master's house* Reading *whb't 'l byt 'dnyk lḥm* with LXX$^{L}$. MT has *whb't whyh lbn 'dnyk lḥm,* "You will bring (your harvest), and it will be food for your master's son" (see the NOTE). But the syntax of the verse, which contrasts the provision of food for the family ("your master's house") with the special provision for "Meribbaal, your master's son" (in the emphatic first position), strongly favors LXX$^{L}$; see Ehrlich 1910:292.

*for them to eat* That is, *w'klw* = *wĕ'ākĕlû,* lit. "and they will eat" (so LXX$^{LMN}$: *kai phagontai*). MT interprets *w'klw* as *wa'ăkālô,* "and *he* (i.e., Meribbaal; see the preceding *Textual Note*) will eat *it.*"

*(Ziba . . . servants)* This parenthesis is disruptive and unnecessary at this point. Though there is no textual basis for excising it, it is almost certainly a marginal note derived from 19:18.

11. *ate* Vocalizing *'kl* as *'ākal* with LXX *(ēsthien).* MT is obliged by its erroneous reading of "at my table" (see the following *Textual Note*) to treat the entire clause as if it were part of the preceding speech of Ziba and to read *'kl* as *'ōkēl;* but "will eat" would require *y'kl* (so MT$^{MSS}$, Vulg.).

*David's table* So LXX$^{BAMN}$. MT "my table" (retained by Ehrlich 1910:293) shows the influence of vv. 7 and 10, and Syr., LXX$^{L}$ "the king's table" looks ahead to v. 13. OL$^{MSS}$, Vulg. "*your* table" reflects an attempt to correct the obvious error of MT while keeping the speech in Ziba's mouth (adopted by Thenius).

## NOTES

9 1. The question of a survivor in the house of Saul is raised by the account of the execution of the Saulids in 21:1–14, which probably once stood before chap. 9. The matter of the original and present arrangements of this material is discussed in the COMMENT as well as the Introduction (LITERARY HISTORY). Veijola (1975:87 n. 43) regards v. 1, which anticipates v. 3, as editorial, the proper introduction to the episode coming in v. 2 (cf. van den Born; Langlamet 1979/81:[86:]208–9).

*whom I may treat loyally.* Hebrew *wĕ'e'ĕśeh 'immô ḥesed.* This act of *ḥesed* has its background in David's relationship to Jonathan, specifically Jonathan's support of David in the perilous days of his departure from Saul's court (cf. especially I Samuel 20). In the present, Deuteronomistically edited, form of the biblical text this connection is made explicit by expansions of the older account of David's rise to power (I Sam 20:11–17,23,40–42; cf. 23:14–18), according to which Jonathan implored David to do *ḥesed* with his family ("if I die, never cut off your loyalty from my house" [I Sam 20:14–15]) and bound him by an oath of Yahweh (I Sam 20:23,42; cf. II Sam 21:7). In the older form of the story, however, I Samuel 20 and II Samuel 9 belonged to different documents, and the reference to David's remarks ("for Jonathan's sake") was more general. The emphasis is on the freely given *ḥesed* of David, who might well have had Meribbaal put to death (cf. 19:29) were he not mindful of having once needed *ḥesed* himself from Meribbaal's father (I Sam 20:8); cf. Sakenfeld 1978:88–90. Note in this regard the threefold repetition of David's motive of "loyalty" *(ḥesed)* in vv. 1,3, and 7, whereby the narrator stresses that it was this motive—and no other—that prompted David to bring Meribbaal into his household. See, further, the COMMENT.

3. *a son of Jonathan . . . a cripple.* Meribbaal was identified and his lameness explained to us in 4:4. As pointed out in the NOTE there, this information may have stood originally here in 9:3 (cf. Josephus, *Ant.* 7.113). The significance of Meribbaal's infirmity is discussed in the COMMENT.

4. *Machir son of Ammiel.* The name has a good pedigree in northern Gilead. In the twelfth century B.C., when the Song of Deborah was composed, Machir seems to have been a tribe occupying the territory between Ephraim and Zebulun (Judg 5:14), which in the developed biblical tradition belonged to Manasseh, which is not mentioned in Judges 5. Evidently Manasseh was originally a clan of Machir that grew powerful and displaced it or, possibly, a rival tribe that drove Machir away (see de Vaux 1978:586–87, 651–52 and bibliography). In any case, the Machirites came to be thought of as a clan of Manasseh (Num 26:29), and in the biblical genealogies Machir is a son of Manasseh (Gen 50:23; etc.) and the father of Gilead (Num 26:29). In this final arrangement the territory of Machir was that part of Gilead said to have been given them by Moses (Num 32:39–40; Deut 3:15), specifically the territory between Mahanaim and the Yarmuk (Sherî'at el-Menâdireh, Map 2) but also including, at least in theory, Bashan (cf. Josh 13:29–31; 17:1). This was the vicinity in which Abiner and Ishbaal established a rump government after Saul's death (cf. the NOTE on "Mahanaim" at 2:13), and it

must have maintained a fierce loyalty to the house of Saul. Our Machir is likely to have shared this sentiment, and it is not surprising to find him harboring the Saulid scion Meribbaal. Nevertheless, Machir will eventually become a supporter of David (17:27). Was he won over by David's "loyalty" to Meribbaal (cf. Sakenfeld 1978:89 n. 114), or is David's surprising support in Transjordan to be explained in some other way? See the COMMENT on § XX.

*Lo-debar.* A city in northern Transjordan, possibly modern Umm ed-dabar (Map 2). Though mentioned in the description of the northern boundary of Gad in Josh 13:26 (read *lō dĕbar* for MT *lidbīr*), Lo-debar was in fact a Manassite or Machirite town maintaining the Saulid loyalty of neighboring cities like Mahanaim and Jabesh-gilead.

7. *all the property of . . . Saul.* We can assume that David took full control of Saul's property in Benjamin and elsewhere after the demise of Ishbaal and the expulsion of the Philistines. Though a family estate was inalienable and hereditary, it could be appropriated by the crown in the absence of a suitable heir; but in this instance an heir is later found and the property is restored (cf. Ben-Barak 1981). Nevertheless, the reassignment is only pro forma. David's future actions will show that he maintains actual control (already in vv. 9–10; cf. 16:14; 19:30).

*you're going to eat your food at my table.* A seat at the king's table represented royal patronage and special favor. Thus in I Kings 2:7 David on his deathbed addresses Solomon in reference to the staunch loyalty of Barzillai (II Sam 17:27; 19:32–39), "As for the sons of Barzillai the Gileadite, treat them loyally *(ta'ăśeh-ḥesed),* and let them be among those who eat at your table!" In I Kings 18:19 we are told that the prophets of Baal and Asherah enjoyed the special patronage of the Samarian court, "eating at Jezebel's table." A particularly relevant example is II Kings 25:27–29 = Jer 52:31–33, where Jehoiachin, the exiled king of Judah and (like Meribbaal) the scion of a defeated royal family, is released from prison by Amel-Marduk (Evil-merodach) and accorded a position of honor at the Babylonian court. Afterwards, we are told, "He ate his food in [Amel-Marduk's] presence from then on [*tāmîd;* cf. II Sam 9:10] for the rest of his life." Compare also Psalm 23, where the psalmist speaks of Yahweh as a gracious king ("my shepherd," v. 1), who sets him a place at his table (v. 5) and permits him to live in his house (v. 6). See, further, the NOTE at v. 10.

8. *a dead dog like me.* Here, as in I Sam 24:15, "dead dog" is a term of extreme self-abasement (cf. I Kings 8:13 [LXX]); in 16:9 it is a term of contempt for someone else. The point is not that a dog is vile or contemptible (*pace* Winton Thomas 1960:417) but that it is insignificant—and a *dead* dog the more so. For "dog," "dead dog," and "stray dog" used similarly in the courtly language of extrabiblical documents from the ancient Near East, see *I Samuel,* pp. 384–85. To the particular expression used here by Meribbaal—*meh 'abdékā kî pānîtā 'el hakkeleb 'ăšer kāmônî,* "What is your servant . . . that you should pay attention to a dead dog like me?"—compare the language of a sixth-century B.C. letter from Lachish (Lachish ostracon 2.4 = *KAI* 194.4): *my 'bdk klb ky zkr 'dny 'bdh,* "Who is your servant, a dog, that my lord should have remembered his servant?" Cf. *miyami anāku kalbu ištēn . . . ,* "Who am I, some dog . . . ?" in a fourteenth-century B.C. letter from Syria (*EA* 202:12–13).

9. *Saul's steward.* Hebrew *na'ar* means "young man" and thus "servant, retainer" or "squire, soldier" (MacDonald 1976; Stähli 1978; cf. the NOTE at 2:14). Though often used in reference to ordinary household servants in a general way (13:17), the term can

connote a specific office of high rank, evidently that of steward or superintendent of the property of an estate. Thus in 19:18 Ziba is called *na'ar bêt šā'ûl,* "the steward of the house of Saul." Here he is called *na'ar šā'ûl,* "Saul's steward," and in 16:1 "Meribbaal's steward." To these titles may be compared those found on Hebrew and Ammonite seals bearing the legend *(l-)*$PN_1$ *nʿr* $PN_2$, "(belonging to) $PN_1$, the steward of $PN_2$"; see Avigad 1976.

10. Ziba is to work Saul's estates and provide for the family with the produce. But Meribbaal will live in Jerusalem under royal patronage and evidently at royal expense. The received Hebrew text gives the impression that Meribbaal is to receive shipments of food from his estate (see the *Textual Note*), and Rainey has seen this as evidence for an administrative system under which royal courtiers were supported by income from their estates, an assumption he then uses to explain the purpose of the Samaria ostraca and certain obscure administrative texts from Ugarit (1967b; 1979). But the force of David's instructions as they appear in the superior Greek text is to emphasize the opposite point, viz. that Meribbaal will be supported at David's expense.

12. *Micah.* According to I Chron 8:34–45 (cf. 9:40–41), Micah became the father of four sons. Our story in its present form shows that both Jonathan (I Sam 20:14–16) and Saul (I Sam 24:21–22) realized that the survival of their family lay in David's hands, and, as it turns out, it is through Meribbaal and Micah, who have now come under David's protection, that the house of Saul will be preserved.

## COMMENT

Long ago, when Jonathan was helping the young David escape from Saul's court, he adjured David to "deal loyally with me; but if I die, never cut off your loyalty from my house. And when Yahweh cuts off each of the enemies of David from upon the face of the earth, if the name of Jonathan is cut off from the house of David, then may Yahweh call David to account!" (I Sam 20:14–16). Now Jonathan is dead, David is king, and David's enemies are "cut off," as the preceding chapter has shown systematically. In other words, the time foreseen by Jonathan has come. David, therefore, acts promptly to exercise "loyalty" (*ḥesed,* vv. 1,3,7) to Jonathan's descendants. In particular, he determines the whereabouts of Jonathan's lame son Meribbaal (cf. 4:4) and sends for him. He formally restores Saul's estate to Meribbaal and gives him a seat at the royal table, a place of honor at court. Henceforth Meribbaal is to live under David's patronage, and "the name of Jonathan" will never be "cut off from the house of David."

These events fit smoothly into the larger story in its present, Deuteronomistically edited, form. There is no reason to believe that I Samuel 20 and II Samuel 9 derive from a single original document—though both may come from the reign of David (see the section LITERARY HISTORY in the Introduction). Nevertheless, a Deuteronomistic hand has made the connection between them explicit by the addition of I Sam 20:11–17,23,40–42 (see *I Samuel*, pp. 16–17,344). As explained in the COMMENT on § XVII, it was also a Deuteronomistic writer who compiled the catalogue of David's wars, in which David's enemies are "cut off," and placed it in the narrative immediately preceding the present passage. As an episode in the Deuteronomistic history, therefore, II Samuel 9 joins with I Samuel 20 to link separate components of the story of David into a narrative unit, while offering, like the episode of David and Michal in 6:20–23, a resolution to issues arising from earlier events in the larger story. In particular, David's relationship to Meribbaal is presented as a sequel to his past relationship to Jonathan and, most especially, the result of a spontaneous initiative of David undertaken in faithful recollection of Jonathan's earnest entreaty.

This suggests that it was also Deuteronomistic editing that separated the story of the Gibeonites' revenge in 21:1–14 from its natural sequel here in chap. 9 and consigned it to an appendix at the end of the materials on the reign of David. The connection between these two passages was first recognized by Klostermann, who has been followed by a large number of commentators (Budde, Schulz, Hertzberg, Caird, de Vaux; cf. also Carlson 1964:198–203). It has been doubted by Smith and others, most notably Gunn (1978:68), who argues that chap. 9 is a sequel not to 21:1–14 but to chaps. 2–4, with particular reference to the death of Ishbaal (cf., already, Segal 1965/66:36–37). But David's question in v. 1 implies that Saul's house is threatened with extinction, not merely that one Saulid, however prominent, has died. Thus, it is very difficult to suppose that the seven Saulids put to death in chap. 21 are alive at the beginning of chap. 9 (Budde). In other words, the events of 21:1–14 are almost certainly *chronologically* prior to those of chap. 9, having taken place early, not late, in David's reign (Budde). Though it may not be possible, as Klostermann supposed, to identify a verbal relic of the editorial separation of these two passages (see the NOTE on "Afterwards" at 21:14), it seems clear that David's question in 9:1 presupposes the events of 21:1–14 and is phrased with reference to them, and it is reasonable, therefore, to assume that 21:1–14 + 9:1–13 once stood in continuous narrative sequence. The separation, then, must have been made by a Deuteronomistic editor who saw David's treatment of Meribbaal in the context of his long-standing relationship to the house of Saul rather than of the suspicious circumstances of the Gibeonites' revenge. The additions to I Samuel 20 and the relegation of II Sam 21:1–14 to an appendix, therefore, were parts of a single redactional effort to stress David's sincerity in his treatment of Meribbaal (Hertzberg) and, at the same time, to reinforce the continuity of the larger history.

It can also be shown that II Samuel 9 represents an introduction to the story that follows in chaps. 10–20 and—passing over the appendices in chaps. 21–24 —I Kings 1 and 2. The two men introduced to us here, Ziba and Meribbaal, will have an important role there (16:1–14; 19:24–30). Moreover, if these chapters (II Samuel 9–20 + I Kings 1–2) are finally concerned with the question of the succession to David, as many scholars have concluded, the identification of the crippled guest in David's household as the sole Saulid heir can be said to contribute to this larger theme. Indeed, Rost's programmatic analysis of this material as a succession narrative identified chap. 9 as the beginning of the main body of the narrative in its present form.

On the other hand, II Sam 21:1–14 + 9:1–13 displays a literary and thematic completeness in itself. It has a clear beginning ("There was a famine in the time of David . . . ," 21:1) and end ("So Meribbaal ate at David's table like one of the sons of the king," 9:11b), followed by a concluding summary (9:12–13). It contributes to the succession question ("Why did Solomon succeed David to the throne?") only in the most general way, but it addresses another question ("Why did David execute the seven Saulids and summon the eighth to Jerusalem?") directly and succinctly. For these reasons it seems preferable to think of 21:1–14 + 9:1–13 as deriving from an originally independent document taken up by the author of I Kings 1–2 in support of his work. Thus, it stands alongside the apology of David (I Sam 16:14–II Sam 5:10) and the story of Abishalom's rebellion (II Samuel 13–20) as part of a corpus of writings from the court of David cited evidentially in support of the apologetic argument of I Kings 1–2 (see the section LITERARY HISTORY in the Introduction; cf. McCarter 1981:361–64). The Solomonic apologist may have found this account of the fate of the Saulids useful because it depicted David as he wanted him to be seen, just but severe (cf. I Kings 2:5–9). Also, the bloodbath that accompanied Solomon's accession might be viewed more generously if David's execution of the Saulids was kept in mind. In any case, the account of Meribbaal's arrival at court provided a needed and convenient introduction to the Meribbaal-Ziba subplot of the story of Abishalom's rebellion. (I do not, however, wish to join Langlamet [1979–81] in reviving the hypothesis of Cook [1899/1900:169–76] that the various Meribbaal elements in chaps. 9, 16, and 19 [cf. 21:7] derive from a single, originally independent document [Cook] or an early editorial expansion of the story [Langlamet]. Still less convincing is the argument of Veijola [1978] for extensive Deuteronomistic expansion in these chapters [in chap. 9, vv. 1,3,6,7,10aεb, and 13], pro-Davidic editing obscuring the fact that, as Veijola believes, Meribbaal was *Saul's* son [cf. 9:7,9,10; 16:3; 19:25; in addition to 21:7] and a contemporary of David. The Meribbaal passages in chaps. 16 and 19 seem organic to their context, as we shall see.)

Considered as an originally independent document from the reign of David, II Sam 21:1–14 + 9:1–13 reveals its purpose readily. It addresses publicly known events—the execution of the Saulids and the summons of Meribbaal—which must have cast the gravest suspicion upon David, especially among Benjaminites. Did David purge the house of Saul in order to secure his own claim to the throne of all Israel? Was Meribbaal, the surviving Saulid heir, a prisoner in David's household? Public appearances lent credence to such suspicions. Our document, however, seeks to explain that, despite appearances, David's behavior was just and honorable. The execution of the seven Saulids was necessitated by the requirements of blood justice arising from Saul's treatment of the Gibeonites (21:1). David had nothing personal at stake in issuing the order of execution; on the contrary, he was acting in the interest of all Israelites to bring relief from the famine (see the COMMENT on § XXXV). As for Meribbaal, he was brought from Jerusalem not as a prisoner but as an honored guest. David summoned him out of loyalty to his past relationship with his father. He restored his family estate to him and gave him a position at court. The modern historian must evaluate David's role in these events in awareness of the favorable slant of the report in 21:1–14 + 9:1–13 as well as the unfavorable predisposition of Benjaminites like Shimei son of Gera, who regarded David as a "bloodstained fiend of hell" (16:7). The Gibeonites' claim on the house of Saul is not likely to have been a pure fiction, but we cannot doubt that David welcomed the opportunity to decimate by legal means a family with a strong claim to his throne. Meribbaal probably did enjoy the status and treatment of an honored member of the court who "always ate at the king's table," language pointing to a position of privilege (see the NOTES at vv. 7,10); but we cannot deny the advantage it was to David to have the sole heir to the house of Saul under his own roof, where he could keep an eye on him. It may be more than accidental, moreover, that the one male Saulid who survived the purge was lame. A man who was lame—or had any physical blemish—could not function as a priest (Lev 21:16–23). We are nowhere told that a blemish excluded a man from becoming king (but see the NOTE at 14:25), but in view of the sacrosanct character of the king's body (cf. the NOTE at 1:14) it seems most unlikely that a man "crippled in both legs" could have been regarded as a qualified candidate for the throne.

Whatever the historical relationship was between David and Meribbaal, their relationship within our story is now established. David is Meribbaal's benefactor and patron as well as the king to whom he owes allegiance. The terms implicit in this relationship will be appealed to more than once as the story continues to unfold.

# XX. THE WAR WITH THE ARAMEAN COALITION (10:1–19)

**10** [1]After this the king of the Ammonites died, and Hanun, his son,
became king in his place. [2]David thought, "I'll treat Hanun son of
Nahash loyally just as his father treated me loyally." So [he] sent
servants to console him over his father.
But when David's servants reached the land of the Ammonites, [3]the
Ammonite leaders said to Hanun, their lord, "Does it seem to you that
David is honoring your father when he sends you comforters? Isn't it
rather to explore the city—to spy on it and look it over—that [he] sends
his servants to you?" [4]So taking David's servants, Hanun shaved off
their beards, cut their skirts in half up to the buttocks, and sent them
away.
[5]When David was told, he had the men met, for they were deeply
humiliated. "Stop over in Jericho," said the king, "until your beards
have grown back; then return."
[6]When the Ammonites saw that they had offended David, [they] sent
away and hired the Arameans of Beth-rehob and the Arameans of
Zobah—twenty thousands of foot soldiers—and the king of Maacah
and the men of Tob—twelve thousands of men. [7]When David heard,
he dispatched Joab with all the soldiers.
[8]The Ammonites marched out and drew up for battle at the entrance
to the gate, with the Arameans of Zobah and Rehob, then men of Tob,
and Maacah remaining apart in the open country. [9]Joab, seeing that
battlefronts were set against him both before and behind, made a selection from all the elite troops in Israel and drew up to meet the Arameans. [10]The rest of the army he put under the command of his brother
Abishai, who drew up to meet the Ammonites. [11]"If the Arameans are
too strong for me," he had said, "you must give me help, and if the
Ammonites are too strong for you, I'll come to help you. [12]Take courage
and we'll exert ourselves on behalf of our people and the cities of our
god! May Yahweh do what seems good to him!"
[13]When Joab and the force that was with him closed in to fight with

the Arameans, they fled from him, [14]and the Ammonites, seeing that the Arameans had fled, also fled from Abishai and went into the city. So Joab returned to Jerusalem from the Ammonite campaign.

### *The Battle of Helam*

[15]When the Arameans saw that they had been routed by the Israelites, they reassembled, [16]and Hadadezer had the Arameans who were across the River brought. They came to Helam with Shobach, the commander of Hadadezer's army, leading them. [17]When David was told, he gathered all Israel, crossed the Jordan, and came to Helam, where the Arameans drew up in front of [him], fought with him, [18]and fled before the advance of Israel. David killed seven hundreds of the Aramean charioteers and forty thousands of their cavalrymen, and he also struck down Shobach, the commander of their army, so that he died there. [19]And when all the vassals of Hadadezer saw that they had been defeated by Israel, they sued Israel for peace and became its vassals, and the Arameans were afraid to help the Ammonites again.

## *TEXTUAL NOTES*

**10** 1. At this point the character of the Septuagintal evidence for the text of Samuel changes radically. $LXX^B$ is no longer a direct witness to the OG text, representing instead the so-called *kaige* recension. $LXX^L$, with all its peculiarities and problems, is now our best source of OG readings. See the section TEXT AND VERSIONS in the Introduction.

3. *the city* Targ. "the land." Cf. I Chron 19:3 and see Talmon 1975:345.

4. *their beards* So LXX. MT has "*half (ḥṣy)* their beards" in anticipation of "cut their skirts in half *(bḥṣy).*"

5. *When David was told* So $LXX^L$: *kai apēngelē tō daueid* = *wygd (wayyuggad) ldwd.* MT (cf. $LXX^{BAMN}$): *wygdw ldwd,* "When they told David." At this point LXX, $4QSam^a$, and I Chron 19:5 add "about the men"; omit with MT. Cf. Barthélemy 1980:24–25.

6. *they had offended David* MT has *nb'šw bdwd,* lit. "they stunk with David," for which I Chron 19:6 offers a more distinctive equivalent, *htb'šw 'm dwd.* LXX *katēschynthēsan ho laos daueid* points to *bwšw 'm dwd,* "the people *('m = 'am)* of David were ashamed."

*and hired . . . thousands of men* The witnesses preserve variant ways of presenting this list. Our translation generally follows that shared by MT and LXX. The fragments of $4QSam^a$ share with Josephus (*Ant.* 7.121) and I Chron 19:6–7 an alternative that, in the form presented by the Chronicler and Josephus, is so elaborated with intrusive materials from 8:3–6 as well as MT's text of the present passage that it is difficult to recover with certainty. The *Textual Notes* that follow draw upon this alternative presentation only where it is possible to be reasonably certain that an authentic variant reading exists. Ulrich (1978:152–56) provides an expert evaluation of the several readings involved and the affinities among them.

*and hired* So MT (cf. LXX): *wyśkrw*. I Chron 19:6 has a different reading of which the first three words are preserved in a fragment of 4QSam$^a$: *'lp kkr ksp lśkr lhm*, "a thousand silver talents to hire for themselves" (cf. also Josephus, *Ant.* 7.121).

*the Arameans of Beth-rehob* So MT (cf. LXX): *'rm byt rḥwb*, lit. "Aram Beth-rehob." I Chron 19:6, Josephus (*Ant.* 7.121), and Ps 60:2 have *'rm nhrym*, "Aram Naharaim," that is, "the Arameans of Mesopotamia."

*and the Arameans of Zobah* Omitted by LXX$^B$.

*foot soldiers* So MT, LXX, to which compare Josephus, *Ant.* 7.121. The chariots and cavalrymen of I Chron 19:6–7 and 4QSam$^a$ may have arisen under the influence of 8:4.

*the king of Maacah* MT, followed by LXX, adds "one thousand of men," on which see Ulrich 1978:155. We omit *'lp 'yš* with I Chron 19:7 and, as space considerations dictate, 4QSam$^a$ (N.B. also Josephus' total of twelve thousand for both Maacah and Tob [*Ant.* 7.121]).

*the men of Tob* So MT: *'yš ṭwb*. 4QSam$^a$ reads this as a man's name, [']*ỵšṭwb*, "Ishtob," to which compare LXX *eistōb*, Syr. *'šyṭwb*, and Josephus (*Ant.* 7.121) *istobon*. See also the NOTE.

At the end of the verse a long passage, absent from MT and those witnesses (here including LXX) dependent on MT, appears in I Chron 19:7 and in a shorter form in the fragments of 4QSam$^a$, which may be reconstructed on the basis of the Chronicles text. I Chron 19:7 makes no mention of "the men of Tob" or the number of troops sent by Maacah and Tob. After referring to "the king of Maacah and his army," it goes on as follows: *wyb'w wyḥnw lpny mydb' wbny 'mwn n'spw m'ryhm wyb'w lmlḥmh*, "And they came and encamped in front of Medeba. And the Ammonites had gathered from their cities, and they came to fight." Space considerations show that if 4QSam$^a$ contained the designation of the number of troops from Maacah and Tob—which seems likely, since the scroll has the reference to Tob (see above)—it cannot also have included the first sentence in the reading from Chronicles just cited. Thus I reconstruct the scroll as follows: [*wbny*] *'mwn n'spw mn h*[*'ryhm wyb'w lhlḥ*]*m*, lit. "And the Ammonites had gathered from their cities, and they came to fight." This leaves space on the scroll before v. 7; it was probably empty (paragraphing; cf. I Chron 19:7–8). We should probably regard this plus, whether in its shorter (4QSam$^a$) or longer (I Chron 19:7) form, as expansive. The reference to Medeba, which seems much too far south (cf. Bright 1972:198 n. 43), is troubling, and, more important, there is no apparent mechanism for its loss. Neither, however, is there an apparent motivation for its insertion or a known source.

7. *the soldiers* The text of MT (cf. LXX$^B$) is conflate, reading *ḥṣb' hgbrym*, "the army, the soldiers," which has been adjusted in LXX$^L$, Syr., Targ., OL, and I Chron 19:8 (*kĕtîb*) to *ṣb' hgbrym*, "the army of soldiers." Read *hgbrym*.

8. *the gate* So MT, LXX$^{BAM}$, Syr. (cf. 11:23). LXX$^{LN}$ and I Chron 19:9 have "the city." Cf. *I Samuel*, the *Textual Notes* at 9:14,18.

9. *seeing* MT (cf. LXX$^{B}$, etc.): *wyr'*, lit. "And (Joab) saw." LXX$^{L}$ reflects *wyr'm*, "And (Joab) saw *them*."

*before* MT *mpnym*, rendered *ek tou kata prosōpon* by LXX$^{(B)}$, in which it is combined with *ex enantias* = *lqr't*, "opposite." In recensional correction to MT, LXX$^{A}$ (correctly) omits *ex enantias*, and LXX$^{LM}$ (incorrectly) omit *ek tou kata prosōpon*.

*the elite troops in Israel* So MT *(kětîb): bḥwry byśr'l*, an archaic construction (GK$^{2}$ §130a) revised by MT *(qěrê)* to *bḥwry yśr'l* (Freedman). LXX$^{L}$ = *bḥwr bny yśr'l*, "the elite troops [collective; cf. I Chron 19:10] of the Israelites."

11. *he had said* So MT, LXX$^{BAMN}$. LXX$^{L}$: "*Joab* had said *to Abishai*." Syr.: "he had said to Abishai *his brother*" (cf. v. 10).

*you must give me help* That is, *whyth ly lyšw'h*, lit. "you must be a help to me" (so MT; cf. LXX$^{L}$). LXX$^{BAMN}$ = *whytm*, etc., "you [plural] must give me help."

*I'll come to help you* So MT (cf. LXX$^{L}$): *whlkty lhwšy' lk*. LXX$^{BAMN}$ = *whyynw lhwšy'k*, lit. "we'll be to help you," i.e., "it will be our task to help you." I Chron 19:12: *whwš'tyk*, "I'll help you."

12. *and we'll exert ourselves* So MT, LXX$^{BAMN}$. LXX$^{L}$: "and we'll exert ourselves *and fight*."

*to him* So MT, LXX$^{BAMN}$. LXX$^{L}$ adds "concerning us."

13. *they fled* So MT (cf. LXX$^{BAMN}$): *wynsw*. LXX$^{L}$ = *wyns 'rm*, "*the Arameans* fled."

14. *So Joab . . . campaign* Reading *wyšb yw'b m'l bny 'mwn yrwšlym*, lit. "And Joab returned from against the Ammonites to Jerusalem," with LXX$^{L}$, OL (cf. I Chron 19:15). Before "to Jerusalem," MT (cf. LXX$^{MN}$) inserts "and (he) came," and MT$^{MSS}$ (cf. LXX$^{BA}$) insert "and *they* (?) came."

15. *When the Arameans saw that they had been routed* So MT, LXX$^{BAMN}$. LXX$^{L}$, OL have "When *the Ammonites* saw that *the Arameans* had been routed" in reminiscence of v. 14.

*by the Israelites* So LXX$^{L}$, Syr.$^{MSS}$: *lpny bny yśr'l*. MT (cf. LXX$^{BAMN}$) has lost *bny* after *lpny*—thus, "by Israel."

16. *and Hadadezer had . . . brought* That is, *wyšlḥ hdd'zr wyṣ'*, lit. "and Hadadezer sent and brought." So MT, LXX$^{LMN}$. LXX$^{B}$: "and Hadadezer sent and *assembled*."

*to Helam* Thenius understood MT *ḥylm* as "their army" (cf. Vulg.); but LXX, Syr., and Targ. take it as a proper noun identical to *ḥl'mh* in v. 17, and this is evidently correct (Ewald 1878:155 n. 2; cf. Wellhausen, Driver).

17. *the Arameans drew up in front of [him]* So MT, LXX$^{B^{mg}ALMN}$. LXX$^{B}$: "David drew up in front of the Arameans" (cf. I Chron 19:17).

18. *and fled* MT has "and *Aram* fled." Omit *'rm* with Syr.$^{MSS}$ (Englert 1949:12) and LXX$^{B}$ (in which it is restored marginally).

*David killed* The figures that follow are those of MT and LXX$^{B}$, but the witnesses differ:

| | | |
|---|---|---|
| MT, LXX$^{B}$: | 700 *rkb* + 40,000 *pršym* | |
| Syr.: | 1,700 *rkb* + 4,000 *pršym* + "a great army" *(w'm' sgy")* | |
| LXX$^{L}$, OL: | 700 *pršym* + 40,000 *rgly* | |
| I Chron 19:18 and Josephus, *Ant.* 7.128: | 7,000 *pršym* + 40,000 *rgly* | |

19. *all the vassals of Hadadezer* MT has *kl hmlkym ʿbdy hddʿzr*, "all the *kings*, the vassals of Hadadezer." LXX is similar, but corresponding to *ʿbdy hddʿzr* LXX[L] (cf. OL) has *hoi symporeuomenoi tō adraazar*, "who traveled with Hadadezer," possibly reflecting *ʿbry hddʿzr* or *hhwlkym* (a variant of *hmlkym?*) *lhddʿzr*. Syr. and one Greek minuscule (d = 107) omit "the kings" in agreement with I Chron 19:19, probably reflecting the primitive situation: *hmlkym* arose as a marginal correction of *hmlʾkym* in 11:1 (see the *Textual Note* there) and found its way into the text at this point.

## NOTES

**10** 1–2. Hanun's father, Nahash, was an enemy of Saul (I Samuel 11) and may have regarded himself ipso facto an ally of David. Outside of the present passage nothing is said of a relationship between David and Nahash except in 17:27, where we are told that a son of Nahash named Shobi was among those who received David in Mahanaim and provided for him during his flight from Abishalom. If this was the act of "loyalty" (*ḥesed*) referred to here, as seems probable, it follows that Abishalom's rebellion, described in chaps. 13–20, was historically prior to the present events. As explained in the COMMENT, we should probably think of Nahash as having allied himself to David during the reign of Saul or Ishbaal to offset the threat Israel posed to Ammon. The language of covenant loyalty (*ḥesed*) found in the present passage suggests that David's dispatch of a delegation to Rabbah was in keeping with an established protocol according to which such embassies were sent at the death of treaty partners in the interest of maintaining covenant relationships intact (Moran 1963a:80). Nahash, says David, "treated me loyally" (*ʿāśâ . . . ʿimmādî ḥesed*), presumably by providing him assistance at Mahanaim. It is therefore David's wish to "treat Hanun son of Nahash loyally" (*ʾeʿĕśeh-ḥesed . . .*), i.e., reassure the new Ammonite king about the continuity of the alliance.

3. *and look it over.* Hebrew *ûlĕhopkāh*, lit. "and *turn* it over," rendered by most recent translators as "and overthrow it." But as Ehrlich pointed out long ago (1910: 294), the verb *hpk* has the meaning "overthrow, destroy" elsewhere only with Yahweh as subject. Here it is probably synonymous with the adjacent verbs *ḥăqôr*, "explore," and *ûlĕraggĕlāh*, "to spy it out," as required by the synoptic parallel in I Chron 19:3, where the order is altered: *laḥqōr wĕlahăpōk ûlĕraggēl*, "to explore [the city], to look [it] over, and to spy [it] out." Thus the Targum Jonathan is correct in rendering *wlhpkh* as *wlmbdqh*, "and discover its secrets," in the present passage.

4. The treatment of David's emissaries finds parallels in gestures of humiliation—whether real, ritual, or symbolic—on other occasions: To the shaving of the beard compare Isa 15:2; Jer 41:5; 48:37; etc.; to the exposure of the buttocks compare Isa 20:4. However, the particular combination here suggests symbolic castration, a peculiarly appropriate punishment for presumed spies in view of the widespread analogue of eyeballs and testicles in myth and folklore. Removal of the beard symbolically deprives a man of his masculinity. Cutting off the skirt may be a palliative for castration, and, in any case, it bares the testicles, and thus—by the same kind of transference that led

Oedipus to gouge out his eyes after discovering that he had been sleeping with his mother—it exposes the "eyes" of the secret spies.

5. *Jericho.* See Map 6. The city (Tell es-Sulṭân) lay near the Jordan, not far from the point at which David's emissaries would have crossed on their return from the Ammonite capital. The most direct road from Jerusalem to Rabbah crossed the river just north of the Dead Sea and proceeded east via Heshbon (cf. Yadin 1955:347).

6–19. According to a number of scholars (Rost 1926:184–91; Flanagan 1972:176; Gunn 1978:65,70) the Aramean war described in these verses had nothing to do with David's conflict with the Ammonites. Thus they regard this section, vv. 6(or 6b)–19, as secondary in its present context, i.e., in its connection to 10:1–15(6a) + 11:1–2 + 12:26–31. I agree with Hertzberg, however, in regarding chap. 10 as a unit. The intervention of the Zobah coalition in the Israelite-Ammonite conflict is not implausible; on the contrary, it is consistent with what seems to have been an Ammonite policy of seeking alliances with Israel's rivals in order to neutralize the Israelite threat, and it is a strategically reasonable move on the part of Zobah in view of the growing conflict of interest in the region between the new Aramean and Israelite powers. See the discussion in the COMMENT.

6. *Beth-rehob.* The city-state is called Rehob in Num 13:21, where it is said to mark the northern boundary of Canaan, and in an Egyptian list of cities conquered by Thutmosis III (*ANET*³ 243). Judg 18:28, where we are told that it controlled the valley in which Dan was built, calls it Beth-rehob. It lay at the southern foot of Mount Hermon and the Anti-Lebanon range (Map 6); the capital city has not been identified. The fact that it is mentioned here before Zobah, the larger state that led the coalition, suggests that Beth-rehob was in some sense the ranking member of the group. This might be explained by reference to the patronymic of Hadadezer *son of Rehob,* the king of Zobah, which has been taken by Malamat and others to indicate that Zobah was ruled by a dynasty from Beth-rehob (see the NOTE on "Hadadezer son of Rehob" at 10:3). Thus Beth-rehob would have had the same relationship to Zobah at this time that Judah had to Israel during the reigns of David and Solomon.

*Zobah.* See the NOTE at 8:3.

*twenty thousands.* The number seems to be intended to refer to the combined infantry of Beth-rehob and Zobah, lending weight to Malamat's theory that the two were joined in a personal union by Hadadezer (see the NOTE on "Hadadezer son of Rehob" at 8:3). Twenty "thousands" (*'elep*) may have contained about two hundred men (cf. the first NOTE at 8:4).

*Maacah.* Along with Geshur (13:37,38) Maacah occupied the Golan, north of Gilead and south of Mount Hermon (Map 6). Maacah lay north of Geshur and thus closer to Beth-rehob and Zobah; and whereas Geshur allied itself to David's kingdom by marriage (2:9), Maacah joined the rival coalition. See, in general, Mazar [Maisler] 1961:21–22,26–27.

*the men of Tob.* "The land of Tob" (Judg 11:3,5; I Macc 5:13) was a small state in northern Transjordan, usually identified with modern eṭ-Ṭaiyibeh, ca. twelve miles southeast of the Sea of Galilee (cf. de Vaux 1978:820 and n. 143). The designation אִישׁ *ṭôb,* "the men of Tob," could be rendered "the *man* of Tob," i.e., the ruler of Tob, as rulers of lesser rank are referred to in Akkadian letters of the second millennium (Jirku 1950); but this usage seems confined to letters addressed to high-ranking kings in which a local ruler, who might elsewhere be called "king," seeks to avoid offense by refraining from calling himself or another local ruler "king."

*twelve thousands.* If our analysis of the textual data is correct (cf. the *Textual Note* on "the king of Maacah"), this number refers to the combined strength of Maacah and Tob, and we should probably think of Tob as subject to Maacah at this time (cf. Boling 1975:197).

8. *the gate.* Presumably of Rabbah, the Ammonite capital, modern Amman, and not Medeba (I Chron 19:7); see the last *Textual Note* at v. 6.

9. Evidently Joab's army marched to Rabbah by the most direct route via Jericho and Heshbon (see the NOTE on "Jericho," v. 5), a tactical blunder that left it with hostile troops on two fronts (Yadin 1955:349–50; cf. Stoebe 1977:243). The best road for a military expedition was that taken later by David, as explained in the NOTE at v. 17.

10. *Abishai.* See the NOTE at 2:18.

12. *the cities of our god.* Hebrew *'ārê 'ĕlōhênû,* reflected uniformly in the textual witnesses. Nevertheless, a number of emendations have been offered: (1) delete *'ry* as a corrupt dittograph of the last two letters of the preceding *b'd* (Schulz, Hertzberg); (2) read *'rwn 'lhynw,* "the *ark* of our god" (Klostermann, Budde, Smith, Nowack, Caird); (3) read *'ry 'lhynw,* "the *altars* of our god"; (4) read *'bdy 'lhynw,* "the *servants* of our god" (Ehrlich 1910:294–95). Giveon (1964) interprets the received text in light of the ancient associations of the cult of Yahweh with the geography of southern Transjordan. Egyptian toponymic lists from the fourteenth and twelfth centuries B.C. refer to a "land of the Shosu," the Egyptian name for the nomads of southern Palestine and Transjordan, called *yhw; (ya-h-wa),* in the vicinity of another "land of the Shosu" called *s'rr,* evidently biblical Seir (Giveon 1971, nos. 6a and 16a; for a discussion, see especially Herrmann 1967 and 1981:76,84). The Mesha stele (*KAI* 181:14–18) shows that Yahweh was still worshiped in the middle of the ninth century in the old Reubenite sanctuary of Nebo (Num 32:3,38), a dozen or so miles southwest of Rabbah. Thus Giveon understands "the cities of our god" to refer to cities with venerable associations with Yahweh in southern Transjordan. "The very ancient tradition of these [cities]," he reasons (1964:416), "made Joab's remarks meaningful for David's warriors in Ammon: by exhorting them to fight for the 'cities of our God' he was arousing the religious feelings of his followers, renewing a very old and sacred tradition."

15–19. Smith followed Winckler (1895–1900:vol. I:139) in regarding vv. 15–19a as secondary, pertaining to a different campaign (cf. Cook 1899/1900:157). The direct participation of David suggests that it may have taken place earlier, before his retirement from the battlefield during the Philistine wars (21:17; cf. Flanagan 1972:176 n. 18). We cannot assume, however, that all conflict with Philistia was over when the war with Zobah broke out or, in particular, that the battle referred to in 21:15–17 had already occurred. As indicated in the NOTE on vv. 6–19 above, I prefer to think of chap. 10 as a unit. Verses 15–19, then, describe a second phase of the same war (cf. Rost 1926:77).

16. *Hadadezer.* The king of Zobah and leader of the Aramean coalition. See 8:3.

*across the River.* As in the case of "the River" in 8:3, some scholars doubt that the Euphrates was originally intended here. Some think of the Jordan, others the Yarmuk (de Groot, van den Born, Stoebe 1977:245), still others the Leontes (Schulz following Jeremias 1930:524). But Arameans were firmly ensconced along the middle and upper

Euphrates and in northwest Mesopotamia by the time of David, and there is nothing implausible about the assumption that Hadadezer recruited help in Transeuphrates (cf. Malamat 1958:100 n. 19; Mazar [Maisler] 1962:102); this is true especially if Malamat's identification of the Aramean king mentioned in Assyrian records contemporary with David as conqueror of territories on the upper Euphrates with Hadadezer (see the NOTE at 8:3) is correct.

*Helam.* The exact location of Helam is unknown. According to Ezek 47:16 (LXX) it lay between Damascus and Hamath (Cornill 1886). If this is correct, it cannot have been far from Hadadezer's principal cities, Tebah and Berothai (8:8; cf. Map 6). But this seems too far north: Shobach's expedition is evidently an offensive thrust into or at least towards Israelite territory. The location of the known cities of I Macc 5:26, where Alema is probably identical to Helam, suggests a site in northern Transjordan. In I Macc 5:26, moreover, Alema is preceded by "in" *(en)* rather than "at" *(eis),* which precedes the other place-names, suggesting that "in Alema" is an attribute of the preceding city, Bosor (Goldstein 1976:301), the location of which is known (Buṣr el-Harîrī, forty to forty-five miles east of the Sea of Galilee on the Transjordanian plateau). It follows that Alema/Helam was a region, not a city, and this is consistent with the description of the battle in vv. 17–18 below, which describes a clash in open country rather than the siege of a city.

17. David intercepts the Arameans in Helam, thus avoiding the predicament of Joab earlier (v. 9). Yadin (1955:347–51) concludes that David must have crossed the Jordan at Adamah (Tell ed-Dâmiyeh) at the southern end of the Valley of Succoth (cf. 11:11) following the best road for a military expedition into Transjordan.

18. *Shobach.* In I Chron 19:16,18 the name, here *šôbak,* is given as *šôpak,* "Shopach." It may be non-Semitic.

19. "From this it is clear that Hadadezer's satellites kept their former political regime and merely exchanged Israelite for Aramean suzerainty." So Malamat (1963:3), who argues (p. 2) that "David took over Hadadezer's realm not only territorially, but also structurally. That is to say, the diverse political entities of Aram Zobah were absorbed by Israel with no change in the status which they previously held—a practice which seems to have been not uncommon in the international relations of the ancient Near East." See also Bright 1976:195.

## COMMENT

This account of David's Aramean war requires commentary of two kinds. It must be discussed first as a historical resource; then its place and literary function in the larger narrative must be assessed.

### *Historical Considerations*

As explained in the NOTE on vv. 1–2, David's words in v. 2 suggest that Nahash, the Ammonite king defeated by Saul in I Samuel 11, was able to maintain his nation's independence from Israel (despite Josephus, *Ant.* 6.80) and, furthermore, that he allied himself to David in his long struggle with the house of Saul. The specific act of "loyalty" *(ḥesed)* David refers to may have been Nahash's dispatch of a delegation led by his son Shobi to receive David at Mahanaim in his flight from Abishalom, which, therefore, must have taken place *before* the present events. But such a gesture presupposes a prior alliance and shows that the Ammonite king recognized a duty to David personally rather than as king of Israel. In all probability, then, the relationship between Nahash and David goes back to the days before David became king of Israel. In view of Ammon's vulnerability to a strong Israelite state, such a relationship was strategically desirable. That is, it was in Ammon's interest to neutralize the power of Saul and Ishbaal by supporting a rival. It is probably in order to renew this relationship with Nahash's successor, therefore, that David sends a delegation to Rabbah to greet the new king and "console him over his father" (v. 2). Times have changed, however. David now rules a united Israel and is himself a threat to Ammonite security. Thus it is consistent with Ammon's earlier policy to reject David's gesture and seek a new alliance to neutralize the power of Israel again.

When we are told in v. 6, therefore, that the Ammonites "hired" a coalition of states led by Hadadezer king of Zobah, we should not be surprised. There is not sufficient cause to deny a historical connection between David's Ammonite war and his battles with the Arameans described in vv. 6–19, which some scholars regard as secondary (see the NOTE). It is unlikely, however, that the Ammonites had the resources to hire such an army as outright mercenaries (cf. Stoebe 1977:244). Surely Hadadezer considered an alliance with Ammon to be in his own interest. Thus we should probably think of the Ammonite incident as the occasion for an inevitable conflict between two new and growing powers. As explained in the COMMENT on § XVII, Zobah had established ascendancy over a number of states north and east of Israel. Hadadezer's power was growing just as David's was. At stake in the clash between Zobah and Israel, then, was political supremacy in Palestine and most of southern and central Syria (cf. Malamat 1958:101; 1963:1).

According to our account, this war took place in three phases. The first battle, which evidently was fought outside the gate of Rabbah (cf. the NOTE at v. 8), is described in vv. 6–15. It was occasioned by the Aramean incursion into southern Transjordan in response to the summons of the Ammonites. It seems to have been only a qualified victory for Israel, Joab having let himself be maneuvered into fighting a battle on two fronts (v. 9) and thus having been too weakened by the battle, we must suppose, to follow up his victory with a siege of the Ammonite capital (cf. v. 14b). The second engagement, described in vv. 15–19, took place in the region of Helam in northern Gilead, where the Arameans, though reinforced by troops from Transeuphrates (v. 16), were isolated from the Ammonites. Israel, now led by David himself (cf. the NOTE on vv. 15–19), won a less equivocal victory, which David followed up with a ceremonial march to the Euphrates (8:3). The final and decisive battle, then, seems to have been that described in 8:3–8 (see the first NOTE at 8:3). It must have taken place in a region formally controlled by Zobah. The result was an Israelite conquest of Hadadezer's coalition and the incorporation of the territories subject to Zobah into David's empire. At this point David was able to concentrate his forces for a siege of Rabbah, described in 11:1 + 12:25–31, and the Ammonite capital finally fell sometime during the following year (cf. 11:1).

### *Literary Considerations*

In all probability this account of David's Aramean and Ammonite conquests (10:1–19 + 8:3–8 + 11:1 + 12:25–31) derives from contemporary (Davidic) annalistic sources (Rost 1926:79; Hertzberg; Whybray 1968:21; etc.). Whether it was drawn from a single report of consecutive events or compounded from two or more archival entries is debated; we have embraced the former position (see the NOTES at vv. 6–19 and 15–19). It remains to inquire into the circumstances of its present location. It does not seem to have had an original connection to any of the other source materials in the Samuel corpus. Flanagan (1972:176) has noted points of contact with the Mahanaim episode in 17:24–29, part of the story of Abishalom's revolt in chaps. 13–20. As we have seen, it is probable that 10:2 refers specifically to the events described in 17:27–29. But this is no more than we expect in documents of more or less contemporary origin, and there is nothing to suggest that the story of the Ammonite-Aramean wars had any original *literary* connection to the story of Abishalom's revolt.

Why, then, and by whom was this war chronicle inserted into the larger account of the reign of David? According to Rost (1926:200–1) and many who have followed him, it was taken from the archives by the author of Rost's Solomonic succession narrative in II Samuel [6] 9–20 + I Kings 1–2 to serve as a framework for his own account of David's adultery with Bathsheba and murder of Uriah in 11:2–12:25. As explained in the COMMENT on § XXI, however, it is unlikely that the David-Bathsheba-Uriah story belonged to the original succession narrative as conceived by Rost or to the Davidic literature that, as we have described the succession narrative, was taken up by the author of I Kings 1–2 in his defense of Solomon. As we shall see, II Sam 11:2–12:25 is a later composition with a prophetic point of view comparable to that of similar materials in I Samuel. If the account of the Ammonite and Aramean wars owes its place in our story to the author of 11:2–12:25, therefore, it must have been drawn from the archives by a prophetic writer who sought it out as a vehicle for his report of the Bathsheba-Uriah affair. According to the tradition he knew, this incident belonged in the context of David's siege of

Rabbah (contra Rost 1926:77), so he selected the appropriate archival entry as a framework. He affixed the whole (chaps. 10–12) to the account of Abishalom's rebellion (chaps. 13–20) as a kind of theological preface. It was his belief that the turmoil described in the latter document was a direct result of David's sin with Bathsheba. In this he may have been guilty of an anachronism, since, as we have noted, the siege of Rabbah seems to have occurred after Abishalom's rebellion. But he was living long after the events and, his interests being theological rather than chronological, he was either unaware of or indifferent to the contradiction involved in his use of his sources. His own composition begins in the following section.

# XXI. THE BATHSHEBA AFFAIR
# (11:1–27a)

**11** [1]When the time of year at which the kings had marched out came
around again, David sent off Joab with his servants and all Israel to
ravage the Ammonites and lay siege to Rabbah. But David himself
remained in Jerusalem.

### *David and Bathsheba*

[2]One evening David got up from his bed and went walking about
on the roof of the palace, and he saw a woman—a very beautiful
woman—bathing. [3][He] sent out inquiries about the woman. "Isn't
she Bathsheba daughter of Eliam," someone said, "the wife of Uriah
the Hittite?" [4]So David sent his agents to get her, and when she came
to him he lay with her. It was the time of her purification, and she
returned home [5]a pregnant woman. She sent someone to inform
David.
"I'm pregnant," she said.

### *Uriah's Furlough*

[6]David contacted Joab: "Send me Uriah the Hittite!" So Joab sent
Uriah to him, [7]and when [he] came to him, David asked if Joab was
well and if the army was well and if the war was going well.
"Yes, well," he replied.
[8]Then David told Uriah, "Go down to your house and wash your
feet!" But when Uriah took his leave of the king, he marched out with
the weapon-bearers [9]and slept at the king's door with his master's
servants; he did not go down to his house.
[10]It was reported to David that Uriah had not gone down to his
house. So David said to Uriah, "Didn't you just arrive from a journey?
Why didn't you go down to your house?"

11 "The ark and Israel and Judah are staying in Succoth," Uriah said
to [him], "and my lord Joab and my lord's servants are encamped on
the battlefield. Then how can *I* go to my house to eat and drink and
lie with my wife? By your very life, I won't do such a thing!"
12 "Stay here today, too," David told [him], "and tomorrow I'll let
you go." So Uriah stayed in Jerusalem that day, and on the next day
13 David invited him to eat and drink with him. He became drunk, but
in the evening he went out and slept in a bed with his master's servants;
he did not go down to his house.

### *The Death of Uriah*

14 In the morning David wrote a letter to Joab and sent it along with
Uriah. 15 In the letter he wrote: "Send Uriah where there is hard fighting,
then withdraw from him, so that he will be struck down and die." 16 So
Joab, as he kept watch over the city, stationed Uriah in a place where
he knew there were powerful men, 17 and when the men of the city came
out to fight with Joab, some of the army of the servants of David fell,
and Uriah the Hittite also died.
18 Joab sent someone to tell David all the details of the battle. 19 He
instructed the messenger as follows: "When you finish relating all the
details of the battle to the king, 20 if he becomes angry 21 say, 'Also your
servant Uriah the Hittite is dead.' "
22 When Joab's messenger came to the king in Jerusalem, he reported
to David everything Joab had sent him [to say]. 23 "The men overpow-
ered us," [he] said to David. "They marched out against us in the field,
and when we drove them back to the entrance to the gate, 24 the arrows
rained heavily on your servants from the wall, and some eighteen of the
king's servants died."
When the messenger finished telling the king all the details of the
battle, David was furious with Joab. "Why did you go close to the city
to fight?" he asked the messenger. "Didn't you know you would be
assailed from the wall? Who slew Abimelech son of Jerubbaal? Didn't
a woman drop an upper millstone on him from the wall when he died
at Thebez? Why did you go close to the wall?"
"Also," said Joab's messenger to the king, "your servant Uriah the
Hittite is dead."
25 Then David said to the messenger, "This is what you are to say to
Joab: 'Don't worry about this, for sometimes the sword devours one

way, sometimes another. Intensify your assault on the city and raze it!' "

## *David's Marriage to Bathsheba*

26When Uriah's wife heard that her husband was dead, she mourned for her lord. 27aThen when the period of grief had passed, David had her brought to his house, where she became his wife and bore him a son.

## *TEXTUAL NOTES*

**11** 1. *the kings* So MT$^{MSS}$, LXX, OL, Targ., Vulg., and I Chron 20:1; cf. Syr. MT has "the messengers." We follow the versions in assuming that the reference is to the marching out *(ṣ't!)* of "the kings" (*hmlkym;* cf. I Chron 19:2) in 10:2. See also the NOTE.

*to ravage the Ammonites* Omitted by Syr.

2. *One evening* Reading *wyhy l'rb* on the basis of LXX$^{BAMN}$ *kai egeneto pros hesperan.* MT, LXX$^{L}$, OL, Syr., etc., have *wyhy l't 'rb* under the influence of *l't ṣ't hml(')kym* in v. 1.

*and he saw a woman . . . bathing* To this clause most witnesses add *m'l hgg,* "from the roof," but in varying positions (MT: "and he saw a woman bathing from the roof"; LXX$^{L}$: "and he saw from the roof a woman bathing"), a sign of its secondary origin. Evidently Syr., which omits the phrase, represents the primitive situation.

3. *Bathsheba* That is, *bat-šeba'* (so MT, Syr.; cf. LXX$^{A}$). LXX$^{BN}$ (cf. LXX$^{LM}$) have *bērsabee,* as if reflecting *bĕ'ēr-šeba',* "Beersheba" (!). In I Chron 3:5 (MT) she is called *bat-šûa',* "Bathshua."

*Eliam* So MT: *'ĕlî'ām,* for which LXX$^{BAMN}$ have *eliab* = *'ĕlî'āb,* "Eliab," LXX$^{L}$ *ēla* = *'ēlā',* "Ela," or *'ēlâ,* "Elah," and Syr. *'ḥyn'm* = *'ăḥînō'am,* "Ahinoam." I Chron 3:5 has *'ammî'ēl,* "Ammiel."

*Uriah the Hittite* Glossed in 4QSam$^{a}$ as *[n]wś' kly yw'b,* "Joab's weapon-bearer," a reading also known to Josephus (*Ant.* 7.131). Cf. v. 9.

4. *and when she came to him* So MT and 4QSam$^{a}$: *wtbw' 'lyw.* LXX *kai eisēlthen pros autēn* reflects *wyb' 'lyh,* "and he went in to her" (cf. v. 24).

*It was the time of her purification* Reading *why' mtqdšt,* lit. "and she was purifying herself" (see the NOTE) with 4QSam$^{a}$. MT (cf. LXX, OL) adds *mṭm'th,* "from her uncleanness," an explicating expansion.

*and she returned* Reading *wtšb* with MT and LXX$^{BAMN}$ *(kai apestrepsen).* 4QSam$^{a}$ *(wtb[w']),* LXX$^{L}$ *(kai apēlthen),* and OL$^{MS}$ *(et intravit)* point to *wtb',* "and she came," which Ulrich (1980:128) prefers. The two verbs stand together in the conflate text of Syr.

5. *a pregnant woman* That is, *wattahar hā'iššâ*, lit. "(and) the woman was pregnant."

*"I'm pregnant"* MT (cf. LXX$^{L}$, OL): *hrh 'nky*. 4QSam$^{a}$ (cf. LXX$^{BAMN}$): *'nwky hrh*.

6. *Joab* At this point LXX$^{BAMN}$ insert *legōn* = *l'mr*, "saying," and LXX$^{L}$ inserts *kai eipen* = *wy'mr*, "and said" (cf. Syr.). Space requirements indicate that 4QSam$^{a}$ shared one of these longer readings.

*Send* MT: *šelaḥ*. 4QSam$^{a}$: *šlḥh* = *šilḥâ* (GK$^{2}$ §48i).

*to him* So LXX$^{L}$, OL, and probably 4QSam$^{a}$, which, though not extant at this point, has insufficient space for the longer reading of MT, LXX$^{BAMN}$, "to *David*." Syr. is doubly long: ". . . the Hittite to David."

7. *and . . . came* MT *wyb'*, of which LXX$^{BMN}$ combine two translations, *kai paraginetai* and *kai eisēlthen* (omitted by LXX$^{AL}$, OL).

*to him* So MT, LXX$^{BAMN}$, Targ. Syr., LXX$^{L}$, OL, Vulg., and MT$^{MSS}$: "to *David*."

*asked* LXX$^{LN}$, Targ.$^{MSS}$ add "him." Syr. adds "David."

*"Yes, well," he replied* That is, *wy'mr lšlwm*, as reflected by LXX$^{L}$ *kai eipen hygiainei* (cf. OL and Josephus, *Ant.* 7.132). This was lost in MT (cf. LXX$^{BAMN}$) before *wy'mr* (homoioarkton) at the beginning of the next verse, and 4QSam$^{a}$ *([hmlḥm]h w[y'mr])* seems to share this shorter, haplographic reading (but cf. Ulrich 1978:187).

8. *took his leave of the king* Lit. "went out from the presence of the king"; so LXX$^{L}$. MT, LXX$^{BAMN}$, Syr.: "went out from the *house* of the king" (in anticipation of v. 9).

*he marched out with the weapon-bearers* MT has *wtṣ' 'ḥryw mś't hmlk*, "and there went out after him a portion from the king," *mś't* being, as Budde says, "a characteristic gift for a guest or dignitary, also probably a dish from the king's table" (cf. Gen 43:34). LXX$^{BAN}$ follow MT, and LXX$^{LM}$, OL, though they point to a different reading, have received enough recensional correction towards MT to render them almost unintelligible. LXX$^{L}$ *kai exēlthen opisō autou (?) ton parestēkoton tō basilei* might mean "and he went out after those who stand by his (?) king," although it seems likely that *autou* is recensional and that we should retroject *wyṣ' 'ḥry hnṣbym lmlk*, "and he marched out after those who guard the king." 4QSam$^{a}$ at this point reads [ ] *'wryh b*[ ], exhibiting confusion between *'ḥry(hw)*, "after (him)," and *'wryh*, "Uriah." Josephus' comment at this point (*Ant.* 7.132) that Uriah slept "with the other weapon-bearers," if it is not simply derived from "with his lord's servants" in v. 9 (as seems unlikely), may point to a variation on LXX *bnṣbym lmlk* from which the reading of MT, *mś't hmlk*, is more easily derived, viz. *bnś'y hklym*, "with the weapon-bearers." I should reconstruct 4QSam$^{a}$ here to read [*wyṣ'*] *'wryh b*[*nś'y hlkym*], "but Uriah marched out with the weapon-bearers." Since *'wryh* is less likely to be original than *'ḥry(w)*, we must correct this on the basis of our analysis of LXX above to *wyṣ' 'ḥry nś'y hklym*. Of our three readings—(1) *wtṣ' 'ḥryw mś't hmlk* (MT), (2) *wyṣ' 'ḥry hnṣbym lmlk* (LXX), and (3) *wyṣ' 'ḥry nś'y hklym*—I regard the last as that from which the others are most likely to have been derived and as providing the most satisfactory sense.

9. *and slept* Or rather, "and *Uriah* slept"; so MT and all versions.

*at the king's door* So LXX$^{BMN}$, Syr. MT, LXX$^{AL}$: "at the door of *the house of* the king."

*with his master's servants* So LXX$^{BAMN}$. MT, LXX$^{L}$, OL, Syr.: "with *all* his master's servants."

10. *It was reported* Reading *wayyuggad* with 4QSam[a] *(wygd)* against MT (cf. LXX) *wayyaggîdû*, "They reported."

*to David* So MT, $LXX^{BAMN}$. $LXX^{L}$ has "to *King* David," and space considerations suggest that 4QSam[a] shared the longer reading.

*that* MT: *l'mr* (cf. $LXX^{L}$, OL). $LXX^{BAMN}$ = *l'mr ky*. OG = *ky*.

*Why* So MT, $LXX^{BAMN}$, Syr. $LXX^{L}$, $MT^{MSS}$: "*And* why."

11. *The ark* So MT (cf. $LXX^{B}$, Targ.): *h'rwn*. $LXX^{N}$ = *hlw' h'rwn*, "Aren't the ark . . . ?" $LXX^{A}$ = *'m h'rwn*, "If the ark. . . ." $LXX^{L}$ = *'m 'rwn h'lhym*, "If the holy ark. . . ." OL = *'rwn yhwh*, "Yahweh's ark. . . ." Syr. = *'rwn bryt yhwh*, "The ark of Yahweh's covenant. . . ."

*how* So $LXX^{L}$: *pōs* = *'yk*. In MT *'yk* was lost before *'ny*. It was restored marginally but found its way into the text in the wrong place, before *wḥy npšk*, "By your very life," as now reflected by $LXX^{BAMN}$ *pōs zē hē psychē sou* = *'yk wḥy npšk*; subsequently the misplaced *'yk* became *ḥyk*, "By your life," by accommodation to what follows (so now MT).

*By your very life* That is, *wḥy npšk*. See the preceding *Textual Note*.

*I won't do such a thing!* That is, *'m ''śh 't hdbr hzh*; so MT (cf. LXX). Syr. *l' 'bd 'n' 'yk hdh* probably reflects *'m ''śh kzh*, "I won't act that way!"

12–13. *and on the next day David invited him* Reading *wmmḥrt qr' lw dwd* with $LXX^{L}$ and Syr. MT, $LXX^{BAMN}$ associate "and on the next day" with the foregoing. We follow Wellhausen, Driver, etc., and JB, NEB, and NJV. In favor of MT's arrangement are Smith, etc. (cf. Simon 1967:215), and RSV. See the NOTE on "today . . . tomorrow," v. 12.

13. *He became drunk* Reading *wayyiškār* on the basis of $LXX^{L}$ *kai emethysthē* and Syr. *wrwy*. MT *(wayšakkĕrēhû)*, $LXX^{BAMN}$ *(kai emethysen auton)*, and $Syr.^{MS}$ *(w'rwy)*: "He (David) got him (Uriah) drunk."

*and slept in a bed* $LXX^{L}$ has *kai ekoimēthē en tē koitē ho oureias*. Omitting the explicit subject, "Uriah," with all other witnesses, we can reconstruct *wyškb bmškb*, which is reflected also by one MS of OL and by Syr. **wdmk bmkmk*, which, however, has become *wdmk* by inner-Syriac haplography. MT (cf. $LXX^{BAMN}$) has *lškb bmškbw*, "to sleep in his bed."

15. *Send* $LXX^{BAMN}$ *eisagage* reflects *hby'*, of which MT *hbw* is a remnant, *'alep* having been lost before the following *'t*. $LXX^{L}$ (cf. OL) *parados* suggests *tn*, "Put" (cf. OL, Vulg. *pōn*[*it*]*e)*, anticipating v. 16.

*where there is hard fighting* Reading *'l hmlḥmh hḥzqh*, lit. "into the hard fighting," on the basis of $LXX^{L}$ *eis ton polemon ton krataion*. $LXX^{BAMN}$ *ex enantias tou polemou tou krataiou* reflects *lqr't hmlḥmh hḥzqh*, "*towards* the hard fighting." MT has conflate prepositions: *'l mwl pny hmlḥmh hḥzqh*, "into the front *('l mwl* or *'l pny)* of the hard fighting." Syr. *br'š ḥyl' dqrb* = *br'š ṣb' hmlḥmh* (?), "at the head of the battle force" (cf. Num 31:14).

*then withdraw . . . struck down* Omitted by $OL^{MSS}$.

16. *So Joab, as he kept watch* Reading *wyhy bšwr yw'b* with 4QSam[a] *(w*[*y*]*hy bšwr* [*yw'b*]*)*. MT (cf. $LXX^{BAN}$) substitutes a more common verb: *wyhy bšmwr yw'b*. $LXX^{LM}$ *perikathēsthai*, OL *obsideret/obsidit*, and Syr. *šr'* reflect *ṣwr* for *šwr*, thus "So Joab, as he *besieged*. . . ." Contrast Ulrich 1978:137–38.

*over* Reading *'l* with LXX *epi*, Syr. *'l*, etc. MT has *'l* for *'l* as frequently in Samuel.

*where he knew* So MT (cf. LXX$^{BAMN}$). LXX$^{L}$ *ton ponounta* seems to reflect *ḥwlh*, "weak"—thus, ". . . a weak place, because there were," etc. (cf. OL *in locum pessimum*).

17. *of the servants of David* So MT (cf. LXX$^{BAN}$): *m'bdy dwd*. LXX$^{LM}$, OL$^{MS}$ reflect *kdbr(y) dwd*, "according to the instructions of David."

*and . . . died* Reading *wymt* with MT (cf. LXX$^{ALN}$). LXX$^{B}$ reflects *wymtw*—thus, ". . . fell and died, and also Uriah," etc.

18. *David* So MT, LXX$^{LMN}$. LXX$^{A}$: "the king." LXX$^{B}$: "King David."

*of the battle* LXX$^{BM}$ add *lalēsai pros ton basilea* = *ldbr 'l hmlk* here after *pantas tous logous tou polemou* = *'t kl dbry hmlḥmh*. This follows the same sequence in the next verse, and we may suppose that its presence here is residual of a haplographic loss, subsequently repaired, by which all but the end of v. 19 fell out.

19. *He* So MT, LXX$^{BAMN}$. LXX$^{L}$, Syr.: "Joab."

20. *if he becomes angry* That is, *whyh 'm t'lh ḥmtw*, lit. "if his anger arises"; cf. LXX$^{L}$. MT: "if *the king* becomes angry."

*angry* At this point in MT (vv. 20–21) we find *w'mr lk*, "and says to you," followed by the entire speech of David that, in our reconstructed text, stands in v. 24. But it is unreasonable to suppose that Joab would anticipate David's remonstrance in every detail. The speech was lost from its original location by haplography, as explained in the second *Textual Note* at v. 24, and because the accident in v. 24 left not even a vestigial reference to David's questioning, a later scribe, seeking to repair the damage by restoring the lost words from another MS, found the present context with Joab's anticipatory remarks to be the most congenial location for them. A defense of MT in vv. 20–24 may be found in Barthélemy 1980:13–15; cf. Simon 1967:218–20.

21. *say* Syr. *'nhw d'mr lk hlyn 'mr lh* = *(whyh) 'm y'mr lk 'lh 'mr lw*, "(and) if he says these things to you, say to him."

In LXX$^{L}$ there follows the entire text of the messenger's speech in vv. 23–24 below. This is contrary to the sense of the passage, however, because Joab at this point is telling the messenger what to say if David becomes angry *after* hearing "all the details of the battle" (cf. v. 19), and it is the messenger's speech that will convey these details. The only detail to be held back is the one that Joab knows will mollify David.

*Also* So MT (cf. LXX$^{L}$): *gm*. LXX$^{BAMN}$ *kai ge* = *wgm*, "*And* also." See the *Textual Note* on "Also," v. 24.

22. *When Joab's messenger . . . Jerusalem* We read *wyb' ml'k yw'b 'l hmlk yrwšlm* on the basis of LXX$^{L}$ *kai paregeneto ho angelos iōab pros ton basilea eis ierousalēm*. LXX$^{BAMN}$ have *kai eporeuthē ho angelos iōab pros ton basilea eis ierousalēm kai parageneto* = *wylk ml'k yw'b 'l hmlk byrwšlm wyb'*, "So Joab's messenger went to the king in Jerusalem, and when he arrived. . . ." MT originally shared the text of LXX$^{BAMN}$ but suffered damage by haplography, a scribe's eye skipping from *yw'b* to *wyb'*. Thus MT reads *wylk hml'k wyb'*, "So the messenger went, and when he arrived. . . ." Cf. Syr., in which *yw'b 'l hmlk byrwšlm* has been removed in approximation to MT but final *wyb'* is lacking.

*everything Joab had sent him [to say]* MT: *'t kl 'šr šlḥw yw'b*. This was part of the material lost from LXX by the long haplography described in the *Textual Note* that follows, and it remains absent from LXX$^{L}$, though in LXX$^{BAMN}$ it has been restored in a slightly different form, viz. *panta hosa apēngeilen* (LXX$^{MSS}$ [cf. OL] *synetaxen*) *autō iōab* = *'t kl 'šr hgyd (ṣwh) lw yw'b*, "everything Joab had *told (commanded)* him."

There follows in LXX a long plus (v. 22+), which, as the following *Textual Note* explains, preserves material lost by haplography in MT.

23–24. Critics since Thenius have recognized that MT is defective at this point and that the long plus of LXX (22+) preserves original material. What seems to have gone unnoticed, however, is that LXX has also suffered a loss, a fact obscured by the recensional insertion of materials from MT, vv. 23 and 24. Even together MT and LXX do not now contain the full reading, but there is enough to permit a restoration that is uncertain only in a few details. We read: [23]*wy'mr hml'k 'l dwd ky gbrw 'lynw h'nšym wyṣ'w 'lynw hśdh wnhlmm 'd ptḥ hš'r* [24]*wykbd 't hḥṣym 'l 'bdyk m'l hḥwmh wymwtw m'bdy hmlk kšmnh 'śr 'yš wykl hml'k ldbr 'l hmlk 't dbry hmlḥmh wyḥr dwd 'l yw'b wy'mr 'l hml'k lmh ngštm 'l h'yr lhlḥm hlw' yd'tm ky tkw mn hḥwmh my hkh 't 'bymlk bn yrwb'l hlw' 'šh hšlykh 'lyw plḥ rkb mn hḥwmh wymt btbṣ lmh ngštm 'l hḥwmh wy'mr ml'k yw'b 'l hmlk gm 'bdk 'wryh hḥty mt* (for the details of specific readings, see the *Textual Notes* that follow). The present condition of MT can be explained on the basis of haplography from the first *hmlk* in v. 24 to the fourth. Thus MT preserves v. 23 almost intact and reads in v. 24, *wyr'w hmwr'ym 'l 'bdk m'l hḥwmh wymwtw m'bdy hmlk wgm 'bdk 'wryh hḥty mt,* "The archers shot at your servants from the wall and some of the king's servants died. And your servant Uriah the Hittite is dead, too." In LXX the haplography involved *'t kl* in the last phrase of v. 22 (see the preceding *Textual Note*) and *'t kl* in v. 24. The resulting text included nothing of v. 23 or v. 24 before *'t kl,* and it preserved everything in v. 24 after *'t kl;* it contained, in other words, vv. 22+ and 24b. In the present text of LXX, however, vv. 23 and 24 have been inserted by way of recensional adjustment towards MT. Because of the defective character of MT itself, the insertion was placed before *wgm 'bdk 'wryh hḥty mt* to approximate the text of MT. The result is an inversion of the original order of the speeches: David becomes angry in v. 22 *before* the messenger has reported the bad news in vv. 23–24a!

23. *They marched out* So MT, LXX$^{BAMN}$, and LXX$^{L}$ (v. 21+). LXX$^{L}$ (v. 23): "*The men* marched out."

*against us* We read *'lynw* with LXX$^{BLMN}$, Syr., Targ. MT, LXX$^{A}$, Targ.$^{MSS}$ have *'lynw.*

*and when we drove them back* Reading *wnhlmm* on the basis of LXX$^{L}$ *kai synēlasamen autous,* "and we drove them back," Syr. *w'ttsymn,* "and we set upon them," and Targ. *whwyn' trdyn lhwn,* "and we were expelling them." MT has *wnhyh 'lyhm,* "and we were against them" (?).

*the gate* So MT, LXX$^{BAMN}$. Syr. and Vulg. have "the city." LXX$^{L}$ in v. 21 has "the city" and is divided here between *tes poleōs,* "the city" ($c_2e_2$) and *tou pylōnos,* "the gate" (bo). To this confusion cf. 10:8.

24. *the arrows rained heavily* Reading *wykbd 't hḥṣym,* lit. "and it was heavy with arrows" (cf. GK$^{2}$ §121ab), on the basis of LXX$^{L}$ *kai katebarynthē ta belē* (cf. OL *et mittebantur graviter sagittae*). MT *(qĕrê),* LXX$^{BAMN}$, and Targ. have *wyrw hmwrym,* "and the archers shot." Syr., omitting "on your servants," has *wšdw hnwn dqymyn,* which seems to reflect *wyrw hrmym,* understood as "and those who were up high *(hārāmîm)* shot," but better "the bowmen *(hārōmîm)* shot."

*some eighteen* That is, *kšmnh 'śr 'yš.* This was lost from MT at the beginning of the haplography described above in the *Textual Note* on vv. 23–24. It is preserved by LXX$^{L}$ (cf. OL) as *hōsei andres deka kai oktō.*

*When the messenger had finished telling the king* Cf. v. 19. We read *wtkl hml'k ldbr 'l hmlk* conjecturally. This part of the text has been lost in all witnesses, but this or something very close to it is required.

*all the details of the battle* This and what follows are preserved by LXX in v. 22+. See the *Textual Note* on vv. 23–24.

*David was furious with* That is, *wyḥr dwd 'l.* So LXX: *kai ethymōthē daueid* (so $LXX^{BAMN}$; $LXX^{L}$ [cf. OL], *orgē daueid* = *'p dwd*—thus, "David's anger [burned at]") *epi* (so $LXX^{L}$; $LXX^{BAMN}$, *pros* = *'l*).

*you would be assailed* Reading *tkw (tukkû)* with LXX *plēgēsesthe.* MT (v. 20) has *yrw,* "they would shoot," to which $LXX^{BAMN}$ in v. 20 have been conformed.

*Jerubbaal* Reading *yrwb'l* with $LXX^{LMN}$ *ierobaal,* Syr. *ndwb'l* [**yrwb'l*] (v. 21; cf. Englert 1949:16). $LXX^{BA}$ have *ieroboam,* "Jeroboam," as in I Sam 12:11, to which they add in v. 21 *huiou nēr,* "son of Ner" (!), as if pointing to a text that had "Abiner" for "Abimelech." MT (v. 21) has *yrwbšt,* another example of the substitution of *bōšet,* "shame," for *ba'al,* understood as "Baal" (see the NOTE on "Ishbaal" at 2:8). Here, however, the received vocalization is *yĕrûbešet* (cf. MT *yōšēb baššebet* in 23:8).

*Also* In $LXX^{BAMN}$ *gm (kai)* has become *wgm,* "*And* also" *(kai ge),* the copula having arisen after the haplography that afflicted MT (and thus by recensional adjustment LXX) joined this statement to the messenger's battle report (". . . some eighteen of the king's servants died, and also your servant Uriah," etc.). The earlier situation is preserved by $LXX^{L}$: *kai* = *gm;* cf. v. 21, where $LXX^{BAMN}$ reflect *wgm* while MT and $LXX^{L}$ preserve *gm.*

25. *Don't worry about this* MT: *'l yr' b'ynyk 't hdbr hzh* (so $LXX^{BAMN}$); cf. $GK^{2}$ §117l. For *'t,* $LXX^{L}$ reflects *'l* (so $MT^{MS}$: *'l* = *'l*).

*and raze it* MT (cf. $LXX^{BA}$) adds *weḥazzĕqēhû,* which we omit with $LXX^{LMN}$. The verb as it stands in MT must be taken as instructions to the messenger, "And encourage him [viz. Joab]!" Syr. *wsḥwpyh,* "and overthrow it," is impossible even if the feminine suffix is substituted *(ḥzqh),* for *ḥzq* in *Pi'el* does not mean "overpower" and in *Qal* does not take a direct object (*pace* Thenius).

26. *Uriah's wife* So MT, LXX. Syr.: "the wife of Uriah *the Hittite*" (cf. v. 6).

*her husband . . . her lord* So MT: *'yšh . . . b'lh.* In LXX the first of these synonyms seems to have been leveled through, in Syr. the second. Before "her husband" MT and LXX specify "Uriah"; omit with Syr.

27. *had her brought* MT *wyšlḥ . . . wy'sph,* lit. "sent and gathered her." $LXX^{L}$ = *wyšlḥ . . . wyqḥ 't btšb',* "sent and took Bathsheba."

## NOTES

**11** 1. A literal translation of the opening clause is "And it was at the return of the year *(litšûbat haššanâ),* at the time of the marching out of the kings. . . ." This is usually understood to mean "In the spring of the year, the time when kings go forth to battle . . ." (RSV), an interpretation that goes back at least to Josephus (*Ant.* 7.129). "The return of the year," wherever it occurs, is taken to mean springtime on the basis of the present passage, since military campaigning began after the onset of the dry season. But the reference here is not to the marching out of kings in general but of some specific kings (*hammĕlākîm,* "*the* kings"). This can only refer to the coalition of Aramean kings summoned by the Ammonites in 10:6 (cf. I Chron 19:9, where they are also called "the kings"). Thus "the return of the year" does not refer to the spring but rather to the coming around again of the time of year at which the Aramean kings marched to the aid of the Ammonites. That is, the siege of Ammon began at a time one year after the beginning of the clash described in 10:8ff. This probably was, as a matter of fact, spring, the time for war and love; but our text does not say so.

We follow Rost (1926:80) and others in regarding this verse as part of the framework in which the story of David and Bathsheba (11:2–12:24) has been inserted. Some scholars who accept the framework theory, however, have emphasized the importance for the David-Bathsheba story of the contrast between the army's departure and David's staying behind (Gunn 1978:70, following Ridout 1971:152–53; cf. Veijola 1979:240); thus they conclude that 11:1 is an original part of the story, not the framework. It seems to me that their premise is correct but not their conclusion. The contrast in 11:1 is indeed important for the subsequent story, but it does not follow that 11:1 comes from the hand of the narrator of 11:2ff. David's decision not to accompany the army is not disgraceful in itself: It may have been made in the spirit of 21:15–17 or for other reasons. It was the author of 11:2ff. who saw the ironic potential in the decision and exploited it. After all, it is not for his failure to accompany the army to war that the king is going to be condemned; it is for what he does at home while the troops are in the field.

*Rabbah.* The Ammonite capital, modern Amman.

2. *from his bed.* It is evening, not night. David must have taken a long afternoon nap.

*the roof of the palace.* David's bed was probably on the roof (cf. I Sam 9:25), which was breezy and cool, a good place for an evening walk.

3. *Bathsheba daughter of Eliam.* It is unusual for a woman's patronymic to be given, especially when she is identified by her husband's name ("the wife of Uriah the Hittite"). This suggests that the identity of Bathsheba's father was significant, although I cannot discover why. According to 23:34 Ahithophel had a son named Eliam, who, like Uriah (23:39), was one of David's warriors. It is taken for granted that this Eliam was Bathsheba's father in the Talmud (Sanhedrin 69b,101a), but we cannot be sure. Eliam is called Ammiel, a variant of the same name, in I Chron 3:5, and the name of the father of Machir of Lo-debar (9:4; 17:27) was Ammiel. According to I Chron 26:5, one of the sons of Obed-edom (6:10) was called Ammiel. But again there is no reason to identify either of these Ammiels with Bathsheba's father.

*Uriah the Hittite.* Uriah was one of David's elite warriors, the Thirty (13:39). It does not follow from his designation as "the Hittite" that he was a mercenary or even a foreigner. The fact that he has a good Yahwistic name (*'ûrîyâ,* "Yahweh is my light") suggests that he was born in Israel. The Hittites were an Anatolian people who established a considerable empire in Syria in the second millennium B.C. After the collapse of the empire at the end of the Late Bronze Age (ca. 1200 B.C.), Hittite civilization survived in a number of small states in northern Syria. The Neo-Hittite states, as they are called, which remained in the time of David, were predominantly Semitic, especially Aramean, in population. It must have been from one of them that Uriah's family came to Israel, and thus, though probably born in Israel and ethnically Aramean, he is called "the Hittite."

4. *It was the time of her purification.* That is, *wĕhî mitqaddešet,* lit. "And she was purifying herself," a circumstantial clause describing Bathsheba's condition at the time of her intercourse with David (Driver; GK[2] §141e). Thus it does not mean "Then she purified herself (viz. from intercourse [Lev 15:18])," as supposed by Keil. As pointed out in the *Textual Note,* many witnesses add *miṭṭum'ātāh,* "from her uncleanness," an explicating expansion based on an interpretation of the text that was probably correct. Bathsheba was ritually cleansing herself after involvement in some kind of uncleanness, in this context almost certainly the ritual impurity of menstruation (Lev 15:19–24). This does not mean, as Guttmann (1964:7) supposes, that David defiled himself by intercourse with a menstruous woman (cf. Lev 15:24) in violation of purity laws (Lev 18:19). The point of the circumstantial clause is rather that Bathsheba's menstrual period was recently over—that is, that the seven days of ritual impurity prescribed in Lev 15:19 were just past—and that therefore (1) her intercourse with David took place at a propitious time for conception (so already Isaac Abrabanel and, among moderns, Nowack, Driver, Smith, Segal, and Hertzberg; cf. the Talmudic tractate Niddah 31b), ovulation ordinarily taking place from ten to fourteen days after the onset of menstruation, and (2) Uriah could not have been the father of the child (Simon 1967:213, citing the eleventh-century French exegete Joseph Kara). Pertinent to the first point is the testimony of pre-Islamic tribesmen cited by Robertson Smith (1966[1907]:132–33 n. 1) that if pregnancy is desired the optimal time for intercourse with a woman is "when she is cleansed from her impurity."

8. *wash your feet.* Often taken to mean no more than "refresh yourself" (Budde, Smith, etc.). But in view of other references to "the feet" (= the genitals) in sexual contexts (Ruth 3:4,7; cf. Ezek 16:25) Isaac Abrabanel was probably right to take this expression as a euphemism for sexual intercourse (Simon 1967:214; so Hertzberg).

10. *a journey.* For *derek,* "way, road, journey," in reference to a military expedition (Judg 4:9; etc.), see the remarks of Greenberg cited by Simon 1967:214 n. 2. He compares the same usage of Akkadian *ḫarrānu* (*AHw,* s.v. *ḫarrānu* 6).

11. To David's frustration the pious soldier insists on maintaining the ritual purity of the battle camp (Deut 23:10–15 [23:9–14]) even on furlough. The warrior consecrated at arms (Josh 3:5) was supposed to maintain a regimen of sexual abstinence, a rule David himself once followed—or pretended to follow—scrupulously (I Sam 20:6).

*The ark.* The contrast to the beginning of chap. 7 is pointed. There (7:1) it was David who thought it wrong to reside in a comfortable house while Yahweh's ark resided "amid curtains." Uriah's oath is almost a paraphrase of the oath attributed to David by the tradition reflected in Ps 132:3–5 (see the NOTE on 7:1 and the COMMENT on § XIII):

I will not enter the shelter of my house,
I will not lie on the mattress of my bed,
I will not let my eyes have sleep,
    or my eyelids slumber,
until I find a place for Yahweh,
    a camping place for Jacob's Bull!

Now, however, David seems perfectly content to remain in his house, and he must be reminded by one of his own soldiers—one he has wronged—that it is not right to lie in one's bed when the ark is in the field. The implications of this irony are explored in the COMMENT on § XXII.

*Succoth.* Interpreting *sukkôt* as a proper noun, as suggested by Yadin [Sukenik] (1955). The rendering "booths" (RSV) is open to a number of objections. The ark was housed in a tent (6:17), not a booth, but "tents" (AV, JB) is an indefensible translation here. Nor did soldiers camp in booths. It is unreasonable, moreover, to think of the commander and the professional soldiers ("Joab and my lord's servants") camping on the bare ground alongside booths used by the rest of the army ("Israel and Judah"). Surely, then, Yadin is correct in reading "Succoth" here (so NJV, NEB [note]) and in I Kings 20:12,16. As he explains (pp. 344–47), the Valley of Succoth, now called the Ghor, had great strategic value to David as a forward base of operations in his campaigns to the east and north. It had short lines of communication to Jerusalem, Rabbah, and Damascus; it had topographical protection from the surrounding rivers, wadis, and mountains; and it was rich in natural resources. The site of the city of Succoth is thought by many to be Tell Deir 'Allā, ca. twenty-five miles northwest of Amman and about a mile north of the Jabbok (Map 6); cf. Shebiit 38d.

*encamped on the battlefield.* For *haśśādeh,* "the field (of battle)," see Yadin [Sukenik] 1955:342 n. 3. While the bulk of the army is stationed in readiness at the forward base of Succoth, the commander and professional soldiers are dug in against Rabbah, i.e., at the front. It is there that Uriah, as one of the Thirty (23:39), thinks he, too, should be.

12. *today . . . tomorrow.* Does David keep this promise? He says he will let Uriah go on the next day but invites him to dinner the next day, and Uriah spends that night in Jerusalem (v. 13), not departing until morning. (Note that adoption of the arrangement of the received Hebrew text, which associates "and on the next day," v. 12, with what it follows rather than what it precedes [the *Textual Note* at vv. 12–13], does not alter this sequence of events or otherwise solve the problem.) The promise is kept only if we assume that David is here speaking to Uriah in the evening and that days are being reckoned from sunset to sunset ("the evening and the morning," Gen 1:5; etc.). Thus Uriah spends the evening of the interview of v. 12 and the next morning in Jerusalem ("today"), goes to the banquet and sleeps with the servants on the evening of the next day (vv. 12–13), and departs in the morning (v. 14) of that same day ("tomorrow").

14–15. Uriah is the carrier of his own death warrant. The normal procedure would be for a messenger to carry the message and read or recite it to Joab, but for obvious reasons this will not do in this situation. David writes the letter personally and Joab reads it to himself—both evidently are literate. It is entirely consistent with poor Uriah's character that he can be relied upon not to look at the letter or, if he cannot read (Ackroyd), have it read to him. On the motif, widespread in world literature, of the messenger carrying his own death warrant, see Gunkel 1921:132. Perhaps the most interesting illustration is found in the *Iliad* (6.168–90), where the Argive king Proteus, suspecting Bellerephon of adultery with the queen, arranges for the young man's death by sending him to Lycia with a coded message asking the Lycian king, Proteus' father-in-law, to put him to death.

16–17. Joab does not follow instructions exactly (Simon 1967:216–17), but he gets the job done.

18–21. This time the message is sent in the usual way (cf. the NOTE on vv. 14–15 above). It is phrased in such a way as to conceal from the messenger, and anyone overhearing his report to David, its real purpose.

24. *Abimelech son of Jerubbaal.* David cites a bit of military history to illustrate the danger of fighting too close to the wall of a city under siege. The story of Abimelech's demise at Thebez in preserved in Judg 9:50–55.

27. *the period of grief.* According to Sir 10:12 mourning lasted seven days, a custom that seems to have been in effect throughout the biblical period (Gen 50:10; Judith 16:24; cf. I Sam 31:13 = I Chron 10:12). The thirty-day periods of grief for Moses (Deut 34:8) and Aaron (Num 20:29) are exceptional.

## COMMENT

The resolution of the Ammonite conflict is deferred in the narrative as our attention is directed away from public affairs to the private life of the king. David does not participate in the siege of Rabbah in person. He remains in Jerusalem, where he sees a beautiful woman bathing and, after ascertaining that she is the wife of one of his elite soldiers, claims her for himself. Bathsheba, unlike the aggressive queen-mother of I Kings 1–2, is a completely passive figure here. Uriah is also passive, inasmuch as he submits wholly to the regimen of a soldier. Ironically, however, it is this very submission that renders him unsusceptible to David's machinations. When David learns that Bathsheba is pregnant, he summons Uriah from the front on the pretext of obtaining news of the war (v. 7). If Uriah sleeps with his wife, the child will be thought to be his. But the staunch fighting man will not indulge himself in domestic pleasures while the rest of the army is in the field. In desperation, then, David solves his problem by contriving Uriah's death in action and, in due course, marrying the widowed Bathsheba.

It is obvious that this chapter is chiefly concerned with the private behavior —or misbehavior—of the king. The events related jolt the reader, who has become accustomed to the mild and generally upright David of the preceding materials. The rabbis were inclined to make excuses for David. Bathsheba, they concluded (Shabbat 56a), was not married to Uriah when David summoned her. Noting the tokens or pledges *(ʿărubbāttām)* David was told to take from his brothers when he visited Saul's battle camp in I Sam 17:18, they surmised that these were things that pledge a man to a woman. Thus everyone —including Uriah—who marched out in the wars of David first wrote a bill of divorce. Nor was Uriah's death unjustified: By disobeying David's order to go to his house, he was rebelling against royal authority and, therefore, was guilty of treason (Shabbat 56a; Qiddushin 43a).

The modern reader, on the other hand, is tempted to inquire with, for example, Cohen (1965) into the psychological motivation for David's conduct. Although not yet an old man, David, it seems, was now too old to accompany his army into the field routinely. It was the crisis caused by this change in his life, says Cohen, that accounts for his behavior: ". . . David felt that his loss of mature powers, with its consequent blow to his self-esteem, struck at the center of his being: his masculinity. . . . [Thus] he had to reassure himself of his manliness, his strength, his power. In this frame of mind he stepped out on the roof at eventide" (1965:146). David's desire for Bathsheba was not born of love, therefore, or even lust, but of a need to reassert his flagging manhood. Love and lust are reserved for young Aminon in chap. 13; David is a victim of "retirement neurosis" (F. Alexander *apud* Cohen 1965:146).

The difficulty with such a plausible analysis is that we have no way of knowing whether it is correct or not. The narrator gives us no clue to David's motives in his conduct towards Bathsheba. Indeed, the absence of such a clue is one of the remarkable aspects of the story (Perry and Sternberg 1968/1969a). David's misconduct is presented bluntly and without explanation, as if any hint of his motivation might mitigate his crime in the mind of the reader (Garsiel 1972; 1973:20). This is in striking contrast to the situation elsewhere in the stories about David. In reading the account of his rise to power, we noted that everything the young man did that might be interpreted as wrong was described in terms carefully chosen to gainsay such an interpretation (cf. McCarter 1980b:499–502). Most often his private motivation was set forth in detail in order to contradict the impression his public deeds might give. Thus, for example, when he left Judah to become a mercenary captain in the Philistine army—an act of treason on the face of it—we were shown that he did so only in despair of a reconciliation to Saul and, more specifically, out of a well-founded fear for his own life (I Sam 27:1). The same pattern is found in the stories of David's later life. In view of the public events recounted in chap. 9, for example, we might suspect that Meribbaal was being put under house arrest were we not specifically informed of David's generous motivation in 9:1. In the chapters that follow, moreover, we shall see further examples of this pattern, whereby possibly contemptible deeds of David are mitigated by reference to some noble or at least innocent motivation. But here in chap. 11 there is nothing corresponding to this pattern. The most egregious behavior possible on the part of a king is attributed to David without a word of mitigation.

It is extraordinary, therefore, that a majority of modern scholars have followed Rost in thinking of chaps. 11–12 as an original part of a document also including chaps. 13–20, where David is guilty of no more serious crime than excessive paternal affection (13:21). Can the narrator who describes David's cold contrivance of the murder of the steadfast and blameless Uriah be the narrator who takes such pains to show David's innocence in the death of the rebel Abishalom (18:5,12–15)? We cannot argue that David's conduct with Bathsheba was so heinous that a writer otherwise favorably disposed to David felt that he could not gloss over the king's misconduct in this case. As we shall see, the author of the account of Abishalom's rebellion in chaps. 13–20 is not simply a chronicler of events. His work represents a carefully designed narrative explanation of David's role in a series of tumultuous and almost disastrous public events. David is depicted as passive, excessively lenient, submissive to the divine will and even to the whims of his family and chief officers. As explained in the COMMENTS on §§ XXIV–XXXIII, it is precisely this passivity that will account for his troubles and also, perhaps, for their resolution. Here in chaps. 11–12, however, David is hardly passive: He is a *taker* (see the NOTE at 12:4).

The king who *takes* is the king of I Sam 8:11–17, about whom the prophet Samuel warned the people. He is the king of the prophetic history that embraces the story of the origins of monarchy in Israel in its present form (*I Samuel*, pp. 18–23 and *passim*). It seems clear that the story of David, Bathsheba, and Uriah—and Nathan!—in II Samuel 11–12 is another contribution from the prophetic hand that introduced, for example, the report of Saul's Amalekite campaign in I Samuel 15, where the king commits a crime (I Sam 15:8–9), comes under prophetic censure (I Sam 15:17–19,22–23,26,28; cf. II Sam 12:7–12), and confesses (I Sam 15:24,30; cf. II Sam 12:13). The verbal and rhetorical parallels between Nathan's speech in II Samuel 12 and the words of Samuel in I Samuel 15 and elsewhere are striking; these are discussed further in the NOTE on 12:7–12. The pattern here, then, is that familiar to us from the prophetic passages of I Samuel but lacking in the oldest materials about David—the story of his rise to power in I Sam 16:14–II Sam 5:10 (exclusive of the appearance of Samuel's ghost in I Sam 28:3–25), the report of the fate of the Saulids in II Sam 21:1–14 + 9:1–13, and the account of Abishalom's rebellion in II Samuel 13–20. Nowhere in the latter materials does a prophet dominate the scene, mediating Yahweh's will to the king, and nowhere in them is David depicted in such opprobrious terms (cf. Flanagan 1972:176).

As we noted in our study of I Samuel, the editorial technique by which the prophetic writer comments on his sources is a simple one. Characteristically he attaches to the older materials, which are left more or less intact, passages from his own hand that present the theological terms in which the old materials are to be understood. Thus, for example, in the story of David's rise to power in its original form the theme of Yahweh's special favor to David provided a theological leitmotif ("Yahweh was with him") according to which David's meteoric rise was explained (McCarter 1980b:503–4). In the process of incorporating this old document into the larger prophetic history, however, accounts of Saul's rejection (I Samuel 15) and David's anointment (I Sam 16:1–13)—both by prophetic mediation—were prefaced to the older document. Thus David's divine favor and uncanny success were now to be understood specifically in light of the notion of the prophet's prerogative on authority of Yahweh to make and unmake kings. Saul is a king rejected by Yahweh and thus denounced by his prophet; David is a man freely chosen by Yahweh to become king (cf. I Sam 13:14) and duly anointed by his prophet. The same editorial technique is in evidence in the present passage. The catastrophic events recorded in the old story of Abishalom's rebellion are interpreted as the working out of Yahweh's word of denunciation of David spoken by Nathan in 12:7b–12 (see the COMMENT on § XXII). This interpretation is offered by the simple procedure of introducing a prophetic writer's account of the Bathsheba affair and David's ensuing audience with Nathan as a preface to the older document.

As to the reliability of this writer's source of information, we can only speculate. That Solomon's mother was once the wife of one of David's elite soldiers is not likely to have been a historical fiction; nor need we doubt that Uriah died in action. The circumstances must have stirred public suspicion at the time, so that the interpretation of the events that our prophetic narrator received from his tradition may ultimately derive from circles contemporary with and hostile to David. It is also possible that the story in 11:1–27 was received intact in the prophetic writer's source and, therefore, that his own contribution is confined to 11:27b–12:26 or even 11:27b–12:15a, which many scholars have thought secondary in relation to 11:1–27a. A conclusion to this question and final remarks on the incorporation of chaps. 11–12 as a whole must be reserved for the COMMENT on § XXII.

# XXII. NATHAN'S PARABLE
## (11:27b–12:25)

11 [27b]Yahweh regarded the thing David had done as wrong, **12** [1]and
[he] sent Nathan to David. When he came to him, he said to him, "Pass
judgment on this case for me. There were two men in a certain city, one
rich and one poor. [2]The rich man had a great many sheep and cattle,
[3]but the poor man had nothing at all except one little ewe lamb, which
he had bought and brought up together with himself and his children.
It ate from his morsel and drank from his cup and slept in his embrace.
It was like a daughter to him.

[4]"A visitor came to the rich man, but he spared taking one of his own
sheep or cattle to fix for the traveler who had come to him. Instead he
took the poor man's ewe lamb and slaughtered it for the man who had
come to him."

[5]David was incensed at the man. "As Yahweh lives," he said to
Nathan, "the man who did this is a fiend of hell! [6]He shall repay the
ewe lamb sevenfold because he did this thing and spared what belongs
to him!"

[7]Then Nathan said to David, "You are the man! This is what Yahweh god of Israel has said: 'It was I who anointed you king over
Israel, and it was I who kept you free from the clutches of Saul. [8]I
gave you your master's daughter and made his wives lie down in your
embrace. I gave you the daughters of Israel and Judah, and if they
were not enough, I would give you that many again. [9]Why did
you treat Yahweh with contempt, doing what he regards as wrong?
You struck down Uriah the Hittite with the sword! You took his
wife as your own wife and killed him with an Ammonite's sword! [10]A
sword, therefore, will never be lacking in your house, because you
treated me with contempt and took the wife of Uriah the Hittite to be
your own wife!' [11]This is what Yahweh has said: 'I'm going to stir up
trouble for you out of your own house. I'm going to take your wives,
before your very eyes, and give them to someone else, and he will lie
with them in the light of the sun itself—[12]for though *you* acted in

secret, *I* shall do this thing in front of all Israel, in front of the sun!' "

[13]Then David said to Nathan, "I have sinned against Yahweh!"

"Yes, but Yahweh has transferred your sin," said Nathan to David. "You won't die, [14]but because you insulted Yahweh in this matter, the child who has been born to you *shall* die."

## *David's Vigil*

[15]When Nathan had gone home, God afflicted the child Uriah's wife had borne to David, and it became sick. [16]David entreated God on behalf of the boy. [He] fasted. He kept going inside and spending the night on the floor. [17]The elders of his house approached him to get him up from the floor, but he refused and would not eat any food with them. [18]When, on the seventh day, the child died, David's servants were afraid to tell him that the child was dead. "While the child was alive," they said, "we spoke to him and he wouldn't listen to us. So how can we tell him the child is dead? He might do something rash!"

[19]David, however, noticed that his servants were whispering together, and [he] realized that the child must be dead.

"Is the child dead?" [he] asked his servants.

"Yes, dead," they replied.

[20]Then David got up from the floor, washed and oiled himself, changed his clothes, and went to the house of Yahweh to worship. When he returned home, he asked for food, and when it was brought to him, he ate.

[21]"What is this thing you've done?" his servants asked him. "While the child was still alive you fasted and wept and kept a vigil, but once the child was dead you got up and ate food!"

[22]"While the child was still alive," he said, "I fasted and wept because I thought, 'Who knows? God might take pity on me and the child might live!' [23]But now that he is dead, why should I fast? Would I be able to bring him back? I'll go to him, but he won't come back to me."

## *The Birth of Solomon*

[24]David comforted Bathsheba, his wife. He went to her and lay with her, and she bore a son. She called him Solomon. But Yahweh loved him [25]and sent instructions through Nathan the prophet that he was to be called Jedidiah by the grace of Yahweh.

## *TEXTUAL NOTES*

**12** 1. *Nathan* So MT. LXX, Syr., MT$^{MSS}$: "Nathan *the prophet.*"

*When he came to him* So MT, LXX$^{BAMN}$. LXX$^{L}$: "When *Nathan* came to *David*" (b = *wb' ntn 'l dwd;* o = *wyb' 'lyw ntn;* $c_2e_2$ = *wyb' 'l dwd ntn*).

*"Pass judgment . . . for me"* Reading *hgyd n' ly 't hmšpṭ hzh* on the basis of LXX$^{L}$ *anangeilon dē moi tēn krisin tautēn* (cf. OL, Vulg.$^{MSS}$). Though this is lacking in MT (cf. LXX$^{BAMN}$), it is hardly secondary. In all likelihood it was followed in MT by an expansive *wy'mr lw,* "and he said to him," a situation that led to haplography *(wy'mr lw hgyd n' ly hmšpṭ hzh wy'mr lw).* Compare the related reading found in two Greek cursive MSS: *anangelō soi dē krisin kai eipen* = *'gydh n' lk mšpṭ wy'mr,* " 'Let me inform you of a case.' *And he said. . . .*"

2. *The rich man had* As pointed out in GK² §126d, we should read *le'āšîr* for MT *lĕ'āšîr,* "*A* rich man had. . . ." Cf. LXX.

3. *and brought up* Reading *wyḥyh* on the basis of Syr. *wḥy' hwt.* MT (cf. OL, Targ.) has two verbs at this point (*wyḥyh wtgdl,* "and brought [her] up and she grew up") and LXX three (*kai periepoiēsato kai exethrepsen autēn kai hēdrynthē* [LXX$^{L}$ *synetraphē*], "and he kept [her] safe and brought her up and she grew up"). The first two verbs of LXX are probably variant renderings of *wyḥyh,* but the short text of Syr. deserves preference.

4. *to the rich man* That is, *lā'îš he'āšîr.* MT *lĕ'îš he'āšîr* is evidently a Masoretic error (cf. GK² §126x).

*for the traveler* MT *l'rḥ.* The reading of LXX is *lnkry,* "for the stranger" (LXX$^{A}$ *tō xenō;* cf. LXX$^{L}$), and the two readings are combined in LXX$^{BMN}$ *(tō xenō [tō] hodoiporō).*

*the poor man's ewe lamb* Reading *'t kbšt hr(')š* with Syr. and LXX$^{BAMN}$ in preference to MT *'t kbšt h'yš hr'š* (cf. LXX$^{L}$).

*and slaughtered it* We read *wyzbḥh* with one MS of LXX$^{L}$ ($c_2$). In other MSS of LXX$^{L}$ (bo; cf. $e_2$) this is combined with the reading of MT, *wy'śh,* "and fixed it" (cf. LXX$^{BAMN}$), which is reminiscent of the previous *l'śwt,* "to fix."

*for the man* So MT, LXX. Syr. repeats "for the traveler" *(l'rḥ' = l'rḥ).*

5. *at the man* MT: *b'yš.* LXX$^{L}$ = *'l h'yš.*

*he* So MT, LXX$^{L}$, Syr. LXX$^{BAMN}$ make the subject explicit.

6. *sevenfold* So LXX$^{BAMN}$. MT, Syr., LXX$^{L}$ (cf. Josephus, *Ant.* 7.150): "*four*fold," in keeping with Exod 21:37 [22:1] (Thenius). Contrast Phillips 1966:243.

*and spared what belongs to him* We read *w'l 'šr lw ḥml* in preference to MT *w'l 'šr l' ḥml,* "and because he had no compassion," as first suggested by Schill (1891) and adopted by Hertzberg, Ackroyd, and others (contrast Simon 1967:231). This emendation is without textual support, but it has much to recommend it. Thus understood, the verb *ḥāmal* has the same meaning in its occurrences in vv. 4 ("but he spared") and 6 ("and spared"). Also, the awkward shift from *'qb 'šr,* "because," to *w'l 'šr,* "and because," is eliminated. To the style of the restored verse Schill compares Gen 22:16.

7. *the man* LXX$^{BAMN}$ add "who did this." Omit with MT, LXX$^{L}$, Syr.

*This is what* Preceded in LXX$^{BL}$ by *hoti* = *ky,* "Because." Omit *ky* with MT, LXX$^{AMN}$, Syr.

*king* MT *lmlk,* read as *lĕmelek.* The same consonantal text is taken by Syr., Targ. as *limlōk,* "to rule over." Cf. the *Textual Notes* on "king" in 2:4 and "over them as king" in 2:7.

*over Israel* Syr. and one cursive MS of LXX have "over *my people* Israel": cf. 5:2,12; 6:21; 7:7,8,10,11,23,24; and the *Textual Note* on "Israel" in 3:18.

8. *daughter . . . wives . . . daughters* That the rest of the verse is concerned with the many women provided David by Yahweh has been obscured in all extant witnesses except Syr. (see below). Yet compare Josephus, *Ant.* 7.151.

*daughter* So Syr.: *bnt* = *bt.* MT has *byt,* "house." LXX$^{L}$ *panta* = *kl,* "everything" (a vestige of *mykl bt,* "Michal, [your master's] daughter"?). The originality of Syr. here was first stressed by Klostermann. Cf. "the daughters," below.

*and made his wives lie down* MT has *w't nšy 'dnyk,* "and your master's wives," a second object of *w'tnh,* "I gave." LXX$^{L}$ *kai tas gynaikas autou* shows that this originally was *w't nšyw,* "and his wives." Syr. (which reads "and your master's wives" with MT) adds *'dmkt* = *hškbty,* "I caused to lie down." There is no apparent mechanism for the loss of *hškbty;* but the superiority of the text of Syr. elsewhere in this verse and the elegantly chiastic prose that this restoration produces is in its favor. Read *w't nšyw hškbty.*

*the daughters* So Syr.: *bnt* = *bnwt.* MT, LXX have "house." Syr. is favored not only by the general context but by the grammar of the sentence: *kāhēnnâ,* "(as many) as they, that many," at the end of the verse calls for a feminine plural antecedent. Contrast Englert 1949:16 and Carlson 1964:152.

*that many* Hebrew *kāhēnnâ,* lit. "(as many) as they." This is repeated in MT, but there is no reflection of *wkhnh* in LXX.

9. *Why* So MT, LXX$^{L}$. LXX$^{N}$ (cf. OL): *kai ti,* "And why . . . ?" LXX$^{B}$: *hoti,* "Because . . ." (cf. v. 10). LXX$^{LM}$: *kai ti hoti,* "Why is it that . . . ?"

*Yahweh* So LXX$^{L}$ and Theodotion (cf. OL: "God"). MT, LXX$^{BAMN}$, Syr. soften the question to "Why did you treat *the word of* Yahweh with contempt?" See, further, the first *Textual Note* on v. 14, where the euphemism in that verse is discussed.

*what he regards as wrong* So MT *(kĕtîb): hr' b'ynw,* lit. "the wrong thing in his eyes" (so LXX, Targ.$^{MSS}$). MT *(qĕrê): hr' b'yny,* "the wrong thing in *my* eyes" (so Targ., Vulg.). Either reading is acceptable: Yahweh himself is speaking, but he has just referred to himself in the third person. Syr., Targ.$^{MSS}$ and one Greek cursive reflect *hr' b'yny yhwh,* "the wrong thing in *Yahweh's* eyes."

*with an Ammonite's sword* Reading *bḥrb lbn 'mwn* on the basis of LXX$^{B}$ *en rhomphaia huiō ammōn.* Other witnesses support *bḥrb bny 'mwn,* "with the sword of the Ammonites."

10. *will . . . be lacking* LXX$^{L}$, Theodotion: *exarthēsetai* = *tkrt,* lit. "will be cut off." MT (cf. LXX$^{BAMN}$): *tswr,* "will turn aside." There is no basis for choosing between these variants.

*me* Omitted by LXX[B].

11. *to someone else* That is, *lr'k* (cf. LXX, Syr., Vulg.), which is plural in MT.

*with them* So Syr. MT, LXX: "with your wives."

12. *the sun* MT *hšmš* (cf. Theodotion, Syr.). LXX = *hšmš hz't*, "*this* sun, the sun *itself*" (cf. v. 11).

14. *Yahweh* As first noted by Geiger (1857:267), the chief witnesses are euphemistic, and the primitive reading, *'t yhwh*, is reflected only in a single Greek cursive MS (c = 376). MT (cf. LXX, OL, Syr., Targ.) has *'t 'yby yhwh*, "*the enemies of* Yahweh." Some of the ancient translators (LXX, Vulg., Symmachus) did not take this as euphemistic, choosing instead to render the preceding verb *(ni'ēṣ ni'aṣtā)* as a causative *Pi'el* (GK[2] §52g), a solution followed by AV ("thou hast given great occasion to the enemies of the LORD to blaspheme") and a few modern interpreters (Hertzberg, Goslinga); but Mulder (1968:110–12) has demonstrated the impossibility of this position on the grounds that *ni'ēṣ* never has such a meaning elsewhere and that in the context it makes no sense to think of David's sin, which is a secret, as having caused Yahweh's enemies—whoever they might be—to blaspheme. Significantly, 4QSam[a] (cf. Coptic) has a different euphemism, viz. *'t [d]br yhwh*, "*the word of* Yahweh," to which compare v. 9. (Note that *BHS* is in error here in its citation of the reading of 4QSam[a]; the apparent *lamed* in the photograph used by de Boer is in fact a shadow behind a small hole in the leather.) Cf. Ulrich 1978:138; Barthélemy 1980:5.

Such euphemisms were not introduced in order to falsify a text but rather out of respect for God and saintly persons (Mulder 1968:109–10). The rabbis were aware of the phenomenon of *lyšn' m'ly'*, "euphemism" (Berakot 11b, etc.), in the Bible, and examples occur in the Talmud (e.g., *śwn'yhm šl yśr'l*, "the enemies of Israel," for "Israel" in Sukkah 29a) and other Postbiblical Hebrew and Aramaic (cf. Dalman 1960:109) texts, and the practice is evidently derived from high antiquity. Yaron (1959) has called attention to an Egyptian example in the so-called Coptos Decree of the thirteenth dynasty, and Anbar [Bernstein] (1979) has discovered a probable example in an Akkadian letter from Middle Bronze Age Mari. Nevertheless, the conclusion of Anbar and Yaron regarding biblical euphemisms of this type requires modification. It is true, as Anbar says, that "it is not necessary to attribute them to later scribes" (p. 111), yet it remains possible that any one of them might derive from a later scribe. In the present case there is no ambiguity: The fact that independent textual witnesses employ *different* euphemisms shows that the primitive text had none. Similarly, in v. 9 the absence of the euphemistic word in some witnesses shows it to be scribal and secondary beyond question. Incidentally, the euphemistic expansion in I Sam 25:22, which is lacking in LXX[BA] (cf. *I Samuel*, p. 394), is also unquestionably late and scribal. In I Sam 20:16, where no textual witness lacks the euphemistic words (*I Samuel*, p. 337), Anbar [Bernstein] is possibly, but not certainly, correct in retaining "*the enemies of* David." As Mulder has noted (1968:113), Samuel seems to have been subject to this kind of scribal tampering more than other parts of the Bible, which may have been accorded a higher degree of sacredness and unalterability. Compare, in this regard, the routine substitution of *bōšet* for *ba'al*, discussed in the NOTE on "Ishbaal" at 2:8.

shall *die* MT *mwt ymwt*, for which 4QSam[a] has *mwt ywmt*, "shall *be put to death*," the standard formula in the Priestly legislation of the Pentateuch (Exod 21:12; Lev 20:2; etc.); cf. also Judg 21:5.

15. *God* So 4QSam^a: *'lwhym* (cf. LXX^L). MT has *yhwh*, "Yahweh" (cf. LXX^BAMN, Syr.), which is too specific, the reference being to divine affliction in general (see the NOTE).

*and it became sick* That is, *wy'nš*, which has been lost in 4QSam^a before the following word, *wybqš* (homoioarkton).

16. *David entreated God* The reading of 4QSam^a, *wybq[š dwy]d mn h'lwhym*, supported by Syr., Targ., is probably to be preferred to that of MT, *wybqš dwd 't h'lhym*. For *h'lhym*, "God," LXX^MSS, Targ., and Vulg. reflect *yhwh*, "Yahweh."

*and spending the night* MT and LXX^A *(kai ēulisthē kai ekoimēthē)* have two verbs here, *wln wškb*, "and he kept spending the night and lying down." LXX^L has *ekatheuden* = *škb*, suggesting that *wškb* stood in the *Vorlage* of OG. LXX^BMN, however, now read *kai ēulisthē* = *wln*, suggesting that at the time they were recensionally conformed to MT, the latter read *wln* (not *wln wškb*). 4QSam^a *([ ]*^ʾ *wyškb)* sides with OG. We may choose, therefore, between the variants *wln* and *wškb*. Tentatively I should read *wln*. At this point 4QSam^a *(bśq)* and LXX^LMN *(en sakkō*; cf. Josephus, *Ant.* 7.154) add "in sackcloth"; omit *bśq* with MT, LXX^BA.

17. *approached him* Reading *wyqrbw . . . 'lyw* on the basis of LXX^L *kai prosēlthon . . . pros auton* and 4QSam^a *wyqṙ[bw . . .] . . . 'lyw*. MT has *wyqwmw . . . ʿlyw*, "stood beside him." Graphic confusion of *reš* for *waw* and *bet* for *mem* was possible especially in the late Hasmonean and early Herodian scripts of the first century B.C. Syr. lacks a correspondent to *'lyw/ʿlyw*; but before *zqny bytw* (where *ep' auton* = *ʿlyw* is placed in LXX^BMN) Syr.^MSS read *klhwn* (thus, "*All* the elders of his house"), and this unique plus is probably, in fact, a corruption of *ʿlwhy* in the Syriac script, in which *ʿē* and *kāph* on the one hand and *nūn* and *yūd* on the other were easily confused.

*eat* 4QSam^a and MT^MSS *brh*, for which MT (erroneously) reads *br'*.

*with them* That is, *'ittām*. 4QSam^a has *'wtm*, to which compare *m'wtk*, "from (with) you," in 24:24.

18. "*While the child was still alive,*" *they said* So MT: *ky 'mrw hnh bhywt hyld hy*. LXX^L = *l'mr ky ʿwd hyld ḥy*, "saying, 'When the child was still alive . . .' " (cf. v. 21).

*we spoke to him* LXX^L adds "to get him up from the ground" (cf. v. 17); omit with MT, LXX^BAMN, Syr.

*So how* MT: *w'yk*. 4QSam^a: *[w]ẏ[k]ḣ*. OL = *wʿth 'yk*, "So *now* how," to which compare the reading of one MS of LXX^L(o): *kai nyn ean* = *wʿth 'm*, "So now *if*."

19. *noticed* Reading *wyśkl* on the basis of LXX^BAMN *kai synēken*. The meaning is that David was alerted by the fact that his servants were whispering among themselves —thus he "noticed, pondered, gave his attention to (the fact) that," etc. MT (cf. LXX^L) has *wyr'*, "saw."

20. *his clothes* MT *(qĕrê) śimlōtāyw* (cf. LXX^BAMN, Syr.). MT *(kĕtîb)* reads *śmltw*, "his cloak."

*food* LXX *arton phagein* reflects *lḥm l'kl*, "food to eat," which originally stood in MT also but was lost after *wyš'l* (homoioteleuton). Syr., however, points to a shorter text, *lḥm'* = *lḥm*.

*and when it was brought to him* MT (cf. LXX^BAMN) has *wyśymw lw lḥm*, "and they set food before him." We omit *lḥm* with Syr.; it probably arose in MT after the loss of *lḥm* in the preceding clause (see above), and its presence in LXX is probably recensional. For *wyśymw* we read *wywśm*, "and it was set (before), brought (to)" (cf. Gen 24:33), with LXX$^{L}$ *kai paratethē.*

21. *While the child was still alive* Reading *b'wd hyld ḥy* with Wellhausen on the basis of LXX$^{L}$ *eti (gar) tou paidiou zōntos,* Syr. *kd ḥy hw' ṭly',* and Targ. *'d drby' qyym.* MT has *b'bwr hyld ḥy* (cf. LXX$^{BAMN}$), "for the sake of the child (when) alive" (Driver).

*and kept a vigil* LXX *kai ēgrypneis* and OL *et vigilasti* reflect *wtšqd,* which was lost in MT after *wtbk* because of the similarity of *dalet* and final *kap.*

*and ate food* LXX adds "and drank (wine)."

22. *God* So Syr., MT$^{MSS}$. MT, LXX: "Yahweh."

*might take pity on me* So MT *(qĕrê): wḥnny (kĕtîb = yḥnny).* LXX has *ei eleēsei me = 'm yḥnny,* "whether (Yahweh) will take pity." Syr. has *'n mrḥm 'lwhy = 'm yḥnn 'lyw,* "whether (God) will take pity upon him (the child)."

23. *he*(1) So MT, LXX$^{BMN}$. LXX$^{AL}$: "the child."

*to bring him back* MT (cf. LXX$^{BAM}$) adds *'wd,* "again"; omit with LXX$^{LN}$ (cf. Syr.).

24. *went* So MT, LXX$^{BAMN}$. LXX$^{L}$: "spoke."

*and lay with her* So MT, LXX$^{BAMN}$. LXX$^{L}$: "and (she) lay with *him.*"

*She called* So MT *(qĕrê),* Syr., Targ. MT *(kĕtîb): "He* (i.e., David) called." See also the NOTE.

25. *by the grace of Yahweh* So MT: *b'bwr yhwh,* the meaning of which is discussed in the NOTE. This is to be preferred as *lectio difficilior* to *bdbr yhwh,* "by the *word* of Yahweh," which appears in MT$^{MSS}$ and seems to be reflected by LXX$^{LMN}$, OL, and Theodotion (but cf. de Boer 1966:27). The translations of Syr. *(mṭly dmry' yddw)* and Vulg. *(eo quod diligeret eum dominus),* "because the Lord loved him," are interpretive.

# NOTES

11 27b. This half-verse is one of three statements (the others are in 12:24 and 17:14) to which von Rad has called special attention (1966:198–201) as the only theologically explicit passages in the succession narrative, in which he, following Rost, would include II Samuel (6;7)9–20 + I Kings 1–2. The purpose of the statement, he says (p. 199), is "to encourage the reader to associate God's judgment on David with the developments which now ensue. If he has taken note of the brief and quite unemotional warning at *II Sam.* XI.27, and then read of the succession of blows which befall the house of David, the reader will know where to look for the explanation of all this piling up of disasters: God is using them to punish the King's sin." Because we have not found chaps. 10–12 to be part of the original Solomonic succession narrative, we must press von Rad's point a step further. The introduction of the story of David and Bathsheba into the larger narrative in a position immediately preceding the old account of Abishalom's rebellion was the contribution of a writer who interpreted the disastrous events of chaps. 13–20 in reference to David's behavior towards Bathsheba and Uriah. Verse 27b, therefore, is the first announcement of Yahweh's displeasure; the very specific indictments in the oracle to follow (especially vv. 9–12) will make the connection explicit. See the COMMENT.

**12** 1–6. Nathan's "juridical parable" (see the COMMENT) seems to be rooted in tribal custom and law. Simon (1967:227–31) cites an account of the bedouin tribes in the district of Beersheba (al-'Ārif 1974[1933]:146–48) for a practice by which it was permissible for a member of a tribe to take a sheep or goat from his neighbor's flock to serve to an unexpected guest. This privilege was accorded, however, only when the host had no stock of his own available. Moreover, among the animals specifically excluded was a "sheep that once had been the pet lamb of the family" (al-'Ārif 1974:146). Seen in this light (and assuming that such customs were very ancient), Nathan's parable highlights David's crime not as an instance of theft but of the abuse of the poor and powerless by the rich and powerful. See also the following NOTE and the COMMENT.

4. *taking . . . took.* As Seebass (1974:205–6) points out, the rich man's crime is not merely an instance of the theft of an animal, which in Israel was a simple tort that would hardly have needed to be brought before the king; it is an instance of *taking,* i.e., the abuse of the poor by the rich, of the powerless by the powerful. The king was supposed to uphold the cause of the powerless and prevent such abuse (Ps 72:2,4,12–14; etc.). In prophetic circles, however, the king was regarded as the *taker* par excellence (cf. Samuel's warning to the people in I Sam 8:11–18 and, on the thematic significance of *taking* in the prophetic account of the origins of the monarchy, *I Samuel,* pp. 213,218), and it is the crime of *taking* that Nathan's parable lays at David's door. See, further, the COMMENT.

5. *a fiend of hell.* Hebrew *ben-māwet,* lit. "a son of death." This expression does not mean "one who is as good as dead" or "one who deserves to die," as commonly supposed. No good parallel for such a meaning exists among the numerous uses of the noun *bēn,* "son." Instead *ben-mawet,* "son of death," and *'îš-mawet,* "man of death" (19:26), should be compared to *ben-bĕlîya'al,* "son of hell," and *'îš-bĕlîya'al,* "man of hell," which mean "fiend of hell" or, more generally, "scoundrel, damnable fellow" (see the NOTES at 16:7; 20:1). Thus I would now read "a fiend of hell" and "hellfiends" in I Sam 20:1 and 26:16 (*I Samuel* [erroneously], "a dead man," and "dead men"). In other words, David, by calling the rich man *ben-māwet,* is characterizing the man's behavior, not condemning him to death. We should not, therefore, suppose that David contradicts himself in v. 6 by demanding a sevenfold restitution after he has imposed a death penalty here ("the man who did this is a dead man") or expressed an opinion that the rich man ought to die ("the man who did this deserves to die"); cf. Phillips 1966:243–44; Seebass 1974:204–5.

6. *sevenfold.* Cf. Prov 6:31. In these two passages the claim for sevenfold compensation "is not to be taken literally and simply means perfect restitution" (de Vaux 1961b:vol. I:160); see the extended discussion of Carlson (1964:152–57). Coxon (1981) stresses the possibility of wordplay in "the subtle intrusion of Bathsheba's name" into the narrative by the reference to "sevenfold" (*šib'ātayim*) restitution. As explained in the *Textual Note,* some witnesses to our text show adjustment to the stipulation of fourfold compensation for the theft of a sheep in Exod 21:37[22:1], and the penalty for a crime of this type in the bedouin law cited by Simon (see the NOTE on vv. 1–6 above) was also fourfold restitution (al-'Ārif 1974:147). In the Talmud (Yoma 22b) the fourfold compensation was related directly to David's case: His punishment was the death of four children, viz. the first child of Bathsheba, Tamar, Aminon, and Abishalom.

7–12. Many of those scholars who follow Rost in thinking of chaps. 10–12 as an original part of a succession narrative containing II Samuel (6;7)9–20 + I Kings 1–2 regard the oracle in vv. 7b–12 as secondary and, according to some, Deuteronomistic (Rost 1926:92–99; von Rad 1966:179; Carlson 1964:157–59; Mettinger 1976:29–30; etc.). They admit, however, that the connection between David's crimes and the troubles looked forward to here is already implicit in the larger account in chaps. 10–12. Moreover, as we have seen, the attitude of chaps. 10–12 as a whole towards the king and their stress on the importance of the prophetically mediated divine word correspond in outlook to certain passages in I Samuel where a prophetic viewpoint is expressed. This is nowhere more clear and explicit than in the present verses, where an angry prophet stands in judgment before a chastened king, just, for example, as in I Samuel 15. The oracle in vv. 7b–12 is dressed out in prophetic speech forms (vv. 7,11; cf. 7:5,8). It opens with an accusatory retrospective on Yahweh's beneficent treatment of David (vv. 7b–8a) comparable to I Sam 15:17–18. The denunciation itself (v. 9) is begun in the interrogative, as in I Sam 15:19, and in both passages the king is accused of having done that which is "evil in Yahweh's eyes," i.e., that which "Yahweh regards as wrong." In both passages, moreover, the king is penitent ("I have sinned," II Sam 12:13; I Sam 15:24,30) when confronted with his crime. Verses 7b–12, then, are not likely to be secondary to the prophetic narrative in chaps. 10–12; on the contrary, they contain a clear expression of its viewpoint, and they contribute directly to its chief purpose, viz. the theological interpretation of chaps. 13–20 (cf. the COMMENT on § XXI). See also the NOTE at vv. 11–12 below.

7. *This is what Yahweh . . . has said.* The prophetic messenger formula; see the NOTE at 7:5.

*I . . . anointed you king.* The reference is to I Sam 16:1–13, the prophetic account of David's anointment by Samuel.

8. *your master's daughter.* Saul's daughter Michal (3:13, etc.).

*his wives.* Nowhere else are we told that David took Saul's wives for himself. Nevertheless, entering the royal harem was a way of claiming the throne (cf. 16:21–22 and, in general, Tsevat 1958b), and it is plausible to suppose that David took over Saul's harem (from Ishbaal?) along with the kingdom. Pointing to the present passage, Levenson and Halpern (1980:507,513–14; cf. Levenson 1978:27) have argued for the identity of Saul's only known wife, Ahinoam daughter of Ahimaaz (I Sam 14:50), with David's wife Ahinoam of Jezreel (I Sam 27:3; 30:5; II Sam 2:2; 3:2); they might have cited the Talmud (Sanhedrin 18a) in support of this argument.

9,10. *the sword! . . . A sword.* Because David was responsible for Uriah's death by the sword, David's family will be ravaged by the sword: His firstborn son, Aminon, will die by the sword (14:23–29); his son Abishalom will take up the sword in rebellion and then die by the sword (18:15); his son Adonijah will die by the sword (I Kings 2:25). Thus David's own sanctimonious words of reassurance to Joab in 11:25 have come back to haunt him: ". . . sometimes the sword devours one way, sometimes another" (cf. Carlson 1964:158).

10,11. *your house . . . your own house.* The future of David's house was a principal theme of chap. 7, and it is of special importance in the present chapter as well. Before, however, we were told of a promise of continuing rule for David's house; here we learn of trouble to arise from David's house. See the COMMENT.

11–12. It has been widely held since the time of Wellhausen (1871:184; 1899:256) that these verses, with their explicit references to future events, are secondary, a reflex of 16:21–22. Seebass (1974:207), however, holds them to be original in their present context, expressing, in fact, the main point of the passage. On this point I agree with Seebass. As explained in the NOTE on vv. 7–12 above, the oracle in vv. 7b–12, with its forecast of trouble for David, is an essential component of the story in chaps. 10–12, and this is especially true of vv. 11–12.

13. *Yahweh has transferred your sin.* The verb *(he'ĕbîr)* means more than "has put away" (RSV). The sin cannot simply be forgotten: It must be atoned for. Thus, if David himself is not to die, the sin must be transferred to someone who will (see Gerleman 1977:133–34). Cf. 24:10 and, on *he'ĕbîr* as "transferred," 3:10.

14. *you insulted Yahweh.* See the discussion in the first *Textual Note* on this verse.

15–23. The story of David's vigil is very strange. David's behavior during the child's illness is like that of a man mourning the dead; but when the child dies, David does not mourn. His explanation in vv. 22–23 is logical but curiously indifferent to conventional rules of behavior. It is difficult to agree with Pedersen (1940:vol. IV:455–57) that David's actions disclose "a revolutionary new attitude in the psychic history of Israel," wherein mourning would no longer be viewed as a spontaneous response to the intrusion of the uncleanness of death into someone's life but rather as having meaning only as an act that might influence Yahweh, or with Brueggemann (1969:489–90) that David is shown by his behavior to be "fully responsible, fully free man, indeed, fully man" because he believed himself "fully trusted by God" in consequence of Yahweh's investment in him in Nathan's oracle in chap. 7. Elsewhere David mourns the dead when they are dead (1:17ff.; 3:31–35; 13:36–37; 19:1), and it would be precarious to regard his behavior in the present episode, which is not part of the oldest literature about David (cf. the COMMENT on § XXI and Conroy 1978:75 n. 134), as indicative of his general attitude towards mourning, still less towards routine cultic or ritual acts as such. Instead, these words are probably to be seen as a rationalistic explanation to his companions for behavior for which the real explanation is different. As Gerleman has pointed out (1977:138), David and his servants have differing views of the death of the child, because David alone knows that it has been foreordained by Yahweh as atonement for David's sin. From the servants' viewpoint David seems to be mourning at the wrong time. From his own viewpoint, however, David is not mourning at all. By his fasting and self-humiliation he is imploring Yahweh to spare the child ("David entreated God on behalf of the boy," v. 16). Whereas it would be illogical to stop mourning when someone dies, it is logical to stop imploring God when one's petition has failed. Thus, behavior that seems strange to his servants seems perfectly reasonable to David. See also the following NOTE.

18. *the seventh day.* The child's illness lasted seven days. Thus David's fasting and self-humiliation also lasted seven days, and since this was the prescribed period of mourning (see the NOTE on 11:27 in § XXI), David could be said to have complied with the conventions of behavior after all, albeit proleptically. This may be a part of the strange logic underlying his actions. Veijola, on the other hand, probably presses the significance of the seven-day period too far. Assuming that the mention of seven days refers to the age of the child, he concludes (1979:242–43) that the period of the child's illness and David's "mourning" corresponded to Bathsheba's period of uncleanness, which, after the birth of a male child, would have lasted seven days (Lev

12:2). Thus when David "went to her and lay with her" (v. 24) Bathsheba was just at the end of her period of purification after uncleanness, the most propitious time for conception, exactly as she was when she conceived the first time (see the NOTE at 11:4). But there is nothing in the text to support Veijola's first assumption (p. 242 n. 47), viz. that the seventh day mentioned in v. 18 was the seventh day of the child's life, or his second assumption (p. 243), viz. that the second pregnancy began one week after the termination of the first. The child may have been several days or weeks old—or more—when it became ill, and a considerable span of time is probably telescoped in v. 24. As Veijola himself admits (p. 243), it is biologically implausible to suppose that Solomon was conceived a week after the birth of his unfortunate brother; nor is Veijola's insistence on the legendary character of the story and its emphasis on *psychological* realism (p. 244) enough to make us more comfortable with such an assumption.

20. *the house of Yahweh.* It is a surprise to find mention of a house of Yahweh in Jerusalem in the time of David. The expression ordinarily refers specifically to a temple, not to a sanctuary in general. Elsewhere, however, our sources are insistent that there was no Yahwistic temple in Jerusalem before the time of Solomon. As we noted, this was a principal concern of Nathan's oracle in chap. 7. Thus we must interpret the present reference to a temple in one of two ways. In agreement with Rupprecht (1977:120 and *passim*), who believes that Solomon's temple was a renovation of an old Jebusite cultic structure taken over by David (p. 102), we might accept the present reference as reliable evidence for a Yahwistic temple of Davidic date that somehow escaped the editorial censorship of later, probably Deuteronomistic, editors, who regarded Solomon's temple as unprecedented. The alternative, which I prefer, is to take the present reference to the house of Yahweh as anachronistic. If David, the dynastic founder, did build a temple, it is difficult to imagine that the tradition would have denied the fact. Why, in other words, would Deuteronomistic writers have handed down a *fiction* that David did not build a temple, while at the same time laboring so earnestly to excuse him for failing to do so (see above, pp. 219–220)? It is much easier to suppose that they were reckoning with the embarrassment of *historical fact.* An anachronism, moreover, is much less surprising here than it would be, for example, in the chapters that follow. Chaps. 13–20, as we shall see, probably derive from Solomonic and, ultimately, Davidic times. In 15:25, however, the shrine of the ark is referred to by the term *nāweh,* "camping place," that is, "tent(!)-shrine" (see the NOTE there). If our interpretation of chaps. 10–12 is correct, the present passage is part of a later compilation of materials composed from a prophetic perspective and dating, perhaps, to the eighth century B.C. (cf. *I Samuel,* pp. 21–23). At this date it would be quite natural to refer to the king entering the house of Yahweh in Jerusalem for worship. Recall, finally, the similar dilemma regarding references to a pre-monarchical temple of Yahweh at Shiloh in I Samuel 1 and 3 (cf. the first NOTE at 7:6); these, too, are materials deriving from prophetic circles (*I Samuel,* pp. 18–19 and 49–101 *passim*).

24. *she bore a son.* The sequence of events as presented gives the impression that both Bathsheba's sons were born during the siege of Rabbah. This is unlikely. There is nothing else to suggest that the siege lasted more than one season's campaign. In all probability the second birth took place some time after the fall of the Ammonite capital. It is not at all surprising that the narrator, having related the story of David and

Bathsheba, should include mention of the birth of the child because of whom their union was important to posterity (cf. Budde). We must also remember the probability that the story of David and Bathsheba was set *secondarily* in the framework of the Aramean-Ammonite war chronicle, as explained in the COMMENT on § XXI. Veijola (1979:238–40), on the other hand, cites the apparent birth of two sons during one season's campaign as evidence for his contention that the story of the first birth was a fiction invented to protect Solomon from the charge of illegitimacy.

*She called him Solomon.* In the time to which our story refers it seems to have been the mother's prerogative to name a newborn child (I Sam 1:20; 4:21; etc.); see Stamm 1960a:287 and Veijola 1979:234 n. 18 for relevant bibliography. But why does Bathsheba call the child *šĕlōmōh?* The explanation given in I Chron 22:19—that Yahweh foretold the name to David as an indication that Israel would have *šālōm,* "peace," during Solomon's reign—stems from a tradition unknown to the author of the present account and irrelevant to the matter at hand. Modern scholarship has attempted to explain the name in a number of ways (see Stamm 1960a:288–89; Gerleman 1973:13). Recently Stamm (1960a) and Gerleman (1973) have related it successfully to a group of names (cf. Stamm 1965) signifying that a child is viewed as a replacement or substitution for a lost sibling or parent. Thus *šĕlōmōh* means "his replacement" (cf. *šillēm,* "make amends, replace, restore") and was given by Bathsheba in reference to the death of her first child or, less likely, her husband. Veijola (1979:234–36), who thinks the story of the first birth was a fiction invented to protect Solomon from charges of illegitimacy, believes the name refers to Uriah. I agree with Stamm (1960a:296) and Gerleman (1973:13) in taking it as a reference to the first child of David and Bathsheba, whose loss was compensated for by the birth of *šĕlōmōh,* "his replacement" (see also Mettinger 1976:30).

25. The idiomatic grammar of this verse has caused confusion among modern translators. Verse 25a reads *wayyišlaḥ bĕyad nātān hannābîʾ wayyiqrāʾ ʾet-šĕmô yĕdîdĕyāh,* lit. "and he sent by the hand of Nathan the prophet, and he called his name Jedidiah." In reference to a divine or royal command, *wayyišlaḥ* followed by another verb—thus, "and he sent and did something"—means "and he had something done" (cf. 3:15; 9:15; 11:27; 14:2; etc.). In a case where *wayyišlaḥ* is followed by *bĕyad PN,* PN is the agent acting on behalf of the subject of *wayyišlaḥ;* thus, compare I Kings 2:25 to the present passage (Schulz). The meaning of v. 25a, then, is "and he had his name called Jedidiah by agency of Nathan the prophet," or, as rendered in our translation, "and sent instructions through Nathan the prophet that he was to be called Jedidiah." For a full discussion of the grammar of this passage, see de Boer 1966.

*Jedidiah.* Hebrew *yĕdîdĕyāh,* lit. "Beloved one of Yahweh." The name is mentioned nowhere else in the Bible, and some have doubted it was Solomon's. Klostermann, for example, thought it was the name of the dead child. If, in fact, it was another name for Solomon, how are we to explain the fact that he had two names? Honeyman (1948:22–23) came to the plausible conclusion that one was a private or personal name and the other a throne name. If this is correct, *šĕlōmōh* must, in view of the considerations presented in the NOTE at v. 24, have been the private name and *yĕdîdĕyāh* the throne name. This is what we should expect: The name given by the parents ought to be the personal name and that given by the dynastic god the throne name. Honeyman argued for the reverse and was thus obliged to assume (p. 23) that Jedidiah was vaguely remembered as another name for Solomon, but, its origin as a private name having been forgotten, it was reinterpreted as "an assurance of divine favor at the time of the child's birth."

*by the grace of Yahweh.* Hebrew *ba'ăbûr yahweh.* Ordinarily *ba'ăbûr* means "for the sake of" or "with respect to"—thus NEB, "for the Lord's sake." Modern translations are characteristically vague, typified by RSV, which, following AV, reads "because of the LORD." De Groot took the expression to mean "because (in this name) Yahweh (is found)." As pointed out by de Boer (1966:27), however, the expression *b'bwr DN* is clarified by its occurrence in the Phoenician Karatepe inscriptions of the late eighth century B.C. (*KAI* 26.I.8; II.6,11–12; III.11), where *b'br DN* must mean something like "by the grace of DN" (cf. Friedrich and Röllig 1970:§252.I.a).

## COMMENT

The description of David's crimes in chap. 11 was straightforward and concise, almost laconic. The narrator offered no word of evaluation or even explanation. Any question of justice that might have arisen in the mind of the audience was left unanswered. David's behavior was never challenged; the king seemed to stand above the law. At the beginning of the present section, however, we are suddenly reminded of a higher law. "Yahweh," we are told, "regarded the thing David had done as wrong" (11:27b). This is the signal that the questions of justice raised by chap. 11 are now to be addressed (cf. Arpali 1968/69). The prophet Nathan arrives at court under the pretext of bringing a case before the king for judgment. He tells the story of a rich man who wrongfully took something from a poor man, and before he is through David has indignantly condemned not only the rich man for taking the poor man's ewe lamb but also —unwittingly—himself for taking the wife of Uriah the Hittite. The prophet goes on to pronounce Yahweh's judgment on the chastened king.

The events of chap. 11, in other words, created a tense and unstable situation. David's behavior was unacceptable, but any response, whether on the part of the narrator or of other characters in the story, was lacking, and ethical questions seemed foreclosed. The audience was left unsatisfied. This closed system is broken open in chap. 12 by means of a *māšāl,* as the story of the poor man's ewe lamb is called in the Talmud (Baba Batra 15b). This particular type of *māšāl* is a judgment-eliciting story of the sort found also in 14:5–11 below as well as I Kings 20:39–40 (cf. Isa 5:1–7). With Simon (1967:220–25) we might call such a story by the *functional* definition of "juridical parable," though this use of the term "parable" may be open to objections from a *formal* point of view (cf. Gunn 1978:40–42; Coats 1981:368–80). A juridical parable is a type of speech that functions to break open a closed system of the sort found here. It presupposes a situation of concealment (Simon 1967:226) or denial, whether of motives or ethical issues, and its purpose is disclosure and exposition.

The way in which Nathan's juridical parable achieves its purpose has been shown most clearly in a paper by Roth (1977), who relies especially on Crossan's studies of story (1975). Roth (p. 8) stresses the problem in the story created by the contrast between David's roles as king and rich oppressor. As king, David is expected to administer justice; as rich oppressor, however, he subverts justice. The parable, too, sets up a tension between what is expected and what happens. According to Crossan (1975:66), "There is in every parabolic situation a battle of basic structures. There is the *structure of expectation* on the part of the hearer and there is the *structure of expression* on the part of the speaker. These structures are in diametrical opposition, and this opposition is the heart of the parabolic event. . . . What actually happens in the parable is the reverse of what the hearer expects." In the case of Nathan's parable, David expects one of the rich man's sheep to be given to the visitor, but the poor man's ewe lamb is unexpectedly given; it is the resulting shock that initiates action and eventually leads to a solution of the problem (Roth 1977:5–6). David the royal judge condemns David the rich oppressor. The closed system is broken open, judgment is elicited, and the tension is resolved.

Roth (p. 9) argues that a new picture of David emerges from this story, one in which the "hidden opposition" in the traditional picture of him is mediated. It seems to me that the ultimate objective of the story in chaps. 10–12 is, as in the case of similar passages in I Samuel, to paint a picture of kings in general rather than David in particular. The tension between what the king is hoped or expected to do and what kings actually do is exploited again and again in the prophetically oriented stories told about Saul, and what emerges there—as here—is a "mediated" view of the royal office. But insofar as the immediate context of II Samuel 10–12 is concerned, Roth is surely correct. These chapters, as we have seen, stand as a preface to the story of Abishalom's revolt in chaps. 13–20. The picture of David in that story is generally flattering. He is not depicted as a paragon, but he is shown to be a good man, and his flaws, as we shall see, are excessive gentleness, leniency, and paternal affection. His troubles are the result of the reckless behavior of those about him. With chaps. 10–12 in place, however, this picture of David is radically modified. His passivity in chaps. 13–20 is counterbalanced by his self-serving willfulness here. Ultimate responsibility for the trouble that arises "out of [his] own house" (12:11) is laid at his own feet.

In the previous two COMMENTS we concluded that the story in chaps. 10–12 derives from the hand of a writer whose perspective was prophetic. Taking an archival report of David's Aramean-Ammonite wars as a framework (10:1–19 + 8:3–8 + 11:1 + 12:25–31), he inserted his own account of David's sin with Bathsheba (11:2–12:24). In composing this account he may have relied on a chain of tradition transmitted in prophetic circles. It seems unlikely, however, that he drew from a written source. A number of scholars (most recently Dietrich 1972:127–29; Würthwein 1974:19–30, especially p. 24; Veijola 1979: 233–34) have followed Schwally (1892:155) in striking the report of Nathan's audience with David as secondary with regard to the surrounding narrative, and it is true that 11:27b–12:15a can be lifted out rather neatly, removing the prophet almost (12:25) entirely from the story. But in view of our earlier observation of the manner in which the tension produced by the moral ambiguity of chap. 11 relies on David's encounter with Nathan for its resolution, it is difficult to imagine 11:2–27a + 12:15b–24 existing in isolation from 11:27b–12:15a. I prefer to think of the David-Bathsheba-Uriah-Nathan sequence (11: 2–12:24) as the wholly original work of a prophetic writer who inserted it into the archival frame and set the finished composition in front of the story of Abishalom's rebellion, which it serves as an interpretive preface.

We are now in a position to see how the words of the oracle in vv. 7b–12 specifically anticipate events described in the chapters that follow. At issue is a sin and its consequences. David has treated "Yahweh with contempt, doing what he regards as wrong" (12:9). He "took" (vv. 9,10) Uriah's wife and was the cause of Uriah's death by the sword. The punishment, therefore, is that "a sword will never be lacking in [David's] house" (v. 10). This looks ahead in a general way to the turmoil to come: As explained in the NOTE at vv. 9,10, David's family will be ravaged by the sword. Similarly, in v. 11a we are told that the trouble to arise from David's house will be set in motion by Yahweh in punishment for David's sin. Verses 11b–12, moreover, are even more explicit—and specific—in their anticipation of subsequent events. Because David lay with Uriah's wife in secret, Yahweh is going to arrange for someone to lie with David's wives in public. This looks ahead specifically to 16:21–22, where Abishalom will enter David's harem. As we shall see, Abishalom does so as a way of publicly asserting his claim to David's place as king, and in the original account of Abishalom's rebellion the episode was included to document that assertion. But in light of vv. 11–12 in the present oracle, the events of 16:21–22 are seen as part of Yahweh's response to David's behavior and a specific component in a scheme of prophecy and fulfilment.

The oracle in vv. 7b–12 is also retrospective. It looks back in v. 7 to David's anointment by the prophet Samuel (cf. I Sam 16:1–13), a necessary legitimating rite in the prophetic view, and to his preservation from Saul. In v. 8 it recalls his marriages to Michal and his other wives. These verses are reminiscent of a similar retrospective that stands in vv. 8–9a of Nathan's earlier oracle in chap. 7. A major theme of that oracle, David's house, is an issue in this one as well. In chap. 7 David was promised an enduring "house," a dynasty, and although we noted evidence there of prophetic reflection on the ancient themes of temple and dynasty, we found nothing in chap. 7 to cast a cloud over the dynastic promise itself: For the prophetic editor of chap. 7 the Davidic dynasty was a given of history. Nevertheless, prophetic thought was suspicious of dynastic succession, inasmuch as it seemed incompatible with Yahweh's appointment of "a man of his own choosing" (I Sam 13:14) as Israel's leader. In the earlier discussion (p. 229), therefore, we anticipated an expression of further reservations about David's house. In the present oracle, then, we hear of David's house as a place of endless strife (v. 10) and a source of trouble for David (v. 11). No doubt prophetic thought saw in the violent character of David's sons an illustration of the risks involved in dynastic succession. Abishalom, in particular, could be said to stand in relation to David as Abimelech did to Gideon, and in chap. 15 below the trees will again make the bramble king (cf. Judg 9:7–20). But the point here is more specific. It is the king himself, not his son or sons, who is responsible for the turmoil to come. The divine promise of a house for David was made in the aftermath of an expression by David of self-denial and concern over the inadequacy of the housing of Yahweh's ark (7:2; cf. Ps 132:3–5). The divine announcement of endless trouble in David's house is made in the aftermath of a demonstration by David of a great capacity for self-indulgence and an apparent indifference to the lodging of the ark. Lest the irony in David's change of attitude be overlooked, the selflessness of the earlier David was pointedly brought to mind in chap. 11 by the exasperating virtue of poor Uriah, who staunchly refused to go to his house while the ark was in the field (see the NOTE on "the ark" at 11:11). The prophetic writer who produced this elaborate story of royal sin (chaps. 10–12) has attempted to show his audience that kings are not selfless and pious men; despite sanctimonious gestures, they are likely to turn out to be self-serving and unscrupulous. Now, in chap. 12, he shows once again that kings are responsible for their deeds to a higher authority. No king who chooses to "treat Yahweh with contempt" can be secure in his position. Not even the solemn promise of a house for David is immune to the sting of the prophetically mediated divine word: The enduring house can become a place of enduring strife.

Considered in still broader perspective, the story in chaps. 10–12 might be described as the birth story of Solomon. But, if so, it seems a strange birth story, to say the least, especially when viewed in comparison to the accounts of the births of heroes like Samuel, Samson, and so on. The circumstances, if not downright sordid, are hardly auspicious. Solomon's nativity, like that of Ichabod (I Sam 4:19–22), is inglorious. Also, as in the case of Ichabod, however, Solomon's birth is not of central interest to the larger story. As we have seen, the climax of the story in chaps. 10–12 comes in 12:7a ("You are the man!"), when the implications of David's deeds are brought to view. The oracle of judgment (vv. 7b–12), David's confession and vigil (vv. 13–17), and the death of the child (vv. 18–23) are denouement. The birth of Solomon (vv. 24–25) is postscript. We have the impression that the narrator reported Solomon's birth as a matter of obligation. Having related the story of David's sin with Bathsheba and its consequences, he could hardly fail to mention the birth of the child who was the chief reason the union of David and Bathsheba was remembered as important. It is erroneous, therefore, to interpret Solomon's birth and the assertion that "Yahweh loved him" (v. 24) as indicating that "the grace of God once again shines out over this child—and so over David, too" (Hertzberg). On the contrary, David, though his sin has been "transferred" and atoned for, remains in *dis*grace as far as the author of chaps. 10–12 is concerned, and David's house is to be a permanent dwelling place for trouble and the sword. The statement that Yahweh loved the second child is a bit of tradition explaining Solomon's other (throne?) name (see the NOTE on "Jedidiah," v. 25) and cannot bear the thematic and theological weight often attributed to it. Nor should we overemphasize the fact, irrefutable in itself, that the story shows that Solomon was not the child of an adulterous union. There is nothing to suggest that the account was designed specifically to show this. From beginning to end it is a story about David, not Solomon (cf. Gunn 1978:82–83); it is concerned with David's deeds and their immediate consequences for him and his family. This also weighs against the more radical hypothesis of Cook (1899/1900:156–57) as recently revived by Veijola (1979; cf. Würthwein 1974:32) that the story of the first child is a fiction crafted in defense of Solomon, who was in fact the child of the adulterous union (see also the NOTES).

Probably, then, II Samuel 10–12 should not be described as Solomon's birth story. This designation is better reserved for II Sam 12:24–25 alone, which stands as an appendix to the larger story that precedes it. That story concludes gloomily in v. 23, with no brighter prospect ahead than trouble out of David's house, and the presence of vv. 24–25 should not be permitted to relieve the gloom the author of 11:2–12:23 has worked so hard to produce. It does not follow from this, however, that we are entitled to pass lightly over the events of vv. 24–25 or to view them in isolation from their context. Within the larger biblical tradition the first appearance of David's heir is no trifling matter. Solomon's birth may be extraneous to the major thematic concerns of the story of David and Bathsheba, but seen in a larger perspective it is a momentous event. This is essentially the paradox of the Book of Ruth, which presents a story of absolute integrity without the concluding genealogical identification of Ruth's son as David's ancestor (Ruth 4:17b–22) but which attains a new significance with the appendix in place. Confronted with such a situation, the reader must avoid (1) reading the story for the sake of the appendix alone—thus letting the tail wag the dog—and (2) overlooking the significance of the appendix. As suggested above, II Sam 12:24–25 may have been added as a matter of obligation by the author of 11:2–12:23, to which it seems to have had no special thematic significance. In itself, however, it is an important passage, and from its perspective 11:2–12:23 *is* significant as background. In contrast to the illegitimate, nameless, and ill-fated child of vv. 15–23, the child of vv. 24–25 is legitimate, twice-named (!), and—as the audience knows—the future king of Israel (Roth 1977:9). It is this last point that shows the inadequacy of our comparison to the story of Ichabod's birth: Solomon was no Ichabod (cf. Matt 6:29 = Luke 12:27). I Sam 4:19–22 does not reverberate beyond the story of the capture of the ark, but II Sam 12:24–25, however incidental to its present context, introduces us to the central figure of I Kings 1–11.

# XXIII. THE SACK OF RABBAH
# (12:26–31)

12 [26]Joab, fighting at Rabbah of the Ammonites, captured the Royal
Citadel. [27][He] sent messengers to David to say, "I've been fighting at
Rabbah, and I've captured the citadel of the water supply. [28]So muster
the rest of the army, encamp against the city, and capture it yourself;
otherwise I'll be the one to capture [it], and my name will be called
there."
[29]So David mustered the entire army, went to Rabbah, and fought
there until he captured [the city]. [30]He took Milcom's crown from his
head: Its weight was a talent of gold, and in it was a precious stone,
which afterwards was upon David's own head. He brought out the spoil
of the city—a very great quantity. [31]He brought out the people who
were in it, ripped [it] with saws and iron cutting tools, and set them to
work with the brick mold. Then, after he had done the same to all the
cities of the Ammonites, David and the entire army returned to Jerusalem.

## *TEXTUAL NOTES*

12 26,27. *the Royal Citadel . . . the citadel of the water supply* That is, *ʿyr hmlwkh . . . ʿyr hmym*, as attested by MT and LXX. In Syr. and Targ. *ʿyr hmym* has been conformed to *ʿyr hmlwkh*, and there is also a tendency among modern critics to resolve the apparent contradiction. Many follow Wellhausen in reading *ʿyr hmym* in both verses. But Wellhausen was mistaken about the graphic similarity of *hmlwkh* and *hmym: yod* was not likely to be confused for *lamed*, still less *mem* for *kap he*. In fact, there is no basis for a challenge to the received text. We must suppose that *ʿyr hmlwkh* and *ʿyr hmym* are two names for the place captured by Joab. Perhaps "the Royal Citadel" was the official name used by the narrator and "the citadel of the water supply" was not a name ("the Citadel of Waters") but rather Joab's descriptive way of identifying its strategic importance to David. See, further, the NOTE.

28. *and capture it yourself* So $\mathrm{LXX}^{L}$: *kai prokatalabou autēn su* = *wlkdh ʾth*. MT has lost *ʾth* after *wlkdh* (homoioteleuton).

30. *Milcom's* MT has *malkām,* "their king" (so LXX[AL]; Josephus, *Ant.* 7.161); while LXX[BMN], preserving two renderings of a single original *(mlkm),* have *melchom* (LXX[B] *melchol) tou basileus,* "Milcom their king." In the case of *malkām,* "their king," the pronominal suffix is without antecedent (Wellhausen, Driver), and it has long been recognized that the correct reading is *milkōm,* "Milcom" (see the NOTE). (O'Ceallaigh [1962:186 n. 2]: "their Molech.")

*and in it was a precious stone* We read *wbh 'bn yqrh* (cf. Syr., Targ.), as in I Chron 20:2. In MT, LXX *(w)bh,* "(and) in it," has been lost; note the repetitive sequence *zhb wbh 'bn* in the original.

*which afterwards was* That is, *wthy,* lit. "and it was" (so MT, LXX, Targ.; Syr. has *w'ttsym,* "and it was *placed*"). The subject must be the stone (so Syr.; the other witnesses are ambiguous), not the crown, which was far too heavy for a human being to wear (see the NOTE on "a talent of gold").

31. *ripped* [*it*] MT has *wyśm,* "and he set [the people to work?]," supported by LXX[BAMN] and Syr. The patently superior reading of I Chron 20:3, *wyśr,* lit. "and he sawed, ripped," is preserved in the present passage by LXX[L] *kai dieprisen* (cf. OL, Targ.). The object is not expressed. It is often taken to be "them," i.e., the people mentioned in the preceding clause (thus OL, explicitly, *illos*), leading to the conclusion that David is torturing his prisoners (cf. Josephus, *Ant.* 7.161). The resumptive use of an independent pronoun in the following clause (*'ōtām,* "them"), however, shows that "them (= the people)" is not the implied object in the present clause. Thus it must be the city itself ("it") that David is ripping up. See, further, the NOTE.

*with saws and iron cutting tools* Reading *bmgrh wbḥrṣy hbrzl,* lit. "with the saw and the cutting tools of iron." After *hbrzl* many witnesses preserve a variant of *bmgrh,* viz. *bmgzr(w)t (hbrzl),* "with axes of iron" (cf. MT, LXX[AL], Targ., and I Chron 20:3; omitted by LXX[BMN], Syr., and a few MSS of MT). Syr., which follows MT in reading *wyśm* for *wyśr* (see the preceding *Textual Note*), makes a quite different interpretation of the circumstances: *w'rmy 'nwn bqwlr' dprzl' wbššlt',* "and he put them into iron collars and chains." O'Ceallaigh (1962:183–84) suggests the reading "And the people who were in her (the city) he brought out and set [*wyśm*] at tearing her down [*bĕmaggĕrāh!*], even with iron crows. . . ."

*and set them to work* MT has *wh'byr,* "and kept causing them to pass (into the brick mold?)"; see the NOTE. In all probability, however, the original was *wh'byd,* lit. "and caused them to labor continually," as first recognized by Hoffmann (1882:66); cf. Exod 1:13; 6:5.

*with the brick mold* We read *wmlbn* with MT *(qĕrê)* and LXX *dia tou plintheiou* (LXX[LMms] *en madebban,* "in Madeba," in consequence of confusion of the Greek majuscules *lambda* and *delta* in a transliteration of *mlbn*). MT *(kĕtîb)* has *bmlkn,* which O'Ceallaigh (1962:185–86) reads *bammālĕkīn,* an Aramaic (!) participial noun meaning, he says, "the Molechs"—thus, "And he made them transgress against ([*h'byr*] i.e., desecrate, violate or destroy) the Molechs" (cf. already Thenius).

## NOTES

12 26,27. *the Royal Citadel . . . the citadel of the water supply.* Hebrew *'îr hammĕlûkâ . . . 'îr hammayim.* Since there is no clear basis for another reading (see the *Textual Note*), we must assume that these are two designations for the same place. Rabbah itself was a royal city inasmuch as it was the residence of a king. But the capture of Rabbah as a whole will come later, v. 29. It follows that *'îr hammĕlûkâ,* "the Royal City" or "the Royal Citadel," must have been a fortified sector *('îr)* of greater Rabbah in the same way that *'îr dāwīd,* "the City (or Citadel) of David," was a fortified sector of larger Jerusalem (cf. the NOTE at 6:10). The name suggests that it was the district of Rabbah that contained the royal palace. But Joab describes it to David as *'îr hammayim,* "the citadel of the waters," suggesting that it also protected the city's water supply. Perhaps Joab captured the royal fortress of Rabbah, which stood atop the steep hill overlooking and protecting the flowing spring fed by the Jabbok (Wadi 'Ammān), which provided the city's water. If this is correct, the task left for David must have been a simple one.

28. *the rest of the army.* Cf. 11:11, the NOTE on "Succoth," where, if Yadin [Sukenik] is correct, the bulk of David's army remained while Joab laid siege to Rabbah with the elite troops.

*and my name will be called there.* If someone's name is invoked over *(niqrā' šem PN 'al)* someone or something, that person or thing is specially associated with him and, in a sense, derives its identity from him, as, for example, in the case of a woman deriving her identity from her husband (Isa 4:1) or a prophet from his god (Jer 15:16). The expression implies rule, dominion (Isa 63:19). In the Bible its primary uses are theological, describing Israel as Yahweh's special people (Deut 28:10; etc.) or referring to the special association with Yahweh of the ark (II Sam 6:2 = I Chron 13:16), the Solomonic temple (I Kings 8:43 = II Chron 6:33; etc.), or the city of Jerusalem (Jer 25:29). In the present case, then, Joab is warning David that if he does not assume personal command of the army for the final siege, Rabbah will be regarded thereafter as Joab's own conquest, not that of the king.

30. *Milcom's crown.* Milcom was the national god of the Ammonites, as we know from the Bible (I Kings 11:33; etc.) as well as Ammonite inscriptions and seals. The reference here is to his cultic image, called simply "Milcom," just as the image of the Philistine god Dagon is called "Dagon" in I Sam 5:2, etc. The word *'ăṭārâ,* lit. "wreath," is used elsewhere in reference to crowns in general as marks of royalty or other distinctions. This one is jeweled (cf. Zech 9:16) and made of gold. Its great weight (see below) suggests that the image was larger than man-size. Horn (1973), who prefers to read "their king" instead of "Milcom" here (cf. the *Textual Note*), has called attention to a group of stone sculptures of crowned heads and one complete statue found in the vicinity of Amman, ancient Rabbah. It is not clear whether these represent gods or kings, but the complete statue is barefoot and, therefore, taken by Horn (p. 179) as a king standing on holy ground. Thus the sculptures may represent crowned Ammonite kings of the first half of the first millennium B.C., as Horn concludes (pp. 179–80).

On the other hand, the crowns find their best known parallels in divine headgear, as Horn points out (pp. 174–75). They are ". . . conical caps or hats similar to those worn by Ba'al or Reshep statues found in Palestine and Syria, with an additional feature, namely a plume or feather attached to each of its two sides" (p. 174); thus they closely resemble the Egyptian *'atef*-crown, worn especially by the god Osiris. This might have been the type of crown David found on the head of the image of Milcom, but it would be somewhat reckless for us to assume so. The stone heads may have come from a gallery of kings, or they may be a series of representations of Milcom; but they are just as likely to be decorative ornaments from an Egyptianizing temple or other public building.

*a talent of gold.* About seventy-five pounds (cf. Horn 1973:172). The weight shows that it must have been the stone, not the crown, that David wore afterwards (cf. the *Textual Note* on "which afterwards").

31. *ripped [it] with saws.* David dismantled the fortifications of the conquered city, a common procedure in siege warfare (cf. II Kings 25:10) intended to make sure that another siege would not soon be necessary. Some of the ancient versions understood v. 31 to refer to tortures imposed by David on the inhabitants of Rabbah ("ripped *them* with saws," etc.), but this interpretation is grammatically improbable (see the *Textual Note*) and most commentators since Klostermann have doubted it; see also Condamin (1898), Goslinga (1959), and Stoebe (1977:245). David is setting up work crews of captives for the economic exploitation of the conquered territory, evidently standard practice for victorious kings (cf. de Vaux 1978:326).

*and set . . . mold.* In view of the preceding NOTE we can conclude that the present statement does not mean "and caused them repeatedly to pass through [*wĕhe'ĕbîr*] the brick kiln." The evidence of Postbiblical Hebrew (Jastrow 756) confirms that *malbēn* means "mold," not "kiln," and a brick mold—a bottomless rectangular box used to make a brick (Hoffmann 1882:53)—was too small for anyone to "pass through" even under torture. At best, then, we might read "and he kept causing them to pass over to the brick mold," i.e., "and consigned them to the brick mold." But it is more likely that we should read "and caused them continually to work [*wĕhe'ĕbîd*] with the brick mold," i.e., "and set them to work with the brick mold" (see the *Textual Note*).

## COMMENT

These verses conclude the long account of David's Ammonite-Aramean war begun in chaps. 8 and 10. As explained in the COMMENT on § XX, this account (10:1–19 + 8:3–8 + 11:1 + 12:25–31) probably derives from contemporary annalistic sources; it was drawn from the royal archives to serve as a framework for the story told in 11:2–12:24. The present section describes the successful conclusion to David's conflict with the Ammonites. When Rabbah fell, Ammon was incorporated into the Davidic empire, where it probably remained until after the death of Solomon (cf. Bright 1972:228).

## XXIV. THE RAPE OF TAMAR
## (13:1–22)

**13** 1This is what happened afterwards. Abishalom son of David had
a beautiful sister whose name was Tamar, and Aminon son of David
fell in love with her. 2Aminon was so upset over his sister Tamar that
it made him sick, for she was a virgin and it seemed to him impossible
to do anything to her. 3Now Aminon had a friend named Jonadab, the
son of David's brother Shimeah. Jonadab was very wise, 4and he said
to [Aminon], "Son of the king, why are you poorly like this morning
after morning? Won't you tell me?"

"It's Tamar," Aminon told him, "my brother Abishalom's sister. I'm
in love with her."

5"Lie down on your bed," Jonadab said to him, "and act sick. Then
when your father comes to visit you, say to him, 'Let my sister Tamar
come and take care of me. Let her fix some food in front of me so that
I can watch; then I'll eat out of her hand.' "

6So Aminon lay down and acted sick, and when the king came to visit
him, Aminon said to [him], "Let my sister Tamar come and make a
couple of hearty dumplings in front of me; then I'll eat out of her hand."

7David sent someone to Tamar at home to say, "Go to your brother
Aminon and fix him some food." 8So Tamar went to her brother Aminon's house, where he was lying down. She took some dough, kneaded
it, formed it into hearty dumplings in front of him, and boiled the
dumplings. 9But when she took the pan and served him, he refused to
eat.

"Get everybody away from me!" [he] cried. Then when everyone had
left him, 10he said to Tamar, "Bring the food into the bedchamber, so
I can eat out of your hand." So Tamar picked up the dumplings she
had made and took them to her brother Aminon in the bedchamber.
11But when she offered him something to eat, he grabbed her.

"Come on, sister!" he said to her. "Lie with me!"

12"Don't, brother!" she said to him. "Don't force me, for such a thing
isn't done in Israel! Don't commit such a sacrilege! 13For my part, where

would I take my shame? And as for you, you would be like one of the outcasts in Israel! So speak to the king! He won't keep me from you!" [14]But he would not listen to her and, overpowering her, he lay with her by force.

[15]Then Aminon felt a very great hatred towards her—indeed, the hatred he felt towards her was greater than the love he had felt for her. "Get up!" [he] said to her. "Go away!"

[16]"Don't, brother!" she said to him. "For this wrong, sending me away, is worse than the other you did me!"

But he would not listen to her, [17]and, summoning the servant who attended him, he said, "Put this woman out, away from me, and bolt the door behind her!" [18b]So his attendant put her out, bolting the door behind her. [18a](She had on a long-sleeved gown, for that is the way the virgin daughters of the king used to dress from puberty on.)

[19]Tamar took ashes and put them on her head. She tore the long-sleeved gown she had on, put her hand on her head, and went away, crying constantly as she went. [20]Her brother Abishalom said to her, "Has Aminon, your brother, been with you? Now hush! He's your brother! Don't take this thing to heart!" So Tamar lived as a desolate woman in the house of her brother Abishalom.

[21]When King David heard about all these things, he was furious; but he did nothing to chasten his son Aminon, because he loved him since he was his firstborn. [22]Abishalom said nothing to Aminon, bad or good, but [he] hated him for having forced his sister Tamar.

## *TEXTUAL NOTES*

**13** 1. *Abishalom* See the *Textual Note* at 3:3.

*beautiful* So MT: *yph*. LXX *kalē tō eidei sphodra* = *ypt mr'h m'd*, "very beautiful in appearance."

*Tamar* So MT *(tāmār)*, LXX$^{AL}$ *(thamar)*, and Josephus, *Ant.* 7.162 *(thamara)*. LXX$^{BMN}$ have *thēmar*, "Temar."

*Aminon* See the *Textual Note* at 13:20.

2. *that it made him sick* Hebrew *lhtḥlwt*, the verb used of *feigned* sickness in vv. 5,6. Some critics have found it necessary to emend the text (without support from the ancient witnesses) to *lḥlwt* (Budde) or some other verb (cf. Ewald 1878:171 n. 1; Ehrlich 1910:301). Klostermann: *lhthll*, "that it drove him crazy."

*and it seemed to him impossible* That is, *wypl' b'ynyw*, lit. "and it was wonderful in his eyes." For *b'ynyw* MT, followed by $LXX^{BAMN}$ (cf. Syr.), has *b'yny 'mnwn*—thus, "and it seemed to *Aminon,*" etc.; the two readings are combined in the text of $LXX^{L}$, where *amnōn* has been added recensionally to *en ophthalmois autou.* Space considerations suggest that $4QSam^{a}$ preserved the shorter reading.

*to do* Syr. has "to *say.*"

3. *Jonadab* So MT *(yônādāb)* and $LXX^{BAMN}$ *(iōnadam/b).* $LXX^{L}$ *(iōnathan)* and $4QSam^{a}$ *([y]hwntn)* have "Jonathan" (cf. Josephus, *Ant.* 7.164), the name of another (?) son of Shimeah mentioned in 21:21 (see the NOTE there).

*Shimeah* MT *šm'h* (= *šim'â*), as in v. 32. $MT^{MSS}$ have *šm'*, as in I Chron 2:13; 20:17; II Sam 21:21 *(qĕrê).* In II Sam 21:21 *(kĕtîb)* it is *šm'y.* In the present passage $4QSam^{a}$ reads *šm'yh.* In I Sam 16:9 and 17:13 MT spells the name *šmh.*

*very wise* So $LXX^{L}$: *phronimos sphodra* = *ḥkm m'd.* MT (cf. $LXX^{BAMN}$) has *'yš ḥkm m'd,* "a very wise man." Space considerations suggest that $4QSam^{a}$ shared the shorter reading of $LXX^{L}$.

4. *to [Aminon]* We read *lw,* "to him," with MT and $4QSam^{a}$ (cf. $LXX^{BAMN}$). $LXX^{L}$ and Syr. have "to *Aminon,*" and making the name explicit is also helpful in English.

5. *to visit you* So $LXX^{L}$: *tou episkepsasthai se* = *lpqdk.* MT and $4QSam^{a}$ (cf. $LXX^{BAMN}$, Syr.) have *lr'wtk,* "to *see* you." It is difficult to choose between these variants. See also v. 6.

*and take care of me* $LXX^{L}$ has *kai parastēketō moi psōmizousa me,* "and stand near me feeding me." This is probably a harmonized conflation of alternate readings, viz. *kai parastēketō moi* = *wtnṣb 'ly,* "stand beside me = take care of me" (cf. I Sam 4:20), and *kai psōmisatō me* = *wtbrny,* "and feed me," the reading of $LXX^{BAMN}$, to which MT adds *lḥm,* "bread." The reading of MT, $LXX^{BAMN}$ anticipates what follows and *wtnṣb 'ly* is probably original.

*some food* So MT (cf. $LXX^{BALN}$): *'t hbryh.* In anticipation of v. 6 $LXX^{M}$ and certain other MSS read *dyo kollyridas* = *šty lbbwt,* "a couple of dumplings."

*in front of me* So MT (cf. LXX): *l'yny,* lit. "before my eyes." Syr. has *ly,* "for me," and Vulg. omits the expression altogether.

*out of her hand* So MT, $LXX^{L}$. $LXX^{BAMN}$, Syr. have "out of her *hands*" (plural). Cf. vv. 6,10.

6. *to visit him* See the *Textual Note* on "to visit you" in v. 5. Here again we follow $LXX^{L}$ *(episkepsasthai auton)* in reading *lpqdw,* "to visit him," against MT, $LXX^{BAMN}$ *lr'wtw,* "to *see* him." Note that in this case $LXX^{L}$ is corroborated by Josephus' use of *skeptomenou* (*Ant.* 7.166).

*come* LXX, Syr. add "to me"; omit with MT.

*her hand* So MT, LXX. Syr. has "out of her *hands*" (plural). Cf. vv. 5,10.

7. *to your brother Aminon* So Syr., $LXX^{L}$ (= *'l 'mnwn 'ḥyk*). MT has *byt 'mnwn 'ḥyk* (cf. $Syr.^{MSS}$, $LXX^{AMN}$), "to *the house of* your brother Aminon" (cf. v. 8). $LXX^{B}$ reflects a text that originally shared the reading of MT but in which *'mnwn* was lost before *'ḥyk* (homoioarkton)—thus, "to the house of Aminon."

8. *She took* So MT, $LXX^{BAMN}$. $LXX^{L}$, OL: "*Tamar* took."

*kneaded it* MT *(qĕrê)* and $MT^{MSS}$: *wtlš* (= *wattāloš*), as in I Sam 28:24 (MT). MT *(kĕtîb): wtlwš* (= *wattālôš* or *wattālûš*), which $4QSam^{a}$ has in I Sam 28:24 (see *I Samuel,* p. 420). Cf. $GK^{2}$ §72t.

9. *the pan* MT *'t hmśrt.* The rare word has prompted much discussion and a few attempts at emendation, but it seems to be firmly attested in Postbiblical Hebrew and Aramaic (independent of references to the present passage) as a term for a pan used in preparing and cooking *ḥălûṭ,* the batter dumplings identified by Targ. with Tamar's pastry in the present passage (cf. v. 7, where Targ. *wtḥlwṭ . . . trtyn ḥlyṭt'* corresponds to MT *wtlbb . . . šty lbbwt,* "and [let her] make a couple of dumplings"). Thus LXX[BAN] *(to tēganon)* and OL *(sartaginen . . . )* render *'t hmśrt* with words denoting cooking pans, and Targ. reads *yt msryt',* which elsewhere in Targ. (Onkelos) translates Biblical Hebrew *maḥăbat* (Lev 2:5; etc.), a shallow cooking pan used in the preparation of cereal offerings.

*had left him* So MT: *wyṣ'w.* LXX, Vulg., MT[MSS], Targ.[MSS] = *wywṣy'w,* i.e., *Hip'il* as in the preceding clause—thus, "Then when they had got everyone away from him. . . ."

10. *your hand* So MT, LXX. Syr., as in vv. 5 and 6, has "your *hands*" (plural).

11. *sister* So MT (cf. LXX[BAMN], Syr.): *'ḥwty,* lit. "my sister," omitted from the *Vorlage* of LXX[L] in a series of four words ending in *-y (bw'y škby 'my 'ḥwty)* or from the Greek text itself in the sequence *met' emou adelphē mou.*

13. *For my part, where* MT *w'ny 'nh.* LXX[L] reflects the loss of *'ny* (homoioarkton).

*where would I take my shame* MT *'nh 'wlyk 't ḥrpty* (cf. LXX[BAMN], Syr.). LXX[L] *pou ouch ēxei to oneidos mou* reflects a variant, *'nh l' tbw' ḥrpty,* "where would my shame not come (with me)."

14. *he* (1) So MT, Syr. LXX: "Aminon."

*he lay with her* MT has *wayyiškab 'ōtāh,* reading *'th* as accusative rather than prepositional *('ittāh).* The prepositional form is *'ôt-* more or less regularly in Jeremiah, Ezekiel, portions of Kings, and rarely elsewhere (cf. 24:24). Occasionally, however, *'t-* following forms of *šākab,* "lie," is read *'ōt-* instead of *'itt-* by the Masoretes in material where *'itt-* is the prepositional form (Gen 34:2; Lev 15:18,24; Num 5:13,19). In all such passages the consonantal text *('t-* not *'wt-)* can be interpreted prepositionally, and in all of them the versions do, in fact, read prepositional forms. This is true in the present case, where the versions reflect *'th* (= *'ittāh*) or *'mh* (so MT[MSS]) and 4QSam[a] has *'th,* unambiguously *'ittāh* in the full orthography of the scroll. How are we to explain the Masoretic treatment of these passages? Was there a special development in the semantic range of *šākab* (cf. GK[2] §117u)? This would not explain why in some passages forms of *šākab* are treated this way and not in others. Perhaps *šākab* has been substituted in these cases for a transitive verb deemed obscene by the scribes. The verb *šāgēl,* a transitive synonym of *šākab,* occurs four times in MT (Deut 28:30; Isa 13:16; Jer 3:2; Zech 14:2), and in each the *qĕrê* substitutes a form of *šākab.* It may be that the same phenomenon has occurred in our passage and those like it (Gen 34:2; etc.). In these cases, then, the *qĕrê* has intruded into the text, but the accusative particle has been preserved in the Masoretic tradition as a vestigial clue to the original reading.

15. *was greater* LXX[B] inserts at this point *meizōn hē kakia hē eschatē ē hē prōtē* = *gdwlh hr'h h'ḥrwnh mn hr'šwnh,* lit., "greater is this latter wrong than the former." This plus arose by mislocation of a marginal annotation to v. 16 (see the third *Textual Note* there).

16. *Don't, brother! . . . For* We read *l' ḥy ky* on the basis of LXX[LMN] *mē adelphe hoti* (cf. OL). MT (cf. LXX[BA]) has *'l* (= *'l*) *'wdt,* "Concerning, on account of," as the

result of graphic confusion of *ḥy* for *wd* and *ky* for *t*. Here we follow Thenius, Wellhausen, and S. R. Driver against the more recent proposal of G. R. Driver (1950:48–49) to read *'al 'ādat* (= *'ādâ*), "Nay, (this great wrong) is more grievous," etc.; cf. Conroy 1978:151.

*she* So MT, OL, Syr. LXX makes the subject explicit.

*this wrong . . . you did me* MT as it stands is unintelligible: *hr'h hgdwlh hz't m'ḥrt 'šr 'śyt 'my lšlḥny*, "(Concerning) this great wrong, (greater?) than the other which you did me, sending me away." LXX$^{LMN}$ (cf. OL) reflect a different reading: *megalē hē kakia hē eschatē hyper tēn prōtēn hēn pepoiēkas met' emou tou exaposteilai me* = *gdwlh hr'h h'ḥrnh mhr'šnt 'šr 'śyt 'my lšlḥny*, "(because) greater is the latter evil than the former that you did me, sending me away." LXX$^{BA}$ have been conformed to the text of MT here, but in v. 15 LXX$^{B}$ has a plus, *meizōn hē kakia hē eschatē ē hē prōtē*, which represents another translation of *gdwlh hr'h h'ḥrnh mhr'šnh* and, evidently, was an old variant in the margin of LXX$^{B}$ preserving the original LXX reading of v. 16. Most critics have rejected the unintelligible reading of MT in favor of the intelligible alternative of LXX on the assumption that the former is a corruption of the latter (Wellhausen). The form of *m'ḥrt* without the article was taken by Wellhausen as indirect support for LXX *hē eschatē* = *h'ḥrnh* or (as he retroverted it) *h'ḥrt* in preference to **mh'ḥrt*, which he supposed to be the necessary form in MT; but probably *m'ḥrt* is correct as it stands, the article being absent because *'ḥrt* governs the following short *'šr* clause, as in the case of *bimqôm 'ăšer* . . . , "the place where," etc., in 15:21 (cf. GK$^{2}$ §§130cd,138g). It seems impossible, moreover, to derive the reading of MT from that of LXX, and it is much more likely that the text of MT points to a variant reading corrupted by fallout from MT's confusion of *'l 'ḥy ky* for *'l 'wdt* (see the *Textual Note* on "Don't, brother . . . For" above). I assume that MT originally had **gdwlh hr'h hz't m'ḥrt*, etc., lit. "(Don't, brother, for) greater is this wrong than the other," etc.; the change of *gdwlh* from a predicate adjective to an attributive took place after the change from *'l 'ḥy ky* (which was followed by a clause) to *'l 'wdt* (which required a nominal phrase as its object). In my opinion, therefore, we must reckon with ancient variants, (A) *gdwlh hr'h h'ḥrnh mhr'šnh 'šr 'śyt 'my lšlḥny*, "greater is the latter wrong than the former that you did to me, sending me away," and (B) *gdwlh hr'h hz't m'ḥrt 'šr 'śyt lšlḥny*, "greater is this wrong than the other that you did me, sending me away." Our translation represents variant B.

*to her* So MT: *lh*. LXX reflects *bqwlh*, as in v. 14.

17. *who attended him* So MT: *mšrtw* (cf. Syr.). LXX has *ton proestēkota tou oikou (autou)*, "who was in charge of the (his) house." Does this reflect *'šr 'l hbyt?*

*he said* LXX, Syr. add "to him." Omit with MT.

*Put* Reading *šlḥ n'* on the basis of LXX$^{LMN}$ *exaposteilon dē*. MT has *šlḥw n'*, but the plural verb, apparently a simple error, is not compatible with the fact that Aminon is speaking to one servant. Note that in LXX$^{BA}$ the LXX plus "to him" (see the preceding *Textual Note*) is preserved alongside the recensionally adjusted imperative, the result being the curious reading *kai eipen autō exaposteilate dē tautēn*, etc., "and he said to him, 'Send [plural!] this woman away. . . .' "

18. The entire verse has been lost from the text of Syr. after v. 17 (homoioteleuton).

*from puberty on* Wellhausen's proposal to emend MT *m'ylym*, "garments" (LXX *tous ependytas autōn* = *m'ylyhn*, "*their* garments"), to *m'wlm* finds support in Josephus, *Ant.* 7.171: "for *in ancient times (tōn archaiōn)* virgins wore," etc. Hertzberg's objection that "a fashion for king's daughters in Israel cannot have been all that old" does not seem cogent if we keep in mind the probability that v. 18a arose as a marginal annotation to the reference to the "long robe" in v. 19 (see the NOTE). The objections of Conroy (1978:151–52), however, are forceful. It is doubtful that *mēʿôlām, "from* ancient times," can mean "*in* ancient times." Conroy follows the suggestion of Klostermann to read *mēʿōllîm,* "from childhood on" (cf., earlier, Eichhorn 1803:vol. II:528). This, or some other noun from *ʿwl/ʿll,* is possible. I prefer, however, to derive the noun from *ʿlm,* "be sexually mature"—thus, *mēʿālôm* or *mēʿālûmîm,* "from puberty."

19. *ashes and put them* So LXX$^{ALMN}$ (cf. OL): *spodon kai epethēken* = *'pr wtśm.* LXX$^{B}$ adds a second *spodon*—thus, *'pr wtśm 'pr,* "ashes and put ashes." MT originally shared the reading of LXX$^{B}$ but lost *wtśm 'pr* by haplography ("Tamar took ashes on her head," etc.). Schulz, Conroy (1978:34 n. 66), and Barthélemy (1980:24) regard the reading of MT as original, a pregnant construction, and interpret the verb in LXX as an explicating expansion.

*her hand* So MT. LXX, Syr., Vulg. have "her hands" (plural), preferred by Driver and others. The evidence is ambiguous: See the NOTE.

20. *Has . . . been* So MT, LXX. Syr. "Has . . . *lain . . . ?*"

*Aminon* The correct vocalization of MT *'mnwn* elsewhere (vv. 1,2, etc.) is *'ămīnôn,* as shown by *'ămînôn* in the present passage, which alone preserves the fuller spelling *('mynwn).* The old, defective spelling *'mnn* led to the traditional mispronunciation *'amnōn,* "Amnon." Cf. the *Textual Notes* on "Abiner" at 2:8 and "Abishalom" at 3:3.

*Now hush!* Cf. OL. MT, followed by LXX, etc., inserts *'ḥwty*—thus, "Now, my sister, hush!"

*Don't take this thing to heart!* MT reads *'l tšyty 't lbk ldbr hzh,* lit. "Don't set your heart (mind) on this thing!" LXX$^{L}$ has *en* = *'l(ʿl)* for *'t* (cf. OL) and interprets *ldbr hzh* as *tou lalēsai ti* = *lĕdabber hazzeh,* "to say anything." LXX$^{BAM}$ (combining two interpretations of *ldbr hzh?*) has *tou lalēsai eis to rhēma touto* (as if *ldbr 'l*[= *ʿl*] *hdbr hzh*), "to speak concerning this thing." We read the text of MT. Alternatively, however, we might suppose the primitive text to have been *'l tšyty ʿl lbk ldbr ʿl hdbr hzh,* "Don't bring (it) to mind by talking about this thing"; MT would then be deemed haplographic *(l[dbr ʿl h]dbr hzh)* and subsequently modified *(ʿl > 't)* in favor of the common idiom *šyt lb l-,* "set the heart on."

*a desolate woman* Reading *šmmh* with LXX$^{BAMN}$, OL, Vulg., and MT$^{MSS}$. MT, LXX$^{L}$, and Syr. have *wšmmh, "and* (was) a desolate woman." Hertzberg supposes that *mrh* preceded this and fell out of the text after *tmr*—thus, "a *bitter and* desolate woman." Many critics have attempted to preserve the *w-* as an example of an emphatic or epexegetical *waw;* see Conroy 1978:152 and GK[2] §§118p,154a(N).

21. *When King David heard* Reading *whmlk dwd šmʿ* with MT, LXX$^{AL}$, OL, and 4QSam$^{a}$ (of which [ ]*šmʿ 'ı*[ ] is extant at this point). LXX$^{BMN}$ = *wyšmʿ hmlk dwd.*

*but he did nothing . . . his firstborn* We read *wl' ʿṣb* (cf. I Kings 1:6) *'t rwḥ 'mnwn bnw ky 'hbw ky bkwrw hw'* on the basis of LXX *kai ouk elypēsen to pneuma amnōn tou huiou autou hoti ēgapa auton hoti prōtotokos autou ēn* and 4QSam$^{a}$ [ *'h*]*bw ky bkwr*[*w* ] (so also OL; cf. Josephus, *Ant.* 7.173). This material is lacking in MT, and notwithstanding Wellhausen's uncharacteristic *non possumus* ("Wie die Lücke in MT. enstand, lässt sich kaum ermitteln"), it seems clear that the loss was haplographic, a scribe's eye skipping from *wl'* at the beginning of the lost passage (v. 21+) to *wl'* at the beginning of v. 22 (homoioarkton). Cf. Barthélemy 1980:3; Ulrich 1980:132.

## NOTES

**13** 1. *Abishalom . . . had a beautiful sister.* After the transitional formula (cf. Conroy 1978:41–42) the story opens *l'bšlwm . . . ,* lit. "Belonging to Abishalom was," etc. The larger story in chaps. 13–20 is concerned principally with Abishalom's revolt, and even though the chief actors in the opening episode (13:1–22) are Tamar and Aminon, Abishalom, as Conroy puts it (1978:26), "overshadows the scene from the very start" (also Schulz, Mauchline). Significantly, then, Tamar is not identified as David's daughter but as Abishalom's sister. "Sister" in this case means *full*-sister. That is, she was a daughter of David and Maacah, Abishalom's mother (3:3). It follows, of course, that she was also Aminon's (half-)sister (v. 2).

*Tamar.* An important name in the family of David. Evidently David's daughter was named for his ancestress, whose story is told in Genesis 38; cf. Ruth 4:18–22; I Chron 2:3–5,9–15; Matt 1:3–6.

2. *it made him sick.*

Seven (days) to yesterday I have not seen the sister,
And a sickness has invaded me.
My body has become heavy,
Forgetful of my own self.
If the chief of physicians come to me,
My heart is not content (with) their remedies;
The lector priests, no way (out) is in them:—
My sickness will not be probed.
To say to me: "Here she is!" is what will revive me;
Her name is what will lift me up;
The going in and out of her messengers
Is what will revive my heart.
More beneficial to me is the sister than any remedies;
She is more to me than the collected writings.
My health is in her coming in from outside:
When (I) see her, then (I) am well.
If she opens her eye, my body is young (again);
If she speaks, then I am strong (again);
When I embrace her, she drives evil away from me—
But she has gone forth from me for seven days!

This is a stanza of Egyptian love poetry (Papyrus Beatty I, verso C iv 6–v 2, trans. J. A. Wilson for *ANET*[3] 468–69) in which a young man expresses his lovesickness in the absence of his "sister," i.e., his lover (cf. Cant 4:9, etc., and the NOTE in v. 11 below). The motif was common in Egyptian poetry, and in view of other direct or indirect Egyptian cultural influences on the courts of David and Solomon, Caspari, and recently Conroy (1978:27 and n. 27 with bibliography), have noted that the original audience of the story of Aminon and Tamar may have known the poetic malady of lovesickness in its Egyptian expression and recognized its symptoms here in a young man who is love-sick for his actual sister. Though Conroy does not mention it, lovesickness became a theme of Hebrew love poetry as well; thus in Cant 5:8 the young woman says:

> I adjure you, daughters of Jerusalem,
> If you find my lover,
> What will you tell him?
> That I am sick with love!

(cf. Cant 2:5, where, however, the "sickness" has another cause, according to Pope 1977:382–83,529).

*impossible.* That is, because she was a virgin, "a hint that, as was proper, unmarried girls, and particularly those of the royal house, would be carefully guarded" (Ackroyd with most commentators).

3. *a friend.* In Judg 14:20 the man called Samson's "friend" was evidently the one who served him as best man in his unsuccessful marriage to a Philistine woman from Timnah. Similarly, in Sumero-Akkadian terminology "friend" *(kuli = ibru)* was a technical term for best man (van Selms 1957:119). Elsewhere in the Bible we find a "friend" acting formally on behalf of a man in his dealings with a woman in Gen 38:20. Thus the term "friend" here may mean more than an intimate acquaintance. Jonadab may have routinely served Aminon as a matchmaker and adviser in affairs of the heart. Van Selms' conclusion (1957:120) that this was the original function of the officer of court called the King's Friend (see the NOTE at 15:37), however, is difficult to assess. It seems to depend heavily on the present passage, inasmuch as this is the only case where the "friend" of a royal person is involved in his dealings with women. The argument would be that as prince Aminon would already have a "friend," who would become "King's Friend" at Aminon's accession to the throne. The language, however, presents a problem: *la'ămīnôn rēa',* "Aminon had a friend," suggests that this man was one friend among others (cf. GK[2] §129c), contrary to what we should expect if he held an official post as Aminon's friend.

*David's brother Shimeah.* Elsewhere "Shimei" or "Shammah" (cf. the *Textual Note);* Shimeah was Jesse's third son (I Sam 16:9; etc.).

*wise.* The English adjective connotes an admirable quality, but in the Bible " 'wisdom' is a purely intellectual and morally neutral quality" (Whybray 1968:58). It was used for attaining goals, whether admirable or not (Mendenhall 1973:172; cf. Ackroyd). We should not be surprised, therefore, to find Jonadab, who uses his wisdom in contemptible ways, called "very wise." He is "wise for doing evil," as the rabbis put it (Sanhedrin 21a). For the same reason it is misleading to translate *ḥākām* as "subtil" (AV), "crafty" (RSV), "shrewd" (NEB, JB; cf. Caird), or "clever" (NJV); cf. Driver; Mendenhall 1973:172 n. 93. Indeed, as Freedman points out to me, "wise" is misleading because of the connotation in English.

4. Aminon's reply is a series of gasping sighs: *'et-tāmār . . . 'ăḥôt 'ăbšālôm 'āḥî . . . 'ănî 'ōhēb.* A somewhat exaggerated effect is achieved by repeated alliteration of *'alep* followed by *-o* and *-a* sounds with a few gutturals thrown in for good measure.

On the language of this verse in general, see Conroy 1978:29 and his citations of Alonso Schökel.

6. *a couple.* For *šětê,* "two," as "a couple, a few," see Ehrlich 1910:301.

*hearty dumplings.* This dish was made from dough that was kneaded and boiled (v. 8) and must, therefore, have been some kind of dumplings or puddings, not "cakes" (so RSV and most English translations). It was boiled in a pan or mold called a *maśrēt* (v. 9), mentioned only here in the Bible but used in rabbinic times for preparing *ḥālûṭ,* a dumpling made by stirring flour in water. The Hebrew name for the dish is *lěbībôt* (rendered *ḥălîṭātā'* by the Targum Jonathan), and this might mean that they were heart-shaped (KB³)—cf. *lēbāb,* "heart." But note the denominative verb *libbēb,* "enhearten," i.e., "give strength, vigor," found in Biblical and Rabbinic Hebrew, not to mention Aramaic cognates. As Pope has shown (1977:478–80), this verb has an erotic sense in its occurrences in Cant 4:9, where it means "ravish" the mind (Pope) or simply "arouse, excite":

> You arouse me, my sister, bride!
> You arouse me with one of your eyes!

In the present passage, then, Aminon asks David for *lěbībôt,* enheartening dumplings, perhaps a traditional food for the sick because of its nourishing quality ("hearty") and digestibility ("boiled"). This seems a reasonable sickbed request on the face of it, but Aminon, by asking that Tamar prepare the dumplings *(tělabbēb . . . lěbībôt),* is privately anticipating more than the restoration of his health, as the use of *libbēb* in Cant 4:9 suggests. Cf. Budde, Brockington.

9. *and served him.* Hebrew *wattiṣṣōq* (or *wattaṣṣīq*) *lěpānāyw,* lit. "and set down [viz. the pan] before him." Josh 7:23 shows that *yāṣaq/hiṣṣîq lipnê PN* means "set before" or "put down in front of." In reference to food, then, it means "serve" (cf. II Kings 4:40,41) like *yṣq b'ap-* in the hippiatric texts from Ugarit (*CTCA* 160[= *UT*⁴ 55].3, 5,9,29; 161[= 56].11,16,20,22). See also the NOTE on "They put down" at 15:24.

*"Get everybody away from me!"* That is, *hôṣî'û kol-'îš mē'ālay,* as in Gen 45:1 and Judg 3:19, "a courtly formula of dismissal" (Conroy 1978:30 n. 45).

11. *sister.* Aminon calls Tamar *'ăḥôtî* because she is his half-sister but also, perhaps, because of the traditional use of "brother/sister" terminology in love poetry. Cf. the NOTE on "it made him sick," v. 2, and the citation of Cant 4:9 in the NOTE on "hearty dumplings," v. 6.

12–13. Tamar's warning is acute and farsighted, and to this extent we are reminded of Abigail's words to David in I Sam 25:24–31. Whereas Abigail's remonstrance was heeded, however, Tamar's will not be.

12. *such a thing isn't done in Israel.* The expression refers to serious violations of custom (Gen 20:9; 29:26) that threaten the fabric of society. Compare, especially, Gen 34:7, where language similar to that of the present verse is used in reference to Shechem's rape of Dinah, a "sacrilege in Israel."

*sacrilege.* Hebrew *něbālâ* is customarily rendered "folly" or "foolishness," but recent studies by Gerleman (1974), Phillips (1975), and especially Roth (1960) have shown this to be inadequate and misleading. It is "a general expression for serious disorderly and unruly action resulting in the breakup of an existing relationship whether between tribes, within the family, in a business arrangement, in marriage or with God. It indicates the end of an existing order consequent upon breach of rules which maintained that order" (Phillips 1975:241). In other words, *nĕbālâ* refers to a violation of the sacred taboos that define, hedge, and protect the structure of society. It is a sacrilege (Roth); cf. Isa 9:16 [9:17]; 32:6. Thus, for example, in the Achan episode in Joshua 7 the private appropriation of taboo objects—items of spoil restricted by the sacred "ban" (*ḥērem)*—is an act of *nĕbālâ* (v. 15), and as a result of their breach of sacred discipline (cf. v. 1, *wayyimʿălû bĕnê yiśrāʾēl maʿal*) the protection afforded the Israelites by their relationship with Yahweh is forfeit (v. 11) and the army falls into disarray and defeat. As Roth notes (1960:406), *nĕbālâ* is used especially of sexual misconduct, including rape (Judg 20:6,10), promiscuity (Deut 22:21), adultery (Jer 29:23), and homosexual assault (Judg 19:23). The "sacrilege" of Aminon is also of this character and, as explained in the COMMENT, its consequences will be far-reaching.

13. *For my part, where would I take my shame?* Conroy (1978:31 n. 51) compares Gen 37:30, where Reuben expresses helplessness and wretchedness in almost identical language ("For my part, where shall I go?"), and a passage in the Beth-shan stele of the Egyptian king Sethos I (ca. 1318–1304 B.C.), where the defeated princes of foreign lands say "Where shall we go?" (*ANET*[3] 253).

*the outcasts in Israel.* See the NOTE at v. 12. Having committed *nĕbālâ,* "a sacrilege," in Israel, Aminon would become *nābāl,* an "outcast," having forfeited his place in the society he endangered. *Nābāl* is traditionally rendered "fool" (cf. the NOTE on "sacrilege" above), but it refers to someone who has severed himself from society by socially destructive behavior and has become an outcast, a moral pariah (see Roth 1960:402–4). Compare the denominative (!) verb **nibbēl,* "treat as a *nābāl,*" i.e., "reject, despise."

*He won't keep me from you!* What does Tamar mean? Does this remonstrance imply that marriage between Aminon and Tamar would have been possible? Intercourse between brother and sister is explicitly forbidden in both Deuteronomic (Deut 27:22) and Priestly (Lev 18:9,11; 20:7; cf. Ezek 22:11) legislation, suggesting that marriage between Aminon and Tamar would be impossible. Pointing to the case of Abraham and Sarah (cf. Gen 20:12), however, some scholars have argued that the prohibition of marriage with a sibling was a late development (Daube 1947:77–79) or that consanguinity was originally thought to exist only with the children of one's mother (de Vaux 1961b:vol. I:19–20). From this it would follow that marriage with the son or daughter of one's father might have been permissible in the time of David. But we cannot be sure. It would be naive to draw straightforward conclusions about prevailing marriage customs from the patriarchal stories, and the laws of Leviticus 18, where marriage to the children of one's father is expressly forbidden (vv. 9,11), seem to presuppose the social structure of the extended family of a patriarchal system and have been thought, therefore, to derive from pre-monarchical times (Elliger 1955). Moreover, even if it could be determined whether the biblical laws forbidding marriage to one's half-brother or half-sister were theoretically in effect in Israel in the time of David, we could not assume that the authority of such rules would have been recognized in Jerusalem, especially in their application to the royal family, and their existence or nonexistence, therefore, would not be conclusive in the interpretation of Tamar's words. There seem to be four possibilities. (1) The laws of Lev 18:9,11 were not in effect in the time of David. In this case Tamar's words are a forthright appeal for reason, and Aminon's crime consists "not in casting his eyes on his half-sister, but in violating her without having contracted a marriage and in contracting no marriage after having violated her"

(Daube 1947:79). (2) The laws were in effect but not recognized in Jerusalem. In this case Tamar's words are, as in the first case, a sincere appeal, and Aminon's crime is rape, not incest (Conroy 1978:17–18 n. 3), though there might be some ambiguity on the last point in the mind of the audience. (3) The laws were in effect in Jerusalem, but their purpose was not to regulate marriage but to prevent casual intercourse with women a man could expect to encounter in his household. In this case Tamar's words are again an appeal for reason, and Aminon is guilty of violating the laws of Leviticus 18 but, because he could have married her, not of committing incest (Phillips 1975:239). (4) The laws were in full effect. In this case Tamar's words, unless she is simply temporizing, imply that David would have been willing to permit the marriage despite its illegality, and Aminon is guilty of both rape and incest. Of these possibilities it is the last that is most defensible. While our sources are very candid about, for example, foreign marriages made by the royal family in the time of the early monarchy, no sibling marriage is mentioned, and it seems probable that some kind of prohibition was in effect. Tamar's assumption that David would be willing to overlook such a prohibition in order to accede to Aminon's request is consistent with what we know of David's attitude elsewhere (v. 21). The story as a whole, with its extraordinary preponderance of sibling references (see the COMMENT), gives the impression that the brother-sister relationship between Aminon and Tamar is of special significance. It is very difficult, moreover, to think of the "sacrilege" Tamar speaks of so emphatically in vv. 12–13 as a simple rape (Wenham 1972:342), since a man who raped an unbetrothed woman was not punished but required only to marry her (Deut 22:28); the rape of Dinah in Genesis 34 was a sacrilege because Shechem was not an Israelite, and the Levite's concubine in Judges 19 was raped to death by a group of men. Surely, then, the sacrilege in the present passage is incest.

15. It was Tacitus (*Agricola* 42.15) who said, "It is human nature to hate those whom you have injured," and according to Max Beerbohm (*Zuleika Dobson,* chap. 13), "Of all the objects of hatred, a woman once loved is the most hateful." A number of poets and psychologists could be cited on the readiness with which love—especially of the acute, grasping variety—turns to hatred and the intensity of the hatred thus produced. Accordingly, most modern commentators have thought it adequate to explain Aminon's sudden change of heart by reference to general truths of human behavior. The rabbis, however, supposed that Aminon hated Tamar because, when he raped her, he became entangled in her pubic hair and injured himself (Sanhedrin 21a).

16. According to Exod 22:15 [22:16], "If a man seduces a virgin who is not betrothed and lies with her, he must make her his wife by paying the bride-price." Similarly, Deut 22:28 says, "If a man meets a virgin who is not betrothed and seizes her and lies with her, then when they are found the man who lay with her will give the young woman's father fifty pieces of silver. She will become his wife because he forced her. He cannot send her away *(šallĕḥāh)* as long as he lives." On such a basis Tamar protests that "sending [her] away" *(lĕšallĕḥēnî)* is a greater wrong than raping her (cf. Carlson 1964:181). "Send away" *(šillaḥ)* is a technical term for the dismissal of a divorced wife (Deut 24:1–4). It is true that Aminon and Tamar are not married (cf. Conroy 1978:33 n. 59), but Tamar implies that they must now become married in view of what has happened and that Aminon has forfeited his right to send her away.

17. *this woman.* Hebrew *zō't,* contemptuously, like *zeh,* "this fellow," in I Sam 10:27; 21:16; etc. (GK[2] §136b). Contrast Caspari.

*away from me.* Hebrew *mēʿālay,* which "itself is contemptuous, implying that the person to be removed is a burden to the speaker" (Conroy 1978:33 n. 60).

18b. *bolting.* For *wĕnāʿal* we should probably read *wĕnāʿōl,* a resumptive infinitive absolute. Comparison with Judg 3:23 shows that a change to *wayyinʿōl,* "and he bolted," is not warranted, and it is unlikely that *wĕnāʿal* is a frequentative, implying fastening with several bolts (GK² §112tt n. 1).

18a. This antiquarian notice arose long after the composition of the story as a marginal comment on the "embroidered gown" mentioned in v. 19. Like the similar notice in I Sam 10:9, it found its way into the text a bit too soon (cf. *I Samuel,* p. 177). It is less disruptive after v. 18b than before it. Here we follow Wellhausen. Contrast Conroy 1978:34.

*a long-sleeved gown.* The meaning of *kĕtōnet passîm,* which occurs only here and in Genesis 37, is uncertain. The traditional "coat of many colors" goes back to the Septuagint's treatment of the phrase in Gen 37:3 as *chitōna poikilon,* "an embroidered (or variegated) frock," which may have been a guess based on one meaning of *pas* in Rabbinic Hebrew, viz. "strip, stripe"—thus *kĕtōnet passîm,* "gown of strips" or "striped gown." Another postbiblical meaning of *pas* was "palm (of the hand)" or "sole (of the foot)"; hence the Septuagint's reading in the present passage, *chitōn karpōtos,* "a frock with sleeves reaching to the wrists" ($LXX^B$), or *chitōn astragalōtos,* "a frock reaching to the ankles" ($LXX^L$). This is the origin of modern translations such as "long robe with sleeves" (RSV). Unfortunately, *pas* is not attested elsewhere in Biblical Hebrew, and we cannot be sure of its ancient meaning. Nor have attempts to explain it on the basis of extrabiblical materials succeeded. Speiser (1964:289–90), for example, compares Akkadian *kitû pišannu,* which he defines as "a ceremonial robe which could be draped about statues of goddesses, and had various gold ornaments sewed onto it"; but the character of the *pišannu*-garment is so obscure (Oppenheim 1949) and the correspondence of *pišannu* to *passîm* so awkward that this avenue of exploration does not seem very promising. More recently Mendenhall (1973:54–55) has called attention to the obscure Ugaritic word *pḏ* (*CTCA* 2[= *UT*⁴ 137].1.19,35) in connection with Hebrew *kātōnet passîm.* He presents a strong argument for identification of *pḏ* and its parallel, *ʿnn,* with Akkadian (*melammū, puluḫtu*) and Hebrew (*kābôd*) terms for the "glory" of a god or king, the refulgent envelope that surrounded the divine or royal body. He then goes on (p. 55) to equate *pḏ* with *kĕtōnet passîm,* "which describes a garment . . . associated with the highest social or political status. In other words, the term does not describe the form of the garment but its social function. It actually is used only of Joseph, who dreams of his brothers bowing down to him, and of Tamar, the princess of the royal house." The chief problem with this proposal is philological: Mendenhall cites no parallel for the presumed correspondence of Hebrew *s* to Ugaritic *ḏ,* which may reflect etymological **ḏ* or even **ṯ* (realized in Hebrew as *z* or *š*) but never to my knowledge **s* (cf. Cross and Freedman 1964) or a non-Semitic consonant realized in Hebrew as *s.* My own solution, which reverts to one of the traditional interpretations of *kĕtōnet passîm,* is more prosaic. Very probably *pas* is identical to *ʾepes,* "extremity." Note the place-name *ʾepes dammîm* in I Sam 17:1, called *pas dammîm* in I Chron 11:13. In Biblical Hebrew *ʾopsayim* means "ankles" unambiguously in Ezek 47:3, the Talmudic form (Yoma 77b) being *ʾapsayim;* and, as already noted, Hebrew *pas* and Aramaic *pissĕtāʾ* (also *pas, passāʾ, pissāʾ*) meant "foot" as well as "hand" in rabbinic times. In Ezek 47:3 *mê 'opsayim*, lit. "water of the ankles," must mean "water extending to the ankles," in view of v. 4, where the water rises to the knees, then the loins (*mê motnayim*). It follows that *kĕtōnet passîm* means "gown extending to the extremities"—i.e., hands *and* feet, since it is plural, not dual—and thus "long gown with sleeves," essentially the reading of the Septuagint and a number of modern translations. Asiatics wearing such garments are depicted in tile decorations from the palace of Ramesses III (1198–1166).

19. *She tore the long-sleeved gown.* Because the garment was customarily worn by virgins (v. 18a), some interpreters have supposed that Tamar tore it as a mark of her lost virginity (Ehrlich 1910:302–3). But the gesture can be explained sufficiently as an expression of grief (1:11; etc.). Rending the clothes was a response to calamities other than death (II Kings 5:7; etc.).

*put her hand on her head.* Placing *one* hand on the head (see the *Textual Note* on "her hand") was another gesture of grief (Conroy 1978:152). At the end of the Egyptian "Story of Two Brothers," for example, the grieving elder brother goes "to his house, with his hand laid upon his head, and . . . smeared with dust" (*ANET*[3], p. 24). In Jer 2:37, on the other hand, Israel under the image of a rejected lover expresses her shame by coming away with both hands on her head (Ehrlich 1910:303).

*went away, crying constantly as she went.* Hebrew *wattēlek hālôk wĕzā'āqâ*, a perfect consecutive coordinated with an infinitive absolute as found elsewhere only in Josh 6:13 (GK[2] §113t). The usual construction coordinates two infinitives absolute (Josh 6:9[!]), as in II Sam 3:16 [MT], but compare 16:13 and the NOTE on "following . . . cursing" there.

20. Whether Tamar lived in Abishalom's household before the rape (Hertzberg) or not (Budde) cannot be determined. In either case, she goes now to her full-brother, the natural leader of her "branch" of the house of David. Hoftijzer (1970a) discerns the outline of a fratriarchal family structure here, thus extending an old theory about patriarchal society (Gordon 1935) to the time of David. But see Conroy (1978:18 n. 5) and, on fratriarchy in the patriarchal age, de Vaux (1978:234–35).

*"Has Aminon . . . been with you?"* A euphemism; cf. Gen 39:10 (Ehrlich 1910:303).

*a desolate woman.* The verb *šāmēm*, "be desolate," refers most often to land that is abandoned and neglected (Isa 49:8; etc.). With respect to a woman it means unmarried (Ehrlich 1910:303), as shown clearly by the ironic contrast in Isa 54:1, where it is said that "the children of a desolate woman (*šômēmâ*) will be more numerous than the children of a married woman." The connection between land and women involved here is that expressed by the clichéd Canaanite complaint about neglected farmland: "My field is like a woman without a mate from lack of plowing" (*EA* 74:17–19; cf. 75:15–17; 81:37–38; 90:42–44).

21. *he was his firstborn.* See 3:2.

22. *said nothing . . . bad or good.* By calling attention to Genesis 31, Hoftijzer (1970a:55–56) has shown that this expression refers not simply to silence but to restraint from hostile action. In Gen 31:24 God tells Laban in a dream not to "say anything to Jacob, good or bad." It is clear in Gen 31:29, however, that Laban feels obliged to refrain not simply from harsh judgment but rather from vindictive action. In the present passage the restraint is self-imposed. Abishalom is biding his time.

*but.* In view of the preceding NOTE, the conjunction *kî* is better taken as adversative/concessive than causative ("said nothing . . . *because* [he] hated him"); so Hoftijzer 1970a:55 n. 6; Conroy 1978:18 n. 6.

## COMMENT

The story of the rape of Tamar and its consequences in chaps. 13 and 14 stands as a prologue to the account of Abishalom's rebellion in chaps. 15–20. The prologue has its own literary integrity (cf. Long 1981), beginning as it does with a detailed report of the violent events that led to Abishalom's exclusion from the court and concluding with an equally detailed description of the process by which his reconciliation to the king was finally achieved. It would be a mistake, however, to conclude that chaps. 13–14 originally existed as an independent narrative centered on Tamar (so Caspari in his commentary as well as 1909:318–24 and 1911:239–42, and recently Delekat 1967:26,29; the criticism of such a conclusion in Conroy 1978:92 is decisive). These two chapters are principally concerned with Abishalom. The opening words, where his name is the first mentioned and Tamar is identified as his sister, show this (see the NOTE at 13:1), as do the facts that the time references in the story (13:23,38; 14:28) attach themselves to his activities (Conroy) and that the only significant interruption in the course of the narrative is a long parenthesis (14:25–27) testifying to his beauty and popularity. All of these things are *praeparatio* for the account of the revolt in chaps. 15ff.

More specifically, chaps. 13–14 provide the knowledge of private matters necessary, in our narrator's opinion, for a correct understanding of the public events recounted in chaps. 15–20. Those events will arise from a clash of personalities presented to us here. First there is Abishalom. He is handsome and winning (14:25), but he is also vindictive and rancorous, not a man to accept the king's kiss (14:33) as a seal of lasting reconciliation after the wrong he perceives his enforced exile to have represented. He is self-willed to a fault and reckless in seeking to gain his own ends (cf. 14:28–32). Then there is David, gentle king and doting father. There is no violence or vengeance in him, but he is carelessly compliant (13:7) and indecisive (cf. 14:1) in dealing with his own family, and his affection for his sons makes him too lenient when punishment is in order (13:21). Finally there is Joab, as usual the foil to David's gentleness (cf. 3:39). He is always ready with a quick solution—for better or for worse—when the king's mildness precipitates a problem. The interaction of these three men in the private events of chaps. 13–14 prepares us fully to understand their roles in the public events to follow.

Most fundamentally, chap. 13 is a story of *nĕbālâ,* "sacrilege." As explained in the NOTE at v. 12, *nĕbālâ* is a violation of the sacred taboos that define and maintain the social structure and, as such, represents a serious threat to the society itself. The particular "sacrilege" committed here is incestuous rape. Although there is no certainty about the legal status of marriage between half-siblings in Davidic Israel (see the NOTE on "He won't keep me from you!" v. 13), our narrator makes it unavoidably clear that incest is an issue by the extraordinary frequency of sibling terms he employs in vv. 1–14 ("brother" and "sister" six times each; cf. Flanagan 1972:180). Thus the particular incident that begins the story of Abishalom's revolt is an act of violence born of excessive love within the royal family, viz. Aminon's rape of Tamar. The immediate result is an act of violence born of excessive hate within the family, viz. Abishalom's murder of Aminon. There is, as Gunn aptly puts it (1978: 100), "excess of love at the beginning, excess of hate at the end." In the process of all this the son, Abishalom, is estranged from the father, David, and will eventually make war on him. The initial sacrilege, therefore, will precipitate the destruction of the entire social unit, the family. And because this particular family is the royal family, the social fabric of all Israel will finally be threatened (chap. 20).

# XXV. THE DEATH OF AMINON
## (13:23–37)

13 [23]Two years later Abishalom had sheepshearing in Baal-hazor near
Ophrah, and he invited all of the king's sons. [24]He went to the king and
said, "Your servant has sheepshearing. Let the king and his servants
go with your servant!"

[25]But the king said to Abishalom, "No, son, we won't all go. We
would just make things more difficult for you." And though [Abisha-
lom] pleaded with him, he would not agree to go.

But when [the king] bade him farewell, [26]Abishalom said, "At least
let my brother Aminon go!"

"Why should he go with you?" said the king. [27]But when Abishalom
pleaded with him, he let Aminon and all the king's sons go with him.

So Abishalom prepared a banquet like a king's banquet. [28]"Be alert!"
[he] instructed his servants. "When Aminon is lighthearted with the
wine and I say to you, 'Strike down Aminon!', then kill him! Don't be
afraid, for I myself have given you the command! Steady yourselves and
be stalwart!"

[29]When Abishalom's servants did to Aminon as Abishalom had instructed, all the king's sons got up, mounted their mules, and fled. [30]But
while they were on the road, the following report reached David:
"Abishalom has slain all the king's sons, and not one of them is left!"
[31]The king got up, tore his clothes, and lay down on the ground; and
all the servants who were standing about him tore their clothes, too.

[32]Then, however, Jonadab, the son of David's brother Shimeah, spoke
up. "My lord the king mustn't think that the servants killed all the
king's sons," he said, "for only Aminon is dead. This happened because
of Abishalom's anger from the time [Aminon] forced his sister. [33]So my
lord the king mustn't take this thing to heart, thinking all the king's
sons are dead. Only Aminon is dead."

[34]Just then the soldier on watch looked up and saw a crowd of people
traveling the Horonaim road on the side of the mountain in the descent,
and [he] came and reported this to the king. "I have seen men," he said,
"on the Horonaim road on the side of the mountain."

[35]Then Jonadab said to the king, "The king's sons have come! It's just as your servant said!" [36]By the time he finished speaking, the king's sons had arrived. They wept aloud, and the king, too, and all his servants wept grievously. [37]He mourned for his son for many days.

## TEXTUAL NOTES

13 23. *Two years later* MT: *lšntym ymym*, lit. "in two years (in) days" (cf. LXX$^{BAM}$: *eis dietērida hēmerōn*), as in 14:28. LXX$^{L}$ *meta dyo etē* = *'ḥry šntym*, "after two years" (cf. OL). Syr.: *l'dn b'dn*, lit. "from season to season (i.e., in one year)."

*Ophrah* MT has *'prym*, "Ephraim," to which LXX$^{BAMN}$ *ephraim* corresponds. LXX$^{L}$ *gophraim*, which shows that the first consonant was *'ayin*, has been partially conformed to the reading of MT (from **gophera* [cf. I Sam 13:17]). See, further, the NOTE.

24. *and his servants* Joüon (1928:308–9) suggests reading *wkl bnyw*, "and all his sons," for MT *w'bdyw*.

*with your servant* So MT (cf. LXX$^{BAMN}$): *'m 'bdk*. LXX$^{L}$, OL, and Vulg. (cf. Josephus, *Ant.* 7.174) share the doubly divergent reading of 4QSam$^{a}$: *'l 'bdẇ*, "*to his* servant."

25. *make things more difficult for you* So 4QSam$^{a}$: *nkbyd 'lyk* (cf. Neh 5:15). MT preserves the older orthography, *nkbd 'lyk*, and interprets *nkbd* as *Qal*—thus, "be a burden on you."

*And though [Abishalom] pleaded* Reading *wypṣr* with 4QSam$^{a}$, LXX *(kai ebiasato/ katebiazeto)*, Syr. *(w'lṣh)*, OL *(cogerat)*, etc. MT has *wyprṣ*, as if "And he broke out (upon him)." For the same metathesis, see v. 27 and I Sam 28:23; II Kings 5:23.

*he* (2) So MT. LXX$^{L}$ has "the king."

26. *let my brother Aminon go* MT adds "with us" *('tnw*; MT$^{MSS}$ *'mnw)*, and LXX$^{L}$ *(met' emou)* and OL *(mecum)*, "with me." We omit both with 4QSam$^{a}$ (*[ylk n]' 'mnwn 'ḥy*), though one might restore *'ty* in the text of the scroll on the assumption of haplography before *'mnwn* (homoioarkton).

*he* So MT, LXX$^{BAL}$. LXX$^{MN}$ and several other MSS make the subject explicit.

*said the king* MT, LXX$^{BAMN}$, and 4QSam$^{a}$ add "to him." Omit with LXX$^{L}$.

27. *pleaded* See the second *Textual Note* at v. 25 above. 4QSam$^{a}$ is not extant at this point, but the other major witnesses read as in the previous case.

*So Abishalom . . . a king's banquet* Reading *wy'ś 'bšlwm mšth kmšth hmlk* on the basis of LXX *kai epoiēsen abessalōm poton kata ton poton tou basileōs* (cf. OL and Josephus, *Ant.* 7.174). Space considerations show that 4QSam$^{a}$ shared this reading, though only *[h]ṁ[l]k* survives on the leather. MT has lost the entire sentence by haplography with the immediately preceding word, *hmlk* (homoioteleuton). See Joüon 1928:309 and, recently, Ulrich 1978:85; 1980:132–33; Barthélemy 1980:3.

28. *then kill* So MT: *wahămittem*. 4QSam$^{a}$ has *wmttm* = *ûmōtattem*, "then dispatch."

*for I myself* Reading *ky 'nky* with LXX^L. MT prefaces this with *hlw',* "Is it not (so) that I myself . . . ?"

*and be stalwart* That is, *whyw lbny ḥyl;* so MT and 4QSam^a (cf. LXX^BAMN). LXX^L, OL reflect *whyw (l)'nšy (eis andras, viri) ḥyl.*

29. *as Abishalom had instructed* So MT: *k'šr ṣwh 'bšlwm.* In LXX, OL, Syr., and Vulg. *k'šr ṣwh lhm 'bšlwm,* "as Abishalom had instructed *them,*" is reflected, and this has led to the loss of *'bšlwm* in LXX^L (homoioteleuton).

30. *one of them* So MT: *mhm 'ḥd* (cf. OL). MT^MSS: *mhm 'd 'ḥd* (cf. LXX^L, Targ.^MS). MT^MSS: *mhm 'yš* (cf. Syr.).

31. *who were . . . their clothes, too* Reading *hnṣbym 'lyw qr'w 't bgdyhm* on the basis of LXX^BAMN *hoi periestōtes autō dierrēxan ta himatia autōn.* MT (cf. LXX^L) has *nṣbym* (LXX^L = *nṣbw 'lyw) qr'y bgdym,* "were standing (stood about him) with torn clothes." OL has *sciderunt vestimenta sua et astabant ei* = *qr'w 't bgdyhm wyṣbw 'lyw,* "tore their clothes and stood about him." In 4QSam^a only the last word survives; it is *bgdyw,* "his (!) clothes," which, unless it is simply an error caused by attraction to *bgdyw* earlier in the verse (so Ulrich 1978:129; 1980:133), indicates that the scroll may have read something like [. . . *qr'w 'yš*] *bgdyw,* ". . . tore, each man his clothes."

32. *Shimeah* MT *šim'â.* Cf. the *Textual Note* at v. 3.

*My lord the king . . . that* Reading *'dny hmlk ky* with LXX, Syr. MT has lost *hmlk ky,* a scribe's eye having skipped from *-ny* to *ky.*

*the servants killed all the king's sons* MT (cf. LXX^BAMN) has *'t kl hn'rym bny hmlk hmytw,* "they (LXX^BAMN "he") killed all the lads, the king's sons," and LXX^L reflects *kl hn'rym bny hmlk mtw* (cf. Syr.), which anticipates v. 33. 4QSam^a has [ ] *hn'rym kwl bny hm*[*lk*]. We might interpret these data as evidence for a doublet (cf. Ulrich 1978:139), *'t kl hn'rym* and *'t kl bny hmlk,* of which the former would be preferable in light of v. 33—thus read *'t kl hn'rym hmytw/hmyt,* "they/he killed all the lads." But the use of *hmyt(w)* with an implicit subject of such remote antecedence is odd, moreover, *hn'rym,* "the lads," in the narrative are the "servants" of Abishalom (vv. 28,29), who do the killing. I prefer, therefore, to read *hn'rym ('t) kl bny hmlk hmytw.* Note that the reading of 4QSam^a might be urged in support of either solution.

*he said* So MT, LXX^BAMN, Syr. LXX^L, OL: "saying."

*This happened because of Abishalom's anger* The original was probably *ky 'l 'p 'bšlwm hyth,* lit. "For it was on account of Abishalom's anger," an idiomatic expression used also in II Kings 24:20 = Jer 52:3 (cf. Jer 32:31) and Jer 24:3. In Jer 24:3, however, MT reads *py* for *'p,* and the same substitution has taken place in MT in the present passage (thus, ". . . according to the command of Abishalom . . ."); in both places LXX reflects the original *'p.* After *hyth* in the present passage MT adds *śwmh* (*kĕtîb,* cf. GK^2 §73f), an insertion in explanation of the idiom ("For it was *determined,*" etc.), which may be deleted with LXX^LM, OL, and 4QSam^a (cf. Ulrich 1980:134). The scroll, which reads [ ]*hyh,* seems, like LXX^LM *(hoti en orgē ēn autō abessalōm)* and OL *(in ira enim est at abessalon),* to understand "Abishalom" as the subject of the verb ("For Abishalom has been in anger [against him] . . .").

[*Aminon*] The name is made explicit in LXX^L.

*his sister* MT, Syr., LXX^BAMN: "*Tamar,* his sister." LXX^L: "his sister *Tamar.*" The variation suggests that the name is secondary.

34. At the beginning of the verse all witnesses read with MT *wybrḥ 'bšlwm,* "And Abishalom fled." The notice anticipates v. 38 and is out of place at this point. Perhaps

it arose as a syntactic variant of *w'bšlwm brḥ* (v. 38), retained marginally and inserted into the text in the wrong place. Wellhausen also strikes these words, which he associates with the duplication and confusion in vv. 37,38 (see below).

*the Horonaim road*(1) . . . *on the side of the mountain*(2) We read *bdrk ḥrnym mṣd hhr bmwrd wyb' hṣph wygd lmlk wy'mr 'nšym r'yty mdrk ḥrnym mṣd hhr.* The text of MT is much shorter in consequence of haplography, a scribe's eye having skipped from *bdrk ḥrnym mṣd hhr* to *mdrk ḥrnym mṣd hhr.* For *ḥrnym* MT has *'ḥryw,* "behind him," but we expect a place-name here, as hinted by the construct form of *mdrk (midderek),* and the reference to "the descent" *(bmwrd)* suggests "Horonaim" (cf. Josh 10:11, where MT has *bmwrd byt ḥrnym* and LXX$^{B}$ *epi tēs katabaseōs hōrōn[e]in* = *bmwrd ḥrnym*), as confirmed here by LXX$^{L}$ *sōraim* and later in the verse by LXX$^{BA}$ *ōrōnēn* and LXX$^{MN}$ *ōran.* The portion of the text missing in MT *(bmwrd . . . hhr)* can be reconstructed from LXX *en tē katabasei kai paregeneto ho skopos kai apēngeilen tō basilei kai eipen andras heōraka* (LXX$^{L}$ *horōn heōraka andras* = *r'h r'yty 'nšym) ek tēs hodou tēs ōrōnēn ek merous tou orous.* Our reconstruction agrees essentially with that of Wellhausen, who, however, would strike the first *mṣd hhr,* the reflection of which in LXX he regards, perhaps correctly, as recensional.

36. *wept grievously* That is, *bkw bky gdwl,* lit. "wept a great weeping" (cf. LXX$^{B}$). MT (cf. LXX$^{ALMN}$) adds *m'd*—thus, "wept a *very* great weeping."

37. Verse 37a reads *w'bšlwm brḥ wylk 'l tlmy bn 'myḥwr mlk gšwr,* "And Abishalom had fled and gone to Talmai son of Ammihur, the king of Geshur" (so MT; see, further, the *Textual Note* on "Geshur" in 13:38). This intelligence is out of place. It probably arose from a correction of v. 38a, which is haplographic in the text of MT, to which other witnesses have been conformed. In a text identical to that of v. 37a, a scribe's eye skipped from *wylk* to *mlk* (homoioteleuton), leaving *w'bšlwm brḥ wylk gšwr,* the present text of v. 38a. This was corrected by supralinear insertion of the longer original, but the correction was incorporated erroneously into the text as v. 37a. The isolation of v. 37b from v. 36, which it originally followed immediately, has caused further confusion in some witnesses, as the two *Textual Notes* that follow explain.

*He* The separation of v. 37b from v. 36 (see the preceding *Textual Note*) left the subject of "mourned" in doubt, and in some witnesses it was made explicit. Thus LXX$^{L}$, OL: "the king"; LXX$^{A}$: "David"; LXX$^{BMN}$ (cf. Syr.): "King David."

*many days* That is, *ymym rbym.* So MT$^{MSS}$, OL, Syr. MT (cf. LXX) has *kl hymym,* "all the while," i.e., while Abishalom was in Geshur. With the separation of v. 37b from v. 36 (see above) it was possible to assume that the son whom David mourned was the absent Abishalom, not the deceased Aminon.

## NOTES

13 23. *Two years later.* Hebrew *lišnātayim yāmîm,* as in 14:28 (also Gen 41:1; Jer 28:3,11 [MT]; cf. Dan 10:2,3).

*sheepshearing. Gōzĕzîm* was a time of festivity as well as work; it was *yôm ṭôb,* lit. "a good day" (I Sam 25:8), i.e., a day of feasting and celebration (see *I Samuel,* p. 397).

Thus, it will not provoke suspicion for Abishalom to invite his father and brothers.

*Baal-hazor near Ophrah.* The modern site is Jebel 'Aṣûr, ca. two miles northwest of eṭ-Ṭaiyibeh, ancient Ophrah (Noth 1966); see Map 7. The ancient name of the latter city was *'oprâ,* "Ophrah" (Josh 18:23; etc.), or *'eprôn,* "Ephron" (II Chron 13:19). It may have been called *'eprayim,* "Ephraim," in later times, this name having replaced the ancient one in some witnesses to our text (see the *Textual Note*), and it has been identified with the "town called Ephraim *(ephraim)*" of John 11:54 (cf. Brown 1966: 441). Nevertheless, it is impossible for us to read "Baal-hazor, which lies within Ephraim (the tribe)," with Schunck (1961:194), who compares other place-names given nearer definition by tribal designations. As Seebass points out (1964:498), the preposition *'im* means "near, in the vicinity of," not "within."

26. *At least.* Here and in II Kings 5:17, *wālō'* (unless, with Matthes [1903:122–23] following Kuipers, it is to be read *wālū',* "Would that . . . !") has the force of "If not, then at least . . ." (cf. GK[2] §159dd).

27. *like a king's banquet.* As in I Sam 25:36, evidently a conventional way of referring to a sumptuous feast. This "banquet" is a *mišteh,* i.e., a drinking-bout, and Abishalom's plan relies on Aminon's enthusiastic participation in the drinking (v. 28).

28. The syntax of this verse is discussed by Joüon (1928:309–10).

29. *mules.* The mule, not the ass or horse, seems to have been the riding animal of royalty in the time of David. Abishalom will ride a mule on the battlefield in 18:9, and Solomon will take the saddle of David's mount, "the king's mule," as a gesture of succession in I Kings 1:33,38,44. If purity laws like Lev 19:19 against hybridizing animals were in effect at this time, these mules must have been imported, and since horses seem to have been scarce in Israel before the reign of Solomon (I Kings 10: 26–29), this seems likely in any case.

30. An exaggerated report of the assassination reaches Jerusalem ahead of the royal party.

31. To these gestures of grief, compare 1:11–12; 3:31–35; 12:16–17.

32. *Jonadab.* Aminon's "friend" seems to have been "wise" (13:3) enough to stay home from Abishalom's party. Here he gives counsel to David, referring rather coldly to the death of the man he served as intimate adviser (see the NOTE on "a friend" at 13:3).

34. *the Horonaim road.* This is not the Moabite city Horonaim of Isa 15:5 and Jer 48:3,5,34 (called *ḥwrnn,* "Hawranen," in the Mesha stele, *KAI* 181:31,32). It is the "two Horons" *(ḥōrōnayim),* i.e., Upper and Lower Beth-horon, modern Beit 'Ur el-Foqa and Beit 'Ur el-Taḥta, lying a couple of miles apart ca. ten or twelve miles northwest of Jerusalem. The royal party must have fled Baal-hazor by way of Bethel and picked up the Horonaim road to Jerusalem near Gibeon. See Map 7.

## COMMENT

Abishalom avenges the violence done to his sister by taking the life of his brother. The incestuous rape reported in the first part of the chapter precipitates, and is compounded by, fratricide. The private and public consequences of these crimes will be grave, as the story of Abishalom's rebellion in chaps. 15ff. shows.

Seizing the occasion of a sheepshearing feast, Abishalom issues an invitation to the royal family that, if accepted, will put them in his power. We cannot be sure that the king's courteous but negative response is cautionary, but it is probable that David already suspects Abishalom's ambition and fears him on that account. It is even less clear, but not impossible, that Abishalom originally meant to kill David too. The request in v. 24 ("Let the king . . . go") may hint that he already has his eye on the throne. In any case, his chief objective in the interview with the king is to maneuver Aminon into a vulnerable position, and in this he succeeds. David does not suspect this dimension of the scheme, as shown by the fact that Jonadab will have to remind him of the rancor Abishalom harbors against Aminon (v. 32b). Again (cf. 13:6–7) David is finally persuaded to grant the request of one of his sons—indeed, he seems to give more than is asked: "At least . . . Aminon" (v. 26) but . . . "Aminon and all the king's sons" (v. 27).

It may be that David was later suspected of complicity in the murder of Aminon. The narrator seems to be exerting himself to show that the king was in no way implicated. We have already been told pointedly that David did no harm to Aminon "because he loved him" (13:21). Here we are shown that David was unaware of Abishalom's real reason for inviting Aminon to Baal-hazor and that, in fact, he let Aminon go along only when pressed by Abishalom. The need for Jonadab's reminder in v. 32b gives further stress to David's innocence of knowledge of the motives of Abishalom. It follows, according to our narrator, that despite his well-known fondness for Abishalom (cf. 18:5; 19:1) David did not abet him in the slaying of Aminon.

Abishalom continues to occupy the center of our attention even when he is offstage in vv. 29ff. David is quick to believe the rumor that "Abishalom has slain all the king's sons" and, as we have said, it is necessary for Jonadab to identify the real deed and its motive to him (v. 32). What, then, was the explanation of events that David had in mind? Perhaps we are to assume that he already suspects Abishalom of a desire for the throne.

# XXVI. ABISHALOM'S RETURN
# (13:38–14:7,15–17,8–14,18–33)

13 [38]Abishalom, meanwhile, had fled and gone to Talmai son of Ammihud, the king of Geshur. When he had been there for three years,
[39]King [David's] enthusiasm for marching out against [him] was spent,
for he was consoled over Aminon's death.

## *The Ruse of the Tekoite Woman*

**14** [1]When Joab son of Zeruiah perceived that the king's mind was on
Abishalom, [2]he had a wise woman brought from Tekoa. "Act as if you
are in mourning," he told her. "Dress in mourning clothes and don't
rub yourself with oil, so that you'll be like a woman who has been
mourning the dead for some time. [3]Then go to the king and speak to
him as follows." Then Joab put the words in her mouth.

[4]So the Tekoite woman went to the king, fell down with her face to
the ground, and, paying homage, said, "Help, O king!"

[5]"What is your problem?" said the king.

"Truly I am a widow woman," she said. "My husband is dead. [6]Your
maidservant used to have two sons, but the two of them got into a fight
outdoors with no one to pull them apart, and one struck the other down
and killed him. [7]And now the whole clan has risen up against your
maidservant! They say, 'Give us the man who struck down his brother,
so that we may kill him for the life of the brother he slew!' So they will
eliminate the heir, and the one ember I have left will be quenched. Then
no name or remnant will be established for my husband on the surface
of the earth!

[15]"Now, then, this is the reason I came to tell the king about this. A
certain kinsman was terrorizing me, and your maidservant thought, 'I'll
speak to the king! It may be that the king will do as his handmaid asks!
[16]Then surely [he] will agree to rescue his handmaid from the grasp of
the man who is seeking to eliminate me and my son together from
Yahweh's estate!' [17]So your maidservant said, 'Let the word of my lord

the king be final, for my lord the king is like an envoy of God in attending to good and evil!' And may Yahweh your god be with you!"

[8]"Go home," said the king, "and I shall render judgment on your case." [9](Also the Tekoite woman said to the king, "Let the guilt fall upon me, my lord king, and upon my father's house! The king and his throne will be innocent!") [10]"As for the man who's been speaking to you," said the king, "bring him to me, and he won't get at you again!"

[11]"Let the king mention Yahweh his god," she said, "that the avenger of blood might not destroy so much! Then they will not eliminate my son."

So he said, "As Yahweh lives, not a hair of your son shall fall to the ground!"

[12]Then she said, "Let your maidservant say something else to my lord the king!"

"Speak," he said.

[13]"Why have you devised such a thing against the people of Yahweh?" she said. "For by reason of the king's having said this thing they become guilty, in that the king does not permit his exile to return. [14]For your son is dead, and as water spilled on the ground cannot be gathered up, so he cannot take up his life again. Yet it seems reasonable to the king to keep his exile away from him."

[18]In reply the king said to the woman, "Don't conceal from me anything I ask you!"

"Let my lord the king speak!" said the woman.

[19]"Is the hand of Joab with you in all this?" said the king.

"By your life, my lord king," said the woman, "it is impossible to turn to the right or the left from anything my lord the king says! For it was your servant Joab who appointed me, and he put all these words in your maidservant's mouth himself! [20]It was in order to put another face on the matter that your servant Joab devised this stratagem, but my lord has wisdom like that of an envoy of God for knowing things on earth."

[21]The king said to Joab, "I am acting according to your advice. Go bring back young Abishalom!"

[22]Joab fell upon his face on the ground, and, prostrating himself, he blessed the king and said, "Today your servant knows that I have found favor with you, my lord the king, for the king is taking the advice of your servant!"

[23]Then Joab got up, went to Geshur, and conducted Abishalom to
Jerusalem. [24]The king said, "He may go over to his house, but he shall
not see my face." So Abishalom went over to his house, but he did not
see the face of the king.
[25]Abishalom! There was no other man in Israel so greatly admired
as he! From the soles of his feet to his scalp he had no blemish. [26]When
he shaved his head—it being at the end of each year when he would
shave [it], for it would be heavy on him, that he would shave [it]—he
would weigh the hair of his head: one hundred shekels by the King's
Weight! [27]Three sons were born to Abishalom, and one daughter, whose
name was Tamar—she was a beautiful woman.

*The Reconciliation*

[28]When Abishalom had lived in Jerusalem for two years without
seeing the face of the king, [29]he sent for Joab in order to send him to
the king; but he refused to come to him. And he sent a second time,
but he refused to come. [30]Then he said to his servants, "Look, Joab's
property is adjacent to mine, and he has barley there. Go set it on fire!"
So Abishalom's servants set the property on fire.
Joab's servants came to him with their clothes torn and said, "The
servants of Abishalom have set the property on fire!" [31]So Joab got up
and came to Abishalom in his house. "Why have your servants set my
property on fire?" he said to him.
[32]"Look," Abishalom told [him], "I sent for you, saying, 'Come here
so I can send you to the king to say, "Why did I come from Geshur?
It would be better for me if I were still there! Now then, let me see the
face of the king! If there is any guilt in me, put me to death!" ' "
[33]When Joab went to the king and informed him, he summoned
Abishalom, who came to the king and prostrated himself to him. Then
the king kissed Abishalom.

## TEXTUAL NOTES

13 38. For the text of v. 38a, see the first *Textual Note* at 13:37.

*Talmai* See the *Textual Note* at 3:3. Here the distribution of witnesses is similar. MT has *talmay*, LXX *tholmai* and variants, OL *tolmi*, and Syr. *twlmy*.

*Ammihud* So Syr., Targ., and MT *(qĕrê): 'ammîhûd* (cf. LXX). MT *(kĕtîb): 'ammîḥûr.*

*Geshur* At this point in v. 37 many witnesses add the equivalent of *b'rṣ ḥylm,* "in the region of Helam" (cf. 10:16,17), which may have arisen as a marginal gloss on "Geshur." Thus LXX$^{L}$ (cf. LXX$^{BAMN}$): *eis gēn chal(l)am(an);* 4QSam$^{a}$: *b*'[*rṣ* . . .]. In v. 38 *gšwr,* everything between it and the preceding *wylk* having been lost (see above), was altered in a few MSS of MT to *gšwrh*—thus, ". . . had gone *to Geshur.*"

39. The text established for the beginning of this verse by Wellhausen is confirmed by the evidence of 4QSam$^{a}$ (see below). The present reconstruction agrees in most details with that of Wellhausen, but our interpretation of the verse is somewhat different. See the NOTES.

*King [David's] enthusiasm . . . was spent* That is, *wtkl (wattēkel) rwḥ hmlk* (see the NOTE), as deduced by Wellhausen and supported by LXX$^{(L)MN}$ *kai ekopasen to pneuma tou basileōs* (cf. Targ., OL$^{MS}$). 4QSam$^{a}$ offers confirmation: [. . . *rw*]*ḥ hmlk.* MT has *wtkl (wattĕkal) dwd hmlk,* "David the king finished . . . ," but the verb is feminine (!), agreeing with *rwḥ,* not *dwd.*

*against* So MT$^{MSS}$, Targ., LXX$^{L}$. MT has *'l,* "to, towards," which, however, should be read *'l,* as often in Samuel.

14 2. *he* So LXX$^{MN}$. MT, LXX$^{BAL}$: "Joab."

4. *went* So LXX, Syr., Vulg., Targ.$^{MSS}$, MT$^{MSS}$. MT: "said."

*"Help, O king!"* So MT, Targ. Syr. (cf. Vulg.): "Help me, my lord king!" LXX: "Help, O king, help!"

5. *she said* So MT, LXX$^{B}$. LXX$^{L}$: "*the woman* said." Syr.: "she said *to him.*"

6. The verse begins with the conjunction in MT (*wĕ-,* lit., "And . . ."), expanded in LXX$^{B}$ to *kai ge* = *wĕgam,* "And also."

*no one to pull them apart* For MT *mṣyl,* "one who pulls apart" (reflected also by LXX$^{BAN}$ [*ho*] *exairoumenos* and Syr. *mpṣyn'*), LXX$^{LM}$ *(ho) syllysōn* (cf. OL *qui dissoluerit*) suggests *mlyṣ,* "mediator, arbiter"—thus, "no arbiter between them."

*one . . . the other* That is, *h'ḥd 't h'ḥd;* so MT. LXX$^{LN}$ reflect *h'ḥd 't 'ḥw,* "one . . . *his brother,*" in anticipation of v. 7. Both readings are reflected by the conflate text of LXX$^{BAM}$: *ho heis ton hena adelphon autou.*

*struck . . . down* Reading *wyk* with LXX, Syr., Targ., Vulg. MT *wykw* (cf. Targ.$^{MSS}$) evidently arose after the preceding plural verb *(wynṣw),* the clause being (erroneously) taken to mean "and they struck *(wayyakkû),* each the other," that is, "and they struck each other"; this was revocalized in view of the sequel ("and killed him") to mean "and he struck him down *(wayyakkô),* the one the other," that is, "and one struck the other down." Here we follow Thenius, Wellhausen, and others against Keil and, recently, Hoftijzer 1970b:419–20 n. 4.

7. *They say* So MT (cf. LXX$^{BAMN}$): *wy'mrw.* LXX$^{L}$ reflects *l'mr,* "saying."

*they will eliminate* So Syr. See Joüon 1928:310–11. MT has "let us eliminate," which is defended by Wellhausen.

*the heir* MT: "*also* the heir." LXX$^{L}$: "*your* heir." Both expansions are found in LXX$^{B}$.

*and the one ember . . . will be quenched* So LXX$^{L}$: *kai sbesthēsetai ho spinthēr* = *wkbth hgḥlt.* The reading of MT is equally acceptable—*wkbw 't gḥly,* "and (they will) quench my ember"—but that of LXX$^{L}$ is better with *'šr hš'rty* (see below).

*I have left* Reading *'šr hš'rty* on the basis of 4QSam[c] *h[š]'rty;* cf. LXX[L] *ho hypoleleimmenos moi* (cf. OL) and Syr. *(d) 'štrt ly,* which suggest *nš'rh ly,* lit. "(who) remains to me." MT has *nš'rh,* "(who) remains." See Ulrich 1979:10–11.

*name or remnant* So MT, LXX[AL], Syr. LXX[BM]: "remnant or name."

15–17. This dislocation is discussed in the NOTE.

15. *this is the reason* MT *'šr,* omitted by one MS of MT and a few other witnesses *(BHS).* LXX[L] seems to reflect *'l 'šr.*

*the king* So LXX[L], Targ.[MS]. 4QSam[c] has an old variant, "my lord" *('dwny),* and the two are inelegantly combined in MT, LXX[BAMN], and Targ.: "the king my lord." Syr. has the usual formula: "my lord the king."

*was terrorizing me* That is, *yr'ny,* read as plural *(yĕrĕ'ūnî)* by MT. But the spelling favors the singular, *yĕrĕ'ēnî.* LXX *opsetai me* suggests *yir'anî* or *yir'ūnî,* "was (were) looking at me."

*your maidservant thought* See MT, LXX[LMN], etc. LXX[BA] "your people will say" is erroneous.

*I'll speak* So MT: *'dbrh n'.* LXX[LMN] (cf. LXX[BA]) have *lalēsatō hē doulē sou* = *tdbrh n' šphtk,* "Your maidservant will speak," as in v. 12.

16. *to rescue* MT *lhṣyl.* LXX reflects *wḥṣyl,* "and will rescue."

*who is seeking* So LXX: *tou zētountos* = *hmbqš,* which (*pace* Barthélemy 1980: 25) was lost in MT after *h'yš* (homoioteleuton). Space considerations suggest that 4QSam[c] had the longer reading (Ulrich 1979:12).

*Yahweh's* So LXX[L], Targ., Theodotion. MT, LXX[BAMN], etc.: "God's."

17. *your maidservant* So MT, LXX[LMN]. LXX[BA]: "the woman."

*Let . . . be* Reading *yhy n'* with LXX *(eiē dē),* OL, Vulg., and MT[MSS]*(BHS).* MT has *yhyh n'.*

*final* MT *lmnwḥh* or *lmnḥh (limnūḥâ;* cf. *BHS),* lit. "a resting, resolution," thus "final"; see the NOTE. LXX, OL, Syr. interpret *lmnḥh* as *lĕminḥâ,* "a gift, sacrifice."

*God* So MT, LXX[BAMN], Syr. LXX[L], OL, Targ.: "Yahweh."

*may . . . be* So MT. LXX, OL, Vulg., MT[MSS]*(BHS): "will* be."

8. *Go home* So MT. The various MSS of LXX add *hygiainousa* = *bšlwm,* "in peace," in a variety of positions, and space considerations suggest that 4QSam[c] shared the reading and order of LXX[L]: "Go home *in peace.*" See Ulrich 1979:11.

*said the king* MT, LXX[LMN], and 4QSam[c] add "to the woman." Omit with LXX[BA] (cf. Syr.).

9. *Let the guilt . . . my father's house!* The elements of the sentence are arranged in several different ways in the various witnesses.

*and his throne* So MT: *wks'w.* LXX[L] *kai ho thronos tou basileōs* = *wks' hmlk,* "and *the king's* throne." 4QSam[c]: *[wks' mmlk]tw,* "the throne *of his kingship*" (cf. Targ. *wkrsy mlkwtyh*).

10. *As for the man who's been speaking to you* MT *hmdbr 'lyk,* construed as *casus pendens* with the clause that follows. LXX[B] reflects *my hmdbr 'lyk,* "Who is the one who has been speaking to you?" LXX[L], OL share the reading of MT, to which they add *dbr*—thus, "Anyone who says *anything* to you."

*bring him* According to Wellhausen MT *wahăbē'tô* should be read *wahăbē'tîw* (< **wahăbē'tîhû).* In LXX[L], OL the *casus pendens* construction has been erased and thus the conjunction does not appear.

*get at* MT *lg't*, for which 4QSam[c] has the more common form *lngw'* (the *n* having been omitted and restored supralinearly).

*you* (2) So MT, LXX[LM], and 4QSam[c]. LXX[BAN] have "him"—thus, "and he won't approach *him* [the remaining son?] again."

11. *the king* So MT, LXX[BAM]. MT[MSS], LXX[LN], OL, Syr.: "*my lord* the king," as in v. 9.

*his god* So LXX[BAM]. In LXX[L], OL "his" has been removed in partial correction towards MT "*your* god." Either reading is acceptable. LXX[N] here reads "Let my lord the king remember his maidservant."

*that . . . so much* Evidently we are to read *mēharbôt* (. . . *lĕšaḥēt*), lit. "from (destroying) excessively," but for *harbôt* MT (*kĕtîb*) inexplicably has *hrbyt* and MT (*qĕrê*) *harbat*. Cf. GK[2] §75ff. Klostermann proposed *mhrpwt*—thus, "that he [Yahweh] not permit the avenger of blood to destroy."

*the avenger of blood* Plural in LXX[L], OL.

*they* LXX[L], OL: "you."

*he said* LXX[LN]: "*the king* said."

*a hair of your son* That is, *miśśa'ărōt* (MT *miśśa'ărat*) *bĕnēk*, lit. "from the hairs of your son" (cf. LXX, Vulg.); one MS of MT has *mś'rwt* (*BHS*) and 4QSam[c] has [*mś'r*]*ẇt*. Syr., Targ., MT[MS] have "from the hair *of the head* of your son."

12. *she said* So LXX[B]. MT, LXX[AMN]: "*the woman* said." LXX[L]: "the *Tekoite* woman said."

*he said* LXX[L]: "*the king* said."

13. *Yahweh* Cf. LXX[L]. 4QSam[c] (*'lẇ*[*hy*]*m*) agrees with MT *'lhym*, "God," which should in any case be *h'lhym* in the expression *'m h'lhym*, "the people of God." Cf. Budde, who compares 1:12 and 6:21 as well as I Sam 2:24.

*For by reason of the king's having said this* MT has *wmdbr hmlk hdbr hzh*. The sense of this seems to be that reflected in our translation, but it is doubtful that this can be derived from the text if *ûmiddabbēr* is taken with the Masoretes as equivalent to *ûmitdabbēr*, as in Num 7:89; Ezek 2:2; 43:6 (Driver, etc.). Instead we follow Budde and others (most recently Hoftijzer 1970b:430 n. 1) in understanding *middabbēr* as *min* + *dabbēr*. Note, however, that LXX[L] has a different reading: *kai ek tou parelthein ton basilea ton logon touton* = *wmh'byr hmlk hdbr hzh*, which Thenius understands as "And yet the king set aside (*ma'ăbîr*) this word. . . ." It is doubtful, though, that *ma'ăbîr* is justified by the evidence or that the syntax will support Thenius' interpretation; we should read instead "And by reason of the king's having put aside (*ûmēha'ăbîr*) this thing . . . ," i.e., "Because the king has excused this thing (viz. the crime of the woman's son)."

*they become guilty* On this interpretation of MT *k'šm*, see the NOTE. LXX[L] *tou enkrateusasthai* seems to reflect *lhšmr*, "to restrain himself," but how this might relate to the rest of the clause is unclear (Thenius: "And yet the king sets aside this word *in refraining* from permitting," etc.).

*his exile* So MT (*ndḥw*) and 4QSam[c] ([*ndḥ*]*ẇ*). LXX[L]: "the one exiled from him" (= *hndḥ mmnw*); cf. v. 14.

14. *For your son is dead* So LXX[L], Theodotion: *hoti tethnēken ho huios sou* = *ky mt bnk*. (The reference is to Aminon; see the NOTE.) In MT this has become a

trite generality: *ky mwt nmwt,* "We must all die" (RSV, NJV); so 4QSam[c] *(k[y' mwt] ṅmwt).*

*so he cannot take up his life again* Again LXX[L] and Theodotion provide the primitive reading: *kai ouk elpi(z)ei ep' autō psychē* = *wl' yś' 'lyw npš* (for *elpizein psychē* = *niśśā' nepeš,* cf. Jer 44:14 [LXX 51:14]). In MT *'lyw* has become *'lhym,* "God"—thus, "and God will not spare life" (cf. the *Textual Note* that follows). LXX[MN], recognizing the error, omit *'lhym,* and LXX[B], perhaps to avoid an impiety, omits *l'* (thus, "and [only] God spares life").

*Yet . . . from him* Reading *wḥšb hmlk mḥšb lndḥ mmnw ndḥ,* lit. "And the king thinks a thought to exile from him an exile," on the basis again of LXX[L]: *kai elogisato ho basileus logismon tou apōsasthai ap' autou apōsmenon* (the other principal MSS of LXX reflect the same text but with loss of *hmlk mḥšb* by haplography). MT has *wḥšb mḥšbwt lblty ydḥ mmnw ndḥ,* "And he [i.e., God; cf. the preceding *Textual Note*] devises plans not to keep an exile away from him." Many critics and translators, endeavoring to derive some satisfactory sense from MT, have followed Ewald in reading *ḥwšb* for *wḥšb*—thus, "And God will not take away the life of one who devises plans not to keep an exile away from him."

18. *In reply . . . the woman* So MT: *wy'n hmlk wy'mr 'l h'šh,* lit. "And the king answered and said to the woman." Ulrich (1979:6,12), on the basis of space requirements and a fragment of 4QSam[a] ([ ] *hi[qw'yt]*), restores 4QSam[c] here as [*wy'n hmlk*] *'t h'šh* [*htqw'yt wywmr*], "And the king answered the Tekoite woman and said. . . ."

19. *with you in all this* So MT, LXX[L], OL. LXX[BAMN]: "in all this with you."

*said the woman* That is, *wt'mr h'šh.* All witnesses are expansive. MT has *wt'n h'šh wt'mr,* "the woman *answered and* said." LXX[BAMN] reflect *wt'mr h'šh 'l hmlk,* "said the woman *to the king,*" the probable reading of 4QSam[c] (Ulrich 1979:12). LXX[L] (cf. OL) reflects *wt'n wt'mr h'šh 'l hmlk,* with which the fragmentary text of 4QSam[a] may be compared (see Ulrich 1979:12)

*it is* For MT *'š,* 4QSam[c] and MT[MSS] have the ordinary *yš* (cf. Targ. *'yt*). See the NOTE.

*in your maidservant's mouth* MT: *bpy špḥtk.* 4QSam[a]: *bpy 'mtk.*

20. *your servant Joab devised* That is, *'śh 'bdk yw'b;* so MT, LXX[MN], and 4QSam[c] (['ś]*h 'bdkh y*[*w'b*]). This is prefaced in LXX[BAL] by *'šr,* which transforms v. 20a into an awkward continuation of v. 19 (". . . he put all these words into your maidservant's mouth himself in order to put another face on the thing that your servant Joab had done, this stratagem").

*this stratagem* Reading *hmrmh hz't* on the basis of LXX[B] *ton dolon touton* for MT *hdbr hzh,* "this thing" (so LXX[ALMN]).

*for knowing things on earth* Reading *ld't 'šr b'rṣ* with LXX[L] *tou gnōnai ta epi tēs gēs* and 4QSam[c] [*ld'*]*t 'šr b'rṣ,* lit. "to know that which is on earth." MT (cf. LXX[BAMN], Syr., Targ., Vulg.) expands and modernizes. The use of *'šr* without *'t* as an accusative in an *independent* relative clause (GK[2] §138e) is archaic and poetic (Isa 52:15; etc.); but the parallel cited by Ulrich (1979:12) from a *dependent* relative clause in *KAI* 181:29 is not relevant.

21. *I am acting* That is, *'śyty,* lit. "I (hereby) do" (GK[2] §106m), to which LXX[BA]

add *soi* = *lk*, "for you" (see the *Textual Note* on "Go bring back" below). A few MSS of MT, LXX, and Targ. have *'śyt (-tā)*, "you have done."

*according to your advice* Reading *kdbrk* on the basis of Syr. *'yk d'mrt* (cf. LXX and Vulg.) and 4QSam[c] *[kdbr]kh* (but Ulrich [1979:6] reads *['t hdbr h]zh*). MT has *'t hdbr hzh*, "(I hereby do) this thing."

*Go bring back* Reading *lk whšb* with $LXX^{LMN}$, OL. MT has *wlk hšb*. 4QSam[c] has *wlk whšb* (cf. $LXX^{A}$). In $LXX^{B}$ *lk* was lost after *kdbrk* (before the recensional addition of *touton* = *hzh*) and restored in the wrong place, before *kdbrk* (cf. the *Textual Note* on "I am acting" above).

22. *prostrating himself* $LXX^{L}$, OL add "to him" (cf. v. 33 [MT]).

*your servant knows* So MT, $LXX^{BAMN}$, and 4QSam[c]. OL (cf. $LXX^{L}$) has "I know."

*for* Expressed by *'šr* in MT (cf. Driver on I Sam 15:15). $MT^{MSS}$ have *ky (BHS)*. LXX *hoti* is ambiguous, but $LXX^{L}$ *kathoti* suggests *k'šr*.

*the king* So MT, $LXX^{L}$. $LXX^{BAMN}$: "*my lord* the king."

*your servant* So MT *(qĕrê)*, $MT^{MSS}$, $OL^{MS}$, Targ., Vulg., and 4QSam[c]. MT *(kĕtîb)* and LXX have "*his* servant." See Ulrich 1979:13.

23. *Then Joab got up* MT *wyqm yw'b*, for which 4QSam[c] has *wy'b*.

25. *Abishalom! There was no other man . . . as he* Reading *gm 'bšlwm l' hyh 'yš kmhw* on the basis of 4QSam[c] *gm 'bšlwm*[ ]; cf. $LXX^{MS}$, $OL^{MS}$. MT has *wk'bšlwm l' hyh 'yš yph*, "And there was no other handsome man (so greatly admired) as Abishalom." See Ulrich 1979:13.

*Israel* So $LXX^{L}$, Syr. MT, $LXX^{B}$, etc.: "*all* Israel."

*admired* MT *lĕhallēl*, lit. "to praise." LXX *ainetos* suggests *mĕhullāl*, "praised" (Smith).

*his scalp* MT *qdqdw*, miswritten *qwqdẇ* in 4QSam[c].

26. [*it*] (2) We omit the pronoun, which stands in MT and $LXX^{BA}$, with $LXX^{LMN}$.

*one hundred* So $LXX^{L}$ and OL. MT, $LXX^{BAMN}$ and 4QSam[c]: "*two* hundred."

*Weight* That is, *'bn*, lit. "stone(s)"; so MT and 4QSam[c]. LXX reflects *šql*, "shekel."

27. *Tamar* So MT (cf. $LXX^{BA}$) and 4QSam[c]. $LXX^{LMN}$, $OL^{MS}$ reflect *ma'ăkâ*, "Maacah," evidently the OG reading. I Kings 15:2 and II Chron 11:20–22 (cf. I Kings 15:10,13) refer to a "Maacah daughter of Abishalom," who married Rehoboam (see the *Textual Note* on the plus below). But is this the same Abishalom (cf. Budde)? Maacah was a common Geshurite name—the name of Abishalom's Geshurite mother (II Sam 3:3) and, indeed, of an adjacent state (II Sam 10:6)—and Abishalom may also have been a common Geshurite name. It is possible that Maacah is the primitive reading here, the name of the beautiful (cf. II Sam 13:1) Tamar having arisen in MT by confusion with Abishalom's sister (so Rosmarin 1933). But I assume that the name Maacah arose in LXX, along with the plus described below, on the basis of an unfounded scribal identification of the daughter of Abishalom son of David with the daughter of an otherwise unknown (Geshurite?) Abishalom mentioned in I Kings 15:2, etc.

*beautiful* So MT: *ypt mr'h*, lit. "beautiful of appearance" (cf. $LXX^{MN}$, OL, Syr.). $LXX^{BAL}$ reflect *yph m'd*, "*very* beautiful."

At this point LXX (cf. OL) adds *kai ginetai gynē tō rhoboam huiō salōmōn kai tiktei autō ton abia* (so LXX^LMN, OL [*abiam*]; LXX^B has *abiathar*), which reflects *wthy 'šh lrḥb'm bn šlmh wtld lw 't 'byh,* "and she became the wife of Rehoboam son of Solomon and bore to him Abijah." The source of this notice is I Kings 15:2 (cf. II Chron 11:20–22). Rosmarin (1933) argues that it is original, having been omitted in MT by way of correction to I Kings 15:2.

29. *he* (1) So OL. Ulrich (1980:142): "possibly the original short text . . . also possibly a stylistic omission." MT, LXX, 4QSam^c: "Abishalom."

*he refused* (1) LXX^L: "*Joab* refused."

*a second time* Preceded in MT and 4QSam^c (cf. LXX^L) by *'wd,* "again"; omit with LXX^BAMN. After "a second time" 4QSam^c adds *'lyw,* "to him."

30. *he* So MT. LXX, OL, Syr.: "Abishalom."

*Joab's property is adjacent to mine* LXX and OL, the various MSS of which show considerable variety in the arrangement of words here, add at one point or another "in the field." Thus, for example, OL suggests "Joab's property is *in the field* adjacent," etc. The addition probably arose from a conflation of variants, viz. *ḥlqt yw'b,* "Joab's property," and *śdh yw'b,* "Joab's field," of which the former is more distinctive.

*adjacent to mine* That is, *'al yādî,* lit. "at my hand, beside me"; so 4QSam^c (*'l y*[*dy*]); cf. MT, LXX^B. LXX^L, OL reflect *'l ydnw,* "beside us."

*Go* MT *lkw* (cf. LXX^BAMN, etc.). LXX^L reflects *lkw n' wr'w,* "Go and see."

*set it on fire* Reading *whṣytwh (wĕhaṣṣîtûhā) b'š* with MT *(qĕrê),* MT^MSS, and 4QSam^c ([*w*]*hṣytwh b'š*). MT *(kĕtîb): whwṣtyh b'š,* probably understood as *wĕhôṣē'tîhū,* "and I shall bring him (i.e., Joab) out with fire." Cf. GK^2 §71.

*property on fire* (1) . . . *property on fire* (2) The repetition of *'t hḥlqh b'š* has caused a long haplography in MT. The text can be restored on the basis of LXX, OL, and 4QSam^c: *'t hḥlqh b'š wyb'w yldy yw'b 'lyw qr'y bgdyhm wy'mrw hṣytw 'bdy 'bšlwm 't hḥlqh b'š.* In retaining this plus we follow Thenius, Klostermann, Smith, and Ulrich (1979:14), against Wellhausen and Budde.

31. *my property* That is, *'t hḥlqh 'šr ly;* so MT (cf. LXX^B). LXX^L reflects *'t śdy,* "my field."

32. *saying* LXX^L adds *hapax kai dis,* "once and a second time." Cf. v. 29.

*let me see the face of the king* So MT (cf. 4QSam^c and LXX^L): *'r'h pny hmlk.* LXX^B reflects *hnh 't pny hmlk l' r'yty,* "the face of the king I have not seen."

*If* So Syr. and MT^MSS *(BHS).* MT, LXX: "*And* if."

*put me to death* MT *wehĕmītānî,* the implied subject of which is "you (David)." LXX^LMN reflect *wĕhūmattî,* "let me be put to death."

33. *and prostrated himself to him* MT (cf. Syr., Targ., Vulg.) has *wyšthw lw* (Syr., Vulg. omit *lw*) *'l 'pyw 'rṣh lpny hmlk,* "and prostrated himself to him upon his face on the ground before the king." LXX reflects *wyšthw lw wypl 'l 'pyw 'rṣh lpny* (LXX^BA = *wlpny*) *hmlk,* "and prostrated himself to him *and fell* upon his face on the ground before the king." 4QSam^c is not extant, but the preceding *wybw',* "came," is preserved, followed by space for thirty to thirty-five letters to the end of the verse (Ulrich 1979:14). Ulrich argues plausibly for reconstructing *wybw'* [*'l hmlk wyšthw lw wyšq hmlk l'bšlwm*], which we have adopted as the primitive reading. The text of MT and LXX appears overcrowded, probably the result of a conflation of variants, viz. *wyšthw lw* and *wypl 'l 'pyw 'rṣh lpny hmlk.* Of these, the former is favored by what Ulrich calls "the ironic literary allusion" in 15:5.

# NOTES

13 38. *Talmai son of Ammihud, the king of Geshur.* Abishalom seeks refuge with his maternal grandparents; see 3:3 and, for Geshur, the NOTE at 2:9.

39. At the beginning of this verse we read the text reconstructed by Wellhausen and confirmed by evidence from Qumran: *wattēkel rûaḥ hammelek lāṣēʾt ʿal ʾăbîšālôm.* This is usually taken to mean "the spirit of the king yearned to go forth to *(ʾel)* Abishalom." But *kālâ* is stronger than "yearn"; it means "be spent"—thus, in Ps 84:3 [84:2] we read *niksĕpâ wĕgam-kālĕtā napšî* . . . , "My soul longs, yea, faints (for the courts of the LORD)" (RSV), and in Ps 143:7 *kālĕtâ rûḥî,* "My spirit fails!" (RSV). I think the meaning here, then, is lit. "the king's enthusiasm for marching out against *(ʿal)* Abishalom was spent." If David longed for Abishalom, Joab's ruse in 14:1ff. would not be necessary. Nor is David's treatment of Abishalom after his return (14:24) consistent with the interpretation that he longs to see him here. The meaning is rather that David is no longer openly hostile to Abishalom and, therefore, ready to be prodded step by step towards a reconciliation.

**14** 1. *the king's mind was on Abishalom.* Again, it is erroneous to suppose that this *(lēb hammelek ʿal ʾăbîšālôm)* implies that David is now favorably disposed towards Abishalom. The meaning is rather that Joab selects a time when he knows that David is thinking about Abishalom, trying (presumably) to decide how to handle the matter.

2–22. The episode of the ploy of Joab and the wise woman that precipitated Abishalom's return was regarded as part of the original succession narrative in the programmatic studies of Rost and von Rad, and its originality is taken for granted in most recent work on the subject as well (Whybray, Gunn, Conroy, etc.). Würthwein, however, who has proposed a new understanding of the succession narrative as an originally anti-Davidic/anti-Solomonic narrative complex that has been given a pro-Davidic/pro-Solomonic slant as a result of a series of editorial revisions (see the Introduction, pp. 13–16), designates II Sam 14:2–22 a "wisdom anecdote" inserted to show Joab's role in Abishalom's recall and thus to transfer the responsibility for the disastrous events to follow from David to Joab (1974:46–47). Würthwein's position has been pressed further by Bickert (1979), who attempts an analysis of the redactional history of the insert, which was based, he says, on a pre-Deuteronomistic "wisdom anecdote" (vv. 2–4aα,4b–7aα,10,11b–12aα,13b,15,18–21), which was expanded by two Deuteronomistic revisions. The first of these (vv. 4aβ,8–9,12aβb,22) was intended to heighten the dignity of the king in relation to Joab and the wise woman, while idealizing David and his throne and removing any attachment of blame to him; it can be attributed to the Deuteronomistic historian. The second revision (vv. 7aβb,11a,13a,14,16–17) offers a theological reinterpretation expressing dynastic and theocratic interests; it derives from a later, "nomistic" Deuteronomist (Smend's DtrN; see p. 7 in the Introduction). I have expressed a lack of confidence in this extreme turn in the source-critical analysis of the Samuel narratives in the Introduction. In the present case one of Würthwein's fundamental reasons for regarding vv. 2–22 as secondary, viz. that 13:39 shows that David was already ready to recall Abishalom without Joab's intervention (1974:46), is based on a common misinterpretation of the text (see the NOTE on 13:39 above).

2. *a wise woman.* In view of what we noted about wisdom in the case of Jonadab (13:3), we must think of it as a tool for accomplishing purposes and attaining goals. It may express itself in a variety of skills and talents, most characteristically in an ability to use speech to achieve desired results. This is clearly the case of the wise women of Samuel. There are three of these. The first is Abigail, who, though not called a wise woman, is praised for her "good intelligence" (I Sam 25:3) and "judgment" (I Sam 25:33); her speech in I Sam 25:24–31, which exhibits a number of points of contact with the present story (Hoftijzer 1970b:424–27; cf. Gunn 1978:42–43), is a carefully designed piece of rhetoric that accomplishes its purpose effectively. The same can be said of the speeches of the wise woman of Abel of Beth-maacah in II Sam 20:16–19 and the wise woman of Tekoa here, in which there are again several points of contact (see Conroy 1978:142 n. 99 and the COMMENT below). "It is self-evident," as Eissfeldt says (1965: 12), "that such men and women, specially skilled in speech, possess a technique which does not depend solely upon a particular gift, but also upon tradition and 'training'; there were in other words certain fixed forms of speech." Thus, we must agree with Hoftijzer (1970b:429 n. 2) against Gevaryahu's contention (1969:11; cf. Budde) that the designation "wise" in the present passage is indicative especially of a skill at uttering lamentations (cf. Jer 9:16). Joab is in need of an actress, not a professional mourner.

*Tekoa.* A village in the Judaean hills about ten miles south of Jerusalem (Map 7); the modern site is Khirbet Teqû'. Tekoa was an agricultural community, perhaps best known as the home of the prophet Amos (Amos 1:1). Presumably Joab went to Tekoa to hire his accomplice because David might recognize a local woman (Ehrlich 1910: 305). There is no reason to suppose that the town had a distinctive wisdom tradition, as argued by Wolff (1964:53–54) on the basis of the present passage and the alleged influence of folk wisdom on the oracles of Amos; on this last point, see the acute remarks of Clements 1975:76–79.

*Joab put the words in her mouth.* Compare Exod 4:15; Num 22:38; and Ezra 8:17 (Hoftijzer 1970b:419 n. 3).

5–7. The woman describes her fictitious plight to David. As Hoftijzer points out (1970b:421–22), she stresses the extenuating circumstances of the case, viz. her widowhood (v. 5) and the fact that the culprit is now her late husband's only heir (v. 7b). Strict justice would require that the son be handed over to the family, but the woman seeks an exceptional ruling from the king.

7. *the one ember I have left will be quenched.* Compare the Old Babylonian expression describing a man with no family as one "whose brazier has been quenched" (*kinūnšu belû, CAD* 2.73; cf. Borger *apud* Hoftijzer 1970b:422 n. 2).

15–17. In our received text and all versions, these three verses stand after the woman drops her mask in vv. 13–14 and before David asks her about Joab's complicity in vv. 18–19. This presents a very awkward sequence of events. As Caird says, "If these verses are not displaced from an earlier part in the story, then she must be trying to cover up the real object of her coming by a voluble reversion to the ostensible object." Even after having tipped her hand, in other words, she attempts to resume the role in order to avoid being too obvious (Thenius); she tries to make what is really her main concern seem a secondary matter (Hertzberg). But, as Budde showed, this will not do. After her words in vv. 13–14 the woman's masquerade is over; she cannot take up the widow woman role again (Ehrlich 1910:308; Hoftijzer 1970b:438). At this point (viz. after v. 14) there remains only the question whether she has tricked the king on her own initiative or someone has put her up to it, and David does not need to be "like an envoy of God" (v. 17) to answer the question and name her accomplice. In its received position, at the beginning of v. 15, the conjunctive element *wĕʿattâ,* "So now," is pointless, since vv. 15–17 have nothing to do with the issues of vv. 13–14. As first recognized by Cook (1899/1900:158 n. 34) and fully set forth by Budde, vv. 15–17 belong between vv. 7 and 8. Having stated her case in vv. 5–7, the woman goes on *(wĕʿattâ)* to explain why she came to the king. Her words, which look like sheer verbosity (Budde: "blosse Schwatzhaftigkeit") after v. 14, are in fact the very articulation of her request, which vv. 5–7 left unexpressed. Verses 15–17 are, in short, a carefully fashioned component of the imposture, hardly "a gush of feminine loquacity" (cf. Hertzberg).

15. *A certain kinsman.* There is disagreement among interpreters of this difficult passage about the meaning of *hāʿām.* Some think it a reference to "the people" in general (Ehrlich 1910:308; Bickert 1979:37). Others (e.g., Hoftijzer 1970b:439) understand it to refer to "the clan" in v. 7 and render it according to the earlier sense of the word, "family, kindred" (cf. Speiser 1960). The latter position is more plausible, especially if we are correct in relocating vv. 15–17 here after v. 7. Thus *hāʿām* is surely related in some way to *hammišpāḥâ,* "the clan," in v. 7. But the two may not be synonymous. Verses 16 and 10 refer to one member of the clan in particular who has been threatening the woman, and both references assume that this man has already been mentioned. Quite probably, then, we should understand *ʿam* in the sense of "kinsman" here, rendering the definite article according to the force explained in GK[2] §126qr—thus, "a certain kinsman," i.e., one member of the clan in particular. In support of this interpretation is the likelihood that the verb "was terrorizing me" is to be read as singular (see the *Textual Note*).

16. *Then surely [he] will agree.* Hebrew *kî yišmaʿ hammelek.* Following a wish introduced by *ʾûlay,* "It may be" (v. 15), such a *kî*-clause probably has the force of an emphatic, corroborative apodosis in a conditional clause (GK[2] §159ee).

*Yahweh's estate.* As Forshey (1975) has shown, *naḥălat yahweh* may refer to the people as well as the land of Israel. Here the woman means that if her son is killed, her family will have no representative among the future generations of Israel. Forshey's suggestion that the use of the expression to refer to the people arose after the loss of the land (i.e., at the time of the Babylonian exile) seems improbable to me. On the contrary, such a usage can only have arisen in a time when the close identification of people and land could be taken for granted. On the other hand, Forshey is probably correct in arguing (p. 52) that the expression in I Sam 26:19 refers primarily to "the political and religious community," not the land (against *I Samuel,* p. 408). An "estate" *(naḥălâ)* was landed property, held inalienably by an individual, whether acquired by inheritance, military victory, or feudal grant. Mythically conceived, Yahweh's estate, land and people, was granted him by the Most High *(ʿelyôn)* at the time of the allotment of nations to the various gods (Deut 32:8 [LXX]) or, alternatively, it was the land won in the conquest.

17. *final.* Hebrew *limnûḥâ.* The interpretation of this as referring to the relief or satisfaction the woman expects from the king's ruling (cf. Hoftijzer 1970b:439–40) lies

behind its rendering in modern translations with terms such as rest, comfort, and relief (RSV, NEB, NJV, JB, etc.). Rather than expressing confidence in a favorable ruling, however, the woman is throwing herself on the mercy of the court with a polite reference to the king's ability to decide justly. By *limnûḥâ* she means that David's word will put the matter *to rest,* and that she is content to accept the *settlement* thus reached.

*the king is like an envoy of God.* Here, in v. 20 below, and in 19:28 the conviction is expressed that King David is as wise and just as a divine being ("an envoy of God," cf. 24:16). In reference to our passage, Mowinckel ([1956]:66) speaks of the endowment of the king with superhuman wisdom as a part of the Israelite ideology of kingship. The evidence of Samuel (II Sam 14:17,20; 19:28; cf. I Sam 29:9 [MT]), however, cannot bear the weight of such a conclusion. As Hoftijzer points out (1970b:440–41), all these comparisons are on the lips of individuals attempting to ingratiate themselves to David. They are rhetorical cunning—flattery not doctrine. The woman seeks to ingratiate herself in the present episode by attributing superhuman wisdom to the king twice, here for his ability to distinguish right from wrong in a case of justice ("attending to good and evil"; cf. Mettinger [1976:242], against Hoftijzer [1970b:441], who takes the expression as merismus, implying omniscience) and, more generally, in v. 20 for his awareness of what goes on about him ("knowing things on earth"; cf. Mettinger 1976:269).

9. A difficult verse, both with regard to its meaning and to its relationship to the verses that precede and follow it (Hoftijzer 1970b:424–28; Bickert 1979:32–36). In view of the fact that the woman is trying to persuade David to make an exceptional ruling on her case—i.e., to set a manslayer free from blood vengeance—the present verse is usually understood as an assurance that she, not David, will suffer any harmful consequences that might arise from such a ruling (Thenius, Keil, Schulz, de Groot, Ackroyd, etc.); it is, in other words, an acceptance of possible guilt ("On me be the guilt!"). Somewhat differently, Hoftijzer (1970b:425–28) takes it as a confession of guilt ("On me is guilt") as a prelude to asking for mercy. Klostermann, by contrast, took it as a complaint about where the burden of guilt will fall ("On me will be the guilt" = "I will be blamed"), an explanation that at least has the virtue of making an intelligible connection with v. 10 ("If anyone says anything to you, bring him to me!"). It seems clear, however, that David's words in v. 10 are a response to the woman's case as she has presented it, not to her words in v. 9. Indeed, what she says here is simply ignored by the king. Nor is v. 9 clearly pertinent to the ongoing conversation. The language is similar, though not identical, to that used by Abigail in I Sam 25:24 at the beginning of her long petition to David. What Abigail says (*bî 'ădônî he'āwôn,* "Let the guilt be mine, my lord!") is probably a fuller version of the conventional entreaty *bî 'ădônî,* used in addressing superiors, especially when taking exception or making a bold request (Exod 4:10,13; Num 12:11; Judg 6:15; etc.); cf. KB³. Thus, we might think of v. 9 as a formulaic prelude to the woman's further request of an oath in v. 11. But the language here (*'ālay 'ădônî hammelek he'āwôn,* etc.) is not precisely that of the conventional formula, and no example of the *bî 'ădônî* formula, including that in I Sam 25:24, is nearly so drawn out and explicit as what we have here. If we take v. 9 as a prelude to v. 11, moreover, we still have the problem of the relationship between vv. 9 and 10. Verse 9, in short, is isolated and disruptive in its present location. Note, further, its concern with the protection of David *and his throne* from guilt, a concern also expressed in 3:28–29, which disrupts its context in a similar way. It is very likely, then,

that we have here in v. 9 another Deuteronomistic expansion, added to protect the house of David from guilt arising from the interview, most especially, perhaps, from David's words in v. 11 with which he unwittingly puts Abishalom under the protection of an oath. This is similar to the position of Bickert (1979:32–36), who, however, also regards vv. 8 and 11a as secondary (cf. the general NOTE on vv. 2–22 above).

11. *mention.* Hebrew *zākar* means "remember" but also, like Akkadian *zakāru,* "mention, call (the name of)"; cf. Jer 23:36 and, for mentioning Yahweh, Jonah 2:8 [2:7] and many other passages. The woman is asking the king to utter Yahweh's name in a binding oath. See de Boer 1962:33; Hoftijzer 1965; 1970b:428 n. 1; contrast Schottroff 1964:168–69.

*the avenger of blood.* Evidently the "kinsman" of v. 15 and the "man" of vv. 16 and 10. Here he is called *gō'ēl haddām.* According to tribal custom "the avenger of blood" had the responsibility of avenging the death of a family member; thus he is a prominent figure in the laws regulating and limiting the traditional blood-vengeance system in Num 35:9–34; Deut 19:4–13; and Joshua 20. As pointed out by de Vaux (1961a:vol. I:12), however, it is surprising to find blood vengeance operative *within* the clan, i.e., against a member of the clan. With de Vaux, then, we might suppose that the clan seeks the life of the woman's son not in vengeance for his brother's blood but to purge the clan of guilt, the mention of the avenger of blood being "abnormal, and . . . used here in a loose sense." But the words of the clansmen in v. 7 above seem to belie this interpretation: "Give us the man . . . so that we may kill him for the life of the brother he slew!"

*As Yahweh lives.* David grants the woman's request that he "mention" Yahweh. A solemn oath of the king now protects the fictitious son of the Tekoite woman and also, as the verses that follow show, his own son Abishalom.

13. On the history of the interpretation of this difficult verse, see Hoftijzer 1970b:429–34. The meaning of the first sentence might be that by excluding Abishalom from Israel the king has devised something against the people by excluding the heir presumptive from their midst (Wellhausen, etc.). Alternatively, it might be that by protecting a fratricide with an oath and thus condemning himself for his treatment of Abishalom he has devised something against the people by putting their king in jeopardy (Budde, etc.). But these interpretations are too subtle. The woman accuses David of devising something against the people directly, not indirectly by peril to the crown prince or the king. Now that the woman's son is protected by a royal oath, his kinsmen can no longer refuse him his place in the clan. Similarly, the kinsmen of Abishalom, "the people of Yahweh," must embrace Abishalom again. But they cannot while the king keeps him in exile. Thus David has put the people under a solemn obligation they are unable to fulfil.

*they become guilty.* Hebrew *kî'āšēm* (MT *kĕ'āšēm,* "he is/they are, as it were, guilty"), the proclitic *kî* particle attached to a verb in the final position, an emphatic construction familiar from Ugaritic (*UT*⁴ §§9.17; 13.51) and Hebrew (Pss 49:16; 118:10,11,12; 128:2; etc.). The subject of the stative verb is usually taken to be the king, but in that case the syntax is awkward, *hammelek* standing in each of the surrounding phrases and especially superfluous in the one that follows. More probably it is the people of Yahweh (*'am yahweh*) who are said to become guilty (so Gevaryahu [1969:26–27], whose interpretation of the meaning is different), for, as we have seen, it is against them that David is accused of having devised something, and it is against his kinsmen that the fratricide is protected by David's oath.

14. *your son is dead.* The woman's argument is that Aminon is dead and David's refusal to end Abishalom's exile cannot change the fact. Joab knows that David is now "consoled over Aminon's death" (13:39) and that he is trying to decide what to do about Abishalom (14:1).

19. *it is.* The particle *'iš* occurs only here in Biblical Hebrew (cf. Mic 6:10, where the text is doubtful), thought it might be the first element in the name "Ishbaal" (see the NOTE at 2:8). It is, however, the standard particle of existence in Ugaritic (*'iṯ*) and Aramaic (*'it[ay]*).

20. *wisdom like that of an envoy of God.* See the NOTE at v. 17.

24. *he shall not see my face.* See the NOTES at 3:13, where it is explained that to "see the face of the king" was a privilege accorded those in favor at court, while exclusion from a personal interview with the king was a sign of disgrace.

25–27. This long parenthesis of testimony to Abishalom's beauty and popularity prepares us for the story of how, by his personal charm, he "stole the hearts of the men of Israel" (15:6) in § XXVII below. It also shows why David found him difficult to resist or reject, even after the revolt (cf. 19:1ff.). Conroy (1978:110) notes further its literary functions of focusing attention squarely on Abishalom and providing an interlude in the course of the narrative during Abishalom's two years of exile. Nevertheless, it has been regarded as secondary by a number of commentators (Klostermann, Budde, Nowack, Dhorme, Schulz, Bressan, van den Born, de Vaux, Caird, Mauchline, Ackroyd).

26. Reference is made to Abishalom's remarkable hair in order to give further illustration of his great beauty; compare the description of the beloved young man in Cant 5:11 with his piled-up locks (cf. Pope 1977:536). In addition to supporting the description of Abishalom's good looks, however, this notice may be intended to prepare the audience for the strange manner of his demise. He will die after being caught by his head in a tree (18:9ff.), and commentators since Josephus (*Ant.* 7.239) have often concluded that his hair was entangled in the branches. See, further, the NOTE at 18:9. Two less likely purposes of the reference to Abishalom's hair should also be mentioned. (1) Long hair suggests strength as well as beauty (Judg 16:15–17), so that v. 26 might be a hint at Abishalom's martial prowess. But there is nothing elsewhere to suggest that he was an accomplished warrior. In any case, the rabbis were probably mistaken in thinking that he was a Nazirite (Nazir 4b). (2) The specific content of David's oath of protection for the fratricide (v. 11) was that not one of his hairs should fall to the ground. Ackroyd wonders if the present notice was introduced under the influence of the oath.

For the grammar of the extraordinarily involved and awkward circumstantial clause, "it being at the end of each year when (*'šr*) he would," etc., see Driver. Joüon (1928: 311) takes *'šr* to mean *'t 'šr r'šw,* "the hair of his head," which he thinks was lost and restored by a marginal abbreviation (!). Subsequent critics seem not to have found this suggestion edifying.

*one hundred shekels.* A shekel weighed a bit less than half an ounce, so that one year's harvest from Abishalom's head weighed two or three pounds. This is quite a lot of hair, especially if it was washed regularly.

*the King's Weight.* This standard, *'eben hammelek,* is not mentioned elsewhere in the Bible. Wellhausen, who regarded the verse as post-exilic, thought the King's Weight was the standard of the Great King of the Persian Empire as distinct from the old Israelite standard. The equivalent Aramaic term, *'bny mlk',* which occurs in the papyri of the Jewish community at Elephantine (Cowley 1923:nos. 5:7, 6:14, and 8:14; cf. p. xxxi), may in fact refer to the Persian standard. But there is no reason to doubt that a royal standard was established and used at the Israelite court during the time of the monarchy (cf. Scott 1959:34; Rainey 1965b:35), as was also done, for example, in Assyria and Babylonia (for the Assyrian "King's Weight," *aban šarri,* see *CAD* 1: 59–60).

27. *Three sons . . . and one daughter.* Contrast the information given in 18:18, and see the NOTE there. The daughter may have been named for her "desolate" (13:20) aunt, and it is for this reason that her name alone of the four children is given (contrast Hertzberg).

33. *the king kissed Abishalom.* The kiss indicates reconciliation and restoration of the royal favor (cf. 15:5, where Abishalom's own kiss intimates royal [*sic*] favor). On the other hand, there is no reason to conclude that it is a gesture of affirmation of Abishalom's right to succeed David, as speculated by Schulz on the basis of I Sam 10:1 (cf. Conroy 1978:103).

## COMMENT

As explained in the COMMENT on § XXIV, chaps. 13–14 provide knowledge of the private affairs of the Israelite court necessary for an understanding of the public events to be recounted in chaps. 15ff. The story of Abishalom's reconciliation with his father in the present section brings this *praeparatio* to its conclusion. The violence of the preceding events is replaced by a fragile harmony in the house of David.

As in chap. 12, David is confronted with an imaginary situation demanding a royal verdict. Again the case is the shadow of a real situation in David's own life, a situation he has been unable to resolve. Blind to the pertinence of the case to himself, he is now able to pass judgment with a sense of justice befitting a king. By this means the stalemate reached at the end of chap. 13 is broken, and the tension building in the royal household abates.

The abatement of tension, however, will be temporary. The resolution apparently arrived at here is false. Permitting Abishalom to return will turn out to have been a mistake. This will become clear quickly in the chapters that follow, and it is a major component of the message of the composition as a whole (chaps. 13–20). Note, in this regard, the effect of the several verbal links between the accounts of David's interview with the wise woman of Tekoa in the present passage and Joab's interview with the wise woman of Abel of

Beth-maacah in chap. 20 (cf. Conroy 1978:142 n. 99). That chapter is a "public epilogue" to the story of Abishalom's revolt, just as chaps. 13–14 constitute a "private prologue," and the two wise-woman scenes stand at either end of chaps. 15–19 in a dramatic inclusion. In both cases the fate of a man who causes trouble for Israel (cf. 20:6) is decided. In both cases the integrity of Israel is involved, that is, there is a question of the elimination of someone from "Yahweh's estate" (14:16; 20:19). In the present case, however, the king's decision sets aside the clan's demand for blood justice in the interest of keeping the Tekoite woman's only heir alive. The effect of this disposition of the woman's sham case is to make possible the return of Abishalom to court. The fratricide will go unpunished under the protection of a royal oath. The result of this subordination of the need of the society—in this case Israel as a whole—for blood justice to the interests of an individual will be a swift unraveling of the social fabric. In the case described in chap. 20, however, the opposite decision will be made. There the concern is not over the elimination of an individual heir from Yahweh's estate, as in 14:16; rather, it is over the elimination of an entire city and, by implication, the society as a whole. As the woman from Beth-maacah puts it, "Why should you swallow up Yahweh's estate?" In chap. 20, then, the individual will be given up for the sake of the group, and the result will be a restoration of harmony. If the verbal echoes of chap. 14 in chap. 20 carry a message, it is that Abishalom should not have gone unpunished, that he certainly should not have been permitted to return to court, a parlous flaw in the fabric of Israelite society.

The story of two brothers who quarrel outdoors, one killing the other, cannot but remind the reader of the Bible of the story of Cain and Abel in Genesis 4 (cf. Blenkinsopp 1966:51; Gunn 1978:43; etc.). We cannot be sure that this old story was in the mind of the author of the story of Abishalom's rebellion, but the correspondences are striking. Note, in particular, the need for the protection of the exiled fratricide, a need met by divine decree in the one case (Gen 4:15), by royal oath in the other (II Sam 14:11). It is where the stories diverge, however, that the account of Cain's fate casts most light on Abishalom's case. Cain is protected by a sevenfold sanction against anyone who harms him, but his exile is not revoked; he remains a wanderer, "cursed with regard to the ground" (Gen 4:11). Abishalom, however, is not only protected by David's oath, he is also brought back to Israel, where his "curse" (if we may call it that) can contaminate others.

It is high testimony to the Tekoite woman's craft that she is able so effectively to command royal sympathy for herself and her son over against the legitimate claims of the clan. More remarkable still is the facility with which she is able to elicit a parallel to the case of Abishalom. One of her two sons struck and killed the other, she says (14:6), when they "got into a fight outdoors with no one to pull them apart." The murder of Aminon, however, was premeditated and carefully planned. Nevertheless, the wise woman, once she has persuaded the king to put her son under the protection of a royal oath, is able even to persuade the king that the exclusion of the fratricide Abishalom from Israel is a danger to "the people of Yahweh" (14:13). And now that the oath is in the air, she is probably correct. At this point Israel is in trouble either way.

In its disregard for larger moral questions and consequences in the interest of the attainment of an immediate goal, the woman's masquerade exhibits what has become familiar to us as the Machiavellian spirit of the sons of Zeruiah (I Sam 26:6–11; II Sam 2:24–30; 16:9–12; 18:10–15; 20:8–10; etc.). Behind the scenes lurks the sinister figure of Joab, manipulating the king and his authority to purposes that he, Joab, thinks good. It may be true, as Gunn suggests (1978:100), that in this instance Joab is acting out of a genuine interest in the welfare of the state. But, if so, he remains nonetheless indifferent to the moral issues involved and, in any case, his efforts lead to disaster, as Gunn admits. Thus David, though not free of blame, is presented as a king sincerely interested in the welfare of his people (14:13–14 + 18–21) but unable to control the reckless sons of Zeruiah (cf. 3:39) and, as always, sentimental and vulnerable where his own sons are concerned. Thus our narrator, before his account of the revolt itself begins, has carefully prepared the way by acquainting us with the personalities of these two principal figures, Joab and David.

As has been the case since the beginning of the story of the rebellion (13:1), however, our attention is centered on the figure of Abishalom. We have come to know him as a rancorous and scheming young man, brooding and sullen (13:22) yet capable of displays of extraordinary personal charm and persuasiveness in the pursuit of his own ends (13:24–27). In the present episode our attention is further concentrated on him by the interlude in 14:25–27, after which we witness a fresh illustration of the single-mindedness with which he promotes his own cause and the abandon with which he resorts to violence. We are now prepared to understand the momentous developments of chap. 15.

# XXVII. THE EVE OF THE REVOLT (15:1–12)

**15** [1]At a later time Abishalom began to make use of a chariot with
horses and fifty men to run before him. [2][He] would get up early and
stand beside the road, and whenever there was anyone who had a suit
to come before the king for judgment, Abishalom would call to him and
say, "What city are you from?"

"Your servant is from one of the tribes of Israel," [the man] would
say.

[3]Then Abishalom would say, "Look, what you have to say is good
and straight, but you will get no hearing from the king. [4]I wish someone
would appoint me as a judge in the land," [he] would say. "Then anyone
who had a suit might come to me, and I would adjudicate it in his
favor." [5]And whenever a man drew near to prostrate himself to him,
he would reach out and embrace him and kiss him. [6]Abishalom dealt
this way with all Israel when they came to the king for a judgment, and
[he] stole the hearts of the men of Israel.

[7]At the end of four years Abishalom spoke to the king: "Let me go
fulfil the vow I made to Yahweh-in-Hebron, [8]for your servant made a
vow when I was living in Aram-geshur, as follows: 'If Yahweh will
bring me back to Jerusalem, I shall serve Yahweh-in-Hebron!' "

[9]"Go in peace!" the king told him. So he arose and went to Hebron.

[10]Abishalom sent agents throughout the tribes of Israel with the
instructions, "When you hear the sound of the shofar, say, 'Abishalom
has become king in Hebron!' " [11]With [him] went two hundred men
from Jerusalem who had assembled and gone in good faith; they knew
nothing of the matter. [12]He had Ahithophel the Gilonite, David's counselor, summoned from his city, Giloh, where he was offering sacrifice.
The conspiracy was strong, and the army with Abishalom grew larger
and larger.

## *TEXTUAL NOTES*

**15** 1–6. The principal verbs in this passage are modal—habitual or durative—a fact obscured in most extant witnesses by the tendency to replace the imperfect or converted perfect verbs with ordinary perfects and converted imperfects. $LXX^L$ reflects the correct forms with Greek imperfects throughout, except in the case of the first verb *(y'śh),* which is preserved correctly only in $4QSam^c$. For further statistics see Ulrich 1979:15.

1. *At a later time* So MT: *wyhy m'ḥry kn* (cf. 3:28), for which $4QSam^c$ substitutes the ordinary expression of transition, *[w]ẏhy 'ḥry kn,* "Afterwards."

*Abishalom began to make use of* So $4QSam^c$: *w'bšlwm y'śh lw* (cf. Josephus, *Ant.* 7.194), for which all other witnesses substitute *wy'ś lw 'bšlwm,* "Abishalom made use of" (cf. I Kings 1:5). See Ulrich 1979:14–15.

2. *beside the road* The witnesses point to a conflation of variants, *'l yd hš'r,* "upon the 'hand' of the gate" (cf. *I Samuel,* the NOTE on 4:13), and *'l hdrk,* arbitrarily chosen here. Thus MT has *'l yd drk hš'r,* and $4QSam^a$ has *'l yd hdrk.* Syr. goes its own way: *'l gb tr'' dmlk'* = *'l yd š'r hmlk,* "beside the king's gate."

*and whenever there was . . . would call* Reading *whyh . . . wqr'* with $4QSam^a$ *(wh[yh] . . . wqr'),* $LXX^L$, and OL in preference to MT (cf. $LXX^B$) *wyhy . . . wyqr'.* Cf. Ulrich 1978:107.

*anyone* $4QSam^a$ (cf. LXX, Targ.): *[k]wl 'yš.* MT (cf. Syr.): *kl h'yš.*

*for judgment* MT: *lmšpṭ.* $4QSam^a$: *'l hmšpṭ.* $4QSam^c$ (erroneously): *mšpṭ.*

*Abishalom . . . to him* MT: *'bšlwm 'lyw* (cf. $LXX^A$). $4QSam^a$: *lw 'bšl[wm]* (cf. $LXX^{BL}$).

2–4. *say . . . would say . . . would say . . . would say* We read *w'mr . . . w'mr . . . w'mr . . . w'mr* on the basis of the imperfect verbs of $LXX^L$. In $4QSam^a$ only the second verb survives on the leather, but it reads *w'mr* correctly. In $4QSam^c$ the first two seem to have survived as *w'mr,* though neither is entirely preserved (see Ulrich 1979:15), while the second two have become *wy'mr . . . wyw'mr.* In $LXX^L$, $4QSam^a$ (*[w'nh h'yš] w'mr*), and $4QSam^c$ (*w'nh [h'yš w'mr]*) the second *w'mr* is expanded to *w'nh h'yš w'mr,* "the man would answer and say." MT (cf. $LXX^{BMN}$) has *wy'mr . . . wy'mr . . . wy'mr . . . wy'mr.*

4. *in the land* So MT, etc.: *b'rṣ.* $LXX^L$ reflects *'l h'rṣ 'l yśr'l,* "over the land, over Israel."

*a suit* Cf. $LXX^L$. MT (cf. $LXX^B$) has a conflation of variants, "a suit and a judgment *(mišpāṭ),*" as if it were "a legal pleonasm" (Conroy 1978:148) or hendiadys for "a just suit."

6. The modal verbs continue in this verse. Read *w'śh . . . wgnb* with $LXX^L$ *kai epoiei* ($LXX^B$ *kai epoiēsen* = *wy'ś) . . . kai idiopoieito* (so $LXX^B$); so probably $4QSam^a$ (*[w'śh . . . ]ẇ[gn]b*). MT has *wy'ś . . . wygnb.*

*the hearts* MT, $LXX^{BA}$, Syr.: *lb* (collective). $LXX^{LMN}$, OL = *lbby.*

*the men* So MT, LXX$^{BAM}$. LXX$^{L}$, OL: "all the men." LXX$^{N}$: "the sons." Syr.: "all the sons."

7. *four years* The impossible *'rb'ym šnh,* "forty years," of MT (cf. LXX$^{BAMN}$) was explained in a variety of ways by the scribes, rabbis, and church fathers (see Thenius, Smith). The reading "four years" is represented by LXX$^{L}$, Syr., Vulg., and Josephus (*Ant.* 7.196), who correctly understands it as a specification of the time that had passed since the reconciliation of David and Abishalom. An alternative solution is to read *'rb'ym ywm,* "forty days," with two MSS of MT (Ehrlich 1910:311; Eissfeldt 1931: 39–40) on the assumption of haplography and erroneous correction. Neither solution is entirely free of difficulties of interpretation; see Conroy 1978:106–7 n. 40. Tentatively I prefer the former. Perhaps the primitive reading was *'rb'-m šnh,* with enclitic *-m.*

*the king* So MT, Syr. (cf. LXX$^{L}$: "the king, *saying*"). LXX$^{BAMN}$: "his father." These two variants have equal claim to originality.

8. *will bring me back* Strengthened by the infinitive absolute *hāšēb,* as reflected by LXX *epistrephōn,* Syr. *mhpkw,* and Targ. *'tb'.* MT *(kĕtîb) yšyb* ("If Yahweh *will bring back,* bring me back"?) and MT *(qĕrê) yāšōb* ("If Yahweh will *again* bring back"?) are both unsuitable.

*Yahweh-in-Hebron* Only LXX$^{L}$ represents "in Hebron," and there is no apparent motive for its loss. It may well be a simple expansion based on v. 7 (cf. Barthélemy 1980:12), but I agree with Smith that it "seems necessary" and that it "may have been left out because it emphasizes the distinctness of the Yahweh of Hebron" (cf. Klostermann, Budde). See the NOTE on "Yahweh-in-Hebron," v. 7.

9. *he arose* LXX$^{L}$: "*Abishalom* arose."

10. *agents* MT *mrglym* (cf. LXX, Syr., Targ., Vulg.). 4QSam$^{c}$ has *myrwšlm,* "from Jerusalem."

*has become king* MT *mālak* (cf. LXX$^{AL}$, Syr.). LXX$^{BMN}$ reflect *mālak melek.*

12. *He had Ahithophel . . . summoned* We read *wyšlḥ wyqr' 't 'ḥytpl* with 4QSam$^{c}$, in which *wyqr'* was at first left out by haplography and then added supralinearly:

[*wyq*]*ṙ'*
[*wyšl*]*ḥ 't 'ḥ*[*y*]*tpl*

In MT *wyqr'* was also lost, but not restored, and the subject was made explicit—thus, *wyšlḥ 'bšlwm 't 'ḥytpl,* "Abishalom sent Ahithophel." LXX$^{LMN}$ reflect *wyšlḥ 'bšlwm wyqr' 't 'ḥytpl,* "Abishalom had Ahithophel summoned," the second verb surviving intact but the name being added as in MT. LXX$^{B}$, in the process of its recensional approximation to MT, stumbled over the assertion that Abishalom, who was not in Giloh, "sent Ahithophel . . . from his city Giloh," and read "send (word) *to* Ahithophel *in* his city" (cf. Syr.); but despite the dative *tō acheitophel,* "to Ahithophel," the title *symboulon* was left in the accusative (Ulrich 1979:16).

*the Gilonite* MT *hgylny;* cf. 23:34. LXX$^{B}$ has *tō thekōnei* = *(l)tqw'y* (?), "the Tekoite," which might be preferred as *lectio difficilior.*

*from his city, Giloh* So MT: *m'yrw mgylh* (cf. LXX$^{LMN}$). LXX$^{B}$ has "*in* his city, Giloh" (see the preceding *Textual Note*). Syr.: "(He sent for ['l] Ahithophel . . .) and brought him *(wdbrh* = *wyb'hw)* from his city, Giloh."

*Giloh* MT *glh.* LXX$^{BA}$ *gōla* points to *gwlh,* an error for *gylh.* LXX$^{L}$ *metallaad* is an error for *megallaad* (confusion of the similar majuscules *tau* and *gamma*), which reflects *mgl'd,* "from Gilead" (cf. the LXX$^{L}$ correspondent of MT *hgylny* in 23:34).

*where he was offering sacrifice* That is, *bzbḥw* (cf. LXX$^{BMN}$), to which MT adds *'t hzbḥym* (cf. LXX$^{AL}$, OL, Syr.).

*was* (2) Reading *whyh* with LXX$^{L}$ *(kai ēn),* OL *(et erat),* and 4QSam$^{c}$ ([*wh*]*yh*) in preference to MT *wyhy.*

*strong* So MT (cf. LXX$^{B}$, etc.): *'mṣ.* LXX$^{L}$ *poreuomenon kai stereoumenon* reflects *hwlk w'mṣ,* "growing stronger and stronger."

## NOTES

**15** 1. *a chariot . . . and fifty men to run.* Appurtenances appropriate to a king (I Sam 8:11). The runners served as a personal escort or bodyguard for the king (I Sam 21:8 [?]; 22:17; I Kings 14:27,28).

4. *a judge in the land.* I doubt if Herrmann (1981:164) is correct in stating that Abishalom, by using the term *šōpēṭ,* "judge," is trying "to associate himself with the best Israelite traditions," i.e., appealing to sectional sentiment in the north and nostalgia for the time of the judges. This interpretation is incompatible with the patently royal connotations of the procurement of a chariot and runners (I Sam 8:1). On the contrary, Abishalom is appealing to the equally venerable, but not distinctively Israelite, tradition of the king as judge, a role that, in his opinion, David is not now playing. Moreover, as explained in the COMMENT, it is unlikely that Abishalom's revolt was confined to the north.

6. *stole the hearts.* Comparison to Gen 31:20 shows that this expression does not mean "captured the affection" but rather "deceived, duped," the heart being the seat of the will and intellect. Smith: "So Absalom *stole the brain* of Israel, *befooled* them." Conroy (1978:106 n. 35) notes that this emphatic final sentence in the paragraph (vv. 1–6) shows the man speaking of justice to be a thief.

7,8. *Yahweh-in-Hebron.* Abishalom's vow was to the Hebronite Yahweh, the local manifestation of the national god worshiped in Abishalom's hometown. Thus the vow cannot be fulfilled in Jerusalem even though Yahweh is worshiped there too. To this formula, DN-in-GN, compare "Dagon-in-Ashdod" in I Sam 5:5 (Freedman) and "Ashtart-in-Sidon" (*'št<rt> bṣd*[*?*]*n*), mentioned on an Ammonite (!) seal of the seventh century B.C. (Avigad 1966:247–51 and pl. 26). Inscribed pithoi of the early eighth century from Kuntillet 'Ajrūd to be published by Zeev Meshel refer to two local Yahwehs with the formula DN of GN: *yhwh šmrn,* "Yahweh of Samaria," and *yhwh tymn/tmn,* "Yahweh of Teman."

8. *when I was living in Aram-geshur.* See 13:38 and, on the Aramean state of Geshur, the NOTE at 2:9. Apart from the transitional phrase in v. 1 ("At a later time"), this verse contains the only direct reference in chap. 15 to the events of chaps. 13–14. For this reason Langlamet (1976b:351), who thinks the account of Abishalom's rebellion did not originally contain the story told in chaps. 13–14, would strike v. 8 as secondary. As explained in the COMMENT on § XXIV, however, the original independence of chaps. 13–14 is unlikely.

10. *the shofar.* See the NOTE at 6:15.

12. *Ahithophel.* The element *tōpel* is otherwise unknown in the Hebrew onomasticon. It seems to mean "foolishness, insipidity," suggesting that *'ăḥîtōpel* might be a deliberate distortion satirizing the man's ill-used wisdom. The actual name, then, will have been something like *'ăḥîpeleṭ*, "Ahiphelet" (cf. *'ĕlîpeleṭ*, "Eliphelet," in 5:16 and 23:34 [Hertzberg; contrast Noth 1928:236]). According to Mazar [Maisler] (1963b:317 n. 1) *tōpel*, like *bōšet* (see the NOTE on "Ishbaal" at 2:8) is a derisive substitute for *ba'al*—thus, *'ăḥîba'al*, "Ahibaal" (so also Carlson 1964:251–52).

*Giloh.* Listed in Josh 15:48–51 among a group of eleven towns in the Judaean hills south of Hebron. The site is unknown. A new suburb of Jerusalem has been given the name of Giloh because of the resemblance of the name of the nearby town Beit Jalah to that of the biblical city; but Ahithophel's home lay much farther south (see A. Mazar 1981:2).

## COMMENT

In preparation for the coup d'etat that takes place offstage at the end of this section, Abishalom sets himself up as king and builds a base of support. His style is flamboyant and characteristically direct. As explained in the NOTE at 15:1, the chariot and runners suggest royalty. In the case of Adonijah, whose self-designation as king is reminiscent—probably deliberately so—of that of Abishalom (McCarter 1981:365), the significance of such a retinue is made explicit. In I Kings 1:5 we are told that "Adonijah son of Haggith had been vaunting himself, saying, 'I am the king!' and he made use of a chariot with horsemen and fifty men to run before him."

Abishalom's treatment of Israelites coming to the capital for litigation of grievances is clearly intended to create a private base of support on which he can rely in the struggle to come. Still brooding, perhaps, on his own recent experience with David, he depicts the king as unresponsive and inaccessible. He represents himself, however, as approachable and sympathetic, and thus he succeeds in beguiling "the men of Israel" (v. 6).

Who are "the men of Israel" to whom Abishalom commends himself in vv. 2–6? Are we to think of all the people here, including Judah, or is only the old northern tribal area, Israel proper, meant? The question touches on the larger issue of the participation of Judah in the rebellion. The terminology is ambiguous, since we are in the period, the time of David, when "all Israel," an old designation of the northern tribes as a whole (2:9; 3:12,21), was being extended to include Judah (Flanagan 1975:108–9), as notably in 17:11. Some scholars still follow Alt (1968[1930]:293–301) in thinking that only Israel proper was involved in the revolt, Judah remaining loyal or neutral (Soggin 1967:75; Flanagan 1975:108–9; Herrmann 1981:164). Others conclude that both Israel and Judah were in rebellion (Noth 1960:201; Weingreen 1969:263; Cohen 1971:96,107; Bright 1972:204; Bardtke 1973; Mettinger 1976:122–23). As we shall see, a number of factors favor the latter position. First, the banner of Abishalom, a son of David born in Hebron (3:3), would be a very unlikely rallying point for a revolt of the northern tribes. Second, it would be extraordinary for someone to arrange to have himself proclaimed "king in Hebron" (v. 10), the traditional capital of Judah (2:1), if he expected only northern support (but see Alt 1968:298 and n. 153; Herrmann 1981:164). Third, we are told that two powerful men of Judah, Ahithophel (v. 12) and Amasa (17:25), were among the leaders of the conspiracy. Fourth, David does not attempt to take refuge in Judah, as we might expect if it was loyal or neutral; instead he flees in the opposite direction. Finally, Hushai's words in 17:11, unless we interpret them as meaning something other than what they seem to mean (see the NOTE there) or strike them as secondary, show that it was possible for Abishalom to muster troops from "all Israel from Dan to Beersheba." For these reasons it seems preferable to think of Judah as having been actively involved in the revolt. Abishalom's intrigues reported in vv. 2–6 of the present passage may nonetheless have been intended primarily to curry favor in the north. He was, after all, a Hebronite by birth (2:3) and could probably rely on a natural constituency in Judah. But there is no reason to assume that his purpose was to incite northern sectional sentiment in his favor (cf. the NOTE on "a judge in the land," v. 4).

It is appropriate to address another historical question at this point. What was the cause of Abishalom's revolt? In considering this question we must keep in mind the fact that the text provides an implicit answer of its own. Our narrator has gone to considerable trouble to show us that the revolt grew out of the interaction of the chief characters in the story, and especially that it was an expression of the ambition and rancor of Abishalom. At a deeper level, we have been shown that the calamity now about to take place arose inevitably from the "sacrilege" of Aminon and the fratricide of Abishalom. Such explanations, however, are not satisfactory for the modern historian. The first is inadequate, inasmuch as it does not explain why Abishalom was able to command a following. The second is simply inappropriate by modern standards. It does not follow from this that the story of Abishalom's revolt is not a historiographical document, as Whybray (1968:11–19) and Gunn (1978: 20–21) conclude. It is historiography in every sense, but its evaluative criteria are not ours.

Our narrator locates the causative factors of historical change in private events and declines, therefore, to give us the information we need to make modern historical judgments (Wellhausen 1957:262). Why was Abishalom able to gain such widespread support for his revolt? Clearly there was a general disaffection with David. It is not surprising that in a document supportive of David we are not told what had made him unpopular. We have already ruled out sectionalist sentiment, which will not surface until chap. 20. Noth (1960: 201), apparently following Alt (1968:293–301), speculates about disapproval of David's policy of imperial expansion, and Weingreen (1969) cites a midrashic interpretation of the superscription of the third [second] verse of Psalm 3 (Tanhuma *Ki tissa* 4) that concludes similarly that David was vilified for his ruthless military campaigns (as well as the Bathsheba affair). Soggin (1967:75), taking his clue from Abishalom's words in vv. 4 and 6, speaks of the erosion of traditional personal freedoms after the imposition of a harsh and incompetent bureaucracy. Bright's analysis of the latter years of David's reign touches on most of the possible issues. He surmises (1972:203–4) that "miscellaneous grievances were abroad upon which clever men knew how to play. While we are not told in detail what these were, there was certainly resentment of the intrusion of the state upon tribal independence, resentment of the burgeoning court and of the privileged position of David's retainers. There were certainly a thousand petty personal jealousies between ambitious courtiers of which we know nothing. There was discontent with the administration of justice (ch. 15:1–6). Moreover, the winning and holding of the empire required Israelite levies to serve year after year, at small profit to themselves and increasingly as mere auxiliaries of David's troops; they probably responded with diminishing enthusiasm, until, in the end, conscription may have been necessary to raise them." As for the revolt itself, Bright concludes (p. 204) that it "seems . . . to have fed on a mass of indefinable grievances."

# XXVIII. DAVID'S FLIGHT FROM JERUSALEM (15:13–16:14)

15 [13]An informant came to David to say, "Abishalom has the hearts of the men of Israel!"

[14]"Arise!" said David to all his servants who were with him in Jerusalem. "We must flee if we're to escape from Abishalom! Go quickly, or he'll soon overtake us, push down the city on top of us, and attack [it] with the edge of the sword!"

[15]"Whatever the king chooses," said the king's servants to him, "we are your servants!"

[16]So the king marched out with all his household at his heels. [He] left ten concubines to keep the house. [17][He] marched out with all his servants at his heels, and they came to a halt at the last house, [18]while the whole army passed on beside him. (All those who were with him —all the officers and warriors—were six hundred men, and they went beside him.)

When all the Cherethites and Pelethites and all the Gittites who had come at his heels from Gath were passing by in front of [him], [19]the king said to Ittai the Gittite, "Why are *you* going with us? Go back and stay with the king, for you're a foreigner and you've gone into exile from your home, too. [20]You came only yesterday: Then shall I dislodge you today to go with us, as I wander wherever I might? Go back! And take your kinsmen back with you! May Yahweh deal loyally and faithfully with you!"

[21]"As Yahweh lives," said Ittai in reply to the king, "and as my lord the king lives, wherever my lord is, there, too, your servant will be, whether it means death or life!"

[22]Then David said to Ittai, "Pass on by!" So Ittai, all his men, and all the children who were with him passed by.

### *The Return of the Ark to the City*

[23]All the land was weeping aloud as the whole army passed by. As the king was crossing the Wadi Kidron, the whole army was passing

before him on the Olive Way in the wilderness, [24]and there, too, were Zadok (with all the Levites carrying the ark of the covenant of Yahweh) and Abiathar. They put down the holy ark until all the army had finished passing by from the city.

[25]Then the king said to Zadok, "Take the holy ark back into the city! If I find favor with Yahweh, he'll bring me back and show it to me along with its camping place, [26]but if he says [to me] 'I don't like you'—well, here I am! Let him deal with me as seems best to him!"

[27]Then the king spoke to Zadok the priest: "Look, you return to the city peacefully, Ahimaaz your son and Jonathan son of Abiathar, your two sons, with you. [28]I'll bide my time in the steppes of the wilderness until word comes from you advising me."

[29]So Zadok and Abiathar took the ark back into Jerusalem and deposited it there, [30]while David made his way up the Slope of the Olives, weeping as he went. His head was bare and he went along barefooted, and the whole army that was with him, each man with his head bare, wept as they went up.

### *An Encounter with Hushai the Archite*

[31]When David was informed that Ahithophel was in the conspiracy with Abishalom, [he] said, "Make Ahithophel's counsel foolish, O Yahweh!" [32]Then, as [he] approached the summit, where God was worshiped, there to meet him was Hushai the Archite with his clothes torn and dust upon his head. [33]"If you travel with me," David told him, "you'll be a burden on me. [34]But if you go back to the city and say to Abishalom, 'Your brothers departed, O king, after the departure of your father, and now I am your servant, O king. Spare my life! I was your father's servant in the past, and now I am your servant!'—then you can frustrate Ahithophel's counsel for me. [35]Zadok and Abiathar, the priests, will be with you there. Report everything you hear from the king's house to [them]. [36]Their two sons are there with them—Zadok's son Ahimaaz and Abiathar's son Jonathan—and you can communicate anything you hear to me through them" [37]So Hushai, the Friend of David, entered the city, just as Abishalom was arriving in Jerusalem.

### *Ziba's Report*

**16** [1]When David had passed a little beyond the summit, there to meet him was Ziba, Meribbaal's steward, with a yoke of saddled asses laden with two hundred loaves of bread, one hundred bunches of raisins, one hundred baskets of summer fruit, and a skin of wine.

[2]"Why do you have these things?" said the king to Ziba.

"The asses are for the royal household to ride," said Ziba, "the bread and summer fruit are for the servants to eat, and the wine is for those who grow faint in the wilderness to drink."

[3]"But where is your master's son?" said the king.

"He's staying in Jerusalem," Ziba told the king, "for he said, 'Today the Israelites are going to give me back my father's kingdom.' "

[4]So the king said to Ziba, "Everything that Meribbaal has is now yours!"

"I am prostrate!" said Ziba. "May I find favor with my lord the king!"

### *The Shimei Incident*

[5]When King David reached Bahurim, out came a man from the clan of the house of Saul, Shimei son of Gera by name, cursing as he came. [6]He hurled stones at David and all his servants, and all the army and the warriors to his right and left. [7]As he cursed [he] said, "Get out of here! Get out of here! You bloodstained fiend of hell! [8]Yahweh has requited you for all the blood of the house of Saul, whose place you took as king! [He] has handed the kingdom over to your son Abishalom! You're in this evil predicament because you're a bloodstained man!"

[9]Then Abishai son of Zeruiah said to the king, "Why should that dead dog curse my lord the king? Let me go over and cut off his head!"

[10]But the king said, "What do you sons of Zeruiah have against me? If someone curses that way, it's because Yahweh has said, 'Curse David!' to him. Who, then, can say, 'Why have you done this?' [11]"Look," said David to Abishai and all his servants, "my own son, the issue of my own body, is seeking my life! How much more so, then, this Benjaminite! Leave him alone and let him curse, for Yahweh has told him to. [12]Perhaps Yahweh will take notice of my affliction and requite me with something good in place of his curse today."

[13]So David and his men marched along the road, with Shimei following alongside on the terrace of the mountain cursing, hurling stones at the flank, and scattering dirt as he went. [14]The king and all his army arrived at the Jordan exhausted, and they refreshed themselves there.

## *TEXTUAL NOTES*

15 13. *the hearts* Cf. MT, etc. Vulg.: "the *whole* heart."

*the men of Israel* So MT, LXX$^{BAMN}$. LXX$^{L}$, Vulg.: "*all* Israel."

14. *We must flee if we're to escape* That is, *wnbrḥh thy lnw plyṭh,* lit. "And let us flee. Then we shall have an escape" (cf. Exod 7:9 and GK² §109h). We follow the text of 4QSam$^{c}$ ([*wnbrḥh*] *thy lnw* [*plyṭh*]) against MT *wnbrḥh ky l' yhyh plyṭh,* "We must flee, for we'll have no escape." Cf. Ulrich 1979:16.

*Go quickly* LXX$^{A}$: "*And* go quickly."

*he'll soon overtake us* MT *ymhr whśgnw,* lit. "he will be quick and overtake us." LXX$^{L}$ *phthasē ho laos kai katalabē hēmas* may reflect *ygy' h'm whśgnw,* "the army will arrive and overtake us."

*push down the city on top of us* MT has *whdyḥ 'lynw 't hr'h,* which can hardly mean "bring disaster upon us" (KB³). Read *wdḥh 'lynw 't h'yr* with LXX$^{L}$ *kai epōsētai eph' hēmas ten polin.*

15. *Whatever* MT: *kkl,* "according to all." LXX$^{L}$, Syr., Vulg. = *bkl,* "in all."

*the king* So LXX$^{L}$. MT has "my lord the king." LXX$^{BAMN}$ have "our lord the king."

*to him* So LXX$^{L}$. MT, LXX$^{BAMN}$: "to the king."

16. *concubines* Cf. MT, LXX$^{AMN}$. LXX$^{BL}$: "(of) *his* concubines." If we read an indefinite with MT, however, we must strike *'ēt* as intrusive from 20:3 (GK² §117d).

*the house* So MT, LXX$^{BAMN}$. LXX$^{L}$: "*his* house."

17–18. As recognized by Wellhausen, the text of LXX in these verses is conflate. LXX$^{B}$ reads [17]*kai exēlthen ho basileus kai pantes hoi paides autou pezē* [*kai estēsan en oikō tō makran* [18]*kai pantes hoi paides autou ana cheira autou parēgon kai pas ho chettei kai pas ho phelетthei*] *kai estēsan epi tēs elaias en tē erēmō* [18]*kai pas ho laos pareporeueto echomenos autou kai pantes hoi peri auton kai pantes hoi hadroi kai pantes hoi machētai hexakosioi andres kai parēsan epi cheira autou kai pas ho chereththei kai pas ho phelеththei kai pantes hoi geththaioi hoi hexakosioi andres hoi ēkontes* (cf. LXX$^{LMN}$) *tois posin autōn ek* (cf. LXX$^{LM}$; LXX$^{B}$: *eis* [cf. I Sam 27:2]) *geth pareporeuonto* (cf. LXX$^{LMN}$; LXX$^{B}$: *kai poreuomenoi*) *epi prosōpon tou basileōs,* reflecting *wyṣ' hmlk wkl 'bdyw brglyw wy'mdw bbyt hmrḥq wkl 'bdyw 'l ydw 'brw wkl hk(r)ty wkl hplty wy'mdw 'l hzyt bmdbr wkl h'm 'brym 'l ydw wkl 'šr 'tw wkl hgdwlym wkl hgbwrym šš m'wt 'yš wyb'w 'l ydw wkl hkrty wkl hplty wkl hgtym šš m'wt 'yš 'šr b'w brglyw mgt 'brym 'l pny hmlk,* "The king marched out with all his servants at his heels, and they came to a halt in the last house, and then all his servants passed on beside him—all the Cherethites and the Pelethites—and they came to a halt beside a certain olive tree in the wilderness, while the whole army passed on beside him. (All those who were with him—all the officers and warriors—were six hundred men, and they went beside him.) When all the Cherethites and Pelethites and all the Gittites who had come at his heels from Gath were passing by. . . ." Everything I have set in brackets in the Greek text is recensional, designed to bring the text in line with that of MT (Wellhausen). Thus, the original LXX version of v. 17b is *kai estēsan epi tēs elaias en tē erēmō* = *wy'mdw 'l hzyt bmdbr,* a variant of MT *wy'mdw byt hmrḥq;* of these, the obscure reference of LXX ("a certain olive tree in the wilderness") may be suspected of anticipating v. 23, and the reading of MT ought probably to be retained. In MT the army marches in v. 17a and David's servants in v. 18a; in $LXX^B$ the situation is reversed. In this case LXX is correct: David and his cortege of courtiers stop while the rest of the army passes them by (Wellhausen). The material concerning the Cherethites, Pelethites, and Gittites at the end of the verse is often also taken as recensional in LXX, but this is not correct. What Wellhausen failed to see was that MT is defective (haplographic). LXX, except for the recensional plus at the beginning, preserves the approximate shape of the primitive text, which was *wyṣ' hmlk wkl 'bdyw brglyw wy'mdw byt hmrḥq* (see above) *wkl h'm 'brym 'l ydw wkl 'šr 'tw wkl hgdwlym wkl hgbwrym šš m'wt 'yš wyb'w 'l ydw wkl hkrty wkl hplty wkl hgtym 'šr b'w brglyw mgt 'brym 'l pny hmlk.* The text of MT was shortened by a haplography involving the repeated sequence *'l ydw wkl.* $LXX^L$ is shorter than $LXX^B$, mentioning the Cherethites and Pelethites only once, and might seem, therefore, to suggest an alternative reconstruction. But this is specious: $LXX^L$ is also haplographic, having lost everything from the first *šš m'wt 'yš* to the second in a text similar to that of $LXX^B$. Note, finally, that the second *šš m'wt 'yš* has been stricken from our reconstructed text. The authority for this is Syr., which surely preserves the primitive situation. The six hundred were David's personal army, raised before he went to Gath (I Sam 23:13; 27:2; 30:9); they were not Gittites.

18. *All those who were with him* Cf. $LXX^B$ (see above). In $LXX^L$ this stands after "all the officers."

*all the . . . warriors* Cf. $LXX^B$ (see above). $LXX^L$: *kai pantēs hoi machētai tou basileōs* = *wkl gbwry hmlk,* "all *the king's* warriors."

*at his heels from Gath* So MT (cf. $LXX^M$). $LXX^L$: "from Gath at his heels."

19. *and* (2)*. . . too* So MT: *wgm;* cf. LXX in the doublet in v. 20. Here LXX reflects *wky,* "and because."

*you've gone into exile* Reading *gālîtā* on the basis of LXX *metōkēkas* (*metanastēseis* in the doublet in v. 20) in preference to MT *gōleh,* "you're an exile." The prepositional phrase *lmqwmk,* "from (!) your home," requires a verb of motion. See the NOTE.

*from your home* MT *lmqwmk;* see the NOTE. LXX, Syr., and Vulg. all translate the preposition as "from," and this is more likely to mean that they read *mmqwmk* (so $MT^{MS}$) than that they correctly interpreted *lmqwmk.*

20. At the beginning of v. 20 $LXX^B$ preserves its own version of v. 20aα. This is followed by a recensional duplicate of vv. 19bβ + 20aα identical to the text of MT. The plus is lacking in the other major MSS of LXX.

*You came* LXX *paragegonas* reflects *b'th* ($LXX^L$ = *b'th 'th,* "*You* [emphatic] came" [dittography?]), expressed in MT by an infinitive construction, *bw'k.*

*shall I dislodge* Reading MT *(qĕrê) 'ănî'ăkā* in preference to MT *(kĕtîb) 'nw'k* (i.e., *'ănû'ăkā;* but *nw',* "totter," is never transitive in *Qal*).

*to go with us* MT: *'mnw llkt.* $LXX^L$: *llkt 'mnw.* In $LXX^B$ *llkt* is not reflected in the first (and older) translation, but it is precisely at this point that the recensional plus was inserted, and it ends with *tou poreuthēnai* = *llkt,* which probably was not lacking in the OG text.

*Go back!* That is, *lk šwb,* lit. "Go, return!" This reading is preserved in $LXX^{LMN}$ *(poreuou kai anastrephe); lk* was lost in MT after *hwlk.*

*May Yahweh . . . with you!* Reading *wyhwh y'śh 'mk ḥsd w'mt* on the basis of LXX *kai kyrios poiēsei meta sou eleon* (LXX$^{L}$) *kai alētheian.* MT has lost *wyhwh y'śh 'mk* by simple haplography after the preceding *'mk* (Wellhausen).

21. *and as my lord the king lives* So MT: *wḥy 'dny hmlk.* LXX$^{L}$ and Syr. (also Symmachus and Theodotion) reflect *wḥy npšk 'dny* (omitted by Syr.) *hmlk,* "and as you yourself live, my lord the king"; cf. I Sam 20:3; 25:26.

The oath is introduced by *kî* (cf. the NOTE on "May God . . . again" at 3:9); so MT *(qěrê),* MT$^{MSS}$ (cf. LXX, Syr.). MT *(kětîb): kî 'im,* "(I can do nothing) except that" (cf. GK$^{2}$ §163d).

*my lord* (2) So LXX$^{BMN}$. MT, LXX$^{AL}$: "my lord *the king.*"

22. *David* So MT. LXX$^{B}$ has "the king," and the two are combined in LXX$^{L}$.

*Ittai* (1) LXX$^{L}$: "Ittai the Gittite."

*Pass on by!* LXX adds *met' emou* = *'ty,* "with me," which probably arose from a duplicate of *'ty,* "Ittai."

*Ittai* (2) So LXX$^{LMN}$. MT, LXX$^{B}$: "Ittai *the Gittite.*"

*all his men, and all the children who were with him* So MT. LXX$^{B}$: "(and) all his *servants,* and all the *force* (*ho ochlos* = *hḥyl* [cf. Syr. *ywrt'*]?) that was with him." LXX$^{L}$: "and all his servants. And *the king* and all his men. . . ." LXX$^{MN}$: "And the king, all his servants, and all the force that was with him. . . ."

23. *weeping* MT *bwkym.* LXX$^{L}$ *eulogountes* reflects *brkym,* "blessing," a graphic error for *bwkym,* which has been added recensionally later in the verse ("blessing aloud and weeping"). The Hebrew letters *w* and *r* were liable to confusion in many scripts of the fourth through first centuries B.C.

*passed by* LXX$^{BMN}$ add "in the Wadi Kidron," which arose as a recensional note, conforming *'t nḥl qdrwn* below to MT *bnḥl qdrwn.* Omit with MT, LXX$^{AL}$.

*crossing the Wadi* That is, *'br 't nḥl;* cf. LXX$^{BM}$. MT has *'br bnḥl,* "passing along *in* the Wadi" (so LXX$^{AL}$; cf. LXX$^{N}$).

*before him on* Reading *'l pnyw 'l* on the basis of LXX$^{L}$ *pro prosōpou autou kata.* MT has *'l pny*—thus, "in front of" or "on the surface of."

*the Olive Way in the wilderness* Reading *drk hzyt ('šr) bmdbr* on the basis of LXX$^{L}$ *tēn hodon tēs elaias tēs en tē erēmō* (cf. OL). MT has *drk 't hmdbr,* and it is evident that *'t* is a corrupt vestige of *hzyt.*

24. *Yahweh* So LXX$^{BAMN}$. MT, LXX$^{L}$: "God."

*and Abiathar* Preserved corruptly in LXX$^{B}$ as *apo baithar,* as if *mbytr* (= *mbytw,* "from his house"?), and in MT as *wy'l 'bytr,* "and Abiathar came up/lifted up (offerings)." In MT this stands later in the verse, after "the holy ark." The cause of the corruption was the late insertion of "(with all the Levites carrying the ark of the covenant of Yahweh)"; see the NOTE. As Wellhausen supposes, there may have been a deliberate editorial attempt—not entirely successful—to remove the non-Zadokite priest Abiathar from the context altogether.

*the holy ark* That is, *'t 'rwn h'lhym,* lit. "the ark of God"; so MT, LXX$^{B}$. LXX$^{L}$: "the ark of the covenant (of Yahweh [one MS])."

25. *the city* LXX$^{AL}$ add *kai kathisatō eis ton topon autēs* = *whwšybw 'l mqwmw,* "and deposit (it) in its place" (cf. I Kings 8:6 and the first *Textual Note* at 6:17 above), which Klostermann and Budde retain.

26. [*to me*] Explicit in LXX$^{L}$. Omit with MT, LXX$^{BAMN}$.

27. *Look* So LXX[L]: *blepe* = *r'h* (LXX[BAMN]: *idete* = *r'w,* "Look" [plural]). MT has *hrw'h,* "Are you (*'th*) watching?" In adopting the LXX reading we follow Budde, Nowack, Dhorme, Schulz, Hertzberg, Goslinga, Caird, and others. MT is accepted by de Groot and Carlson (1964:173–75), who follow Arnold (1917:93) in taking it as a rhetorical question: "Are you a seer?" i.e., "You are no seer!" MT *hărô'eh* is emended to *hārō'eh* by Keil (". . . the priest, 'O seer, you . . .' ") and Klostermann ("You are an oracular priest . . ."). Hoftijzer (1971:608–9) interprets the consonantal text of MT as a formulaic idiom meaning "Pay attention!" or the like. Wellhausen and Ehrlich (1910:313) read *hr'š,* "the chief (priest)," etc.

*Ahimaaz* Prefaced in LXX[L] by *idou* = *hnh* or *r'h,* "Look."

28. The verse begins with *hnh* (or *r'h,* LXX[L] *idou*), lit. "Look" but best left untranslated. MT has *r'w* (cf. LXX[BAMN]), "Look" (plural).

*bide my time* So MT (cf. LXX[B]): *mtmhmh.* LXX[L] has *prosdechomai hymas,* "I shall receive you."

*in the steppes of the wilderness* MT *b'rbwt* (so *qĕrê* [cf. LXX]; the *kĕtîb* is *b'brwt,* "in the passes") *hmdbr;* cf. 17:16. LXX[L] has *epi tes elaias en tē erēmō* = *'l hzyt bmdbr,* "beside a certain olive tree in the wilderness" (cf. the *Textual Note* to vv. 17–18).

29. *the ark* So LXX[B]. MT, LXX[ALN], Syr.: "the ark of God."

*and deposited it* Reading *wayyōšeb* on the basis of LXX[B] *kai ekathisen.* MT has *wayyēšĕbû* (cf. Syr. *wytbw*), "and they remained." LXX[L] *kai anestrepsen* reflects *wayyāšob,* "and it (?) went back." Smith suggests *wayyēšeb* (cf. Syr.[MSS] *wytb*), "and it remained."

30. *the Slope of the Olives* So MT, LXX[BAL]. LXX[MN] (cf. Josephus, *Ant.* 7.202): "the slope of the Mount of Olives." See the NOTE.

*weeping as he went* MT *'lh wbwkh.* In LXX, *anabainōn kai klaiōn* (LXX[AMN]) was left out of LXX[B] after *elaiōn,* "Olives" (partially restored in LXX[L]).

31. *When David was informed* We read *wldwd hwgd,* lit. "And it had been told to David." MT has *wdwd hgyd,* "And David had told," but *wldwd* is attested by MT[MSS], LXX[LMN], Syr., Targ., Vulg., and 4QSam[a] ([*w*]*ldwy*[*d*]), and *hwgd* (so MT[MS]) is supported by LXX[BAMN], Syr., Targ., and Vulg.

*Ahithophel* So MT. LXX[BLMN] and Vulg. reflect *gm 'ḥytpl,* "Ahithophel, too."

*Make . . . foolish* MT *sakkel,* reflected by LXX[L] as *mataiōson.* LXX[B] *diaskedason* reflects *hāpēr,* "Frustrate," which anticipates v. 34 below and 17:14.

*Yahweh* So MT, at the end of the speech, and Syr., at the beginning. LXX[B] reflects "Yahweh, my god" at the end of the speech, and LXX[L] has this at the beginning.

32. *Then, as [he] approached* Reading *whyh dwd b'* with LXX[BAMN] *(kai ēn . . .)* in preference to MT *wyhy dwd b'* (cf. LXX[L], OL).

*the summit* MT *hārō'š,* taken by LXX as a proper noun. Targ. and Vulg. reflect *r'š hhr,* "the summit of the mountain" (cf. Josephus, *Ant.* 7.203). Syr. has *dwkt' ḥd',* "a certain place."

*where God was worshiped* So MT: *'šr yštḥwh šm l'lhym,* lit. "where one would prostrate himself to God" (cf. LXX[B], etc.). LXX[L], OL (cf. Josephus, *Ant.* 7.203) reflect *wmštḥwh šm lyhwh,* "and prostrated himself there to Yahweh" (cf. Caspari).

*God* So MT, Syr., LXX[BAM]. LXX[LN], OL, Targ., and Vulg. reflect "Yahweh."

*there* That is, *whnh,* "and behold" (MT, LXX[B], etc.). LXX[L] reflects *(w)hnh šm,* "and behold *there.*" Syr. *w't' lwth* suggests *wyb' 'lyw,* "(Hushai the Archite) came to him," instead of *whnh lqr'tw* (MT).

*Hushai the Archite* Glossed in LXX and OL as "David's friend" (cf. Josephus, *Ant.* 7.203); see v. 37.

33. *David* LXX[L]: "the king."

34. *Your brothers . . . and now* We read the text of a long LXX plus lost from MT by haplography. LXX[B] reads *dielēlythasin hoi adelphoi sou kai ho basileus katopisthen mou dielēlythen ho patēr sou kai nyn,* reflecting *'brw 'ḥyk whmlk 'ḥry 'br 'byk w'th,* understood to mean, "Your brothers departed, and the king after me departed—your father—and now." (LXX[L] shows an attempt to improve this awkward interpretation by reading *'ḥry 'br* after *'byk*—thus, "Your brothers departed, and the king, your father, after me departed." The reading of LXX[B] appears in LXX[L] as part of a plus after v. 36.) But this makes little sense. The plus as understood by the LXX translators is obscure and, probably for this reason, has not commended itself to modern critics. The picture changes, however, when it is recognized that *'ḥry 'br 'byk* is not to be read *'aḥăray 'ābar 'ăbîkā* with LXX but *'aḥărê 'ăbôr 'ăbîkā,* "after your father departed" or "after the departure of your father." The conjunction before *hmlk,* which (like the other *hmlk* in the verse) is vocative, is secondary. Thus *'brw 'ḥyk hmlk 'ḥry 'br 'byk w'th* means "Your brothers departed, O king, after the departure of your father, and now. . . ." This was lost in MT by homoioarkton before the succeeding *'bdk.*

*Spare my life!* LXX *eason me zēsai* probably reflects *ḥyny,* of which a variant, *'ḥyh,* "Let me live!" led to the defective reading of MT, *'hyh,* "I am."

*in the past* So LXX, Syr. MT: "*and* in the past."

*and now* Rendered twice by LXX[BAL].

*then you can frustrate* MT *whprth* (cf. LXX[BAMN]). LXX[L] (cf. Syr.) = *whpr* (imperative).

35. At the beginning of the verse we read *whnh* with LXX (cf. Syr.). MT has *whlw'.*

*from the king's house* So MT (cf. LXX[BA]): *mbyt hmlk.* LXX[MN] = *mpy hmlk,* "from the king's *mouth.*" LXX[L] = *m'm (para) hmlk,* "from the king."

36+. At this point LXX[L] adds a misplaced duplicate of portions of v. 34: *kai ereis tō abessalōm dielēlythasin hoi adelphoi sou kai ho basileus katopisthen mou dielēlythen ho patēr sou kai egō artiōs aphigmai kai egō doulos sos* = *w'mrt l'bšlwm 'brw 'ḥyk (w)hmlk 'ḥry 'br 'byk w'ny m'z b'yty* (cf. v. 20) *w'ny 'bdk,* "and you will say to Abishalom, 'Your brothers departed, O king, after the departure of your father. And I arrived in the past, and I am your servant.' "

37. *Hushai* LXX[AL] add "the Archite."

*Jerusalem* LXX[L] adds *kai acheitophel met' autou* = *w'ḥytpl 'tw,* "and Ahithophel was with him." See 16:15.

**16** 1. *Meribbaal* See the *Textual Note* at 4:4. In the present passage (vv. 1,4) Meribbaal is called *mĕpî-bōšet,* "Mephibosheth," by MT (cf. LXX[BAMN]) and *memphibaal* = *mpyb'l,* "Mippibaal," by LXX[L].

*one hundred* (1) So MT, LXX[BA]. LXX[LMN]: "an ephah."

*one hundred* (2) So MT, LXX[BA]. LXX[MN]: "an ephah." LXX[L]: "two hundred" (cf. I Sam 25:18).

*baskets of summer fruit* MT *qyṣ* (cf. GK[2] §134n). LXX[LMN] *(palathai/ōn)* reflect *dblym,* "date-cakes," perhaps read also by LXX[BA] (*phoinikes,* as if *tmr,* "palm [branches]"[?], but possibly *dblym,* "[fruit of the] date-palm").

2. *asses* LXX[L] (cf. OL): "*saddled* asses."

*the bread* Reading *whlḥm* with MT *(qĕrê)* and all the versions. MT *(kĕtîb): wlhlḥm.* The erroneous *lamed* arose from mechanical repetition of the initial *lamed* of the preceding words (Thenius, Wellhausen, citing Maurer).

*summer fruit* LXX has "date-cakes," as in v. 1 (LXX$^{L}$: "date-cakes and raisins").

*those who grow faint* MT: *hy'p* (cf. LXX$^{L}$). LXX$^{BAMN}$ = *hy'pym.*

3. *But* The conjunction is omitted by LXX$^{L}$.

*for* LXX$^{L}$: "and."

*the Israelites* So MT$^{MSS}$: *bny yśr'l,* also reflected by Syr. and one MS of LXX$^{L}$ (o). MT has *byt yśr'l,* "the house of Israel"—thus, perhaps, "Today they are going to give me back the house of Israel, my father's kingdom."

4. *May I find* So MT: *'mṣ'.* LXX$^{L}$ = *mṣ'ty,* "I have found."

*with* That is, *b'ny,* "in the eyes of" (cf. LXX$^{L}$). MT has *b'nyk,* "in *your* eyes."

5. *reached* Reading *wyb'* with LXX$^{BAMN}$ *kai ēlthen.* MT (cf. LXX$^{L}$) has *wb',* which might be interpreted as a participle ("As King David was coming to Bahurim . . ."), but in such a case we should expect a different word order *(whmlk dwd b' 'd bḥwrym).* Cf. GK$^{2}$ §§112tt,113t.

6. *He hurled* So MT *(wysql),* LXX$^{MN}$. LXX$^{BAL}$ continue with participles *(wmsql).*

*his servants* So LXX$^{L}$, Syr. MT, LXX$^{BAMN}$: "*King David's* servants."

*his right and left* So MT. LXX: "the (LXX$^{BA}$ "his") right and left of the king."

8. *whose place you took as king* MT *'šr mlkt tḥt(y)w* (cf. LXX$^{LMN}$). LXX$^{BAMmg}$ reflect *ky mlkt tḥtyw,* "because you took his place as king."

*You're in this evil predicament* So MT: *whnk br'tk,* lit., "And behold yourself in your evil" (cf. LXX$^{BAMN}$). LXX$^{L}$, OL reflect *wyr' lk 't r'tk,* "And he (Yahweh) has caused you to see this misfortune of yours."

9. *dead dog* MT *hklb hmt* (so LXX$^{BAMN}$). LXX$^{L}$ *ho kyōn ho epikataratos* reflects *hklb h'rwr,* "*accursed* dog."

10–11. This passage is highly repetitious. We may have here an elaborate repository of variants and blended corrections arising from attempts to repair an accident in the text of a single long speech. If this is the case, the primitive text may be irrecoverable. It is also possible, however, that David spoke twice in the primitive text and the repetition, therefore, is authentic and must be interpreted as such. Our translation reflects this latter alternative. The two verses exhibit a strong tendency towards conflation in any case, as the *Textual Notes* that follow show.

10. *the king said* LXX$^{LMN}$ add "to Abishai."

*you sons of Zeruiah* Cf. MT, LXX$^{BAMN}$, Syr. Only one son of Zeruiah is present (viz. Abishai), and LXX$^{L}$, therefore, reads a singular. But as in 19:23, David is referring to his general relationship to his violent nephews. See the NOTE.

*If . . . because* We read *kh yqll wky* with MT *(qĕrê)* and LXX$^{BAMN}$ (contrast Langlamet 1979/81:395–98). In LXX, however, this is preceded by a reflection of *whnḥw lw w-,* "Leave him alone and," an anticipation of v. 11 found also in Syr. and Vulg. Here MT *(kĕtîb)* has *ky yqll wky,* and LXX$^{L}$ reflects *ky (dioti) yqll ly ky.*

*can say* LXX$^{L}$ *(autō = lw)* and LXX$^{N}$ *(pros auton = 'lyw)* add "to him."

11. *Abishai* LXX$^{L}$: "Joab" (!).

*Leave him alone* Singular in LXX$^{L}$, which would be appropriate in v. 10 (cf. the *Textual Note* on "If . . . because"), but not here.

*for Yahweh has told him to* That is, *ky 'mr lw yhwh* (so MT, LXX$^{BAMN}$). LXX$^{L}$

and Syr. reflect the word order of v. 10: *ky yhwh* (Syr. = *h'lhym*) *'mr lw,* to which Syr.$^{MSS}$ add *dṣḥ' ldwyd* = *qll 't dwd,* "Curse David!" (cf. v. 10).

12. *my affliction* Reading *b'nyy* with MT$^{MSS}$, LXX, Syr., and Vulg. (cf. I Sam 1:11; etc.). MT *(kĕtîb): b'wny,* "my guilt." MT *(qĕrê): b'yny,* "my eye" (cf. Targ.). This is listed by the Masoretes among the so-called *tiqqûnê hassōpĕrîm,* "the emendations of the scribes." See Levin (1978:73 n. 11), who regards both *b'wny* and *b'yny* as deliberate alterations of *b'yn(y)w,* "with his own eyes" (cf. already Geiger 1857:324–35).

*and requite* Cf. LXX$^{BAMN}$, Syr., Vulg. MT: "and Yahweh will requite."

*his curse* So MT, LXX (LXX$^{A}$ "*this* curse," erroneously). Syr. and MT$^{MSS}$ *(kĕtîb):* "*my* curse" *(BHS).*

13. *his men* So MT, LXX$^{BA}$. LXX$^{MN}$: "all his men." LXX$^{L}$: "all the men with him."

*cursing, hurling . . . as he went* The original was probably *hālôk wĕqallēl wĕsaqqēl* (cf. LXX$^{BAMN}$), lit. "going and cursing and hurling," but the second and third infinitives have become finite verbs *(. . . wyqll wysql)* in MT, a most awkward construction. In Syr. these verbs are also finite, but the problem does not arise because *hlwk* is missing (cf. Snaith 1945:18).

*at the flank* We read *mṣdw,* lit. "from his side," with LXX$^{BAMN}$ *ek plagiōn autou.* LXX$^{L}$ and Vulg. reflect *'lyw,* "at him." MT repeats *l'mtw,* "alongside him" (MT$^{MSS}$ *mzh l'mtw* [*BHS*]), which Langlamet (1979/81:402–6) retains.

14. *his army* So LXX$^{B}$. MT, LXX$^{LMN}$, Syr., Targ., and Vulg. read "the army (that was) with him."

*at the Jordan* Missing in MT and most other witnesses. Some designation of place is, however, "imperatively demanded" (Driver; cf. Wellhausen, Smith). One MS of LXX$^{L}$ has *para ton iordanēn* = *'l hyrdn,* "beside the Jordan" (cf. Josephus, *Ant.* 7.210: *epi ton iordanon*) after *eklelymenoi* = *'ypym,* "exhausted," and 17:22 shows this to be the correct spot. Perhaps *'l hyrdn* preceded *'ypym* in the text of MT and was lost by homoioarkton. Joüon (1928:312) suggests changing *'ypym* to *'d hmym,* "to the water." Other suggestions are listed by Snaith 1945:19. See also Langlamet 1979/81:406–12.

## NOTES

15 13. *the hearts of the men of Israel.* That is, their minds. The meaning of the message is that Abishalom has deluded the Israelites and thus captured their loyalty, not necessarily their affection (though he probably has that, too). See the NOTE on "stole the hearts," 15:6.

16–17. The beginning of v. 17 recapitulates the beginning of v. 16 after the circumstantial clause about the concubines. "All his servants" (v. 17a) is equivalent to "all his household" (v. 16a). The mention of the concubines is preparatory to 16:21–22. Langlamet (1976b:352) would strike vv. 16b–17a as secondary for two reasons: (1) He does not think the concubine episode in 16:21–22 was an original part of the story of Abishalom's revolt (cf. Langlamet 1977), and (2) he reads the (inferior) text of the received Hebrew (MT) of v. 17a, according to which it was "all the army" that marched out after David in contradiction to v. 16a (cf. Cook 1899/1900:162,176).

18. *six hundred men.* According to Mazar (1963b:314) "the size of regular regiments in Israel and Philistia" (cf. I Sam 13:15; etc.). Is the present reference to the six hundred men who followed David before he became king (cf. I Sam 23:13; 25:13; 27:2; 30:9)? The point may be that they alone remain loyal now that his kingship has been taken away.

*the Cherethites and Pelethites.* The royal bodyguard, who probably followed David from Ziklag. See the NOTE at 8:18.

*the Gittites.* While living in Ziklag, David served in the army of the king of the Philistine city of Gath (I Samuel 27), where he won the loyalty of this contingent of Gittite mercenaries. On the location of Gath, see Rainey 1975.

19. *Ittai the Gittite.* The commander of the Gittite force and one of David's staunchest supporters. In the battle in the Forest of Ephraim he will stand alongside Joab and Abishai as commander of a third of David's army (18:2). His name, *'ittay,* may be compared to Hittite *atta-* and Hurrian *attai,* both "father" (Laroche 1966:47,241,337; Gelb, Purves, and McRae 1943:207), an onomastic element common at Ugarit (Gröndahl 1967:221–22); the change **'attay* > *'ittay* conforms to a standard Northwest Semitic pattern of dissimilation. A Semitic origin of the name, hypocoristic of the type *'ittô-DN,* "DN is with him," is also possible. For other possibilities, see Delcor 1978: 411–13.

*from your home.* Hebrew *limqômékā.* The preposition means "to" or "at," but with an appropriate verb of motion—like *gālîtā,* "you've gone into exile," here (cf. the *Textual Note*)—the required sense in English is "from." Compare our adoption in the COMMENT on § XIII of Hillers' translation of *limnûḥātékā* in Ps 132:8 as "from your resting place." On the present passage, cf. Carlson 1964:170.

20. Sakenfeld (1978:1–8) draws a happy parallel to Ruth 1:8, where Naomi bids farewell to Ruth and Orpah with a wish that Yahweh might "deal loyally" with them, and Ruth, like Ittai, refuses to return. On the loyalty of Yahweh to an individual, see the NOTE at 7:15. On the collocation of "deal loyally and faithfully" *(ḥesed we'ĕmét),* see Sakenfeld 1978:32–34, where she shows that the combination has the force of "be sure to do *ḥesed.*"

23. *the Wadi Kidron.* The valley between the city and the Mount of Olives to the east; see Map 3. The Kidron was a traditional boundary of Jerusalem (I Kings 2:37), so that at this point David can be said to have left the city.

*the Olive Way.* Hebrew *derek hazzayit* (see the *Textual Note*), a road leading up the Slope of the Olives (v. 30) and over the crest to Bahurim (16:5).

24. *Zadok . . . and Abiathar.* David's two chief priests. See the NOTES at 8:17.

*(with all . . . of Yahweh).* Most commentators agree that the mention of the Levites here is secondary, the contribution of a late, possibly Deuteronomistic, editor who insisted that the holy object must have had an appropriate retinue of Levites (contrast, however, Ehrlich 1910:313). Compare, for example, the Levites added by the Chronicler (I Chronicles 15) to the party David organized to bring the ark into Jerusalem (II Samuel 6). Compare also I Sam 6:16.

*They put down.* Hebrew *wayyaṣṣîqû,* for which we might have expected *wayyaṣṣîgû,* as in 6:17. But this form receives support from (1) its occurrence in Josh 7:23 (*wayyaṣṣîqūm,* "and they put them down"), (2) the use of Ugaritic *yṣq b'ap-* to describe the placing of solid foods in front of a horse in the hippiatric texts (*CTCA* 160 [= *UT*⁴

55].3,5,9,29; 161 [= 56].11,16,20,22), and the comparable use of Biblical Hebrew *yāṣaq/hiṣṣîq lipnê PN* in reference to serving foods, as explained in the first NOTE at 13:9, and (3) the use of the passive participle *mūṣāq* to mean "fixed in place" in Job 11:15 (cf. 22:16) and Rabbinic Hebrew (Jastrow 590). Taken together, the evidence suggests that *yṣq*, "set," is less likely to be a semantic extension of *yṣq*, "pour out," than a dialectal variant of *yṣg*, "set"; cf. Gordon 1965:413–14 (§19.1141).

25–26. Würthwein (1974:43) assigns these verses, together with v. 29, to his "pro-David" redaction, while Langlamet (1976b:352) considers them part of his "theological-sapiential" redaction (see the Introduction, p. 14). According to Veijola (1975:46), they derive from the hand of the Deuteronomistic historian; but the language is not Deuteronomistic (cf. Langlamet 1976a:124). It is true that David is cast in a favorable light here, but, as explained in the COMMENTS on §§ XXIV–XXXIII, I regard the original story of Abishalom's rebellion to have been favorable to David. Langlamet's remark on the duplication in the beginnings of vv. 25 and 27, therefore, does not seem to me to be sufficient evidence to strike vv. 25–26 as redactional.

25. *its camping place.* Hebrew *nāwēhû*, "a specific designation of a tent shrine" (Cross 1973:125, in reference to *nĕwê qodšĕkā*, "your holy encampment," in Exod 15:13). On *nāweh*, "camping place," see Edzard 1959; Malamat 1962:146; 1971:16–17. Contrast Rupprecht 1977:93–95.

28. *the steppes of the wilderness.* The Jordan Valley north of the Dead Sea. The royal party will stop on the west bank (16:14) and await word from Jerusalem (17:15ff.).

30. *the Slope of the Olives.* This probably refers to the steep ascent of the second (Jebel eṭ-Ṭûr) of the three summits of the Mount of Olives, which rose east and northeast of Davidic Jerusalem. It is possible, though, that *ma'ălê hazzêtîm*, "the Slope of the Olives," was an older name for *har hazzêtîm*, "the Mount of Olives," which is not attested before the post-exilic period (Zech 14:4 [*bis*]).

31. David's petition to Yahweh is given great stress by von Rad (1966:200). David utters these words as he climbs the Slope of Olives. When he reaches the top, a place of worship (v. 32), he will find, as if in answer to his prayer, a man who "can frustrate Ahithophel's counsel" (v. 34). All of this looks ahead to the report of Hushai's masquerade in 17:5–14.

Langlamet, who, like Würthwein (1974:33–42), regards 17:5–14 as part of a pro-Davidic redaction of the succession narrative, considers the present verse (along with most of v. 34) to be secondary; see Langlamet 1976b:352–53 and especially 1978:59–61. David's prayer, says Langlamet, anticipates the frustration of Ahithophel's counsel (cf. 17:14b) in the work of a redactor who sought to demonstrate the divine control of the events leading to the rejection of Abishalom in favor of Solomon.

32. *the summit, where God was worshiped.* The only known place of worship on the Mount of Olives was the so-called Mount of Corruption *(har hammašḥît)* of II Kings 23:13, where foreign gods are said to have been honored at the instigation of Solomon's foreign wives. But the Mount of Corruption was probably the southern limit of the Mount of Olives, whereas David, on his way to Bahurim (16:15), seems to be crossing the middle summit, as explained in the NOTE at v. 30. Was "the priestly city of Nob" (I Sam 22:19) located atop the Jebel eṭ-Ṭûr (cf. Voigt 1923; Albright 1932b:413)?

*Hushai the Archite.* The name *ḥûšay* may belong to a common type that indicates ethnic origin, suggesting that the family came from *šûaḥ*, "Shuah" (*sic!*; cf. *ḥûšā* [I

Chron 4:4] = *šûḥâ* [I Chron 4:11], *ḥûšîm* [Gen 46:23] = *šûḥām* [Num 26:42]), either the Aramean state called Shuhu on the right bank of the Middle Euphrates or the Edomite or Arabian tribe alluded to in Gen 25:12 (cf. Albright 1927/28). Hushai's family, however, is now part of the Archite clan of Benjamin, who are said in Josh 16:2 to occupy the territory southwest of Bethel. The father of Baana, one of Solomon's prefects, is also called Hushai (I Kings 4:6), probably the same man.

37. *the Friend of David.* Hebrew *rēʿeh,* "friend," occurs only in reference to important royal officials (II Sam 15:37; 16:16; I Kings 1:8 [cf. LXX$^{L}$, Josephus, *Ant.* 7.346]; 4:5), apart from Prov 27:10, where the text is uncertain *(qĕrê: rēaʿ).* The usual word for "friend" is *rēaʿ.* The use of the less common word (cf. GK[2] §§84ai,93ll) lends plausibility to the suggestion of de Vaux (1939:403–5; 1961b:vol. I:22–23) that the title *rēʿeh hammelek,* "the Friend of the King," is based on the Egyptian honorific *rḫ nsw,* "acquaintance of the king." The suggestion gains support from the probability that other Egyptian titles were used at David's court (see the NOTES on "remembrancer" and "scribe" at 8:16,17) and the fact that this title seems to have been known in fourteenth-century B.C. Jerusalem (cf. *ru-ḫi šarri* in *EA* 288:11). If this identification is correct, we should probably assume that the title was first used as an honorific, as in Egypt, later becoming the designation of an officer of state, a sort of privy counselor (Donner 1961:270–71), as its inclusion in the list of Solomon's officials (I Kings 4:5) implies. Note also that although "friend" is not a correct translation of *rēʿeh* (< *rḫ,* "acquaintance"), it probably came to be understood this way in Hebrew, as suggested by Abishalom's ironic play on Hushai's title in 16:17 below and the identification of Hushai as *rēaʿ* (!) *hammelek,* "the Friend of the King," in I Chron 27:33. See, further, in addition to the studies by de Vaux cited above, Donner 1961 and Bright 1976:203–4. Van Selms, who doubts the connection with the Egyptian title (1957:121–22), finds the origin of the office in the function of a man's "friend" as a romantic counselor and best man, for which he is able to cite both Sumero-Akkadian and biblical evidence. Of "the king's friend," then, he concludes (p. 120): "Perhaps he was originally consulted in matters of marriage and family relations only, but from there to the position of intimate counselor on matters of state is only a step." But see the discussion of Mettinger 1971:63–70.

**16** 1–14. Cook (1899/1900:169) considered these two incidents to have been drawn from an independent document concerned with David's relationship to the house of Saul (see the COMMENT on § XIX); originally, he believed, the story of Abishalom's revolt, which took place *before* David began to rule over all Israel, made no mention of this concern. Langlamet (1979/81:481–82), though he does not agree about the chronology of the revolt, also regards 16:1–14 as standing outside the horizon of the story of the revolt (cf. 1976b:353). In his opinion both incidents (vv. 1–4 and 5–14) are to be grouped with the other "Benjaminite episodes" (9; 19:17–31; etc.), which derive from an originally independent and unified source. Würthwein (1974:43–48) considers the report of the second incident (vv. 5–13) to have arisen in the process of pro-Davidic editing.

1. *Ziba, Meribbaal's steward.* On Ziba and Meribbaal, see chap. 9, where Ziba is called "Saul's steward," an office discussed in the NOTE at 9:9.

3. These charges will be refuted in 19:27–29 by Meribbaal, who will accuse his steward of slander.

5. *Bahurim.* The Benjaminite town identified in the NOTE at 3:16 with Râs eṭ-Ṭmîm, east of Mount Scopus.

*a man from the clan of the house of Saul.* In I Sam 10:27 Saul's clan is identified as Matri *(maṭrî),* "the humblest clan of all the tribe of Benjamin" (I Sam 9:21). Evidently Shimei is also a Matrite.

*Shimei son of Gera.* Gera was a Benjaminite clan (Gen 46:21; cf. I Chron 8:3,5), and it is sometimes supposed that the designation *ben-gērā'* here indicates Shimei's membership in the clan of Gera, to which Ehud son of Gera (Judg 3:15), then, must have also belonged. But, as noted above, Shimei seems rather to have been a Matrite. Gera, a short form of *gēr-DN,* "client of DN," was a common Northwest Semitic name occurring in Egyptian records of the Twentieth Dynasty (Albright 1934:14), in Phoenician (Benz 1972:298–99), in Samaria Ostracon 30 (*ANET*[3] 321), and in Arad Ostracon 64 (Aharoni 1981:200 and pl. 2 [*gry*]). I assume, then, that "son of Gera" is simply what it seems to be, the patronymic of Shimei (and probably of Ehud), not in this case a clan designation.

7. *You bloodstained fiend of hell!* That is, *'îš haddāmîm wĕ'îš habbĕlîya'al,* lit. "man of blood and man of hell." A "man of blood" is a man who has shed blood, a "bloodstained man" (v. 8), or perhaps, more generally, any wicked man or criminal (Pss 5:7 [5:6]; 26:9; 55:24 [55:23]; 59:3 [59:2]; 139:19; Prov 29:10; cf. Ezek 24:6,9; Nah 3:1). Hebrew *ben/'îš bĕlîya'al* probably does not mean "son/man of worthlessness," that is, "worthless fellow" (BDB 116), but rather, like *ben/'îš mawet* (cf. 12:5), "man/son of hell," that is, "hellfiend" or even "damnable fellow" and thus "scoundrel" (20:1). The composite word *bĕlî-ya'al* probably means "(place of) not-coming-up," that is, "hell" (Cross and Freedman 1953:22 n. 6), although Winton Thomas (1963) derives it from *bl',* "swallow"—hence, "Swallower" (preferred also by Dahood 1965b:105). In any case it refers to "hell, the underworld," as shown conclusively by its use in 22:5, where it is parallel to "death" and "Sheol."

8. *the blood of the house of Saul.* Because Shimei is not more specific, we cannot tell whether he is cursing David for his execution of the seven Saulids at Gibeon (21:1–14), which probably took place early in David's reign (see the COMMENTS on §§ XIX, XXXV), or for the deaths of Abiner and Ishbaal (§§ VI, VII), for which David's enemies must have held him accountable (cf. McCarter 1980b:501–2). It is even possible that public suspicion implicated David, who was attached to one of the Philistine armies that fought in the battle of Mount Gilboa, in the deaths of Saul and Jonathan (cf. McCarter 1980b:500–1).

9. *Abishai son of Zeruiah.* See the NOTE at 2:18. Like all the sons of Zeruiah, Abishai is always ready with a swift and severe solution to a problem. He seems, in particular, to regard the prompt execution of an adversary as the most convenient way out of any awkward situation (I Sam 26:8–11; II Sam 16:9–12; 19:21–23; 21:17).

*that dead dog.* For this expression of contempt, see the NOTE at 9:8. Abishai is remarking on the presumption of Shimei—whom he regards as trash, riffraff, a "dead dog"—in cursing the king himself. This unpleasantry, he says, is not necessary; it can easily be brought to an end.

10–12. David's reply is repetitious, and the text of vv. 10–11 is troubled (see the *Textual Note*). Veijola (1975:33) regards vv. 11–12 as Deuteronomistic anticipation of the execution of Shimei in I Kings 2:8,44–45. Verse 12, however, looks forward to "something good" for David, not to retribution on Shimei, whose execution will take place after David's death. These verses (10–12) correspond in tone to David's reply to Abishai in I Sam 26:9–11. Both passages exhibit David's piety towards the god of Israel and forbearance in dealing with the house of Saul. Thus they tend to strengthen his claim on the Israelite throne, and they belong, in all probability, to the earliest form of each narrative. The meaning of David's reply in the present passage can be paraphrased as follows. It is obvious from the circumstances of David's flight that he is now living under the impact of a curse. He is in exile from his home and his own son has become his enemy. All this must reflect the divine will. It is hardly surprising, therefore, that Yahweh should put a curse against David in the mouth of a Benjaminite. Nor would it be proper or possible to change things by slaying Shimei. Instead, the attitude that David takes is one of patience and trust in Yahweh. He hopes for "something good" in return for the curse he must now endure; this evidently looks ahead to his restoration. See, further, the COMMENT.

10. *What do you . . . have against me?* That is, *mallî* [*mâ* + *lî*, GK² §§37bc] *wĕlākem*, lit. "What do you and I have (between us)?" exactly as in 19:23. Comparison with other passages (Judg 11:12; I Kings 17:18; II Chron 35:21) shows that this most often means, "What issue or grievance is there between us that you should want to harm me?" Thus David is saying to Abishai here and in 19:23, "What do you sons of Zeruiah have against me, that you continuously cause me trouble?" David's point is that it would be disastrous for him to take Abishai's advice. A good discussion of this idiom, which occurs as a Semitism in John 2:4 (Snaith 1945:14), can be found in Brown 1966:99, though I cannot agree with his interpretation of the present passage as meaning "This is not *our* concern."

13. *following . . . cursing.* Hebrew *hālôk wayqallēl*, an infinitive absolute coordinated with an imperfect consecutive, as in I Sam 19:23. See GK² §113t, *I Samuel*, p. 329, and, in the present volume, the NOTE at 13:19.

## COMMENT

When news of the revolt reaches the king, he immediately departs, marching out of the capital city with his private army to seek safety in the wilderness.

This description of David's flight from Jerusalem might be subtitled "Many Meetings." Beginning with his arrival at the last house in the outskirts of the city (15:17), David has a series of important encounters as he crosses the Kidron (15:23), makes his way up the Mount of Olives (15:30) and over the summit (16:2) to Bahurim (16:5), from which his company winds down finally to the Jordan (16:14). Along the way, at stages in the journey, David meets Ittai the Gittite (15:18b–22), the priests Zadok and Abiathar (15:24–29), Hushai the Archite (15:31–37), Ziba, the steward of Meribbaal (16:1–4), and the Benjaminite agitator Shimei (16:5–13).

Each of these meetings prepares the reader for some part of the story to follow, the issue immediately at stake being loyalty or disloyalty to David in the struggle to come. Ittai and his men, for example, show themselves staunch in their allegiance despite their foreign birth. Ittai will command a third of David's army in the battle in the Forest of Ephraim (18:2). Zadok and Abiathar, too, are prepared to go into exile with David, but he sends them back. They—and more especially their sons Ahimaaz and Jonathan—will play important roles in the little drama of advising and strategy presented in 16:15–17:23, roles anticipated by David's instructions to them here in 15:27–28. Similarly, Hushai, who will play the key role in that drama, is introduced to us here for the first time. As we shall see, the rebels' disregard for the advice of Ahithophel will predetermine the outcome of the battle in the Forest of Ephraim, and it is in David's conversations with Zadok and Hushai in the present episode that an effective plan for subverting the counsels of Abishalom is formulated. The meetings with Ziba and Shimei, on the other hand, look beyond the battle to the king's return to Jerusalem. David's final disposition of the case of Meribbaal in 19:25–31 will be based in part on the testimony Ziba gives here; similarly, the pardon of Shimei in 19:17–24 will be granted against the background of his behavior here.

*David Under the Curse*

At the same time that he is preparing us for events to come, however, the narrator is working out the central thematic issue of his account of Abishalom's revolt. He is fashioning a structure of responsibility, blame, and divine censure that becomes increasingly visible as the story goes along. In David's attitude towards the disposition of the ark and the chief priests we see a king prepared to submit fully to the divine will. We can speak of David's trust in Yahweh if we want. The main point, however, seems to be his resignation to Yahweh's will, whatever it might be. "Let him deal with me as seems best to him!" he says (15:26). The reader is naturally caught up in this attitude of patient resignation and finds himself as willing as David to see in the resolution of the story a demonstration of what the divine will actually is. This attitude is reinforced by the narration of the Shimei incident, in which David again shows himself ready to submit to whatever Yahweh has in store. In this case the king's resignation is set in high relief by the contrasting example of one of the always precipitate sons of Zeruiah. As at other times, "David is prepared to allow that the kingdom is not his to grasp or cling to but lies in the hands of others to give" (Gunn 1978:102). Again this passivity on David's part guides the reader in his own judgment: Events will show what Yahweh has in mind.

If events reveal the divine will, however, what can be concluded from the present situation? The king is marching into exile, but his flight seems sometimes to have the character of a religious pilgrimage rather than a strategic military retreat (Gressmann). He submits to the ordeal with humility. It is as if he is the object of severe divine disapproval. Indeed, as many commentators stress (Caspari, etc.), details of the narrative suggest that his journey over the Mount of Olives was made as an act of penance: "All the land was weeping aloud," (15:23) and as for the king himself, "His head was bare and he went along barefooted" (15:30). Ackroyd sees in these details evidence that "the story of an actual rebellion is being told under the influence of forms which belong to worship, in which the humiliation and triumph of the king are celebrated not as historical events but as indications of the king's relationship to God" (cf. Psalm 89, especially vv. 39–46 [38–45]). I prefer to interpret the penitential character of the procession as evidence that David—and the narrator—understood his exile from the city as a situation to which a penitential response was somehow appropriate.

This is consistent with David's attitude towards Shimei. The Benjaminite curses him, and he is resigned even to this. "Leave him alone and let him curse," he says (16:11). Nor does he deny the validity of the curse. "If someone curses that way, it is because Yahweh has said, 'Curse David!' to him" (16:10). In other words, David himself admits that Shimei is cursing him because "Yahweh has told him to" (16:11). It follows that David's penitential behavior is an acknowledgment that his exile should be interpreted as evidence of a curse under the impact of which he has come. This does not mean that he accepts the interpretation of the curse made by Shimei in 16:8 (see the NOTE there). If the curse had arisen from David's shedding of Saulid blood, he could hardly hope, as he does in v. 12, that "Yahweh will take notice of my affliction and requite me with something good in place of [Shimei's] curse."

Why, then, *is* David cursed? David himself does not seem to know. Consistent with his behavior elsewhere in the story of Abishalom's revolt, his posture is one of acceptance and patience. He acknowledges the curse, humbles himself, and hopes for "something good" to come of it in the end. The reader of the larger story has been prepared to interpret David's troubles as the result of the crimes reported in chap. 11 (see the COMMENT on § XXII); but now we are concerned with the older story of Abishalom's revolt (chaps. 13ff.) and the interpretation the original narrator made of the situation. It is uncharacteristic of the original narrator to be as direct and explicit as the prophetic author of chap. 12. In the older story, therefore, the reasons for the curse are implied in the events themselves without recourse to interpretive passages like 12:7–12. Nevertheless, the reasons are clear. All of this began with the "sacrilege" *(nĕbālâ)* committed by Aminon. As in Joshua 7 and elsewhere, the result of such a sacrilege is general disaster (cf. the NOTE at 13:12). The disaster might have been averted if the king had punished the perpetrator of the sacrilege, but the just king yielded to the devoted father (13:21). In consequence, the incestuous rape was complicated by fratricide, and the disastrous sequence of events began.

David, then, is implicated in the causes of the trouble, but he is not directly responsible. Direct responsibility falls upon Abishalom. The gradual resolution of the crisis thus begun will, accordingly, bring hardship to David, doom to Abishalom, and, as we shall see, the narrator will permit—not constrain—his audience to see in this resolution the operation of divine justice. Indeed, this quiet providence is already shown to be at work in the present material. By his exile and humiliation David has suffered the consequences of his implication in the events of chaps. 13–14. It seems, in fact, that his penalty is paid, for at the moment his fortunes reach their low point with the intelligence that Ahithophel has defected to the enemy (15:31), he utters a prayer to Yahweh and his fortunes begin to change (von Rad 1966:200). At that moment he reaches the summit of the Mount of Olives, a place "where God was worshiped," and finds Hushai there (15:32). Hushai is quite literally the answer to a prayer, for it is he who will defeat the counsel of Ahithophel, thereby predetermining, as we have said, the outcome of the showdown in the Forest of Ephraim. To be sure, this will be a result of careful planning by David, Hushai, and others. But it will not result *only* from human planning; lest the reader be confused on this crucial point of interpretation, the narrator will insert an uncharacteristically forthright interpretive parenthesis into his account of the rejection of Ahithophel's counsel (17:14b) as a reminder of Yahweh's oversight of these events. But we are getting ahead of the story: The counsel of Ahithophel and its rejection by Abishalom are reported in the material to follow.

# XXIX. THE COUNSEL OF AHITHOPHEL (16:15–17:23)

16 [15]Abishalom and all the men of Israel had arrived in Jerusalem,
and Ahithophel was among them.

### *The Arrival of Hushai*

[16]When Hushai the Archite, the Friend of David, came to Abishalom, Hushai said to Abishalom, "Long live the king!"
[17]"Is this your loyalty to your friend?" said Abishalom to Hushai.
"Why didn't you go with your friend?"
[18]"I didn't," said Hushai to Abishalom, "because him whom Yahweh
and these people and all the men of Israel have chosen—to him I belong
and with him I'll stay! [19]And in the second place, whom should I serve
if not [David's] son? Just as I served your father, so I am now in your
service!"

### *Ahithophel's Counsel*

[20]Then Abishalom spoke to Ahithophel. "Give us your counsel! What
shall we do?"
[21]"Go to your father's concubines, the ones he left to keep the house,"
said Ahithophel to Abishalom. "Then all Israel will hear that you've
become odious to your father, and everyone on your side will gain
strength." [22]So a tent was pitched for Abishalom on the roof, and
Abishalom went to his father's concubines in the sight of all Israel.
[23]In those days the counsel Ahithophel gave was regarded as if the
word of God had been consulted; all of [his] counsel to Abishalom was
regarded this way, just as it had been to David. **17** [1]And Ahithophel
said to Abishalom, "Let me choose twelve thousands of men and go in
pursuit of David tonight. [2]I'll come upon him when he is weary and his
guard is down. I'll surprise him, so that the entire army that is with him
will desert and I can attack the king alone. [3]Then the entire army will

come back to you, as a bride comes back to her husband. You seek the
life of only one man, so the entire army can be at peace." 4This plan
seemed sound to Abishalom and all the elders of Israel.

*The Double-dealing of Hushai*

5Then Abishalom said, "Summon Hushai the Archite, and let's hear
what he has to say." 6And when Hushai came to [him], Abishalom said
to him, "This is what Ahithophel has advised. Shall we act on his
advice? And if not, advise us yourself!"
7"This time," said Hushai to Abishalom, "the counsel Ahithophel
has given is not good. 8You know," [he] said, "that your father and his
men are crack soldiers and that they are embittered, like a bear bereft
in the wild or a sow snared in the wild. Your father is a warrior: He
won't spend the night with the army; 9he'll be hidden in a pit or some
other place. And when the army falls in the first engagement, anyone
listening will hear it and think, 'There has been a rout of the army that
follows Abishalom!' " 10Even if he is a stalwart man with the heart of
a lion, he'll grow faint with fear, for all Israel knows that your father
is a crack soldier and that those who are with him are stalwart men.
11"Instead, I myself must offer counsel as follows: Let all Israel, from
Dan to Beersheba, gather about you, as many as the sands of the sea,
so that you personally may travel among them. 12We'll come upon
[David] in one of the places where he can be found and descend upon
him as fog descends over the ground; and of him and the men with him
not even one will be spared. 13If he withdraws into a city, all Israel will
bring ropes to that city and drag it down into the wadi until not a pebble
can be found there!"
14Abishalom and all Israel thought that the counsel of Hushai the
Archite was better than the counsel of Ahithophel. (For Yahweh had
ordained that the counsel of Ahithophel should be frustrated, so that
[he] might bring misfortune upon Abishalom.)

*Hushai Informs David*

15Then Hushai said to Zadok and Abiathar, the priests, "This is how
Ahithophel counseled Abishalom and the elders of Israel, and this is
how I myself counseled them. 16Quickly now, send word to David as
follows: 'Don't spend the night in the steppes of the wilderness, but

cross over immediately, or else disaster will befall the king and the
entire army that is with him!' "
[17]Now Jonathan and Ahimaaz were waiting in En-rogel—a maidservant would come and give them information, and they would go and
report it to King David—for they could not risk being seen entering the
city. [18]But a soldier saw them and told Abishalom. So they both left
quickly and went to the house of a man in Bahurim who had a well in
his yard. They got down into it, [19]and the wife took a cover, stretched
it over the mouth of the well, and spread groats over it, so that nothing
would be noticed. [20]Then when Abishalom's servants came to the
woman's house and asked her where Jonathan and Ahimaaz were, [she]
told them, "They went on in the direction of the watercourse." Though
[the men] sought them, they found nothing, and so they returned to
Jerusalem.
[21]After they left, [Jonathan and Ahimaaz] climbed out of the well and
went and made their report to King David. "Arise," they told him,
"and cross the water quickly, for this is how Ahithophel has given
counsel against you!" [22]So David and the entire army that was with him
arose and crossed the Jordan, so that by the morning light there was
not a straggler who had not crossed the Jordan.

## *The Death of Ahithophel*

[23]Ahithophel, when he saw that his counsel was not acted upon,
harnessed his ass and went up to his home in his own city. Having given
instructions concerning his estate, he hanged himself and died. He was
buried in the tomb of his father.

## *TEXTUAL NOTES*

16 15. *the men of Israel* So LXX$^{B}$. MT (cf. LXX$^{L}$) has "the army *(h'm),* the men of Israel."

16. *to Abishalom* LXX$^{L}$ adds *eis tēn polin* = *'l h'yr,* "to the city."

"*Long live the king!*" Repeated in MT, Syr., Targ., and Vulg. LXX has *zētō ho basileus* = *yḥy hmlk* only once (so MT$^{MSS}$). One could argue for haplography in LXX or, as assumed here, dittography in MT.

18. *and these people* So MT, LXX$^{BAMN}$, etc. LXX$^{L}$ *ho laos autou,* "and *his* people," is probably an inner-Greek error for *ho laos houtos* (so LXX$^{B}$, etc.); cf. v. 14 (LXX$^{B}$)

*to him* So MT *(qĕrê),* LXX, etc.: *lw.* MT *(kĕtîb): l'.*

19. *whom should I serve* MT *lmy 'ny "bd* (cf. LXX$^{B}$, etc.). LXX$^{L}$ *tinos egō doulos* and Syr. *dmn 'n' 'bd'* reflect *lmy 'ny 'bd,* "whose servant am I?" Ehrlich (1910:315), plausibly but without textual support, reads *"br* for *"bd*—thus, "to whom should I *cross over* (i.e., transfer my allegiance) . . . ?" Joüon (1928:312) suggests *"md,* also changing the preceding *lmy* to *lpny*—thus, "before whom should I stand?" (see Ehrlich's suggestion on "I served" below).

*if not [David's] son* MT *hlw' lpny bnw* (cf. LXX). Syr. has *l' hwt b'ydy (hd'),* as if reflecting *l' thyh bydy (z't),* "this is not in my hands (under my control)."

*I served* All witnesses reflect *'bdty,* which is awkward before *lpny* (Snaith 1945:21) and for which Ehrlich (1910:315), again without textual support but with a second from Joüon (1928:312), would read *'mdty,* "I stood (before)"; cf. I Kings 18:15; etc.

*your father* Reading *'t 'byk* with MT$^{MSS}$, LXX$^{L}$. MT (cf. LXX$^{BAMN}$) has *lpny 'byk.*

*in your service* So MT (cf. LXX$^{B}$, etc.): *lpnyk.* LXX$^{L}$ reflects *'mk,* "with you."

21. *the house* LXX$^{AMN}$: "*his* house."

*you've become odious* MT *nb'št,* for which LXX has *katēschynas,* reflecting *hbyšt,* understood as "you've put (your father) to shame." But *hbyšt* probably arose from a defective spelling of *hb'yšt,* a *Hip'il* variant of *nb'št* with a similar meaning (cf. I Sam 27:12).

*and everyone . . . will gain strength* So MT: *wḥzqw ydy kl 'šr 'tk,* lit. "and the hands of all who are with you will be strong." LXX$^{L}$ has *kai kratēsousin hai cheires sou kai pantōn tōn meta sou,* which might reflect an original longer reading, *wḥzqw ydyk wydy kl 'šr 'tk,* "and your hands and the hands of all who are with you will be strong," shortened by haplography in MT. I assume, however, that LXX$^{L}$ reflects a conflation of variants, viz. *wḥzqw ydyk* and *wḥzqw ydy kl 'šr 'tk.*

22. *his father's concubines* LXX$^{L}$: "all his father's concubines."

23. *In those days* So MT (cf. Syr., Vulg.): *bymym hhm.* LXX reflects *bymym hr'šnym,* "in *former* days."

*had been consulted* We read *yš'l,* lit. "one used to consult," with MT *(kĕtîb).* MT *(qĕrê)* has *yš'l 'yš.* Cf. Nedarim 37b.

**17** 1. *Let me choose* So MT, Syr. LXX *(emautō)* and Vulg. *(mihi)* add *ly,* "for myself."

*twelve* So MT, LXX$^{BAMN}$, Syr., and Vulg. LXX$^{L}$ (cf. Josephus, *Ant.* 7.215): "ten."

3. *will come back* Cf. LXX$^{L}$, OL. MT: "I'll bring back."

*as a bride . . . one man* MT is defective here and, as first recognized by Thenius (so Wellhausen, Ewald [1878:183], Klostermann, Driver, Budde), the primitive text is to be recovered from LXX. LXX$^{L}$ (cf. LXX$^{B}$, OL) reads: *kathōs epistrephei* (LXX$^{B}$: *hē) nymphē pros ton andra autēs plēn psychēn andros henos,* from which we may restore *kšwb (h)klh 'l 'yšh rq npš 'yš 'ḥd.* As Thenius showed, MT suffered further corruption after being shortened by haplography involving *'yš(h)* and *'yš*—thus, *kšwb hkl* (MT$^{MSS}$: *kl) h'yš 'šr.* The objection of Ehrlich (1910:315), recently restated by Barthélemy (1980:27–29), that the collocation of *kallâ,* "bride," with *'îš,* "husband," instead of *ḥātān,* "bridegroom," is "unhebräisch" strikes me as forceless. Are we to believe that a newly married man, *ḥātān,* was not also called *'îš* in regard to his bride until after the wedding week? Barthélemy argues (p. 28) that the eight days during which a bride was properly *kallâ* would be insufficient time for her to become estranged from her husband and return to him. But here Barthélemy has missed the point of the metaphor: From the point of view of the conspirators, the army with David is properly the new bride of the new king = husband, Abishalom.

*so the entire army* Read *wkl h'm* with MT$^{MSS}$, LXX, Syr., Vulg., and Targ.$^{MSS}$. MT has *kl h'm*.

5. *Summon* Singular in MT; plural in LXX, Syr., and Vulg.

*Hushai* Preceded by *gm* in MT and LXX. We omit *gm* with MT$^{MSS}$, Syr.

At the end of the verse MT adds *gm hw'*, "he, too" (emphatic, GK² §135f), which we omit with LXX$^{L}$.

6. *to him* LXX$^{L}$: "to Hushai." In most witnesses *l'mr* follows, but it is probably to be omitted with MT$^{MSS}$, Syr., and a few other witnesses.

*This . . . advised* So MT: *kdbr hzh dbr 'ḥytpl*. LXX$^{L}$ reflects *kdbr hzh 'šr dbr 'ḥytpl*, to be read as indirect discourse, ". . . (spoke to him) about the thing that Ahithophel had advised."

*And if not* So MT$^{MSS}$ (cf. LXX, Syr.): *w'm 'yn*. MT has *'m 'yn*, "If not. . . ." LXX *hē pōs* probably reflects *'m 'yk*, "Or (?) how (do you advise us)?"

7. *the counsel* So MT, LXX$^{L}$. LXX$^{BAMN}$: "*this* counsel."

8. *said* LXX$^{L}$, Vulg.: "said *again*."

*his men* LXX$^{L}$: "the men with him."

*crack soldiers* MT *gbrym*, "strong men, crack soldiers," for which LXX seems to have read *gbrym m'd (sphodra)*, "*very* strong men."

*or a sow snared in the wild* This has fallen out of MT because of haplography ("in the wild . . . in the wild"). It can be restored on the basis of LXX$^{B}$ *kai hōs hys tracheia en tō pediō* = *wkḥzyrh rksh* (= *rĕkūšâ?*) *bśdh*. If the two metaphors are old variants, the sow has better claim to originality than the bear, which has parallels (see the NOTE).

9. *he'll be hidden* That is, *hnh hw' nḥb'*. Before *hnh* LXX adds the conjunction; omit with MT. After *hnh* MT adds *'th*, "even now"; omit with OL and one MS of LXX$^{L}$.

*the army* So LXX$^{L}$: *ton laon* = *h'm*. MT has *bhm*, "(some) among them" (?).

*will hear it* Followed in LXX$^{MN}$ by *kai pataxei* = *whkh*, "and he (?) will defeat (them)."

11. *Instead . . . as follows* Reading *ky kh y'ṣ 'nky y'ṣty* on the basis of LXX$^{B}$ *hoti houtōs symbouleuōn egō syneboueusa*. MT *ky y'ṣty* is haplographic *(ky . . . 'nky)*.

*about you* Omitted by LXX$^{N}$. MT (cf. LXX$^{BA}$) has *'lyk*. LXX$^{LM}$ reflect *'lyk*.

*as the sands of the sea* MT *kḥwl 'šr 'l hym*, lit. "as the sand that is beside the sea." MT$^{MSS}$, Targ.$^{MS}$ have the standard expression *kḥwl 'šr 'l śpt hym*, "as the sands that are upon the shore of the sea" *(BHS)*.

*among them* MT has *bqrb*, understood as *baqrāb*, "into battle"; but *qĕrāb* is probably an Aramaism and late. Most critics read *bqrbm* on the basis of LXX$^{(B)}$ *en mesō autōn*. We should probably, however, read *bqrbw* (the antecedent being *kl yśr'l*), the final *-w* having been lost before the initial *w-* of the following word.

12. *upon* (1) Cf. LXX$^{ALMN}$, Syr., Targ., Vulg. MT, LXX$^{B}$: "to."

*the men* Cf. LXX$^{BMN}$. MT, LXX$^{L}$ (cf. LXX$^{A}$), Syr.: "*all* the men."

13. *can be found* So MT, LXX$^{L}$, OL, and Vulg. *(nmṣ')*. LXX$^{BAMN}$, Syr., and Targ. has "is left" *(nš'r)*.

14. *all Israel* Cf. LXX$^{L}$, OL, Syr. MT, LXX$^{BAMN}$, Vulg., Targ.: "all *the men of* Israel."

*the counsel of Ahithophel* (1) LXX$^{B}$: "the *good* counsel of Ahithophel."

*the counsel of Ahithophel* (2) MT, LXX$^{AMN}$: "the *good* counsel of Ahithophel." OL (cf. LXX$^{L}$): "the counsel of Ahithophel *and the counsel of Abishalom.*"

At the end of the verse LXX$^{BA}$ add *panta,* "all" (as if "every misfortune"), which is out of place here. Omit with MT, LXX$^{LMN}$.

15. *Hushai* So MT, LXX$^{AL}$, OL. LXX$^{BMN}$: "Hushai *the Archite.*"

*the priests* Omitted by OL, which may preserve the primitive situation at this point.

*the elders of* Syr.: "all."

16. *Quickly now, send word* That is, *w'th šlḥw mhrh whgydw,* lit. "And now, send quickly and inform." LXX$^{L}$ *kai nyn speusantes apangeilate* seems to reflect a shorter and perhaps superior reading: *w'th mhrw hgydw,* "And now, quickly inform."

*David* So MT, LXX$^{BAMN}$, and Syr. LXX$^{L}$: "to the king." OL: "to King David."

*in the steppes* MT *b'rbwt* (cf. LXX). Several MSS of MT have *b'brwt,* "in the passes" *(BHS);* cf. 15:28.

*cross over immediately* We read *'br mhr* on the basis of LXX$^{BAMN}$ *diabainōn speuson* (cf. LXX$^{L}$: *diabēthi ta hydata* = *'br hmym,* "cross over the waters"; cf. vv. 20, 21). MT has an alternative with its own claim to originality: *'bwr t'br,* "you must cross over."

17. *entering* So MT: *lbw'* (cf. LXX$^{B}$, etc.). MT$^{MS}$: *wlbw',* "*or* entering" (cf. LXX$^{L}$, Syr., Vulg.).

18. *Bahurim* So MT: *bḥwrym* (cf. LXX$^{BAMN}$, etc.). LXX$^{L}$ *baithchorrōn* suggests *byt ḥrwn,* "Beth-horon."

*who had* MT *wlw,* lit. "and belonging to him (was)." LXX$^{L}$ reflects *wl'yš,* "and belonging to *the man* (was)."

19. *the mouth of* So MT$^{MSS}$ *(py),* LXX$^{L}$, OL, Syr., Targ., and Vulg. MT *(pny),* LXX$^{BAMN}$: "the surface of."

20. *in the direction of the watercourse* MT is obscure, reading *mykl hmym.* The assignment of a meaning like "water-channel" to *mîkal* is arbitrary (cf. Driver). The versions offer indirect help at best, but Barthélemy's attempt to interpret all the versional readings as interpretations of MT (1980:26–27) is forced. LXX$^{B}$ has *mikron tou hydatos,* "a little bit of water," but the original scribe wrote *meikron tou hydatos,* suggesting that *m(e)ikron* arose from a transliteration of an obscure Hebrew original; that is, *mykl* may have been rendered *meichal,* which became *mikron* in an attempt to make Greek sense of it (cf. 16:1, LXX$^{L}$). OL and Josephus (*Ant.* 7.226) suggest that the woman is saying that the two young men stopped by for water (OL *prendere aqua*) and then went on, but v. 21 shows that "the water" probably refers to the Jordan. LXX$^{L}$ has *speudontes* (cf. OL, Vulg.$^{MSS}$), "hurrying," upon which we might suspect the influence of v. 21 *(mhrh 't hmym);* but there is nothing here corresponding to *hmym* (a point on which the note in *BHS* is misleading). In view of MT *mykl hmym,* it is graphically most likely that *speudontes* reflects *mbhlym,* confusion of *k* and *b* being common in scripts of the fourth through first centuries B.C. This suggests that MT's reading may derive from an original **mybl hmym,* from which LXX$^{L}$ *mbhlym* also arose. Tentatively, I read *miyyĕbal hammayim.* For *yābāl,* "(water)course," see Isa 30:25 and 44:4.

Josephus (*Ant.* 7.227) amplifies the woman's speech, adding that "She predicted that if they pursued them promptly they would overtake them." Here we detect the influence of Josh 2:5 on Josephus or his *Vorlage.*

21. *they told him* So LXX$^{LMN}$, OL, Syr. (cf. Vulg.). MT, LXX$^{BA}$, Targ.: "they told *David.*"

22. *there was not . . . the Jordan* So MT: *'d 'ḥd l' n'dr 'šr l' 'br 't hyrdn,* lit. "until one did not lag behind who had not crossed the Jordan." LXX$^{L}$ (cf. OL) is different: *heōs tou mē apokalypthēnai ton logon houtōs diebēsan ton iordanēn* = *'d blty h'dr dbr kh 'brw 't hyrdn,* "until not a thing was left behind. Thus they crossed the Jordan."

23. *his ass* So LXX, Syr., and Vulg. MT: "*the* ass."

*the tomb of his father* LXX$^{AL}$: "the *house* of his father."

## NOTES

16 16. *the Friend of David.* See the NOTE at 15:37.

*"Long live the king!"* As shown by de Boer (1955), Lipiński (1965:352), and Mettinger (1976:131–37), the expression *yĕḥî hammelek,* lit. "May the king live!" is not merely a wish for the well-being of the king. It is an acclamation by which royal authority is officially recognized and assented to; according to Mettinger it is actually an elliptical form of an oath of allegiance. In any case, it is uttered here with exquisite irony. Abishalom assumes the sentiment is directed at him, whereas Hushai is secretly thinking of David. (Compare David's similarly sly words to Achish of Gath in I Sam 29:8.)

17. *your loyalty.* Hebrew *ḥasdĕkā,* on which see the NOTES at 2:5,6; 9:1; 10:1; and, with regard to the present passage, Sakenfeld 1978:31–32. Abishalom, says Sakenfeld, "perceives Hushai's abandoning of David as the failure to do *ḥesed.* Yet by this ingenious turn of phrase the narrator of course suggests to the reader that Hushai's action is in fact his *ḥesed* for David. David's life depends on Hushai's act of *ḥesed.*" So also Conroy 1978:114.

*your friend* (bis). If we are correct in concluding that Hushai was called "the Friend of David" (v. 16) as an honorific title, as explained in the NOTE at 15:37, we must conclude with de Vaux (1961b:vol. I:123) that Abishalom here, by twice referring to David as Hushai's "friend," is making a sarcastic play on words.

18. Hushai pretends to believe Abishalom to be king by divine election as well as popular acclamation ("him whom Yahweh . . . and all the men of Israel have chosen"). On the equation of popular acclaim with divine choice, see Schmidt 1970:180–81,187.

19. *And in the second place.* Hebrew *wĕhaššēnît,* uncommon or unique in such a use in the Bible (cf. Conroy 1978:133 n. 75), but compare the common use of *šanīta(m)* with the same force in Amarna Akkadian (Caspari).

21–22. By claiming the royal harem Abishalom publicizes his claim to the throne (cf. Tsevat 1958b). Compare, in this regard, Solomon's reaction to Adonijah's request for Abishag, the last woman to sleep in David's bed (I Kings 2:22–23), and the possibility that David himself took over Saul's harem (see the NOTE at 12:8). In 12:11

3. *as a bride comes back to her husband.* See the *Textual Note* on "as a bride . . . one man." A "bride" *(kallâ)* is a young woman recently married or about to be married. Ahithophel's metaphor describes the army with David as a bride taken away from her new husband, the new king Abishalom. Given a chance, says the wise man, she will return willingly. In view of what we know of the loyalty of men like Ittai (15:19–22), however, we must doubt that the wise man is correct. Ahithophel turns out to be foolish in attributing his own fickleness to other men, and, ironically, it is the loyalty of Hushai, who seems fickle but is not, that will defeat Ahithophel's counsel.

5–14. Würthwein (1974:33–35,40–42) and Langlamet (1976b:353–54; 1978:67–74; cf. Cook 1899/1900:163–64) regard these verses, together with vv. 15b and 23, as secondary, part of the pro-Davidic redaction they believe this material to have undergone; see the NOTES at 16:21–22 and 14:2–22, with which Langlamet finds a number of points of contact in the present passage. Mettinger (1976:29) considers vv. 5–14 to be Deuteronomistic.

7–10. Hushai's arguments against Ahithophel's plan are specious. He says that, like a wild animal, David will be more dangerous if cornered (v. 8a). A sudden night attack will fail because David, a member of the warrior elite *('îš milḥāmâ),* will not sleep on the open field with mere troops *(hā'ām)* but in some special and hard-to-find place (vv. 8b–9a). Because of the reputation of David's army (v. 10b), moreover, anyone overhearing the clash of troops at night would assume that Abishalom's forces had been bested (v. 9b). The only result of Ahithophel's plan would be to start a panic among Abishaom's own supporters (v. 10a)!

7. *not good.* Not good for David! Again Hushai's sly words cut two ways. Cf. Conroy 978:114.

8. *like a bear bereft in the wild.* Cf. Hos 13:8; Prov 17:12. The sow metaphor, owever, is unparalleled (cf. Ps 80:14 [80:13]), and Wellhausen doubts it is Hebraic.

11–13. Hushai's plan, which he knows will give David time to organize his defenses, that Abishalom will wait until he can muster the entire army available to him (v. 1a), that Abishalom himself will lead the army (v. 11b), and that they will fall upon avid en masse and annihilate his force (v. 12). He advises, in other words, taking time r a call-up of the conscript army of "all Israel, from Dan to Beersheba." There is no ason to hurry, he implies, because with an army of that size Abishalom will be able overwhelm David wherever he might go, even into a fortified city. The effect of the option of this plan will be to permit David to rest (cf. 16:14), to obtain provisions his army (17:27–29), to organize his forces (18:1–2a), and, perhaps most importly, to select the terrain on which the battle will be fought (18:6). In the Forest of hraim the advantage of the superior numbers Abishalom here elects to muster will minimized, as we shall see.

1. *all Israel, from Dan to Beersheba.* Hushai's description of the forces available Abishalom is important evidence for the position adopted in the COMMENT on XVII that not only Israel but also Judah was involved in the revolt. Those historians hold that Judah remained loyal or neutral must regard the description as secondor illusory. According to Alt (1968:298 n. 152), for example, it arises from "political algia," and Flanagan (1975:108–9) calls it "a deliberate and theatrical exaggera-." I take it to be original and to mean what it says. Abishalom can, at least oretically, call up a huge army of tribal militia from both Judah and Israel. The

—which, as we have seen (the COMMENTS on §§ XXI, XXII), probably
later, prophetically oriented introduction to the story of Abishalom's
incident was anticipated as retributory for David's sin with Bathsheba. I
however, that the present verses (along with v. 23 and the words "
counsel!" in v. 20) are secondary to the story of the revolt itself, as argued
(1977; 1978; cf. 1976b:353) following Würthwein (1974:36) and ul
(1899/1900:162–64,176).

It was Cook's position that two originally independent accounts of
of Ahithophel's counsel have been combined in our story, a conclusio
close examination of the events that ensue in chap. 17, where Coo
contradictions. We are told that Hushai's counsel, which calls for a d
of the army, was taken. But at certain points it seems that Ahithop
immediate night attack has been adopted after all (17:16,21). Simil
argues for redactional expansion. According to the original narrative
been instructed by David to frustrate Ahithophel's counsel (15:34), do
the counsel, which was *accepted* by Abishalom, to David in time f
To this, says Würthwein, a later redactor added David's prayer t
counsel be made foolish (15:31), together with the present verses (
show Ahithophel giving counsel that is, in Würthwein's opinion, foo
ary is Hushai's advice (17:5–14), counseling a delay in the departur
its acceptance by Abishalom. The purpose of the secondary materia
is to cast David in a favorable light by showing that Yahweh was c
met's position is somewhat different. He, too, finds pro-Davidic edi
but he relates the prayer in 15:31 directly to the rejection of Ahit
favor of Hushai's in 17:5–14. The present verses, 16:21–22, he as
redaction (cf. 1978:69–73). Budde, in criticism of Cook, and Gun
criticism of Würthwein, have shown that the unevenness of the narr
as to require the postulation of multiple sources or redactions
correct in concluding that there is nothing foolish about the advi
The NOTES that follow will show how I interpret the problema

21. *you've become odious to your father.* Compare I Sam 13:3–4
shofar to publicize the fact that the Israelites had become odious c
begun to stink") to the Philistines. The signal used to publicize
is no more subtle, especially since the shofar has already been

23. *the word of God.* That is, a divine oracle, which seems in t
obtained through the use of an ephod and the sacred lots, as
at 5:19.

**17** 1–4. The soundness of Ahithophel's plan lies in its em
David's army is weary and disorganized, not yet ready to wit
even a moderate force. Ahithophel, therefore, wants to att
vulnerable. He knows that, given minimal time, David, an expe
warrior, will be able to organize a formidable force of his ow
secure. We may wonder if Ahithophel underestimates the loy
army in expecting them to desert in the face of a sudden attack
But we shall not find out: The counsel of Ahithophel will fi
of that of Hushai.

cliché "from Dan to Beersheba," as a merismatic description of greater Israel (see the NOTE at 3:10), occurs elsewhere in Samuel in Deuteronomistic (II Sam 3:10) and prophetic (I Sam 3:20) contexts, but in II Sam 24:2,15 and the present passage it derives from Davidic times.

*as many as the sands of the sea.* Cf. Judg 7:12; I Sam 13:5; I Kings 4:20; 5:9; etc.

12. *as fog descends upon the ground.* Fog (*ṭal*) is not used elsewhere in the Bible in a military metaphor. Conroy (1978:125 n. 46), however, calls attention to the comparison of the cavalry of the Sons of Light to "clouds or banks of fog" in the War Scroll from Qumran (1QM12:9; 19:12). There, as here, the allusion is to the enveloping of the enemy by an enormous number of troops.

14. *(For Yahweh . . . upon Abishalom.).* This parenthesis is the last of three theologically explicit passages (11:27; 12:24; and 17:14) stressed by von Rad (1966:199–200) as crucial to the interpretation of the succession narrative (see the NOTE at 11:27b [§ XXII]). The reader is reminded of David's fleeting prayer in 15:31, "Make Ahithophel's counsel foolish, O Yahweh!" As explained in the COMMENT on § XXVIII, the meeting with Hushai at a place "where God was worshiped" (15:32) immediately after this prayer was believed by the narrator to have been providential, not accidental (von Rad; cf. Gunn 1978:108–9). Here was a man who could fulfil David's wish and "frustrate Ahithophel's counsel" (15:34). Abishalom's fatal choice of counsel, then, was divinely influenced in order, again, "that the counsel of Ahithophel should be frustrated." As explained in the COMMENT below, therefore, this parenthesis is crucial to an understanding of the story of Abishalom's revolt: It shows once and for all what Yahweh has in mind. Compare the similar parenthesis at the end of I Sam 2:25; its interpretive significance for the ark narrative is comparable to that of the present parenthesis for the story of Abishalom's revolt (cf. Miller and Roberts 1977:70).

15–16. The words of David's informants here and in v. 21 present a problem of interpretation. Hushai, having reported on Ahithophel's counsel and his own (17:15), sends David an urgent warning to cross the Jordan immediately (17:16). When Jonathan and Ahimaaz convey the message to David, the gist of it is the same: "Cross the water quickly" (17:21). This urgency might suggest that Ahithophel's plan, which called for an immediate march against David (17:1), was accepted after all. Thus it would lend support to a source-critical reconstruction of the story in which the counsel of Hushai in 17:5–14 and the allusions to it in 17:15b and 17:23 are regarded as derived from another source or added by a redactor (see the NOTES at 15:31 and 17:5–14). It would follow that in the primary story Ahithophel's advice was accepted, and Hushai, whose role was that of an informer only, reported the plan to David in time for him to escape. I wonder, however, if the urgency of the message to David is incompatible with the story of the counseling contest as it stands. If Ahithophel's plan had been accepted, it is doubtful that Hushai could have helped David at all. Ahithophel's march was to take place immediately ("tonight," 17:1), and although a swift runner would probably have been able to reach David ahead of Ahithophel's army, there would have been little time to alert the troops and no hope of marching them across the river before the enemy arrived. Hushai's plan gains a few days for David, but still there is no time to waste. Moreover, Hushai has learned from Ahithophel that David's present position is vulnerable. It is not surprising, therefore, that he urges him to break camp immediately and move into more secure terrain. It is true that Hushai's counsel is not mentioned in v. 21, where the report of Jonathan and Ahimaaz is recorded. But there is no reason to assume that the narrator is reporting the entire message at that point. It is customary in biblical narrative to summarize or otherwise abbreviate details already known to the audience. The message to David is already reduced to summary form in Hushai's report to the priests in vv. 15–16. In v. 21, then, we have a summary of a summary, and only the most important parts of the message remain. The principal things Hushai wants to convey to David are the vulnerability of his present position, as revealed by the words of Ahithophel, and the need for swift defensive action. The summarized message in v. 21, therefore, mentions Ahithophel's counsel and urges David to act ("Cross the water quickly").

15. *Zadok and Abiathar.* The two priests were left in Jerusalem precisely for the purpose they serve here. See 15:27–28.

16. *the steppes of the wilderness.* Where in 15:28 David told Zadok he would be waiting for news (cf. 16:14). Hushai stresses the vulnerability of this position revealed by Ahithophel's counsel and urges David to cross immediately to the east bank, putting a natural barrier between him and the vast army Abishalom is mustering.

*or else disaster will befall the king.* Hebrew *pen yĕbulla' lammelek.* Recent Hebrew lexicography distinguishes between *bl'* I, from **bl',* "swallow," and *bl'* II, from **blġ,* "reach, attain, arrive at." The evidence of Arabic *balaġa* suggests that *bl'* II in *Pi'el* might mean "cause (a message) to reach" and thus "inform," and KB[3], following Jacob (1912:287), would render the *Pu'al* here and in Job 37:20 as "be informed"—thus, "or else the king . . . will be informed." But Hushai probably would not refer to Abishalom as the king when speaking to David, and the expression "the entire army that is with him" ought, as in v. 2, to refer to David's army. Arabic *balaġa* refers to exertion, to extreme or excessive action, often with a sense of affliction. Thus Guillaume (1962:321) compares the form of the present passage to the use of *balaġa* in a similar impersonal passive construction to refer to the extreme affliction of the subject—thus, "or else disaster will befall the king." Our translation follows Guillaume. The alternative is to follow G. R. Driver (1934:52) and most translators in taking *yĕbulla'* from *bl'* I in a metaphorical sense—"or else the king . . . will be swallowed up."

17. *Jonathan and Ahimaaz.* The sons of Abiathar and Zadok, implicitly designated as messengers by David in 15:27.

*En-rogel.* A spring southwest of the City of David in the Wadi Kidron, just south of its junction with the Wadi Hinnom (Map 3). It marked one point on the boundary of the tribal territories of Benjamin and Judah (Josh 15:7; 18:16). The modern site is Bîr Ayyûb, "Job's Well."

*would come and give . . . would go and report.* The verbs are frequentative (GK[2] §112k and n. 4) "and express how communication was *regularly* maintained between David and his friends in the city" (Driver). The previous errands thus implied must have taken place while David was making his way towards the Jordan (cf. 15:31), for there has been insufficient time for repeated trips since he arrived there, and this is evidently the first message since Abishalom's arrival in Jerusalem (cf. Budde).

18–20. Compare to this little episode the more elaborate story of Rahab and the spies in Joshua 2. Two spies in danger of being discovered are harbored by a woman, who successfully deceives and turns away their pursuers. In Josh 2:6 the men are hidden on the roof with stalks of flax spread over them; in the present passage they are hidden in a well with groats spread over them. See, in general, Gunn (1976:223–25; 1978: 44–45), who speaks of the influence of a traditional story pattern here. Contrast Van Seters (1976b:27–28), who argues for a direct literary dependence of the present passage on Joshua 2. I agree with Gunn that we have a traditional story pattern here, but I do not see this as evidence that the primary reason for the composition of the larger story was entertainment, or that the story is a product of what Gunn calls "oral-traditional composition." This is a case of the influence of a traditional story pattern on the composition of an original *literary* work.

18. *Bahurim.* See 16:5 and the NOTE at 3:16. Maps 3,7.

19. *groats.* That *hārīpōt,* which occurs only here and in Prov 27:22 (with reference to something crushed with mortar and pestle), means groats, grits, or polenta was the opinion of the rabbis (Jastrow 367). The Targum Jonathan renders the word *dĕqīlān* = *dĕqîqān* (?), "pounded grits" (Jastrow 319), and the Vulgate expands helpfully, *quasi siccans ptisanas,* "as if drying barley-groats." One Greek translation ($LXX^{B}$), however, attempts no rendering *(araphōth),* and another ($LXX^{L}$) reads *palathas,* "cakes of preserved fruit." In retaining the received form we follow Schulthess (1905) against Koehler (1922), who proposes *ḥărîpôt,* a term for grains of sand added to barley for grinding purposes (?).

20. *in the direction of the watercourse.* That is, towards the Jordan; see the *Textual Note.*

21. The report the young men make to David is recorded here in summary form. See the NOTE on vv. 15–16 above.

23. Matthew may have had the death of Ahithophel in mind when he fashioned his report of the suicide of Judas (Matt 27:5); Acts 1:18, obscure as it is, does not seem to allow that Judas hanged himself. The motifs of the betrayal, the son of David, and the ascent of the Mount of Olives are all there in Matthew. Gethsemane, where Jesus was betrayed, cannot have been far from the place on the Slope of the Olives where David stood when he learned that Ahithophel had betrayed him (15:30–31).

*his own city.* Giloh (see 15:12).

## COMMENT

Having taken his leave of the king to whom his loyalty truly belongs, Hushai hurries to Jerusalem to express a pretended loyalty to the new king. It seems that Abishalom is completely taken in by the imposture of the Friend of David (16:16), for Hushai quickly finds himself deep in the counsels of the enemy. The task assigned him by David, to "frustrate Ahithophel's counsel" (15:34), is a formidable one. When Ahithophel states an opinion, we are told, it is ordinarily accepted straightway, "as if the word of God had been consulted" (16:23). And, indeed, Ahithophel's advice to Abishalom is given with oracular authority and clarity of vision. None of Abishalom's followers hesitates to accept it (17:4). Nevertheless, Hushai is equal to the task. As explained in the

NOTE on 17:1–14, Ahithophel recognized that success for Abishalom depended less on numerical superiority than timing. He knew that David was vulnerable now, but that if given time to organize he would be difficult to defeat. Thus Ahithophel's plan called for immediate action. Hushai is able to counter this by insisting on caution and safety in numbers, neither of which is appropriate to the circumstances (see the NOTE on 17:11–13). He persuades Abishalom to delay—a fatal mistake. Using a messenger system devised for the purpose earlier (cf. 15:27–28), Hushai and the loyal priests of Yahweh send word to David, who is able to cross the Jordan to safety (17:22) and, eventually, to organize his defenses (18:1).

In this episode we stand at the midpoint in the story of Abishalom's revolt. As explained in the COMMENT on § XXVIII, much of the account of David's sorrowful march into exile in the preceding material was preparatory. In particular, the encounters with Zadok and Abiathar in 15:24–29 and Hushai in 15:31–37 were described in anticipation of the present episode. Moreover, the course of future events, as recounted in chaps. 18–20, is, to a large extent, set by what happens here. The outcome of the battle in the Forest of Ephraim is decided in advance by Abishalom's choice of counsel here. This episode, then, is central, pivotal to the story in chaps. 13–20.

The centrality of the counseling contest of Ahithophel and Hushai gives further stress to what we have already noticed about the narrator's interpretive parenthesis in 17:14b (see the COMMENT on § XXVIII). There we are told that Abishalom's fateful choice of counsel was made because "Yahweh had ordained that the counsel of Ahithophel should be frustrated, so that [he] might bring misfortune upon Ahithophel." It follows that the resolution of the story —the quelling of the revolt and the restoration of David—will be a reflex of the divine will, and David's attitude of resignation to the course of events as reflective of Yahweh's purposes is going to be vindicated.

# XXX. DAVID'S ARRIVAL IN MAHANAIM (17:24–29)

17 [24]Abishalom crossed the Jordan, all Israel with him, David having arrived at Mahanaim.

### *Amasa*

[25]Amasa had been put in charge of the army by Abishalom in place of Joab. Amasa was the son of a man named Ithra the Ishmaelite, who had gone to Abigail daughter of Nahash, the sister of Zeruiah, Joab's mother. [26]Israel and Abishalom encamped in the land of Gilead.

### *A Reception Committee*

[27]When David arrived in Mahanaim, Shobi son of Nahash from Rabbah of the Ammonites, Machir son of Ammiel from Lo-debar, and Barzillai the Gileadite from Rogelim [28]had brought sleeping couches with embroidered covers as well as bowls and ceramic jars with wheat, barley, flour, roasted grain, broad beans, lentils, [29]honey, the curd of the flock, and the cheese of the herd. They offered these things to David and his army to eat, for they thought the army would have become famished, exhausted, and parched in the wilderness.

## *TEXTUAL NOTES*

17 24. *all Israel* So $LXX^{A}$, Syr. MT, $LXX^{BLMN}$: "all *the men of* Israel."

25. *Ithra* That is, *yitrā'* (so MT; cf. Syr., Targ., Vulg.). The various MSS of LXX and OL point directly or indirectly to *yeter,* "Jether," as the name is given in I Chron 2:17. These are longer and shorter forms—both probably "correct"—of the same name. Compare the similar variation in the name of Moses' father-in-law in, for example, Exod 4:18 *(yeter . . . yitrô);* cf. Levenson and Halpern 1980:511–12.

*the Ishmaelite* So $LXX^{A}$ and I Chron 2:17 *(hyšm''ly).* Here MT has *hyśr'ly,* "the

Israelite" (so LXX[BL], OL) and LXX[M] has *ho izraēlitēs* = *hyzr"ly*, "the Jezreelite," preferred by Levenson and Halpern (1980:511–12).

*Abigail* The name should be read *'ăbîgayil*, as in I Chron 2:17, as shown by LXX *abeigaian*, OL *abigael*, Targ. *'bygyl*, and Vulg. *abigail* in the present passage. The spelling of MT, *'bygl* (vocalized *'ăbîgal*, "Abigal," by the Masoretes), reflects a pronunciation with contraction of the diphthong, *-gêl*. The *kĕtîb/qĕrê* distinction in 3:3, *'bygl/'ăbîgayil*, is to be explained in the same way. Cf. the frequent spelling *yrwšlm(-lêm)* for *yĕrûšālayim*.

*daughter of Nahash* This is an apparent error, but there is no reliable textual witness to contradict it. As Zeruiah's sister, Abigail was Jesse's daughter (cf. I Chron 2:16). A number of Greek MSS, including LXX[LMN], actually read *iessai*, "Jesse," in place of *naas*, "Nahash," here; but this is a result of secondary correction. It is quite possible that *bt nḥš*, "daughter of Nahash," arose from a misplaced duplicate of *bn nḥš*, "son of Nahash," in v. 27 below (Wellhausen). The text as it stands makes sense only if Nahash is the *mother* of Abigail and Zeruiah, which is improbable (Wellhausen), or if Nahash is the name of an earlier, deceased husband of Jesse's wife (Hertzberg); see the NOTE.

*the sister of Zeruiah* Cf. I Chron 2:16. Here LXX[BA] have "the brother of Zeruiah"; but though Zeruiah had at least seven brothers (I Chron 2:13–15), none was named Nahash.

26. *Israel and Abishalom* So MT. LXX[BA]: "*All* Israel and Abishalom. LXX[MN]: "Abishalom and all Israel." LXX[L], OL: "Abishalom and all *the men of* Israel."

*the land* Omitted by LXX[N].

27. *Shobi* So MT: *wšby*, lit. "and Shobi" (cf. LXX[LM], OL). In LXX[B] the conjunction is taken as part of the name: *ouesbei*.

28. *had brought sleeping couches with embroidered covers* Cf. LXX[B]: *ēnenkan deka koitas kai amphitapous* = *hby'w 'śrt mškb wmrbdym*, "had brought ten beds and embroidered covers." That we should read *'rśt ('aršōt miškāb)*, "couches," for *'śrt*, "ten," was first recognized by Klostermann (cf. Syr., where *'rst' wtšwyt'* probably corresponds to *'rśt [w]mškb*). Of the reading adopted here *(hby'w 'rśt mškb wmrbdym)* only *mškb* appears in MT. The verb, however, is necessary, supported by Syr. and Vulg. as well as LXX, and favored by Wellhausen, Budde, Dhorme, Schulz, Hertzberg; cf. Driver, Nowack. We should probably explain the text of MT as the result of haplography from *mrglym* at the end of v. 27 to *mrbdym*; *mškb* returned through partial restoration (cf. Wellhausen, Budde). In many witnesses (LXX[MN], OL) the conjunction is omitted before the translation of *mrbdym*, which is thus construed adjectivally (". . . embroidered sleeping couches"). For a defense of MT, see Barthélemy 1980:22; Conroy 1978:54 and n. 27, 153.

*bowls* MT *sappôt*. LXX: "*ten* bowls." In Syr. and Vulg. this was eliminated recensionally by scribes who were anxious to reduce the list to the numerical equivalent of MT but who did not understand the correspondence of the various translations and originals.

At the end of the verse MT adds a second *wqly*, "and roasted grain," which can be omitted on authority of LXX and Syr.

29. *the curd of the flock* Reading *wḥm't ṣ'n* on the basis of Syr. *wḥ'wt' d'n'*. MT has *wḥm'h wṣ'n*, "curd and flocks (goat meat?)."

*They offered* Reading *wygyšw* with LXX *kai prosēnenkan* in preference to MT *hgyšyw*, which arose after the loss of the previous verb.

*and his army* So LXX$^{L}$. MT: "the army that was with him."

*they thought* That is, *'mrw*, lit., "they said," the usual way of expressing (private) motivating thoughts; so MT and most witnesses. LXX$^{BA}$: "he (David) said."

# NOTES

17 24. On the syntax of this verse, see Conroy 1978:53 and n. 20.

25. Würthwein (1974:46 n. 80) and Langlamet (1976b:354) would strike this verse as secondary on the grounds that it disrupts the narrative flow of vv. 24 and 26 and that Amasa will not be mentioned again in connection with the coming battle. They regard the introduction of the Amasa theme (17:25; 19:14; 20:4–5,8–13; I Kings 2:5–6,31b–33) a part of the pro-David/anti-Joab redaction they identify in the larger story (see the Introduction, p. 14). Conroy (1978:42 n. 2, 48), however, notes that the details of Amasa's identification are useful at this point to give additional stress to the familial character of the conflict.

*Amasa.* A ranking military officer, a member of David's own family (cf. 19:13), and evidently a leading citizen in Judah. His recruitment represents important support for the revolt in the south. Note that later, to appease the people of Judah after the revolt is quashed, David himself will put Amasa in charge of the army (19:13).

*Ithra the Ishmaelite, who had gone to Abigail.* As explained in the *Textual Note*, the evidence for the gentilic of Amasa's father is ambiguous; he may have been called "the Israelite," which makes no sense, or "the Jezreelite," i.e., a resident of the Judean town southwest of Hebron. The latter seems entirely fitting at first glance, and it is defended by Levenson and Halpern (1980:511–12), who argue ingeniously that Ithra was the real name of the man called Nabal, "Fool," in I Sam 25:3 and *passim*. Levenson and Halpern, however, do not discuss the extraordinary way in which the relationship between Ithra and Abigail is described. He "had gone to" *(bā' 'el)* her, we are told. She is not called his wife here or in I Chron 2:17, and it is clear they were not married in the usual sense. Either Amasa was the illegitimate issue of a casual liaison or, more likely, he was the child of a special type of relationship comparable to the *ṣadiqa* marriage of the ancient Arabs, according to the terms of which the woman remained with her children in her parents' home and received periodic visits from the man (Smith, Hertzberg). Compare, in this regard, Samson's marriage to a Philistine woman in Timnah (Judges 14). Amasa's father, then, was an Ishmaelite, but Amasa himself was in fact a member of his mother's family, the house of Jesse.

*Abigail.* See I Chron 2:16,17. Levenson and Halpern (1980:511) raise the possibility that this Abigail, David's sister, is identical to the Abigail of I Samuel 25, who became David's wife and the mother of his obscure second son, Daluiah (3:3): "There are only two Abigails in the entire Hebrew Bible, one the wife of David and one the sister. What is the probability that the only two people of this name would be not only contemporaries but sisters-in-law?" As explained in the preceding NOTE, it is unlikely that Ithra can be identified with Nabal, and this lessens the probability that the two Abigails were identical, though it remains possible.

*daughter of Nahash.* Abigail's patronymic may be a scrap of textual flotsam (see the *Textual Note*). If it is authentic, we must suppose with Hertzberg that Nahash was the name of an earlier husband of Jesse's wife, to whom she bore Abigail and Zeruiah. Names compounded with *nāḥāš,* "snake," were not uniquely Ammonite (10:2; 17:27); the name *naḥšôn,* "Nahshon," in fact, had an excellent pedigree in this part of Judah (I Chron 2:10,11; Ruth 4:20).

*Zeruiah, Joab's mother.* David's sister (I Chron 2:16).

26. *Israel and Abishalom.* The order is anomalous. Mauchline suggests plausibly that this emphasizes Abishalom's decision to accompany his army, a point at issue in the counseling duel of Ahithophel and Hushai (17:11). Conroy (1978:54,141) thinks it may imply an insult to Abishalom. Caspari supposes that Abishalom at first stood here alone, Israel being added as seemed to befit the word "encamped." I think Caspari's solution, which does not explain the odd word order, is backward. The original text said "Israel encamped," but since the identity of "Israel" in this material is apt to be ambiguous at times, some helpful ancient added "and Abishalom."

27–29. Again, Langlamet (1976b:355) regards these verses as secondary preparation for 19:32–40. He argues that they disrupt the continuity between vv. 24 + 26 and 18:1.

27. *Shobi son of Nahash from Rabbah.* On the Ammonite king Nahash, see the NOTE at 10:1–2. There we were told that he was succeeded by his son Hanun. Shobi is mentioned only in the present passage. In the COMMENT on § XX I took the position that the siege of Rabbah described there took place sometime after the resolution of Abishalom's rebellion. Accordingly, the providing of food to David in the present passage by Shobi son of Nahash, who is probably still alive, may be the gesture of "loyalty" *(ḥesed)* referred to by David in 10:2.

*Machir son of Ammiel of Lo-debar.* See the NOTES at 9:4. Once a loyal supporter of the house of Saul and the patron of Meribbaal, Machir is now loyal to David. See the COMMENT.

*Barzillai the Gileadite from Rogelim.* "Gilead" is ordinarily a geographic designation (cf. the NOTE at 2:9), but here it seems to refer to a tribe or other ethnic unit, as in Judg 5:17, where it stands between Reuben and Dan in an old war song. On the question of a tribe of Gilead, see de Vaux 1978:574–76 and the bibliography cited there. The site of the Gileadite town of Rogelim is unknown (Bersînyā? [Map 7]). In return for his good treatment of David here, Barzillai will receive an invitation to Jerusalem after the rebellion is quelled (19:33–40). Although he will declare himself too old for life at court, his sons will eventually take their places at Solomon's table (I Kings 2:7). For the possible identification of this Barzillai with the father of Adri(el) the Meholathite, husband of Saul's daughter Merob, see the NOTE at 21:8.

29. *the curd of the flock, and the cheese of the herd.* Hebrew *wĕḥem'at ṣō'n ûšĕpôt bāqār,* interpretation of which has been hampered by textual corruption (discussed in the *Textual Notes*), the unrecognized parallelism, and the presence of the hapax legomenon *šĕpôt.* The verb *špy in Postbiblical Hebrew and Aramaic (Jastrow 1615) means tilt, strain, or pour out liquid, slowly leaving the sediment. Thus *šĕpôt* is probably a product of some such process, and the parallel here with "curd" suggests "cheese" or the like. The Arabic evidence elicited by Wetzstein (1883:276–78; cf. BDB,

Mauchline) for a translation like "cream" is vitiated by the lack of correspondence in the sibilants of the Hebrew (*š* < **š* or **ṯ*) and Arabic (*š* < **ś*) words in question.

*would . . . parched.* Three perfect verbs, not adjectives (Joüon 1928:312).

## COMMENT

David is received warmly in Mahanaim by a delegation of local worthies bringing field provisions for his army. It is historically noteworthy that this Transjordanian area, which was the seat of Ishbaal's government in his long struggle with David (cf. 2:8–9), is the one place David can find haven and support for his struggle against Abishalom. In the case of Shobi, we may think of an Ammonite policy of neutralizing the larger Israelite army (which Abishalom now controls) by supporting David or speculate on an alliance between David and Nahash, Shobi's father, dating from the time of their mutual antagonism to Saul (on both possibilities, see the COMMENT on § XX). But it is surprising to find Machir, once the guardian of Meribbaal (9:4), and Barzillai of Gilead—an old stronghold of Saulid sympathy—supporting David with such enthusiasm.

We must, however, keep in mind the point of view of the narrator of the story of Abishalom's revolt. If he was not also the author of the story of David's rise to power in I Sam 16:14–II Sam 5:10 and the account of the execution of the Saulids in II Sam 21:1–14 + 9:1–13, he was at least in sympathy with the viewpoint expressed in both of those compositions, which are intended to show that David deserved the sympathy and loyalty of past followers of the house of Saul. Our narrator did not, in other words, accept the truth of Shimei's accusations in 16:8, as we have seen. It was his view, instead, that David should be embraced by even the most zealous followers of Saul. He will attempt to demonstrate the validity of this position by his account of David's treatment of Shimei and Meribbaal in 19:17–31, and this may be the reason for his emphasis on the loyal spontaneity of Machir and Barzillai here (cf. 19:32–40). The modern historian may suspect that David's support in Transjordan was born of fear of the army he brought with him rather than loyalty to his person, but the author of the present episode is intent that we should think otherwise.

# XXXI. THE BATTLE IN THE FOREST OF EPHRAIM
## (18:1–19:9abα$\beta$)

**18** [1]David mustered the army that was with him, setting captains of thousands and captains of hundreds over them. [2][He] divided the army into three parts, one third under the command of Joab, one third under the command of Abishai son of Zeruiah, Joab's brother, and one third under the command of Ittai the Gittite.

Then the king said to the army, "I, too, shall march out with you!"

[3]"You mustn't march out," they said, "for if we retreat, no one will pay attention to us, and if half of us die, no one will pay attention to us. But you are like ten thousands of us! So it is better for us for you to be in the city to help."

[4]"I'll do what seems best to you," the king told them. So [he] stood atop the gate as the entire army marched out by hundreds and thousands. [5]And [he] instructed Joab and Abishai and Ittai as follows: "Protect young Abishalom for me!" The entire army was listening when the king instructed all the commanders concerning Abishalom.

[6]Then the army marched out into the field to confront Israel, and there was a battle in the Forest of Ephraim. [7]The army of Israel was routed there before the advance of the servants of David, and the slaughter that day was great—twenty thousands! [8]The fighting was scattered over the surface of the whole region, and the forest consumed more troops that day than the sword.

### *The Death of Abishalom*

[9]Abishalom was far ahead of the servants of David, riding on his mule. But as the mule went under the tangle of a certain large terebinth, [Abishalom's] head caught in the terebinth, and he was left hanging between the sky and the ground as the mule under him went on ahead. [10]Someone who saw him reported it to Joab.

"I just saw Abishalom hanging in a tree!" he said.

[11]"If you saw him," said Joab to the man who was making the report,

"why didn't you strike him to the ground? Then I'd have been obliged to give you ten pieces of silver and a belt!"

[12]But the man said to Joab, "Even if I felt the weight of a thousand pieces of silver upon my palm, I wouldn't lay a hand on the king's son! For within our hearing the king instructed you and Abishai and Ittai, 'Be careful of young Abishalom!' [13]Otherwise I would have been dealing recklessly with my own life; for nothing is hidden from the king, and you were stationed some distance away."

[14]"I won't dally with you this way!" said Joab. He took three sticks and struck them against Abishalom's chest while he was still alive in the tree, [15]and ten soldiers, Joab's weapon-bearers, surrounded Abishalom and killed him.

### *The Cairn of Abishalom*

[16]Then Joab blew on the shofar, and the army turned back from its pursuit of Israel, for Joab held [it] in check. [17]They took Abishalom, cast him into a large pit in the forest, and heaped up over him a very large pile of stones, while all Israel fled, each man to his tent. ([18]When Abishalom was still alive, he erected a pillar for himself in the Valley of the King, for he said, "I have no son by whom my name might be remembered." So he called the pillar by his own name. It is called "Abishalom's Monument" even today.)

### *The Report of Abishalom's Death*

[19]Then Ahimaaz son of Zadok said, "Let me run to the king with the news that Yahweh has set him free from the power of his enemies!"

[20]"You won't be a bearer of news today," said Joab. "You'll bear the news some other day, but today you won't bear news." This was because the king's son was dead. [21]Then Joab said to a certain Cushite, "Go tell the king what you've seen!" So the Cushite bowed to Joab and set out.

[22]Again Ahimaaz son of Zadok spoke to Joab. "Whatever the situation, let me run, too—after the Cushite!"

"Why should you run, my boy?" said Joab. "You'll have no reward for going." [23]But [Ahimaaz] said, "Whatever the situation, let me run!" So he said, "Run!" and Ahimaaz ran along the Circuit Road, passing the Cushite.

[24]David was sitting between the two gates, and the watchman on the
roof of the gate went to the wall, looked out, and saw a man running
towards him alone. [25]So the watchman shouted to inform the king. "If
he is alone," said the king, "there is news on his lips!" But as he drew
closer, [26]the watchman saw another man running.

When the watchman on the gate shouted to say, "There's another
man running alone!" the king said, "This one is bringing news, too!"

[27]Then the watchman said, "I can see that the first man runs like
Ahimaaz son of Zadok."

"He's a good man," said the king, "and it's because of good news that
he comes!"

[28]When Ahimaaz drew near, he greeted the king and prostrated
himself before [him] with his face to the ground. "Blessed be Yahweh
your god," he said, "who has delivered up the men who raised their
hands against my lord the king!"

[29]"Young Abishalom is all right?" said the king.

"I saw a great commotion," said Ahimaaz, "when Joab, the king's
servant, was sending your servant off; but I don't know what it was."

[30]"Go take your place over there," said the king. So he went over and
stood.

[31]Then the Cushite arrived. "Let my lord the king receive the news,"
he said, "that today Yahweh has set you free from the power of all those
who rose up against you."

[32]"Is young Abishalom all right?" said the king to the Cushite.

"May all the enemies of my lord the king and all who rise up against
you in malice be like that young man!" said the Cushite.

### *David Mourns for Abishalom*

**19** [1]Then the king began to tremble. He went up to the upper room
of the gate and wept, and as he wept he said, "My son, Abishalom! My
son, my son, Abishalom! Would that I had died instead of you! Abishalom, my son, my son!"

[2]Joab was told that the king was weeping and mourning over Abishalom. [3]The victory that day turned into mourning for the entire army
when [they] heard that the king was grieving over his son. [4]The army
stole into the city that day just as a humiliated army steals in when they
have fled in battle. [5]As for the king, he had covered his face, and he cried
in a loud voice, "My son, Abishalom! Abishalom, my son!"

### *Joab's Intervention*

[6]Then Joab came indoors to the king. "Today," he said, "you've mortified your servants, who saved your life this very day, as well as the lives of your sons and daughters and the lives of your wives and concubines, [7]by loving those who hate you and hating those who love you! Indeed you've made it clear today that officers and servants are nothing to you—for you know that if Abishalom were alive today, we'd all be dead! Then things would seem right to you! [8]Now then, get up, go out there, and placate your servants! For, by Yahweh, I swear that if you don't go out there, not a man will stay with you tonight, and this will be worse for you than anything that has happened to you from your childhood until now!"

[9]So David got up and took his seat in the gate, and when [they] were told that the king was sitting enthroned in the gate, the entire army presented themselves to [him].

## *TEXTUAL NOTES*

**18** 1. *the army* So MT, LXX$^{BA}$, Syr. LXX$^{LMN}$, OL: "the *entire* army."

2. *divided . . . into three parts* Reading *wyšlš* on the basis of LXX$^{L}$ *kai etrisseuse* (cf. OL). MT (cf. LXX$^{BAMN}$) has *wyšlḥ*, "sent," which Conroy (1978:153) defends by appeal to Arad ostracon 24 (cf. Lemaire 1973:14; Aharoni 1981:48). If it is the case, as seems probable, that the broken context of lines 13–14 of this ostracon refers to a transfer of troops with the words *wšlḥtm 'tm rmtnġ[b by]d mlkyhw*, "and you shall send them to Ramoth-negeb under the command of Malkiyahu," it is also the case that this is a special situation, a dispatch of troops from one garrison to another, to which the present passage is not analogous. David is not *sending* his army anywhere: He is mustering it and organizing it for the coming battle. From a text-critical standpoint, moreover, it is incredible to suppose that *wyšlš* arose from *wyšlḥ* and not the reverse. Nor does it seem necessary, with Joüon (1928:312–13), to add *wytn*, "and he put," after *wyšlš*.

*the king* So MT, LXX$^{L}$. LXX$^{BAMN}$: "David." OL: "King David."

At the end of v. 2 and the beginning of v. 3 Syr. omits everything from "I, too," to "for." Evidently a scribe simply skipped a line of his text.

3. *march out* OL adds "into battle."

*they said* So LXX$^{BAMN}$. MT, LXX$^{L}$, OL, and 4QSam$^{a}$ (*[wy'mr] h'm*): "the army said."

*no one will pay attention to us* (bis) We read *l' yśym lnw lb . . . l' yśym lnw lb*. The first occurrence is supported by LXX$^{L}$ *(ou stēsetai en hēmin kardia)* and OL *(non stabit in nobis cor nostrum),* which have been conformed to MT in the second occurrence. The second occurrence is confirmed by the extant fragments of 4QSam$^{a}$: *[l' yśy]m lnw lb.* MT (cf. LXX$^{B}$) twice has *l' yśymw 'lynw ('lynw) lb,* "they will not pay attention to us." See Ulrich 1978:107–8; 1980:138–40.

*if half of us . . . to us* Omitted by homoioteleuton after the preceding statement by Syr. and a few MSS of MT and LXX.

*But you* So LXX$^{BAN}$ (= *ky 'th*). MT (cf. LXX$^{LM}$, OL, Syr.): "For now" *(ky 'th)* —thus, "For now there are ten thousands like us."

*But you . . . of us!* The reading of LXX$^{L}$ here, shared by Theodotion, is obscure: *(hoti) kai nyn aphairethēsetai ex hēmōn hē gē deka chiliasin* = *(ky) gm 'th ykrt mmnw h'rṣ 'śrh 'lpym,* "For even now the land will be cut off from us, ten thousands." OL is similar to this, reflecting *ky gm 'th ykrtw (separentur) mmnw 'śrh 'lpym,* "For even now ten thousands will be cut off from us."

*it is better for us for you to be* So LXX$^{L}$: *kalon estin hēmin tou einai se* = *ṭwb (yhyh) lnw hywtk.* MT: *ṭwb ky thyh lnw,* "it is better that you be for us. . . ."

*in the city* So LXX = *b'yr.* MT has *m'yr,* "from the city." Conroy (1978:153–54) conjectures that the original was *b'yr* with the sense of "*from* the city," the more usual preposition for "from" having been substituted in MT. This is unlikely. The preposition *bĕ-* sometimes requires the translation "from" in conjunction with verbs of motion, but not in a situation of the present kind. Moreover, *m'yr* ought to be *mn h'yr* or *mh'yr.* This shows that the text of MT arose by graphic confusion of *b* for *m,* a common error especially liable to occur in scripts of the late Hasmonean and early Herodian periods.

*to help* So MT *(qĕrê): l'zwr.* MT *(kĕtîb): l'zyr.* In LXX$^{B}$ the *kĕtîb* and *qĕrê* of MT are reflected in a double translation: *boētheia tou boēthein.* LXX$^{L}$ reflects *l'zwr lnw,* "to help us."

At the end of the verse, Syr., the text of which is seriously disturbed here, adds a sentence: "And David's servants said to him, 'Pray let us go out and quickly fight with them!' "

5. *Protect* See the NOTE.

*was listening* So 4QSam$^{a}$: *šm'ym.* MT: *šm'w,* "listened."

6. *the army* So MT. LXX: "the *entire* army."

*the field* So MT, LXX$^{L}$, OL, and 4QSam$^{a}$ *([h]śdh);* cf. Josephus, *Ant.* 7.236. LXX$^{BAMN}$: "the forest."

*Ephraim* So MT. LXX$^{L}$ *(maainan)* and LXX$^{A^{mg}}$ *(maenan)* have "Mahanaim." See also the NOTE.

7. *the slaughter* MT, Syr. add a second *šm,* "there." Omit with LXX. Contrast Hertzberg, Conroy 1978:154.

*twenty thousands* Twenty-five, according to OL. LXX adds *andrōn* = *'yš,* "men." In LXX$^{L}$ the figure is preceded by *kai piptousin* = *wyplw,* "and (twenty thousands) fell."

8. *The fighting* MT adds "there." Omit with LXX$^{L}$ (cf. Syr.).

*was scattered* MT *(kĕtîb): npṣwt* (but *BHS: npṣyt* [?]) = *nĕpûṣôt* (cf. Isa 11:12). MT *(qĕrê): npwṣt* = *nāpôṣet.* Either reading is acceptable.

*the whole region* So MT: *kl h'rṣ.* LXX$^{LMN}$, OL = *kl hy'r,* "the whole *forest.*"

*than the sword* That is, *m'šr 'klh hḥrb,* lit. "than those whom the sword consumed." After *'klh*, LXX[BMN] add *b'm*, "of the soldiers," in reminiscence of *l'kl b'm* earlier.

9. *was far ahead of* We read *wygdl . . . lpny* on the basis of LXX[L] *kai ēn megas . . . enōpion*. MT has *wyqr' . . . lpny*, usually interpreted to mean, "chanced to meet." But the point is that Abishalom was about to escape when the branch stopped him and allowed Joab and the rest to catch up.

*riding* That is, *whw' rkb*, lit. "and he was riding"; so LXX[L] and 4QSam[a] *(whw' [rwkb])*. MT: "and *Abishalom* was riding."

*caught* MT *wyḥzq* (cf. LXX[LMN]). LXX[B] has *kai ekremasthē* = *wytl*, "hung," in anticipation of the next clause.

*and he was left hanging* MT has *wytn (wayyuttan)*, "and he was set," which, as long recognized, is to be corrected to *wytl*, as reflected by LXX *kai (an)ekremasthē* (cf. Syr., Targ., Vulg.). This is now confirmed by 4QSam[a]: *wytl*.

*hanging* LXX[L] adds "in the tree" (cf. v. 11).

10. *Someone* Reading *'yš* with 4QSam[a] for MT *'yš 'ḥd*, "One man."

11. *making the report* MT adds "to him." Omit with LXX[B], Syr.

*strike him* MT adds "there." Omit with LXX[B], Syr.

*ten pieces of silver* So MT: *'śrh ksp*. Instead of "ten," LXX[LMN], Josephus (*Ant.* 7.240), and 4QSam[a] (*[ḥm]šy[m]*; cf. Ulrich 1978:108–9) have "fifty." A few witnesses (LXX[L], etc.; cf. Targ.) seem to read *šqly* before *ksp*—thus, "ten (fifty) silver shekels."

12. *Be careful* MT *šimrû-mî*, which critics have dealt with in one of two ways. Many (Budde, Smith, etc.) would read *lî*, "for me, for my sake," for *mî* on authority of the versions; but *lî* can be impeached as reminiscent of v. 5. Others (cf. GK[2] §137c) attempt to read *mî* as an indefinite—thus, "Be careful, whoever you might be . . ."; but such a construction is without good parallel (cf. Driver). I prefer to retain *mî*, understood as an enclitic particle. Though the existence of enclitic *-m* in Biblical Hebrew is now generally acknowledged, its vocalization is unknown. The present instance suggests that in direct speech it was pronounced *mî*, as in Akkadian.

13. *Otherwise . . . recklessly* So MT: *'w 'śyty . . . šqr*. LXX[B]: *mē poiēsai . . . adikon* = *m'śwt . . . šqr*, "(Be careful of young Abishalom) so as not to deal recklessly (with his life)." LXX[L]: *kai pōs poiēsō . . . adikon* = *w'yk "śh . . . šqr*, "And how can I deal recklessly (with my own life) . . . ?"

14. *"I won't dally with you this way!"* So MT: *l' kn 'ḥylh lpnyk*, lit. "Not thus shall I tarry (*'ōḥîlâ*) before you!" LXX[L] (cf. LXX[A], Vulg., Targ.) has *dia touto egō arxomai enōpion sou* = *lkn ('nky) 'ḥlh lpnyk*, "Therefore I shall begin (*'āḥăllâ*) before you!" The latter is preferred by Budde, G. R. Driver (1962:133), and others.

*He* So MT. LXX: "Joab."

*sticks* According to Thenius we should read *šlḥym*, "darts," with LXX[B] *belē* in preference to MT *šbṭym*, "sticks" (so Wellhausen, Smith, Budde, Driver, Caspari). But we follow the interpretation of G. R. Driver (1962:133–34) and read MT; see the NOTE.

17. *They took* Reading *wyqḥ* with LXX in preference to MT *wyqḥw*. The antecedent subject is *h'm*, "the army." LXX[LMN] have "*Joab* took."

*a large pit* LXX[BAL] combine two translations of *'l (h)pḥt (h)gdwl*, viz. *eis chasma mega* and *eis ton bothynon ton megan*. The second is identical to MT and recensional. The first is probably primitive in both form (indefinite) and position (before "in the forest"). If the definite article is original, we must read "a certain large pit" (GK[2] §126qr) or "the large pit," assuming the place was well known (Dhorme).

*and heaped up* MT has *wyṣbw,* "and erected," which is appropriate to a monument (v. 18) but not a pile of stones. Accordingly, Budde would restore *wyqymw,* "and raised up," the verb used in the analogous passages Josh 7:26 and 8:29 (see the NOTE). But Joüon (1928:313) has recognized the primitive reading in our passage. Read *wyṣbrw* (cf. Vulg.).

18. *When . . . pillar* The witnesses preserve variants, which are both represented by the conflate (and corrupt) text of LXX$^{B}$. One variant, which is found in MT, reads *w'bšlm lqḥ wyṣb lw bḥyw 't mṣbt 'šr,* lit. "And Abishalom took and erected for himself during his life the pillar that is. . . ." A second variant is reflected by LXX$^{LMN}$: *kai abessalōm (de) eti zōn elaben kai estēsen (he)autō stēlēn* = *w'bšlm 'wd ḥy lqḥ wyṣb lw mṣbh,* lit. "And Abishalom, when still alive, took and erected a pillar. . . ." Klostermann and Budde used the conflate text of LXX$^{BA}$ to develop a text in which *David* erected the pillar for Abishalom.

*I have . . . my name* LXX$^{B}$: "He has . . . his name" (indirect discourse).

*by his own name. It is called* These words *('l šmw wyqr' lh)* fell out of LXX$^{B}$ after "So he called the pillar" *(wyqr' lmṣbt).*

19. *said* LXX$^{L}$ and Syr.$^{MSS}$ add "to Joab."

*Let me run . . . with the news* Reading *'rwṣh n' 'bśrh,* lit. "Let me run, let me carry the news," with LXX$^{L}$ *dramōn dē euangelioumai* and Syr. *'rhṭ 'sbrywhy.* MT (cf. LXX$^{B}$, etc.) has *'rwṣh n' w'bśrh,* "Let me run *and* carry the news."

*the king* LXX$^{L}$: "King David."

*has set him free* MT *špṭw,* lit. "judged him." LXX$^{BA}$ omit "him."

20. *said Joab* So LXX$^{L}$. MT: "said Joab *to him.*"

*but today* So MT: *whywm hzh.* LXX = *wbywm hzh,* "But *on* this day."

*This was because* So MT *(qĕrê): ky 'l kn,* lit. "For it was because. . . ." LXX$^{L}$ reflects *ky* alone, which might be considered superior by virtue of its shortness. MT *(kĕtîb): ky 'l (kn* having fallen out before the following *bn),* as if "For it (the news) would be concerning the king's son (who is) dead" (cf. Syr.).

21. *Go tell* So MT. MT$^{MSS}$, LXX$^{L}$: "Go and tell."

*the Cushite* In its second occurrence in this verse in MT *kwšy* appears without the article, as if it were a name, "Cushi"; in its other occurrences in vv. 21–32 of MT it has the article. LXX, Syr., Vulg., and Targ. treat it as a name throughout. Note also the superscription to Psalm 7: "A shiggaion of David, which he sang to Yahweh because of the words of Cushi (so LXX; MT 'Cush'), a Benjaminite."

*and set out* So LXX$^{B}$: *kai exēlthen* = *wyṣ'.* MT (cf. LXX$^{L}$, Syr. v. 22): *wyrṣ,* "and ran."

22. *You'll have no* That is, *wlkh 'yn;* so MT (cf. LXX$^{L}$). LXX$^{B}$ *deuro ouk estin soi* presupposes approximately the same text with *(w)lkh* interpreted two ways.

*reward for going* MT *bśwrh mṣ't.* The second word is vocalized *mōṣē't,* perhaps understood as "(no news [*bĕśôrâ*]) finding (= *mōṣe'et*) anything" or "(no news) bringing (= *môṣē't*) anything" (Driver). But *bĕśôrâ* by itself can mean "reward" (cf. 4:10). Thus the LXX gloss (?), *eis ōphel(e)ian* = *lbṣ,* "for gain," is unnecessary, and *mṣ't* should not be interpreted to refer to finding or bringing in something. Wellhausen's proposal to read *mūṣē't,* "(no reward) will be found (for you)," is accepted by Budde and others (cf. Targ. *mtyhb*). I prefer to read *miṣṣē't,* lit. "from going forth" (cf. *wyṣ'* in v. 21 [LXX]). Joab is saying that Ahimaaz has nothing to gain *from going.* The sense of LXX *poreuomenō*, though it appears at first glance to point to *lĕhōlēk* (Klostermann), is close to our interpretation of *mṣ't*.

23. *But [Ahimaaz] said* We read *wy'mr*, which is missing in MT but necessary (contrast Thenius, Keil, and Conroy 1978:70 n. 109). It is preserved by LXX$^{BA}$, Syr., and Vulg. LXX$^{LMN}$ reflect *wy'mr 'ḥym'ṣ*, "But Ahimaaz said," and it is also necessary to make the subject explicit in English. Possibly the longer reading fell out of MT after *mṣ't* at the end of the preceding verse.

24. *towards him alone* Reading *lbdw lpnyw* with LXX *monos enōpion autou*. In MT *lpnyw* has dropped out after *lbdw*.

25. *If he is alone* So MT. LXX$^{L}$: "If he *runs* alone."

26. *on the gate* So LXX$^{L}$: *epi tēn pylēn* = *'l hš'r*. LXX$^{B}$ *pros tē pylē* reflects *'l* (= *'l*) *hš'r*, which in MT is interpreted as *'el haššō'ēr*, "to the gatekeeper."

*another* Cf. LXX, Syr., Vulg., Targ.$^{MS}$. MT lacks *'ḥr*, so that the watchman repeats the final words of v. 24 exactly *(hnh 'yš rṣ lbdw)*.

27. *and . . . because of* MT has *w'l* for *w'l* (cf. LXX$^{B}$), as often in Samuel. LXX$^{L}$ *hyper* reflects *'l*, without the conjunction (see the *Textual Note* that follows).

*he comes* So MT: *wybw'* (cf. LXX$^{B}$). LXX$^{L}$ reads *yby'* and interprets David's words as "He's a good man because of the good news *he brings*."

28. *drew near* Reading *wyqrb* on the basis of LXX$^{L}$ *kai prosēlthen* and LXX$^{M}$ *kai prosēgagen*. MT (cf. LXX$^{BAN}$) has *wyqr'*, "shouted," which Schulz and Conroy (1978:72 n. 115) prefer.

*who raised* So MT: *'šr nś'w* (cf. LXX$^{ALMN}$). LXX$^{B}$ has *tous misountas* = *'šr śn'w* (or *hśn'ym*), "who hated," which does not fit the statement as presently constituted. It presupposes a reading such as *'šr sgr bydk 't h'nšym hśn'ym 't npš 'dny hmlk* (cf. LXX$^{MSS}$ *psychen tou kyriou mou to basileōs*), ". . . who has delivered into your hand the men who hate the soul of my lord the king."

29. *I saw* So MT: *r'yty*. LXX$^{L}$ (cf. Josephus, *Ant.* 7.25) reflects *šm'ty . . . 'ḥry*, "I heard . . . behind me."

*when . . . off* Reading *bšlḥ yw'b 'bd hmlk 't 'bdk* with LXX$^{LN}$ (cf. Vulg.). MT has *lšlḥ 't 'bd hmlk yw'b w't 'bdk*, "for sending the king's servant, Joab, and your servant."

*what it was* MT *mh*, to which LXX adds *šm*—thus, "what was *there*."

30. *and stood* So MT, LXX$^{BA}$. LXX$^{MN}$: "behind him." LXX$^{L}$: "and stood behind him."

31. *he said* So Syr., Vulg. MT: "*the Cushite* said." LXX: "he said *to the king*."

*you . . . you* Syr.: "him . . . him."

32. *against you* LXX$^{BAMN}$, Vulg.: "against *him*."

**19** 1. *tremble* So MT: *wyrgz* (cf. LXX$^{B}$ *kai etarachthē*). LXX$^{L}$ has *kai edakrysen* = *wydm'* (?), "Then the king began to *weep*."

*as he wept* So LXX$^{LMN}$: *en tō klaien* = *bbktw*. MT: *blktw*, "as he *went*."

2. *Joab was told* So MT, LXX$^{BAMN}$. LXX$^{L}$, Syr.: "They told Joab."

*and mourning* Reading *wmt'bl* with Syr., Targ., and MT$^{MSS}$ *(BHS)*. MT has *wyt'bl*, "and he (Joab?) mourned." In LXX both verbs are finite.

4. *humiliated* So MT, etc.: *hnklmym*. LXX$^{L}$ *ēttēmenos kai ētimōmenos* = *hḥtym whnklmym*, "shattered and humiliated."

5. *and he cried* So LXX$^{L}$, Syr., Vulg. MT: "and *the king* cried."

*my son* Cf. LXX. MT adds another "my son" (cf. v. 1).

6. *indoors* That is, *hbyt(h);* so MT, LXX, Syr.[MSS]. The word is omitted by Syr., which may preserve the primitive situation at this point.

*your servants* So LXX[L]. MT: "*all* your servants."

*your life* LXX[BA]: "you."

*and concubines* LXX[L]: "and *the lives of* your concubines."

7. *Indeed you've made it clear* That is, *ky hgdt;* so MT (cf. LXX[LM]). LXX[BAN] = *wtgd,* "And you made it clear."

*you know* So LXX[L]. MT: "*I* know."

*if* So MT *(qĕrê)* and 4QSam[a] *([w]lw): wlw* (cf. LXX, Targ.). MT *(kĕtîb): wl'*—thus, "Abishalom is *not* alive today."

*today* (2) Cf. LXX[L]. Placed at the beginning of the clause in MT ("I know today that . . .").

*we'd all be dead* That is, *wklnw mtym,* into which MT inserts another *hywm,* "today" (omit with LXX[L], Syr.). In LXX[BAL] and Syr. the conjunction is omitted, perhaps reflecting the primitive situation.

8. *I swear* LXX[LN]: "*they* have sworn."

*that if you don't go out there* Reading *ky 'm 'ynk ywṣ'* with LXX and 4QSam[a] *(ky 'm 'y[nk ywṣ']).* In MT, *'m* has fallen out. At this point LXX[B] adds another *sēmeron* = *hywm,* "today" (omit with MT, etc.), and LXX[L] adds *eis apantēsin tou laou* = *lqr't 't h'm,* "to meet with the army"; both expansions have influençed OL.

*and this will be worse for you* So MT: *wr'h lk z't.* The text of LXX is conflate, combining the OG reading *(kai epignōthi seautō* = *wd'h lk,* "and know for yourself") with that of MT *(kai kakon* [LXX[L]: *cheiron*] *soi* = *wr'h lk);* cf. Barthélemy 1963: 121–22; Ulrich 1978:145–46.

9. *in the gate* (bis) LXX[L]: "*upon* the gate."

*and when [they] were told* We read *wygd (wayyuggad) lkl h'm,* lit. "and it was told to the entire army." MT has *wlkl h'm hgydw,* "and to the entire army they told," and LXX[BAMN] reflect *wkl h'm hgydw,* "and the entire army told."

## NOTES

**18** 2. *three parts.* Threefold division of an army is a strategy used elsewhere in attacking a battle camp (Judg 7:16; I Sam 11:11) or, in one case, a city (Judg 9:43). Perhaps, then, the battle (v. 6) began with a raid by David's army on Abishalom's camp (cf. 17:26). It may be, however, that such a division of an army was simply traditional, unrelated to specific strategies; so Boling (1975:147) and Conroy (1978:55 n. 33), both following Mendenhall (1958:57–58 n. 32), who cites antecedents at Mari.

*Abishai.* It might seem unnecessary to identify Abishai, who has appeared as recently as 16:9–12, as "Joab's brother." But the narrator uses every occasion possible to stress the role of Joab in the events to follow (Conroy 1978:56).

*Ittai.* See 15:18b–22.

2–4. *Then the king . . . the king told them.* The dialogue between David and the army (vv. 2b–4a) is regarded by Würthwein (1974:44–45) and Langlamet (1976b:355) as secondary, a part of the pro-Davidic editing they believe the story to have undergone. Noting the similarity to 21:17, Langlamet concludes that the present verses were introduced by a redactor who wanted to emphasize David's absence from the battle. I agree that the dialogue is reported to emphasize David's absence while also showing that he did not stay away out of fear; but I regard it as part of the original account of Abishalom's revolt (so Conroy 1978:44 and n. 3).

3. *ten thousands.* Hebrew *'ăśārâ 'ălāpîm,* "ten *'elep*-contingents" or "thousands," not *'ăśeret 'ălāpîm,* "ten thousand" (Ehrlich 1910:318). In either case the force of the hyperbole is clear.

5. Compare 3:35–37. These two passages are examples of apologetic writing in its most forthright vein. We are shown that David wanted Abishalom treated leniently, further evidence of the king's irenic disposition and affection for his son. Moreover, he expressed his wishes clearly to the commanders, including Joab, and the "entire army" were witnesses. Responsibility for Abishalom's death, therefore, can be placed squarely on Joab's shoulders when the events of vv. 9–15 are reported. Blame is thus removed entirely from David, and he is shown to be worthy of the loyalty of Abishalom's followers in the aftermath of the revolt.

*Protect.* Hebrew *lĕ'aṭ* is apparently intended as a prepositional phrase (cf. BDB, KB[3]) meaning "Deal gently." This was doubted by Haupt (1926), however, who denied the existence of a noun *'aṭ,* "gentleness." He derived the word from *lwṭ,* "cover, veil," and read *lôṭ* (< **lāṭ*), an infinitive absolute used as an imperative (GK[2] §113bb). It seems probable that some form of *lwṭ* is intended (cf. *lā'aṭ* for *lā'ṭ* = *lāṭ,* "he had covered," in 19:5 below), perhaps **lū(')ṭ,* a simple imperative. The sense of "cover" and thus "protect" is favored by the paraphrase *šimrû,* "Be careful of," in v. 12.

*young Abishalom.* David's use of *na'ar,* "young (man)," in reference to Abishalom here and in vv. 12, 29, and 32 below is demonstratively affectionate (Budde, Schulz, Conroy 1978:48; contrast Caspari). As elsewhere, the narrator is intent upon keeping David's love for his son before us.

6. *the Forest of Ephraim.* Since the battle clearly took place in Transjordan, a question arises about a district east of Jordan with the name of a tribe west of Jordan. Noth (1960:201) identifies the battleground as "the wood hill country in the central land east of Jordan south of the Jabbok," a region originally settled, he concludes (pp. 60–61), by settlers from Ephraim west of Jordan (so Hertzberg). This is possible but not certain; see de Vaux 1978:788–89.

7. *twenty thousands.* About 100 to 280 men according to the figures given in the NOTE at 6:1.

8. *The fighting was scattered.* Compare I Sam 14:23+ in the description of the battle of Michmash Pass (cf. *I Samuel,* the *Textual Note* at 14:23b).

*the forest consumed more troops . . . than the sword.* Clearly the Forest of Ephraim was "not an orderly tree-planted area, but rough country with trees and scrub and uneven ground, dangerous terrain for both battle and flight" (Ackroyd). By delaying in Jerusalem on Hushai's advice, Abishalom permitted David to cross the Jordan (17:16) and choose for the battleground the forests of Gilead, which could be compared even to those of Lebanon for density (Jer 22:6; Zech 10:10), and where the numerically superior force of Abishalom's conscript army would be at a disadvantage against David's more skilled private army, with its considerable experience of guerrilla warfare.

9. Josephus (*Ant.* 7.239) interpreted Abishalom's predicament as follows: "Borne along at a gallop, he was bounced up by the unsteady motion, so that his hair became entangled in a shaggy tree with large, widely overhanging branches, and he was left hanging in this odd way." The Talmud (Sotah 9b) understands the text in a similar way, adding the moralizing interpretation that because Abishalom gloried in his hair he was hanged by it. Many modern commentators doubt that Abishalom's extraordinary head of hair (14:26) is involved here, and in fact the text does not say so (Caird, Ackroyd). We might suppose, then, that the young man is trapped by the neck in a fork of crossed branches (cf. G. R. Driver 1962:131). Other commentators, however, think the hair may be involved after all (Bressan, van den Born, Hertzberg, McKane, Goslinga). Surely Conroy is correct when he suggests (1978:44 n. 4) that the narrator had the connection to 14:26 in mind and intended the reader to "draw a contrast between promise and pride on the one hand and humiliation and doom on the other."

*his mule.* As explained in the NOTE at 13:29, the mule was the royal saddle animal in the time of David, and the symbolic force of Abishalom's unmuling in the present passage ought not be overlooked (Alonso Schökel). As Conroy puts it (1978:60), "The mule was a royal mount; losing his mule Absalom has lost his kingdom."

*the tangle.* The noun *śôbek,* which occurs only here, can be explained by reference to Arabic *šabaka,* "entangle, intertwine." It refers to the tangled branches of the terebinth.

*a certain large terebinth.* Hebrew *hā'ēlâ haggĕdôlâ.* Unless a particular well-known tree is meant (Kirkpatrick)—thus, "*the* large terebinth"—the article has the force described in GK² §126qr. The *'ēlâ*-tree might be a terebinth or an oak or something else (see bibliography in Conroy 1978:61 n. 58).

*between the sky and the ground.* That is, in midair, as in 24:16. See Rosmarin (1932) and Levine (1975; 1976:97).

10–14. These verses are regarded by Würthwein (1974:43–48) and Langlamet (1976b:355) as secondary, part of the pro-David/anti-Joab redaction they suppose the story to have undergone. Langlamet finds vv. 14 and 15 incompatible: If Abishalom had three darts in his heart (see the NOTE at v. 14), it would hardly have been necessary to finish him off. In the original account, Langlamet concludes, Abishalom was killed by the ten soldiers; vv. 10–14 were inserted to lay the blame more directly at Joab's door. If G. R. Driver's interpretation of v. 14 is followed, however, the difficulty of vv. 14–15 is removed (see below). In any case, our interpretation of the story of Abishalom's revolt as an originally pro-Davidic document assumes that Joab's ruthlessness was a primitive and essential component of the narrative.

14–15. As noted above, the rabbis saw Abishalom's arboreal suspension as an appropriate consequence of his pride in his hair. They conclude similarly (Sotah 9b) that it was because he cohabited with his father's *ten* concubines (16:22; cf. 15:6) that he was pierced with *ten* lances and that it was because he stole *three* hearts—the heart of his father, the heart of the courts of justice, and the heart of Israel (cf. 15:16)—that he was struck in the chest (heart!) with *three* sticks. The interpretation I have adopted, however, is that of G. R. Driver (1962:133–34; cf. NEB). If Joab "took three darts in his hand, and thrust them into the heart of Absalom" (RSV, v. 14), ten soldiers would hardly have been required to dispatch him (v. 15), even granting that this was a responsibility of a warrior's weapon-bearers (I Sam 14:13). It seems better to understand the three *šĕbāṭîm* of v. 14 as a bunch of stout sticks that Joab struck *(tq')* against Abishalom's chest *(lēb)* in order to dislodge him from the tree. Once on the ground Abishalom was at the mercy of Joab's men. An alternative explanation offered by Hertzberg also avoids contradiction of v. 15: three darts, not spears, thrust in Abishalom's chest started a flow of blood that marked him for death. Thus understood, v. 14b$\beta$ ("while he was still alive in the tree") might better be grouped with v. 15 than v. 14 (so already Thenius). In any case it is clear that Joab deliberately arranged for Abishalom to die at the hands of an entire platoon, so that no individual (certainly not himself!) could be named the killer.

16. *the shofar.* See the NOTE at 6:15.

*held [it] in check.* Hebrew *ḥāśak . . . 'et-hā'ām,* lit. "held the army (i.e., David's troops) in check." According to Thenius, however, Joab's restraint of the army is already indicated by the first part of the verse. The meaning here, he says, is that Joab "spared (i.e., wished to spare) the army (i.e., the Israelite forces of Abishalom)." Either meaning of *ḥāśak* is acceptable, and Thenius' interpretation has found some support (Klostermann, etc.); but it presents the difficulty that, thus understood, the two references to "the army" in the verse, neither of which is further defined, have different meanings.

17. *a large pit . . . a very large pile of stones.* This is the burial of an accursed man. Compare: (1) Josh 7:26, where Achan, having been stoned to death for his sacrilege (Josh 7:15), is buried under "a large pile of stones"; (2) Josh 8:29, where the king of Ai, having been hanged on a tree, is thrown into a pit (LXX) and covered with "a large pile of stones"; and (3) Josh 10:27, where five enemy kings, having been put to death and hanged from trees, are thrown into a cave, the mouth of which is then covered with large stones. Abishalom is accursed as a fratricide and rebel, and he too was hanged on a tree (cf. Deut 21:23). Mythically speaking, it is the fate of the rebel who would *ascend* the throne that he will *descend* into the pit. In the Judaeo-Christian tradition one could mention Isa 14:12–15 and the myth of the fall of Lucifer. In Aegean tradition the Giants, in consequence of their revolt against the Olympians, are buried beneath huge stones (islands!), and the rebellious monster Typhon, after being pummeled to exhaustion by the lightning bolts and hailstones of Zeus (cf. Josh 10:11; 7:25), winds up buried beneath Mount Aetna.

*each man to his tent.* See the NOTE at 19:9 (§ XXXII).

18. This parenthesis is evidently a late redactional notice introduced to identify a monument well known in the time of the redactor who added it ("even today"); cf. Caird; Carlson 1964:138 n. 4, 187; Langlamet 1976b:355; Ackroyd; Conroy 1978:64–66 and nn. 84–87. The implied connection between "Abishalom's Monument," obviously a memorial stela of some kind, and the "large pile of stones" of v. 17 is spurious—indeed, it is silly. Moreover, the statement that Abishalom had "no son" is in direct contradiction to 14:27, where we are told he had three sons. Thenius—followed by Schulz, Hertzberg, Gunn (1978:33), and others—concluded that Abishalom's three sons died young, a possibility for which he found support in the absence of their names from 14:27, in contrast to the naming of their sister Tamar. A few commentators (Smith, Kennedy, Mauchline; cf. Caird) consider 18:18 primitive and 14:27 late.

*a pillar for himself.* In connection with this passage Cassuto (1939:126–27) and others (see bibliography in Conroy 1978:65 n. 88) have called attention to *CTCA* 17

[= *UT*[4] 2 Aqht].1.27,45; 2.16, where it is implied that in Ugaritic society the ideal son was "one who erects the stela of the 'god' of his father," that is, his father's shade or ghost (*'l'b;* cf. I Sam 28:13 and the interpretation of Job 12:6 offered in *I Samuel,* p. 421). Since Abishalom has no son to do this, he must do it "for himself." He wants to be sure that he will be remembered and also, perhaps, that his shade will receive offerings (cf. Deut 26:14).

*the Valley of the King.* In Gen 14:17 this name appears as a gloss on the Valley of Shaveh, possibly another name for the Wadi Kidron (15:23) or a part of it. The traditional site is immediately east of the City of David at the foot of the Mount of Olives, where there is a Hellenistic or Roman period tomb popularly known as "Absalom's Tomb"; but there the wadi *(naḥal)* is too narrow to be called a valley *('ēmeq).* Accordingly the King's Valley is usually located at the confluence of the Kidron and the Valley of Hinnom, south of the City of David (or some other place entirely). It may be that the royal family owned property there.

*"Abishalom's Monument."* Hebrew *yad 'ăbīšālōm;* on *yad,* "stela, monument," see the NOTE at 8:3 and, in general, Delcor 1967:230–34.

19. *Ahimaaz son of Zadok.* Cf. 15:27,36. Evidently Ahimaaz remained with David's army after the events recounted in 17:17–21. Having carried bad news before, he now wants a chance to carry what he thinks is good news.

20–21. Joab refuses to let Ahimaaz carry the news. The reason is the death of Abishalom. Ahimaaz knows nothing of this, as he says in v. 29 below. (Verse 20bβ, "This was because the king's son was dead," is not a part of Joab's answer to Ahimaaz, who is not a liar or coward, as v. 29 would then imply; it is an explanation of the narrator.) Joab could inform Ahimaaz of Abishalom's death, but Ahimaaz, as one of those staunchly loyal to David and not under Joab's sway, could not be expected to react favorably or to make the official report in the positive way Joab wants (cf. v. 32b). Thus Joab appoints another runner, a member of the army, who can be relied upon to report the victory *and* the death of Abishalom as good news. There is no reason to suppose the fact that this fellow is a Cushite to have special significance. The designation suggests that his ancestry was Ethiopian or Nubian, and a few commentators (Dhorme, de Vaux) conclude that his black skin was a signal to David of the bad news he was carrying. But, clearly, both Joab and the Cushite thought the news was good and wanted the king to think so too. The tradition behind the superscription to Psalm 9 held that the Cushite ("Cushi," see the *Textual Note* at v. 21) was a Benjaminite, and this is not impossible: Cushi, father of the prophet Zephaniah, was a great-grandson of Hezekiah (Zeph 1:1); presumably Cushi's mother was an Ethiopian—thus he was *kûšî,* a Negro, and at the same time a Judahite.

22–23. Ahimaaz insists on going despite Joab's attempts to dissuade him. Excited about the victory and unaware of the death of Abishalom, the young man wants to be the first to tell the good news to the king. Joab, being who he is, cannot comprehend such innocent enthusiasm. "You'll have no reward for going," he says, mistakenly attributing to Ahimaaz the sort of motive that would stir his own enthusiasm. When the young man persists, Joab's patience, which is never very resilient (cf. v. 14), gives way, and the conversation ends on a brusque monosyllable, *rûṣ,* "Run!"

22. *my boy.* Not in this case an expression of affection (*pace* Conroy 1978:70 and n. 106). The tone of *bĕnî,* lit. "my son," on Joab's lips is condescending, patronizing, or at least ironic.

*reward for going.* Hebrew *bĕśôrâ miṣṣē't;* see the *Textual Note.* As in 4:10, *bĕśôrâ* means "reward" not "news" (so Ehrlich 1910:321).

23. *the Circuit Road.* The Circuit or Kikkar *(hakkikkār)* was the valley of the lower Jordan. The Cushite, we must assume, has set out on a direct, overland route to Mahanaim, which lay not far away to the north of the battlefield, and he will have rough going all the way because of the hills and dense undergrowth. Ahimaaz chooses the "longer but better road" (Hertzberg), probably the major local artery, along the Jordan Valley.

27. *a good man . . . good news.* Compare I Kings 1:42, where Adonijah will welcome Jonathan son of Abiathar with the words, "Come in, for you are a stalwart man *('îš ḥayil),* and it must be good news that you bring *(wĕṭôb tĕbaśśēr)!*" Probably *'îš ṭôb,* "a good man," here has something of the connotation of *'îš ḥayil,* "a stalwart man," there, viz. that the messenger is loyal to the cause (cf. the NOTE at 2:7); on "good(ness)" as a term of political loyalty, see *I Samuel,* p. 322. David, in other words, recognizes the runner as a man staunchly loyal to him, not one of Joab's lackeys, and assumes that the news is good. In a way he is correct: Ahimaaz has come to report good news and knows nothing else. But there is bad news to follow.

**19** 7. *those who hate you . . . those who love you.* On love and hate as terms of political loyalty, see *I Samuel,* the NOTES on 16:21 and 20:17 and the references there (see additional bibliography in Conroy 1978:78 n. 151). David's mistake—if it *is* a mistake—is permitting his natural human love to take precedence over the love he officially owes to his loyal subjects as their king. This is an excellent example of the conflict between David the father and David the king that runs throughout the story of the revolt, as shown most clearly by Gunn (on the present passage see 1978:103). The audience is inclined, as usual, to sympathize with David, for the commonplace wisdom of loving one's friends and hating one's enemies seems both callous and inadequate at this point (cf. Delekat 1967:30, who compares the Sermon on the Mount). Still, the truth of what the hard-boiled Joab is saying is also undeniable. Viewed in terms of political realities, the shoes of David's love are on the wrong feet. Moran (1963a:81) compares *EA* 286:18–20, where the king of Jerusalem reports having said to an officer of the king of Egypt, "Why do you love the Apiru but hate the governors?"

9. *sitting enthroned.* That *yōšēb* has this connotation here was recognized by Caspari. For a list of Ugaritic and biblical parallels, see Dahood in Fisher 1972:264–65 (cf. Schoors in Fisher 1972:115), to which add the text published in *Ugaritica V,* III.3 (RS 24.245).

## COMMENT

The outcome of Abishalom's revolt is decided in a single battle. David has had time to organize his forces, a consequence of Abishalom's fatal choice of counsel (§ XXIX). The army marches out of Mahanaim in three companies, passing in review before the king, who, on the advice of his troops, has elected to stay away from the battlefield. Battle is joined in the tangled Forest of

Ephraim, where the superior might of the conscript army of all Israel is neutralized in favor of David's more experienced and canny professionals (cf. the NOTES at 17:11–13 and 18:8). David's victory is decisive: The partisans of Abishalom fortunate enough to escape both the sword and the forest (cf. 18:8) flee to their homes (19:9bγ [§ XXXII]), and the rebellion simply evaporates.

At the center of this section stands the account of the death of Abishalom (18:9–15), and the reader's attention is centered on Abishalom's death, its causes and consequences, throughout the section. As the troops are marching out of Mahanaim, David instructs his three generals very clearly: "Protect young Abishalom for me!" (18:5). He says this standing "atop the gate" (v. 4) in full hearing of everyone, and the narrator, not wanting to take the chance that his audience might overlook the point, states explicitly, "The entire army was listening" (v. 5). When Abishalom falls into the hands of Joab's troops, we are reminded of David's instructions by the report of a conversation between Joab and the soldier who reports Abishalom's entrapment to him (18:10–14a). Nevertheless, Joab, acting solely on his own authority, has Abishalom dispatched straightway.

It is clear that the narrator is working very hard here to show his audience that David was not responsible for the death of Abishalom. As always in chaps. 13–20, David appears as a gentle man and loving father, referring to his murderous rebel son—whom he knows to be seeking his life (16:11)—with obvious affection as "young Abishalom" (see the NOTE at v. 5). His order of protection for Abishalom is reported so pointedly (18:5) and repeated so specifically (18:12) that we cannot doubt it is regarded by the narrator as of primary importance. The narrator is attempting to evoke sympathy for David, probably addressing himself to former supporters of Abishalom's cause in the aftermath of the revolt. David loved Abishalom, says the narrator. Abishalom's killing was not David's doing—indeed, it was done against his specific orders, publicly issued. David was absent from the battlefield (v. 3). It was Joab, acting independently and in deliberate violation of his orders, who had the young man put to death. If Joab did so on the basis of a careful appraisal of the situation and a fear of the long-range political consequences of sparing Abishalom's life, we are not told this. We can assume, if we want, that Joab was drawing upon his keen sense of political pragmatism and his Machiavellian sense of public morality. But for the narrator Joab is, as usual, only a foil. He is important because the audience's acquaintance with his behavior will exonerate David. When the audience has been made aware of what actually took place on the day of the battle in the Forest of Ephraim, they will understand that David is not to be blamed for Abishalom's death and, therefore, that he has not forfeited his claim on the loyalty of those Israelites who followed Abishalom.

The account of the report of Abishalom's death to David and his reaction (18:9–19:9abαβ) restates and reinforces the narrator's argument as just defined. David's eagerness for tidings is clearly shown by his close attention to news from the road. His optimism (cf. v. 27) is ironic and pitiful. The news will not be good for him, even though his army has won a battle and quelled the rebellion. David is concerned only for the welfare of Abishalom. He offers no reaction at all to the news of victory given by the two messengers in 18:28 and 18:31. Instead he asks immediately if Abishalom is all right (18:29,32). Similarly, he is so overcome with grief at the news of Abishalom's death that he ignores his responsibilities to his troops entirely. He is inconsolable. His lament is loud and long and, again, witnessed at least indirectly by the entire army (19:3). In fact, the army, insulted and humiliated by the king's demonstrative grieving over the fallen enemy, is on the point of desertion when Joab, again coarsely pragmatic and wholly unsentimental, intervenes and brings David back to his senses.

The scene closes with David "sitting enthroned in the gate" of Mahanaim (19:9). He is king once again. Now he must return and reclaim the throne in Jerusalem.

# XXXII. DAVID'S RETURN TO JERUSALEM
## (19:9bγ–20:3)

19 [9]Israel had fled, each man to his tent. [10]The entire army was
complaining to all the staff-bearers of Israel. "It was the king who saved
us from all our enemies," they said, "and he was the one who rescued
us from the clutches of the Philistines. But now he has fled from the
land and from control of his kingdom, [11]and Abishalom, whom we
anointed over us, is dead in battle. Why, then, do you have nothing to
say about bringing back the king?"
When the things all Israel was saying reached the king, [12][he] sent
word to Zadok the priest: "Speak to the elders of Judah as follows:
'Why are you the last to bring the king back to his house? [13]You're my
kinsmen! You're my bone and my flesh! Then why are you last to bring
back the king?' [14]And to Amasa say, 'Aren't you my bone and my flesh?
Now then, may God do thus and so to me and thus and so again, if you
are not the commander of my army in place of Joab from now on!' "

### *Arrival at the Jordan*

[15]Then all the men of Judah were like one man in their resolve, and
they sent word to the king: "Come back, you and all your servants!"
[16]So the king started back and reached the Jordan as the Judahites were
arriving in Gilgal, having come down to meet the king and conduct
[him] across the Jordan. [17]Also Shimei son of Gera, the Benjaminite
from Bahurim, hurried down with the men of Judah to meet King
David, [18]a thousand men from Benjamin with him. But Ziba, the steward of the house of Saul, and his fifteen sons and twenty servants waded
through the Jordan ahead of the king [19]and did the work of bringing
the king across and doing the things he wanted done.

### *Shimei Pardoned*

Shimei son of Gera, falling down before the king as he crossed the
Jordan, [20]said to [him], "Let my lord not think of wrongdoing! Don't

think back to the wrong your servant did on the day my lord was marching out of Jerusalem! Let the king not take it to heart! [21]For your servant knows that I was at fault—but, look, today I came, first of all the house of Joseph to come down to meet my lord the king!"

[22]Then Abishai son of Zeruiah spoke up. "Shouldn't Shimei be put to death on this very spot?" he said. "For he cursed Yahweh's anointed!"

[23]"What do you sons of Zeruiah have against me," said David, "that you should become my adversary today? Shall anyone be put to death in Israel today? Don't you know that today I begin to rule over Israel?" [24]Then the king said to Shimei, "You shall not be put to death!" and gave him his oath.

*Meribbaal*

[25]Also Meribbaal son of Jonathan son of Saul had come to meet the king. He had not cut his toenails or trimmed his mustache or even washed his clothes from the day the king left until the day he returned safely. ([26]When he came to Jerusalem to meet with the king, the king said to him, "Why didn't you go with me, Meribbaal?"

[27]"My lord king!" he said. "My servant let me down: For your servant said to him, 'Saddle me an ass, so I can ride on it and go with the king!'—for your servant is lame. [28]And he slandered your servant to my lord the king. But my lord the king did what I thought was good —like an envoy of God! [29]For though all the men of my father's house were nothing but fiends of hell to my lord the king, you set your servant among those who eat at your table. From whom, then, could I have better treatment?"

But when he cried out to the king, [30]the king said, "Why do you talk so much? I have spoken: You and Ziba shall divide the property!"

[31]"Let him take it all," said Meribbaal to the king, "since my lord the king has come home safely!")

*Barzillai*

[32]Also Barzillai the Gileadite had come down from Rogelim. He went along with the king to see him off from the Jordan. [33]Barzillai was a very old man—eighty years old—and he had provided for the king while he was staying in Mahanaim, for he was a very important man.

[34]"Come along with me," said the king to Barzillai, "and I'll provide for your old age in Jerusalem with me."

[35]But Barzillai said to the king, "How many days would I have there, that I should go up with the king to Jerusalem? [36]I'm now eighty years old. Do I know right from wrong? Can your servant taste what I eat and drink? Can I hear the songs of men and women? Then why should your servant become a burden on my lord the king? [37]It is just a short distance that your servant will go along with the king, so why should the king give me a reward such as this? [38]Let your servant go back, so that I can die in my own city near the grave of my father and mother! But here is your servant Chimham: Let him go along with my lord the king, and treat him as you think best!"

[39]"Chimham shall go along with me," said the king, "and I'll treat him as I think best, and anything else you choose to ask of me—I'll do that for you, too!"

[40]When the entire army crossed the Jordan, the king stayed behind. He kissed Barzillai and blessed him. Then [Barzillai] went back home, [41]and the king crossed over to Gilgal. Also Chimham crossed over with him.

### *Dissension in the Ranks*

The entire army of Judah was marching along with the king, and also half of the army of Israel. [42]Then all the men of Israel came to the king and said to [him], "Why have our brothers, the men of Judah, stolen you away and conducted the king and his household across the Jordan along with all of David's men?"

[43]The men of Judah gave this reply to the men of Israel: "Because the king is closely related to us! And why are you angry about this? Have we eaten any of the king's food? Has he given us a gift? Has he brought us a present?"

[44]"We have ten shares in the king!" said the men of Israel in reply to the men of Judah. "And furthermore we, not you, are firstborn! So why have you slighted us? And why weren't we given priority because of what we said about bringing back our king?"

The men of Judah were more stubborn in the things they said than the men of Israel, **20** [1]and a scoundrel named Sheba son of Bichri the Benjaminite, who happened to be there, blew on the shofar and said: "We have no share in David and no estate in the son of Jesse! Every man to his tent, Israel!" [2]So all Israel left David to follow Sheba son of Bichri, while the men of Judah accompanied their king from the Jordan to Jerusalem.

## *The Fate of the Concubines*

[3]When David reached his house in Jerusalem, [he] took the ten concubines he had left to watch the house and put them in a guarded cell, where he provided for them but did not visit them. They were confined until the day they died, widows while alive.

## *TEXTUAL NOTES*

19 10. *complaining* Reading *nlwn* with LXX$^{LM}$ *gongyzontes*. MT has *ndwn*, a unique *Nip'al* of *dyn*, meaning "in a state of mutual strife (with)" (?); cf. Driver.

*the staff-bearers of Israel* See the NOTE.

*the king* So MT, Syr. LXX and 4QSam$^{a}$ *(hmlk dwẏ[d])* have "King David."

*from all* MT has *mkp*, "from the clutches of." In LXX$^{B}$ (cf. LXX$^{L}$) this is combined with *mkl*, "from all," preserved alone in LXX$^{M}$. Evidently *mkl* was the OG reading, and it is preferable to *mkp*, which anticipates the language of the subsequent clause.

*and from control of his kingdom* That is, *wm'l mmlktw*, lit. "and from (being) over his kingdom"; cf. LXX$^{MN}$. Again this is the OG reading, combined in LXX$^{BAL}$ with that of MT, *m'l 'bšlm*, "from [?] Abishalom," which is shown to be inferior by its anticipation of the next word in the text (*w'bšlm*, "and Abishalom," v. 11) and by the awkward construction of *mē'al* with a proper noun (Klostermann).

11. *and Abishalom* Omitted in LXX$^{B}$ by haplography; cf. the preceding *Textual Note*.

*whom we anointed over us* LXX$^{L}$ adds *eis basilea* = *lmlk*, "as king."

*When . . . the king* This sentence *(wdbr kl yśr'l b' 'l hmlk)* is preserved here in its proper place in LXX, OL, and, as space considerations require, 4QSam$^{a}$ (see Ulrich 1978:89). In MT it was lost after the preceding sentence by homoioteleuton *(lhšyb 't hmlk . . . 'l hmlk)* and restored erroneously after *lhšyb 't hmlk* in v 12 (hence the repetition of *'l bytw*, "to his house," at the end of v. 12 in MT). As Thenius recognized long ago, however, it is necessary in the earlier position to explain David's actions in v. 12.

12. *to Zadok the priest* So 4QSam$^{a}$: *'l ṣdwq hkw[hn]*, uniquely. All other witnesses support MT in reading *'l ṣdwq w'l 'bytr hkhnym*, "to Zadok and Abiathar the priests."

At the end of the verse MT adds *wdbr kl yśr'l b' 'l hmlk 'l bytw*, a displaced correction of the loss in v. 11 of MT (see the *Textual Note* on "When . . . the king," v. 11), to which most other witnesses have been recensionally corrected. In Syr. the displaced plus continues with a rough equivalent of v. 12a.

13. At the end of this verse, after ". . . to his house," $LXX^L$ adds a translation of *wdbr kl yśr'l b' 'l hmlk,* which stands after the same words in v. 12 in most witnesses. See the *Textual Notes* on "When . . . the king" in v. 11 and at the end of v. 12.

14. *And to Amasa say* Reading *wl'mś' t'mr(w)* with MT, LXX. Syr., however, has *w'mr l'ms',* "And he (David) said to Amasa"; a case for this reading could be made.

*Now then* So LXX: *kai nyn* = *w'th,* which has fallen out of MT after *'th.*

15. *Then . . . resolve* Lit. "Then the heart of every man of Judah was inclined like one man." The verb is *wyṭ,* which we read as *wayyēṭ* with Targ. *(w'tpny)* and $MT^{MSS}$ *(BHS);* cf. Budde. MT (cf. LXX) has *wayyaṭ,* "*And he inclined* [transitive] the heart of every man," etc., the subject being understood as David or, perhaps, Amasa (so explicitly in $LXX^L$).

*to the king* LXX, Syr., and Vulg. reflect *l'mr,* "saying," before the speech that follows.

16. *the Judahites* That is, "Judah"; so MT. LXX: "the men of Judah."

*having come down* Reading *lrdt* with $MT^{MSS}$ *(BHS)* and $LXX^L$ *(katabēnai);* cf. v. 21. MT has *llkt,* "having gone."

17–19. The correct arrangement of these verses was recognized by Wellhausen. The first clause of v. 18 belongs with what precedes it, v. 17, not with what follows it. Shimei and his men arrive with the men of Judah (v. 17) and wait for the king on the west bank. Only Ziba and his family wade through the Jordan *ahead of* David (v. 18). This is why Ziba has brought such a large retinue—he wants to ingratiate himself with the king—and David's decision in v. 30 suggests that he succeeds.

18. *waded through* MT has *wṣlḥw,* "and they kept wading through" (?), but Wellhausen saw that this should be *ṣlḥw,* the initial *w-* having been repeated from the end of the previous word, *'tw.* $LXX^B$ resolved the problem of tense by reading *kai kateuthynan* = *wyṣlḥw,* "and they waded through." $LXX^L$ *kai apostellousin epi* reflects *wyšlḥw 'l,* "they sent (word) across." On the meaning of *ṣlḥ* see the NOTE.

19. *and did the work* At the beginning of the verse LXX preserves the OG reading of several words, after which the MT equivalent has been supplied recensionally in all MSS except $LXX^L$. We follow LXX *kai eleitourgēsan tēn leitourgian* in reading *wy'bdw h'bdh* (cf. Syr.). From this we might restore *wy'brw h'brh,* "and crossed the ford" (cf. Targ. and Vulg.), which stands closer to MT *w'brh h'brh,* "and the ford (?) kept crossing" (cf. Wellhausen, Driver). But the verb, in view of the two infinitive phrases that follow and specify it ("bringing . . . across . . . doing"), must refer to work in general, not crossing alone.

*the king* Cf. LXX (OG). MT: "the king's house."

*before the king* So MT, Syr., $LXX^A$. $LXX^{BLMN}$: "*on his face* before the king."

20. *Let my lord not think of wrongdoing!* So LXX (= *'l yḥšb 'dny 'wn*). MT: *'l yḥšb ly 'dny 'wn,* "Let my lord not reckon (my) wrongdoing *to me!*"

*my lord was marching out* So $LXX^B$: *ho kyrios mou exeporeueto* = *'ădōnî yōṣē'.* MT has *yāṣā' 'ădōnî-hammelek,* "my lord the king marched out" (so $LXX^L$; cf. $LXX^{AMN}$).

21. *to come down to meet* MT *lrdt lqr't.* $LXX^L$ *eis katabasin* seems to reflect *'l mwrd,* "to the descent (of my lord the king)."

22. *"Shouldn't Shimei be . . . ?"* LXX^L: "Shimei should be . . . !"

23. *Shall anyone . . . today?* The first word should probably be read *hhywm* (cf. LXX^LMN). In MT the statement begins *hywm* and in LXX^BA *hywm l'* ("No one shall be," etc.).

*in Israel* So MT, LXX^L, OL. LXX^BAMN: "*from* Israel."

*Don't you know that* Reading *(h)lw' yd'tm ky* on the basis of LXX^L *ouk oidate hoti* (cf. Josephus, *Ant.* 7.266). MT: *ky hlw' yd'ty ky,* "For don't I know that." LXX^B: *hoti ouk oida ei* = *ky l' yd'ty 'm,* "For I don't know if."

*I begin to rule* That is, *'mlk 'ny;* cf. LXX. MT: *'ny mlk,* "I am king." See the NOTE.

25. *Meribbaal* See the *Textual Note* at 4:4.

*son of Jonathan son of Saul* Cf. LXX^LMN, Syr. MT seems to have suffered haplography: *bn* [*yhwntn bn*] *š'wl,* "son of Saul"; but one could argue for the originality of this reading *(bn š'wl* = a member of Saul's family). LXX^B reflects *bn bn š'wl,* "*grand*son of Saul," a scribe's correction.

*cut his toenails* MT *'śh rglyw,* lit. "done his feet," rendered twice by LXX (Thenius) as *etherapeusen tous podas autou,* "cared for his feet," and *ōnychisato,* "done his nails," to which LXX^L adds *tas cheiras autou* = *ydyw,* "his hands"—thus, "cared for his feet or done his fingernails" (cf. JB). See, further, the NOTE.

*safely* MT *bšlwm,* to which LXX^L adds *'l yrwšlm,* "to Jerusalem," which might be original, having fallen out after *bšl(w)m.*

26. *When he came to Jerusalem* Only a few minuscules of LXX support a reading like "And he had come *from* Jerusalem (to meet the king)," favored by Thenius and Wellhausen. See the NOTE on vv. 26–31.

27. *he said* So MT. LXX, Syr.: "Meribbaal said to him."

*to him, 'Saddle* Reading *lw ḥbšh* with LXX (cf. Vulg.) for MT *'ḥbšh,* "I'll saddle." See Thenius, Wellhausen.

28. *did . . . God* MT and LXX diverge in arrangement and sense here. MT has *kml'k h'lhym w'śh hṭwb b'ynyk,* "is like a messenger of God. Then do that which is good in your eyes!" LXX^B reflects *'śh hṭwb b'yny kml'k h'lhym,* lit. "did that which was good in my [!] eyes—like a messenger of God," after which the equivalent of the second sentence of MT has been added recensionally. The LXX version is preferable: As the following verse shows, Meribbaal is saying that his opinion of David was one of gratitude and admiration and thus implying that he would on no account have behaved as Ziba claimed.

29. *From whom, then* Reading *myd my* on the basis of LXX^LMmg *ek cheiros tinos* in preference to MT *mh,* "What (further right [?] do I have . . .)."

*he cried out* We read *wyz'q* with LXX^LMmg *(kai eboēsen).* MT (cf. LXX^B) has *wlz'q(y),* "by crying (that I should cry) further to the king."

30. *said* MT, LXX^BAMN, Syr. add "to him." Omit with LXX^L.

*Why do you talk so much?* That is, *lāmmâ tarbeh dĕbārêkā,* lit. "Why do you multiply your words?" (cf. Job 34:37; Eccles 10:14). For *tarbeh,* which is reflected by LXX^L *plēthyneis,* MT has *tĕdabbēr*—thus, *lmh tdbr 'wd dbryk,* "Why do you keep saying your words?" We omit *'wd,* present in both MT and LXX^L, with Syr. and LXX^N

32. *went along* That is, *wy'br,* which was taken to mean "crossed over" by a scribe who added *hyrdn,* "the Jordan" (Wellhausen), creating an awkward duplication ("the Jordan . . . from/at the Jordan") here. The same thing has happened in v. 37.

*from the Jordan* So LXX$^{L}$ = *myrdn.* It is also possible, though less defensible, to read *byrdn,* "at the Jordan," or *'t hyrdn* (cf. MT$^{MSS}$, LXX$^{B}$), "(to send him [over]) the Jordan," but not *'t byrdn* (MT), an artificial combination of the two (Wellhausen).

33. *while he was staying* MT has *běšîbātô,* evidently intended as equivalent to *běšibtô* (LXX *en tō oikein autou, en tō kathēsthai autou*). The spelling *bšybtw* is less likely to represent an authentic form than to reflect, as recognized by Wellhausen, the influence of *śybtk,* "your old age," which stood in the following verse in the *Vorlage* of LXX and may have appeared marginally in MT.

34. *your old age* So LXX *(to gēras sou)* and OL *(senectutem tuam): śybtk.* MT has *'tk,* "you."

35. *How . . . there* We read *kmh ymym yhyw ly šm* on the basis of LXX$^{L}$ *posai hēmerai esontai moi ekei.* MT is quite different: *kmh ymy šny ḥyy,* "How many are the days of the years of my life?" We can see that (1) *šm* and *šny* and (2) *yhyw* and *ḥyy* correspond graphically, but a full explanation of the divergence and a firm determination of priority elude us.

36. *Do I know* So MT (cf. LXX$^{L}$). LXX$^{AMN}$: "Don't I know" (cf. Syr.).

*taste* LXX: "*still* taste." LXX$^{MN}$ *gnōsetai,* "recognize," is an inner-Greek corruption of *geusetai* (so LXX$^{BAL}$) = *yṭ'm* (MT).

*hear* So LXX$^{L}$. MT: "*still* hear."

*become a burden* So MT *(yhyh . . . lmś').* LXX$^{L}$ (cf. Syr.): "be a burden" *(= yhyh . . . mś').* MT has *'wd,* "still," before *lmś';* omit with LXX$^{L}$.

37. *just a short distance* So MT: *km'ṭ.* LXX$^{L}$ *hoti oligon* suggests *ky m'ṭ,* "Because . . . a short distance."

*will go along* That is, *y'br.* The extant text in all major witnesses reflects *y'br . . . 't hyrdn,* "will cross the Jordan." See the second *Textual Note* at v. 32.

38. *go back* So MT: *yāšob-nā'* (cf. LXX$^{L}$). LXX$^{B}$ *(kathisatō)* and Syr. *(npwš)* have "remain," reading the same consonantal text as *yēšeb-nā'.*

*near* MT *'m.* LXX$^{L}$ *kai taphēsomai en* reflects *w'qbr b-,* "and be buried in."

*Chimham* LXX$^{LMN}$, Syr. add "my son" before or after the name. The name appears in MT as *kimhām,* reflected in LXX$^{B}$ as *chamaam;* see the NOTE. LXX$^{LM}$ *acheinaam* (as if *'ḥyn'm,* "Ahinoam") arises from **(a)chimaam.* Syr. *bmhm* is the result of an inner-Syriac error involving the graphically similar letters *bet* and *kap.*

39. *said the king* LXX$^{L}$ adds "to him."

*as I think best* So LXX$^{LMN}$, Syr. MT: "as *you* think best" in reminiscence of v. 38.

40. *stayed behind* So LXX$^{LMN}$: *histēkei* = *'md.* MT has *'br,* "crossed over"; but David does not cross until v. 41.

[*Barzillai*] The name is supplied in LXX$^{L}$, and it is also necessary in English. But the shorter text of MT is superior.

41. *Chimham* MT *kimhān* (here only), possibly by dissimilation (Freedman).

*was marching along* So LXX$^{BAMN}$ = *'brym.* MT *(kĕtîb): wy'brw,* "and they marched along." MT *(qĕrê): he'ĕbîrû,* "conducted (the king) along" (cf. LXX$^{L}$).

43. *The men of Judah* Cf. LXX$^{L}$. MT: "*All* the men of Judah." Syr.: "All the *house* of Judah."

*the men of Israel* Syr.: "and were saying to the house of Israel." LXX$^{L}$: "the men of Israel and said"; cf. v. 44.

*Has he given . . . a present?* So LXX$^{(L)}$: *ē doma (d)edōken hēmin* (omitted by

LXX$^{BAMN}$) *ē arsin ēren hēmin* = *'m mtn ntn (lnw) 'm mś't nś' lnw.* As Wellhausen concluded, the text of LXX might instead reflect a double translation of MT *'m nś't nś' lnw,* but I assume that MT has lost *mtn ntn lnw 'm* by haplography (homoioarkton); the change from *mś't* to *nś't* in MT is secondary.

44. *And furthermore . . . firstborn!* That is, *wgm bkwr 'ny mmk,* lit. "And also firstborn am I, rather than you!" So LXX: *kai prōtotokos egō ē su;* OL: *et primogenitus ego sum quam tu.* In MT this was corrupted to *wgm bdwd 'ny mmk,* "And also *in David* I am more than you!" a translation of which has been added recensionally to the text of LXX. The mutilation of *bkwr* to *bdwd,* understandable graphically, was prompted by the slogan in 20:1.

*And why . . . what we said* MT has *wl' hyh dbry r'šwn ly,* lit. "And my word was not first to me." This is usually taken to mean "Wasn't my word first . . . ?" that is, "Didn't I speak first (about bringing the king back)?" But there is no textual support for emending *wl'* to *hl'* (Smith, etc.), and in any case *ly* is superfluous to such an interpretation. The clause can be taken as continuing the force of the preceding *wmdw'*: "So why have you slighted us, and (why) was my word not first . . . ?" But the result is contrary to fact—the Israelites *were* first to speak about bringing David back (vv. 10–11)—and *ly* remains unexplained. The solution lies in the text of LXX$^{BAMN}$, which reflects not *wl' hyh* (LXX$^{L}$ *kai ouk egeneto*) but *wl' nḥšb (kai ouk elogisthē).* With this reading in place the clause can be taken as a continuation of the previous question ("So why . . . ?"), and the purpose of *ly* becomes clear. Read *wl' nḥšb dbry r'šwn ly,* lit. "And (why) was my word not reckoned to me as prior" (to which LXX$^{BMN}$ add *tou iouda* = *myhwdh,* "[prior] to Judah"), that is, "And why was I not given priority because of what I said . . . ?"

**20** 1. *his tent* So MT, LXX$^{L}$. LXX$^{BAMN}$: "your tent."

2. *all Israel* So LXX$^{BL}$. MT: "all *the men of* Israel." Syr.: "all the *sons* of Israel."

3. *the ten concubines* LXX: "*his* ten concubines." Cf. the *Textual Note* at 16:13.

*the house* LXX$^{L}$: "*his* house."

*widows while alive* Cf. LXX: *chērai zōsai* = *'almānôt ḥayyôt* (Wellhausen, Budde); see the NOTE. MT has *'almānût ḥayyût,* "the widowhood of life" (?). Targ. *'rmln db'lhwn qyym,* "widows of their living husband," shows an interpretation of the text similar to the one we have adopted.

## NOTES

19 9. *each man to his tent.* This part of the story line is now resumed from the end of 18:17, where we were told that "all Israel," i.e., Abishalom's army, "fled each man to his tent." This expression, "each man to his tent," is a cliché referring specifically to the demobilization of an army: Judg 7:8; 20:8; I Sam 4:10; 13:2; II Sam 18:17; 19:9; 20:1 (cf. II Chron 10:16),22; II Kings 14:12 = II Chron 25:22. In some of these passages (I Sam 4:10; II Sam 18:17; 19:9; II Kings 14:12 = II Chron 25:22) it refers more specifically to the flight home of a defeated army.

10. *the staff-bearers of Israel.* See the *Textual Note* at 7:7, where we adopt the

suggestion of Reid (1975) to revocalize *šibṭê yiśrā'ēl*, "the tribes of Israel," as *šōbĕṭê yiśrā'ēl*, "the staff-bearers of Israel." See also 5:1, where "the staff-bearers of Israel" stand in the position of "the elders of Israel" in 5:3 (Reid 1975:20). The change is probably to be made in the present passage, too, though Reid does not cite it. The army is urging the ruling elders of Israel, not the tribes as a whole, to reconsider their position towards David.

12–14. Judah, where the revolt began (15:10) and from which its leadership was principally drawn (Ahithophel, Amasa, Abishalom himself), evidently was slower than Israel in reclaiming David as its king. David's message is directed at this problem. Because he is himself a Judahite, he says, the elders of Judah—"my bone and my flesh" —should not lag behind the staff-bearers of Israel in renewing his kingship. As a conciliatory gesture—obviously aimed at those who had supported Abishalom—he states his intention to appoint Amasa, Abishalom's chief general (17:25), in place of Joab, Abishalom's executioner, as commander of his army. On Amasa's parentage and position in Judah, see the NOTES at 17:25.

16. *Gilgal.* An important Benjaminite shrine and place of sacrifice near Jericho and the Jordan; the modern site is unknown. Cf. Map 7.

17–31. This material concerns David's relationship with the house of Saul. Cook (1899/1900:169) regarded it as secondary, part of the originally independent document he supposed to have consisted of parts of chaps. 9, 16, and 19 (cf. the COMMENT on § XIX and the NOTE at 16:1–14). Similarly, Langlamet (1976b:355–56; 1979–81) considers most of this material editorial expansion of the original story of the revolt. Specifically, he lists as secondary 19:17–40,41ab$\alpha\gamma$, and 42b$\delta$ (see also the NOTE at 20:3) and argues for an original connection between 19:16 and 19:41b$\beta$.

17. *Shimei.* See 16:5–13, the events of which are alluded to by Shimei in v. 20 below.

18. *a thousand men from Benjamin.* Unless the meaning is "a thousand of men," i.e., an *'elep*-contingent (see the NOTE at 6:1), this is probably an exaggeration. As elsewhere, the narrator is eager to emphasize the loyalty of former followers of Saul to David (cf. the COMMENT on § XXX).

*Ziba.* See 16:1–4 and, for background, 9:2–11.

*waded through the Jordan.* Hebrew *wayṣallĕḥû hayyardēn*, the meaning of which can be clarified by reference to Aramaic *ṣallēḥ*, "cleave, split; penetrate, pass through." The sense here is either that Ziba's party actually split the Jordan, i.e., dammed it up so David could cross dryshod, or, more likely, that they waded in and conveyed the royal party across on their shoulders.

21. *first of all the house of Joseph.* Unless this can be read "before all the house of Joseph" (de Vaux 1978:643), which is unlikely, we are to think of "the house of Joseph" in the most general sense, a reference to all the northern tribes in contrast to "the house of Judah" (2:7,10,11); cf. Josh 18:5. In a stricter sense Shimei, a Benjaminite, was not of the house of Joseph (Josh 17:17; etc.).

22–23. Veijola (1975:34) regards these verses as secondary, deriving from the hand of the Deuteronomistic historian. They provide a rationale for Solomon's execution of Shimei (cf. I Kings 2:8–9,44–46), which was lacking in the original text of the present passage as Veijola conceives it (19:19b–21 + 24), by implying that David might have put Shimei to death on some other day. Rost (1926:101–2), though he considered the verses an original part of the succession narrative, also understood them to look forward to Solomon's execution of Shimei. But see Conroy (1978:103), who argues that within the story of Abishalom's revolt the case of Shimei is closed in this passage. I agree with Conroy. While there is no doubt that the author of I Kings 1–2 found support for Solomon's treatment of Shimei in the Shimei subplot of the story of Abishalom's revolt (II Sam 16:5–13; 19:17,19b–24), it is also clear that the narrator of the original story wanted to stress David's leniency and generosity towards the Benjaminite agitator. Nor would it be necessary for an editorial hand to insert vv. 22–23 in order to point out the culpability of what Shimei did—which is not in doubt—or to illustrate further the ruthlessness of the sons of Zeruiah.

22. *Abishai.* Abishai's role is reminiscent of the part he played in 16:9ff.

*he cursed Yahweh's anointed.* On the sacrosanct character of the man anointed king at Yahweh's behest, see 1:14 as well as I Sam 26:9; 24:6.

23. *What do you . . . have against me . . . ?* Hebrew *mah-lî wĕlākem,* on which see the NOTE at 16:10. David's point is that an execution on the day of his coronation would be wrong (see the following NOTE) and, therefore, that Abishai's proposal actually imperils him.

*Shall anyone be put to death . . . today?* This passage, taken together with I Sam 11:13–15, suggests that a coronation was accompanied by a general amnesty. David becomes king today, albeit for the second time, and no one is to be executed (cf. Schulz; Macholz 1972:170; Mettinger 1976:119). The granting of a coronation day amnesty, if there was such a practice, may have had less to do with the crowning of the new king than the passing of the old king, under whom the criminals were condemned (cf. Num 35:25,28; Josh 20:6 [Macholz 1972:170 n. 18]).

25. *cut his toenails.* Hebrew *ʿāśâ raglāyw,* lit. "done his feet." The interpretation of this as "washed his feet" is criticized by Joüon (1928:314), who proposes to change *raglāyw,* "his feet," to *rōʾšô,* "his head," in the sense of *chevelure* (Lev 10:6; etc.), comparing (n. 2) the collocation of clothes, hair, and mustache in Lev 13:45. Weill (1929:212) thinks the text of Josephus (*Ant.* 7.267) also favors reading *rōʾšô.* Most modern English translations, however, have retained *raglāyw* and rendered the expression "dressed his feet" or something similar, following AV (RSV, NEB; cf. JB). Our interpretation (cf. NJV, "pared his toenails") is that made by the rabbis (Yebamot 48a) on the basis of Deut 21:12, where *ʿāśâ* is used of the nails and an action mentioned in regard to the head is cutting the hair. According to Yebamot 103a, on the other hand, v. 25 is euphemistic.

26–31. David will not reach Jerusalem until 20:2–3, and the text does not say, "When he (Meribbaal) came *from* Jerusalem" (cf. NJV). Accordingly, some critics (Budde, Caspari, Hertzberg) regard *yrwšlm,* "(to) Jerusalem," as secondary or misplaced. Conroy (1978:98 n. 11) thinks *yrwšlm* can mean "from Jerusalem" as it stands. I doubt this. In any case, the syntax—*wayhî kî bāʾ yĕrûšāla(y)im,* "When he came to Jerusalem" (not *wayyābōʾ yĕrûšālayim,* "And he came to/from Jerusalem")—suggests that the conversation is to be thought of as taking place in the future. Verses 26–31, in other words, record a conversation that took place sometime after the events of the immediate context, when Meribbaal returned to (!) Jerusalem. These words are placed here because they provide the logical resolution of the issues raised by the mention of Meribbaal's presence among the reception party.

27. *let me down.* Hebrew *rimmānî,* which, as noted by Thenius, does not mean

"deceived me" in this context. Instead it retains its more radical meaning suggesting harm resulting from the failure of something or someone relied upon. As in Lam 1:19, it has the sense "left me in the lurch" (Thenius).

*lame.* See 4:4; 9:3,13.

28. *like an envoy of God.* Routine flattery. See the NOTE at 14:17.

29. *my father's house.* The house of Saul, Meribbaal's grandfather (4:4; 9:3).

*fiends of hell.* Hebrew *'anšê-māwet,* lit. "men of death" (cf. I Kings 2:26). See the NOTE at 12:5.

*those who eat at your table.* See the NOTE at 9:7.

30. *I have spoken.* Hebrew *'āmartî,* the force of which is "I (hereby) declare" (GK[2] §106i). Is David's decision "Solomonic," as Hertzberg describes it, or is it simply equivocal? It is difficult, perhaps impossible (cf. Ackroyd), to decide whether Ziba was lying in 16:1–14 or Meribbaal is lying here. David's verdict suggests that he at least does not know. It may be that Meribbaal's response to the king's decision in v. 31 shows that he is the truthful one (cf. I Kings 3:26–27). Perhaps we should assume that David is persuaded of Meribbaal's sincerity but still moved by Ziba's recent service (vv. 18–19).

32. *Barzillai.* See 17:27.

36. *Do I know right from wrong?* Knowledge of right and wrong, i.e., moral discernment, is what distinguishes animals and children from adult human beings and gods, as the Eden myth shows. By referring to his loss of this knowledge Barzillai is saying he has become like a child in his old age (cf. Deut 1:39; Isa 7:15,16). But it is not moral discernment he has lost. It is something else accompanying the transition from childhood to adulthood, viz. sexual potency; cf. Gen 3:7, where sexual awareness comes with the knowledge of right and wrong, or Gilgamesh 1.4,29,34 (*ANET*[3], p. 75), where wisdom and understanding come with sexual experience. Barzillai's rhetorical question, in other words, is a polite way of saying that he has outgrown his sexual powers and that because of this—and the loss of his other sources of pleasure—he could not expect to enjoy himself at court.

38. *Chimham.* This odd name, *kimhām,* has been explained by Noth (1928:25 and n. 5) by reference to Arabic *kamiha,* "change complexion, become pale" (cf. Ps 63:2 [63:1]?), as meaning "of pale complexion." But who is this "Paleface"? Is he Barzillai's son, as many Greek and Syriac MSS assert (cf. the *Textual Note*)? If so, he is presumably among the sons of Barzillai commended to Solomon by David on his deathbed in I Kings 2:26.

42. The complaint of the Israelite army is that it is the Judahite army that has claimed the honor of first receiving the king (vv. 15–16). The reader knows this is because of the hesitation of the Israelites (v. 11a) and David's overture to the Judahites (vv. 11b–14).

43–44. The details of the quarrel reflect differing attitudes towards King David. The men of Judah speak of the king as a particular individual, a man from Judah who is "closely related" to them (cf. v. 13). The men of Israel, on the other hand, speak of the king as the king, the particular man in office at present being of no concern to them. Thus they claim a greater interest in the king—ten shares (for the ten northern tribes) to Judah's one—and rights of seniority as "firstborn," a reference to the time before the incorporation of Judah into "all Israel" (see Flanagan 1975).

*food . . . a gift . . . a present.* The men of Judah say they have received no special favors that the men of Israel should resent. Or are they insisting they were not bribed?

44. *what we said.* That is, to the staff-bearers of Israel; see vv. 10–11.

**20** 1. *a scoundrel.* Hebrew *'š bĕlîya'al;* see the NOTE on "You bloodstained fiend of hell!" at 16:7.

*the shofar.* The shofar was also used to signal Abishalom's rebellion (15:10) and Saul's revolt against the Philistines (I Sam 13:3). Cf. the NOTE at 6:15.

Sheba's slogan, "no share in David and no estate in the son of Jesse," will be taken up again at the time of the schism after the death of Solomon. See I Kings 12:16.

*Every man to his tent.* See the NOTE at 19:9 above.

3. Langlamet (1976b:356; 1977), following Cook (1899/1900:167,169,176) in regarding the concubine theme as secondary to the original story of Abishalom's revolt, would strike this verse along with 15:16b–17a and 16:21–22.

*the ten concubines.* See 15:16. Now that these women have been illegally claimed by Abishalom (16:21–22), they must be put away.

*widows while alive.* We follow Wellhausen in taking "living widows" (see the *Textual Note*) to mean "widows of living men"—in this case widows of the living man David. The other possibility, also noted by Wellhausen, is that "living widows" means "vigorous widows," i.e., "widows in the prime of life" (NEB).

## COMMENT

The account of David's return journey to Jerusalem has two aspects, which coexist with some tension. This is, on the one hand, the record of a series of meetings reminiscent of the meetings of the outward journey (§ XXVIII). The meetings on David's flight raised questions and concerns, inviting the audience to look ahead with some anxiety to the events to come. The meetings of David's return offer reassurance, representing the resolution of many of the earlier concerns, such as the defection of Meribbaal and the threats of Shimei. In one sense, then, the present section contains a spirit of resolution. At the same time, however, there is a spirit of renewed conflict here. The circumstances and events of the return of the king precipitate an outbreak of sectional hostility that will have to be resolved before the kingdom can finally be regarded as secure.

The first of the meetings is with Shimei. The meeting with Shimei on David's flight was the last in that series (16:5–13), taking place after David had crossed the summit of the Mount of Olives, where the other meetings occurred, and reached the village of Bahurim, Shimei's home. At that time Shimei grievously cursed David. Now, however, he is first to welcome the king home, declaring himself at fault for his prior behavior. He receives a royal pardon from David. Here, as elsewhere, the narrator stresses David's leniency and generosity towards the former followers of the house of Saul and the reciprocal loyalty they feel for David. "A thousand men from Benjamin" came to receive David, we are told (19:18), and David, for his part, granted Shimei a full pardon. According to the author of I Kings 1–2, who was eager to offer justification for the bloodbath that accompanied Solomon's accession, David later demanded that Shimei should be punished (I Kings 2:8–9); but there is no hint in the story of Abishalom's revolt that the decision rendered here is not final (cf. the NOTE at 19:22–23).

The next meeting is with Meribbaal. As explained in the NOTE, the conversation reported in 19:26–31 seems to have taken place later in Jerusalem. We are shown, nevertheless, that despite his lameness Meribbaal came to the Jordan, disheveled and unkempt like a man whose servant has "let him down" (19:27) or a loyal subject grieving for his exiled sovereign. Meribbaal's behavior seems to convince David that Ziba's earlier accusations (16:3) were false. Ziba himself, however, has rallied his entire family, hurried to the Jordan, and waded across to David with his sons and servants, leaving the rest of the reception party behind (19:18b–19a). He is most eager to be of help and to ingratiate himself with the king. David settles this contest of obsequiousness by declaring it a draw.

The undercurrent of conflict that qualifies the optimistic tone of these meetings arises from sectional jealousy. As explained in the COMMENT on § XXVII, there seems to have been both northern and southern support for Abishalom's rebellion. Now that David is returning, however, there is a rivalry between Israel and Judah for priority in bringing him back. At first the Israelites vacillate (19:9–11), prompting David, who may have wondered if anyone would welcome him, to appeal directly to Judah. The appeal is made on the basis of kinship (19:13), and the desired result is achieved, "all the men of Judah" (19:15) endorsing the king's return with enthusiasm.

David must have concluded later, however, that the appeal to his kinship with the Judahites was a mistake, for it seems to have promoted the sectional conflict that ensued. The sight of Judah conducting David towards Jerusalem provokes Israel, somewhat belatedly, to think of protecting its interests in the king. A quarrel breaks out in the two armies, with Judah claiming priority of place because David is a kinsman (19:43) and Israel claiming priority because he is king of Israel, of which the northern tribes represent the older and larger part (19:44). The result is, finally, the defection of the Israelite army under the leadership of a dissident from the Ephraimite hills (20:21) named Sheba.

Despite the apparent movement of the narrative towards a reentry of Jerusalem and a resolution of conflict, therefore, this section ends amid turmoil and uncertainty. Sheba's revolt is potentially more disastrous even than Abishalom's (cf. 20:6). How this new problem is resolved is the subject of the section that follows.

# XXXIII. SHEBA'S REVOLT
## (20:4–22)

20 [4]The king said to Amasa, "Call up the men of Judah for me in three
days; then report here." [5]So Amasa went to call up Judah, but he was
late for the appointment that had been made for him. [6]So David said
to Abishai, "Now Sheba son of Bichri is going to cause us more trouble
than Abishalom did. Now then, take your master's servants with you
and chase after him. He might find himself some walled cities and cast
a shadow over our eyes." [7]So Abishai called out after him Joab, the
Cherethites and Pelethites, and all the warriors, and they marched out
of Jerusalem in pursuit of Sheba son of Bichri.

### *The Assassination of Amasa*

[8]They were near the big rock that is in Gibeon, and Amasa was
coming towards them. Joab was dressed in his tunic, and over it he was
girded with a sword strapped to his hip in its sheath; but it slipped out
and fell. [9]"Are you well, brother?" [he] said to Amasa, grasping
Amasa's beard with his right hand to kiss him. [10]Amasa was not on
guard against the sword that was in Joab's hand. He struck him with
it in the belly, so that his entrails spilled out on the ground; and though
he did not strike him a second time, he died.

Then Joab with his brother Abishai went on in pursuit of Sheba son
of Bichri, [11]but one of Joab's soldiers stayed behind with [Amasa] and
said, "Whoever favors Joab and whoever is on David's side, after Joab!"
[12]But Amasa was weltering in gore in the middle of the highway, and
the man saw that the entire army stopped. So he moved Amasa off the
highway into the field and covered him with a blanket, for he could see
that anyone who came upon him would stop. [13]When he had removed
him from the highway, all the men went on by after Joab in pursuit of
Sheba son of Bichri.

### *The Siege of Abel of Beth-maacah*

[14][Sheba] passed through all the tribes of Israel to Abel of Beth-
maacah, and all the Bichrites assembled and entered [the city] behind

him. [15]The entire army that was with Joab came and laid siege to him
in Abel of Beth-maacah. Intending to pull down the wall, they cast up
a siege-mound against the city, so that it stood against the bulwark.
[16]Then a wise woman called from the wall. "Listen! Listen!" she said.
"Tell Joab to come closer so that I can speak to him!" [17]Then when he
had drawn near to her, [she] said, "Are you Joab?"
"I am," he said.
"Listen to what your maidservant has to say!" she said.
"I'm listening," he said.
[18]"In the past," she said, "they had a saying, 'Let them inquire in
Abel and Dan whether [19]that which the architects of Israel ordained has
been carried out!' You're trying to destroy one of Israel's mother cities!
Why should you afflict Yahweh's estate?"
[20]"I'll be damned if I'm going to afflict anything or destroy anything!"
said Joab in reply. [21]"It's not like that. A man from the Ephraimite
highlands, Sheba son of Bichri, raised his hand against King David.
Give us him—by himself—and we'll go away from the city."
So the woman told Joab, "His head will be thrown to you over the
wall." [22]Then she spoke wisely to the entire city, and they cut off Sheba
son of Bichri's head and threw it to Joab. He blew the shofar, and [the
army] dispersed from him, each man to his tent. Joab himself returned
to the king in Jerusalem.

## *TEXTUAL NOTES*

20 6. *Abishai* Syr. (cf. Josephus, *Ant.* 7.281) has "Joab," which Wellhausen considered original.

*Now then* So $\mathrm{LXX}^{AL}$ = *w'th*. MT has a variant of this, viz. *'th*, "You." Both variants are reflected in the conflate text of $\mathrm{LXX}^{B}$.

*take . . . with you* Reading *qḥ 'tk* with $\mathrm{LXX}^{BLMN}$, Syr. In MT *'tk* has been lost before the following *'t*.

*He might find* Emending *pn mṣ'* to *pn ymṣ'* ($\mathrm{GK}^2$ §107q, n. 3). Cf. Driver.

*and cast a shadow over* MT has *wĕhiṣṣîl*, "and snatch away," rendered *wnḥṭṭ*, "and tear away," by Syr. Ewald (1878:193 n. 1) was the first to recognize that $\mathrm{LXX}^{B}$ *kai skiasei*, "and shade, cover," understands the verb as denominative from *ṣēl*, "shadow." We follow LXX, therefore, in reading *wĕhēṣēl*. See also (S. R.) Driver's discussion of alternative interpretations (to which add G. R. Driver 1962).

7. *Abishai called out after him Joab* No single witness is entirely acceptable, yet, oddly enough, a survey of them suggests several acceptable readings. MT has *wyṣ'w*

*'ḥryw 'nšy yw'b,* "There went forth after him (viz. Abishai) the men of Joab," etc. LXX^B reflects *wyṣ' 'ḥryw w'nšy yw'b,* "He (viz. Abishai) went forth after him (viz. Sheba) along with the men of Joab," etc., the reading adopted by Driver. But we require a reference to Joab himself at this point, and it is likely that *'nšy,* "the men of," is a corruption of *'bšy,* "Abishai." LXX^L reflects *wyṣ'q (kai parēngeilen;* cf. I Sam 10:17) *'ḥry 'bšy 't h'm wyw'b,* "He (viz. David) called out after Abishai the army, including Joab," etc. With a glance at this reading Smith, Budde, and many others would restore *wyṣ'w 'ḥry 'bšy yw'b,* "There went forth after Abishai Joab," etc., a plausible solution. Nevertheless, the verb of LXX^L, *wyṣ'q,* is clearly preferable to *wyṣ'w,* especially in view of the occurrence of *wyṣ'w* later in the verse We cannot adopt the entire reading of LXX^L, however, for *'t h'm,* "the army," is surely secondary, and it seems unlikely that David would do the mustering. Read, therefore, *wyṣ'q 'ḥryw 'bšy ('t) yw'b.*

*the Cherethites and Pelethites* LXX^L has lost "the Cherethites" and seems to understand *hplty (phelti)* as *palṭî,* "Palti(el)" (cf. I Sam 25:44 and II Sam 3:15); but Paltiel, if involved at all, is probably carrying a firebrand at Sheba's right hand. The corruption is probably inner-Greek.

*and they marched out* Omitted by LXX^L.

8. *in Gibeon* So MT: *bgb'wn.* LXX^L *'l hgb'h,* "upon the hill."

*Joab was dressed . . . and fell* MT has *wyw'b ḥgwr mdw lbšw w'lyw (kĕtîb: w'lw) ḥgwr ḥrb mṣmdt 'l mtnyw bt'rh whw' yṣ' wtpl,* "And Joab was girded in his tunic—his clothing—and over it the belt of a sword strapped on his hip in its sheath. And when he went forth, it fell." The combination *mdw lbšw,* "his tunic, his clothing," is suspicious, and reading **medew* or the like for *middô*—thus, "the tunic of his clothing" (cf. LXX)—is little better. Note also the repetition of *ḥgwr,* especially striking if we read the second as *ḥāgûr,* "was girded," with LXX instead of MT *ḥăgôr,* "the belt of." Budde would strike the second *ḥgwr,* but it is the first that is wrong: One is dressed *(lbš)* in a tunic *(mdh;* cf Driver and I Sam 17.38) and girded *(ḥgr)* with a sword. Moreover, LXX^L *(periekeito)* and OL *(indutus erat)* seem to read *lbwš* for *ḥgwr* in the first clause. Thus we read *wyw'b lbwš mdw.* For *w'lyw,* "and over it," OL (cf. LXX^L) reflects *'lyw w-,* "upon him, and"; we follow MT here. For *whw' yṣ',* "and he went forth," read *why' yṣ'h,* "but it (the sword) came out" (cf. LXX^B, OL). Thus we follow Josephus' understanding of the passage: "He (Joab) went to meet him (Amasa), Joab being girded with a sword and dressed in a tunic. As Amasa was coming forward to greet him, he artfully made the sword fall, as if of its own accord, out of the sheath. Picking it up from the ground as he grasped Amasa by the beard with his other hand as if to kiss him, he killed him with an unforeseen thrust to the belly" (*Ant.* 7.284). It is strange, however, that we have nothing in the biblical text to explain how the fallen sword got from the ground to Joab's hand, where it turns up in v. 10. Klostermann's two-sword interpretation has received approval from a number of critics: *wyw'b ḥrb bydw mtḥt lbwšw* (cf. Judg 3:16) *w'lyw ḥgwr ḥrb . . . ,* "And as for Joab, a sword was in his hand under his clothes, and upon him (outside) he was girded with a sword," etc.; but the textual evidence will hardly support this. In Syr. the problem does not exist: The sword is strapped on Joab's hip "like a dagger" (*'yk glb'* = *kt'r* [?] for *bt'rh,* "in its sheath"), and "as he went forth, his hand fell over his sword" (as if, *whw' yṣ' wtpl ydw 'l ḥrbw*), i.e., concealing it. This is tempting; but how is the loss of *ydw 'l ḥrbw* to be explained?

10. *against the sword* That is, *mḥrb* (cf. LXX^L, Syr.). MT: *bḥrb*, "*by reason of* the sword" (BDB).

*in the belly* The preposition was probably *'l* (LXX^L *epi*), as in 4QSam^a: *'l hḥmš*. MT has *'l*. Cf. 3:27.

*spilled out* With Joüon (1928:315) we read *wayyiššāpěkû* (cf. LXX^B, Syr.) in place of MT *wayyišpōk* ("and he [Joab] spilled his [Amasa's] entrails out on the ground").

11. *with [Amasa]* We read *'lyw* with MT. LXX^L and OL make the name explicit.

*Whoever . . . and whoever* That is, *my 'šr . . . wmy* (cf. LXX), for which MT has *my 'šr . . . wmy 'šr*. 4QSam^a: *my ['šr] ḥpṣ byw'b wmy ld[wyd]*.

12. *gore* LXX^L: "*his* gore."

13. *him* LXX^L: "Amasa."

*the men* So MT. LXX^BAMN: "the men *of Israel*." LXX^L: "the army."

14. *to Abel of Beth-maacah* As in v. 15 (MT), *'blh byt m'kh*. Here MT has "to Abel *and* Beth-maacah." LXX^B: "to Abel *and to* Beth-maacah." LXX^L: "*and* Abel *and* Beth-maacah."

*and all the Bichrites* Reading *wkl hbkrym* with LXX^B *kai pantes en charrei* in preference to MT *wkl hbrym*, "and all the *Berites* (?)," LXX^L *kai pasai hai poleis* = *wkl h'rym*, "and all the *cities*," and Vulg. *omnesque viri electi* = *wkl hbḥrym*, "and all the *picked warriors*."

*assembled* Reading *nqhlw* with LXX *exenklēsiasthēsan* in preference to MT *(qěrê) wyqhlw*, "and they assembled."

*behind him* Preceded in MT by *'p*, on which see Driver and, for bibliography, Conroy 1978:118 n. 15.

15. *Intending* MT has *mštyḥm*, apparently "causing destruction," but ingeniously explained by Ewald (1878:195 n. 1) as a denominative from *šaḥat*, "pit"—thus, "digging a pit." LXX^L *enenooun* and Targ. *mt'štyn*, however, point to *mḥšbym*, tentatively adopted here (cf. Syr., Vulg.).

*against the city* The preposition is *'l* (LXX^L *epi*), not *'l* (MT).

16. *the wall* So LXX^B, Syr. MT, LXX^L: "the city."

*to come . . . to him* That is, *lqrb . . . 'lyw* (cf. LXX^L), treated as direct discourse in MT: *qrb . . . 'lyk*, "Come . . . to you!"

17. *when he had drawn near* So MT: *wayyiqrab*. LXX^L: "when *Joab* had drawn near." LXX^B: "when someone had brought (him) near" *(kai prosēngisen = wayyaqrēb)*.

*she said* So LXX^L. MT: "she said *to him*."

"*I'm listening*" LXX^L: "I'm listening. Speak!"

*he said* So MT, LXX^L. LXX^B: "*Joab* said."

18. *she said* Followed in MT by *l'mr*. Omit with LXX^L.

*they had a saying* That is, *dbr* (= *dābār*) *ydbrw*, lit. "they used to say a saying"; cf. LXX. In MT *dbr* is understood as an infinitive absolute *(dabbēr)*.

*in Abel* MT *b'bl*, for which Syr. has *bnby'*, "of the prophet."

18–19. *and Dan . . . carried out* MT has *wkn htmw* (= *hētammû*) *'nky šlmy 'mwny yśr'l*, "and that way they reached a conclusion. I am one of (?) the peaceful ones of the trusted ones of Israel." The original reading of LXX, into which the equivalent of MT's reading has been recensionally introduced in LXX^BA (cf. Barthélemy 1963: 72,132–33), was *kai en dan ei exelipon* (LXX^L *exel[e]ipen*) *ha ethento hoi pistoi tou is-*

*raēl* = *wbdn htmw* (= *hătammû*) *'šr śmw 'mwny yśr'l,* "and in Dan whether that which the trusted ones of Israel ordained has been carried out." Most critics, following the lead of Ewald (1878:195 n. 2), adopt the reading of LXX in preference to the obviously troubled text of MT. Recently, however, Barthélemy (1980:31–33) has mounted a vigorous defense of MT, arguing that LXX represents either a simplifying translation of a difficult Hebrew text or a translation of a simplified Hebrew text. But the awkwardness of MT remains. Can *hētammû* stand as an intransitive verb? Can the association of *'ănōkî* with a plural construct sequence refer collectively to the people of Abel, as Barthélemy implies? Nor are his objections to the text of LXX convincing. It is true, as he says, that *'ămûnê yiśrā'ēl,* "the trusted ones of Israel" (Pss 12:2 [12:1]; 31:24 [31:23]), ought to be those who obey the laws, not those who ordain them; but read *'ămônê yiśrā'ēl,* "*the architects* of Israel" (see the NOTE). The variation of *śmw* and *šlmy* (< **šlmw*), which also troubles Barthélemy, is to be explained by reference to the other examples of the interchange of *śym* and *šlm* cited by Talmon (1975:347; cf. the first *Textual Note* at 2:20 in *I Samuel*). Our translation assumes that LXX reflects the original text. Our interpretation is explained in the NOTES.

20. *I'll be damned* That is, *ḥlylh ly* (cf. $LXX^{LMN}$, OL, Syr.). MT repeats *ḥlylh* (dittography).

21. *Sheba son of Bichri* MT adds *šmw,* "(is) his name." Omit with $LXX^{L}$.

*over the wall* So MT: *b'd hḥwmh.* $LXX^{L}$ = *m'l (apo) hḥwmh,* "*from* the wall."

22. *Then she spoke . . . to the entire city* Reading *wtdbr 'l kl h'yr* with LXX *kai elalēsen pros pasan tēn polin,* to which a translation of MT's text—*wtbw' h'šh 'l kl h'm,* "Then the woman went to all the people"—has been added recensionally. Wellhausen compares the interchange of *wt'mr* and *wtb'* in 14:4.

*He blew* $LXX^{L}$: "*Joab* blew."

[*the army*] Explicit in $LXX^{L}$.

*from him* MT has *m'l h'yr,* "from the city." In $LXX^{BA}$ a rendering of this was added recensionally to *ep' autou,* the OG reading. MT is reminiscent of v. 21. Read *mmnw.*

## NOTES

20 7. *the Cherethites and Pelethites.* See 8:18; 15:18.

8–13. Würthwein (1974:45–46) and Langlamet (1976b:356; cf. Cook 1899/1900: 167–68) consider the material about Amasa's assassination (including 17:25; 19:14; 20:4–5) to be secondary, part of the pro-David/anti-Joab redaction they believe the story to have undergone. At the end of v. 13 Langlamet notes a "reprise" of the end of v. 7.

8. *the big rock . . . in Gideon.* Pritchard (1960:6) has suggested that this "big rock" might be the "big high place" at Gibeon (Map 8) where Solomon offers sacrifices in I Kings 3:4. Blenkinsopp (1972:7,63) tentatively identifies it with the large stone set up as an altar by Saul after the battle of Michmash Pass (I Sam 14:33–35).

14. *Abel of Beth-maacah.* The site, Tell Abil, lies ca. twelve miles north of Lake

Huleh, just east of Tell Dan (v. 18); see Map 8. This may have been the Abel *('u-bi-ra)* conquered by Thutmosis III in the fifteenth century B.C. (Albright 1934:39 [VI.B.1]). It was certainly the "Abilakka" conquered by Tiglath-pileser III in the eighth century B.C. (*ANET*³, p. 253; cf. I Kings 15:29). It was also taken by Ben-hadad I of Damascus during the reign of Baasha early in the ninth century B.C. (I Kings 15:20 = II Chron 16:4). The regional or clan designation Beth-maacah ("the house of Maacah") is interesting. Did Abel have a traditional connection with the kingdom of Maacah (10:6)?

*all the Bichrites.* That is, all the fellow clansmen of Sheba *son of Bichri.*

16. *a wise woman.* See the NOTE at 14:2. The woman has been chosen to represent the people of Abel in the parley by reason of her skills of speech and persuasion.

18. *Let them inquire.* The beginning of the old saying, *šā'ōl yěšā'ělû*, is grammatically strange. There are a few parallels for a *Pi'el* verb strengthened by a *Qal* infinitive absolute (see Driver), but the *Pi'el* of *š'l* with this meaning is otherwise unattested.

*in Abel and Dan.* Adjacent cities at the northern extreme of Israel proper (cf. the NOTE at v. 14 above). The woman defends Abel as a model city. Here and in Dan, she says, one could expect to find the intentions of the founding fathers of Israel cherished and faithfully performed. Why, then, would Joab harm Abel?

19. *the architects of Israel.* I take *'ămōnê* (MT *'ěmûnê*) *yiśrā'ēl* to be the original shapers of Israel, the founding fathers. (Compare *'āmôn*, "architect," in Prov 8:30, where Wisdom is personified as a master craftsman accompanying God at the time of the construction of the world, and note Biblical Hebrew *'ommān*, "master craftsman," in Cant 7:2 and Aramaic *'mn*, "architect, craftsman.") The reference is not to some specific group, such as the patriarchs, but to the ancient worthies in general from whom Israelite society was inherited.

*one of Israel's mother cities.* Lit. "a city and a mother in Israel." For Phoenician *'m*, "mother (city), metropolis," see Tomback 1978:22–23. Malamat (1979) connects Hebrew *'ummâ*, a tribal designation (Gen 25:16; Num 25:15), Ugaritic *'umt*, a kinship term, and Old Babylonian *ummatum*, a military unit, with *'ēm*, "mother"; all originally referred to the "mother unit of a tribe." He understands the "city and mother" of our passage not as mother city but as "city and family/clan."

*afflict.* For this meaning of Hebrew *bāla'* see the NOTE at 17:16.

20. *A man from the Ephraimite highlands.* For the rabbinic conceit that Sheba, Micah, a man who kept his own Levite in his house in the Ephraimite hills (Judges 17–18), and Nebat, the Ephraimite father of Jeroboam (I Kings 11:26), were one and the same man, see Sanhedrin 101a.

## COMMENT

"Revolt" may be too strong a term for this incident. We were told in 20:2 that "all Israel" followed Sheba when he abandoned David's entourage at the Jordan. But the present section shows that no organized rebellion emerged from the withdrawal of the Israelite forces. We have the impression that Sheba "passed through all the tribes of Israel" (v. 14) more or less alone, finding support only among Bichrites, members of his own clan. "All Israel" seems to have gone home. The city of Abel opened its gates to the rebel, but the conclusion of the story suggests that he found no deep sympathy there.

Most historians of Israel have concluded that Sheba's expression of dissent was significant not because it provoked a revolt of serious proportions but because it exposed a dangerous weakness in the structure of the kingdom. As Bright says (1972:205), it revealed the fragility of the union David had achieved. Thus there was reason for David's fear that Sheba might "cause us more trouble than Abishalom did" (v. 6): Whereas Abishalom's revolt threatened the king, Sheba's threatened the kingdom itself. The Sheba incident showed that the allegiance of the northern tribes to the house of David had become tenuous. David had won the loyalty of Israel by force of his personal skills and charm, but he maintained it after Abishalom's rebellion only by force of arms (cf. Herrmann 1981:165–66). In the larger historical perspective, therefore, the Sheba incident was important because it foreshadowed the final lapse of Israelite loyalty to the Davidic throne that occurred after the death of Solomon. The connection between these events is dramatized in the Bible by the adoption of Sheba's slogan "We have no share in David and no estate in the son of Jesse!" by the rebellious Israelite army in I Kings 12:16. We may not accept the rabbis' flat identification of Sheba with Nebat, the father of Jeroboam (see the NOTE at v. 20), but we can recognize a sense in which Sheba's dissent engendered Jeroboam's secession.

The resolution of the Sheba incident brings to a close the larger account of Abishalom's revolt in chaps. 13–20. One might argue, with support from some of the older literary critics, that the events of chap. 20 were unrelated to Abishalom's revolt. But it is historically plausible that sectional strife should break out in the aftermath of a national trauma of such proportions, and chap. 20 is a well-integrated part of the larger literary unit. As Conroy points out (1978:141–42), the appearance of the wise woman of Abel in the present chapter reminds the audience of the wise woman of Tekoa in chap. 14; and the connection between these two chapters, which is reinforced by a number of verbal parallels (Conroy 1978:142 n. 99), is one of the principal unifying features of the larger story. As pointed out in the COMMENT on § XXVI, the masquerading wise woman of chap. 14, who has been told by Joab what to do (14:33), persuades David to set aside the interests of the society as a whole in favor of the interests of one man, and the result is a rebellion. In the present chapter the wise woman of Abel, who tells Joab what to do, counsels the sacrifice of one man in the interests of the society as a whole, and the result is the prevention of a rebellion. A resolution of the social chaos precipitated by the reception of the fratricide Abishalom at court is resolved by the execution of a man who would lead the Israelites in a war against their brothers (cf. 19:42).

Note, finally, that the apologetic character of the story of Abishalom's revolt, which is written in such a way as to invite sympathy for David among those who had followed Abishalom, continues in the present episode. The subject of the apology in this case is the death of Amasa. He had been among the leaders of the revolt (17:25) and was evidently a man of great influence and popularity in Judah (see the NOTES at 17:25). After the revolt was quelled, David appointed him commander of the royal army in place of Joab (19:14), a gesture that secured for David the renewed loyalty of the Judahite army (19:15). This much was public knowledge. A few days later, however, when the king was securely on his throne in Jerusalem, Amasa was slain. There must have been widespread outrage among those men of Judah who, moved by David's appointment of Amasa, had conducted the king back to Jerusalem. The outward appearance of the events suggests treachery on the part of David. The author of our account, however, is intent, as usual, upon showing us that David was innocent of wrongdoing. We are shown that David assigned Amasa an urgent task that fell within the responsibilities of his new position. When Amasa was slow to accomplish this task, the welfare of the nation was imperiled. This was why David turned to Abishai, and it was Abishai, not David, who brought Joab into the affair (v. 7). David, then, had nothing to do with the assassination of Amasa. This was the work of Joab, acting on his own initiative and motivated by his usual sense of ruthless expediency, probably augmented in this case by envy and injured pride.

# XXXIV. DAVID'S CABINET (II)
# (20:23–26)

20 [23]Joab was in charge of the whole army of Israel. Benaiah son of Jehoiada was in charge of the Cherethites and the Pelethites. [24]Adoniram was in charge of the labor force. Jehoshaphat son of Ahilud was herald. [25]Shausha was scribe. Zadok and Abiathar were priests. [26]Ira the Jairite was also a priest of David.

## *TEXTUAL NOTES*

A tendency to correct towards the list in 8:16–18 is felt throughout this list.

20 23. *of Israel* Omitted by LXX$^{MN}$, MT$^{MSS}$ in correction towards 8:16 (cf. *BHS*).

*Jehoiada* MT *yhwyd'* (cf. LXX$^{ALMN}$, OL, etc.). LXX$^{B}$ has *acheilouth* = *'ḥylwd*, "Ahilud," the patronymic of Jeshoshaphat the herald (v. 24), whose name follows Joab immediately in 8:16.

*the Cherethites . . . the Pelethites* So MT, LXX$^{B}$, etc.: *hkrty* (so MT [*qĕrê*], MT$^{MSS}$; MT [*kĕtîb*]: *hkry;* LXX$^{B}$ *tou cheleththei* [LXX$^{AMN}$: *tou chereththei*]) . . . *hplty* LXX$^{L}$ and Theodotion have *tou plinthiou* . . *tous dynastas* (Theodotion: *dynatous*) = *hmlbn . . . hgbwrym*, "the brick kiln (cf. 12:21) . . the warriors" (?).

24. *Adoniram* Reading *'dnyrm* on the basis of MT$^{MS}$, LXX$^{BAMN}$ *(adōn[e]iram)*, and Syr. *('dwnyrm);* cf. I Kings 4:6. MT (cf. Josephus, *Ant.* 7.293) has *'drm*, "Adoram"; cf. I Kings 12:18. LXX$^{L}$ (cf. OL) has *iezedran* (cf. *ieddouran*, the LXX rendering of *hdwrm* at 8:10).

*the labor force* MT *hms* (cf. LXX$^{BAMN}$, etc.). LXX$^{L}$ (cf. Josephus, *Ant.* 7.293) reflects *hmsym*, "the labor forces."

*Jehoshaphat* LXX$^{L}$ (cf. OL) has *saphan*. LXX$^{Mmg}$ has *yōad*.

*Ahilud* LXX$^{L}$ (cf LXX$^{M}$, OL) has *achithalaa*.

*herald* So LXX (cf 8:16). MT has "*the* herald."

25 *Shausha* See the *Textual Note* at 8:17 for the evidence in favor of *šawšā'* Here MT *(kĕtîb)* has *šy'* and MT *(qĕrê) šĕwā'* (so MT$^{MSS}$, Targ.) LXX$^{BA}$ have *i(ē)sous* (cf. LXX$^{Mmg}$). LXX$^{LMN}$ have *sousa* (cf. OL; Josephus, *Ant.* 7.293; Targ.$^{MS}$). Syr. has *šry'* (cf. 8.17 [MT]).

*scribe* So MT, LXX$^{LMN}$ (cf. 8.17). LXX$^{BA}$ have "*the* scribe."

26 *Ira* That is, *'îrā'*: so MT (cf. LXX$^{BAN}$). LXX$^{L}$ *iōdae* suggests *yĕhôyādā'*. Be-

naiah's patronymic (v. 23), which (unlike *'îrā'*) is a pedigreed priestly name (cf. II Kings 11:4; Neh 12:10; etc.).

*the Jairite* MT *hayyā'îrî* (cf. LXX$^{BAN}$). LXX$^{MN}$ *ho iether* and Syr. *(dmn) ytyr* exhibit confusion with another Ira, viz. the Jattirite in 23:38 (see the *Textual Note* there).

## NOTES

20 24. *Adoniram.* Identified further in I Kings 4:6 as "son of Abda" (MT *'abdā'*). Adoniram seems to have continued in office throughout the reign of Solomon (I Kings 4:6; 5:28 [5:14]) and into at least the beginning of the reign of Rehoboam (I Kings 12:18 [LXX]; cf. II Chron 10:18).

*in charge of the labor force.* Captives of war were committed to enforced labor (Deut 20:11; cf. II Sam 12:31), and a similar treatment was accorded the surviving non-Israelite population of Palestine after the arrival of Israel (Josh 16:10; 17:13; Judg 1:28,30,33,35). Solomon, especially, is said to have exploited this latter source of labor (I Kings 9:21 = II Chron 8:8) and even to have imposed enforced labor on "all Israel" (I Kings 5:27 [5:13], doubted by Noth 1960:211). To what extent David did so is unknown. This force of slave or conscript labor was called *mas,* a term that first appears ($^{\text{LÚ.MEŠ}}$*MA.AZ.ZA*$^{\text{MEŠ}}$) in a fourteenth-century B.C. letter from a king of Megiddo to the king of Egypt (Thureau-Dangin 1922:97, lines 23,25; cf. line 14) with reference to forced labor gangs in the Valley of Jezreel (cf. Gen 49:15; *ANET*$^{3}$, p. 485). The title *'al hammas,* "(officer) in charge of the labor force," is used in the Bible only of the officials of David, Solomon, and Rehoboam—in fact, apparently only of Adoniram (see the preceding NOTE). But we know the office continued throughout the monarchical period: A seventh-century B.C. Hebrew seal published by Avigad (1980) belonged to a certain Pelaiah son of Mattithiah, whose title was *'šr 'l hms.* A useful discussion of the title and the institution of the *mas* is found in Mettinger 1971:128–39.

26. *Ira the Jairite.* Jair was the eponymous ancestor of the inhabitants of a region called Havvoth-jair, "the villages of Jair," in Gilead (Num 32:41; Deut 3:14; Josh 13:30; I Kings 4:13; I Chron 2:22,23). Presumably Havvoth-jair is Ira's homeland. Blenkinsopp (1969a:156), however, raises the possibility that he might be a Jearite, i.e., from Kiriath-jearim (cf. the NOTE at 21:19), where the ark was housed before being brought to Jerusalem (6:2; I Sam 7:1,2).

*also.* There is no mention in this list of other priests, and yet v. 26 begins *wĕgam,* "And also." Klostermann concluded from this that David's sons, identified as priests in 8:18, were originally listed here before Ira.

*a priest of David.* The rabbis concluded that the famine of chap. 21 was connected to David's honoring a private priest (Erubin 63a). In the time of David, however, there seems to have been no objection to the king's maintenance of a private priest even if, like Ira, he was not a Levite.

## COMMENT

This list duplicates that in 8:16–18 with a few changes. It is, according to many scholars (Noth 1960:210–17; cf. 1981:56; Bright 1972:201; 1976:202; Herrmann 1981:161; etc.), from the late years of David's reign, the previous list deriving from the early years. The reasons for this conclusion seem to be two, viz. the position of the two lists in the present Book of Samuel and the presence in the second list alone of Adoniram, who continued in office under Solomon (see the NOTE).

It seems more likely, however, that the two lists derive from a single source and that the duplication is a relic of the literary history of the material (cf. already Budde). As explained in the COMMENT on § XIX, 21:1–14 may once have stood before 9:1–13 as part of a single document. A Deuteronomistic editor excised 21:1–14 and he or a later editor consigned it to an appendix. It was in the course of the removal of 21:1–14, which in its original position before 9:1–13 was attached to and immediately followed the list of David's cabinet officers, that the duplication 8:16–18 = 20:23–26 arose (Kapelrud 1955:113, citing Mowinckel).

If 20:23–26 and 8:16–18 are variants of one original list, which has priority? Smith and Caird cite evidence favoring 20:23–26. The order is more logical: military officers (Joab, Benaiah), palace officials (Jehoshaphat, Shausha), priests (Zadok, Abiathar, Ira). There is an obvious motive for the omission of Adoniram, viz. the desire to protect David from the sort of reproach leveled against Solomon for his use of enforced labor. Evidently, then, the present list (20:23–26) preserves the more primitive form of the roll of David's chief officers.

# XXXV. THE GIBEONITES' REVENGE
# (21:1–14)

**21** [1]There was a famine in the time of David year after year for three years, and David sought an audience with Yahweh. "There is bloodguilt upon Saul and upon his house," said Yahweh, "because he put the Gibeonites to death."

[2]So the king summoned the Gibeonites and said to them— (Now the Gibeonites were not part of the people of Israel—they were part of the remnant of the Amorites, but the Israelites had sworn an oath to them —and Saul, in his zeal for the people of Israel and Judah, tried to exterminate them.) [3]So David said to the Gibeonites, "What can I do for you? In what way can I make amends, that you might bless Yahweh's estate?"

[4]"We have no claim of silver and gold against Saul and his house," [they] told him, "and it is not for us to put anyone to death in Israel."

"What do you want?" he said. "For I'll do it for you!"

[5]So they said to the king, "The man who set himself against us and persecuted us, who meant to eradicate us from having a place anywhere in the territory of Israel—[6]let us be given seven of his sons, so that we may crucify them to Yahweh-in-Gibeon on the mountain of Yahweh."

"I'll do it," said the king. [7]The king spared Meribbaal son of Jonathan son of Saul because of the oath of Yahweh that was between them, between David and Jonathan son of Saul, [8]but [he] took the two sons that Rizpah daughter of Aia had borne to Saul, Armoni and Mippibaal, and the five sons that Merob daughter of Saul had borne to Adri son of Barzillai the Meholathite. [9]He handed them over to the Gibeonites, who crucified them on the mountain, the seven of them lying prostrate together. They were put to death in the days of Ziv at the beginning of the barley harvest.

### *Rizpah's Vigil*

[10]Rizpah daughter of Aia took sackcloth and spread it out for herself on the crag from the beginning of the harvest until the waters poured

down on them from the sky, letting no flying bird molest them during the day or wild beast at night. [11]When David was told what Rizpah daughter of Aia, Saul's concubine, had done, [12][he] went and got the bones of Saul and his son Jonathan from the lords of Jabesh-gilead, who had stolen them from the plaza in Beth-shan, where the Philistines hung them at the time [they] defeated Saul on Gilboa. [13]From there [David] brought up the bones of Saul and his son Jonathan, gathering up the bones of the men who had been crucified, too. [14]He buried the bones of Saul and Jonathan in the territory of Benjamin in a chamber of the tomb of Kish, [Saul's] father. Everything the king commanded was done, and afterwards God accepted supplication on behalf of the land.

## *TEXTUAL NOTES*

**21** 1. *a famine* LXX$^{L}$: "a famine *in the land.*"

*bloodguilt upon Saul and upon his house* Reading *'l š'wl w'l bytw dmym* in preference to MT *'l š'wl w'l byt hdmym,* which exhibits an incorrect division of words in the older orthography (**. . . byth dmym).* LXX, though conflate and corrupt, points to the correct arrangement. See the *Textual Note* that follows.

*bloodguilt . . . because he put . . . to death* So MT: *(h)dmym 'l 'šr hmyt.* The troubled text of LXX is to be explained as follows. The OG probably read *hē adikia dia tou thanatōsai auton* = *h'wn 'l hmytw,* "the guilt because of his slaying," preserved in this form in one MS of LXX$^{L}$ (cf. Chrysostom). In other MSS of LXX$^{L}$ we find *hē adikia dia to thanatō haimatōn thanatōsai auton.* The inserted words, *thanatō haimatōn,* represent a "correction" of *thanatōsai auton,* made under the influence of a text similar to MT *'l bytw dmym,* viz. *'l myt dmym,* "because of bloody death." The recensional process has gone further in LXX$^{B}$, where *thanatōsai auton* has been deleted and *peri hou ethanatōsen* (= MT *'l 'šr hmyt*) added in its place.

2. *the king* So MT, LXX$^{L}$. LXX$^{B}$: "King David."

*part of the people of Israel* That is, *mbny yśr'l,* lit. "from the children of Israel." LXX$^{B}$: "(. . . the Gibeonites were not) the Israelites."

*part of the remnant* MT *mytr,* rendered *apo tōn kataloipōn* (LXX$^{L}$) or *ek tou leimmatos* in LXX. In LXX$^{BAMN}$, however, *leimmatos* has become *haimatos*—thus, "from the blood."

*had sworn an oath to them* LXX$^{L}$ adds *mē apolesai autous* = *lblty 'bdm,* "not to destroy them." One could argue for haplography by homoioteleuton *(lhm . . . 'bdm),* but the shorter reading is acceptable (cf. Josh 9:15,18,19,20) and probably ought to be given preference.

*in his zeal for the people of* That is, *bqn'tw lbny* (so MT), to which LXX$^{L}$, however, offers a shorter alternative: *en tō zelō (tou israēl . . .)* = *bqn't,* "in (= by means of?) the zeal (of Israel . . .)."

*tried* MT *wybqš,* for which LXX$^{L}$ and Theodotion *(kai estēse[n])* seem to have read *wyqm,* "arose."

*to exterminate them* Reading *lklwtm* on the basis of LXX$^{L}$, Theodotion *syntelesai autous* in preference to MT *lhkwtm,* "to slay them." Cf. Num 25:11.

3. *that you might bless* Reading *wbrktm* with LXX$^{BAL}$ *kai eulogēsete.* MT (cf. LXX$^{MN}$ *kai eulogēsate*) has *wbrkw,* "and bless"—the imperative "used instead of the more normal voluntative, for the purpose of expressing with somewhat greater force the intention of the previous verb" (Driver).

4. *in Israel* So MT, LXX$^{BA}$. LXX$^{LMN}$: "*from all* Israel."

"*What do you want?*" We read *mh ('tm) tḥpṣw* with LXX$^{L}$ *ti hymeis thelete* and Vulg. *quid . . . vultis.* LXX$^{B}$ reflects *mh 'tm t'mrw,* "What do you say?" MT has *mh 'tm 'mrym,* "What are you saying?"

*he said* So MT. LXX$^{AL}$, Syr., Vulg.: "he said to them."

*For I'll do it* Reading *w'śyty* with LXX (cf. Vulg.) in preference to MT *'śh,* "I'll do it."

5. *The man who* So MT: *h'yš 'šr* (cf. LXX$^{LMN}$). LXX$^{B}$ = *h'yš,* "The man." 4QSam$^{a}$: *'yš '[šr],* "A man who."

*set himself against us and persecuted us* We read *klh 'lynw wyrdpnw* on the basis of LXX$^{B}$ *synetelesen eph' hēmas kai ediōxen hēmas.* MT *klnw,* "exterminated us," is impossible and obviously defective.

*who meant to eradicate us* Reading *'šr dmh lhšmydnw* in preference to MT *'šr dmh lnw wnšmdnw.* As recognized by Wellhausen, *lnw wnšmdnw* is a corruption of *lhšmydnw;* the two readings stand side by side in the conflate text of LXX. The treatment of the first verb in v. 6 in 4QSam$^{a}$ shows that the scroll, though not extant at this point, also read *wnšmdnw* (see the *Textual Note* that follows). For *dmh* LXX reads *rmh (parelogisato),* "dealt treacherously."

6. *let us be given* That is, *yntn lnw (= yinnatēn lānû),* lit. "let it be given to us"; so MT *(kĕtîb).* MT *(qĕrê) has ytn lnw (= yuttan-lānû),* reflected also in LXX$^{B}$ *(dotō hēmin)* but understood as *yittēn lānû,* "let someone give us." LXX$^{L}$ and Targ. follow MT in reading the verb as passive, but they eliminate the synesis by reading a plural, *ytnw* (Targ.) or *wntnw* (LXX$^{L}$, Targ.$^{MS}$), "let (seven of his sons) be given." The OG, preserved in LXX$^{AMN}$ *(dote hēmin),* seems to have read *tnw lnw,* "give us" (imperative). 4QSam$^{a}$ is similar: *wnttm l[nw],* "and give us." Those witnesses in which the conjunction is prefixed to the verb (LXX$^{L}$, 4QSam$^{a}$) are probably following the LXX interpretation of *nšmdnw* in v. 5 as *našmīdennû,* "we shall eradicate him (from having a place . . .)," rather than *nišmadnû,* "we have been eradicated" (MT); thus the verb here would be the *second* in the apodosis of the sentence and would require the conjunction.

*in-Gibeon on the mountain of Yahweh* Following Wellhausen, we read *bgb'wn* (LXX$^{BA}$) *bhr yhwh.* MT has *bgb't š'wl bḥyr yhwh,* "in Gibeah of Saul, the chosen one of Yahweh." When **bĕhar,* "on the mountain" (cf. v. 9), was mistaken as *bĕḥîr* or *bĕḥûr,* "the chosen one," *š'wl* arose as a gloss and *gb'wn* became *gb't* in view of I Sam 11:4; 15:34; and Isa 10:29.

"*I'll do it*" That is, *'ny 'tn,* lit. "I'll give (them)," to which LXX$^{L}$ adds "to you."

7. *Meribbaal* See the *Textual Note* at 4:4.

*that was between them* LXX[L]: "that they had sworn between them."

*between David* So MT, LXX[L]. LXX[B]: "*and* between David."

8. *Rizpah daughter of Aia* Glossed in LXX[M] and a few other MSS as "Saul's concubine" (cf. v. 11).

*Mippibaal* That is, *mippî ba'al*, "out of the mouth of Baal," which appears in MT as *mĕpîbōšet* and LXX as *memphibosthe* = *mippî bōšet*, "out of the mouth of shame." See the *Textual Note* on "Meribbaal" at 4:4 and, for the euphemistic substitution of *bōšet* for *ba'al*, the NOTE on "Ishbaal" at 2:8.

*Merob* MT has *mykl*, "Michal," but we know that Michal was childless (6:23) and that Adri(el) was Merob's husband (I Sam 18:19). LXX[LN] *(merob)* and MT[MSS], therefore, are correct in reading *mrb*, "Merob" (cf. LXX[M], Syr., Targ.). LXX[B] agrees with MT, but the fact that it renders *mykl* as *michal* instead of the usual LXX *melchol* (3:13, etc.) shows that it is recensional and suggests (*pace* Barthélemy 1980:18–19) that *merob* was in fact the OG rendering. Thus *merob* cannot have been derived from I Sam 18:19, which was lacking in OG (cf. *I Samuel*, pp. 299–309). For the pronunciation of the name, see *I Samuel*, the *Textual Note* at 14:49. A defense of MT's reading ("Michal") may be found in Glück 1965. For the rabbinical explanations of the contradiction in MT between 2:23 and 21:8, see Sanhedrin 21a.

*Adri* The full name, *'dry'l* (I Sam 18:19), is attested in MT, LXX[MN], and Syr. But a shortened form, *'dry*, is suggested by LXX[BAL] and must be original here. Many of these witnesses (LXX[LN], Syr.) support an alternative name, viz. *'zry('l)*, "Azri(el)" (so MT[MSS]).

9. *the seven of them* So MT *(qĕrê): šb'tm*. MT *(kĕtîb): šb'tym*, "seven times." LXX[LMN] = *hšb'h*, "the seven," to which is prefixed *ekei* = *šm*, "there," which might be defended as primitive, having fallen out of MT before *šb-*.

*Ziv* MT has *qṣyr br'šnym*, "harvest, on the first (days)," probably a corruption of *hqṣyr hr'šwn*, "the former harvest," which arose as follows: The following word, *btḥlt* (see below), was written *mtḥlt* (so MT *kĕtîb*) in anticipation of v. 10; subsequently the *m-*, obviously out of place, was associated with the preceding word, which thus became *hr'šn(y)m;* but *b-*, introduced marginally as a correction of *mtḥlt* (cf. MT *qĕrê*), found its way into the text in the wrong place. As shown by Brock (1973), however, LXX[L] *zeiōn* points to a shorter and obviously superior reading. We should not be misled by *zeiōn*, "spelt." Spelt was harvested *later* than barley: Brock compares Exod 9:31–32. Instead *zeiōn* is a Hellenized transliteration of the month name *zw*, "Ziv"; cf. I Kings 6:37, where MT *zw* is rendered *ziou* by LXX[L]. See, further, the NOTE.

*at the beginning* So MT *(qĕrê): btḥlt*. See the preceding *Textual Note*.

10. *Rizpah daughter of Aia* LXX[L] adds "Saul's concubine." Cf. v. 11.

*on the crag* The preposition is *'l* (cf. LXX[LMN], Syr., Targ., Vulg.). MT (cf. LXX[BA]): *'l*.

*from the beginning* So MT (cf. LXX[L], Syr., Targ., Vulg.): *mtḥlt*. MT (cf. LXX[BAMN]): *btḥlt*, "*at* the beginning."

*the harvest* LXX, in reminiscence of v. 9, reads "the *barley* harvest."

*on them* MT *'lyhm*, which will have been written *'lyhm* in some MSS according to the common variation of these prepositions in Samuel (cf. the *Textual Note* on "on the crag" above). It was probably the interpretation of *'lyhm* as *'lhym* that led to the reading *(my) 'lhym,* "(the waters) of God," reflected by LXX$^{LMN}$, OL (adopted as original by Klostermann).

At this point LXX$^{L}$ (cf. OL) adds *kai exelythēsan kai katelaben autous dan huios iōas ek tōn apogonōn tōn gigantōn* = *wyšbm dn bn yw'š mylydy hrp'ym,* "and they (the wild beasts?) grew weary, and Dan son of Joash, one of the votaries of the Rephaim, captured them." The same notice appears after v. 11 in LXX$^{B}$. It derives from a marginal correction of the corrupt text of vv. 15–16 below (see the *Textual Note* there). Perhaps it found its way into the text at this point because of the reference to birds *('wp),* as if, "when they flew away *(wy'pw* = *wayyā'ūpû),* Dan son of Joash . . . captured them").

11. *what* LXX$^{LMN}$: "everything that."

12. *the lords of* So MT: *b'ly.* LXX$^{LM}$ = *'nšy,* "the men." LXX$^{BAN}$ = *'nšy bny,* "the men of the sons of." See the *Textual Note* at 2:5.

*the plaza* So MT (cf. LXX$^{BA}$). LXX$^{LMN}$ (cf. Targ.): "the walls," as in I Sam 31:12.

*Beth-shan* LXX$^{B}$ omits "-shan."

13. *[David] brought up* We read *wy'l* with MT, etc. In LXX$^{L}$ the subject is made explicit, and this is also necessary in English.

14. *He buried* So LXX$^{AL}$. MT: "*They* buried."

*Jonathan* Cf. Syr. MT: "Jonathan *his son.*" LXX$^{LMN}$: "Jonathan and the bones of those who had been crucified." LXX$^{B}$: "Jonathan and those who had been crucified."

*accepted supplication* So MT: *wy'tr.* LXX$^{L}$ reflects an alternative: *kai exilasato* = *wykpr,* "regarded (the land) as atoned for," as in Deut 32:43.

## NOTES

**21** 1. *David sought an audience with Yahweh.* On the expression *biqqēš 'et-pĕnê yahweh,* lit. "seek the face of Yahweh," see García de la Fuente (1968), who cites Babylonian and Hittite parallels showing that the underlying concept in "seeking the face" of a deity is that of an audience with a god in his temple comparable to an audience with a king in his palace. Compare, in this regard, the Hebrew expression "see the face of the king," discussed in a NOTE at 3:13. Thus, in Biblical Hebrew to "seek the face of the king" was to seek an audience with him, to seek his counsel (II Chron 9:23). To "seek the face of Yahweh" was to seek Yahweh's counsel, especially in time of danger or disaster (Hos 5:15; II Chron 7:14). Thus, as García de la Fuente says, it means to seek divine succor (Pss 27:8 [*bis*]; 105:4 = I Chron 16:11), and this is the meaning in the present passage. It is clear from what follows that seeking an audience with Yahweh involved, in this case, the obtaining of an oracle (Malamat 1955:9 n. 2), though translations such as "consulted Yahweh" (JB) or "inquired of the Lord" (NJV) are too explicit (cf. Vulg. *et consuluit David oraculum Domini!*); the rabbis inferred from Num 27:21 that David was using the Urim and Thummim here (Yebamoth 78b). Presumably David inquired of Yahweh in Jerusalem, but it is possible that he, like Solomon at a later time (I Kings 3:4–15a), went to Gibeon for his divine audience (Hertzberg, etc.).

*Saul . . . put the Gibeonites to death.* There is no mention elsewhere in the Bible of a slaughter of Gibeonites instigated by Saul. Attention naturally falls on the massacre perpetrated by Saul that we do know about, viz. that of the priesthood of Nob (I Sam 22:6–23). The rabbis (Yebamoth 78b) interpreted the words of the oracle to imply that by slaughtering the priests of Nob, for whom the Gibeonites were "hewers of wood and drawers of water" (Josh 9:23,27), Saul had eliminated the Gibeonites' source of food and water, thus indirectly causing their death. A number of modern scholars have attempted to distinguish the Nob of I Samuel 21 and 22 from the place referred to in Isa 10:32 and Neh 11:32 and identify it instead with the sanctuary in Gibeon (von Schlatter 1893:246–48; Poels 1897:282–90; Bruno 1923:69–75; Hertzberg 1929:177–81; Hylander 1932:286,291–92; Brinker 1946:160). Thus it would be possible to associate the words of the present oracle directly with the slaughter of the priests of Nob, which, according to I Sam 22:19, extended to all the inhabitants of the city (Bruno 1923:75–87; Hertzberg 1929:177–78). But this hypothesis has not found wide support; see the balanced discussion of Blenkinsopp 1972:67–71. Still more problematic is the attempt of van den Born (1954:201–14) to identify the Gibeah of Judges 19 and 20 with Gibeon and relate the events recorded there to Saul's attempt to put the Gibeonites to death. It is safest to assume that the present oracle refers to events not recorded elsewhere in the Bible. Saul "in his zeal for the people of Israel" (v. 2) tried to exterminate the Gibeonites. His motive for doing so may have been, as Malamat suggests (1955:10), concern over the security risk represented by the Gibeonite cities, a group of non-Israelite enclaves on Israel's western border (see the following NOTE). The situation of these cities effectually cut Israel in half (Blenkinsopp 1972:56), and a Philistine-Gibeonite alliance such as Cazelles postulates (1955b:170) would have been disastrous for Saul (cf. Malamat 1955:10).

2. *(Now the Gibeonites . . . to exterminate them.).* On Gibeon in general see the NOTE at 2:12. In addition to Gibeon, the Gibeonites lived in Chephirah, Beeroth (cf. 4:2), and Kiriath-jearim (Josh 9:17). They were non-Israelites, "part of the remnant of the Amorites," i.e., the pre-Israelite inhabitants of the land. The story of the ruse by which they entered into a treaty with Israel, thereby saving themselves from destruction in the conquest, is told in Joshua 9. It is because of Saul's violation of this treaty, we are told, that the famine has taken hold of the land. Saul's guilt, then, is not the result of shedding blood as such—he shed the blood of many peoples—but of shedding the blood of a people protected by treaty oaths. On this point see Malamat (1955:9), who is probably correct in doubting the conclusion of Smith, Caird, and others that this parenthesis was added secondarily. Veijola (1975:108) regards vv. 2b and 7 as Deuteronomistic.

4. *it is not for us to put anyone to death.* The Gibeonites' predicament, as they express it, seems to be this. As resident aliens (*gērîm;* cf. Blenkinsopp 1972:34) protected by oath they are empowered to make certain pecuniary claims ("silver and gold") against Israelites to protect their interests. They are not, however, protected by blood-feud laws like native Israelites (cf. Blenkinsopp 1972:136 n. 31). Therefore, since their claim against the house of Saul arises from a blood grievance rather than any financial claim, they are helpless. For this interpretation see, for example, Cazelles 1955b:165. A strong but not, perhaps, decisive objection to this interpretation is that, thus understood, the two *'ên lānû* clauses in the verse have different idiomatic meanings (cf. Pedersen

1940:vol. II:383–84,532). The alternative is to read "we have no claim on the life of anyone (else [i.e., other than Saul and his house]) in Israel."

6. *so that we may crucify them.* Hebrew *wĕhôqa'ănûm*, the meaning of which is uncertain. Apart from the present passage, *hôqîa'* occurs only in Num 25:4, where it also describes a form of execution "in the sun." The rabbis (Sanhedrin 34b) took it to mean "hang," and the Greek translation of the present passage, *kai exēliasōmen*, suggests crucifixion in the sun (cf. *neged haššemeš*, Num 25:4). This remains the most plausible interpretation, though we need not go so far as Heller (1966:75–76), who thinks Gibeon was a center of sun worship (cf. Dus 1960) and concludes that the Saulids were crucified in honor of the sun god. In *Qal* the verb once refers to the dislocation of Jacob's thigh (Gen 32:26), and Kapelrud (1955:119–20; 1959:300–1), following Koehler, takes *hôqîa'* to mean "expose (with arms and legs broken)." Another line of reasoning concludes that *hôqîa'* describes ritual dismemberment (cf. Cazelles 1955b:167–70), a technical term for punishment of covenant violations (Polzin 1969). In view of the statement in v. 9 that the seven Saulids *fell* (*wayyippĕlû*, here rendered "lying prostrate") together, a case might be made for returning to the understanding of *hôqîa'* favored by Robertson Smith (1969:419 n. 2). Noting Arabic *waqa'a*, "fall," which in the II- and IV-forms means "let fall, cast or hurl down," he concluded that *hôqîa'* refers to execution by hurling down. In any case, it is clear that the execution is of a special kind and that an important part of it is the exposure of the bodies of the dead. With regard to this, Fensham (1964:100) points out that exposure of the corpse was part of the punishment for a treaty violation elsewhere in the ancient Near East.

*Yahweh-in-Gibeon.* That is, the Gibeonite Yahweh, the local manifestation of the national god. See the NOTE on "Yahweh-in-Hebron" in 15:7,8.

*on the mountain of Yahweh.* Presumably the Gibeonite high place of I Kings 3.

7. This verse is secondary, having been introduced after the separation of 9:1–13 from 21:1–14. In the original account (21:1–14 + 9:1–13) David learned of Meribbaal's existence only after the death of his seven kinsmen.

8. *Rizpah daughter of Aia.* Saul's concubine, who was the subject of the quarrel between Abiner and Ishbaal in 3:7–11.

*Merob daughter of Saul.* See I Sam 18:17–19.

*Adri son of Barzillai the Meholathite.* Adri is called by his longer name, Adriel, in I Sam 18:19. The name of his father is given only in the present passage. Is he the Barzillai of 17:27 and 19:31–40? We cannot be sure, but it is quite possible. The Barzillai who assisted David at Mahanaim was a Gileadite from the unidentified town of Rogelim. Adri is also a Gileadite; specifically, he is a Meholathite, and the town of Abel-meholah lay a few miles east of Jabesh-gilead at modern Tell Abū Kharaz.

9. *in the days of Ziv.* See Brock 1973. The month of Ziv is mentioned elsewhere only in I Kings 6:1,37. Ziv in the old Canaanite calendar corresponds to Iyyar in the Babylonian month nomenclature later adopted by the Jews. It was the second month (April–May) of the agricultural year, the time of the barley harvest.

10. *until the waters poured down . . . from the sky.* Did Rizpah's vigil last until the coming of the November rains? It seems more likely that an unseasonable, late spring or summer rain is meant, coinciding with the end of the famine and accompanying drought. Cf. Hertzberg.

12. *the bones of Saul and his son Jonathan.* See I Sam 31:12–13, where we are told that the men of Jabesh burned and buried the bones of Saul and Jonathan. Thus, it can be no more than ashes that David here recovers.

## COMMENT

Like the other six units of material in 20:23–24:25, this section is a self-contained composition with no direct relationship to what precedes or follows it. As explained in the COMMENT on § XIX, chap. 9 was probably a sequel or conclusion to 21:1–14 before the separation of the original literary unit (21: 1–6,8–14 + 9:1–13) by a Deuteronomistic editor. Thus the present section was consigned to an appendix at the end of the book or simply omitted, only to be restored out of sequence by a later editor.

The original narrative unit described the execution of the house of Saul in payment of a debt of bloodguilt and the preservation of the line of Jonathan by David's patronage of Meribbaal. A famine had afflicted Israel for three years when David learned that its cause was an attempt by Saul to exterminate the Gibeonites, a non-Israelite enclave living in a group of cities north of Jerusalem. The Gibeonites were protected by an oath sworn in the time of Joshua (Josh 9:3–27), and Saul's attack on them was a violation of the treaty of the sort the tribal chiefs had warned against long before: "Now that we have sworn an oath to them by Yahweh, god of Israel, we must not harm them. We must carry through on this and let them remain alive, so that wrath won't be upon us because of the oath we swore to them" (Josh 9:19–20). The famine was the expression of this divine rage or wrath *(qeṣep),* and it could be averted only by the death of the offending party. Thus the surviving male members of the house of Saul were crucified "on the mountain of Yahweh" in Gibeon, and the famine ended.

A number of scholars have found evidence in this account for David's assimilation of Canaanite religious practices (Cazelles 1955b; etc.). In particular, Kapelrud (1955; 1959) argues that the central issue of the story is the relationship between the king and fertility, and that the execution of the Saulids is a royal sacrifice. Because of the king's implicit responsibility for the fertility of the land, he says (1955:116–17; 1959:299), the famine cast David in a bad light. It was clear to David that a sacrifice was in order, and "For the sake of fertility a sacrifice of the highest rank was necessary" (1959:300). Kapelrud points to other biblical examples of royal sacrifice in times of extreme emergency, notably II Kings 3:26–27, where the sacrifice of the firstborn son of the king of Moab brings a great divine rage *(qeṣep)* upon Israel, saving a Moabite city from an Israelite siege. II Kings 16:3 and 21:6 show that this practice was not unknown in Judah itself. David, however, did not choose his own son for sacrifice; still less did he propose himself as a victim. He chose the descendants of Saul. According to Kapelrud, he made this choice for two reasons: (1) He knew that the death of the Saulids would represent a legitimate royal sacrifice; and (2) he had political reasons for wanting them out of the way. Kapelrud (1955:120; 1959:301) considers the time of the sacrifice—"at the beginning of the barley harvest"—an important detail: "Here a direct line of connection is drawn between the sacrifice of the royal family, famine and drought."

Kapelrud's treatment is limited by its disregard of the reason for the execution offered by the text itself. The Saulids are crucified in propitiation of divine wrath arising from the violation of a treaty sanctioned by solemn oaths. This is no grandiose gesture of royal sacrifice comparable to a king's immolation of his infant son. It is a matter of propitiatory justice, of restitution exacted upon those who bear the guilt for a gross breach of a divinely sanctioned oath. Thus the discussions of our passage by Malamat (1955) and Fensham (1964) are much more instructive. Fensham (p. 20) shows that exposure of the dead body of a transgressor was part of the punishment for treaty violations elsewhere in the ancient Near East. Malamat's treatment brings into focus the central issue of a past crime transmitting its burden of guilt to the present generation. He succeeds in locating this issue within a known tradition of ancient Near Eastern historiography. He is able to demonstrate a common doctrine of causality in Hittite and Israelite literature according to which a national disaster (famine, plague, etc.) might arise from a past violation of a treaty oath. The primary Hittite texts are the so-called "plague prayers" of the fourteenth-century king Muršiliš II (*ANET*[3], pp. 394–96). These prayers, addressed to the Hittite storm god, describe a severe plague that has been raging in Hatti for years. Muršiliš says that he has consulted an oracle and learned the cause of the plague. During his father's reign there was a peace treaty between Hatti and Egypt sanctioned by oaths to the Hittite storm god. His father violated this treaty by repeatedly attacking Egyptian troops. The plague first broke out among prisoners brought back from one of these raids, and it has been ravaging Hatti ever since. Muršiliš now hopes to avert the scourge by admitting his guilt. "It is only too true," he says, "that man is sinful. My father sinned and transgressed against the word of the Hattian Storm-god, my lord. But I have not sinned in any respect. It is only too true, however, that the father's sin falls upon the son. So, my father's sin has fallen upon me." Muršiliš also mentions his propitiatory offerings and, with reference to the innumerable Hittites who have died in the plague, offers to make any kind of further restitution the storm god might require.

The biblical story of the Gibeonites' revenge shares the historiographical outlook of the plague prayers of Muršiliš. The central figure in each account is a king who is trying to discover the cause of a national disaster—a famine, a plague—and thus a way to avert it. The two documents have a common doctrine of causality which traces the present-day disaster to a past violation of treaty oaths. The famine arose in Israel because the former king, Saul, violated the oath sworn to the Gibeonites in the days of Joshua. The plague broke out in Hatti in consequence of the former king's violation of the oath sworn in ratification of a peace treaty with Egypt. In each case it fell to the succeeding king to find the means of restitution for these past crimes. In each case the god before whom the oaths of ratification were sworn—Yahweh, the Hittite storm god—had to be appeased.

Generically, however, the story in II Sam 21:1-14 and the plague prayers of Muršiliš differ. The Hittite texts are prayers, addressed to the storm god and presumably intended to placate him. The Israelite text is a third-person narrative, and it is intended to sway a human audience. As Kapelrud and others have stressed, the near extermination of the male descendants of Saul, any one of whom might have become a claimant to the throne, represented a great political gain for David. Similarly, the permanent residence of the one remaining Saulid, Meribbaal, in Jerusalem, where his activities could be carefully watched, contributed greatly to the security of David's throne. It is not difficult to imagine the public reaction to these events at the time they occurred. It would have been quite natural for David's contemporaries to conclude that the massacre of the Saulids and house arrest of Meribbaal were ruthless actions of the king undertaken for personal political gain (cf. Bright 1972:203). Many, especially those with past loyalties to the house of Saul, must have been in sympathy with Shimei's characterization of David as a "bloodstained fiend of hell" (16:7). The present account (21:1-14 + 9:1-13), however, addresses these suspicions with an attempt to allay them. There is no denial of the publicly known events: David did order the execution of the seven Saulids and he did summon Meribbaal to Jerusalem. Nevertheless, the account shows that the death of the sons of Rizpah and Merob was required by Yahweh in restitution of Saul's violation of a sacred oath. David did not act out of malicious self-interest. On the contrary, his actions were those of a king sincerely concerned for the welfare of the land. His purpose was to alleviate the famine, and in this he succeeded. Similarly, Meribbaal's status in Jerusalem is shown to have been that of a guest, not a prisoner. David invited him to join the royal table company (9:7) as a gesture of loyalty to his own past relationship with Jonathan, Meribbaal's father (see the COMMENT on § XIX). Thus David actually emerges from this account as a benefactor of the house of Saul! It was he who saw to it that Saul, Jonathan, and the seven sons of Rizpah and Merob received an honorable burial in their ancestral tomb (21:1-14a). It was he who provided the one surviving Saulid with an honored place at court.

We have no way of assessing the success of this apologetic document in allaying the suspicions of David's subjects. The Shimei incident (16:5-14), if it occurred later than the promulgation of our account, suggests that the suspicions remained. The modern historian is also likely to read the argument for David's innocence with caution. Most would probably agree with Kapelrud that David acted out of a mixture of religious and political motives, addressing the powers of his office to a genuine public need but also manipulating the situation to his private advantage.

## XXXVI. THE VOTARIES OF RAPHA
## (21:15–22)

21 [15]Once again the Philistines fought a battle with Israel, and David
went down with his servants to fight the Philistines.

### *Dodo Son of Joash*

David became exhausted, [16]and Dodo son of Joash, one of the votaries of Rapha, captured him. His helmet weighed three hundred bronze
shekels, and he was girded with armor. He intended to kill David, [17]but
Abishai son of Zeruiah came to his aid, striking down the Philistine and
killing him.

Then David's men swore, "Don't march out to battle with us any-
more! You mustn't put out the lamp of Israel!"

### *Saph*

[18]After this there was another battle with the Philistines at Gezer. It
was then that Sibbecai the Hushathite slew Saph, one of the votaries
of Rapha.

### *Goliath the Gittite*

[19]Then there was another battle with the Philistines at Gob, and
Elhanan, a Jearite from Bethlehem, slew Goliath the Gittite, the shaft
of whose spear was like a weavers' heddle rod.

### *The Six-fingered Giant*

[20]Then there was another battle in Gath. There was a giant who had
six fingers on his hands and six toes on his feet—a total of twenty-four!
—and he, too, was devoted to Rapha. [21]He defied Israel, and Jonathan
son of Shimeah, David's brother, slew him.

22 These four were devoted to Rapha-in-Gath, and they fell by the hands of David and his servants.

## *TEXTUAL NOTES*

21 15. *with his servants* So MT: *w'bdyw 'mw*, lit. "and his servants with him." $LXX^{L}$: "and his *men* with him."

15–16. *David* (2) . . . *him* The defective text of MT can be repaired on the basis of the displaced marginal plus that stands before v. 11 in $LXX^{L}$ and after v. 11 in $LXX^{BA}$. MT has *wy'p dwd wyšbw bnb 'šr bylydy hrph*, "David became exhausted. And Jishbo *(wĕyišbô)* of Nob, who was among the votaries of Rapha. . . ." In v. 11+ LXX reads *kai exelythēsan kai katelaben autous dan huios iōa(s) ek tōn apogonōn tōn gigantōn*, a marginal correction of the reading in vv. 15–16, which found its way into the text in the wrong place. This yields a clear text: *wy'p dwd wyšbw (wayyišbēw* < **wayyišbēhû;* cf. Cross and Freedman 1952:50 and n. 28) *ddw* (cf. $LXX^{L}$ *dadou* in v. 16) *bn yw'š mylydy hrph*. The confusion in MT arose when *ddw* fell out of the text after *wyšbw* (homoioteleuton). The resulting *bn yw'š* was read *bnb 'šr* under the influence of *bgwb* in vv. 18,19 (for which $MT^{MSS}$ read *bnwb*).

16. *His helmet* very doubtful. MT *qênô*, "his . . . ," is unique, and no satisfactory interpretation has been proposed. Most modern translators implicitly follow LXX *tou doratos autou* in reading "his spear" (JB; cf. NEB, NJV, etc.). One might read *qānô*, "his (spear)shaft," apparently with Targ. *swpnyh;* compare Ugaritic *qnm*, "reeds (to be made into arrows)" (*CTCA* 17.6,23); but spear *shafts* are not made of bronze (Nowack). Syr. has *(d)šrynh* = *šrywnw*, "his cuirass" (cf. I Sam 17:5). Provisionally we follow Klostermann, Smith, Budde, and Nowack in reading *qwb'w* (cf. I Sam 17:38).

*shekels* MT *mšql* is evidently a mistake for *šql(ym)* (so $LXX^{L}$; cf. $LXX^{B}$) under the influence of *mšqlw* earlier in the verse.

*armor* The witnesses reflect variants, none of which gives an intelligible meaning. MT has *ḥdšh*, "new(ness)," hence Syr. and Vulg., "a new *sword*," as if *hrb ḥdsh;* cf. Leibel (1958/59), who takes *ḥdšh* alone as "sword." Targ. *'spnyqy ḥdth*, "a new girdle," indirectly supports the reading of $LXX^{LM}$, $OL^{MS}$, and Theodotion, viz. *parazōnēn* = *ḥgwrh*, provisionally adopted here. The solution may lie behind $LXX^{B}$ *korynēn*, "a club, mace." What Hebrew original does this reflect?

17. *came to his aid* So MT: *wy'zr lw*. $LXX^{L}$ *kai esōse ton daueid* reflects *wywšy' 't dwd*, "saved David."

*swore* MT adds "to him." Omit with LXX, Vulg.

18. *Gezer* Cf. $LXX^{LMN}$. We read *gzr*, "Gezer," as in I Chron 20:4. MT has "Gob" and $LXX^{B}$ "Gath," anticipating vv. 19 and 20, respectively.

*Sibbecai* So MT, which reads *sbky* as *sibbĕkay*. The vocalization *sĕbōkay*, "Sebocai," is attested by $LXX^{MN}$ (cf. $LXX^{BAL}$) *sobochai* and $LXX^{MN}$ *sabouchei* in 23:27.

*the Hushathite* MT *haḥûšātî*. $LXX^{L}$ = "the Hittite."

*Saph* MT *sap*, for which I Chron 20:4 has *sippay*, probably a longer form of the same name. The reading *spy* is indirectly attested by LXX$^{LMN}$, which read *tous episynēgmenous* = *'spy*, "the ones rounded up (from the votaries of Rapha)."

*one of the votaries* Reading *mylydy* (cf. LXX$^{L}$) as in I Chron 20:4. MT has *'šr bylydy*, "who was among the votaries."

19. *Gob* So MT: *gwb*. LXX has *rhob* (or *rhom*), a result of confusion of the Greek majuscules *rho* and *gamma*.

*a Jearite from Bethlehem* MT has *bn y'ry 'rgym byt hlḥmy*, "son of Jarre-oregim the Bethlehemite." Omit *'rgym* with LXX$^{LMN}$ and I Chron 20:5. We read *y'ry (yĕ'ārî)*, "the Jearite," for *bn y'ry* for the following reasons: (1) Elhanan's patronymic is given as *dwdw*, "Dodo," in 23:24; (2) the form *y'ry* suggests a gentilic; and (3) Bethlehem, Elhanan's home, is closely associated with Kiriath-jearim, "the city of the Jearites" (see the NOTES). We must suppose that *byt hlḥmy* is either a gloss on *y'ry* or, as I assume, an adjusted form of an original *(m)byt lḥm* (cf. 23:24); cf. OL and Coptic.

*from Bethlehem . . . Goliath* That is, *mbyt hlḥm 't glyt* (cf. MT and see the preceding *Textual Note*). I Chron 20:5 has *'t lḥmy 'ḥy glyt*, "Lahmi, the brother of Goliath," a scribal error with the effect of harmonizing this notice with I Samuel 17. See Driver.

20. *another battle* LXX$^{L}$ adds "with the Philistines."

*a giant* MT has *'yš mdyn (kĕtîb)/mdwn (qĕrê)*, "a man of Midian/Madon," or, perhaps, "a man of strife" or "a quarrelsome man" (cf. Jer 15:10; Prov 26:21) or even "a champion, gladiator, monomachist." It is more likely, however, that the primitive reading was *'yš mdh*, "a man of (great) stature, a giant," as in I Chron 20:6 (cf. 23:21 below and I Chron 11:23).

21. *Jonathan* So MT, the major Greek uncials, and I Chron 20:7. Syr. and a group of cursive MSS of LXX have "Jonadab," as in 13:3. Evidently Jonathan and Jonadab were brothers.

*Shimeah* See the *Textual Note* at 13:3. Here MT *(qĕrê)* has *šm'h* (but MT [*kĕtîb*]: *šm'y*; cf. LXX$^{B}$). LXX$^{L}$ reflects *šm'*, as in I Chron 20:7.

22. *in-Gath* A corrupt duplicate of *bgt*, viz. *byt*, "a house," has caused confusion in the text of LXX.

## NOTES

21 16. *the votaries of Rapha*. The Hebrew expression is *yĕlîdê hārāpâ*. This has traditionally been understood to refer to descendants *(yĕlîdê)* of the Rephaim, legendary giants of the past (Gen 14:5; 15:20; Deut 2:10–11,20; 3:13; Josh 12:4; 13:12; 17:15; etc.). Recently, however, Willesen (1958a, 1958b) and L'Heureux (1974, 1976, 1979) have challenged the assumption that *yālīd* refers to physical descent. In fact, it seems to be used in deliberate preference to *bēn*, "son," to connote membership in a group attained by some other avenue than birth (cf. L'Heureux 1976:83). It refers especially to a slave or servant who provides military service, as suggested by Gen 14:14 (de Vaux 1961b:vol. I:219). According to Willesen (1958b:210; cf. 1958a:328) a *yālīd* was a slave "dedicated to the deity who was head of the social unit into which he was admitted

by consecration." L'Heureux is somewhat more cautious, concluding that the *yĕlîdê hārāpâ* were members of a military group into which one was admitted not by birth but by "adoption, initiation, or consecration" (1976:84). Willesen (1958a:331) explains *hrph* as a Greek word, viz. *harpē*, "sickle, scimitar." The *yĕlîdê *harpē*, then, were "the Corps of the Scimitar," an elite group of Philistine warriors of which the scimitar was the emblem. L'Heureux (1976:84–85) understands the *yĕlîdê hārāpâ* as "the votaries of Rapha," an elite group of warriors devoted to *hārāpā'* (cf. I Chron 20:6,8), a divine epithet meaning "one who is in a healthy condition" (euphemistically for an underworld deity?) and applied in Ugaritic literature to a number of gods. One god in particular is called *rp'u*. He appears as the patron of an elite military-aristocratic group called *rp'um* (L'Heureux 1974:266–70; Jirku 1965). In our translation we follow L'Heureux. The god to whom members of this "cultic association of warriors" (L'Heureux) devoted themselves was, more specifically, "Rapha-in-Gath" (see the NOTE at v. 22).

17. *Abishai son of Zeruiah.* See the NOTE at 2:18.

*You mustn't put out the lamp of Israel!* Presumably a perpetually burning lamp was a symbol of endurance and prosperity, though there is no good parallel for this expression elsewhere in Biblical Hebrew. The idea expressed in v. 17b is essentially that of 18:3.

18. *Gezer.* Gezer, west of Jerusalem in the direction of the Philistine plain, was an Israelite-Philistine border city, a natural site of conflict. See Map 9.

*Sibbecai the Hushathite.* The village of Hushah (I Chron 4:4) lay in the Judaean hills a few miles southwest of Bethlehem (Map 9); the modern site is Ḥūsān (cf. Elliger 1935:44). It is possible that Sibbecai was one of the Thirty; see the *Textual Note* on "Mebunnai the Hushathite," 23:27.

19. *Gob.* Mentioned only here in the Bible (cf. the *Textual Note* on "Gezer," v. 18), omitted in the parallel in I Chron 20:5, and unknown in extrabiblical sources.

*Elhanan, a Jearite from Bethlehem.* "The city of the Jearites" *(qiryat-yĕʿārîm)* was Kiriath-jearim, but the connections between the inhabitants of that city and those of Bethlehem are well known (see p. 176). Just as there were Ephrathites in both cities, so evidently there were Jearites.

*Goliath the Gittite.* This giant, the shaft of whose spear was "like a weavers' heddle rod" (cf. I Sam 17:7), was identified in tradition with an anonymous Philistine slain by David (I Samuel 17). See *I Samuel*, the NOTE on "Goliath" at 17:4, for details and alternative theories. Deeds of obscure heroes tend to attach themselves to famous heroes, and there is no doubt that the tradition attributing the slaying of Goliath to Elhanan is older than that which credits the deed to David. The contradiction in the tradition was eliminated in the targumic and midrashic literature by identifying David with Elhanan (cf. Pákozdy 1956:257 nn. 2,3). This harmonizing solution seems to have been introduced into modern scholarship by Böttcher (1863:233–35), but it has become especially associated with Honeyman (1948:23–24), who concluded that "David" was the throne name of a man whose personal name was "Elhanan." Although this position continues to find adherents (von Pákozdy 1956; Ahlström 1959:37; cf. Bright 1972:-188), its critics seem to have the stronger case (Stamm 1960b:167–68,182; Stoebe 1967:215–16; cf. *I Samuel*, p. 291); it is no longer possible, in any case, to argue that *dāwīd* was a *title*, comparing Mari Akkadian *da-wi-du-um* ("defeat," not "high chief"; cf. Tadmor 1958). See, in general, Hoffmann 1973:168–206.

*like a weavers' heddle rod.* See *I Samuel,* the NOTE at 17:7.

21. *Jonathan son of Shimeah.* On David's brother Shimeah or Shammah (I Sam 16:9), see 13:3. Evidently Jonadab, the wise guy of chap. 13, was Jonathan's brother, though the ancient witnesses to our text show a tendency to identify them.

22. *Rapha-in-Gath.* Hebrew *hārāpâ* is probably equivalent to *hārāpā'* (I Chron 20:6,8). It is a divine epithet meaning "the Hale One," comparable to Ugaritic *rp'u* (*rapa'u/rapi'u,* "the Hale One," or *rāpi'u,* "the Healer"; see Parker 1972; Cross 1973: 20–22; L'Heureux 1979:215–18). The latter is used of a number of gods, but there is one god in particular called *rp'u.* Because of the associations of the Ugaritic *rp'um* and the biblical Rephaim with the underworld, it is likely that "the Hale One" had a chthonic character and that the epithet was euphemistic. The worship of Rapha continued in the time of David, and one of its centers, it seems, was the Philistine Gath. The Philistine champions defeated in the stories in the present section were cultically devoted to the Gittite Rapha (cf. "Yahweh-in-Hebron," the Hebronite Yahweh of 15:7, and "Yahweh-in-Gibeon," the Gibeonite Yahweh of 21:6).

## COMMENT

These four brief episodes constitute a unit in that each describes a victory of one of David's warriors over a Philistine champion and, more specifically, each of the enemies is said to belong to a cultic association of warriors called the votaries of Rapha. The section as a whole may derive from an ancient archive. Attempts to determine the reason for its present position (cf. Hertzberg) will probably not succeed. It was deposited among a miscellany of unrelated items at the end of the story of Abishalom's revolt, awaiting integration into the book. On chronological grounds it ostensibly belongs in the context of David's Philistine wars (5:17–25), but no editor took it up and put it there, and it remains without context.

# XXXVII. A PSALM OF DAVID
## (22:1–51)

**22** [1]David addressed the words of this song to Yahweh at the time Yahweh rescued him from the grasp of all his enemies, including Saul. [2]He said:

Yahweh!
My cliffside stronghold,
who keeps me secure!
[3]My divine crag,
in whom I find shelter!
My sovereign peak of safety,
my lofty refuge,
from violent men he saves me!

[4]Derided, I cried "Yahweh!"
I called for help from my enemies.
[5]The breakers of death engulfed me,
the torrents of hell shocked me,
[6]the cords of Sheol encircled me,
the snares of death waylaid me.
[7]In my distress I cried "Yahweh!"
I called for help to my god.
In his temple he heard my voice,
my call for help was in his ears.
[8]He took notice, and the earth shuddered,
the foundations of the mountains trembled,
they groaned because he was angry.
[9]Smoke went up from his nostrils,
a devouring fire from his mouth,
glowing coals flared from him.
[10]He spread open the sky and came down,
a rain cloud beneath his feet.
[11]Mounting a cherub he flew,
he swooped on the wings of the wind.

12He set darkness about him,
his covert was the sieve of the waters.
13From the brightness before him flared
hail and glowing coals.
14Yahweh thundered from the sky,
Elyon roared.
15He launched arrows and scattered them,
shot lightning bolts and made them rumble.
16The channels of the sea were exposed,
the foundations of the world were laid bare
by Yahweh's roar,
by the blast of his nostrils.
17Reaching from the heights he took hold of me,
drew me out of the deep water.
18He rescued me from my powerful enemies,
from my foes—for they were too strong for me.
19They waylaid me on the day of my ordeal,
but Yahweh was a support for me.
20He brought me out into the open,
he drew me out because he preferred me.
21Yahweh dealt with me according to my innocence,
he treated me according to my blamelessness.
22For I had kept the ways of Yahweh,
I had not strayed wickedly from my god.
23All his judgments were in front of me,
I had not removed his statutes from me.
24I had been faultless towards him,
I had carefully avoided guilt.
25So Yahweh treated me according to my innocence,
according to my blamelessness in his sight.

26With the loyal you are loyal,
with the guiltless you are guiltless,
27with the pure you are pure,
but with the perverse you are devious.
28You—a humble people you will vindicate,
but the eyes of the exalted you will bring low.

29You are my lamp, Yahweh,
my god, who sheds light on my darkness.

30 With you I can leap a gully,
with my god I can jump a wall.

31 The god whose dominion is complete—
[the decree of Yahweh is pure silver—]
he is a sovereign for all who seek refuge with him.
32 For who is a god but Yahweh?
Who is a crag but our god?
33 The god who girded me sturdily
and mapped out complete dominion for me.
34 Stationing my legs like tree trunks,
he made me stand upright;
35 programing my hands for fighting,
he shaped the bows of my arms.

36 You bestowed on me the gift of your victory,
and your conquest made me great.
37 You made my stride long beneath me,
and my ankles did not falter.

38 When I pursued my enemies,
I destroyed them;
I did not turn back
    until they were finished.
39 When I smashed them,
    they did not get up;
They fell beneath my feet.
  40 You girded me sturdily for fighting,
  making my foes cower beneath me
  41 and offering me the nape of my enemies.
  My adversaries—I struck them down!
42 They cried for help,
    but there was no one to save them,
to Yahweh,
    but he did not answer them.
43 I ground them like the dirt of a path,
like mud in the streets I mashed them.
44 You freed me from the conflicts of the army
and set me at the head of the nations.
A people I did not know served me,
45 by the hearing of the ear they obeyed me.

46 Foreigners abased themselves to me,
they came fettered by their collars.

47 As Yahweh lives,
  Let my god be blessed!
  Let my safe crag be high!
48 The god who gave me vengeance,
subduing people at my feet
49 and taking me away from my enemies.
Yes, you lifted me up from my foes,
you protected me from violent men.
50 Therefore I extol you among the nations,
I sing praise to your name:
  51 The one who magnifies the victories of
    his king,
  who deals loyally with his anointed,
  with David and his descendants forever.

## *TEXTUAL NOTES*

**22** 2. *He said* A rubric is inserted before the poem in some witnesses ($LXX^B$: *ōdē*, "A Song"; $LXX^M$: *ōdē daueid*, "A Song of David"; Syr.: *tšbwḥt' ddwyd*, "A Song of David"; etc.). $LXX^L$ and Syr. open the poem in the manner of Ps 18:2, viz. *'rḥmk yhwh ḥzqy*, "I love you, Yahweh, my strength (and my trust [Syr.])!" The variation in the opening words is discussed at length by Schmuttermayr (1971:32–37).

*My cliffside stronghold* That is, *sl'y wmṣdty*, lit. "my cliff and my stronghold." For *wmṣdty*, "and my stronghold," $LXX^L$ has *ek thlipseōs mou* = *mṣrty*, "from my distress."

3. *My divine crag* That is, *'ly ṣwry*, lit. "My god, my crag," as in Ps 18:3 (cf. LXX, Vulg., Targ., $Syr.^{MSS}$). MT has *'lhy ṣwry*, "The god of my crag." Here and throughout the psalm LXX avoids a literal translation of *ṣwr*, "crag, mountain," as a divine epithet. $LXX^L$ here and elsewhere reads *plastēs*, "creator," which accords with the haggadic treatment of the epithet as if from the root *yṣr*, "form, shape," with its rabbinic by-form *ṣwr* (cf. Berakot 5b, on Job 18:4, etc.).

*my lofty refuge* That is, *mśgby wmnwsy*, lit. "my lofty place and my place of refuge." For *mśgby* $LXX^L$ has *monōtatos emoi*, evidently reading *lbd ly*, "mine alone."

*from violent men he saves me* MT has *mš'y mḥms tš'ny*, "my savior, from violence you save me." This is a corruption of *mš'y mḥmsym yš'ny*, "my savior, from violent men he saves me," the text reflected by $LXX^L$ (. . . *ex asebōn sōsei me)*. There is no other second-person verb in the first twenty-five lines of the poem, and confusion of final *-m* with *t* was possible in scripts of many periods. Syr. preserves an intermediate form in which the *m* was associated with the following word but not read as *t*: . . . *mn* *ʿwlʾ wprwgy* = *mḥms wmšʿny,* ". . . from violence and the one who saves me." The reconstructed line, *mšʿy mḥmsym yšʿny,* is evidently conflate: *mšʿy* and *yšʿny* are variants, and though there is little basis for choosing between them, we might impeach *mšʿy* for its conformity to the pattern of the previous *m*-prefix nouns. Thus we strike *mšʿy* (so Dhorme, Schulz) and read *mḥmsym yšʿny.*

The last four words of v. 3, *wmnwsy mšʿy mḥms tšʿny* (see above), are lacking in Psalm 18, and some critics (Gunkel 1926:68; cf. Smith) regard them as superfluous and secondary. Cross and Freedman (1953:21–22 n. 2) find variant texts, not wholly reconstructible, underlying vv. 2–4. In particular, they consider *mḥms tšʿny,* "from violence you save me," a variant of *mʾyby ʾwšʿ,* "from my enemies I am saved," in v. 4. See, in general, Schmuttermayr 1971:37–40.

4. *Derided* MT reads *mhll* as *mĕhullāl,* "praiseworthy," understood in reference to Yahweh. The word is treated by LXX in Ps 18:4 as *mĕhallēl,* "offering praise," understood in reference to the psalmist. But in view of Ps 102:9 [102:8], where *mhlly* is parallel to *ʾyby,* and for the sake of the parallelism in the present verse, we should probably read *mĕhōlal,* "treated as a fool, derided," if not *mimmĕhōlĕlay,* "from my deriders." Thus the colon is semantically and structurally equivalent to that at the beginning of v. 7, which resumes its force after vv. 5–6.

*I called for help* All witnesses reflect *ʾwšʿ,* "I was saved," but for the sake of the parallelism with *ʾqrʾ,* "I cried," we should probably read *ʾšwʿ.*

5. At the beginning of the verse MT has *ky.* Omit with Ps 18:5.

*breakers* So MT: *mšbry.* Syr., $MT^{MSS}$: *ḥbly,* "cords," as in Ps 18:5.

6. *Sheol* So MT, $LXX^{L}$. $LXX^{B}$: "death."

7. *called for help* MT again has *ʾqrʾ,* "cried," but LXX, Syr., and Vulg. all reflect different verbs. Thus we should probably follow Ps 18:7 in reading *ʾšwʿ* (Cross and Freedman 1953:23 n. 9).

*was in his ears* MT *bʾznyw.* Syr., like Ps 18:7, conflates this with a variant, *lpnyw tbwʾ,* "came before him" (cf. Vulg.). For a somewhat different interpretation of the evidence see Cross and Freedman 1953:23 n. 13.

8. *He took notice* MT *(kĕtîb): wtgʿš,* "(The earth) shuddered"; MT *(qĕrê): wytgʿš,* "He (Yahweh) shuddered." But this verb occurs later in the verse, and LXX *epeblepse* (also in Coptic and Armenian), attached to the beginning of the verse, suggests an alternative, viz. *wybṭ.* Perhaps *wtgʿš* arose as a marginal variant of *wtrʿš,* "quaked," and was erroneously introduced into the text in place of *wybṭ.*

*the mountains* So Syr. *(ṭwrʾ)* and Vulg. *(montium): hrym,* as in Ps 18:8. MT has *hšmym,* "the skies."

*they groaned* So $LXX^{L}$: *kai ephōnēsen* = *wyhgw.* MT has *wytgʿšw,* "they shuddered," as earlier in the verse.

*he was angry* So MT: *ḥrh lw.* $LXX^{B}$ (cf. Syr., $LXX^{L}$) = *ḥrh yhwh bhm* (Syr. = *ʿlyhm*), "Yahweh was angry with them."

9. *a devouring . . . mouth* That is, *wʾš mpyw tʾkl* (MT), lit. "and a fire from his mouth was devouring." For *mpyw* $LXX^{L}$ and Syr. read *mpnyw,* "from his face." For *tʾkl* $LXX^{L}$ reads *tʾkl ʾrṣ,* "was devouring the earth."

11. *a cherub* So MT. LXX: "cherubim" (preferred by Cross and Freedman 1953:24 n. 28).

*he swooped* Reading *(w)yd'* with Syr., Vulg., and Targ., as in Ps 18:11. MT has *wyr',* "he appeared," by confusion of *r* and *d.* Compare Deut 14:13, where MT reads *hr'h* for LXX/Samaritan *hd'h.*

12. *about him* Preceded by *strw,* "his hiding place," in LXX *(apokryphēs autou)* and Syr. *([l]gnyh),* as in Ps 18:12. Presumably *strw* arose as a marginal gloss on or variant of *sktw/swkw* below, possibly on the basis of Ps 27:5 (Schmuttermayr 1971:71).

*his covert* So LXX, Syr. = *sktw* (so Ps 18:12) or *swkw* (so $MT^{MSS}$). MT has *skwt,* "booths."

*the sieve of the waters* We follow MT in reading *ḥšrt mym* against $LXX^{B}$ and Ps 18:12, which have *ḥškt mym,* "the *darkness* of the waters" ($LXX^{L}$ = *[wy]ḥśk myw,* "and he withheld his waters"). See, further, the NOTE.

After *ḥšrt mym* MT has *'by šḥqym,* "thick masses of clouds" (so Ps 18:12). $LXX^{B}$ *epachynen en nephelais aeros* seems to reflect *'bh ('ibbâ) b'by šḥqym,* "He thickened (it) with dark masses of clouds," representing two interpretations of *'b-.* It has been noted that *'by šḥqym* does not fit metrically with what precedes it (Cross and Freedman 1953:25 n. 34), but attempts to combine it with the lightning imagery that follows produce awkward results (cf. Cross 1973:159 and n. 61). In all probability this extraneous phrase, *'by šḥqym,* arose as a gloss on *ḥšrt mym,* the obscure phrase that precedes it (G. R. Driver 1957:155–56; so Bardtke 1969:1099).

13. *flared/hail and glowing coals* Reading *b'rw brd wgḥly 'š.* MT has *b'rw gḥly 'š,* having lost *brd w-* after *b'rw.* $LXX^{L}$ preserves *brd w-,* but for *b'rw* reads *'brw,* "passed on"; this is also the reading of Ps 18:13, where *'brw* is prefixed by a corrupt duplicate, *'byw,* "his clouds" (cf. Feigin 1950:43)—thus *'byw 'brw brd wgḥly 'š,* "his clouds passed on (with) hail and glowing coals."

15. *shot lightning bolts* Variants are reflected here. MT *brq,* "lightning," probably arose from one variant, viz. *(wy)brq brq,* "he flashed lightning" (so $LXX^{LMN}$). Ps 18:15 has another, viz. *wbrqym rb,* "he shot lightning bolts," attested for II Sam 22:15 by Syr. *(wbrq'* [plural] *'sqy = wbrqym rbh).* $LXX^{L}$ reflects a combination of these variants in corrupt form: *wybrq brq bbrd,* "and he flashed lightning with hail." In favor of the second variant *(wbrqym rb[h])* are the suspicion of the influence of Ps 144:6 on the first and the occurrence of the rare verb *rbb/rbh,* "shoot (a bow)" (cf. Gen 21:20 and 49:23 in addition to **rab,* "archer," in Jer 50:29; Job 16:13; and Prov 26:10).

16. *The channels of the sea* That is, *'pqym ym.* The *-m* after *'pqy* is enclitic. It confused the scribes, who edited it out (II Sam 22:16) or associated it with *ym*—thus, *'pqy mym,* "the channels of water" (Ps 18:16). See Patton 1944:12; Cross and Freedman 1950:294 and 1953:17,26 n. 41; Hummel 1957:93; Freedman 1960:102–3.

*by Yahweh's roar* So MT: *bg'rt yhwh.* Ps 18:16 has *mg'rtk yhwh,* "by your roar, Yahweh," which shows the influence of Pss 76:7; 104:7 (cf. 80:17[80:16]).

*by the blast* MT has *bnšmt rwḥ,* which $LXX^{L}$ shows to be a conflation of variants. We omit *rwḥ* with $LXX^{L}$ *(apo pnoēs).*

*his nostrils* Ps 18:16: "*your* nostrils," as in the case of "roar" above.

18. *from my powerful enemies* We read *mē'ōyĕbay 'ōz,* lit. "from my enemies of power" (cf. Dahood 1965b:110). The rare but well-established phenomenon of a genitive following a suffixed noun ($GK^{2}$ §128d) led to the reinterpretation of this expression

as *mē'ōyĕbî 'ōz*, "from my powerful enemy," in MT, but the translations of the versions and the parallel (*miśśōnĕ'ay*, "from my foes") point to the plural. In LXX^L the confusion was resolved by a rearrangement of the text: *m'z 'yby*, "from the power of my enemies."

20. *He brought me out* We read MT *wyṣ' . . . 'ty*. LXX reflects *wyṣ'ny*, as in Ps 18:20, but the emphatic pronoun is distinctive and, as explained in the NOTE, essential to the meaning of the verse.

21. *according to my blamelessness* That is, *kbr ydy*, lit. "according to the cleanness of my hands." For *kbr* LXX^L reflects *kbd*—thus, "He returned to me *the honor* (= wealth?) of my hands." Cf. v. 25.

22. *strayed wickedly from* So MT: *rš'ty m-* (see the NOTE). LXX^L = *rš'ty b'yny-*, "acted wickedly in the eyes of."

23. *I had not removed . . . from me* So LXX^L: *ouk apostēsetai ap' emou* = *l' 'syr mny*, as in Ps 18:23. Emendation of *mny* to *mmny* with Cross and Freedman (1953:27 n. 55) is unwarranted: *mny* is a well-attested poetic form. MT has *l' 'swr mmnh*, "I had not departed from it (his statute [sing.]?)."

24. *towards him* So MT: *lw*. LXX^L, Vulg., and Syr. reflect *'mw*, "with him," as in Ps 18:24 (cf. Dahood 1965b:111–12).

25. *according to my blamelessness* Reading *kbr ydy*, lit. "according to the cleanness of my hands," with LXX, Syr., and Vulg., as in Ps 18:25. MT is defective as a result of confusion of *r* and *d*: **kbr* [*yd*]*y* > *kbry*, "according to my purity." Similarly, LXX^L has *doxasmos mou* = *kbdy* (< **kb*[*r y*]*dy*) before the LXX reading cited above. Cf. v. 21.

26. The textual confusion in this verse is the result of haplography and correction in a highly repetitive quatrain (vv. 26–27); it is to be explained as follows. The primitive text, reflected in our translation, read:

*'m ḥsyd tthsd*
*'m nqy tnqh*

MT lost the second bicolon by haplography when a scribe's eye skipped from *'m n-* in *'m nqy* to *'m n-* in *'m nbr* in v. 27. The defective text was then corrected imperfectly. Instead of *'m nqy tnqh* a variant, *'m tmym ttmm*, was introduced, probably under the influence of v. 24. Moreover, as often happens, a duplicate arose at the point of insertion, *nbr* being preserved both before and after it. The awkward sequence *nbr tmym* then became *gbr tmym* (cf. Ps 18:26). Thus, in MT we read, "With the loyal you are loyal,/with the faultless warrior *(gibbôr tammîm)* you are faultless." LXX^L preserves the primitive reading, except that the equivalent of MT's second semicolon has been inserted recensionally between the first and second semicola. The original second semicolon, *'m nqy tnqh*, is rendered unambiguously *meta athōou athōos esē* by LXX^L, *athōos* being used elsewhere to translate only forms of *nqh*. Note that the LXX of Ps 18:26 also preserves this original translation, though it has been adjusted to the pattern of MT by the insertion of *andros* (= *gbr*) before *athōou*, as if *athōou athōos esē* = *tmym ttmm*.

27. *you are devious* Reading *ttptl*, as in Ps 18:27. MT has *ttpl*, "you are ignominious," but it can probably be said of the author of this poem, as it is of Job, that "He did not ascribe ignominy *(tiplâ)* to God" (Job 1:22). The translations of LXX^BMN and Syr. employ verbs cognate to the substantives preceding them, suggesting a variant

*t'qš,* "you are perverse." One could argue that this arose in conformity to the pattern of the three preceding semicola, as I assume, or, conversely, that *t'qš* was regarded as blasphemous by a scribe, to whom *ttptl* was more acceptable (though the verbs seem to have been synonymous).

28. *You* Reading *w't* (= *wĕ'attā* in archaic orthography; Cross and Freedman 1953:28 n. 62) with MT (cf. I Sam 24:18; Ps 6:4; Job 1:10; Eccles 7:22; Neh 9:6). LXX *ky 'th,* "For you" (so Ps 18:28), anticipates v. 29.

*but the eyes of the exalted* MT has *w'ynyk 'l rmym,* "but your eyes are on the exalted." The texts of LXX^L and Ps 18:28 show that *'l* is secondary, added after *'ynyk* arose by confusion of final *-m* and *-k* from *'ynym* (so LXX^B, Ps 18:28). The primitive reading was *w'yny-m rmym,* but the enclitic *-m* confused the scribes, who deleted it (= *w'yny rmym,* so LXX^L) or revised *rmym* to an adjective (= *w'ynym rmwt,* "but the exalted eyes"; cf. Syr.).

29. *You are my lamp* So MT: *'th nyry.* LXX^LMN reflect *'th t'yr nry,* "You *light* my lamp," as in Ps 18:29. The expansion, *t'yr,* probably arose from a marginal variant of *y/tgyh* below.

*my god* Reading *'ly* on the basis of LXX *moi* (!) or *'lhy* on the basis of Ps 18:29 for MT *wyhwh,* "and Yahweh."

*who sheds light on* That is, *ygyh,* a relative clause without a relative pronoun (GK² §155f); so MT. LXX^L reflects *tgyh,* "*you* shed light on" (so LXX in Ps 18:29).

30. *I can leap a gully* See the NOTES.

*I can jump a wall* So MT: *'dlg šwr,* rendered *exaloumai hōs moschos,* "I can jump like a bull" (as if *šwr* = *šôr*), by LXX^L (!).

33. *who girded me* Reading *m'zrny* with 4QSam^a (cf. LXX^L, OL, Syr., Vulg., and Ps 18:33). MT has *m'wzy,* "is my refuge." LXX^B *ho krataiōn me* suggests *m'zzny,* "who strengthened me," though the verb is not elsewhere attested in *Pi'el* (Prov 8:28?).

*and mapped out* Perhaps the obscurity of this stich is the result of the defective spelling of *wyt'r,* lit. "and he traced," as *wytr* (cf. *wtzrny,* v. 40), interpreted by MT as *wayyattēr,* "and he searched out (?)," and replaced in Ps 18:33 by the *lectio facilior wytn,* "and he set, established."

*dominion for me* That is, *drky;* so MT *(qĕrê),* LXX, and Ps 18:33. MT *(kĕtîb): drkw,* "*his* dominion" (cf. v. 31).

34. *my legs* So MT *(qĕrê),* as in the versions and Ps 18:34. MT *(kĕtîb):* "*his* legs."

*like tree trunks* Reading *kĕ'ēlôt,* "like trees, terebinths," for MT *kā'ayyālôt,* "like does, hinds."

*upright* So MT: *'l bmwty* (cf. 4QSam^a: [. . . *b*]*mty*), lit. "on my backs, haunches." See 1:19.

35. *he shaped* MT *(w)nḥt* (see the NOTE). LXX^L at this point betrays the influence of I Sam 2:4: *kai ouk ēsthenēse* = *wl' ḥth,* "and (the bow of my arm) was not shattered."

*the bows of my arms* Reading *qšt zr'ty* with LXX^L *toxon brachionos mou* (so Nowack, Schulz). MT has *qšt nḥwšh zr'ty*—thus, "(He shaped) my arms as a bow *of bronze.*" This would be entirely appropriate. The "bow of bronze" of Job 20:24 is not a bow made of bronze or with bronze ornamentation or reinforcement (de Vaux). Nor is it necessary to think of "bow" in such a context as synecdoche (G. R. Driver 1951:248) or (better) metonymy for "arrowhead." Couroyer (1965) has shown that "bronze," a symbol of strength elsewhere (Jer 1:18; Job 6:12; 40:18; etc.), refers to the great strength of the bow (cf. Pope 1973:153). Thus *nḥwšh* would fit the sense of the present passage well. But the shorter text of LXX$^L$ deserves preference, and the stich is too long metrically with the word in place. It may have arisen under the influence of Job 20:24 (Segal 1914/15:219). Since the parallel, *yāday*, "my hands," is plural, we should probably retain the plural vocalization of MT, *zĕrō'ōtāy*, "my arms." Perhaps *qšt* should be read *qāšōt*, "bows" (cf. *I Samuel*, the *Textual Note* on 2:4, and Dahood 1965a:15), referring to the bows (*el*bows!) of the two arms. But "the bow (MT *qešet*) of my arms," referring to the sweep of the two arms together as bow-shaped, is also possible.

36. *the gift* See the NOTE.

*your victory* MT *yš'k*, for which LXX reflects *yš'y*, "*my* victory." In Ps 18:36, too, MT has "your . . ." and LXX "my. . . ." 4QSam$^a$ reads *yš'k*.

At this point LXX$^L$ and Syr. reflect *wymynk ts'dny*, "Your right hand supported me," as in Ps 18:36. On the conflate text of LXX$^L$, see Ulrich (1978:140). These words are lacking in the text of MT, however, and also in the usually full text of 4QSam$^a$, and although Ulrich speaks of haplography here (Cross and Freedman [1953:31 n. 82]: "accidentally dropped out"), I should argue for the originality of the shorter text (cf. Nowack, Dhorme, Bardtke 1969:1100).

*your conquest* Reading *'nwtk*, as in Ps 18:36 (see the NOTE). MT has *'ntk*, "your response." Wellhausen's conjecture, *'zrtk*, "your help," now turns up in 4QSam$^a$. It is a (graphic) variant of *'nwtk*, and the latter must be preferred by reason of its relative obscurity.

37. *my stride . . . beneath me* So MT: *ṣ'dy tḥtny*. In LXX$^L$ a reading proximate to that of MT has been inserted before an older rendering of the verse. In the older text LXX$^L$ reads at this point *oligotētes exestēsan me* = *ṣ'rym ḥtny*, "insignificant men dismayed me." 4QSam$^a$ omits "beneath me."

*and . . . falter* MT *wl' m'dw qrsly*, for which the older translation in LXX$^L$ (see above) reads *kai ouch hypestēsan me hoi hypenantioi* = *wl' 'mdw qwmy ly*, "and those who arose against me did not stand" (cf. Ulrich 1978:102). In 4QSam$^a$ only the very beginning of this stich survives *(wl[']),* and there is also the beginning of a supralinear addition *(wl')*. Ulrich's conjecture that the scroll preserved the two readings also combined in LXX$^L$ is credible.

38. *I destroyed them* So MT, 4QSam$^a$, and all witnesses to the text of Samuel: *w'šmydm*. Ps 18:38 has a variant, *w'śygm*, "I overtook them."

*until they were finished* So 4QSam$^a$: *'d klwtm*, lit. "until finishing them," as in Ps 18:38. LXX reflects a variant (rendered twice by LXX$^L$): *'d ('šr) 'klm*, "until I finished them." MT is conflate, embracing both variants in a harmonized text: *'d klwtm w'klm*, "until they were finished. And I finished them. . . ." See, further, the *Textual Note* that follows.

39. *they did not get up* MT *wl' yqwmwn*, for which Syr. and Targ. reflect *wl' yklw qwm*, "they were not able to get up," as in Ps 18:39. It is possible that *yklw* arose from a marginal indication of MT's variant, *'klm*, at the end of the preceding verse (see above) or, alternatively, that *'klm* arose from a marginal *yklw*.

40. *You girded me* MT is defective: *wtzrny*. 4QSam$^a$ reads *[w]t'zrny*, as in Ps 18:40. One is tempted to read *tazzīrēnī*, "You sanctified me (for battle)," omitting *ḥyl* as reminiscent of v. 33.

*sturdily* MT *ḥyl,* lit. "with strength," to which LXX^L *(dynamin)* adds *kai agalliasin* = *wgyl* (?), "and rejoicing," a corrupt variant (cf. Ps 65:13).

41. *I struck them down!* 4QSam^a: *'ṣmytm,* as in Ps 18:41 (cf. LXX^L). MT: *w'ṣmytm.* LXX^B = *w'mytm,* "and I *killed* them."

42. *They cried for help* So LXX = *yšw'w,* as in Ps 18:42. MT has *yš'w,* "They looked."

*no one to save them* So MT and 4QSam^a: *'yn mšy'.* LXX^B *ouk estin boēthos* suggests *'yn mšw',* "no cry for help."

*to Yahweh* So MT and 4QSam^a: *'l yhwh,* interpreted by LXX^L as "God Yahweh." In Ps 18:42 *'l* has become *'l,* "because of" (?), rendered "the Most High" by Dahood (1965b:117).

43. *like the dirt of a path* 4QSam^a has [*k'pr 'l*] *pny 'rḥ,* which shows the primitive reading to have been *k'pr 'rḥ,* as conjectured by Wutz (1925). In MT (cf. LXX^B) this has become *k'pr 'rṣ,* "like the dirt of the earth." In LXX^L and Syr. it has become *k'pr 'l pny rwḥ,* "like dirt (dust) on the face of the wind," as in Ps 18:43. Dahood's suggestion (1965b:117) to vocalize *rwḥ* as *rewaḥ*—thus, "in the square" (cf. the NOTE on "on the wings of the wind," v. 11)—also saves the parallelism, but it does not explain the reading of II Sam 22:43.

*I mashed them* MT combines two variants: *'dqm 'rq'm,* "I crushed them, I mashed them." The first of these is reflected alone in LXX^B, but in LXX^L it has become *'r(y)qm,* "I poured them out" (but see G. R. Driver 1936:173–74), as in Ps 18:43. We follow 4QSam^a in reading *'rq'm* alone.

44. *the conflicts of the army* Reading *mērîbê 'ām,* as in Ps 18:44. In the MT of II Sam 22:44 *'m,* "the people, army," has become *'my,* "my people," possibly by "actualization" towards the events of David's life (cf. Schmuttermayr 1971:169–70). LXX^B reflects *'mym,* "the peoples"; cf. the variation in Ps 144:2 between *'my* (MT) and *'mym* (MT^MSS, Syr., Targ., Vulg.). Witnesses to *'m* in II Sam 22:44 include LXX^L, Syr., and Targ. The reading *mryby* is supported by MT and Syr. in II Sam 22:44 and indirectly by LXX^L (= *mrby,* understood as *mērabbê,* "from the leaders [of the army]"). In light of *mērībĕbôt 'ām,* "from the myriads of the army," in Ps 3:7 [3:6], some critics would restore *mēribbô 'ām* (Ehrlich 1910:339; Rehm) or *mērībĕbôt 'ām* (Kraus 1963:139; cf. Bardtke 1969:1101) here.

*and set me* So LXX^L *(ethou me)* and Syr. *([w]t'bdny): tśymny,* as in Ps 18:44. MT has *tšmrny,* "and protected me."

*at the head of the nations* MT *lr'š gwym.* LXX^L = *l'wr gwym,* "as the light of the nations" (!); cf. Isa 42:6; 49:6. Cf. Nowack.

45–46. The text of these verses is confused in all witnesses. The major witnesses read as follows:

MT: *bny nkr ytkḥšw ly*
*lšmw' 'zn yšm'w ly*
*bny nkr yblw*
*wyḥgrw mmsgrwtm*

Ps 18:45–46: *lšm' 'zn yšm'w ly*
*bny nkr ykḥšw ly*
*bny nkr yblw*
*wyḥrgw mmsgrwtyhm*

4QSam$^{a}$: *lšm*[*' 'zn yšm' ly*]
[*bny nkr ykḥšw ly*]
*l' yḥgrw mmsrwtm*

(On the reconstruction of the scroll, cf. Ulrich 1978:109–11.) The simplest explanation of the data assumes *bny nkr y(t)kḥšw ly* and *bny nkr yblw (ly)* to be variants. Thus both II Sam 22:45–46 and Ps 18:45–46 are conflate. 4QSam$^{a}$ preserves a shorter text, but *l'* is probably a replacement for *bl,* a corrupt vestige of a marginal indication of *yblw* (Ulrich). The arrangement of MT was probably like that of the psalm at one time, but *bny nkr ytkḥšw ly* was lost by haplography and restored in a different position. We read:

*lšm' 'zn yšm'w ly*
*bny nkr ytkḥšw ly*
*yḥgrw mmsgrwtm.*

For further details see the *Textual Notes* that follow.

46. *abased themselves* MT *ytkḥšw,* for which Ps 18:46 has *ykḥšw* (cf. Deut 33:29).

*they came fettered* MT has *wyḥgrw,* "and they girded themselves" (?), evidently understood as "and they came halting" by LXX$^{B}$ (*kai sphalousin,* "and they stumbled") and LXX to Ps 18:46 (*kai echōlanan,* "and they limped") in light of Postbiblical Hebrew *ḥgr,* "limp, be halt." LXX$^{L}$ *elytrōthēsan,* "they were released," is difficult to explain; Ulrich (1978:111) guesses that it might represent an interpretation of *yḥgrw* as "they were *un*girt"—hence 4QSam$^{a}$ *l' yḥgrw,* "they were *not* girt" (see the *Textual Note* above on vv. 45–46). The reading of Ps 18:46, *wyḥrgw,* is made attractive by its very obscurity; it is adopted here. The translation is discussed in the NOTE.

*by their collars* That is, *mmsgrwtm* (so MT and Ps 18:46); see the NOTE. 4QSam$^{a}$ has *mmsrwtm,* "by their bonds" (so LXX$^{L}$: *ek tōn desmōn autōn*). In Ps 18:46 LXX has *apo tōn tribōn autōn* = *mmslwtm,* "from their highways" (!).

47. *my god . . . my safe crag* The witnesses differ in the placement of the parallel words *'lhy,* "(my) god," and *ṣwr(y),* "(my) crag." In Ps 18:47 we read "my crag . . . the god of my safety" (cf. LXX$^{MN}$ in the present passage). In MT (II Sam 22:47) and the LXX of Ps 18:47 the two words are read together in the second position ("my god, my safe crag"); but while MT has "my crag" in the first position, the LXX of Ps 18:47 has "my god." No witness preserves the arrangement we read (*'lhy . . . ṣwr yš'y*), but the context (". . . be high") favors it. Note that for *ṣwry* (in the first position) LXX$^{L}$ reads *ho plasas me* = *hyṣrny,* "the one who created me" (cf. Syr. *mḥylny* [?]).

48. *The god* Combined in LXX with the variant "Yahweh."

*who gave* Expressed by a participle in MT *(hntn)* but in LXX$^{L}$ *(hos edōken)* and 4QSam$^{a}$ *(['šr] ntn)* by a finite verbal clause. The latter is prosaic (Freedman).

*subduing* The original reading is preserved in 4QSam$^{a}$: *wmrdd* (cf. LXX$^{L}$); cf. Ps 144:2. This has become *wmwryd,* "bringing down," in MT (MT$^{MS}$: *wmryd*) and evidently *mysr,* "disciplining," in LXX$^{B}$ *(paideuōn).* Ps 18:48 displays a variant, *wydbr,* "and he subdued" (cf. G. R. Driver 1930:284), as in Ps 47:4.

49. *and taking me away* So MT: *wmwṣy'y* (cf. LXX$^{B}$). LXX$^{L}$ = *ywyṣy',* "and he took me away." Syr. = *wmplṭy,* "and rescuing me" (cf. Ps 18:49).

*Yes* Reading *'p* for MT *w-,* "And," as in Syr. and Ps 18:49. LXX$^{L}$ places *'p* earlier: "from the wrath *('p)* of the enemies," etc.

*you lifted me up* LXX$^{L}$, Syr.$^{MSS}$ = "*he* lifted me up."

*from my foes* MT *wmqmy,* for which LXX[L] reflects *wmmqwmy,* "from my place."

*you protected me* Reading *tnṣrny* with LXX[L] *(dietrēsas)* and 4QSam[a] *([t]n̊ṣrny).* MT has *tṣylny,* "you saved me."

*from violent men* That is, *m'yš ḥms* (collective); so Syr., Ps 18:49, and according to space requirements, probably 4QSam[a]. MT (cf. LXX) has *m'yš ḥmsym,* as in Ps 140:2.

50. The divine name occurs at least once in this verse in all witnesses, but the variety of its location shows it to have been original nowhere. It probably arose from the reference to "your name," for which LXX[L] reads "the name of Yahweh." In MT and LXX[B] it stands before "among the nations," and in LXX[L] and Syr. it stands after (so Ps 18:50).

*I sing praise* MT *'zmr,* for which LXX[L] reads *'zkr,* "I bring to mind, remember."

51. *The one who magnifies the victories* We read *mgdl yšw't.* The first word can be interpreted as *magdīl,* "The one who magnifies" (so MT [*kĕtîb*], LXX, and Ps 18:51 [*magdîl*]), or *migdal,* "The tower" (cf. Prov 18:10; here MT [*qĕrê*] has *migdôl,* which occurs elsewhere only as the name of a city [Exod 14:2, etc.]). The second word can be read *yĕšû'ōt,* "victories" (so MT and Ps 18:50 [*yĕšû'ôt*]; cf. LXX[B]) or *yĕšû'at,* "safety" (so LXX[L] and 4QSam[a] [*yšw't*]). In view of the predominant theme of the latter part of the poem, "The one who magnifies the victories" seems better than "The tower of safety" (cf. vv. 2–3).

*with David* Followed in LXX[L] by a variant, *eis genea* = *ldwr,* "with (his) generation" (= *ldwr wdwr,* "from generation to generation," parallel to *'d 'wlm,* "forever"?).

## NOTES

A preliminary note on the spelling practices represented by the text of the psalm is in order. The orthography of II Samuel 22 is generally conservative in comparison to that of Psalm 18 in particular and to Masoretic usage as a whole. One especially striking feature has been stressed by Cross and Freedman (1953:16). Several times in the poem the vowel *ô* contracted from an original diphthong *aw* is spelled without *w: mš'y* and *tš'ny* in v. 3; *mqšy* in v. 6; *msdwt* in v. 16; and *mšy'* in v. 42. The first two of these are not extant in the text of Psalm 18, but the three that are extant are spelled with *w: mwqšy* in v. 6; *mwsdwt* in v. 16; and *mwšy'* in v. 42. One of the five survives in the text of 4QSam[a], and it is written defectively: *m̊šy'* in v. 42. There are two further probable examples of defective spelling of *ô* < **aw* in the MT of II Samuel 22: *yblw* (= **yōbīlû;* cf. Klostermann, Nestle 1896:324, and Cross and Freedman 1953:33 n. 103) in v. 46; and *mryd* (= **mōrîd,* preserved in the Aleppo Codex of MT but not the Leningrad Codex; cf. the *Textual Note* on "subduing," v. 48, and Cross and Freedman 1953:34 n. 109) in v. 48. Elsewhere there are five cases of *aw* or *ô* < **aw* for which the full spelling is used: *mwt* in v. 5; *mwt* in v. 6; *mwsdwt* in v. 8; *twšy'* in v. 28; and *mwṣy'y* in v. 49; *qwly* in v. 7, *qwlw* in v. 14, and *ywm* in v. 19 are ambiguous (cf. Cross and Freedman 1952:24,50,53). II Samuel 22, therefore, preserves a stage in the development of orthographic practices at which the indication of medial *ô* < **aw* by *w* has not yet been leveled through the text, as it has in Psalm 18. The surprising aspect of this is that there seems to have been no stage in the development of the spelling of *Judaean* Hebrew when **aw* was not represented by *w*. In pre-exilic Judaean Hebrew *aw* remained uncontracted in all positions and thus was consistently represented by *w* (Cross and Freedman 1952:57; Freedman 1962:89), as recently confirmed by the publication of the Hebrew inscriptions from Arad (cf. Aharoni 1981:142). We know little of the spelling practices of the fifth and fourth centuries, but in third-century orthography, when **aw* had contracted to *ô* in unstressed positions, the sound was represented by *w* with general consistency. On the other hand, *ō* not derived from **aw* was not consistently represented by *w* in this later period (cf. Freedman 1962). This suggests that the representation of *ô* < **aw* by *w* was a survival of historical spelling and thus that there never was a time when *ô* < **aw* was not represented by *w* in Judaean Hebrew. If the defective spellings of II Samuel 22 are Judaean in origin, therefore, they must represent an artificial and deliberately archaizing orthography deriving from a time after the contraction of diphthongs. We know of no such orthography. In view of considerations of this kind, Cross and Freedman postulated a *northern* origin for our psalm (1953:16; cf. Freedman 1962:89). In Israelite Hebrew the diphthong *aw* was contracted in all positions (Cross and Freedman 1952:57). Assuming, then, that the cases noted above in which *ô* < **aw* is represented by *w* are secondary modernizations, we should suppose the orthography of II Samuel 22 to be pre-exilic and Israelite. It follows that the author of the psalm was a northerner, or at least that the psalm passed through the hands of an editor who spoke the northern dialect. This hypothesis, though attractive, remains tentative. Our evidence is too meager to rule out the existence of an archaizing orthographic tradition in early post-exilic Judah, and the data of II Samuel 22 need to be cast against the background of a book-by-book statistical analysis of Masoretic orthography as a whole.

**22** 1. The psalm is identified with events in David's life, as in Psalms 3, 7, 18 (= II Samuel 22), 34, 51, 52, 54, 56, 57, 59, 60, 63, and 142. In contrast with the other cases, however, II Samuel 22 = Psalm 18 is not related to a specific incident but rather to Yahweh's ongoing protection of David, his rescue of David from "Saul and all his enemies" throughout his life. According to Dahood (1965b:104, the reference is even more general, viz. to David's rescue from "Sheol (*šĕʾōl* for *šāʾûl*, 'Saul') and all his enemies."

2–3. In the opening section of the psalm Yahweh is praised under the image of a place of refuge high on a rocky hillside. The psalmist makes frequent use of hendiadys, best resolved in English: "my cliff and my stronghold" = "my cliffside stronghold"; "my god, my crag" = "my divine crag"; "my sovereign [see below] and my peak of safety" = "my sovereign peak of safety", "my height and my refuge" = "my lofty refuge." The concept of Yahweh as a "crag" or "mountain" *(ṣûr)* offering refuge and safety is common (Isa 17:10; Pss 31:3–4 [31 2–3], 71:3, and often). More generally, though, Yahweh is "the crag of Israel" *(ṣûr yiśrāʾēl)*; cf. II Sam 23:3 and Isa 30:29, where *ṣûr*, "crag," is virtually a synonym for *ʾĕlōhîm*, "god." Compare also such archaic proper names as *ṣûrîʾēl*, "El is my crag" (Num 3:35); *ṣûrîšadday*, "Shaddai is my crag" (Num 1:6; etc.); and *pādâ ṣûr*, "the Crag has ransomed" (Num 1:10; etc., cf Noth 1928.129–30), as well as *haṣṣûr*, "the Crag," used as an independent divine title in passages like Hab 1:12 (cf Deut 32:4,18,37; etc.). "Many of the most important

Anatolian and Northwest-Semitic deities of the second millennium B.C. were deified mountains—a fact which . . . explains why *ṣûr,* 'mountain' . . . appears so often in such an archaic poem as [Deuteronomy 32] in the meaning 'god, God,' as well as why it has the same sense in several Hebrew personal names of the Mosaic period" (Albright 1961:23). Elsewhere in the present poem, therefore, when we find *ṣûr,* "crag," parallel to *'ēl,* "god" (vv. 32,47), we need not think specifically of the image of a lofty place of refuge invoked here. In other words, *ṣûr* is another general designation for a divine being.

3. *My sovereign.* Hebrew **mĕgānî* (MT *maginnî,* "My shield"), on which see the NOTE on "shield" at 1:21. It might seem prudent to retain "shield" in a context of shelter and protection like this. But *mgny* stands in this stich in the position of *'ly,* "My god" ("My divine [crag]"), in the last. Moreover, *māgān,* "sovereign," *is* a term of protection. Fundamentally it seems to designate one who bestows (feudal) gifts (see the NOTE on "the gift of your victory," v. 36, and Dahood 1965b:16–17) and thus a suzerain who provides protection to his vassals in return for service. Thus Yahweh is called "a sovereign for all who seek refuge with him" in v. 31, where the parallel stich refers to the completeness of his "dominion" *(darkô).*

4. The psalmist invokes divine help against his enemies, a common motif in the Psalter: 3:2 [3:1]; 7:2 [7:1]; 17:10 [17:9]; etc.

*I cried . . . I called.* Hebrew *'eqrā' . . . 'iwwāšēa'.* Here and often throughout the poem prefixed verb forms express past actions, contrary to the standard pattern of Hebrew prose. Study of the Ugaritic verb has shown that the prefixed form "was the common, generally used verb form in old Israelite poetry, as in old Canaanite poetry, and that its time aspect was determined by the context" (Cross and Freedman 1953:20).

5–6. Compare Ps 116:3 and especially Jonah 2:6–7a [2:5–6a]. The psalmist likens his distress to entrapment at the watery entrance to Sheol, the Underworld. On this imagery in general see McCarter 1973.

5. *hell.* That is, *bĕlîya'al,* "(the place of) not coming up," on which see the NOTE at 16:7 and, on the present passage, Cross and Freedman 1953:22 n. 6. The parallelism here of *bĕlîya'al* to *mawet,* "death," and *šĕ'ōl,* "Sheol, the Underworld," confirms this interpretation against that which understands *bĕlîya'al* as "worthlessness."

6. *Sheol.* A common biblical designation for the shadowy abode of the dead. For the derivation of *šĕ'ōl,* "place of interrogation," see McCarter 1973:408 n. 20 and bibliography cited there.

7. *his temple.* For *hêkāl,* "temple," used of Yahweh's *heavenly* dwelling, see also Pss 11:4 and 138:2 (?), cited by Patton (1944:21); cf. Mic 1:2.

8. The quaking of the earth (Ps 77:19 [77:18]), mountains (Isa 5:25), or foundations of the earth (Isa 24:18) is a standard cosmic response to the approach of Yahweh in archaic and archaizing biblical poetry. Compare especially Judg 5:4–5 and Ps 68:9 [68:8] in addition to extrabiblical passages cited at v. 14 below. In this context "the earth" probably refers to the netherworld, as argued by Dahood 1965b:106; cf. Tromp 1969:23–46.

*they groaned because he was angry.* The third stich of the verse is suspected of being a gloss by many interpreters; cf. Cross and Freedman 1953:23; Schmuttermayr 1971:62; and Bardtke in *BHS,* p. 1099. But, as shown in the *Textual Notes,* the verb *htg'š,* "shuddered," the repetition of which has raised suspicions (cf. Cross and Freedman

1953:23 n. 18), was not used again here in the original, and the chiastic pattern of the tricolon favors retaining the stich:

> He took notice, and the earth shuddered . . ,
>
> they groaned because he was angry.

9. In his anger Yahweh breathes fire like the monster Leviathan in Job 41:12. Elsewhere, too, Yahweh vents his wrath by breathing fire (Isa 66:15; Ezek 21:36 [21:31]; 22:31; 36:5; 38:19; etc.) and smoke (Deut 29:19 [29:20]; Isa 65:5; Pss 74:1; 80:5 [80:4]). In vv. 13ff. below, the fiery language becomes part of the larger thunderstorm imagery that pervades this section of the poem.

10. *He spread open the sky.* Yahweh spreads apart the sky like a warrior spreading open the flaps of his tent. The verb *nāṭâ/hiṭṭâ,* used only here and in Ps 144:5 in such a context, might also mean "bend down, incline"—thus, "He bowed the heavens" (RSV). However, in view of Isa 63:19, "You tore open *(qāra'tā)* the sky (and) came down," the first interpretation is more likely (Cross and Freedman 1953:24 n. 23; Cross 1973:159 n. 59).

10–11. Elsewhere Yahweh is described as a sky-rider (Ps 68:34 [68:33]), who employs a cloud chariot to fly on the wings of the wind (Ps 104:3; cf. Isa 19:1). If the standard emendation or interpretation (cf. Dahood 1968:136) of *rōkēb ba'ărābôt* in Ps 68:5 [68:4] as "he who rides on the clouds" is correct, we have there a direct parallel to the common epithet of Ugaritic Baal Cloudrider (*rkb 'rpt;* see citations in Patton 1944:20).

11. *Mounting.* For the preferability of rendering *rkb* in this sense rather than "riding" or "traveling," see the discussion and bibliography in Schmuttermayr 1971: 64–66.

*a cherub.* A mythological creature, probably in the form of a winged lion with a human head, i.e., a winged sphinx (Albright 1938). "Seated-upon-the-Cherubim" was a cultic epithet of the Shilonite Yahweh, envisioned as an enthroned monarch; see the NOTE at 6:2. Here Yahweh is thought of as swooping through the sky astride (?) a cherub.

*on the wings of the wind.* Dahood (1965b:107) argues that *bknpy rwḥ* means not "on the wings of the wind" *(rûaḥ)* but "on the wings of broadness" *(rewaḥ),* i.e., "on wings outstretched."

12. *his covert.* Hebrew *sukkātô* (see the *Textual Note*). Compare Job 36:29:

> Can anyone understand the billowing clouds,
> the thunderings of his covert *(sukkātô)?*

*the sieve of the waters.* Hebrew *ḥašrat mayim,* the meaning of which was correctly understood by the rabbis (Taanit 9b) in light of Postbiblical Hebrew *ḥāšar,* "sift, distill through a sieve." It is confirmed by the Ugaritic noun *ḥṯr,* "sieve" (*CTCA* 6 [= *UT*⁴ 49].2.32). In Arabic the same verb *(ḥaṯara)* means "become solid, thick, viscous; coagulate; curdle"; this suggests an alternative rendering of *ḥašrat,* viz. "(place of) condensation." In any case, this cosmic structure is the celestial rain cloud. Perhaps it was called a sieve because rain falls to earth from it in small drops; see, in general, Feigin (1950), who, however, is mistaken in his preference (p. 42) for "the sieve of the skies" to "the sieve of the waters" *(šmym* for *mym).*

13. To the rain-cloud imagery is now added flashing lightning and hail. The mode

of theophany is the thunderstorm, as often in older biblical poetry. See Cross 1973: 156–63.

14. For the voice of the storm god as thunder, see, for example, *CTCA* 4 [= UT⁴ 51].5.70–71, *wtn qlh b'rpt šrh l'arṣ brqm,* "(Baal) will sound his voice in the clouds, flashing lightning bolts to the ground"; *EA* 147:14–15, ". . . who utters his cry in the sky like Adad, and the whole earth quakes from his cry." See Schoors in Fisher 1972:23–24. The motif is also common in biblical poetry: Isa 30:30–31; Jer 10:13 = 51:16; Joel 4:16 [3:16]; Amos 1:2; Pss 29:3–9; 46:7 [46:6]; 68:34 [68:33]; 77:18–19 [77:17–18]; 104:7; Job 37:4 (cf. Joel 2:11). In prose: Exod 9:22–35 (cf. 19:16; 20:18); I Sam 7:9–10 (cf. 12:17–18).

*Elyon.* The "Most High" of the gods, to whom all the gods (Yahweh included originally: cf. Deut 32:8 [LXX, OL, Symmachus, 4QDt^q]) were subordinate (Ps 82:6), was identified by the Israelites with their god, and *'elyôn* has become an epithet of Yahweh in the biblical literature (Pss 7:18 [7:17]; 47:3 [47:2]). Elsewhere *yahweh* and *'elyôn* stand in parallelism in Pss 21:8 [21:7]; 83:19 [83:18]; 87:5–6; 91:9; 92:2 [92:1]; etc.

15. Like Zeus and the Ugaritic Baal, Yahweh hurled thunderbolts at his enemies: Hab 3:11; Pss 77:19 [77:18]; 97:4; 144:6 (cf. Zech 9:14; etc.).

*them . . . them.* The arrows, not the enemies, who will first appear in v. 18 (Duhm 1899:54; Dahood 1965b:109).

16–17. Compare vv. 5–6. Yahweh's roar lays bare the bottom of the sea, where the psalmist is entrapped at the gates of the Underworld. From there, "in the deep waters," Yahweh rescues him.

*The channels of the sea.* Hebrew *'ăpîqê-m( ) yām;* the enclitic *-m( )* particle is discussed in the *Textual Note.* Patton (1944:29,34,35) cites *CTCA* 3[= *UT*⁴ 'nt].4(E).14–15 and 17[= 2 Aqht].6.48: *'apq thmtm tgl(y).* Comparison of the biblical "channels of the sea" to the Ugaritic "channels of the double-deep" is apt, but in the Ugaritic passages the verb refers to opening a tent flap, not to exposing the bottom of the sea. For *'apq thmtm* alone, see also *CTCA* 4[= *UT*⁴ 51].4.22; 6[= 49].1.6.

*the foundations of the world.* Hebrew *mōsĕdôt tēbel,* to which Patton (1944:29) compares *môsĕdê 'ăreṣ* in Ps 82:5 and *msdt 'arṣ* in *CTCA* 4[= *UT*⁴ 51].1.41, both "the foundations of the earth." To this list we can add *môsĕdê 'ăreṣ* in Isa 24:18; Jer 31:37; Mic 6:2; and Prov 8:29; *môsĕdôt hā'ăreṣ* in Isa 40:2; *môsĕdê hārîm,* "the foundations of the mountains," in Deut 32:22; and *môsĕdê dôr wādôr,* "the eternal foundations," in Isa 58:12.

*Yahweh's roar.* Hebrew *ga'ărat yahweh,* on which see May 1955:17 n. 32; Dahood 1965b:110; and Cross 1973:159 n. 63.

18–19. The imagery of thunderstorm and raging waters gives way to a more direct mode of expression. It is no longer the subterranean "snares of death" (v. 6) that have "waylaid" the psalmist but rather his enemies.

19. *the day of my ordeal.* See McCarter 1973 for the background to this expression.

20. *into the open.* Compare Ps 31:9 [31:8]: "You did not hand me over to an enemy;/you made my feet stand in the open *(bammerḥāb).*" *Hammerḥāb,* "the open," refers to broad space with plenty of room. In the present passage, then, *lammerḥāb* means "into the open" and refers to Yahweh's rescue of the psalmist from his tight predicament. Dahood (1965b:111) and Tromp (1969:47), however, understand *hammerḥāb* as "the broad domain," a designation of the netherworld, and translate, "He

brought me out of the broad domain." Dahood renders Ps 31:9 [31:8], "You did not put me into the hand of the Foe, nor set my feet in the broad domain," understanding the particle *lō'* as negating both verbs (1965b:189). In the case of the obscure occurrence of *merḥāb* in Ps 118:5, however, Dahood finds a reference not to the netherworld but to Yahweh's celestial abode (!); see Dahood 1970:156. The two occurrences of *(ham)merḥāb* outside of the Psalter weigh against Dahood's interpretations. In Hab 1:6 *lĕmerḥăbê-'ereṣ* refers to the Babylonians' march "abroad" to capture lands not rightfully theirs, and in Hos 14:16 Yahweh is said to shepherd Israel *kĕkebeś bammer-ḥāb,* "like a lamb in the open," i.e., "in a wide pasture" (cf. Andersen and Freedman 1980:377).

*me . . . because he preferred me.* The first pronoun is emphatic, and the phrase *kî ḥāpēṣ bî* indicates not only affection but preference (20:11). The psalmist asserts that Yahweh rescued *him* (and not someone else) because of a preference for him over others —in particular, we may assume, over the enemies of vv. 18–19.

21–25. In these verses the psalmist boasts of his innocence and purity. Notice the repetition in vv. 21 and 25. This forms a chiastic inclusion (Schmuttermayr 1971:99) and marks off the section as a compositional unit within the poem. I am inclined, moreover, to agree with the earlier literary critics (Duhm 1899:54; Briggs 1906:145; Segal 1914/15:211–13; etc.) and, recently, Veijola (1975:120–24) in regarding vv. 21–25 (or at least vv. 22–25) as an expansion. There is distinctive Deuteronomistic language here. To "keep the ways of Yahweh" *(šāmar darkê yahweh)* in v. 22, compare Judg 2:22 (reading *darkê* for MT *derek* with Targ.), and for "the ways of Yahweh" see Deut 8:6; 10:12; 11:22; 19:9; 26:17; 28:9; 30:16; Josh 22:5; I Kings 2:3; 3:14; 8:58; 11:33,38; II Kings 21:22. The "judgments" and "statutes" of v. 23 are among the most familiar of Deuteronomistic clichés (cf. Weinfeld 1972:337–38). Contrast Weiser (1962:192–93), who argues that these features are not necessarily Deuteronomistic (cf. also Schmuttermayr 1971:95–99). See, further, the COMMENT.

22. *strayed wickedly from.* A pregnant construction: *lō' rāša'tî mē'ĕlōhāy,* lit. "I had not acted wickedly (turning away) from my god." Cross and Freedman (1953:27 n. 53) follow Albright in doubting the legitimacy of such a construction and restore *lō' pāš-a'tî . . . ,* "I have not *rebelled against . . . ,*" comparing II Kings 8:20,22. For similar reasons Dahood (1965b:111) would associate the *m* of *m'lhy* with *rāša'tî* as enclitic and read *'ĕlōhāy* as vocative: "(I) have not been guilty, O my God." But *rāša'* occurs only nine times in *Qal,* and it seems too bold, therefore, to reject *rāša' min-* because it is not found elsewhere. Moreover, similar pregnant constructions involving *min-* with other verbs abound (GK[2] §119xy and especially 119ff.).

27. *with the pure you are pure.* Hebrew *'im-nābār tittābar.* Zorell (1928), troubled by the contrast in v. 27 after the synonymous parallelism of v. 26, compares Arabic *nabara,* "raise," which, when used of the voice, can describe either insolent or imperious behavior. He suggests a translation like "with the proud you deal with harsh severity."

30. *I can leap.* The text reads *'ārûṣ,* "I can run"; but this could be construed with an object only very awkwardly, and the meaning would have to be "I can rush toward, against" or the like (Schmuttermayr 1971:109). Conjectures for interpreting *'ārûṣ gĕdûd* include "I can run (= go on) a raid" (KB[3]) and, reading *'ārîṣ* for *'ārûṣ,* "I can put a raiding party to flight" (Fleet 1931). The suggestion of Kimchi to derive the verb

from *rṣṣ*, "crush," has been revived by Smith, Nowack, Dhorme, and others. But the parallelism of *'adalleg*, "I can jump," is strongly against all of these possibilities (Schmuttermayr 1971:110). I think the solution lies in a different direction. With recognition of the meaning of *gĕdûd*, "gully" or "fence" (see below), and in view of the parallel, *'ădalleg-šûr*, "I can jump a wall," it seems very likely that *'rwṣ* is a simple corruption of *'dwṣ*, "I can leap," a rare verb attested elsewhere only in Job 41:14. Confusion of *resh* and *dalet* is so common as hardly to require comment (cf. the *Textual Notes* on "he swooped," v. 11, and "according to my blamelessness," v. 21).

*a gully*. Hebrew *gĕdûd*. For the meaning "gully" compare Ps 65:11 [65:10], where *gĕdûdêhā*, "its (the earth's) gullies," is parallel to *tĕlāmêhā*, "its furrows"; the verb *hitgōdēd* means to make incisions *(gĕdûdôt)* in one's flesh. A possible but less likely meaning of *gĕdûd* is "wall," on which see KB³. In any case, emendation to *gādēr*, "wall," in violation of the principle *lectior difficilior preferendum est* is out of the question.

31. Something is wrong in this verse. Cross and Freedman (1953:29 n. 67) compare the first line to that of Deut 32:4:

> The crag whose work *(pā'olô)* is perfect,
> for all his deeds *(derākāyw)* are just.

They ask if a similar second line might have fallen out of our poem. They also note Prov 30:5, which is almost identical to the second and third lines of the present verse:

> Every decree of God *('ĕlôah)* is pure silver;
> he is a sovereign for those who seek refuge with him.

I think it is most likely that our second line is intrusive, a scribal importation from Prov 30:5 (so Dhorme, Hertzberg, de Vaux, and many Psalms commentators); cf. also Bardtke 1969:1100.

*dominion*. This meaning of *derek*, corresponding to Ugaritic *drkt*, is now widely recognized. See Dahood 1954 and, for bibliography, 1965b:2.

*pure silver*. Hebrew *ṣĕrûpâ*, "pure, refined." "Silver" is implied; cf. Akkadian *ṣarpu*, "refined (silver)," and *ṣurruppu*, "refined" (attested only of silver).

*a sovereign*. Hebrew *māgān* (MT *māgēn*), on which see the NOTE at v. 3.

32. The "monotheistic formula" found here appears in other literature first in the seventh century (Eichrodt 1961:vol. I:221), and it becomes common only later still. The language suggests a late date: *mibbal'ădê*, "but, apart from," occurs elsewhere only in Josh 22:19, a late passage in Joshua (Noth 1981:117 n. 18) and Deutero-Isaiah (cf. Hartmann 1961:235). In fact, such a lyrical outburst of monotheistic sentiment reminds us more of Deutero-Isaiah (43:11; 44:6,8; 45:21) than anything else. It is not likely to have been a part of the original form of our poem (cf. Segal 1914/15:213). Indeed, we can probably identify the source of the expansion: Isa 45:5, where we read "I am Yahweh and there is no one else! Apart from me there is no god!" followed by "I gird you . . . ," to which compare v. 31 below.

33–46. A number of key terms in these verses have gone unrecognized or unexplained, with the result that the passage appears in most modern translations as a rather obscure description of Yahweh's equipping the psalmist for war, as the expression "gird sturdily" or "gird with strength (= armor)" in vv. 33 and 40 might suggest, and bringing him victory. In fact, however, the imagery is richer and more extravagant.

Yahweh *creates* the psalmist, fashions him as an efficient and powerful fighting machine capable of subduing the earth. Verse 33 introduces both themes, the creation of the warrior and the subjugation of the earth. In vv. 34–35 the divine manufacture of the psalmist is described. Yahweh first forms two powerful legs and positions a warrior's body atop them (v. 34). Then he attaches the hands and arms (v. 35), tuned for fighting. The newly built fighting man is then granted a march of conquest (v. 36). Set in motion (v. 37) with long, steady strides, he subdues his enemies (vv. 38–43) and takes his position as an imperial ruler (vv. 44–46).

33. *who girded me sturdily.* Hebrew *mĕʿazzĕrēnî ḥāyil.* Compare the ironic reversal in I Sam 2:4 between the mighty, whose "bows" (elbows, arms; see below) are shattered (?) or paralyzed with fear *(ḥattîm),* and the feeble, who are "girded with strength" *(ʾāzĕrû ḥayil).* To gird with strength is to wrap stoutly, sturdily. It refers here to Yahweh's manufacture (!) of the body of the psalmist as a tightly wrapped and powerfully muscled instrument of war. This half-verse, then, introduces the theme of the divine manufacture of the psalmist-warrior in vv. 34–37.

*and mapped out.* Hebrew *wayyĕtāʾēr,* spelled defectively in the received text as *wytr* (= **wayyĕtā*[ʾ]*r*). The verb is used twice in Isa 44:13 with reference to a woodworker's use of a line and compass to trace out the design of his handiwork. It is generally acknowledged to underlie the corrupt text of Num 34:7,8,10, where it refers to mapping out geographical boundaries. It probably occurs in Hab 3:6 in the same defective spelling found in our passage: "He (Yahweh) stood and surveyed *(wymdd)* the earth./ He looked and mapped out *(wyt*[ʾ]*r)* the nations." In the present passage it refers to Yahweh's mapping out a universal dominion for the psalmist, and it thus introduces the theme of vv. 38–46 below.

*complete dominion for me.* Hebrew *darkî tāmîm,* lit. "my dominion (as) complete." On *derek,* "dominion," see the NOTE at v. 31 above.

34. *upright.* Hebrew *ʿal bāmôtay,* lit. "on my backs, haunches." As explained in the NOTES at 1:19 and 1:25, where David eulogizes Saul and Jonathan as having been slain "on your backs," that is, "standing upright" like warriors, the expression "stand on one's 'backs' *(ʿal bāmôt-)*" is an idiomatic way of referring to upright posture. Here the psalmist says that Yahweh, having given him legs like two powerful tree stumps, set his body atop his *bāmôt,* his hips and calves. Compare Hab 3:19: "Yahweh girded me (read *ʾzrny* for MT *ʾdny*) sturdily: he set my legs like tree trunks, and he caused me to walk *(yadrīkēnî)* upright *(ʿal bāmôtay).*"

35. *he shaped.* Hebrew *nīḥat.* Dahood (1965b:114) aptly compares *CTCA* 2.4 (= *UT*[4] 68).11 and 18, but he speaks of lowering weapons into the hands of a warrior. An important meaning of the verb *nḥt* is not cited in the standard Hebrew and Ugaritic lexicons. The clue is Arabic *naḥata,* which means "hew, shape, dress (stone or wood)," etc.; cf the noun *naḥt,* which refers to woodwork, stonework, or sculpture. In Hebrew and Ugaritic *nāḥat (Qal)* and *nḥt* (G) mean "descend." The Hebrew verb occurs once (Ps 38.3 [38 2]) in *Nipʿal* with the sense "penetrate, sink in." Hebrew *nīḥat (Piʿel)* and Ugaritic *nḥt* (D) do not mean simply "bring down, lower" but "*press* down, engrave, grave" and thus "fashion, shape, grave." This is clear in the Ugaritic passage cited above, where it is said of Kothar, the craftsman god, that he "fashioned *(ynḥt)* a pair of clubs" for Baal—precisely what we expect of the Canaanite Hephaestus. On the other hand, to say that "Kothar lowered/brought down a pair of clubs" makes little

sense. In the present passage we are told that Yahweh, still under the image of a divine craftsman fashioning a sturdy warrior, "shaped *(nīḥat)* the bows of my arms." That this is the meaning of the verb here has already been recognized by Reider (1952:114), who translates "fashions my arms into bows of brass." Compare, finally, Ps 65:11 [65:10], where God sends rain upon the earth, "Drenching its furrows, carving out *(naḥēt)* its gullies *(gĕdûdêhā;* cf. v. 30 above)." Other studies of this verb are reviewed by Schmuttermayr 1971:141–45, to which we may now add Couroyer 1981.

*the bows of my arms.* The word "bows" (or "bow") refers to the *shape* or *form* of the psalmist's arms, not to an archer's weapon. Yahweh fashions his arms as bows. Each hand (*yad,* the palm and wrist) is tuned for fighting. Each arm (*zĕrôa',* the strong part of the arm to the shoulder) is a mighty bow (*el*bow!).

36. *the gift of your victory.* Hebrew *mĕgan yiš'ékā.* The noun *māgān* is to be understood in light of Ugaritic *mgn,* "gift," and the verb *mgn,* "give." Compare Akkadian *magannu,* "(freely given) gift," an Indo-Iranian loanword by way of Hurrian. The Canaanite word must derive from Akkadian; so, too, Aramaic *maggān,* "gratuitously, in vain" (= Akkadian *ina/ana magāni*), and even Arabic, *majjan,* "gift." Hebrew **miggēn,* "give," occurs in Gen 14:20; Isa 64:6 (LXX); Hos 11:8; and Prov 4:9. The term seems originally to have had to do with the granting of feudal gifts; thus it may be related to Phoenician-Hebrew *mgn,* "sovereign, suzerain" (cf. vv. 3,31), i.e., one who bestows feudal gifts.

*your victory . . . your conquest.* The word *'anwātĕkā* has been interpreted in many ways (cf. Schmuttermayr 1971:148–52). Dahood (1965b:116) is surely correct to stress the parallelism of *yiš'ékā* and *'anwātĕkā* and insist on interpreting the latter in light of the verb **'nw,* "subdue, conquer." The Phoenician inscription of Azitawadda from Karatepe illustrates the meaning well: "And I conquered *(w'n)* powerful lands which all the kings who were before me had not conquered *(bl 'n)*" (*KAI* 26A I.19; *ANET*[3], pp. 653–54).

37. *beneath me.* Hebrew *taḥtēnî,* a form occurring only in this poem (vv. 37,40,48) in Biblical Hebrew. In Psalm 18 it is replaced by the conventional form, *taḥtáy,* in each occurrence. In both Ugaritic and Phoenician, prepositions are sometimes augmented with *n* before pronominal suffixes or (rarely) even nouns (Gordon 1965 §12.9; Segert 1976 §51.26), a phenomenon occurring regularly in Biblical Hebrew only in the case of *min-,* "from." To *taḥtēnî* compare especially Phoenician *tḥtn* (= *taḥtēnī*) in the Kilamuwa inscription (*KAI* 24.14) and *tḥtnm* on the sarcophagus of Eshmunazor (*KAI* 14.9).

38–39. *they were finished . . . I smashed them.* The Ugaritic verbs *mḫṣ,* "smash," and *kly,* "finish off," occur in parallel in *CTCA* 5[= *UT*' 67].1.27–28; 19[= 1 Aqht].4.196–97,201–2 (Patton 1944:40). Elsewhere (*CTCA* 2.4[= *UT*' 68].9; 3[= 'nt].2.7–8) *mḫṣ* stands parallel to *ṣmt,* "destroy," leading Dahood (in Fisher 1972:258) to speak of a poetic inclusion in vv. 39–41: "I smashed them . . . I destroyed them." See the NOTE at v. 41b below.

40–41a. The foes of the warrior-psalmist cower in submission. In v. 41a in particular, Dahood (1965b:116) identifies "the image of the victor placing his foot on the neck of the vanquished, as represented on reliefs and described in literary texts." He compares Josh 10:24, Exod 23:27, and Isa 51:23, to which we may add Gen 49:8.

41b. *My adversaries—I struck them down!* Should this be associated with what precedes or what follows? In favor of grouping it with the foregoing lines is the apparent parallelism of vv. 40b ("my foes"), 41a ("my enemies"), and 41b ("My adversaries"). In favor of grouping it with the following lines is the first-person verb, which looks ahead to v. 43. Note also that *'aṣmîtêhem,* "I struck them down" (on the meaning of *ṣmt* see Held 1959, especially p. 172 n. 56), resumes the force of *'emḥāṣēm,* "I smashed them," in v. 39; these verbs stand parallel in *CTCA* 2.4[= *UT*[4] 68].9 (cf. 3[= 'nt].2.7–8):

> Your enemies, O Baal—
> your enemies you will smash *(tmḫṣ)!*
> You will strike down *(tṣmt)* your foes!

"This means that, although standing apart, the paired verbs create an inclusion. The ancient listener or reader would doubtless have recognized the parallel brace and mentally linked the separated cola together" (Dahood in Fisher 1972:vol. I:80; cf. p. 258). By this technique the second-person passage in vv. 40–41a with its somewhat different theme (the surrender of enemies) is isolated, and the principal theme of vv. 38–43 (the slaying of enemies) is picked up from v. 39.

46. *they came fettered by their collars.* Hebrew *wayyaḥrĕgû mimmisgĕrôtām.* The verb *ḥrg* seems not to have meant "tremble (with rage or fear)" (cf. BDB, KB[3]), an interpretation relying heavily on Mic 7:17 (". . . they will squirm [*yrgzw*] because of their collars"), but rather "be straitened" or even "be paralyzed" (Arabic *ḥarija,* "be tight; be straitened, confined"; cf. Targumic Aramaic *ḥrgt mwt',* "rigor mortis" [!]). The noun *misgĕrôtām,* lit. "their rims" and thus "their neck stocks, collars," is probably the plural of *masgēr,* which BDB and KB[3] take as "dungeon" but which Ps 142:8 (*masgēr napšî,* "the *masgēr* of my neck" [!]) shows to have meant "(neck) stock, collar" like Biblical Hebrew *sûgar* (cf. Rabbinic *sûgār,* "dog collar"), a loanword from Assyrian *šigāru,* "neck stock." The reference, then, is to conquered foreigners cringing before the psalmist and immobilized by reason of *(min-)* the stocks or collars they wear on their necks.

47. *As Yahweh lives.* The standard oath formula, *ḥay yahweh.* Arguing for a precative translation on the basis of the rest of the verse, Dahood (1965b:118) renders "May Yahweh live!" citing Ewald and comparing *CTCA* 10[= *UT*[4] 76].2.20, *ḥwt 'aḫt,* "May you live, O my sister!" See also the discussion of Schmuttermayr 1971:182–87.

51. This verse contains a final word of praise, as v. 50 leads us to expect (Ehrlich 1910:340). However, the specificity with which Yahweh is praised as David's benefactor has raised questions about the originality of the verse. Some of the earlier commentators thought the verse as a whole to be an addition intended to give the psalm closer application to the context identified in v. 1 (Nowack, etc.). More common, however, is the view that only v. 51c, "with David and his descendants forever," is secondary (Duhm 1899:59; Cross and Freedman 1953:34 n. 116; etc.), an "actualizing" plus from the pen of the redactor who inserted the poem here (cf. Schmuttermayr 1971:199). Veijola (1975:120–24) argues that v. 51c, along with vv. 1 and 21–25, reflects the touch of a Deuteronomistic hand. Nevertheless, the language seems appropriate to an old royal psalm. As Cross and Freedman point out (1953:34 n. 116), *mĕšîḥô,* "his anointed," uses a term found frequently in the oldest sources of Samuel (I Sam 26: 9,11,16,23; II Sam 1:14,16; 19:22) and poses no obstacle to an early date for v. 51. The rest of the terminology in v. 51bc is that of the ancient (Solomonic) promise of kingship to David underlying II Samuel 7, viz. vv. 11b–12 + 13b–15a (cf. pp. 224–25):

1) *ʿōśeh ḥesed*, "who deals loyally." Cf. 7:15 and the NOTE there on Yahweh's *ḥesed*, special "favor" or "loyalty" that maintains the family of David on the throne.

2) *zarʿô*, "his descendants." Cf. *zarʿăkā*, rendered "your offspring" in 7:12.

3) *ʿad ʿôlām*, "forever." As in 7:13b (cf. 7:29). 7:16 is Deuteronomistic.

The terminology of v. 51, then, is that of Nathan's oracle and related passages. This might mean (1) that v. 51 is an original part of the psalm, which (therefore) must stem from circles at the Jerusalem court or, conversely, (2) that v. 51 (or at least v. 51c) is an addition based on Nathan's oracle intended to associate a psalm that was *not* from the Jerusalem court with the house of David. In the preliminary NOTE on orthography and in the COMMENT we reckon with the possibility of a northern (Israelite) origin of the psalm. If this is correct, we shall have to bracket v. 51 (or at least v. 51c) as secondary.

## COMMENT

This psalm comes down to us in two versions, II Samuel 22 and Psalm 18. There are no structural or compositional differences between the two, and it is certain that they stem from a single original poem. The several divergences that do exist are scribal in origin and correspond to the categories of change that take place in the transmission of any ancient text (modernization of grammar and spelling, scribal errors, glosses, etc.). The presence of a doubly attested poem in the received text of the Bible affords a special advantage to students of the transmission of the text, and a relatively small number of such poems exist (Pss 14 = 53; 40:13–17 = 70; 57:8–12 = 60:7–14 = 108; Ps 96:1–13 = I Chron 16:22–33; Ps 105:1–15 = I Chron 16:8–22; Ps 106:1,47–48 = I Chron 16:34–36). Of these only II Samuel 22 = Psalm 18 is thought to contain poetry of high antiquity. Our psalm, therefore, has attracted a great amount of scholarly attention. A full review of the literature before 1971 can be found in the balanced study of Schmuttermayr.

### *Structure*

"Like the two spires of a cathedral the two parts of the mighty hymn soar to heaven" (Weiser 1962:187). The psalm extols Yahweh with praise and thanksgiving throughout, but it does divide naturally into two parts. The first, vv. 2–20, describes the psalmist's rescue from his enemies under the image of raging waters. Its dominant theme is the storm theophany of Yahweh. The second part, vv. 29–51, describes the psalmist as a mighty warrior who conquers distant lands. Yahweh is praised as the psalmist-warrior's creator and the author of his victories. The intervening material, vv. 21–28, consists of an assertion of the psalmist's innocence and purity (vv. 21–25) followed by the quotation of "an old gnomic quatrain" (Cross and Freedman 1953:28 n. 60) (vv. 26–27) and a brief reference to Yahweh's just reversal of human fortunes (v. 28).

Some interpreters have concluded that the psalm is an amalgamation of two (or more) originally independent songs (Schmidt 1934; Baumann 1945/48:132; Michel 1960:49; etc.). Others deny this (Weiser 1962:186; etc.). Still others leave the question open (Cross and Freedman 1953:21). The presence of Deuteronomistic language in vv. 21–25 (see the NOTE), the major part of the verses that bind the two parts of the psalm together, suggests that the unity of the psalm may be editorial. The quatrain quoted in vv. 26–27 may be quite ancient (cf. Albright 1969b:25), but it does not relate directly to the principal themes of either of the two main sections of the psalm. The same can be said of v. 28. These transitional verses (21–28), together with the monotheistic formula of v. 32 (if it is not a still later addition [see the NOTE]), may have been introduced by the editor who added the psalm to the appendix of the Samuel corpus. By thus combining two old poems he produced a whole with direct application to the two dominant aspects of the then extant David tradition, viz. David's vindication from his enemies (Saul, Abiner, Ishbaal, Abishalom) and his foreign conquests. The first poem (vv. 2–20) was an old song of deliverance; it had no royal aspect before it was joined to the second poem (cf. Baumann 1945/48:136). The second poem (vv. 29–31 + 33–50 [51ab?]) was a royal victory song.

### *Provenience*

The presence of Deuteronomistic language in the linking segment indicates that the psalm as a whole probably does not predate the seventh century. This provides only a *terminus ante quem*, however, for the two major parts, which can have been much older. Before the Qumran discoveries showed that the psalm already existed in fully developed form in the pre-Christian period, a number of scholars believed it to be Maccabean in date (Duhm 1899:59; Spoer 1907:155). A few have continued to defend a post-exilic date (Tournay 1956: 167). Most now agree, however, that the poetry of the psalm is consistently archaic, as shown by comparison to Ugaritic poetry, early biblical poetry, and (by contrast) later biblical poetry with sporadic archaizing features (cf. Schmuttermayr 1971:23–24). The pioneer study in this respect was that of Cross and Freedman (1953), who identified archaic elements of language, theme, and prosody throughout the poem. Most of the more recent commentators on Samuel (Hertzberg, van den Born, Goslinga) and Psalms (Weiser 1962:186; Kraus 1963:141) support an early date. Many would agree specifically with Freedman (1976:96), who now assigns the psalm to the tenth century in agreement with biblical tradition (cf. Albright 1969b:25 [tenth]; Robertson 1972:155 [eleventh–tenth]; Schmuttermayr 1971:24 [tenth–ninth]).

The insertion of the psalm along with 23:1–7 here at the end of the Samuel corpus suggests that it may have been regarded as old and venerable and that it had a traditional association with David surpassing that of the pseudepigraphical David songs in the Psalter. There is, however, no internal support of the sort displayed by the lament in chap. 1 for assuming Davidic authorship. One or both of the major parts of the psalm may have been composed as early as the time of David, and it is unlikely that either postdates the ninth century; but as a whole the psalm is a product of the seventh century or later. There is some reason, moreover, to think that it was composed by an Israelite, i.e., a speaker of the northern dialect (see the preliminary NOTE on orthography above).

In view of these considerations we can tentatively reconstruct the literary history of II Samuel 22 = Psalm 18 as follows. The two poems in vv. 2–20 and vv. 29–31 + 33–50 (51ab?) were composed early in the monarchical period, possibly in the northern kingdom. In seventh- or sixth-century Judah these two old poems were known and held in high regard, and their antiquity was recognized. At least the second poem, the royal victory song, had come to be associated with David. The psalm of deliverance may also have been assigned Davidic authorship. At that time the two poems were combined by an editor who inserted between them vv. 21–28, which reflect the Deuteronomistic theology of the day. The superscription in v. 1 and the reference to "David and his descendants forever" in v. 51c (if not v. 51 as a whole) were also added at this time. The result was a long poem of praise and thanksgiving applicable to the two aspects of the David tradition found in the Deuteronomistic history, viz. deliverance from enemies and military conquest. Along with the "Last Words of David" (23:1–7), the psalm was included in the appendix to the stories of David. This appendix seems to have been compiled after the composition of the Deuteronomistic history; cf. Noth (1981:125 n. 3) and Veijola (1975:120–24), who thinks the two poems were edited and put in their present position by the "nomistic" Deuteronomist (DtrN; contrast Mettinger 1976:281). See also the Introduction, pp. 18–19.

# XXXVIII. THE LAST WORDS OF DAVID
(23:1–7)

23 [1]These are the last words of David:
The utterance of David son of Jesse,
the utterance of the man God established,
the anointed of the god of Jacob,
the darling of the stronghold of Israel.
[2]"Yahweh's breath spoke through me,
his word was upon my tongue.
[3]The god of Jacob spoke to me,
Israel's crag said:
'One who rules justly among men
ruling in the fear of God,
[4]is like the light of a morning at sunrise,
a morning too bright for clouds,
when because of a rain there is verdure from the earth.'
[5]Surely my house is like this with God!
For he has given me a perpetual covenant
fully set forth and secured.
But the man who shows no regard for me,
he who does not favor me,
will not sprout [6]and will not grow up.
They are like uprooted thorns, all of them.
For they cannot be held in the hand,
[7]and a man cannot touch them,
except with an iron or wooden tool—
in the fire they will be burned up!"

## *TEXTUAL NOTES*

23 1. *oracle* (bis) In both cases LXX *(pistos)* and OL *(fidelis)* reflect *n'mn*, "secure, faithful." Read *n'm* with MT.

*God established* Reading *hqym 'l* with 4QSam[a] *(hqym 'l)* and LXX[L] *(hon anestēsen ho theos)*. MT has *hqm 'l*, "established on high," which Barthélemy (1980:35) defends by comparison to Num 24:3,15. It has been suggested that *'l* represents the divine name *'al* or *'ēlī*, "the Most High" (Nyberg 1938:378,383; Driver 1938:92–93; cf. Bewer 1942:47–48; Richardson 1971:260–61; cf. already Dhorme [= *'elyôn* abbreviated]); but in view of the frequent interchange of the prepositions *'l* and *'l* in Samuel (22:42; etc.), it is safer to read *'l* here (so Cross 1973:52 n. 31, 234 n. 66).

*the stronghold* MT has *zmrwt*, which Mettinger (1976/77:151) takes as an "intensive plural," comparing *bĕhēmôt*, "the beast par-excellence"; but the singular, *zmrt*, "stronghold," has textual support. It is preserved in the texts of LXX[B] and OL, which, however, understand it as "the song." For the translation see the NOTE.

3. *Jacob* So LXX[L], OL. MT has "Israel."

*to me* MT *ly*, for which Syr. reflects *wly*, "and to me," and LXX[L], OL *by*, "through me" (cf. v. 2). According to *BHS*, *ly* is omitted by MT[MSS].

*One . . . God* The text of LXX[B] is seriously confused. It reads *parabolēn eipon en anthropō pōs krataiōsētai* (so LXX[M]; LXX[B]: *krataiōsēte*) *phobon christou*, apparently reflecting *mšl 'mr* (= *'ōmār* [Wellhausen]) *b'dm 'yk tmšl yr't mšyḥ*, "a parable. I said among mankind, 'How will the fear of the anointed be grasped?' " The primary corruption seems to have arisen from graphic confusion involving **ṣdq*, which was mistaken for *'k t-*: *ṣ* and *'*, *d* and final *k*, and *q* and *t* were all easily confused, especially in the scripts of the fourth and early third centuries. As Wellhausen suggests, *'mr* is probably a mistake for *'dm*, *en anthrōpō* being a secondary correction towards MT. *Christou* might be the contribution of a Christian scribe (Wellhausen). More likely, however, it is a corruption of *ischyrou*, "the Mighty One," the LXX[L] translation of *'l* in v. 5, under the influence of *christon theou* in v. 1. Note *(kai) en theou* at the beginning of v. 5 in LXX[B], a marginal correction of *phobon christou* to *en phobou theou* that found its way into the text in the wrong place. Underlying the troubled text of LXX[B], then, is a reading not substantially different from that of MT: *mšl (b)'dm ṣdq mšl (b)yr't 'l*.

*One who rules* The primitive text had *mšl*, preserved in its second occurrence below by 4QSam[a]. It is interpreted (correctly) by MT as *môšēl*, "One who rules." As noted above, LXX[B] understands *mšl* in its first occurrence as *māšāl*, "a parable." LXX[L] *(arxon)* takes it as an imperative, *mĕšōl*, "Rule!" Cross (1973:235 n. 70) prefers this, but it is inconsistent with v. 2 ("*through* me") and, more importantly (since v. 2 may be secondary [see the NOTE]), it creates difficulties in the syntactic relationship between vv 3 and 4.

*the fear* MT *yr't* is possibly to be prefixed with *b-* (so MT[MSS], LXX[L], OL, Syr., Targ., and Vulg.); but cf. Richardson 1971:262; Cross 1973:235 n. 71.

*God* We should probably read *'l*, as in vv. 2 and 5, for MT *'lhym* (cf. LXX[LMN]; LXX[A], OL: "Yahweh"), as hinted by the curious reading of LXX[B], *christou*, "(the) anointed one." See the *Textual Note* on "One . . . God" above.

4. This verse provides the predicate of v. 3b (contrast Mettinger 1976/77:148–49), a fact obscured by the introduction of *w-*, "and," at the beginning of v. 4 in MT. Richardson (1971:262) calls this "The *waw emphaticum*," but it is shown to be secondary by LXX[L], OL, Syr., and Vulg., all of which omit it.

*a morning too bright for clouds* MT *bqr l' 'bwt mngh*, lit. "a morning without clouds from (= because of) brightness." In LXX[B] *'bwt* was misread as the verb *'br* and supplied with a subject—thus, *to prōi ou kyrios parēlthen ek phengous* = *bqr l' yhwh* *'br mnghwt* (cf. Isa 59:9), "a morning (when) Yahweh did not pass by from (its) light," a syntactical abomination (< **bqr l' yhyw 'bwt mngh?*).

*when because of a rain* We read *mmṭr* with MT, lit. "from rain." MT^MSS have *wmmṭr* (so Syr.), "and from rain." LXX^L and OL reflect *kmṭr*, "like rain" (= "when as if from a rain"?). LXX^B reflects *wkmmṭr*, "and as from rain" (= *ûkĕmō māṭār*, "and like rain"?; cf. Freedman 1971:329).

5. *set forth* MT *'rwkh*, which in LXX^L is read as *'d kh (heōs ōde)*. This is preceded in LXX^L by *sōsai me* = *lhwš'ny* (?), "to save me," and it is followed in OL by the same addition *(salvare me)*. Note that below, in place of MT *yš'y*, "my help, salvation," LXX^L has a different reading. It may be that the addition here arose from a recensional correction in the margin there.

*But the man . . .* The key to this difficult passage is recognition of the repetition of the negative particle *bl/bly* underlying the present readings of the principal witnesses. Note that where MT has *kl ḥpṣ*, "every delight," LXX^L reflects *l' yḥpṣ*, "he will not take delight." The original must have been *bly ḥpṣ*, "one who does not take delight (in), favor": In MT *bly* was misread as *kl*, while in LXX^L *bl-* was replaced by its more common synonym *l'* and *-y* associated with *ḥpṣ*. Similarly, MT reads *l'* before *yṣmḥ* while LXX^L reflects *kl*; the original must have been *bl*. It follows that we should also read *bly š'y*, "one who does not show regard for me," for MT *kl yš'y*, "all my help" (thus recovering a better parallel to *bly ḥpṣ*, "one who does not favor me") and redivide *bly'l* at the beginning of v. 6 as *bl y'l*. The result is a symmetrical tricolon structurally reminiscent of v. 4 (syllable = count in parentheses):

| | |
|---|---|
| *ky bly š'y* | (5) |
| *wbly ḥpṣ by* | (6) |
| *bl yṣmḥ wbl y'l* | (6) |

*the man who shows no regard for me* Reading *bly š'y (šō'î)* for MT *kl yš'y*, as explained in the preceding *Textual Note*. LXX^L *panta ton antitheton moi* seems to reflect *kl śm 'ly*, which should be read *bly šm' ly*, "one who does not obey me," a variant of *bly š'y*.

*he who does not favor me* Reading *wbly ḥpṣ by* for MT *wkl ḥpṣ ky*, as explained above. According to *BHS*, *by* has the support of MT^MSS.

*will not sprout* Reading *bl yṣmḥ* for MT *l' yṣmyḥ*, as explained above. LXX^L *pantes hoi anatellontes* seems to reflect *kl hṣmḥym*.

6. *and will not grow up* Reading MT *wbly'l* as *wbl y'l*, as explained above. LXX^L seems to omit this word, but *kai hoi loipoi*, "and the rest," may be an error for *kai hoi loimoi* = *wbly'l* (understood collectively, as the passage would require), the majuscules *pi* and *mu* being easily confused.

*like* So LXX^BL: *k-*. MT has *b-*, "in, among." Confusion of *bet* and *kap* is rampant in this poem.

*uprooted thorns* So MT: *qwṣ mnd*. LXX^L *apomygma lychnou*, "the snuff of a lamp," may reflect *qwṣ* (cf. KB³) *mnr(h)* (= *minnēr* or *mĕnōrâ*) or perhaps *qnb nr* (cf. Postbiblical Hebrew *qĕnîbâ*, "snuffing [of a wick]")—thus, "They are like the snuff of a lamp, all of them, for they cannot be taken (cf. *mlqḥym*, "snuffers") in the hand. . . ."

*all of them* MT *kullāham* is, according to de Boer (1957:55), a combination of *kullĕhem* and *kullām*; the former is the older form and probably original here.

7. *cannot touch* So MT: *yiggaʿ*, understood by LXX[B] as *yīgaʿ*, "weary himself with." LXX[L] *ekleipsei* (cf. OL) suggests *ygwʿ*, "will perish" (all but one MS of LXX[L] actually read *ekthlipsei*, "will squeeze," a secondary adjustment towards the lampwick-snuffing interpretation). The negativity of the verb, made explicit in LXX, is derived from the *l*ʾ in the preceding colon.

*except* MT has *yml*ʾ, understood as *yimmālēʾ*, "he will be filled." Most commentators since Thenius (who cites de Wette) take this to mean "he will arm himself," on the basis of *wĕyēhûʾ millēʾ yādô baqqešet* in II Kings 9:24, understood as "And Jehu filled his hand (= armed himself) with a bow." I doubt this is possible. In any case, LXX[L] *ean mē* (cf. OL) preserves a superior reading, viz. *ʾm l*ʾ, "if not, unless, except."

*with an iron or wooden tool* That is, *brzl wʿṣ*, lit "(with) iron or wood." In some witnesses (e.g., Syr.) "with" is explicit. LXX[L] *sidēros kai xyla diakopsē/ei autous* suggests "(unless) iron or wood splits them"; but, in fact, *kai xyla* and *diakopsei* probably reflect variants, viz. *wbʿṣ* and *ybṣʿ*. We might conjecture the original form of this colon to have been *ʾm lʾ bgrzn ʿṣ*, "except with a wooden ax," but despite Syr. *(d)nrgʾ* the evidence is too meager to emend *brzl w-* to *bgrzn* (cf. Mowinckel 1927:40).

At this point MT adds *ḥnyt*, "a spear"—thus, *ʿṣ ḥnyt*, "the wood (= shaft) of a spear." LXX[L] and OL (cf. Syr.) have no equivalent of this. It arose from *ʿṣ ḥnytw*, "the shaft of whose spear," in 21:19 (cf. I Sam 7:17). A factor contributing to the conflation of these two verses may have been *mnd*, "uprooted," in v. 6 above, an obscure word read by some witnesses as *mnr* or *mnwrh*; cf. *mnwr*, "heddle rod," in 21:19.

*burned up* At the end of the verse MT adds *bšbt*, which might mean something like "on the spot"; LXX reflects *bštm*, "their shame." De Boer (1957 55) thinks *bšbt* might mean "in calm air." But note the textual confusion surrounding the name "Jeshbaal" in the following verse, where the readings *bšbt* and *-bšt* are attested. The extra word here probably arose from a marginal note there (cf. Driver)

# NOTES

**23** 1. *The utterance of David.* The poem opens.

*nĕʾūm dāwīd ben-yīšay*
*ûnĕʾūm haggeber hēqîm ʿēl.*

The same formula opens the oracles of Balaam in Num 24:3,15:

*nĕʾūm bilʿām bĕnô bĕʿōr*
*ûnĕʾūm haggeber šĕtūm hāʿāyin*

The utterance of Balaam son of Beor,
the utterance of the man whose eye is flawless.

Compare also the opening of the so-called "Sayings of Agur" in Prov 30:1: *dibrê ʾāgûr ben-yāqeh . . . nĕʾūm haggeber*, "The sayings of Agur son of Jakeh . . . the utterance of the man . . ."; the text of Prov 30:1, however, is very uncertain.

*the man God established.* Hebrew *haggeber hēqîm ʿēl*, which refers to the divine inauguration of David's kingship. Although elsewhere the verb *hēqîm* is used of Yahweh's raising up heirs for David (programmatically in 7:12 above; cf. I Kings 15:4; Jer 23:5; 30:9), it is also used of the elevation of a man without royal ancestry to the throne (I Kings 14:14). The present case is, strictly speaking, an example of the latter usage, although we should note that the expression would also be appropriate as a reference to any future "David" (cf. Jer 30:9), any Davidic heir.

*the darling of the stronghold of Israel.* Hebrew *nĕʿîm zimrat yiśrāʾēl,* traditionally understood as "the sweet one of the songs (MT *zĕmîrôt*) of Israel," that is, "the sweet psalmist of Israel" (AV), and a similar interpretation has recently been defended on the basis of Ugaritic cognates (Tsumura 1976). Because it is parallel to "the god of Jacob," however, a majority of recent interpreters understand *zimrat yiśrāʾēl* as a divine epithet and *nĕʿîm* as a title of gods and heroes known also from the Ugaritic texts, where it means "beloved one, darling" (*CTCA* 14.2[= *UT*⁴ Krt].4,61; 15[= 128].2.20; 17 [= 2 Aqht].6.45). In explanation of *zimrat* most interpreters (Richardson 1971:261; Mettinger 1976/77:149–51; etc.) compare **ḏmr,* "store up, protect." This root is reflected in (1) Amorite *zimri-,* "protection" (or, perhaps, "strong one"); (2) Ugaritic *ḏmr,* which refers to a class of troops and in more recently published texts occurs with the meaning "strength, protective power" (*Ugaritica V,* Text 2 [RS 24.252]; cf. Borger 1969:3–4); (3) Arabic *ḏimr, ḏamir,* "brave man," and *ḏimar,* "cherished, protected, sacred property"; (4) Old South Arabic *ḏmr,* "protect," *ḏmr,* "protection," and *mḏmr,* "strong man"; and probably (5) Akkadian *ṣimru = zimru,* "treasure," and *ṣ/zummurru,* "collect." Its occurrence in Biblical Hebrew in the expression *ʿazzî wĕzimrāt(î),* "my strength and my stronghold," used in reference to Yahweh (Exod 15:2; Isa 12:2; and Ps 118:14) has been long recognized (Gaster 1936/37:45; Cross and Freedman 1955:243; Parker 1971:377–78). Probably, however, Hebrew *zimrâ* does not mean "strength" or "protection" abstractly; rather, it refers concretely to a "stronghold" or "storehouse." Compare *mizzimrat hāʾāreṣ* in Gen 43:11, which does not mean abstractly "from the strength (= the choicest fruits) of the land" but rather "from the local *storehouse.*" Thus *zimrat yiśrāʾēl* may refer to Yahweh as the "stronghold (place of protection) of Israel," and the epithet *zimrâ* may be compared to *mĕṣûdâ,* "stronghold, fortress" (22:2), *miśgāb,* "lofty place (of refuge)" (22:3), *mānôs,* "place of refuge" (22:3), etc. A slightly different nuance, which I prefer, is "stronghold (place of storage), storehouse," a reference to Yahweh as protector and guarantor of the welfare of the land.

2. In this verse David represents himself as a prophet. The *māšāl* in vv. 3b–4 thus becomes a message for the people of Israel in general, not just a message to David, as v. 3 alone would suggest. The notion that David was a prophet has no parallel in the early literature. It arose at a later time when psalms attributed to David were being given prophetic interpretation (cf. Acts 2:30). We might conclude, as many earlier interpreters did (see the COMMENT), that the poem as a whole is a very late composition. But the significant signs of lateness are confined to this verse. Only here does David appear as a prophet (*nĕʾūm,* v. 1, means "utterance" [cf. Arabic *naʾama,* "make a sound, vocalize"], often a divine utterance and thus secondarily "oracle"). Here, too, occurs the only word in the poem that might be suspected of entering the Hebrew language fairly late, viz. *millâ,* an Aramaizing (?) synonym of *dābār,* "word," which occurs elsewhere only in the poetry of Job, in Pss 19:5 [19:4], 139:4, and in Prov 23:9.

Verse 2, moreover, is easily removed from our poem, v. 3a providing a suitable introduction to the *māšāl* without it. I assume, therefore, that v. 2 is a late insertion, intended to transform Yahweh's message to David into a message addressed to Israel as a whole and, thus, a prophecy for later generations to heed.

3. *Israel's crag.* For *ṣûr,* "crag, mountain," as a designation of a god, see the NOTE at 22:2–3.

*the fear of God.* The expression denotes the awe of the worshiper in the presence of the numinous, but it connotes proper religious devotion in general, even with a suggestion of obedience to divine statutes and customs. The last aspect is especially apparent in the Deuteronomic and Deuteronomistic use of the expression (cf. the passages cited in Weinfeld 1972:332). Similarly, in the wisdom literature, with which the present poem has many points of contact (cf. Budde, de Boer 1957:49–50), the "fear of God" is virtually synonymous with the "knowledge of God" (cf. Prov 9:10), concrete knowledge of divine commandments (see, in general, H.-P. Stähli in *THwAT* 1:766–78). The king who rules in the fear of God, then, is one who rules in accordance with religious principles and whose royal authority is grounded in religious devotion.

4. The meaning of the metaphor as I understand it (see the *Textual Notes*) is that a just king, ruling in accordance with religious principles, is like the sun on a cloudless morning, which by its light causes the rain-drenched earth to turn green. There is an implicit connection between the grass (*deše',* "verdure"), which sprouts in response to the sun's rays, and the loyal subjects of the king, who flourish under his rule. This is shown by the contrasting example of the disloyal subjects of vv. 5–7, who will not "sprout" and "grow"; for them the sun, i.e., the king, will bring death rather than life when in the "fire," the blaze of the sun, "they will be burned up" (cf. Mal 3:19 [4:1] and the Egyptian literature cited below).

The prosodic analysis of the verse accepted here is that of Freedman (1971), Mettinger (1976/77:152–53), and others. The received Hebrew text associates *minnōgah* with the last colon—thus, "from (= because of) the brightness, from (= after) rain," etc. But as Freedman and Mettinger have pointed out, *minnōgah,* "from (= because of) brightness," and *mimmāṭār,* "from (= because of) rain," stand in grammatical chiasm at the end and beginning of the second and third cola. The verse is a symmetrical tricolon (syllable = count in parentheses):

*k'wr bqr yzrḥ šmš* (6)
*bqr l' 'bwt mngh* (6)
*mmṭr dš' m'rṣ* (6)

Freedman understands the chiasm to involve *kĕ'ôr* as well as *minnōgah* and *mimmāṭār.* He translates as follows:

And [he shall be] like the light
on a morning at sunrise
more brilliant than a morning
without clouds
[better] than rain [upon] the
grass of the earth *(dš'-m 'rṣ)*

The elaborate chiasm of *k'wr//mngh//mmṭr* is poetically appealing but grammatically bewildering. How can *mngh* mean "more brilliant than" or *mmṭr* "better than rain"?

Mettinger's treatment follows from his understanding of *kēn* in v. 5 to mean "so, thus" in resumption of the metaphor in v. 4. He associates *kĕ-* at the beginning of v. 5 with *kēn*, after the pattern of *ka'ăšer . . . kēn*, "just as . . . thus," in prose (cf. Mettinger 1976/77:148–49). The initial *kĕ-* serves all three cola of v. 4, each of which he takes as a different simile. Thus:

> And as the sun shines forth at daybreak,
> [as] a morning without clouds after dawn,
> [as] after rain grass [comes] from the earth—

Just as morning follows dawn and grass follows rain, says Mettinger, so the prosperity of David's house follows the granting of the covenant. In finding a triple simile here, Mettinger comes close to the subtle and somewhat forced interpretation of de Boer (1957:52–53), who understands v. 4 as three proverbs pointing to necessary connections among things in human experience (morning and sunrise, morning clouds and the coming of day, rain and vegetation). These, says de Boer (p. 54), prepare for the assertion of v. 5 that the covenant made by God with David is proof that David's house must be just *(kēn)* towards God. Mettinger's three similes, like de Boer's three proverbs, seem improbable to me. Surely the point of the *māšāl* is that when the sun shines on the rain-watered earth at dawn, green plants spring up. There is only one metaphor.

5. *Surely.* On emphatic **lū* or **lā*, "surely," often concealed by Masoretic *lō'*, "not," see Richardson 1971:263; Cross 1973:235 with bibliography in n. 74. Nyberg (1938:381–82) retains the negative sense, concluding that David's "house" is Israel, which is not in a right *(kēn)* relationship to God. Many translators preserve the negative by treating the sentence interrogatively.

*like this.* Hebrew *kēn*, which might mean "thus, so, like this," as I suppose, or "just, right" (Nyberg 1938:381–82; de Boer 1957:153; Cross 1973:236; etc.), even "legitimate" (cf. Akkadian *kīnu*), but probably not "firm" (Carlson 1964:256; cf. Richardson 1971:259 ["established"]), which would be *nākôn* (7:16). In rendering *kēn* as "like this," we follow Mettinger (1976/77:153–54). The referent of *kēn*, however, is not just v. 4, as Mettinger concludes, but the *māšāl* in vv. 3b–4 as a whole: " 'One who rules justly . . . is like the light. . . .' Surely my house is like this with God!" That is, I and my family are, in God's opinion (see the following NOTE), rulers like the one in the *māšāl*.

*with.* Hebrew *'im*, with the meaning "in the estimation of," as in 6:22 and, more particularly, in I Sam 2:26.

*a perpetual covenant.* This colon might also be read "For the Eternal One *('ôlām)* has given me a covenant" with Freedman (*apud* Richardson 1971:263; cf. Cross 1973:236 n. 78; Freedman 1976:73–74), but I take *bĕrît 'ôlām* as the covenant with David mentioned in Pss 89:20–38 [89:19–37]; 132:12; Isa 55:3 (where the reference to David is probably a gloss); Jer 33:17,20–22; II Chron 13:5; 21:7; etc. Though the specific combination *bĕrît 'ôlām* occurs in none of these passages (Freedman 1976:74), it is clear in all of them that the covenant *(bĕrît)* exists in perpetuity (*'ad-'ôlām*, etc.). A *bĕrît 'ôlām* is a legal contract without a specified term, i.e., one that exists in perpetuity (cf. Weinfeld 1970:199). The content of this covenant is, presumably, the grant of kingship and dynasty made to David in chap. 7.

*fully set forth and secured.* This is, as Driver explains, "an expression borrowed probably from legal terminology, and intended to describe the *bryt* as one of which the terms are fully and duly set forth (comp. the forensic use of *'rk* in Job 13,18 al. *to state in order* or *set forth pleadings*), and which is secured by proper precautions against surreptitious alteration or injury."

*shows no regard for me . . . does not favor me.* Hebrew *bělî šō'î ûbělî ḥāpēṣ bî* (see the *Textual Note*). Both verbs are used commonly of loyal regard (*šā'â,* Exod 5:9; 17:8,11; 31:1; 32:3 [preceded by *lō'* = *lū'*]; Ps 119:117) and favor (*ḥāpēṣ,* II Sam 20:11; etc.). What follows, then, describes the fate of those not loyal to the king.

5–6. *will not sprout . . . grow.* That is, in contrast to the "verdure from the earth" of v. 4, implicitly the loyal subjects of David. The Hebrew here is *bal yiṣmaḥ ûbal ya'al,* as explained in the *Textual Notes.* For *'ālâ,* commonly used of vegetative growth, compare Gen 40:10; 41:5,22; etc.; in Deut 29:22 it follows *ṣāmaḥ,* "sprout," as in the present passage, and in Isa 32:13 and Hos 10:8 it is used with *qôṣ,* "thorns."

6. *uprooted thorns.* Hebrew *qôṣ mūnād.* De Boer (1957:55) understands *mūnād* as "thrust away" in the sense of "shunned, avoided," and many other interpretations have been proposed. But the basic meaning of *nûd* is "move out of place," and with reference to plants it seems to mean "be uprooted." Thus in Isa 17:11 we are told that the harvest of a carefully planted garden "will be uprooted" *(nād* for MT *nēd),* and in I Kings 14:15 we read: "Yahweh will smite Israel, just as a reed is uprooted *(yānûd)* by water, and he will uproot *(wěnātaš)* Israel from this good soil he gave to their fathers."

7. *the fire.* That is, the blaze of the sun. The rule of a lawful king is like the life-giving warmth of the sun for crops (= the king's loyal subjects), but it is like the death-dealing heat of the sun for thorny weeds (= the disloyal).

## COMMENT

The traditional swan song of David is a short poem with a four-part structure. First, there is an introduction (v. 1) identifying David as the speaker and describing him as the favorite of the god of Israel. Second, there is a wisdom saying or *māšāl* (vv. 2–4), which has an introduction of its own (vv. 2–3a) stating that it was spoken by Yahweh's spirit *through* David (v. 2, which is probably secondary [see the NOTE]) and that it was spoken by Yahweh *to* David (v. 3a). The *māšāl* itself (vv. 3b–4) extols the rule of a just king. The third part (v. 5abα) is an assertion by David that God *('ēl)* regards his house as one that provides this kind of rule, as his gift of a perpetual covenant to David shows. Part four (vv. 5bβ–7) concludes the poem by threatening those disloyal to David with ruin.

The central metaphor of the poem is the comparison, drawn in the *māšāl* in vv. 3b–4, of a just ruler to a bright morning sun that causes green vegetation to spring from rain-watered ground. The effects of the just king's rule, in other words, are like the beneficial influence of the sun's rays. The sprouting grass alludes at least implicitly to the loyal subjects of such a king: The king "who rules justly among men" (v. 3) is like the sun that shines on the grass (v. 4)

—both men and grass will thrive. The metaphor is resumed at the end of the poem. Those who are *not* loyal to David are like thorny weeds. They will not thrive. For them, torn from their roots (*mŭnād,* v. 6), the heat of the sun will bring destruction, not prosperity.

The king under the image of the sun is a widespread motif in the royal ideologies of the ancient Near East. It has a particularly Egyptian flavor. Praise of the shining of the solar god-king as the source of vegetative growth and human welfare is a commonplace of Egyptian literature. In a Middle Kingdom hymn to Amon-Re, for example, the king is adored as:

> The lord of rays, who makes brilliance . . . ,
> Who extends his arms to him whom he loves,
> (But) his enemy is consumed by a flame.
> (*ANET*[3], p. 365)

Solar terminology was also applied to the Hittite king, whose common title was "the Sun." Thus, in the Amarna letters the Egyptian king is called "my Sun(-god)" by his Asiatic vassals, and in Ugaritic correspondence the title "Sun" is used in addressing both the Hittite and Egyptian sovereigns. In the prologue to the Code of Hammurapi the Babylonian king is said "to rise like the sun over the black-headed (people), and light up the land"; he is "the sun of Babylon, who causes light to go forth over the lands of Sumer and Akkad" (*ANET*[3], pp. 164–65). The application of solar imagery to the king in our poem, therefore, has a strong tradition behind it (cf. Mowinckel [1956]:227 and n. 3). Still, it is unusual in Israelite literature. Ps 84:12 [84:11], though it refers to Yahweh rather than a human being, is comparable because it describes him as a divine *king,* calling him *šemeš ûmāgān* (MT *māgēn;* cf. the NOTE at 22:3), "Sun and Sovereign," i.e., a divine suzerain who "bestows favor and honor," showing that "Sun" was also a royal title in Israel. "Sun" may also mean "king" in Mal 3:20 [4:2], which prophesies the coming of a "rightful Sun" (*šemeš ṣĕdāqâ),* a legitimate king (!). Indeed, Mal 3:19–20a [4:1–2a], though a post-exilic passage looking forward to the coming of a future king, displays many parallels to our passage:

> For the day is coming, blazing like a furnace, and all who are arrogant and all who do evil will be stubble! The day to come will burn them up, says Yahweh Sabaoth, leaving them neither root nor branch! But for you who fear my name a rightful Sun will shine forth with healing in its wings!

In contrast to Malachi's oracle, however, our poem speaks of the royal house as a living institution, not an object of hope in the future. II Sam 23:1–7, then, is to be dated in the monarchical period. Moreover, its traditional assignment to David is by no means impossible—two other poems preserved in II Samuel are almost certainly Davidic in date (1:19–27; 3:33–34)—and a number of scholars favor a Davidic date for our poem (Procksch 1913; Segal 1914/15: 225–27; Hertzberg; Richardson 1971:257; Cross 1973:237 and n. 81; Freedman 1976:96). Others place it slightly later, in the time of Solomon (Caquot 1963:218; Ishida 1977:108). Mowinckel (1927:57–58), however, assigns it to the reign of Hezekiah or Josiah, and Nyberg (1938:384–85) relates its content to issues current at the time of the fall of Samaria in 722–721. Mettinger (1976:257–59) concludes that it can be no earlier than the late years of the monarchy, his chief objection to an early date being the occurrence of the expression *bĕrît 'ôlām*, "perpetual covenant," which he finds elsewhere no earlier than the seventh century. Among the early commentators the poem was regarded as "rather late" (Nowack), "comparatively late" (Smith), or "very late" (Budde). Davidic authorship was denied, as Nowack says, "by almost all exegetes." The indications of lateness cited included the view of David as a songwriter, said to lie behind the introduction (Nowack), the similarities of thought to wisdom passages like Psalm 1 and Prov 30:1–31:9 (Budde), the notion of David as a prophet (Nowack), and, more generally, the presence of late vocabulary and thought (Smith, who is not more specific).

Almost all commentators agree that it is very difficult to assign a date to this poem. I cannot deny this. It seems to me, however, that those who favor an early date have the better argument. The objections of Smith, Budde, and Nowack are not decisive. Wisdom motifs are timeless. The introduction of the poem has nothing in common with the tradition of assigning anonymous psalms to David in prose rubrics (cf. 22:1): "The utterance of David," etc., is an organic part of this poem. David is presented as a prophet only in v. 2, which is superfluous and quite possibly secondary (see the NOTE). I can find no "late" vocabulary here, unless it be *millātô*, "his word," again in v. 2. There was a tendency to give a vaticinal and messianic interpretation to the poem among its later interpreters, as its treatment in the Targum Jonathan shows (cf. de Boer 1957:47). Such an interpretation may have affected its rendering into Greek (cf. "the fear of the anointed" in v. 3, cited in the *Textual Note* on "One . . . God") and, if v. 2 is indeed secondary, its present shape in the received Hebrew text. The assessment of Smith, Budde, and Nowack could be said to stand within this ancient interpretive tradition.

As for Mettinger's emphasis on *bĕrît 'ôlām*, "perpetual covenant" (see above), we must keep in mind the fact that the other occurrences of this precise expression, which, as he says, are no earlier than the seventh century, do not refer to the covenant with David (cf. Freedman 1976:74). However, the *concept* of the perpetual covenant with David is found in passages like Pss 89:29 [89:28] *(lĕ'ôlām . . . bĕrîtî)* and 132:12 *(bĕrîtî . . . 'ădê-'ad)*, and many scholars would not accept Mettinger's judgment that these passages are very late. A decision on this point depends, finally, on a full evaluation of Mettinger's larger argument for dating the application of the term *bĕrît* to the contractual relationship between David and Yahweh to the Exile (Mettinger 1976:275–90, especially pp. 282–83), an evaluation we cannot undertake here.

On the other hand, there are positive indications of an early date. As explained in the NOTES, the opening of the poem finds its only clear parallel with the Balaam oracles in Numbers 24, which are widely recognized as very ancient (Albright 1944; see also Wilson 1980:147–50 with bibliography in n. 27). The divine epithets are consistent with an early date (Freedman 1976: 73–75). There is no trace of Deuteronomistic language. Tentatively I should assign II Sam 23:1–7 to the early monarchical period, perhaps to the time of David. If this is correct, the Egyptian flavor of the poem's central metaphor might be accounted as another bit of evidence for Egyptian influence on the courts of David and Solomon (cf. the NOTES in § XVIII and von Rad 1962:vol. I:40–42).

# XXXIX. A ROSTER OF DAVID'S WARRIORS
# (23:8–39)

23 [8]These are the names of David's warriors.

## *The Three*

Jeshbaal the Hachmonite was chief of the Three. He brandished his
spear over eight hundred slain at one time.
[9]After him among the three warriors was Eleazar son of Dodo the
Ahohite. He was with David when the Philistine defied them at Pas-
dammim. When the Philistines gathered there for battle, Israel withdrew; [10]but he held his ground and slew Philistines until his hand grew
tired and stuck to his sword. Yahweh brought about a great victory that
day, and then the army crept back to him—only to strip [the slain]!
[11]After him was Shamma son of Agee the Hararite. The Philistines
assembled at Lehi, where there was a plot of ground filled with lentils.
The army fled from the Philistines, [12]but he took up a position in the
plot and held it, defeating the Philistines. Yahweh brought about a
great victory.

## *Three of the Thirty*

[13]Three of the Thirty marched down at harvest time and joined David
in the stronghold of Adullam, a clan of Philistines having encamped in
the Valley of Rephaim. [14]At that time David was in the stronghold, and
there was a Philistine outpost in Bethlehem.
[15]David felt a yearning and said, "O, for a drink of water from the
well in the gate at Bethlehem!" [16]So the three warriors infiltrated the
Philistine camp, drew some water from the well in the gate at Bethlehem, and carried it to David. But he refused to drink it. Pouring it out
to Yahweh, [17]he said, "I'll be damned, Yahweh, if I'll do this! Shall I
drink the blood of the men who went? For they brought it at the risk
of their lives!" So he refused to drink it.
These are things the three warriors did.

*Abishai and Benaiah*

18Abishai, Joab's brother, was chief of the Thirty. He brandished his
spear over three hundred slain, but he did not have a place among the
Three. 19He was honored above the Thirty, and he became their commander. But he did not attain to the Three.
20Benaiah son of Jehoiada was a stalwart man from Kabzeel, who had
done many deeds. He slew the two sons of Ariel in Moab. He went
down into a pit and slew a lion on a snowy day. 21He slew a giant
Egyptian. The Egyptian had a spear in his hand, but [Benaiah] marched
down against him with a staff. He wrenched the spear from the Egyptian's hand, and killed him with his own spear.
22These are the things that Benaiah son of Jehoiada did. He did not
have a place among the three warriors. 23He was honored above the
Thirty, though he did not attain to the Three, and David set him in
charge of his bodyguard.

*The Thirty*

24Joab's brother Asael was among the Thirty.
Elhanan son of Dodo from Bethlehem.
25Shammah the Harodite.
Elika the Harodite.
26Helez the Paltite.
Ira son of Ikkesh the Tekoite.
27Abiezer the Anathothite.
Sibbecai the Hushathite.
28Zalmon the Ahohite.
Mahrai the Netophathite.
29Heldai son of Baanah the Netophathite.
Ittai son of Ribai from Gibeah of the Benjaminites.
30Benaiah the Pirathonite.
Hiddai from the wadis of Gaash.
31Abial the Beth-arabathite.
Azmaveth the Bahurimite.
32Eliahba the Shaalbonite.
Jashen the Gizonite.
Jonathan son of 33Shamma the Hararite.

Ahiam son of Sachar the Urite.
34 Eliphelet son of Ahasbai the Maacathite.
Eliam son of Ahithophel the Gilonite.
35 Hezrai the Carmelite.
Paarai the Archite.
36 Igal son of Nathan, the commander of the army of the Hagrites.
37 Zelek the Ammonite.
Nahrai the Beerothite, the weapon-bearer of Joab son of Zeruiah.
38 Ira the Ithrite.
Gareb the Ithrite.
39 Uriah the Hittite.

Thirty-seven in all.

## *TEXTUAL NOTES*

23 8. *Jeshbaal* The name *yešba'al* (see the NOTE) is preserved in LXX$^{L}$ *(iesbaal)* and OL *(iesbael)*. In MT it became *yešbōšet* (LXX$^{B}$ *iebosthe*) by substitution of *bōšet*, "shame," for *b'l*, "Baal" (see the NOTE on "Ishbaal son of Saul" at 2:8); this was corrupted to *yōšēb baššebet*, "Josheb-bassshebeth," as MT now reads. I Chron 11:11 has *yāšob'ām*, "Jashobeam."

*the Hachmonite* MT *tḥkmny* is an error for *bn ḥkmny*, Jeshbaal's patronymic as it appears in I Chron 11:11 (cf. I Chron 27:32); graphic confusion of *bn* and *t* was possible in scripts of the fourth and third centuries B.C., decreasingly likely in the second century and later. LXX$^{L}$ *huios thekemanei* (cf. OL) points to this reading, though the name has been "corrected" towards MT. *Bn ḥkmny* is a conflation of variants, viz. *bn ḥkmn*, "son of Hachmon," and *hḥkmny*, "the Hachmonite" (cf. "the Ahohite" below); we read the latter. Cf. LXX$^{B}$ *ho chananaios*, which suggests *hḥnny*, "the Hananite."

*the Three* MT has *haššālīšī*, "the officers" (?). But how is the ending *(-ī)* to be explained? One could read *haššělīšī*, "the Third" (cf. v. 18 [MT]), with LXX$^{BAMN}$ and Syr. I Chron 11:11 offers *haššālīšîm*, "the officers" *(qěrê)*, and *haššělôšîm*, "the Thirty" *(kětîb)*. The context, however, requires us to read *haššělōšâ*, "the Three," with LXX$^{L}$ (cf. Vulg.); cf. Wellhausen.

*brandished his spear* This is the reading of I Chron 11:11: *'rwr ('t) ḥnytw*. MT has *'dynw h'ṣny (kětîb: h'ṣnw)*, evidently understood as a name ("Adino the Ezenite"), and LXX$^{B}$ reflects a conflation of the two. It is remotely possible that *'dynw h'ṣnw* is a graphic corruption of *'rwr ḥnytw*, but it seems very unlikely, especially in view of *'rwr 't ḥnytw* in v. 18. This suggests that the primitive reading is more closely approximated by MT, which, however, will not yield to interpretation. LXX$^{L}$ *diekosmei tēn diaskeuēn autou/autōn* and OL *adornavit adornationem suam* seem to reflect *'dh ('t) 'dyw*, "decked himself with ornaments." Syr. has *(šmh) gdḥw gbr' dnḥt wqṭl*, "(His name was) GDḤW, the warrior who felled and slew . . . ," evidently a double rendering (cf. LXX[B]); *gdḥw* is probably an inner-Syriac error for *'dynw*, but the rest is completely opaque. Vulg. has *(quasi) tenerrimus ligni vermiculus*, "(like) a very tender little wood worm," which is quaint but not enlightening. Targ. has *(w)mtbyb 'l ydy mwrnytyh*, "fighting (?) repeatedly with his spear," to which compare Josephus' reading (*Ant.* 7.308), *pollakis . . . empēdōn*, "repeatedly springing (upon)"; both seem to understand the first word as *'ōdennû*.

*eight hundred* So MT, LXX[B]. LXX[L], OL, Josephus (*Ant.* 7.308): "nine hundred." I Chron 11:11: "three hundred" (cf. v. 18).

*slain* So MT: *ḥll*. LXX[B] = *ḥyl*, "troops."

9. *warriors* Reading *hgbrym* with LXX[L], as in I Chron 11:12. MT has lost *h-* after the preceding word *(hšlšh)*; it is supplied by the *qĕrê*.

*Eleazar* LXX[B], OL: "Elhanan" (cf. v. 24).

*Dodo* So MT *(qĕrê)*: *dōdô* (cf. LXX[B] and I Chron 11:12). MT *(kĕtîb)*: *ddy* = *dōday* (cf. LXX[L]).

*the Ahohite* MT *bn 'ḥḥy* is a conflation of *bn 'ḥḥ* and *h'ḥwḥy* (I Chron 11:12); we read the latter. LXX[B] has *huios sousei* = *bn šwšy* (?), "son of Shoshi." LXX[L] omits (haplography?).

*He was* So LXX[L] (cf. I Chron 11:13) = *hw' hyh*. The omission of these words from MT is difficult to explain, but they are necessary to the sense of the verse.

*when the Philistine . . . Philistines* The original reading was *bḥrpm hplšty bps dmym whplštym*. MT reads *bḥrpm bplštym*, having lost everything from *hplšty* to *hplštym* by haplography. LXX[L] agrees with I Chron 11:13 in reading *bps dmym (en serran) whplštym*, the result of a different haplography, from *b-* to *b-*.

*withdrew* MT *wy'lw* (cf. I Kings 15:19; II Kings 12:19 [12:18]), understood as "marched up" by LXX[L] (cf. LXX[MN]), which adds *pro prosōpon autōn* = *lqr'tm*, "to meet them."

10. *crept back* So MT: *yšbw*, understood as *yāšūbû* (cf. LXX[L]). LXX[B] interprets the same reading as *yāšĕbû*, "remained."

*only* MT *'k*, evidently read as *'d*, "toward," by LXX[L] *(eis)* and Vulg. *(ad)*; not rendered by Syr.

[*the slain*] Made explicit in Syr., Targ., Vulg.

11. *Shamma* So MT: *šammā'*. MT[MSS]: *šmh* (cf. vv. 25,33). LXX: *samaia(s)* = *šmy'*.

*the Hararite* Reading *hhrry* for MT *hrry* (cf. v. 33). LXX[BA] *ho harouchaios* (cf. LXX[MN]), LXX[L] *ho harachi*, and OL *arucius* all point to *hhrky*, "the Harukite" (?).

*at Lehi* MT *lḥyh* is to be read *leḥyāh* with LXX[LM] *epi siagona* and OL *ad maxillam* (cf. Josephus, *Ant.* 7.310).

12. *victory* LXX[L] adds "on that day," as in v. 10.

13. *Three* So LXX, Syr., Targ. Vulg., as in I Chron 11:15. MT has "Thirty."

*the Thirty* Followed in MT by *r'š*, "the thirty chiefs" (?). Perhaps this was added to clarify the relationship of these three men to the Three on the one hand and the Thirty on the other—thus Vulg. *tres qui erant principes inter triginta* (cf. Targ.). Omit *r'š* with LXX[B], Syr.

*at harvest time* So MT: *'l* (= *'l*, cf. I Chron 11:15) *qṣyr*. LXX[L] reflects *'l hṣwr*, "to the crag" (cf. I Chron 11:15), which is adopted by most critics. We should not, to be sure, think of David as involved in a harvest at Adullam (*'l qṣyr*, "*to* the harvest"), but a reference to the time of year (*'l qṣyr,* "*upon* the harvest, at harvest time") is perfectly in order.

*the stronghold* Reading *mṣdt* for *m'rt,* "the cave," with Wellhausen. See *I Samuel,* the *Textual Note* at 22:1.

15. In LXX$^{BALM}$ the last half of v. 14 is repeated after v. 15.

16. *he refused* LXX$^{L}$, MT$^{MSS}$: "*David* refused."

17. *Yahweh* LXX$^{L}$, Syr., Targ., MT$^{MSS}$: *myhwh,* "from, by Yahweh" (cf. I Chron 11:19: *m'lhy*).

*Shall I drink . . . their lives!* There is confusion in all witnesses. MT is defective: *hdm h'nšym hhlkym bnpšwtm,* "Is it the blood of the men who went at the risk of their lives?" To this LXX adds *piomai* = *'šth*—thus, "Shall I drink . . . lives?" But if this was the primitive text, it is difficult to see how *'šth* was lost in MT. I Chron 11:19 has *hdm h'nšym h'lh 'šth bnpšwtm ky bnpšwtm hby'wm,* "Shall I drink the blood of these men with their lives? For at the risk of their lives they brought it!" Clearly the first *bnpšwtm* should be struck as a duplicate. The evidence suggests that the primitive text of II Sam 23:17 read *hdm h'nšym hhlkym 'šth ky hby'wm bnpšwtm.* In MT *'šth ky hby'wm* was lost by haplography (homoioteleuton). LXX represents a partial correction.

18. *Joab's brother* MT adds "the son of Zeruiah." Omit with LXX$^{L}$ (cf. I Chron 11:20).

*the Thirty* So Syr., though this may be a correction *ad sensum.* The chief witnesses read "the Three" or "the third" (cf. v. 8), but as Wellhausen and Driver have shown, we must read *hšlwšym* here.

*three hundred* LXX$^{L}$, OL: "*six* hundred" (cf. Josephus, *Ant.* 7.315).

*but he did not have a place* That is, *wĕlō' śīm,* lit. "but he was not set." MT has *wlw šm,* "and he had a name." Read *wl'* as in I Chron 11:20 with MT$^{MSS}$.

19. *He* So LXX$^{B}$: *ekeinos* = *hw'.* MT has *hky.* LXX$^{L}$ reflects *mšnym* (cf. I Chron 11:21), which may represent a "correction" of *mn hšlšh,* "above the Three," to "above the two (others)." See the following *Textual Note.*

*the Thirty* Reading *hšlšym* with Syr. The other witnesses have "the Three," as in v. 18.

20. *a stalwart man* We read *'yš ḥyl.* MT has a double reading: *bn 'yš ḥyl* (so *qĕrê*), "the son of a stalwart man"; cf. *bn 'yš ymyn* in I Sam 9:1, and see Talmon 1960:165–66. We omit *bn* with LXX$^{BAMN}$. For *ḥyl* MT *(kĕtîb)* has *ḥy,* which LXX$^{B}$ reads as *hw' (autos),* while LXX$^{L}$ renders *'yš ḥy* as *iessai.*

*the two sons* So LXX$^{BALN}$ = *šny bny.* MT has lost *bny* by haplography.

21. *giant* Reading *'yš mdh* (cf. 21:20), as in I Chron 11:23 (where it is glossed, "five cubits [tall]"). In II Sam 23:20 this was misread as *'yš mrh* and the spelling corrected to *'yš mr'h* (so MT [*qĕrê*]; cf. LXX), "a man of [imposing?] appearance," which became *'šr mr'h* in MT *(kĕtîb).*

*a spear* LXX adds *hōs xylon diabathras,* "like the wood of a ladder" (= *k'ṣ m'lh?*), and I Chron 11:23 adds *kmnwr 'rgym,* "like a weavers' heddle rod" (cf. II Sam 21:19).

*a staff* So MT. LXX has "the spear," thus understanding the Egyptian as the subject of the clause (explicitly so in LXX$^{L}$: "and *the Egyptian* marched down against him with *his* spear").

22. *He did not have a place* See the *Textual Note* at v. 18.

23. At the end of this verse LXX inserts, as an introduction to the list in vv. 24–39, "And these are the names of the warriors of David the king" (cf. v. 8).

24. *son of Dodo* That is, *bn ddw* (MT), rendered twice by LXX^B as "son of Dodo" and "(son of) his uncle."

*from Bethlehem* MT lacks "from." It is supplied by LXX^LAMN (cf. LXX^B), Targ., Vulg., and I Chron 11:26.

25. *Shammah* So MT: *šammâ,* for which MT^MSS read *šm'* (cf. vv. 11,33). LXX^L = *šmy'.* LXX^MN = *šmwt,* as in I Chron 11:27 (cf. the combined reading *šmhwt* in I Chron 27:8).

*the Harodite* So MT: *hḥrdy,* for which I Chron 11:27 has *hhrwry* (cf. vv. 11,33).

*Elika the Harodite* Omitted by LXX^B, Syr., and I Chron 11:27 (homoioteleuton).

26. *the Paltite* So MT: *hplṭy* (cf. Syr.). LXX^ALMN reflect *hplwny,* "the Pelonite," as in I Chron 11:27.

27. *Sibbecai* MT has *mbny,* the result of two graphic errors, viz. confusion of *kap* and *nun* (thus LXX^L *sabanei* = *sbny,* the intermediate form) and confusion of *samek* and *mem.* Read *sbky* with LXX^LMN, as in 21:18 and I Chron 11:29. See, further, the *Textual Note* at 21:18. For the name *mbn(y)* on an eighth-century Hebrew seal from Shechem, see Zeron 1979.

*the Hushathite* LXX^L: "the Hittite" (cf. 21:18).

28. *Zalmon* The relationship of MT *ṣalmôn* to I Chron 11:29 *'îlay* is not clear.

29. *Heldai son of Baanah the Netophathite* Lost in LXX^B by haplography after "Mahrai the Netophathite."

*Heldai* The reading *ḥldy,* found in I Chron 27:15 (cf. I Chron 11:30), is supported by LXX^L *allan,* an inner-Greek error for **aldan* by confusion of the majuscules *delta* and *lambda.* MT *ḥlb,* "Heleb," arose by graphic confusion of *dy* and *b.*

30. *Benaiah* Lost in LXX^B after "the Benjaminites."

*the Pirathonite* LXX^B reads "the Ephrathite" and then omits everything before "Azmaveth" in v. 31 (partially restored in v. 39+).

*Hiddai* MT *hdy (hidday),* read as *hadday* by LXX^L *(addai)* and LXX^B *(adaoi)* in v. 39+. LXX^MN *(ouri)* read *hwry,* as in I Chron 11:32.

31. *Abial the Beth-arabathite* MT has *'by 'lbwn h'rbty,* "Abi-albon the Arabathite." LXX^MN (cf. LXX^B in v. 39+) have *abiēl huios tou arabōthitou* = *'by'l bn h'rbty,* "Abiel son of the Arabathite" (cf. I Chron 11:32). Taking a clue from Klostermann, we can recover the original from which both readings arose, viz. *'by'l* (or *'byb'l;* cf. Wellhausen; Mazar [Maisler] 1963b:316 n. 4) *bt h'rbty,* "Abial the Beth-arabathite." See, further, the NOTE.

*the Bahurimite* MT has *habbarḥūmî* and I Chron 11:33 *habbaḥărûmî,* but the correct reading is almost certainly *habbaḥūrîmî.*

32. *Jashen* That is, *yāšēn.* To this MT prefixes *bny,* evidently the result of dittography after the preceding word, *hš'lbny* (cf. Elliger 1935:31 n. 4). We omit *bny* with LXX^L *(iassai).* In I Chron 11:34 *bny ysn* has become *bny hšm,* "sons of the name," i.e., "famous men."

*the Gizonite* The gentilic has been lost in MT. In LXX^L it is *ho gounai,* which reflects *hgwny,* "the Gunite." I Chron 11:34 has *hgzwny,* "the Gizonite." Confusion of *zayin* and *waw* was common, and we cannot doubt that *hgwny* arose from *hgzny* (cf. LXX^MN^ *ho gōyni* = *hgwwny* [!] < *hgzwny*) and not the reverse, *zayin* being much the rarer letter, despite the fact that Gizon is not otherwise known. Guni is a clan name in Naphtali (Num 26:48), which is geographically too remote here, as Elliger points out (1935:53–54). He offers the plausible conjecture *hgmzny*, "the Gimzonite." Gimzo lay a few miles southeast of Lydda (II Chron 28:18), not far from Shaalbim.

*son of* Omitted by MT. Read *bn* with LXX^LMN^ and I Chron 11:34.

33. *Shamma* Reading *šammā'* with MT^MSS^. MT has *šammâ*, but Jonathan's father is probably the hero of v. 11, not v. 25. I Chron 11:34 has *šāgē'*, "Shagee"; cf. *šammā' ben-'āgē'*, "Shamma son of Agee," v. 11, and see Elliger 1935:32 n. 5.

*the Hararite* So MT, LXX^MN^, and I Chron 11:34. LXX^B^ reflects "the Hararite," as in v. 25. LXX^L^ *arachei* suggests *hrky* (cf. I Chron 4:12).

*Sachar* So LXX^L^: *sachar-* = *śākār*, as in I Chron 11:35. MT has *šārār* (cf. LXX^BMN^). MT^MSS^ and LXX^A^ *([s]arad)* have *šārād* (cf. Syr. *'šdd*).

*the Urite* In LXX a doublet or fragment of the preceding patronymic has been prefixed to the gentilic. Thus, for example, LXX^B^ has *saraoureitēs* for **sar[ar] aoureitēs* = *šrr h'wry*, "Sharar the Urite." The correct gentilic may have been *h'wry*. In MT this has become *h'rry* by confusion of *waw* and *reš*, and in I Chron 11:35 it has been further corrupted to *hhrry*, "the Hararite," the gentilic of the preceding name in the list.

34. *Eliphelet* So MT: *'lyplṭ*. I Chron 11:35 has *'lypl*. Omitted by LXX^L^.

*Ahasbai* After *'ḥsby* MT inserts *bn*, a corrupt dittograph of *-by*. LXX^L^ omits *bn*. LXX^B^ had *asbei tou* = *'ḥsby h-*, "Ahasbai the . . . ," before its recensional approximation to MT by the insertion of *huios tou*—thus, *asbeitou huios tou*. . . . In I Chron 11:35–36 the name is corrupt *('wr ḥpr)*, but *bn*, "son of," is absent.

*the Maacathite* So MT: *hm'kty*. LXX^L^ *makarthei* reflects *(h)mkrty*, as in I Chron 11:36.

*Eliam* So MT: *'ly'm*. LXX^B^ = *'ly'b*, "Eliab." LXX^L^: *ho thalaam* (?). I Chron 11:36 omits "Eliam son of" (homoioteleuton).

*Ahithophel the Gilonite* MT *'ḥytpl hglny*, for which I Chron 11:36 has *'ḥyh hplny* (< *'ḥytp[l hg]lny*).

35. *Hezrai* Reading *ḥṣry* with LXX and MT *(qĕrê)*. MT *(kĕtîb)* has *ḥṣrw*, as in I Chron 11:37.

*Paarai* So MT (cf. LXX^AL^): *p'ry*, for which I Chron 11:37 has *n'ry* by confusion of *pe* and *nun*.

*the Archite* We read *h'rky* (so MT^MSS^; cf. LXX^B^ *-oerchei* = *ho erchei*, LXX^A^ *ho arachei-*), for which MT has *h'rby* by confusion of *kap* and *bet* and I Chron 11:37 has *(bn) 'zby* by confusion of *reš* and *zayin*. Omitted by LXX^LN^. For a defense of MT see Elliger 1935:58–59.

36. *Igal son of* So MT: *yg'l bn*, for which LXX^L^ *iōēl adelphos* reflects *yw'l 'ḥy*, "Joel brother of," as in I Chron 11:38.

*the commander of the army* We read *rb ṣb'* (cf. LXX^B^ *apolydynameōs*, LXX^A^ *pollysdynameōs*), for which MT has *mṣbh* (as if "from Zobah") = *mṣb'*, "from the army of" (cf. LXX^MSS^ *apo dynameōs*), and I Chron 11:38 *mbḥr* (as if "Mibhar") = *mbḥry*, "from the elite troops of." We may suppose that *rb ṣb'* and *mbḥry* were ancient variants.

*the Hagrites* We read *bny hgry*, which has become *bny hgdy* in MT; but "Bani [MT *bānî*] the Gadite" is doubtful, and "the Gadites" would be *bny gd* ("the sons of Gad"), while *bny hgry* ("the sons of Hagri") is correct for "the Hagrites" (cf. the NOTE). I Chron 11:37 preserves *hgry* but reads *bn* for *bny*, having interpreted *mbḥr(y)* as a name —thus, "Mibhar son of Hagri." In the present passage LXX$^{LMN}$ agree with I Chron 11:37, while Syr. goes its own way, reading *b'n' dmn gd* = *b'nh hgdy*, "Baanah [cf. v. 29] the Gadite."

37. *Nahrai* So MT: *nḥry*, as in I Chron 11:39. So LXX$^{L}$ *(-n araia)*. LXX$^{MN}$ (cf. LXX$^{B}$) have *gelōrai* (< Greek **gedōrai* < Hebrew **gdwry* < **gḥry* < *nḥry*). See also the following *Textual Note*.

*the weapon-bearer* So MT *(qĕrê)* and LXX$^{BAMN}$, as in I Chron 11:39. Plural, according to MT *(kĕtîb)* and LXX$^{L}$. If we retain the plural, we must read *wḥry*, "Horai," for *nḥry*, "Nahrai"—thus, "Zelek the Ammonite and Horai the Beerothite, the weapon-bearers of Joab," etc.

38. *the Ithrite* (bis) So MT: *hayyitrî*, which Thenius and others (cf. Elliger 1935: 62–63 and n. 189) would read *hayyātīrî*, "the Jattirite" (cf. I Sam 30:37; etc.). In place of the second occurrence LXX suggests a slightly different name: LXX$^{B}$ *eththenaios* (cf. LXX$^{L}$ *iethem*) = *ytny* (?), and Syr. has *(d)mn lkyš* = *hlkyšy*, "the Lachishite" (!).

39. After v. 39 LXX$^{B}$ adds as vv. 40–41 a duplicate of portions of vv. 30–31. See the *Textual Note* on "the Pirathonite," v. 30.

## NOTES

23 8. *Jeshbaal*. Hebrew *yĕšba'al* (see the *Textual Note*), which means "Baal exists." It brings to mind the Ugaritic verses " 'Al'iyan Baal lives! The Prince, Lord of Earth, exists *('iṯ)*!" (*CTCA* 6[= *UT*$^{4}$ 49].3.8–9), and the Ugaritic Akkadian name *i-ši-$^{d}$Ba'al* (RS 12.34 + 12.43.25; cf. *PRU III*, pl. IX and p. 193; see Moran 1954). It may be that Jeshbaal's family worshiped Baal (Hadad), but *ba'al*, "the Lord," might also refer to Yahweh in this period (cf. the NOTE on "Ishbaal" at 2:8). According to I Chron 27:2 (where he is called "Jashobeam" as in I Chron 11:11; see the *Textual Note*) Jeshbaal's father was Zabdiel, a descendant of Perez and thus a remote kinsman of David (Ruth 4:18–22). In the same passage we are told that Jeshbaal was in charge of the first of the twelve monthly divisions into which David's army was divided according to the Chronicler's scheme.

*the Hachmonite*. According to I Chron 27:32, Jehiel, another Hachmonite, was the caretaker of David's sons.

9. *Eleazar son of Dodo*. According to I Chron 27:4 (LXX), Eleazar was in charge of David's military division for the second month.

*the Ahohite*. Hebrew *hā'ăḥōḥî* (see the *Textual Note*), presumably designating Eleazar as a member of the clan descended from *'ăḥôaḥ*, "Ahoah," a son of Benjamin's firstborn son Bela (I Chron 8:4); contrast Elliger 1935:45–46. Another famous Ahohite is listed among the Thirty below (v. 28). Cf. also I Chron 11:29.

*Pas-dammim*. The Ephes-dammim of I Sam 17:1, the site of David's victory over a Philistine champion confused in the tradition with Goliath of Gath, who was slain by David's hero Elhanan (21:19). The modern site of Ephes-dammim may be Damun (see the map in *I Samuel,* p. 283).

11. *Shamma son of Agee.* The father of Jonathan, one of the Thirty (v. 33).

*the Hararite.* Elliger (1935:54–56) compares the place-name *a-ra-ru* in *EA* 256 (*ANET*³, p. 486), one of several cities in the southern Golan that rebelled against Egypt early in the reign of Akhenaton. It is precarious, however, to clarify the obscure by reference to the obscure, and others identify Amarna *a-ra-ru* with biblical Aroer (24:5; cf. Albright 1943:14 n. 38). I prefer to think of the Hararites as an otherwise unknown *mountain* clan.

*Lehi.* Where Samson slew a thousand Philistines with the jawbone *(lĕḥî)* of an ass (Judg 15:9–19). The site was in Judah (Judg 15:9), perhaps near Beth-shemesh. See Map 9.

13–17a. The theme of the little story told here—the search for a drink of water for the king at the risk of the lives of his followers—has a number of general parallels in world literature and folklore. See Hull 1933.

13. *Three of the Thirty.* These three are not *the* Three of vv. 8b–12, although confusion on this point may account for the inclusion of the story in vv. 3–17a at this point. These three warriors are members of the Thirty, on whom see the NOTE at v. 24.

*harvest time.* Hot, dry weather, when rain is not expected and kings become thirsty.

*the stronghold of Adullam.* This old fortress city (modern Tell esh-Sheikh Madhkûr), some sixteen miles southwest of Jerusalem (Josh 15:33–35; cf. II Chron 11:7), was the rallying point of David's private army during his early days as an outlaw leader in the countryside of Judah; see I Sam 22:1. It is probable that the episode in vv. 12–17a belongs to that period and not to the time of David's kingship (see the NOTES at v. 14). Mazar [Maisler] (1963b:315 n. 4) doubts the text, arguing that a site nearer Bethlehem than Adullam is required by the story: "The intention here is to a place near Bethlehem, most certainly a fortified camp of David, which suffered from a lack of water." Probably, however, David's desire for water from Bethlehem is prompted more by homesickness than thirst. He may well have had ample water where he was. The point of the story is that the too loyal soldiers act recklessly in response to their leader's idle, nostalgic remark. If David's army had no water, the infiltration of the Philistine camp to obtain it would have been a militarily sound operation, and David's reaction in vv. 16–17 would make no sense. See the NOTE at v. 15 below.

14. *David was in the stronghold.* Compare the reference in I Sam 22:4 to "the time David was in [his] stronghold." The present reference places the episode of vv. 13–17a early in David's career, when he was an outlaw chief and a fugitive from Saul or, at latest, during his rule over Judah in Hebron, when he may have continued to use Adullam as a base of operations. See also the NOTE at 5:17.

*there was a Philistine outpost in Bethlehem.* Another indication that the episode belongs early in David's career, after he left Saul's court but before he became a Philistine mercenary (I Sam 27:1), or possibly during his reign over Judah in Hebron and, in any case, before the victories described in 5:17–25.

15. It is "harvest time" (v. 12), and David is thirsty; but his "yearning" is probably less a result of thirst than nostalgia. It is not just "a drink of water" that he yearns for

but "a drink of water from the well in the gate of Bethlehem," his hometown. He longingly remembers the draughts that quenched the harvest-time thirsts of his childhood.

*Pouring it out to Yahweh.* On sacrificial water libations in Israel see *I Samuel,* p. 144. Here, however, David is not offering water; he is pouring out blood (see below).

17. David's reaction is not ungrateful. On the contrary, by refusing to drink he acknowledges his mistake in idly wishing for water from his hometown and shows that he has no wish to imperil loyal soldiers to indulge his whims. Because the three men risked their lives for the water, he says, it is blood and must be poured out on the ground in accordance with religious laws (cf. Lev 17:10–13; Deut 12.23–24).

*These . . . did.* This notice refers to and concludes the section on the deeds of the Three in vv. 8b–12 (cf. the notice concluding the exploits of Benaiah in v. 22a). The insertion of the episode in vv. 13–17a obscures the reference (cf. Wellhausen).

18. *Abishai.* See the NOTE at 2:18.

19. *he did not attain to the Three.* Cf. v. 18. Our translation of this statement *('ad-haššělōšâ lō'-bā')* suggests that it means that Abishai never achieved the rank of the Three (cf. de Vaux, explicitly: "Mais il n'égala pas les Trois"). On the basis of comparison to the wording of military lists from Alalakh, Tsevat (1958a:127), followed by Pohl (1959:298–99) and Vogt (1959), concludes that the statement is simply a conventional way of indicating that Abishai is not to be thought of as included in the list of the Three just given; that is, he says, the language "does, in itself, not connote grading or appreciation."

20–23. Benaiah was captain of the Cherethites and Pelethites, the royal bodyguard (8:18; 20:23), and in the reign of Solomon he replaced Joab as commander of the army (I Kings 2:35). According to I Chron 27:5–6 he—or his son Ammizabad—was in charge of David's military division for the third month. The present section (vv. 20–23) is the subject of a study by Zeron (1978), who notes the special treatment accorded Benaiah in the list in contrast to other warriors who were more prominent during David's reign. He concludes (p. 27) that the finished list was probably published during the reign of Solomon when Benaiah was commander of the army. Zeron's comparison (pp. 25–26) of Canaanite and Egyptian accounts of heroic exploits is instructive for study of the Benaiah pericope and for the hero stories in 21:15–22 and 23:8–23 in general. Compare, for example, the account in the Egyptian story of Si-nuhe of Si-nuhe's victory over a Syrian champion in single combat (*ANET*³, p. 20).

20. *a stalwart man.* Hebrew *'îš ḥayil,* which refers to bravery, strength, and especially loyalty (cf. 2:7; 13:28; and *I Samuel,* the NOTE at 10:26,27a).

*Kabzeel.* A town in the extreme south of Judah near Arad and Beersheba (Map 9); cf. Josh 15:21.

23. *he did not attain to the Three.* See the NOTE at v. 19 above.

24. *Asael.* See 2:18–23. The death of Asael provides a *terminus ante quem* for this version of the roster. Elliger (1935:34) thinks the Asael entry, which differs slightly in form from the rest of the roster, is secondary, added to complete the list of the three sons of Zeruiah. According to I Chron 27:7, Asael was in charge of David's military division for the fourth month.

*the Thirty.* In his study of the list of David's warriors Elliger (1935:66–67) cites a Theban inscription describing a feast at the coronation of Ramesses II when the king was praised by, among others, a group of thirty men whom Elliger identifies as the king's bodyguard, a royal cortege of thirty soldiers. If there was such a "host of thirty" at Pharaoh's court three centuries before the time of David, Elliger concludes, the fraternity of the Thirty at David's court might be another example of the influence of Egyptian institutions on the early Israelite monarchy (cf. the NOTES on "remembrancer" and "scribe" at 8:16,17). Mazar [Maisler] has challenged this conclusion on the grounds that the number thirty "is to be found in the pre-monarchic Israelite tradition, where there is frequent mention of thirty companions, or sons, who were associated with a charismatic personality or with the head of a clan" (1963b:310). Among the groups of thirty cited by Mazar (Judg 10:4; 12:9; 14:11; I Sam 9:22; I Chron 11:42), however, only one has a clear military character, and it, a group of thirty Reubenites in I Chron 11:42, is part of the Chronicler's expansion of the present list. Thus the evidence for a pre-Davidic history of the institution of the Thirty is meager: Elliger's Egyptian parallel is suggestive but inconclusive, and Mazar's biblical parallels are specious. The issue remains in doubt.

*Elhanan.* The slayer of Goliath; see 21:19, where Elhanan is identified as a Jearite. Elliger (1935:34 n. 10) questions the identification of these two Elhanans.

25. *Shammah.* Probably to be identified with Shamhuth the Izrahite of I Chron 27:8 (see the *Textual Note*), where it is said that he had charge of David's military division for the fifth month.

*the Harodite.* Elliger (1935:39–40) discounts a connection with the Spring of Harod near Jezreel (Judg 7:1). Following G. Dalman, he points to Khirbet el-Ḥarēḏān, a few miles southeast of Jerusalem, known as Beth Harudu in the Roman period. "Lizards' Ruin" (cf. Arabic *ḥaraḏin,* "lizards") would derive its name from wordplay on the ancient name. See Map 9.

*Elika.* The name *'ĕlîqā'* means "God has vomited" (cf. Noth 1928:40 n. 1) unless Zadok (1977) is correct in revocalizing it *'ēl-yāqâ,* "God has guarded."

26. *the Paltite.* A member of the Calebite clan descended from Pelet (I Chron 2:47) or an inhabitant of Beth-pelet, a town in the extreme southern district of Judah near Beersheba (Josh 15:27). The clan and the town might be associated; cf. Elliger 1935: 41–43. See Map 9.

*Ira.* According to I Chron 27:9 Ira was in charge of David's military division for the sixth month.

*the Tekoite.* On Tekoa see the NOTE at 14:2 and Map 9.

27. *Abiezer.* According to I Chron 27:12, Abiezer had charge of David's military division for the ninth month.

*the Anathothite.* Anathoth (Râs el-Kharrubeh, near the modern village of 'Anâtâ, three miles north-northeast of Jerusalem) was a priestly city in Benjamin, where Abiathar was banished by Solomon (I Kings 2:26) and the prophet Jeremiah was born (Jer 1:1). See Map 9.

*Sibbecai.* The hero of 21:18. According to I Chron 27:11, Sibbecai was in charge of David's military division for the eighth month. From the same passage we learn that he, like Mahrai (v. 28), was a Zerahite, a member of the Judahite clan that traced its descent to Zerah (Num 26:20; cf. I Chron 2:6).

*the Hushathite.* The town of Husha, modern Ḥûsān, lay southwest of Bethlehem. See Map 9.

28. *the Ahohite.* See v. 9 above.

*Mahrai.* According to I Chron 27:13, Mahrai was in charge of David's military division for the tenth month, and like Sibbecai (v. 27) was a member of the Judahite clan of the Zerahites.

*the Netophathite.* The site of the ancient town of Netophah is Khirbet Bedd Fālûḥ, southeast of Bethlehem (see Map 9), not far from the 'Ain en-Nāṭûf, a spring that preserves the ancient name.

29. *Heldai.* According to I Chron 27:15, Heldai was in charge of David's military division for the twelfth month. We are also told there that he was a member of the Kenizzite or Calebite clan that traced its ancestry to the "judge" Othniel (I Chron 4:13; cf. Josh 15:15–19; Judg 1:11–15; 2:7–11).

*Gibeah of the Benjaminites.* The home of Saul (I Sam 9:1–2; etc.). See Map 9.

30. *Benaiah.* Not the better known Benaiah of vv. 20–23, who was from Kabzeel. Benaiah the Pirathonite was, according to I Chron 27:14, in charge of David's military division for the eleventh month.

*the Pirathonite.* The town of Pirathon was the home of the "minor judge" Abdon (Judg 12:13–15). It was an Ephraimite town (cf. I Chron 17:14), perhaps Far'âtā, ca. five miles southwest of Shechem. See Map 9.

*the wadis of Gaash.* Mount Gaash (Josh 24:30 = Judg 2:9) lay south of Timnath-heres, which was about fifteen miles southwest of Shechem. See Map 9.

31. *Abial.* That is, *'ăbî-'al,* which means "My (divine) father is 'Al." On the divine name *'al,* "the High One," see Nyberg 1938; Dahood 1965b:45–46.

*the Beth-arabathite.* A town on the Judah-Benjamin border (Josh 15:6; 18:18), possibly el-Gharabeh, southeast of Jericho (cf. Josh 18:22). See Map 9.

*Azmaveth.* The name *'azmawet* "Death is strong," evidently with reference to the god Death (cf. the name *'ăḥîmôt,* "Ahimoth," meaning "My [divine] brother is Death," in I Chron 6:10); contrast Noth (1928:231 n. 6), who reads *'azmôt* (cf. LXX) and takes it as the name of an unknown plant. Comparing *mt 'z,* "Death is strong," in *CTCA* 6 (= *UT*' 49).6.17,18,20, Freedman suggests to me that the name might be a quotation from the Canaanite epic (cf. the NOTE on "Jeshbaal," v. 8). It occurs as the name (Azmaveth or Beth-azmaveth) of a place near Jerusalem in Ezra 2:24 and Neh 7:28; 12:29. According to I Chron 27:25, a certain Azmaveth son of Adiel, perhaps the Azmaveth of our passage, had charge of David's treasuries.

*the Bahurimite.* On the village of Bahurim see the NOTE at 3:16 and Map 9.

32. *the Shaalbonite.* The city is called Shaalbim in Judg 1:35 and I Kings 4:19 and Shaalbin in Josh 19:41–42, where it is grouped with Ajalon and Beth-shemesh. These two cities are grouped with a city called Selebi in Jerome's commentary on Ezek 48.22, and Elliger (1935:50–53) deduces from this that the modern site is Selbît, three miles northwest of Ajalon and eight miles north of Beth-shemesh. See Map 9.

*the Gizonite.* As explained in the *Textual Note,* the reading is very uncertain. No town or clan by this name is known.

33. *Shamma the Hararite.* See v. 11.

*the Urite.* See the *Textual Note.* If the reading is correct, perhaps *hā'ûrî* designates Ahiam as a descendant of the Judahite Uri, father of Moses' craftsman Bezalel (Exod 31:2; 35:20; etc.).

34. *the Maacathite.* We need not look to the Aramean kingdom of Maacah (10:6)

or even to the region of Beth-maacah near Dan (20:14–15). There was a Judahite clan of Maacathites, with which I Chron 4:19 associates Eshtemoa, ancestor of the town south of Hebron (Elliger 1935:56–57). Eliphelet comes from this area. See Map 9.

*Eliam son of Ahithophel the Gilonite.* On Ahithophel see 15:12,31 and § XXIX *passim.* This Eliam and Eliam the father of Bathsheba may be the same man; see the NOTE at 11:3. Giloh is identified at 15:12. See Map 9.

35. *the Carmelite.* Carmel lay south of Hebron in Judah (Tell el-Kirmil); see Map 9. It was the site of David's encounter with Nabal and Abigail in I Samuel 25.

*the Archite.* A clan located in northwest Benjamin, south of Bethel. The most famous Archite was Hushai (15:32).

36. *the Hagrites.* Transjordanian nomads living east of Gilead. According to I Chron 5:10,19–22, Reuben and the other Israelite tribes conquered the Hagrites and occupied their territory "until the exile," but Ps 83:7 [83:6] suggests that hostilities with the Hagrites continued into the monarchical period. David seems to have won the loyalty of a number of them. The unit commanded by Igal is probably a foreign mercenary army like Ittai's Gittites (cf. 15:18). According to I Chron 27:30, a Hagrite named Jaziz had charge of David's flocks.

37. *the Beerothite.* On Beeroth see the NOTES at 4:2–3 and Map 9.

38. *the Ithrite.* Apparently the Ithrites were the chief indigenous clan of Kiriath-jearim (I Chron 2:53). Like the Beerothites they were probably Hivite in origin (cf. Josh 9:17 and see Mazar [Maisler] 1963b:319 n. 1).

39. *Uriah the Hittite.* The husband of Bathsheba, chaps. 11–12 *passim.*

*Thirty-seven in all.* This is an editor's computation, but it is difficult to discover how it was reckoned. The roster of the Thirty in vv. 24–39 has thirty names as I read it. Adding the Three (vv. 8b–12) and Abishai and Benaiah (vv. 18–23) brings the total to thirty-five. If the editor read two names in v. 36, as in the received Hebrew text, his total was still only thirty-six. It may be that thirty-seven was reached by counting Joab (v. 37), as Elliger supposes (1935:36). But there are other places a thirty-seventh name might have been found ("Adino the Ezenite" in v. 8 [see the *Textual Note* on "brandished his spear"], etc.), and because we do not know the condition of the text at the time the editor made his computation, it is futile to try to guess what he meant. See, further, the COMMENT.

## COMMENT

This list of David's warriors falls naturally into three parts. First (vv. 8b–12 + 17b), the Three are identified and their exploits summarized. The vignette in vv. 13–17a is out of place, having been inserted by an editor who wrongly associated the three anonymous warriors who fetch water for David with the Three. The second part (vv. 18–23) names Abishai and Benaiah. Both were "honored above the Thirty" (vv. 19,23)—and Abishai was the commander of the Thirty—but neither attained to the Three (vv. 19,23). These two, in other words, stood somewhere *between* the Three and the Thirty in rank. The third part (vv. 24–39a) is a list of the Thirty.

It is often assumed, however, that all the warriors named, including the Three, Abishai and Benaiah—perhaps even Joab—belonged to the Thirty. This is possible since, as Elliger points out (1935:36–37), the Thirty was an institution, not just a reckoning of the list, and its membership must have changed from time to time with deaths, replacements, etc. Thus we might interpret the first thirty names, beginning with Jeshbaal, as the original roster (cf. Mazar [Maisler] 1963b; Hertzberg). Elliger (1935:47) notes that the first ten warriors in the list after Asael (v. 24) come from Judah, most from towns within a narrow radius of Bethlehem; the next ten are from farther north. Thus we might think of an early core of warriors, later expanded as David's power grew. The three warriors in vv. 33–35, notes Elliger (1935:59–60), are from southern Judah. This brings the total to twenty-three. By adding the Three, as well as Abishai, Benaiah, and Asael, we reach twenty-nine, and Joab makes thirty (cf. Hertzberg). This, we might conclude, was the original roster. The names in vv. 36–39, some of which come from east of the Jordan, are later replacements made after the eastward expansion of David's power. Mazar [Maisler] (1963b:318–19) follows this interpretation but identifies the common feature of the names at the end of the list (vv. 36–39) more precisely: All are of non-Israelite origin, whether foreign (Hagrite, Ammonite) or indigenous (Hivite [Beerothite, Ithrite], Hittite). He concludes (p. 319) that they "were perhaps added on to the Thirty to serve as officers over foreign mercenary units in David's army."

Against such an interpretation is the absence of any indication that the Three was a subgroup of the Thirty, and the fact that Abishai and Benaiah are said to be *min-haššělōšîm nikbād*, lit. "honored more than the Thirty," that is, "honored above the Thirty" (vv. 19,23). This might be taken to mean "honored more than *the rest of* the Thirty," but there is no reason to think so unless it be the fact that Abishai was commander of the Thirty. The entry *baššělōšîm*, "among the Thirty," after Asael's name in v. 24, followed by a list of names without further specification as to membership, shows that the roster of the Thirty begins with Asael. There must have been changes in the membership from time to time, but this roster represents the membership as it stood when the list was made, not a retrospective list of all who held membership at any time in David's reign.

There does seem to be a geographical arrangement in the roster, though it is not so strict as Elliger supposes. Among the first ten names after Asael there is at least one non-Judahite by Elliger's own reckoning (Abiezer from Anathoth) and a second by mine (Zalmon the Ahohite). The next six, from Ittai to Eliahba, are from Benjamin, Dan, and Ephraim. The next three are uncertain, though Jonathan and Ahiam are probably from Judah. Eliphelet, Eliam, and Hezrai are from southern Judah, but Paarai is a Benjaminite. The geographical distribution in vv. 24–35, then, shows a tendency for places closer to Bethlehem to appear earlier in the list, but the pattern is not as strict as we should expect if geography were the chief organizing principle. The pattern of the list as a whole—the Three, then two between the Three and the Thirty, then the Thirty—shows that its organizing principle is rank. This is probably the case within the roster of the Thirty as well. We should expect soldiers from towns close to Bethlehem to rank high in seniority and influence. Those from more remote areas stand farther down the list. Non-Israelites naturally fall at the end in the official hierarchy.

The geography of the list also attests to its antiquity. There is no anachronistic "all Israel" veneer here. Apart from the mercenaries in vv. 36–39, the warriors whose homes can be identified come only from Judah and tribal territories immediately adjacent to the north, viz. Benjamin, Dan, and Ephraim. A number of Transjordanian names appear in the Chronicler's supplement to the list (I Chron 11:41b–47), but this only serves to highlight the limits of the original list, of which the Chronicler's version must be a later expansion (cf. Mazar [Maisler] 1963b:319–20). It seems clear that the list in the form that appears in II Samuel 23 derives from an early point in David's career. That it predates his accession to the northern throne is shown by the geography and by the presence in the list of Asael (v. 24), who died in David's war with the house of Saul (2:18–23). The list can be no later than David's Hebron period, and it might be as early as the wilderness period—note the absence of Ittai and his Gittites and of the Cherethites and Pelethites, all of whom became attached to David while he was in the service of Achish of Gath.

# XL. THE CENSUS PLAGUE
## (24:1–25)

**24** [1]The wrath of Yahweh was kindled against Israel again, and he
incited David against them, saying, "Go count Israel and Judah!"
[2]So the king said to Joab and the commanders of the forces that were
with him, "Make the rounds of all Israel from Dan to Beersheba and
take a census of the people, so that I'll know [their] number."
[3]"May Yahweh your god add to the people a hundred times their
number while you look on!" said Joab to the king. "But why does my
lord the king want such a thing done?" [4]But Joab and the commanders
of the forces were constrained by the king's command, and [they] went
out from their interview with the king to take a census of the Israelite
people. [5]After crossing the Jordan, they began from Aroer and the city
in the wadi of the Gadites near Jazer [6]and went by way of Gilead and
the region beneath Hermon to Dan. Then they skirted Sidon, [7]went by
Fort Tyre and all the Hivite and Canaanite cities, and came out in the
Negeb of Judah at Beersheba.
[8]At the end of nine months and twenty days they returned to Jerusalem, having made the rounds of the whole country. [9]Joab presented the
statistics of the census of the people to the king: In Israel there were
800,000 men who drew the sword, and in Judah 500,000 men.
[10]Afterwards, however, David was conscience-stricken because he
had counted the people. "I've sinned greatly in what I've done," [he]
said to Yahweh. "But now, Yahweh, transfer your servant's guilt, for
I've been very foolish."
[11]When David got up in the morning, the word of Yahweh had come
to Gad, David's seer: [12]"Go tell David, 'Yahweh has spoken as follows:
"There are three things I can impose upon you. Choose one of them,
and I'll do it." ' " [13]So Gad came to make his report to David. He said
to him, "Shall three years of famine come upon your land? Shall you
flee before your enemy for three months while he pursues you? Or shall
there be three days of plague in your land? Now think it over and
decide. Which reply shall I make to the one who sent me?"

14"All of them are very difficult for me," said David to Gad, "only let me fall by the hand of Yahweh, for his mercy is great, and not by the hand of man!"

15So Yahweh unleashed a plague in Israel from morning until dinnertime. The scourge spread among the people, and seventy thousand of
[them] died from Dan to Beersheba. 16But when the envoy extended his
hand towards Jerusalem to destroy it, Yahweh was content with the damage, and he said to the envoy who was wreaking destruction among the people, "Enough now! Relax your hand!"

Yahweh's envoy was poised near the threshing floor of Araunah the Jebusite. David looked up, and he saw Yahweh's envoy poised between the ground and the sky with his sword drawn in his hand, which was stretched out towards Jerusalem. David and the elders fell on their faces, covering themselves with sackcloth.

17When he saw the envoy slaying the people, David spoke to Yahweh. "I'm the one who sinned," he said. "I, the shepherd, did wrong. But these people, the sheep, what have they done? Let your hand be upon me and my father's house!"

18That same day Gad came to David and said, "Go set up an altar
to Yahweh on the threshing floor of Araunah the Jebusite." 19So
David went up according to Gad's instructions, as Yahweh had commanded.

20Araunah glanced down and saw the king and his servants coming towards him with their features concealed. Araunah was threshing wheat, and when David reached [him], Araunah looked up and saw him. He ran out from the threshing floor and prostrated himself before the king with his face to the ground.

21"Why has my lord the king come to his servant?" said Araunah.

"To buy the threshing floor from you," said David, "to build an altar to Yahweh, so that the scourge can be averted from the people."

22"Let my lord the king take whatever he chooses," said Araunah to
David, "and offer it up. Look, the ox will do for the holocaust, and the
threshing sledges and harnesses for the wood! 23I give it all to my lord
the king!" Then Araunah said to the king, "May Yahweh your god respond favorably to you!"

24"No," said the king to Araunah, "I must buy [it] from you for a
price. I won't offer costless holocausts to Yahweh my god!" So David
bought the threshing floor and the ox for fifty silver shekels. 25[He] built
an altar to Yahweh there and offered holocausts and communion offer-

ings. Then Yahweh accepted supplication for the land, and the scourge was averted from Israel.

## TEXTUAL NOTES

**24** 1. *The wrath of Yahweh* So MT. LXX$^{L}$. "The wrath of God." I Chron 21:1: "Satan" (see the NOTE).

2. *and the commanders* Reading *w'l śry* with LXX$^{L}$ (cf. I Chron 21:2). MT has *śr*—thus, "to Joab, the commander," etc. Note v. 4 and the plural imperative *pqdw*, "take a census," later in the present verse.

*with him* LXX$^{L}$ adds "in Jerusalem."

*Make the rounds* Reading *šwṭw* (pl.) for MT *šwṭ*; cf LXX$^{L}$.

*of all Israel* We read *bkl yśr'l*, into which MT inserts *šbṭy* ("of all *the tribes of* Israel") and to which LXX$^{LMN}$ append "and Judah."

*take a census* Reading *pqdw* (pl.) with MT (cf. LXX$^{L}$); LXX$^{B}$ reflects *pqd* (sing.).

*so that I'll know* Preceded in LXX$^{L}$ by *kai enenkate pros me* = *whby' 'ly*, "and bring (the information) to me," as in I Chron 11:2.

3. *May . . . add* Reading *ywsp* with LXX$^{L}$, Syr., and Vulg., in preference to MT *wywsp*.

*your god* So MT, LXX$^{AMN}$. Omitted by Syr.$^{MSS}$ and one MS of LXX$^{L}$. Other MSS of LXX$^{L}$ have "*their* god." LXX$^{B}$ has "God."

*the people* So MT, LXX$^{BAL}$. LXX$^{MN}$: "*your* people." One MS of LXX$^{L}$ has "*his* people," as in I Chron 21:3. See also the following *Textual Note*.

*their number* That is, *khm wkhm*. In LXX$^{ALMN}$ *wkhm* has fallen out (so I Chron 21:3). Vestiges of *wkhm* have given rise to the readings "your *(-k)* people" and "his *(-w)* people," cited in the preceding *Textual Note*.

4. *from their interview* That is, *lpny*, lit. "before, in the presence of," which, like *l-* (cf. 22:20), can be translated separatively. LXX$^{L}$ *ek prosōpou*, Syr. *mn qdm*, and Vulg. *a facie* reflect the more common *mlpny*.

5. *they began from . . . and* Reading *wyḥlw m- . . . wmn* on the basis of LXX$^{L}$ *kai ērxanto apo . . . kai apo*. MT has *wyḥnw b- . . . ymyn*, "they encamped in . . . south of."

*of the Gadites near Jazer* MT has *hgd w'l y'zr*, while LXX$^{L}$ reflect *hgdy w't y'zr*. The original reading was probably *hgdy 't/'l y'zr*. The *w-* of MT arose from *-y*; it was added recensionally to LXX$^{L}$. The prepositions *'t*, "near," and *'l*, "alongside," are variants.

6. *beneath Hermon* The problem here is very difficult, and we follow the exquisite argument of Skehan (1969). MT *tḥtym ḥdšy* is unintelligible. LXX$^{L}$ has *chettieim kadēs*, from which Wellhausen, following Hitzig and Thenius, reconstructed *hḥtym kdšh*, "(to the region) of the Hittites, to Kadesh." This reading has found wide acceptance, though there is disagreement as to whether Kadesh (Ḳedesh) of Naphtali (Tell Qades near Lake Huleh) is meant (Klostermann) or Kadesh on the Orontes. Well-

hausen favored the latter on the grounds that Kadesh of Naphtali is off the route and too far south for an ideal boundary. His argument against the southern Kadesh is strong, but the northern Kadesh is, as Skehan puts it (1969:44), "simply and totally too far north." Evidently the reading of LXX$^{L}$ is an ancient guess. LXX$^{B}$ offers even less help, reading *thabasōn,* to which is added, recensionally (?), *hē estin nadasai.* From *thabasōn* one might restore *tbṣ . . . ,* "Thebez," but Thebez (Ṭubâṣ, northeast of Shechem) is farther off the route than Kadesh of Naphtali, and Skehan is probably right in deriving *thabasōn* from **thaathabasōn* (or **thaathamasōn*). We are reduced to conjecture, and Skehan's (derived ultimately from Ewald 1878:162 and n. 3) is best. Assuming a rare (Isa 3:10) confusion of *š* and *m,* he reads *ḥrmwn* for *ḥdšy,* citing a series of passages (Deut 3:8; 4:48; Josh 11.3,17; 13:5; etc.) in support of "a very strong presumption as to what should be the northeastern turning point" (p. 47). Thus he reads *tḥt ḥrmwn,* which we adopt with one small change: *tḥt mḥrmwn,* "beneath Hermon."

*to Dan* Reading *'d dn* with LXX$^{L}$ *(heōs dan).* LXX$^{B}$ reflects three ways of expressing this: *eis daneidan kai oudan* < **danei* + *eis dan* + *heōs dan* = *dnh* + *'l dn* + *'d dn.* MT has *dnh y'n,* the second word being probably a corrupt vestige of a conflation similar to that of LXX$^{B}$.

*they skirted* So LXX: *kai ekyklōsan* = *wysbbw* (so Syr ; cf. Targ., Vulg.). MT has *wsbyb.*

*Sidon* Reading *'t ṣydwn* with LXX$^{L}$ for MT *'l ṣydwn.* LXX$^{AL}$ add *tēn megalēn*—thus, *'t ṣydwn rbh,* "Greater Sidon" (Josh 11:8; 19:28).

9. *800,000* So MT. LXX$^{L}$: "900,000" (cf. Josephus, *Ant.* 7.320). I Chron 21:5: "1,100,000."

*men* (1) So MT$^{MSS}$ (cf. LXX$^{MN}$): *'yš,* as in I Chron 21:5. MT has *'yš ḥyl,* "stalwart men."

*500,000* LXX$^{L}$: "400,000" (cf. Josephus, *Ant.* 7.320). I Chron 21:5: "470,000."

*men* (2) So MT: *'yš.* LXX *andrōn machētōn* = *'nšy gbwrym,* "warriors." I Chron 21:5 has *'yš šlp ḥrb,* "men who drew a sword."

10. *Afterwards . . . because he had counted* MT has *'ḥry kn spr,* for which we must read either *'ḥry spr (sěpôr),* "after the counting of" (cf. LXX$^{B}$, Syr.) or *'ḥry kn ky spr* (cf. LXX$^{L}$). MT is more easily understood on the assumption that the latter reading was original. For the text of I Chron 21:6–7 see the NOTE.

*in what I've done* MT *'šr 'syty,* to which LXX$^{ALMN}$ add *'t hdbr hzh*—thus, "in that I did this thing"—as in I Chron 21:8.

11. *Gad, David's seer* So LXX$^{L}$ (cf. I Chron 21:9). Syr.: "Gad the prophet." MT (cf. LXX$^{BAMN}$): "Gad the prophet, David's seer."

12. *impose upon you* MT *nṭl 'lyk* (cf. Lam 3:28 [Thenius]), for which I Chron 21:10 has *nṭh 'lyk,* "offer" [?], preferred by Wellhausen.

13. *He said to him* After this LXX$^{BLMN}$ add *eklexai seautō genesthai,* "Choose (for yourself to come to pass)"; cf. v. 12.

*three* So LXX, as in I Chron 21:12. MT has "seven."

*your land* (1) We can read *lk . . . h'rṣ* with LXX$^{L}$ or *'rṣk* with MT$^{MSS}$ but not *lk . . . 'rṣk* with MT.

*before* So MT: *lpny.* LXX$^{L}$ *ek prosōpou* reflects *mpny,* "from (before)," as in I Chron 21:12.

*your enemy* The following *whw'*, "while he," shows that MT *ṣryk*, "your enemies," should be *ṣrk* (cf. Syr.).

*in your land* Instead of *b'rṣk* (so MT) LXX[L] reads *b'rṣ w-*, "in the land? And. . . ."

14. *All of them* Reading *kullô* with LXX[B] *pantothen* and OL *undique*. In MT *klw* has fallen out after *ly*.

*for me* At the end of the sentence LXX[LMN] add *kai ta tria* = *whšlšh*, "and the three (things)," which is ungrammatical in this position. Probably *hšlšh* was a variant of *klw* (see above); cf. I Chron 21:13 (LXX).

*only* So LXX[L] (cf. OL): *plēn* = *'k*, which in other witnesses has fallen out before *'plh*, "let me fall" (homoioarkton).

*let me fall* So LXX. MT has "let *us* fall" here but "let *me* fall" below. Syr.: "It is better for us that we should fall . . . but let us not fall."

*and not* That is, "and let me not fall." See above.

15. At the beginning of the verse LXX[BALM] (cf. OL[MS]) have a long plus: *kai exelexato heautō daueid ton thanaton kai hēmerai therismou pyrōn* = *wybḥr lw dwd 't hdbr w(yhy b)ymy qṣyr ḥṭym*, "So David chose the plague. And in the days of the wheat harvest. . . ." This does not appear in I Chron 21:14, and there is no apparent motivation for its loss in MT. We must suspect the main clause of being an interpretive expansion of v. 14. The final clause *(wymy qṣyr ḥṭym)* is, as it stands, grammatically unrelated to anything adjacent; it, too, may have arisen as a gloss (on *'t mw'd*, "the appointed time" [MT]?) in anticipation of v. 20 (cf. Fuss 1962:152–53).

*dinnertime* MT has *'t mw'd*, which is usually taken to mean "the time appointed" (Nowack, Goldman, etc.), in reference to the three days' limit of v. 13. Caspari compares the use of *mw'd* in 20:5, and Rupprecht (1977:7 n. 12) adds Exod 9:5; Pss 75:3 [75:2]; and 102:14 [102:13]. Schmidt (1933:82) and Schmid (1970:246) think it means "the time of the (cultic) assembly." Ehrlich (1910:345) emends the text to *'lwt hmnḥh*, "(until) the sacrifice was offered up," comparing I Kings 18:36 and II Kings 3:20. For "the time appointed" we should expect *'ēt hammô'ēd* or *hā'ēt hammû'ād* but not *'ēt mô'ēd*. Moreover, LXX *hōras aristou* points to *'t s'd*, which is unquestionably preferable. Confusion of *s* and *m* was especially easy in scripts of the third and second centuries. Graphic confusion was also responsible for the reading of Targ., which reflects *'t bw'r* (< *mw'd*), "the time of burning." For the translation of *'t s'd* see the NOTE.

*The scourge . . . people* So LXX: *kai ērxato hē thrausis en tō laō* = *wyḥl hmkh b'm*, lit. "and the scourge caused sickness *(wayyāḥel)* among the people." This was lost in the text of MT before the following *wymt* (homoioarkton).

16. *the envoy* So MT, LXX[AL] (see the NOTE). LXX[B]: "the envoy of God." OL: "the envoy of Yahweh."

*Yahweh's envoy* LXX[L]: "God's envoy."

*was poised near* Reading *'md 'm* with 4QSam[a] *('wmd '[m])* and I Chron 21:15.

*Araunah* So MT *(qĕrê): (h)'rwnh*. MT *(kĕtîb): h'wrnh*. I Chron 21:15: *'rnn*. 4QSam[a]: *['r]n'* (cf. *'rn'*, v. 20). The reading of the name is discussed in the NOTE.

*David looked . . . Jerusalem* This passage, known from I Chron 21:16, is preserved in 4QSam[a]: *wyś' [dwyd 't 'ynyw wyr' 't ml'k yhwh 'wmd byn h]'rṣ wbyn [hšmy]m wḥr[b]w šlwph bydw [nṭwyh 'l yrwšlm wypl dwyd whzqnym 'l pn]yhm mt[ksym bśq]ym.*

I Chron 21:16 differs in reading *mksym* for *mtksym* and in reading *'l pnyhm* after *mksym bśqym*. The entire passage was lost in MT when a scribe's eye skipped from *wyś' dwd* to *wy'mr dwd* at the beginning of v. 17. See Cross 1961:141 n. 40a; Ulrich 1978:156–57.

17. *I, the shepherd, did wrong* So 4QSam^a: [']*ṅky hr'h ḣr'ty* (= *hārō'eh hărē'ōtî*). Cf. (in addition to LXX^L, OL, and Josephus [*Ant.* 7.328]) I Chron 21:17: *hārēa' hărē'ôtî*, "I indeed did wrong." In MT *hr'h* has fallen out, and *hr'ty* has become *h'wyty* by confusion of *reš* and *waw* and metathesis. Cf. Shenkel 1969:81; Ulrich 1978:86; 1980:143–44.

18. *said* MT adds "to him." Omit with LXX^L and 4QSam^a.

*Araunah* So MT *(qĕrê)*: *'rwnh*. MT *(kĕtîb)*: *'rnyh*. I Chron 21:18: *'rnn*.

20. On first inspection the text of I Chron 21:20–21 seems repetitious, presenting two statements that Araunah looked and saw ([1] *wyšqp* [> *wyšb*] . . . *wyr'* . . . [2] *wybṭ* . . . *wyr'*) David; we might suppose that the second statement arose in correction of the first, which is corrupt. On the other hand, there is a logical progression in the longer text. Araunah glanced down (**wyšqp*) and saw the approaching party, but he did not recognize them because their features were concealed (*mtḥb'ym*) and he was preoccupied with his threshing. When David came to the place where Araunah was (*'d 'rnn*), however, Araunah was able to get a better look (*wybṭ*) and recognized him. 4QSam^a, moreover, seems to preserve the longer reading in expanded form. The scroll may be reconstructed as follows: *wyšq̇ṗ* [*'rn' wyr' 't hmlk w't 'bdyw b'ym 'lyw mtḥb'ym mtksym*] *bśqym w'rn' dš ḥṭyṁ* [*wyb' dwyd 'd 'rn' wybṭ 'rn' wyr' 't dwyd w't 'bdyw mtk*]*sym bśqẏṁ b'*[*ym 'lyw wyṩ'*. . . . This differs from the text of I Chron 21:20–21. First of all, the scroll preserves the correct verb at the beginning, *wyšqp*. In I Chron 21:20 this has become *wyšb*, and the entire opening clause is corrupt: *wyšb 'rnn wyr' 't hml'k* (LXX = *hmlk*) *w'rb't bnyw 'mw*, "Araunah turned and saw the envoy (the king), his four sons who were with him (concealing themselves . . .)." The correspondences of *wyšb* to *wyšqp*, *hml'k* to *hmlk*, *w'rb't* to *w't 'bdyw*, and *'mw* to *'lyw* (cf. Ulrich 1978:158) suggest that the original of *bnyw* was not *'brym* (so II Sam 24:20) but *b'ym*; indeed *b'ym*, which is the more usual verb for an approaching party, was probably the primitive reading, *'brym* having arisen after *'bdyw*. 4QSam^a also differs from I Chron 21:20 in inserting *mtksym bśqym* after *mtḥb'ym*. This is probably an epexegetical expansion drawn from v. 16, intended to explain the concealment of the features of David's party by reference to the sackcloth they were wearing. The expansion in 4QSam^a of *dwyd* in the last clause to *dwyd w't 'bdyw*, etc., has no correspondent in I Chron 21:21; it is probably secondary. The short text of MT in II Sam 24:20, however, evidently arose from an expanded text of the type of 4QSam^a. A scribe's eye skipped from the first *b'ym 'lyw* to the second, resulting in a large loss of material; the change from *b'ym 'lyw* to *'brym 'lyw* was subsequent. According to these considerations, then, the primitive text of II Sam 24:20a is to be reconstructed as follows: *wyšqp 'rwnh wyr' 't hmlk w't 'bdyw b'ym 'lyw mtḥb'ym w'rwnh dš ḥṭym wyb' dwd 'd 'rwnh wybṭ 'rwnh wyr' 't dwd*.

*from the threshing floor* Reading *mn hgrn*, as in I Chron 20:21, for which II Sam 24:20 has *'rwnh*, "Araunah."

21. *said David* LXX^L adds "to him."

22. *and offer it up* So MT: *wy'l*, to which LXX adds "to Yahweh." Many MSS of LXX reflect *wy'ś*, as in I Chron 21:23. The verb is omitted by Syr.

23. *I give it all to my lord the king!* MT has *hkl ntn 'rwnh hmlk lmlk,* lit. "Everything Araunah gives, O king, to the king!" or "Everything Araunah the king gives to the king." The second possibility ("Araunah the king") has led to the interpretation of the verse as evidence that Araunah was the Jebusite king of Jerusalem, a conclusion reached already by Martin Luther in his notes on the passage (cf. Rupprecht 1977:11 n. 13); see Ahlström 1961:117–18 and the hypothesis of Rupprecht discussed in the COMMENT. Note, however, that *hmlk* is lacking in LXX, OL, Syr., Targ., and Vulg.$^{MSS}$. This suggests not that *hmlk* should be removed but rather that *lmlk* arose in correction of *hmlk,* replacing it in some MSS and combined with it in a conflate text in others. Thus, we must account for *hkl ntn 'rwnh hmlk.* I suggest that the primitive reading was *hkl ntty* (so I Chron 21:23; cf. Gen 23:11) *l'dny hmlk.* When *'d(w)ny* was misread as *'rwnh* (cf. Wellhausen), the grammar was adjusted accordingly *(ntty l- > ntn),* leaving *hkl ntn 'rwnh hmlk,* to which *lmlk* was attached as explained above. Many critics follow another solution proposed by Wellhausen: *hkl ntn 'bd 'dwny hmlk lmlk,* lit. "Everything the servant of my lord the king gives to the king!" Hertzberg posits the loss of an entire clause: *hkl ntn 'rwnh lmlk wy'mr hmlk l'rwnh l' ttn lmlk,* " 'All this Araunah gives to the king.' And the king said to Araunah, 'You shall not make a gift to the king' " (Hertzberg's translation); but it is difficult to see how this explains the present evidence.

*respond favorably to you* So MT: *yrṣk,* for which Wellhausen, without textual support, would read *wyrṣny;* cf. Budde: "The verb is too weak for David." Thus (?) LXX$^{B}$: *eulogēsai se = ybrkk,* "bless you." But this is not a question of Yahweh's general favor to or acceptance of David; the issue is rather his favorable reception of the prepared offering (cf. Hos 8:13; Jer 14:12 [cf. v. 10]; Ezek 43:27), as understood by LXX$^{L}$ *(prosdexetai para sou)* and OL *(accipiat a te).*

24. *from you* MT *m'wtk,* for the usual form *m'tk* (so MT$^{MSS}$). See the *Textual Note* on "he lay with her," 13:14.

25. *offerings* At this point LXX (cf. OL) adds *kai prosethēken salōmōn epi to thysiastērion ep' eschatō(n) hoti mikron ēn en prōtois = wywsp šlmh 'l hmzbḥ 'ḥryt ky qṭwn hyh br'šwnh,* "And Solomon added to the altar later, for it was small at first."

*accepted supplication* So MT: *wy'tr,* as in 21:14. LXX$^{L}$ *hileōs egeneto* may reflect *wyslḥ,* "pardoned."

## NOTES

**24** 1. *The wrath of Yahweh.* In the story as it has come down to us the cause of Yahweh's wrath is not given. It is, to use Caspari's expression, "anger for an unknown reason" (cited also by Hertzberg). And, in fact, the cause may not have been known. The king ordered a census, thus imperiling the people (see below), and the order was given, we are told, on divine instigation. The result was a terrible plague. The conclusion was inevitable, therefore, that Yahweh was angry with Israel. In the course of the literary growth of the account, however, attention was focused on David's responsibility and guilt (see the COMMENT). The result is that in the final form of the story Yahweh incites David to order the census (v. 1), then offers him a choice of three dire punishments for having done so (vv. 11–13)! It is no wonder that the Chronicler (or his tradition) resolved the contradiction by substituting Satan for the wrath of Yahweh in v. 1 (I Chron 21:1)! Note also the Chronicler's plus at the end of v. 9 (I Chron 21:6–7), discussed in the NOTE on vv. 10–14 below.

*again.* This nuance, achieved by the verbal syntax *(wayyōsep . . . haḥărôt),* effects a link with 21:1–14, another story of divine wrath, its consequences, and appeasement. The two accounts have a number of features in common, and most of the earlier literary critics agreed with Thenius in viewing chap. 24 as having originally been a sequel to 21:1–14. Many (Wellhausen, Budde, Dhorme) assumed the two passages were connected before the insertion of the materials in 21:15–23:39 separated them. Compare Hertzberg, who agrees about the original connection but suggests that chap. 24 was removed to the end of the book because it looks ahead to Solomon and the temple. Fuss, however, has effectively challenged the consensus (1962:146–49). He acknowledges the structural similarity between the two passages but argues that this similarity is a function of the content. The structure shared by the two accounts was dictated, he says, by ancient patterns of thought about disasters of the kind both accounts describe. I agree with Fuss's conclusion that the connection between the two passages is editorial, but I think he goes too far in designating v. 1 as a whole as redactional (Fuss 1962:149; cf. Rupprecht 1977:6). The narrator of chap. 24 is generally sympathetic to David, showing his audience that David did what was required to fend off the plague. Verse 1 shows that the census was not David's idea in the first place, and it is the only place that David's responsibility for the census is mitigated. It is probable, then, that v. 1 is substantially original, having been revised by an editor (from *wayyiḥar 'ap-yahweh bĕyiśrā'ēl . . . ?*) in order to achieve an editorial link with its context when it was placed at the end of the book (for the reasons given by Hertzberg, as noted above).

*he incited David against them.* For the notion of a god "inciting" *(hēsît)* one man against another, see I Sam 26:19, where it is implied that the proper course of action in such a situation is to soothe the god with an offering. See also Job 2:3, which refers to Satan's inciting Yahweh against Job.

*count Israel and Judah.* David is told to conduct a census. By doing so he will put Israel in grave danger (as Yahweh intends), for by counting the people he will create the risk of a plague. The connection between census and plague is discussed in the COMMENT.

3. Compare 19:6–8. The positive side of Joab's hard-boiled pragmatism is shown to its best advantage here, where he is a voice of reason. In this case, however, his advice does not prevail.

5–7. Joab's route is illustrated by Map 10. The itinerary skirts the boundaries of the kingdom, and we are evidently to assume that everything within this radius was also counted. Herrmann (1981:157), however, thinks David counted only the outlying regions "to form a picture of the total number of troops in the contingents from those areas which had newly come under his dominion." Fuss (1962:156) thinks an idealized boundary description was added to the text later, and it is true that the description of the route is missing from the parallel in I Chron 21:4. Nevertheless, Noth (1960:192) considers this an accurate picture of the boundaries of the Davidic kingdom. If so, it shows that the administrative reorganization imposed during the reign of Solomon, as reflected in I Kings 4:7–9, had already begun in the time of David (Alt 1968:210–11; Mazar [Maisler] 1960:71).

5. *Aroer.* The census begins at the city which lay at the southern extreme of the land east of Jordan, captured by the Israelites from the Amorite king Sihon at the beginning of the conquest (Deut 4:48; Josh 12:2); it was thus the southeast boundary of the kingdom. The site is 'Arâ'ir on the north bank of the Arnon (Wâdī el-Môjib).

*the city in the wadi of the Gadites near Jazer.* The text is not certain. The unnamed town evidently lay on the bank of "the wadi of the Gadites," apparently the Jabbok (Nahr ez-Zerqā), near which was Jazer on the Israelite-Ammonite border (Num 21:24 [LXX]).

6. *Gilead.* See the NOTE at 2:9.

*the region beneath Hermon.* As explained in the *Textual Note,* we follow Skehan (1969) in restoring *taḥat mēḥermôn* here, the expected northeast turning point. Compare Deut 3:8; 4:48 ("from Aroer . . . as far as Mount Sirion, that is, Hermon"); Josh 11:3,17; 13:5; etc.

*Dan.* The traditional northern boundary of the kingdom (cf. v. 2).

*they skirted Sidon.* The city itself lay some distance north of the route, and Phoenicia as a whole is probably meant here (cf. Noth 1960:192 n. 3).

7. *Fort Tyre.* According to Noth (1960:192) *mibṣar-ṣōr* refers to fortified, mainland Tyre (as distinct from the island city) here and in the Naphtali boundary description in Josh 19:29. But we hardly expect Tyre to be included in the census, and it is more likely that Fort Tyre was a fortress on the Israelite-Phoenician border. In any case it represents the northwest turning point of Joab's route.

*all the Hivite and Canaanite cities.* Alt (1968:289; cf. pp. 210–11,314): "This can only mean the towns of the western plains which, although neither Israelite nor Judean, were nevertheless equally obliged to provide troops and thus must have been allied to the kingdoms and possessed the same rights" (cf. Bright 1976:198; Herrmann 1981:156–57).

*Beersheba.* The traditional southern boundary of the kingdom (cf. v. 2).

9. *the statistics.* A total figure of 1,300,000 able-bodied fighting men is much too high. Albright (1925) argued that the prototype of the census lists in Numbers 1 and 26, where the total is about 600,000, was the Davidic census, the numbers in II Samuel 24 having been distorted by confused scribes. This total (ca. 600,000), he says, originally included men, women, and children. This is obviously a very fragile hypothesis. If the "thousands" (*'ălāpîm*) are taken as *'elep*-units, however, then, using the figures calculated by Mendenhall (1958:63) for Numbers 1 (5 to 14 men per unit), we arrive at a figure of 6,500 to 18,220 men eligible for conscription. Compare the much smaller number available to Saul in I Sam 11:8: 300 "thousands" from Israel and 30 "thousands" from Judah (1,650 to 4,620 men; cf. *I Samuel,* p. 107).

10–14. As explained in the COMMENT, these verses were probably not part of the original account. In the text as it stands, David's sudden change of heart is inexplicable. The problem is solved by an expansion in the text of I Chron 21:6–7, where we read, in a position corresponding to the end of II Sam 24:9, "But Levi and Benjamin were not counted among them, for David's instructions were abhorrent to Joab. God was displeased because of this, and he smote Israel."

*David was conscience-stricken.* Cf. I Sam 24:10.

*transfer your servant's guilt.* Cf. 12:13. Here again the meaning of the verb *(ha'ăbernā')* is "transfer," not simply "take away." David requests a way to save his life by transferring his guilt to someone or something else. Yahweh accedes to the request and gives him three choices (vv. 11–13).

11. *Gad.* Last mentioned in I Sam 22:5, where he seems to have accompanied David on his flight from Saul's court. In II Chron 29:25 he is referred to as "the royal seer" *(ḥōzēh-hammelek)* in contrast (?) to "Nathan the prophet" *(hannābî');* but cf. I Sam 22:5.

13. *the one who sent me.* Yahweh.

14. *by the hand* (bis). Not "*into* the hand." Cf. 21:22 and see Ehrlich 1910:344.

*the hand of Yahweh.* According to Hertzberg, "David merely decides against the second punishment ['the hand of a man'] and leaves it to the Lord to decide between the first and the third." But Ehrlich (1910:345) argues that only plague is entirely "by the hand of Yahweh," since famine is also caused by the siege of a city. The decisive indicator, however, is the use of the expression "the hand of Yahweh," which is a standard biblical way of referring to plague (I Sam 5:6; etc.), with extensive Near Eastern parallels (Roberts 1971).

15. *dinnertime.* Hebrew *'t s'd* (see the *Textual Note*), lit. "the time of sustenance, nourishment." The verb *s'd* means "sustain," most often with food (Gen 18:5; Judg 19:5,8; I Kings 13:7; Ps 104:15). In Talmudic Hebrew the nouns *sā'ōd* and *sĕ'ûdâ* mean "meal, dinner." The present expression, then, probably refers to the time of the evening meal. Thus the plague raged for one day before it reached Jerusalem. In the original account it continued there (v. 16b; cf. vv. 21,25), but according to the present form of the story (cf. the COMMENT) Yahweh relented and stayed the hand of his envoy at this point, thus ending the plague two days early (v. 16a).

16. According to the present form of the story, Yahweh relents and stops the plague at this point, before David's supplicatory offerings are made on the new altar. But v. 16a ("But when . . . 'Relax your hand!' "), is probably secondary (see the COMMENT). Note that "the envoy" *(hammal'āk)* is referred to as if he had been mentioned before: We expect him to be identified as *mal'ak yahweh,* "Yahweh's envoy," as in v. 16b, the first time he appears.

*Yahweh's envoy.* A *mal'āk,* "envoy, messenger" (Greek *angellos,* hence "angel"), was a divine being, an agent through whom Yahweh's will was carried out. The agent of the plague in Exodus is called *hammašḥît,* "the destroyer" (Exod 12:23), and in the present passage the agent is called *(h)ammal'āk hammašḥît bā'ām,* "the envoy who was wreaking destruction among the people" (v. 16a). It was the opinion of Gressmann that a pre-Israelite (Jebusite) cultic legend involving a theophany and the erection of an altar lies behind the present account. Thus, recent interpreters assume that behind the envoy lies a non-Israelite god (Fuss 1962:162–63; Schmid 1970:246; Rupprecht 1977:10), perhaps a plague god like Resheph (Schmid). I think the traditional associations of Yahweh with plague are so strong (cf. *I Samuel,* p. 126) as to make this unlikely. See, further, the COMMENT.

*between the ground and the sky.* That is, in midair. See the NOTE at 18:9.

18. *the threshing floor.* A threshing floor was a traditional site of theophany (Judg 6:37; cf. II Sam 6:5) and a place where divine messages are received (II Kings 22:10; I Sam 14:2,18–19 [cf. *I Samuel,* the NOTE on 14:2]). At Ugarit, too, it was a place of

theophany (*CTCA* 17[= *UT*[4] 2 Aqht].5.4ff.) and divination (19[= 1 Aqht].1.19ff.). It does not follow from this, however, that the threshing floor of Araunah was already a place of worship before David built an altar there (Ahlström 1961:115–19); cf. Rowley 1967:77 n. 4.

*Araunah.* The name is non-Semitic. It is often thought to be related to the Hurrian word *ibri-* or *iwri-*, "lord, king" (cf. Gelb, Purves, and McRae 1943:210). Note, in this regard, the spelling in its first occurrence in v. 16 (MT [*kĕtîb*]), *h'wrnh* with the definite article, as if it meant "the lord," a title rather than a name; but it occurs commonly as an element in Ugaritic names (Gröndahl 1967:224–25). Elsewhere in the chapter, however, the name appears as *'ărawnâ*. This has been compared by Rosén (1955) to Hittite *arawa(nni)-*, "free," an adjective designating a freeman or aristocrat in legal texts from the Hittite empire. The element *arawi-* occurs in Hittite names at Ugarit (Gröndahl 1967:272); note especially the name spelled alphabetically as *'arwn* and syllabically as *ar-wa-nu*. It has been argued that Araunah was a member of the old Hurrian ruling aristocracy and the pre-Israelite king of Jerusalem (*h'wrnh*, "the king," v. 16), either David's predecessor (Ahlström 1961:117–18) or an ancient, semilegendary king (Rupprecht 1977:10–11); cf. the first *Textual Note* at v. 23. According to Fuss (1962:164), he is a fiction, a creation of the author of the story of David's purchase, who knew the site as "the threshing floor of Araunah" and derived the man's existence from the name. I assume that Araunah was a pre-Israelite citizen of Jerusalem, a Jebusite of Hurrian or Hittite ancestry, who sold David a threshing floor.

*the Jebusite.* See the NOTE at 5:6.

21–24. The conversation between David and Araunah recalls Abraham's negotiation with the "Hittites" (i.e., pre-Israelite inhabitants) of Hebron in Gen 23:3–16.

## COMMENT

At Yahweh's instigation David conducts a census of Israel and Judah. In consequence a plague breaks out among the people and thousands die. Order is restored when David, having seen the divine agent of pestilence wielding his sword against Jerusalem, erects an altar on the spot and makes propitiatory offerings.

### *Census and Plague*

Why should the taking of a census produce a plague? The present account in the form we have it indicates that the census was a sin of the king (v. 10) and the plague, therefore, was a punishment for sin (v. 13). This was certainly the view of the prophetic circles in which the final form of the account derives (see below). The census was a sin (perhaps) because of the administrative innovations it implied, viz. fiscal reorganization and military conscription (cf. Bright 1972:201,246; Cross 1973:227,240). Such observations, however, beg the larger question of the relationship between census and plague, because, prophetic theology aside, there was an "ancient taboo of counting heads" (Sanders 1962). Independently of the present passage, for example, Exod 30:11–16 provides for a "life's ransom" (*kōper napšô,* v. 12) for every Israelite counted, "so that there will not be a scourge *(negep)* among them when you count them." Thus we must first seek an explanation of the old religious belief in the connection between census and plague.

Speiser (1958) has attempted to provide such an explanation by drawing on information about the census from the Bible and from the archives of the Middle Bronze Age city of Mari in northwestern Mesopotamia (cf. Kupper 1950; 1957:23–29). Noting that census taking involved ritual purification in both Mari and Israel, Speiser asks what the cultic element in the census might be. He finds the answer in the practice of taking names and keeping written records, concluding (1958:24):

> There must have been a time when the Near Easterner shrank from the thought of having his name recorded in lists that might be put to unpredictable uses. Military conscription was an ominous process because it might place the life of the enrolled in jeopardy. The connection with the cosmic "books" of life and death must have been much too close for one's peace of mind. It would be natural in these circumstances to propitiate unknown powers, or seek expiation as a general precaution.

Useful as Speiser's study is, his conclusion is not entirely convincing. It is not clear that name taking was a part of the Israelite census: In Num 4:32, which Speiser cites (p. 23), *bĕšēmôt,* "by names," seems to be added precisely because the case is exceptional. Moreover, Speiser does not give attention to the rules of purification regarding military service, conscription for which was, as he notes, the primary purpose of the census. By retracing some of the ground charted out by Speiser, we shall arrive at a somewhat different destination.

At Mari the noun *tēbibtum* and related terms, which ordinarily refer to cultic purification, were used to refer to the census (Kupper 1950; Speiser 1958; cf. Kupper 1957:23–29). In Israel, as we have seen, anyone enrolled in the census was required to pay a "ransom," *kōper,* a term elsewhere referring to ritual purification from the unavoidable or excusable contamination with guilt of a person in a situation requiring purity (Lev 17:11; Num 8:19; 18:22–23; etc.; cf. Milgrom 1976a:80). To be enrolled in a census, therefore, one had to be ritually purified. In the absence of such a purification, a plague could result, exactly as in Num 8:19, where the Levites who attend the sanctuary are described as "making ransom for" (*lĕkappēr ʿal;* cf. Exod 30:15) the Israelites, so that a plague *(negep)* will not break out if they encroach on the sanctuary, another violation of rules of purity. Plague, in other words, could result if purity regulations were not carefully followed. The half-shekel *kōper* of Exod 30:12, then, was a precaution against a breach of purity laws. But what were the purity laws to which an Israelite enrolled in the census was subject?

It is widely acknowledged that "the major purpose of the census in the ancient world was always to lay the basis for levying taxes and registering men for military service" (Bright 1976:198; cf. Mendenhall 1958:53–54). The biblical materials show clearly that the census was expected to provide an estimation of available military manpower. According to Num 1:2–3 (cf. Exod 30:14) the Israelites to be enrolled in the census were males twenty years old or older, "everyone able to march with the army *(kol-yōṣē' ṣābā')*." In David's census, too, it was "men who drew the sword" who were counted (v. 9). Now military duty was a sanctified occupation involving a complex set of laws of purity: A soldier was consecrated before battle (Josh 3:5), the battle camp was kept ritually clean (Deut 23:10–15 [23:9–14]), etc. Once enrolled in a census, therefore, an Israelite was subject to military rules of purity. Any infraction could lead to disastrous results. This is the reason that David's census order put Israel in jeopardy. The onset of the plague suggests that taboos were violated, as would be almost inevitable in a general enrollment. Was the precautionary half-shekel *kōper* paid? If such a provision was in effect in the time of David, it must have been neglected, as Speiser supposes (1958:22).

### *Literary History*

The connection between census and plague mentioned in Exod 30:12 suggests that in the original version of our story the census was followed spontaneously by an outbreak of pestilence. Yet we are told that Yahweh offered David a choice of disasters (v. 13). This is only one of several inconcinnities that the reader of chap. 24 will observe. A series of questions arises as the story unfolds. Is Yahweh's anger (v. 1) or David's sin (v. 10) responsible for the plague? That is, is the plague a punishment for some unnamed offense in Israel or for David's sin in taking the census? If the latter is the case, as vv. 10ff. seem to state clearly, how can this be reconciled with the statement in v. 1 that Yahweh incited David to order the census? What moved David to repent of the census in v. 10 *before* the plague began? Did Yahweh stop the plague before it reached Jerusalem (v. 16a) or did it continue (vv. 16b–17)? Did it stop when Yahweh was satisfied that the punishment was sufficient (v. 16) or when he heeded David's supplication after the erection of the altar (v. 25)? Did David build this altar in response to his vision of the divine envoy on the threshing floor (v. 16b) or in obedience to the command of Yahweh delivered by Gad (vv. 18–19)?

Generally speaking, scholars have not been inclined to attempt to resolve these questions by positing parallel strands running through the account (so Schmid 1955:175; but cf. Schmid 1970:245–46) or attempting to isolate extensive Deuteronomistic revisions (so Veijola [DtrG: vv. 1,19b,23b,25bα; DtrP: vv. 3–4a,10–14,15aβ,17,21bβ,25bβ]; see the Introduction to the present volume, p. 7). Instead they have spoken of (1) later insertions in an originally unified account and/or (2) a side-by-side combination of two or more originally independent episodes into a single, composite narrative. Many agree with Smith in considering vv. 10 and 17 secondary. Fuss, however, in consequence of a detailed study of the chapter (1962), goes much further, concluding that the original form of the narrative contained only vv. 2,4b,8–9,15aαb, 17*,18,19*, and 25. This, he says (p. 162), was an old account of Davidic-Solomonic date written to gloss over the fact that the altar in the temple was pre-Israelite in origin and to associate its foundation with David. To this, the rest of the chapter accumulated from the tradition in the course of a long history of literary growth. Fuss's conclusions are accepted by Haag (1970: 136–37). Schmid (1970:245–50) divides the chapter into three originally independent accounts: (1) the census story in vv. 1–11a, which is historically grounded; (2) the plague story in vv. 11b–17, which revolves about the folktale motif of the choice of three punishments and the theophany of the plague god; and (3) the altar story in vv. 18–25, an etiological narrative. Rupprecht (1977: 1–13) adopts a scheme close to that of Schmid but with significant differences in detail. Striking vv. 1 and 3–4a as redactional, he confines the census story to vv. 2 + 4b–9. The second part centers on Gad; it originally contained vv. 11–15, v. 10 being redactional. The third part, the altar etiology, consists of vv. 16 + 18–25, v. 17 being from the hand of the redactor who inserted vv. 1,3–4a, and 10. Schmid and Rupprecht agree with Fuss that the main interest of the story is the altar and its Davidic origin. Following the lead of Gressmann, they see the theophany in vv. 16–17 as a relic of an old Jebusite cult legend the Israelite story is designed to replace (cf. the NOTE on "Yahweh's envoy," v. 16). According to Fuss (1962:62–63), this was not a part of the original Davidic-Solomonic story; it came in later from the tradition, having continued to be nurtured in Jerusalem. Rupprecht (1977:10–11), however, thinks elements of the Jebusite legend were built into the Israelite altar etiology from the start. He concludes (pp. 12–13) that it was originally Araunah who —in a very ancient Jebusite legend comparable to the stories of patriarchal altar-building in Genesis (which he thinks are also non-Israelite in origin)— had the vision of the god on the threshing floor. Schmid (1970:246) speaks of an original theophany of a plague god such as Resheph. Dietrich (1977:61–62), though he questions details of the arguments of Fuss and Rupprecht, considers the presence of an underlying Canaanite tradition probable.

### *The Prophetic Version of the Story*

Yahweh's own associations with plague are so well documented, however (cf. *I Samuel*, p. 126), that it is difficult to doubt that the threshing-floor theophany is an original and primitive Israelite component of the story. It may be that David was originally said to have seen Yahweh himself—the envoy having come into the story later to protect the divine transcendence—but surely it was the theophany that led David to acquire the site and erect an altar there. On the other hand, the divine message transmitted through Gad (vv. 17–18) seems designed to shift the initiative from the king to the prophet—or rather to "the one who sent" the prophet (cf. v. 13). This is the pattern throughout the story wherever the questions of interpretation listed above arise: The passages involving Gad obscure or confuse the issue by their strong tendency to discredit the king and stress the independence of divine initiative. Thus, in v. 1 we are told that Yahweh incited David to order a census, and by the end of v. 9 this has been done. Now we expect the plague to break out. But before it does (v. 15), there is a long retarding passage in which David declares himself a sinner and receives a visit from Gad, who presents him with a choice of punishments (vv. 10–14). Thus we lose sight of the divine instigation of the census, and the responsibility for what is about to happen—originally a consequence of an unnamed provocation of Israel against Yahweh—is laid entirely at David's feet. In v. 15 the plague begins and in vv. 16b–17 it has reached Jerusalem and will rage until David erects the altar and appeases Yahweh. In v. 16a, however, it is stayed preemptively by Yahweh. This difficulty, too, can be traced to an overlay of prophetic theology: Yahweh is shown to act on his own initiative, not in response to a cultic gesture. Note, finally, that although we expect David to erect the altar promptly in response to his theophanic vision in v. 16b, we find instead that he first declares himself a sinner (again) and pronounces doom on his family (v. 17), and then proceeds with the altar only after having been authorized to do so by Yahweh speaking through Gad.

This prophetic theology is familiar to us from the stories of Samuel and Saul in I Samuel and from the prophetic components of II Samuel 7 and 11–12. The present form of II Samuel 24 can be explained by positing the same kind of literary activity we found in those passages. To the original story of the census plague a prophetic writer added vv. 10–14,16a, and 17–19. As in chap. 7, he was concerned to show that the initiative for the erection of the altar came from Yahweh, not David, and his generally suspicious attitude towards the king led him to offer a revised interpretation of the cause of the census and (thus) of the plague. Furthermore, he probably maintained objections to the institution of a census as such, inasmuch as it made possible royal innovations—military conscription, fiscal reorganization, taxation—of the sort to which prophetic thought objected (cf. Bright 1972:201,246; Cross 1973:227,240).

### *The Present Location of the Chapter*

We should not, however, suppose that it was this prophetic writer who set the story of the census plague at the end of the Samuel corpus and, by manipulation of v. 1 (see the NOTE on "again," v. 1), related it to the story in 21:1–14. This was done very late in the literary growth of the book, probably after the formulation of the Deuteronomistic history (cf. Noth 1981:124–25 n. 3). It originally stood somewhere else in the materials about David's reign, perhaps in connection with the account of the conquest of Jerusalem in 5:6–10 or with the story of the arrival of the ark in chap. 6 (cf. Budde), or perhaps with chap. 7 (cf. Caspari). The reason it was relocated was the belief that the altar erected by David on the threshing floor of Araunah was the altar of holocausts of the temple in Jerusalem. Thus the story of the origin of this altar looks beyond the reign of David towards Solomon's erection of the temple. This connection is not made explicit in Samuel–Kings, however, and its historicity has been doubted (Galling 1962:97; see, further, below). But the Chronicler states explicitly that the temple was built on the threshing floor of Ornan (II Chron 3:1), as Araunah is called in Chronicles, and corresponding to v. 25 of the present passage Chronicles has a much longer passage (I Chron 21:26–22:1):

> David built an altar to Yahweh there and offered holocausts and communion offerings. He invoked Yahweh, who answered him with fire from the sky upon the holocaust altar, consuming the holocaust (LXX). Then Yahweh spoke to the envoy, and he returned his sword to its sheath. At that time, when David saw that Yahweh answered him on the threshing floor of Ornan thc Jebusite, he made sacrifice there. Yahweh's tabernacle, which Moses had made in the wilderness, and the holocaust altar were at that time on the high place in Gibeon, but David had not been able to go before it to inquire of God because he was terror-stricken by the sword of Yahweh's envoy. So David said, "*This* is the house of the god Yahweh, and *this* is the holocaust altar for Israel!"

### *The Character of the Original Document*

It is clear, therefore, that the story of the census plague functioned in post-exilic tradition as an etiology for the holocaust altar in the Solomonic temple. This was a natural conclusion to reach in an age when the association of David with another nearby altar, a "high place," would not have been expected. It provides the holocaust altar in the temple with an origin consonant with the apparent implication of the law of the altar in Exod 20:24 that Yahweh was to select the site of an altar himself. In the older version of our story in Samuel–Kings, however, no explicit connection is made between David's altar and the temple site, as we have noted, and we cannot be sure that the traditional identification of Araunah's threshing floor with the temple site was ancient or accurate. I am not inclined, moreover, to see the original account of the census plague as primarily etiological in character. It is true that vv. 16–25 are structurally similar to etiological narratives like, for example, those of the stone pillar at Bethel (Gen 28:11–22) and the altar at Ophrah (Judg 6:11–24). But there are important differences. The David of Samuel–

Kings is not a Jacob or a Gideon, remote figures of the legendary past. With a few exceptions, such as the account of his victory over Goliath, most of the materials in which David appears in Samuel are historiographical, not legendary, in character, often corresponding to known genres of ancient Near Eastern historiography. Moreover, the apparently etiological character of vv. 16–25 is less clear when one looks at the chapter as a whole. Seen in its totality, chap. 24 is primarily concerned with *the plague,* its cause (the census), and solution (the altar). It is not impossible that a fairly late etiological legend has come into the text here (cf. the Sela-hammahlekoth etiology in I Sam 23:24b–24:1), having been combined with a plague story, as many scholars suppose. In my judgment, however, the original purpose of the story was to give an official account of the plague, the erection of the altar being described to show how the plague was finally averted. This interpretation suggests itself when the primitive document, as we have reconstructed it above, is summarized.

According to the original story (vv. 1–9 + 15 + 16b + 20–25) Yahweh was enraged at Israel because of some crime not named in the account as it has come down to us. He therefore incited David to order a census and thus to put Israel in danger of a plague. David sent Joab out to count the fighting men "from Dan to Beersheba" (v. 2), and when the census was complete a plague broke out "from Dan to Beersheba" (v. 15). When the divine agent of the scourge reached Jerusalem, David looked up and saw him hovering in midair near the threshing floor of a certain Araunah. The king therefore went to the Jebusite, purchased the site, and erected an altar there. Yahweh was appeased by the offerings and the scourge was lifted.

Like other public documents from the time of David (the story of David's rise to power, the story of Abishalom's revolt, the story of the execution of the Saulids [21:1–14 + 9:1–13]), the original account was sympathetic to the king and apologetic in tone. It was addressed to an audience who certainly knew that David had ordered the census, despite the risk it was traditionally believed to represent, and who probably knew that Joab had objected to the plan. When a severe plague broke out in the land, therefore, there must have been widespread public bitterness, if not open denunciation, of the king for having brought grief to the people. The published account, however, offered a favorable view of the king's actions. It made no attempt to deny that David ordered the census—this was public knowledge—but it explained that he was "incited" to do so by Yahweh. Its chief purpose, moreover, was to show that David was responsible for stopping the ensuing plague by erecting an altar and appeasing the angry god. Thus David was presented not as a king who had brought grief to the people but, on the contrary, as a king who had saved them from grief.

# LIST OF MAPS



*Maps by Rafael Palacios*

MAP 1.

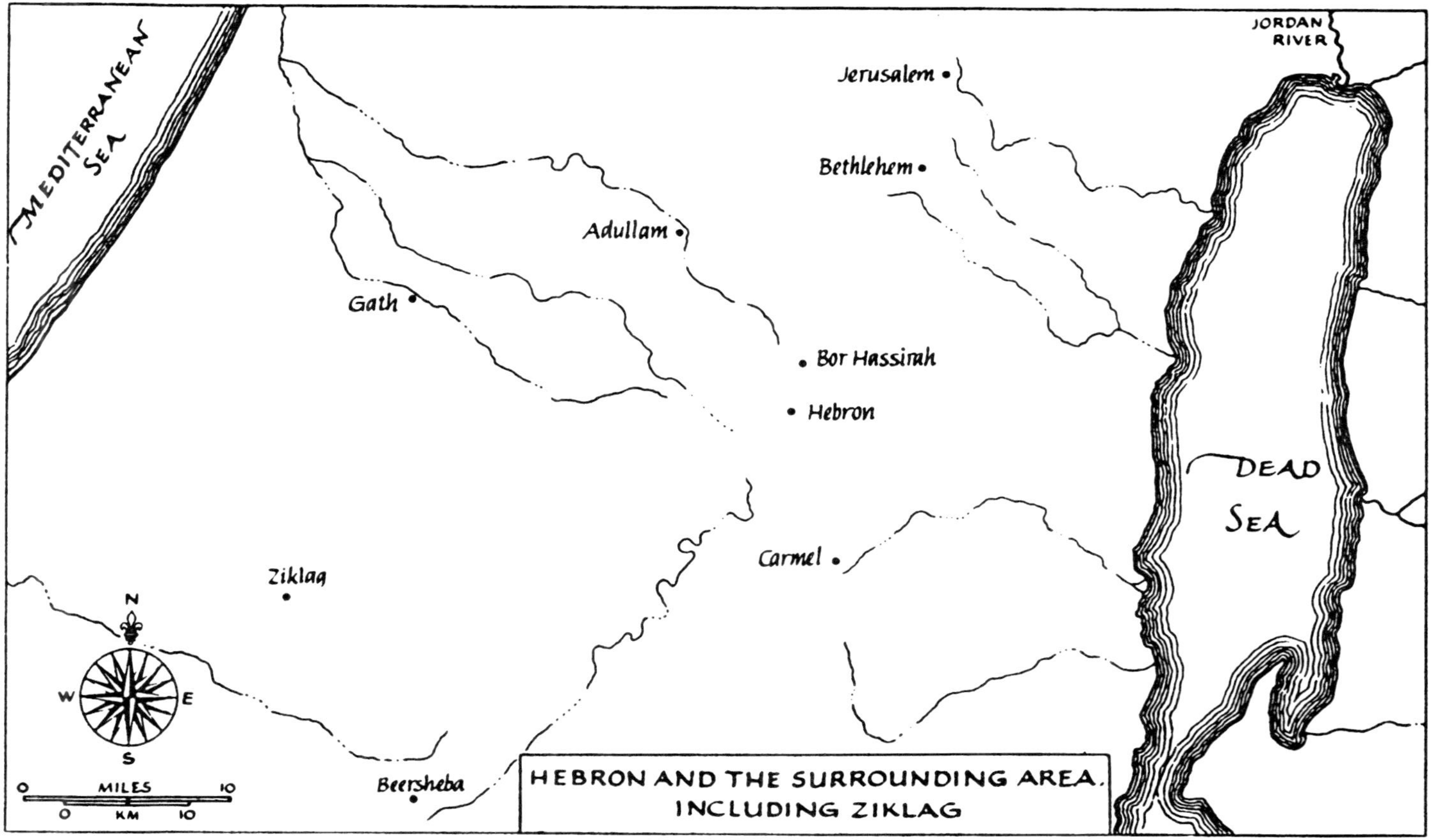
MEDITERRANEAN
SEA
JORDAN
RIVER
Jerusalem
Bethlehem
Adullam
Gath
Bor Hassirah
Hebron
DEAD
SEA
Carmel
Ziklag
N
W
E
S
0
MILES
10
0
KM
10
Beersheba
HEBRON AND THE SURROUNDING AREA,
INCLUDING ZIKLAG

MAP 2.

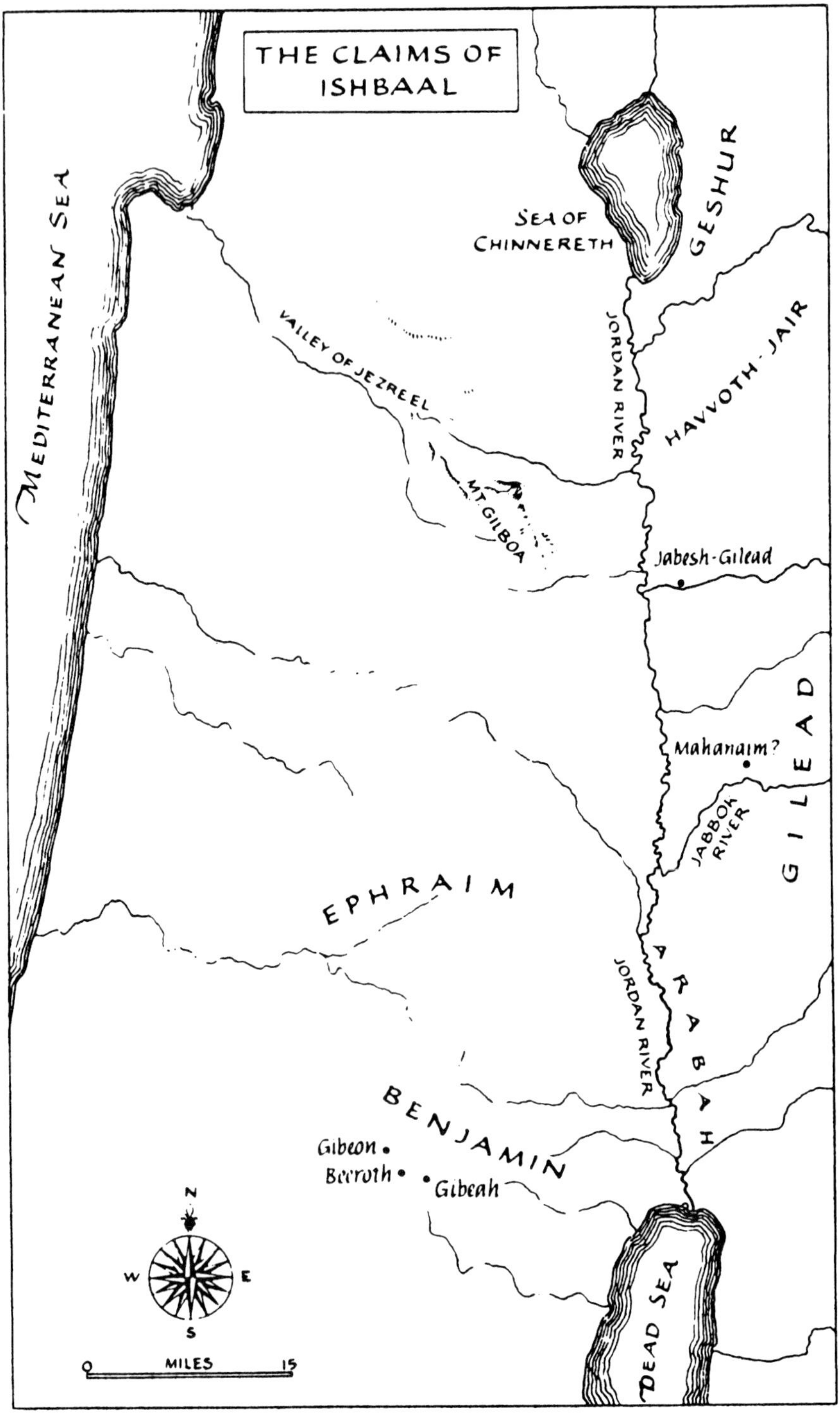
THE CLAIMS OF ISHBAAL
MEDITERRANEAN SEA
SEA OF CHINNERETH
GESHUR
VALLEY OF JEZREEL
JORDAN RIVER
HAVVOTH-JAIR
MT. GILBOA
Jabesh-Gilead
GILEAD
Mahanaim?
JABBOK RIVER
EPHRAIM
ARABAH
JORDAN RIVER
BENJAMIN
Gibeon
Beeroth
Gibeah
DEAD SEA
N
W
E
S
0
MILES
15

MAP 3.

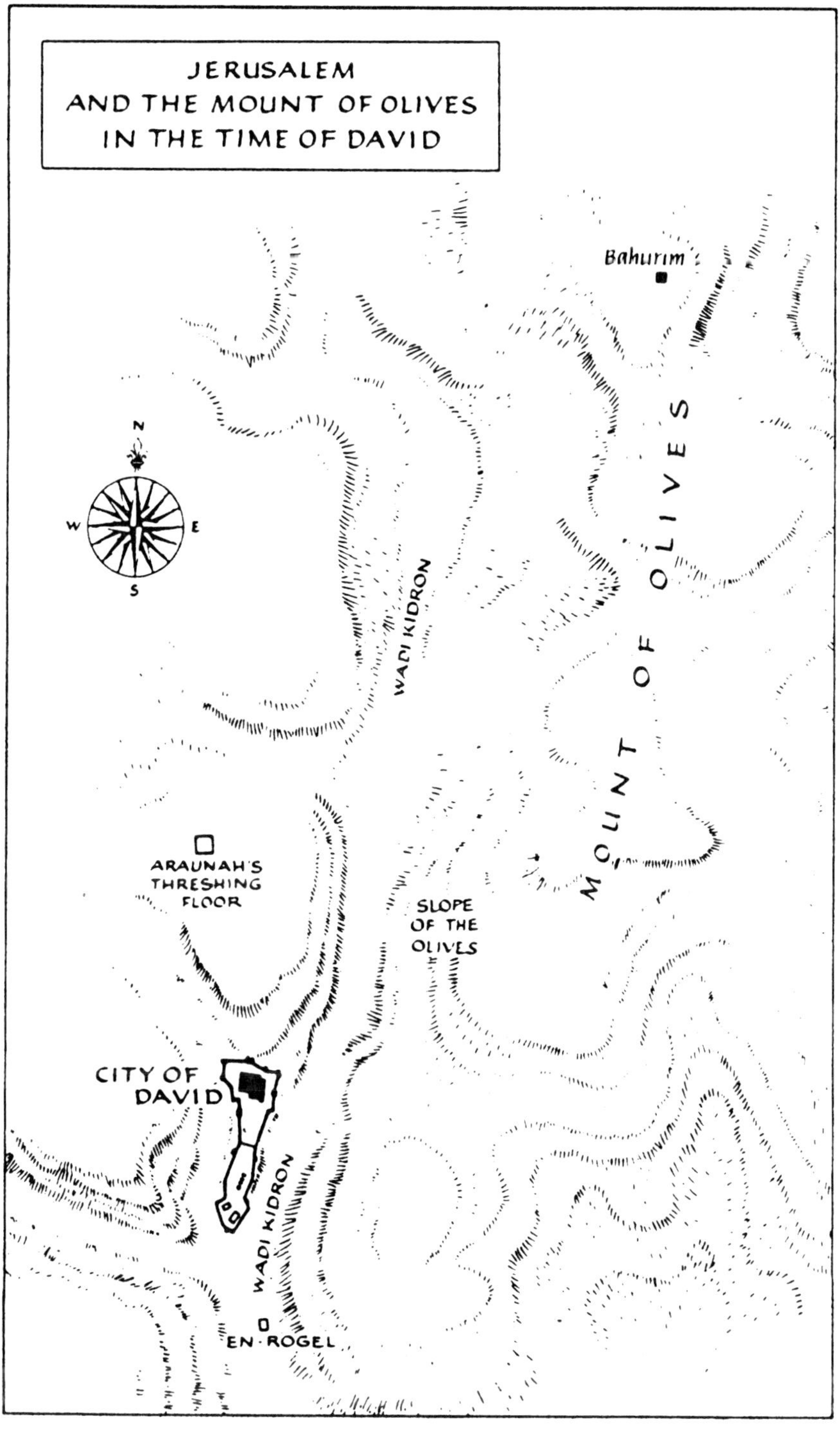

JERUSALEM
AND THE MOUNT OF OLIVES
IN THE TIME OF DAVID
N
W
E
S
Bahurim
MOUNT OF OLIVES
WADI KIDRON
ARAUNAH'S
THRESHING
FLOOR
SLOPE
OF THE
OLIVES
CITY OF
DAVID
WADI KIDRON
EN-ROGEL

MAP 4.

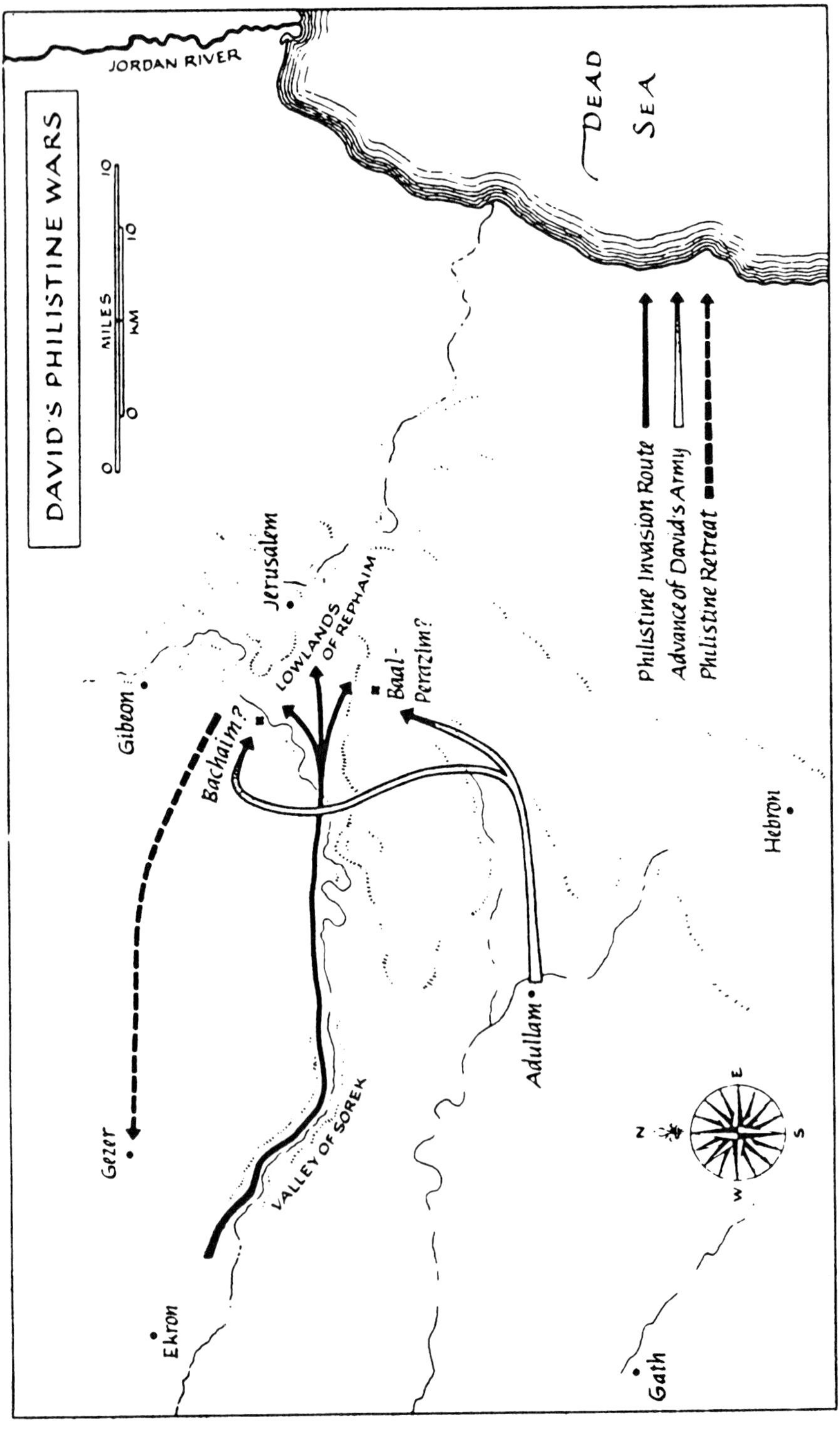
DAVID'S PHILISTINE WARS
0
10
MILES
0
10
KM
JORDAN RIVER
DEAD SEA
Jerusalem
Gibeon
LOWLANDS OF REPHAIM
Baal-Perazim?
Bachaim?
Philistine Invasion Route
Advance of David's Army
Philistine Retreat
Hebron
Adullam
VALLEY OF SOREK
Gezer
Ekron
Gath
N
E
S
W

MAP 5.

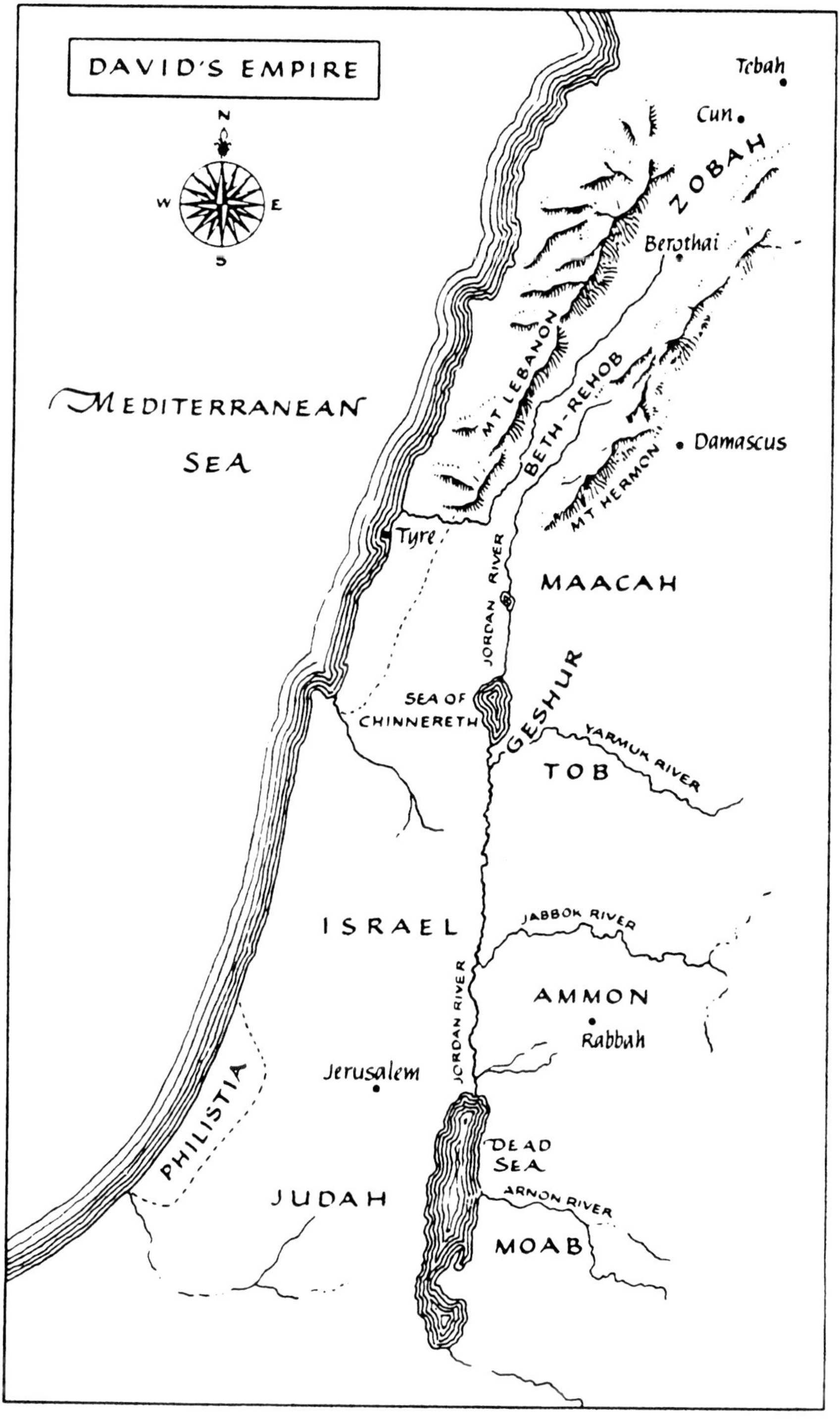

DAVID'S EMPIRE
N
W
E
S
Tebah
Cun
ZOBAH
Berothai
MT LEBANON
BETH-REHOB
MEDITERRANEAN
SEA
Damascus
MT HERMON
Tyre
JORDAN RIVER
MAACAH
GESHUR
SEA OF
CHINNERETH
YARMUK RIVER
TOB
ISRAEL
JABBOK RIVER
AMMON
Rabbah
JORDAN RIVER
Jerusalem
PHILISTIA
DEAD
SEA
ARNON RIVER
JUDAH
MOAB

MAP 6.

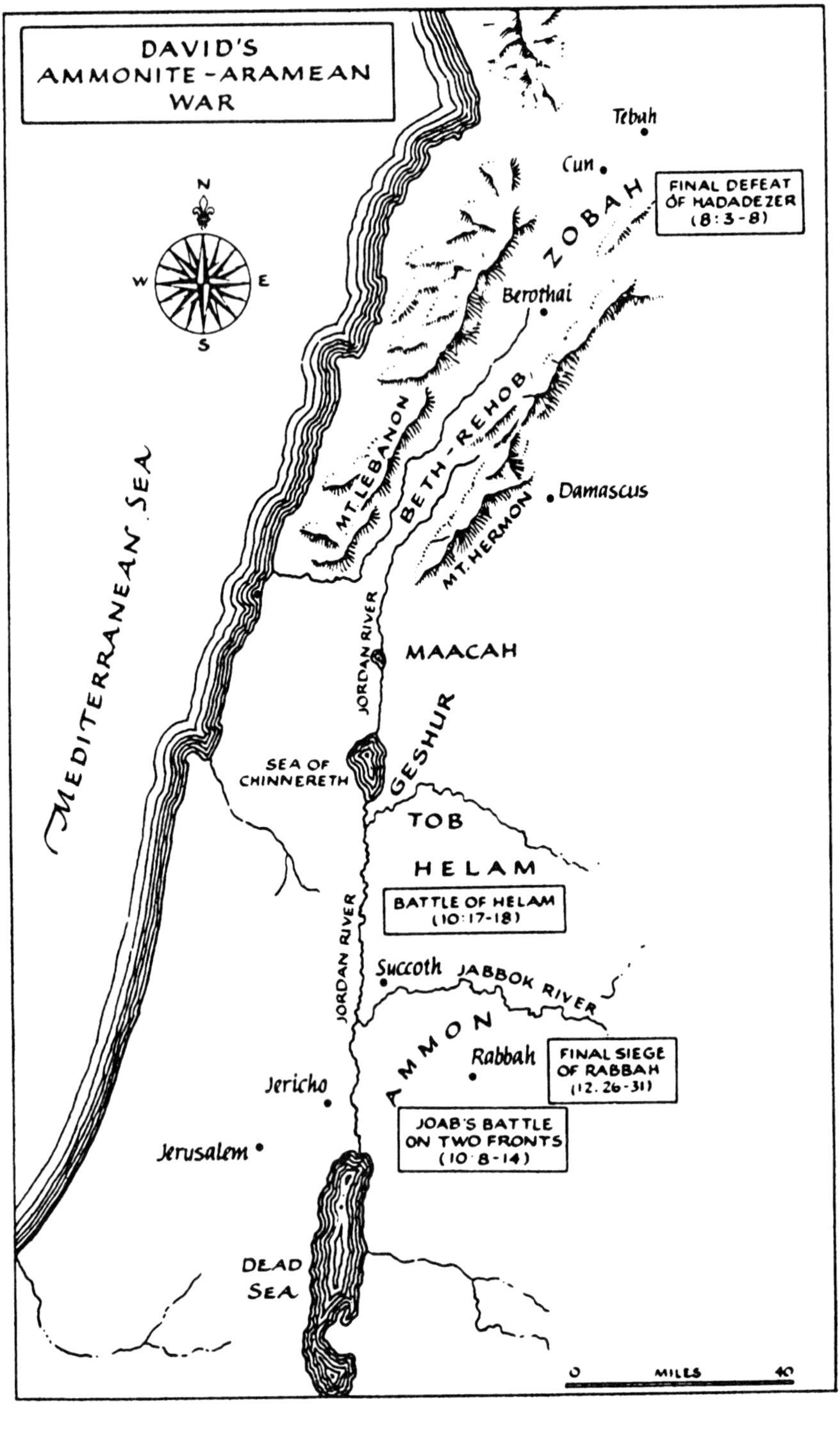

DAVID'S AMMONITE-ARAMEAN WAR
N
W
E
S
Tebah
Cun
FINAL DEFEAT OF HADADEZER (8:3-8)
ZOBAH
Berothai
BETH-REHOB
MT. LEBANON
Damascus
MT. HERMON
MEDITERRANEAN SEA
JORDAN RIVER
MAACAH
GESHUR
SEA OF CHINNERETH
TOB
HELAM
BATTLE OF HELAM (10:17-18)
JORDAN RIVER
Succoth
JABBOK RIVER
AMMON
Rabbah
FINAL SIEGE OF RABBAH (12.26-31)
Jericho
JOAB'S BATTLE ON TWO FRONTS (10·8-14)
Jerusalem
DEAD SEA
0 MILES 40

MAP 7.

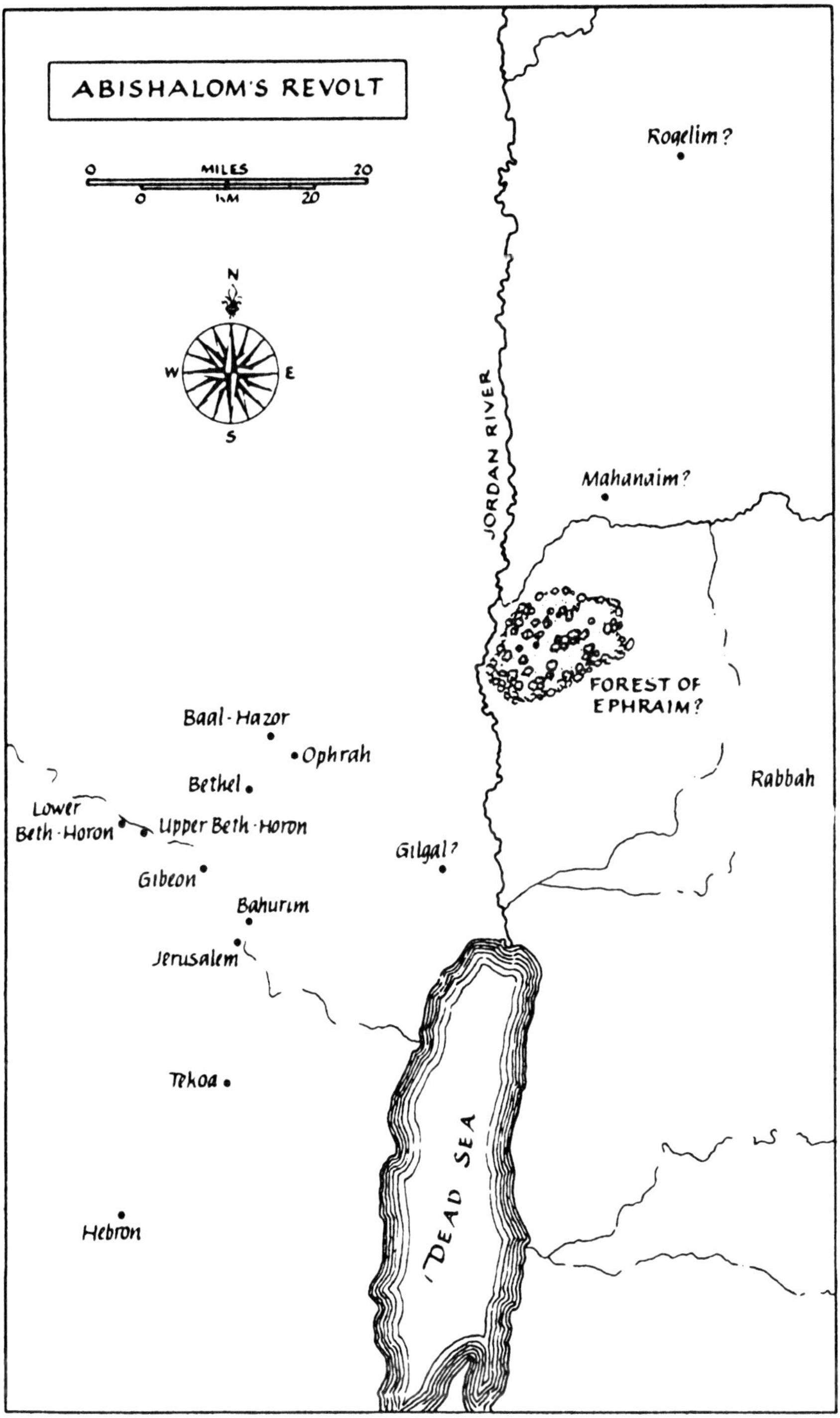
ABISHALOM'S REVOLT
0 MILES 20
0 KM 20
N
W
E
S
JORDAN RIVER
Rogelim ?
Mahanaim ?
FOREST OF EPHRAIM ?
Baal-Hazor
Ophrah
Bethel
Lower Beth-Horon
Upper Beth-Horon
Gibeon
Bahurim
Jerusalem
Gilgal ?
Rabbah
Tekoa
Hebron
DEAD SEA

MAP 8.

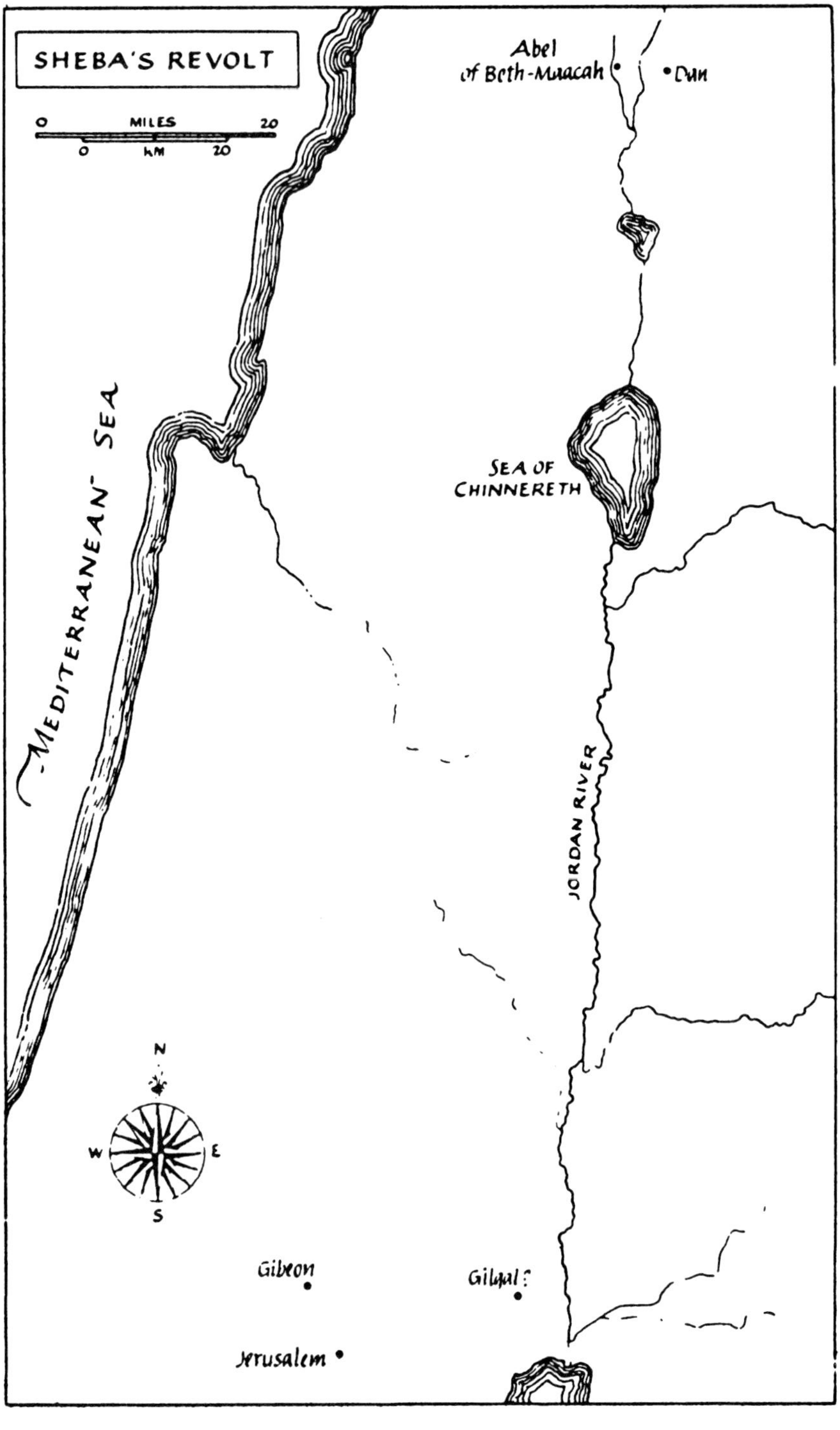
SHEBA'S REVOLT
0 MILES 20
0 KM 20
Abel of Beth-Maacah
Dan
SEA OF CHINNERETH
MEDITERRANEAN SEA
JORDAN RIVER
N
W
E
S
Gibeon
Gilgal?
Jerusalem

MAP 9.

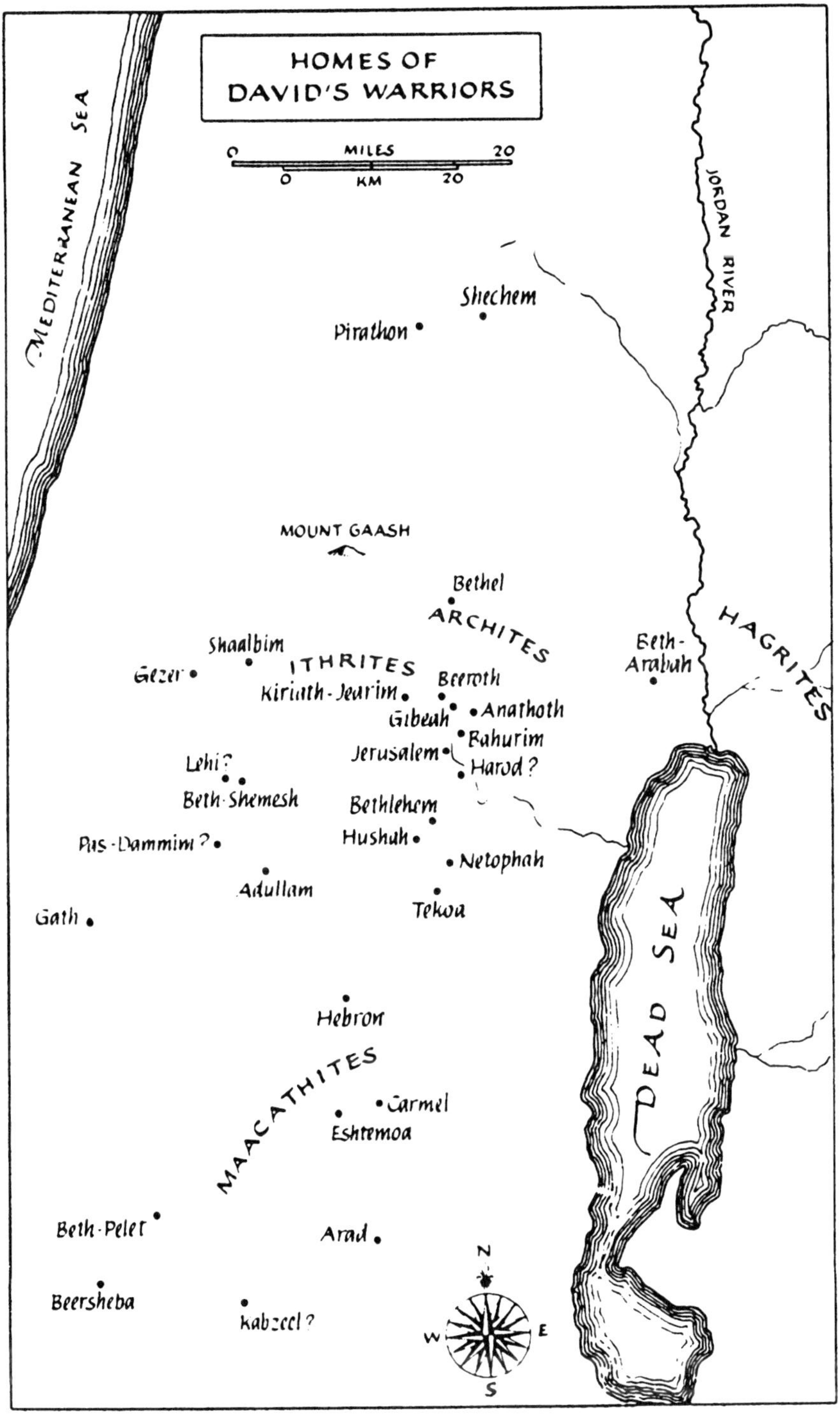

HOMES OF DAVID'S WARRIORS
0 MILES 20
0 KM 20
MEDITERRANEAN SEA
JORDAN RIVER
Shechem
Pirathon
MOUNT GAASH
Bethel
ARCHITES
Shaalbim
ITHRITES
Gezer
Kiriath-Jearim
Beeroth
Beth-Arabah
HAGRITES
Gibeah
Anathoth
Bahurim
Jerusalem
Harod ?
Lehi ?
Beth-Shemesh
Bethlehem
Pas-Dammim ?
Hushah
Netophah
Adullam
Tekoa
Gath
DEAD SEA
Hebron
MAACATHITES
Carmel
Eshtemoa
Beth-Pelet
Arad
Beersheba
Kabzeel ?
N
W
E
S

MAP 10.

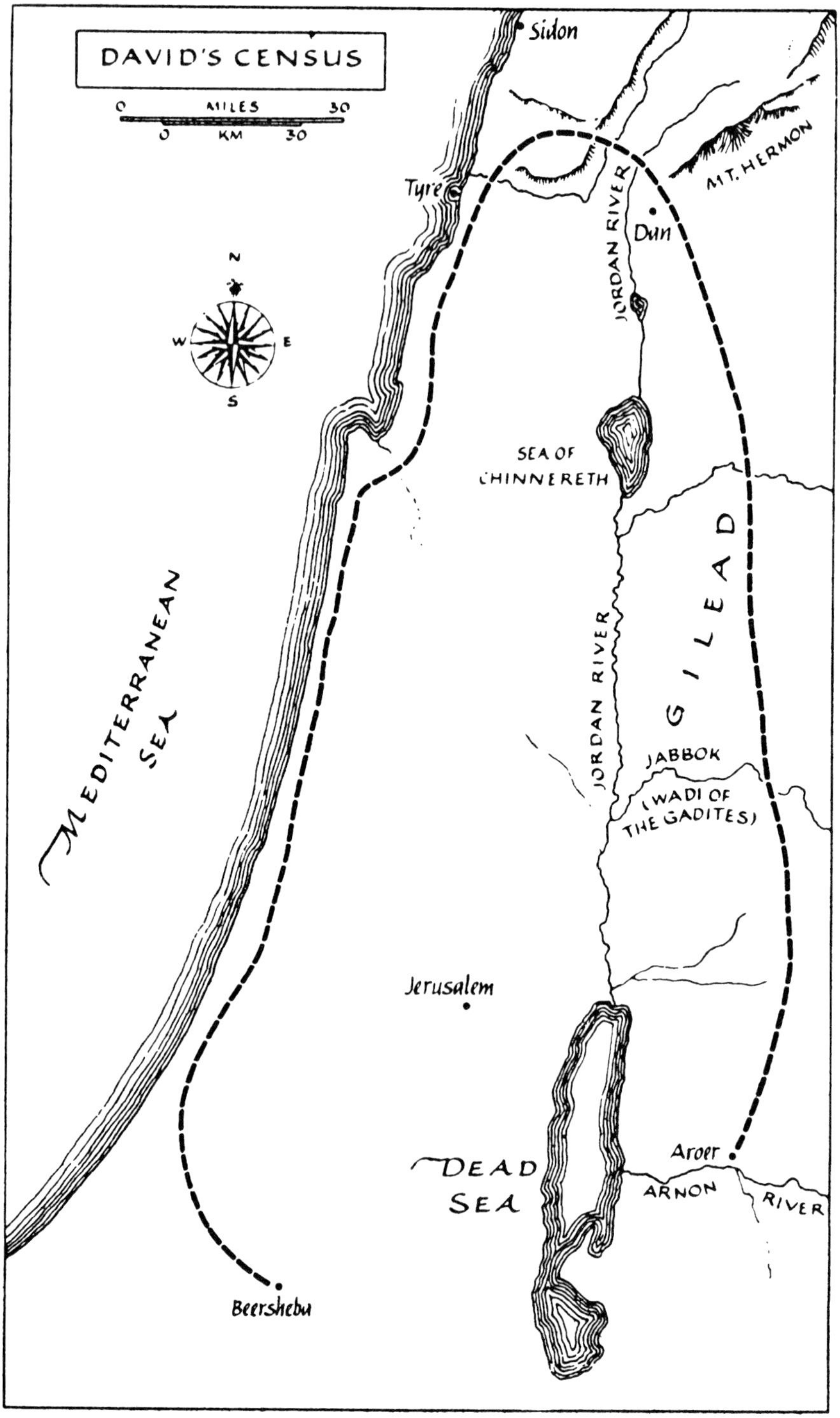
DAVID'S CENSUS
0 MILES 30
0 KM 30
N
W
E
S
Sidon
Tyre
Dan
MT. HERMON
JORDAN RIVER
SEA OF CHINNERETH
GILEAD
JORDAN RIVER
JABBOK
(WADI OF THE GADITES)
MEDITERRANEAN SEA
Jerusalem
DEAD SEA
Aroer
ARNON RIVER
Beersheba

# INDEX OF BIBLICAL REFERENCES, INCLUDING APOCRYPHA AND RABBINIC LITERATURE

Versification of English Bibles, where it differs from that of the received Hebrew text (MT), is indicated in square brackets.

# INDEX OF AUTHORS

Lightning Source UK Ltd.
Milton Keynes UK
UKOW04f0458281115

263689UK00002B/78/P

9 780300 139518